汉外双向全译实践系列教程

汉英

黑龍江大學出版社
HEILONGJIANG UNIVERSITY PRESS

图书在版编目(CIP)数据

汉英双向全译实践教程 / 黄忠廉，郑淑明主编. --
哈尔滨：黑龙江大学出版社，2012.10(2018.10 重印)
汉外双向全译实践系列教程 / 黄忠廉总主编
ISBN 978-7-81129-520-7

Ⅰ. ①汉… Ⅱ. ①黄… ②郑… Ⅲ. ①英语-翻译-教材 Ⅳ. ①H315.9

中国版本图书馆 CIP 数据核字(2012)第 176521 号

汉英双向全译实践教程
HANYING SHUANGXIANG QUANYI SHIJIAN JIAOCHENG
黄忠廉　郑淑明　主编

责任编辑　安宏涛　张春珠
出版发行　黑龙江大学出版社
地　　址　哈尔滨市南岗区学府路 74 号
印　　刷　哈尔滨市石桥印务有限公司
开　　本　787×1092　1/16
印　　张　24.5
字　　数　650 千
版　　次　2012 年 10 月第 1 版
印　　次　2018 年 10 月第 3 次印刷
书　　号　ISBN 978-7-81129-520-7
定　　价　45.00 元

《汉外双向全译实践系列教程》编写委员会

《汉英双向全译实践教程》编写组

主　编:黄忠廉　郑淑明

副主编:杜洪峰　张　晔　张文英　蒙博涵

编撰者:(以姓氏拼音为序)

崔雪波　杜洪峰　黄峻峰　黄忠廉　李　威　李凤敏

李凤英　李家春　李明明　蒙博涵　孙跃鹏　邬明晶

熊　俊　岳铁艳　张　丹　张　力　张　晔　张红芸

张文英　张小川　赵子明　郑淑明

双向·全译·实践(代总序)

何谓全译？基本译能是什么？基本译理有哪些？如何突出实践？实践与实用和实际关系如何？全译教程如何一本多用？如何满足不同层次不同性质的教学要求？此类问题,《汉外双向全译实践系列教程》尝试解答。

本套教程以实践需求为导向,以基本译能训练为目标,以全译研究为基础,重点突出三大特点:

第一,双向。突出双向,旨在促进汉外互译。本科翻译教学重双向实践能力,汉外互译能力于习译者好比飞机双翼,缺一不可。汉译外并非外译汉的简单逆归,二者若能互动互学,必将事半功倍。

本套教程可实行双轨制,可先外汉再汉外,也可互译齐教,平行推进,好比田里种稻,一年双季,两次收获。双向教程虽讲求双重,但有侧重。视具体情况或重外译汉,以打好基础;或在外译汉基础上偏重汉译外,满足译才培养当下之急需。汉外互译双向可生双效,比如外译汉之后自行回译,反之亦然;400 个基本词可以双向记忆,实为 800 词;比读体悟,也可试着回译,更能深入体悟汉外互译之妙,如此这般,效果翻番。

第二,全译。突出全译,旨在奠定基本翻译技能。全译是整个翻译能力训练的基础,只有真枪实弹扎实地训练全译能力,才可拓展其他翻译能力,比如摘译、编译、译述、仿作等变译能力。

所谓全译训练,即在全译基本知识指导下,立于篇章的高度,辗转于词句之间,训练对译、增译、减译、转译、换译、分译、合译等成套的全译七法,体悟全译发生发展过程。整个教程训练完毕,将习得和学得全套方法,遇到翻译不会怯生,能较快地发现传达原文内容的译法,至此习译者的全译意识已初步建立。当然,全译技能并不等于全能,译无止境,还要靠毕业后更多专门的实战训练。

第三,实践。突出实践,重在按话题训练。专业翻译教学的本质是实践性的,实践可以与实际和实用接轨。本科全译课的实质就是基于翻译基本知识,根据习译者的实情,选择实用的材料,保证学生足数的时间和内容,对习译者进行实足的训练。而双向全译教程的目标无非是坐实于汉外互译实践,依据学生实际,讲究实用价值,凸显现实话题,完成适量的实践训练。

本套教程以中专、专科、本科、非外语专业、MTI、自考等层次学生为教学对象,从社会对译才需求的现象出发,训练 30 个话题,实事求是,从其全译实践中导出对全译的基本认识。这种训练分层设计内容,将技能落到实处,译者译得脚踏实地,教者教得循序渐进。相信译者一定会获得译的实感和实学,教者也会看到教的实绩和实效。

黄忠廉　许钧

2012 年夏

编法·教法·学法（代前言）

要想一年半载入得译门，必经严格的科班训练。

以“编法·教法·学法”代前言，旨在与习译者共享学得和习得全译艺术、领悟全译之道。翻译是实践的艺术，翻译能力的提高离不开日积月累的实践演练，多译、多比和多思才是硬道理，是习译者的不二法门。

《汉英双向全译实践教程》将翻译、娱乐、休闲、医疗、保健、婚姻、家庭、历史、文化、旅游、资源、环保、新闻、媒体、贸易、商品、广告、交通、通信、工农业、企事业单位、经济、管理、政治、外交、科学、技术、法律、教育、文学、艺术、体育等32个话题编入21课，充分体现了社会对译才的现实需求、由浅入深的教学梯度、由易到难的教学进度、学习兴趣逐步发展。整个教程以全译实践为主、以全译基本知识和方法导入为辅，意在通过72学时（一学期每周4学时；两学期每周2学时）的汉英互译实战演练，训练近30 000汉字的翻译量，培养学生的汉英互译技能与全译意识。实践证明，经过这一训练，在专业八级考试、专业和非专业考研中翻译题易得高分，在求职翻译面试中能获得佳绩，毕业后做翻译更能快速上手。

编　法

导译　每课开篇阐明话题及其所涉的内容，交代全译的重点或难易顺序，或话题的全译特色等。

课前练笔　专为学生练笔设计，体现实践性和实用性。每课材料3—5篇/片，全教程80余篇/片，汉英互译约1 250汉字，每篇/片为一台阶，以叙述性和议论性为主，逐级增加难度，按由短至长、由易到难梯级排列，供不同性质、不同层次、不同学校的教师和中专、专科、本科、研究生、自考、自学等各类习译者自由选择。

课前批评　每课英汉互译各一篇，全教程共42篇。要求学生课前进行分析，仔细揣摩，学会分析别人的译作，学会欣赏找差距，学会批评练思辨。

全译知识　21个全译知识点包括定义、分类、单位、过程、策略、原则、标准、规律、对译、增译、减译、转译、换译、分译、合译、科技全译、文学全译、艺术翻译、全译批评、翻译腔、翻译工具等。整个知识紧随实践训练之后，讲究系统性、实用性和基础性，突出全译通则，不刻意与每课的话题相对应。每课一种知识，只作简明阐释，当用例时，则少而精，略作分析。

全译窍门　每课配以窍门5个左右，全教程约100个。窍门是全译基本知识的有益补充，力求短小精悍，以点代面，力求选出最常见、最有趣、最有用、最典型、习译者必须了解或容易忽视的全译技巧；多数窍门说理精短，有例佐证。

话题词汇　话题词目每课约400条，全教程共8 000余条，以基本词汇为主、缩略语为辅,含最基本、最常用、最有特色的词语以及少量的常用表达式,时兴词语酌情选入,要求具有科学性和基础性,以增进习译者相应的学识与学养。力求覆盖话题的主干内容,以彰显其知识体系,也满足译者建立基本词库的要求。

比读体悟 双语对照的短文或片段,每课4—6篇,全教程近100篇。本部分首先供自学者用,其次供有余力的学生课余自学,为其提供各领域丰富的专业对照读物,在比读之中深入体悟全译之道。

课后练习 练习形式有三种。其一是分析题,即结合每课的话题、全译知识和窍门分析全译问题;每课3个,全教程共60多个。其二是实训题,即课后练笔的园地,英译约150汉字的篇幅,汉译约200词的篇幅,与“课前实践”共计约1 600汉字量。其三是思考题,既具理性又比较有趣,是与每课话题、全译知识和窍门相关的问题,旨在推动研究性学习,每课15个左右,全教程近300题。

教 法

灵活利用教材 教材编写的顺序并非教与学的顺序。30多个话题可供教师选择,教学实际周数为16—18周,教师有较大的选择空间。弄清每课的话题与全译的关系之后,“课前练笔”是教学重点,每次课90%的时间用于全译训练与讨论,10%用于全译知识归纳或窍门欣赏;时间不够时,知识与窍门可以自学。训练中涉及新窍门,则可及时补充。“话题词汇”由学生识记。

课前巧作安排 不同学校的教师可根据学生层次和水平,从“课前练笔”中选择1—3篇/片,要求课前译好,以便课堂讨论。“课前批评”可视学生水平灵活取舍。此外,课前要求学生阅读开篇有关话题与全译的介绍、本课或相关课的全译知识和窍门。为切实达到练笔的实效,教材不附带参考译文,有需要者可向出版社或编者索取。

课堂引导讨论 翻译是最容易上得盎然有趣的课程。教学得法,教、学定能相长。课前抽点(随机或指定)学生或抄译于黑板,或用PPT演示,或口头译出,让学生简述翻译过程,即如何译、为何译、有何得意、有何疑惑。教师则组织讨论各种译案,旁证说理,简明点化,指出错误,肯定不同译法的适用度。讨论一定要掌控进度与节奏,鼓励自由发言,兼顾点名调动,促进全班互动起来,以达教学目的。全译教学的重点不在语言或文化知识,而在于语际转化和跨文化交际规律以及全译意识的培养,具体是双语、双文化特点的对比及其转化艺术的分析。每次上课伊始,可用两分钟、抽两人简述上次课的译后心得和对全译知识的认识。

课后整理思考 要求学生准备两个练习本,单双周轮流使用。课后“实训题”可与“课前练笔”一起讨论,时间充裕也可做在本上。“分析题”和“思考题”可供有余力的同学做。还有一种新型的练习形式:整理译文写心得。要求学生结合课堂讨论整理自己的译文,鼓励学生坚持己译,用相应的符号标出不同之处。更重要的是写译后心得,写法多样,或有感而发,或系统总结,促进学生学会总结,学会思考,善于发现,敢于表达。老师重点批阅学生译文的不同之处和译后心得。

学 法

预习与练笔 每课学习之前,必须了解话题与全译的关系,熟悉话题所涉及领域、内容、文本特色以及全译的重难点，必要时了解相关背景知识，做到心中有数、有备而译。译前多读原文，准确理解，把握原作特色；多读汉语平行文本，熟悉话题及其语言特点；动笔试译，多查词典和参考书，多作同义词、短语、句式的比较与选择，多发现、总结习译中的重难点、疑惑点、优缺点。尽量写下初/粗译，要大胆试译，疑难处可以空着，将自己的灵感或思考写在相应的地方，以便课堂讨论。

知识与窍门　全译知识、话题词汇与全译窍门可在译前预习，也可在译后总结。既要善于通过实践总结全译知识与窍门，更要学会用译理分析译例，学会检视己译与他译之优劣得失，能举一反三，即学即用，力求理论分析与实战演练互补，译艺习得与译道领悟并进。

"话题词汇"提供了相当数量的词汇和表达式，对于习译者，"无他，熟记尔"，必要时可查阅文献或网络搜索。只有在译前译后苦练"背"功，建立庞大的知识库，才能在习译以及未来的全译实践中少花时间翻词典、查资料，磨刀不误砍柴工。

讨论与体悟　有老师指导参与课堂讨论是习译者难得的机会。课堂上直抒己见，可道心声；与同窗切磋，可开茅塞；听老师分析，如醍醐灌顶。讨论之中通过生生互动和师生互动，可品译之美，可习译之艺，可悟译之道。

自学者虽无上述便利，也可在全译知识与窍门指导下，先自译"比读部分"的原文，再与右边的译文比较；还可把所给的译文回译，从中体味互译规律以及双语的特点。若有可能，还可将译文与译语文献比读，从中体味译之理，不仅可以领略全译艺术，还可以扩大相关话题的知识面。也可通过邮件、BBS、QQ 群等手段跨越时空进行交流。在校生若有余力，如此训练，多多益善。

巩固与提高　课后"实训题"，学有余力者课堂上可与"课前练笔"一并讨论，一来可循序渐进地加大实践量，二来可巩固课前实践所形成的译感，以便温故而知新。"分析题"有助于巩固与反思所学的内容，提高分析能力，指导全译实践，可供有余力的习译者选做。"思考题"则为本专科学生小科研和研究生毕业论文提供参考性选题，为社会上需要写作中小型翻译论文者提供思路，促其从中获得启迪，拓宽选题视野。

无论课堂讨论之后，还是自译与他译对比之后，都建议写译后心得。译后所感的对象包括：习译感受、正误比较、巧妙译法、双语比较、转化规律、多种译法比较、译中某类语言或文化现象小结、老师的点悟、同窗的启发、己译之优劣等等。这种心得，能写出译感，写出信心，写出对全译的爱。每课小有收获，坚持半年必有大获，一生从译也就能自我解"惑"！读后感或写于所感对象之下，或置于其后括号内，或独撰于整个译文末尾，或在译文中标上序号而分条撰写于文末。

读后感既可能是现象描写式总结，即就事论事，进行最简单的归类或小结，培养自己的问题意识和思考能力；也可能是提升抽象式总结，即在描写式总结基础上，进一步总结，上升为对全译基本知识和各种窍门的认识。

本教程编写单位及作者按课序分别为：黑龙江大学黄忠廉（第 1 课）、大庆师范学院张小川（第 2 课）、东北林业大学蒙博涵（第 3 课）、东北林业大学张丹（第 4 课）、吉林华桥外国语学院赵子明（第 5 课）、牡丹江大学张红芸（第 6 课）、黑龙江工程学院邬明晶（第 7 课）、黑龙江大学李家春（第 8 课）、哈尔滨工程大学岳铁艳（第 9 课）、绥化学院李凤英（第 10 课）、东北农业大学张力（第 11 课）、东北农业大学孙跃鹏（第 12 课）、哈尔滨工业大学郑淑明(第13课)、哈尔滨理工大学张文英/吉林大学(珠海)李凤敏(第14课)、哈尔滨师范大学张晔(第15课)、长春理工大学黄峻峰(第16课)、黑龙江大学杜洪峰(第17课)、黑龙江东方学院李明明(第18课)、湖北工程学院熊俊(第19课)、延边大学崔雪波(第20课)、黑河学院李威(第21课)。黄忠廉负责整个教程的设计、审读与统稿,执笔"全译知识";郑淑明负责全书初稿的审读;杜洪峰协助整个统稿工作;四位副主编分头审读了部分书稿。

本教程是教育部人文社会科学重点研究基地黑龙江大学俄罗斯语言文学与文化研究中心2008年度重大项目"(俄汉)全译转化机制及其应用研究"成果之一。

目录

第1课 全译探微

导译

学习翻译一般建议由英汉全译入手,汉译英或紧随其后,或同期进行,口译则略晚于笔译。有时间有余力则可以开设变译课,也可自学。由此可见,全译是最基本的翻译技能。全译技艺可以学习,分为学得和习得。所谓译艺学得,是指经过科班的全译教学系统地掌握全译之道;要学得译艺,得通过老师教授,体味语际转化的高妙,明白自己的缺陷,系统训练技能,掌握翻译基本知识;通过课堂讨论,集思广益,取长补短,查漏补缺,扩大翻译视野,开阔翻译思路。所谓译艺习得,是指经过一定的全译实践自然领悟全译之道;要习得译艺,得通过自译,历经语际转化之苦,由译生痛,痛定而乐,享受两种思维磨砺之乐;通过比读,见人之长,明己之短,看到高手之译,惊叹之余,欲与他人试比高,看到拙劣之译,修改之后,引以为戒可加勉。

全译是语际转化的艺术,在词语转换、句序重组之际自需相应技法与对策。勿因技小而不为。技巧切不可小觑,以为是低层次,须知由技而可致于艺,无技便无艺。技之精者近乎道。油翁注油,"无他,唯乎熟尔";庖丁解牛,无他,唯理同尔,二者都精乎艺。而刘谦施魔,更是完全靠"技"靠"术";熟能生巧,神乎其技,令人惊叹。术的有无与高低,关乎艺的文野与精粗。要做好翻译,须重技巧的悟得与妙用。

全译之能,并不能仅仅指望几十学时的教与练,而是长期经验的积累和日夜苦练的结晶。勤练,善学,多思,译能必定日有所进。一句话,译精于勤而成于思。

1 课前练笔

1.1 环保

中国政府高度重视保护环境,认为保护环境关系国家现代化建设的全局和长远发展,是造福当代、惠及子孙的事业。中国政府将环境保护确立为一项基本国策,在推进经济发展的同时,采取一系列措施加强保护环境。特别是近年来,中国政府坚持预防为主、综合治理、全面推进、重点突破,着力解决危害人民群众健康的突出环境问题;坚持创新体制机制,依靠科学进步,强化环境法制,发挥社会各方面的积极性。经过努力,环境污染和生态破坏加剧的趋势减缓,部分流域污染治理初见成效,部分城市和地区环境质量有所改善,全社会保护环境意识进一步增强。

1.2 The Family Car

The Moto 1 100 is a small family car. It has a small engine which is in the front. The engine has a capacity of 1 100 cubic centimeters. It is a front wheel drive can. The gear level is on the floor. There are seats for four or five people. It has four front forward gears and a reverse. It has a maximum speed of about 130 km per hour. One advantage of this is that it has very low fuel consumption.

1.3 A Room with a View

She fixed her eyes wistfully on the tower of the palace, which rose out of the lower darkness like a pillar of roughened gold. It seemed no longer a tower, no longer supported by earth, but some unattainable treasure throbbing in the tranquil sky. Its brightness mesmerized her, still dancing before her eyes when she bent them to the ground and started towards home.

1.4 I Have a Dream

Five score years ago, a great American, in whose symbolic shadow we stand signed the Emancipation Proclamation. This momentous decree came as a great beacon light of hope to millions of Negro slaves who had been seared in the flames of withering injustice. It came as a joyous daybreak to end the long night of captivity.

But one hundred years later, we must face the tragic fact that the Negro is still not free. One hundred years later, the life of the Negro is still sadly crippled by the manacles of segregation and the chains of discrimination. One hundred years later, the Negro lives on a lonely island of poverty in the midst of a vast ocean of material prosperity. One hundred years later, the Negro is still languishing in the corners of American society and finds himself an exile in his own land. So we have come here today to dramatize an appalling condition.

2 课前批评

2.1 二马

她要是个中国妇人，我一定跟她明说："我爱你！"可是，对中国妇人就有这样胆气吗？马威！马威！你是个乏人，没出息！不想了！好好念书！父亲不成，我再不成，将来怎办！谁管将来呢，现在叫我心不疼了，死也干！……

眼前水流着，鸟儿飞着，花在风里动着；水，鸟，花，或者比她美，然而人是人，人是肉作的，恋爱是由精神上想不透，在肉体上可以享受或忍痛的东西；压制是没用的！（老舍）

Erma

"If Mary were Chinese I'd certainly go to her and say, 'I love you.' But would I really have that much nerve with a Chinese girl? Ma Wei," he reproached himself, "you're a wasted, hopeless fool! Don't think about it, just concentrate on the books, if I get as mucked up as Father then what'll become of us! Oh, but who cares about the future — just want to know how to stop this aching in my heart now, even if it means death, I don't care."

He looked at the scene in front of him , the stream flowing, birds flying, flowers swaying in the breeze. And he told himself that the water, the birds, the flowers were perhaps more beautiful than Mary. But people were after all human, made of flesh and blood, and love was something that couldn't be explained sway rationally. It was something the flesh could either rejoice in or suffer through, it was pointless to try to repress it.（尤利叶·吉姆逊 译）

2.2 Lexicography

Lexicography provides at its best a joyful sense of busyness with language. One is immersed in the details of languages as in no other field. Sometimes the details are so overwhelming and endless they sap the spirit and depress the mind. Often at the end of a hard day's work one realizes with dismay that the meager stack of finished work one has accomplished has an immeasurably slight impact on the work as a whole. As I hope the readers of this work will come to understand, dictionaries do not sprint into being. People must plan them, collect information, and write them. Writing takes time, and it is often frustrating and even infuriating. No other form of writing is at once so

词典编纂

词典编纂最能使人产生与语言打交道的快感。有别于其他领域，编者埋头于语言材料，材料有时浩如烟海，耗力费神。往往是辛苦一天，才发觉薄薄的几页只是九牛一毛，好不沮丧。所以，我相信本书的读者会明白，词典编纂并非一蹴而就。他们要先制订计划，查找材料，方能编写。编纂不仅费时，还常让人受挫，甚至恼怒。词典编纂与其他写作不同，既要富于空想，又要脚踏实地；虽不需才华横溢

quixotic and so intensely practical. Dictionary making does not require brilliance or originality of mind. It does require high intelligence, mastery of the craft, and dedication to hard work. If one has produced a dictionary, one has the satisfaction of having produced a work of enduring value.

或思维敏捷，但更求智力高超，精于编纂，甘于吃苦。编出一部词典，创下长久的价值，就会收获一份欣慰。（黄忠廉 译）

知识 3 全译知识 翻译概说

3.1 翻译

翻译是人或/和机器将甲语文化信息变化为乙语以求信息量相似的智能活动和符际活动。

依动词的“主体+方式+行为+客体+因果/目的+属性”义素可对其作出分析：

翻译的主体即译者主要是人，机译出现后，机器也成了翻译主体或其中一部分。最恰当的翻译主体表示法应是“人或/和机器”，表明翻译是人或机器单独完成的行为，也可是合作完成的行为，如机助人译、人助机译等。

翻译的方式/工具是用译语，译语用来将原语文化信息再次表达出来的过程，具有工具性。

翻译行为的轴心是“变化”。“译即易，谓换易言语使相解也。”（贾公彦《周礼·义疏》）“易”即“变化”，由“变”“化”构成。“变”，指因译语读者需求与原作的大矛盾而对原作施以“变通”，包括增、减、编、述、缩、并、改、仿等八大变通策略；“化”，指因原作内容与译语形式的小矛盾而对原作内容施以“转移”，对原作形式施以“化解”，包括对、增、减、转、换、分、合等七大化解策略，两个行为核心分别对应变译和全译两大翻译策略。

翻译的客体或对象是原文，即原语所表达的文化信息，而非原文的表达工具——原语。

翻译的目的包括两个：变译追求译前译后信息量不同程度的相似，全译追求译前译后信息量的极似，二合一，可构成翻译的总目的：求得译作与原作信息量相似。

翻译的类属仍是一种行为，包括智能活动和符际活动。前者可将人译与机译尽收其中，因为机器同人一样具有“某些智慧和才能”。后者不仅涉及语言符号，还涉及图表、音乐等其他符号，用“符际活动”更具概括性和普适性。

3.2 全译

全译是人或/和机器用乙语转化甲语文化信息以求信息量极似的智能活动和符际活动。

全译是译者用译语转化原作以求信息量极似的翻译活动。

以上是全译的繁式和简式定义，不妨用最简单的译例予以证明。

①I'm a student.

【汉语人译Ⅰ】:我是一名/个大学生。

【汉语人译Ⅱ】:我是个/名大学生。

【汉译人译Ⅲ】:我是大学生。

【汉译人译Ⅳ】:我学生。

【汉语人译Ⅴ】:我是男/女生。

【汉语人译Ⅵ】:我男/女生。

【汉语机译Ⅰ】:我是一个/名学生。

【汉语机译Ⅱ】:我是个/名学生。

【汉语机译Ⅲ】:我是学生。

全译的主体、方式/工具、客体、类属四者与“翻译”相同,特别之处有二:

第一,目的上求信息量极似,即尽可能地传达原作的信息,包括内容、形式及其统一体即风格。例中的机译已相当不错地传达了原作信息,“我是一个/名学生→我是个/名学生→我是学生”与原文越来越近似,由形似走向意似,最终走向风格似。

第二,行为上求转化。转化可分解为“转换”和“化解”,重在转换,转移原文内容,用译语更换原语形式,旨在求化。转换成功,即可求化。如例中人译有超越机译之处:机译所能人译都能,人译还能根据语境由欧化走向汉化,由书面走向口语,由共性走向性别;用汉语“代词+名词”表示判断,如“我男/女生”虽为口语,却含古汉语句法的味道。

3.3 回译实践

英汉互译是一种双向实践,具有回译的功效,习译者可通过自译或比读材料开展回译,更能体味全译之妙。从自译或他译译回原语,与原文逐句相较,可察出异同。坚持英汉回译,单向翻译时理解并不透彻的双语现象,通过回译则能深刻地领悟词、语、句的表达作用,通过句式甚至是篇章的转化可以掌握双语的思维模式,不仅可习得全译技能,还可品到双语的写作风格,嗅到双语的味道。如:

②【原文】:伯父家盖房,想以它垒山墙,但苦于它极不规则,没棱角儿,也没平面儿;用錾破开吧,又懒得花那么大气力,因为河滩并不甚远,随便去捎一块回来,哪一块也比它强。(贾平凹)

【英译/原文】:When Uncle's family was building a house, we thought of using it to pile up a side of the house wall. This proved to be impossible, however, since the rock was of an extremely irregular shape, possessing neither sharp right angles nor any smooth, flat surfaces. We could have used a chisel to break the rock up, but no one could be bothered to expend such a great deal of effort over it; the riverbank was only a short distance away, and any old rock that we brought back from there would have been easier to use than this one.

【回译】:伯父家盖房子时,我们曾想到用它垒一面墙,但最后还是没能用上,因为这块岩石外形太不规则,既没有尖利的直角,又没有光滑的平面。我们用凿子凿开它吧,可是没人愿费那么大气力。河边没多远,我们随便从那儿搬运一块石头回来都比用这块岩石省劲。(见王克非,2003)

汉语原文65字,汉语回译104字,回译比原文多出39字,增幅达60%,即汉译英时发生了英语扩增,导致回译相应地扩增。原因在哪儿?根本原因是汉译英趋繁而译者又不能像原文作者那样善于从简表达。原文中"伯父家盖房"是"想以它垒山墙"的时间背景,回译时见 when 就译作"(当)……时(候)";原文上下文暗示"我们"要垒墙,英译补出,回译时也照之译出了;一个"但苦于"蕴含了石头不中用与其外形的不足,存有因果关系,汉语的空灵害得英译几近添加了一个小句"但最后还是没能用上",把结果交代得明明白白;即使是接着解释原因,也少不了用表示原因关系的连词 since、表示并列关系的连词"neither… nor …",不料回译时译者一一坐实外显,对将过来:"因为"、"既……也……"。再说词和语,"极不规则,没棱角儿,也没平面儿"经由英译回到汉语,成了"外形太不规则,既没有尖利的直角,又没有光滑的平面"。

经过回译与剖析,汉简英繁的特点自现,对汉译英如何趋繁、英译汉如何趋简的规律也会悟得一二。

4 全译窍门

4.1 意一言多

翻译首先是"意一言多"的行为,即面对大千世界不同语言表达同一对象。"意一"指原作所表达的内容;"言多"指表达这一内容的多种语言。人类思维的共性决定了能对同一事物具有大致相同的表达能力,特性决定了表达手段的差异。若用 M 指代意义,L 指代语言,"意一言多"的行为可表示为图 1。

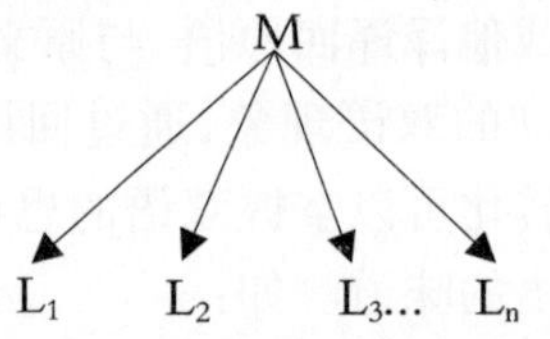

图 1 意一言多

③ 我要给阿 Q 做正传,已经不止一两年了。(鲁迅)

【译文Ⅰ】:For several years now I have been meaning to write the true story of Ah Q.(杨宪益、戴乃迭 译)

【译文Ⅱ】:Вот уже год или два, как я собираюсь написать подлинную историю А-Q.(罗果夫 译)

译文Ⅰ是英译,译文Ⅱ是俄译。英俄语是同属印欧语系的亲属语言,两种译文句型虽然有别,但语序基本相同,几近对译,双双有别于原文因为汉语属于汉藏语系。

4.2 意一形多

翻译其次是"意一形多"的行为,即面对大千世界同一对象可用同一语言的不同手段表达。"意一"仍是原作所表达的内容,"形多"则是同一语言表达这一内容的多种形式。同一民族的思维方式决定了能对同一事物具有大致相同的表达能力,但个体差异和语言资源的丰简决定了表达手段的多样性。面对原文,尤其是文化内涵较深的词句,修养深厚的译者,沉吟之际常会想到各种译案,再多中选一,既凭理性,更凭直觉。若用 M 指代意义,F 指代形式,“意一形多”的行为可表示为图 2。

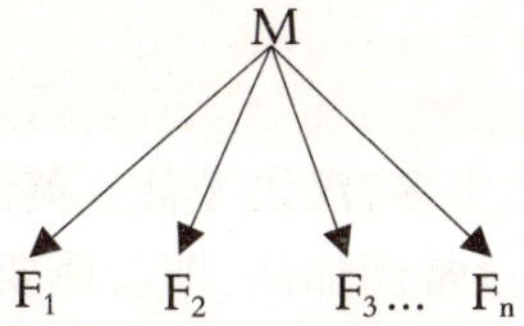

图 2 意一形多

④ Feminists feel that it is an invasion of their privacy to be obliged to indicate via the title "Mrs." or "Miss" whether or not they are married.

【原译】:女权运动者们认为,人们称呼她们,使用 Mrs.(太太)或 Miss(小姐)的称呼,不得不表明她们已婚或未婚,这种做法是对她们私事的一种侵犯。(黄汉生、顾孟耀 译)

【试译Ⅰ】:女权运动者认为,称呼她们 Mrs. 或 Miss 以表明她们婚否,这侵犯了隐私。

【试译Ⅱ】:女权派认为称呼“太太”或“小姐”以明婚否强人所难,侵犯了隐私。

【试译Ⅲ】:女权派认为“太太”或“小姐”之称区分了婚否,这强行侵犯了隐私。

【试译Ⅳ】:女权派认为称“太太”或“小姐”强行区分婚否侵犯了隐私。

原译未译出 to be obliged to,行文不简,同时“女权运动者”虽已固化,但可简称“女权派”,“派”指立场、见解或作风、风气相同的一些人,据此“持不同政见者”可译作“异见派”。试译Ⅰ两次译出“她们”;英语原词留用,会欺负不懂外文者;同样未译出 to be obliged to。试译Ⅱ译出了原意,符合汉语;试译Ⅲ和试译Ⅳ将 to be obliged to 转换视角译作“强行”,前者比后者更简洁。

4.3 转义化形

如全译定义所言,全译活动的轴心是转化,即转移内容,更换形式,化解原文内容与译语形式之间的矛盾。遇上双语思维相同,可对应译出,思维相异,则需调整,或扩充,或压缩,或转换,所有这一切都见之于形,化之于形,换言之,形随意化。如:

⑤ The block of flats has nine-storey, he lives on the eighth floor or the top floor.

【原译】:这座公寓有 9 层楼,他住在 8 楼或顶层楼。

【改译】:这座公寓有 9 层楼,他住在 9 楼或顶层楼。(何炳威 译)

【试译Ⅰ】:这座公寓有 9 层,他住 9 层,即顶层。

【试译Ⅱ】:这座公寓有 8 层,他住 8 层,即顶层。

关于楼层,英美说法有别。本例为英式英语,据之理解 the ground floor 为“一楼”,the first floor 为“二楼”,依此类推,the eighth floor 应为汉语的第九楼,若取英国文化视角,原译八九矛盾,会让不懂英国文化的读者云遮雾障,要么取改译或试译Ⅰ,要么取试译Ⅱ。试译Ⅱ取美国文化的视角,first floor 从平地那层楼算起,比较简单,那么原文就是八层楼,这种思维与汉语相同。这是文化内涵的转移,也是语义的转移。此外,原译基本上是对译,除了虚词外,基本上逐词对过;改译是对译夹有因文化内涵而发生的换译,即将 eighth 换译为“9”;试译Ⅰ同改译,但未将 or 译作表选择关系的“或”,而换译为表判断关系的"即",从原文语义来看,or 实为等同关系;试译Ⅱ则是从美语出发将 nine 换译为"8"。由例可知,处理的似乎是个别的词,面对的却是两种文化。

4.4 汉译趋简

语言讲究经济简练,以少许胜多多,汉语尤甚。英译汉要从英语的重形转向汉语的重义,形式选择常用减法,语义容量常用加法,即汉译要重于意而简于形。换言之,汉译时要注意少用介词、连词、代词等,少用或不用关联手段,善用紧缩句、连动句等,利用语境简省,靠语序表达语义,突出意合的特点。诚如孔子所言:"辞达而已矣。"言辞能表达意义就足够了,言简而意丰。如:

⑥ In the doorway lay at least twelve umbrellas of all sizes and colors.

【原译】:门口放着一堆雨伞,少说也有十二把,五颜六色,大小不一。(连淑能用例)

【试译】:门口少说也放了十二把雨伞,五颜六色,大小不一。

英语句子虽不算长,却脉络清楚,若照搬汉译为"在门口至少放了各种颜色各种大小的雨伞十二把"已是拗口,若是译作"在门口少说也放了五颜六色、大小不一的十二把雨伞",也是尾大不掉,转折不灵。试译则充分利用语境,能省则省,如表方位,"门口"前不用介词"在";再如 sizes and colors 限定前面的"雨伞",汉译则不必一一提前,而是单独成句;相应地,译尺寸和颜色也不用加"雨伞",凭语境可承前省略,发挥汉语流水句的作用。

4.5 英译趋繁

汉英分属两大语系,往往扞格难通。翻译时,要善入善出,去"隔"会通,关键不仅在遣词,更在造句和行文。与英译汉相反,汉译英则要趋近比汉语繁复的英语,经常要使用形合手段,如介词、连接词、代词和副词等关系词,词缀变化,词类的形态变化(如名词、代词的性、数、格,动词的时、体、态,语气,人称和物称,形容词、副词的比较级、最高级)等。如例②后半部分理解时要在大脑中变得繁复:

(我们)用錾破开(它)吧,(但是我们)又懒得花那么大气力(做这件事),因为河滩(离这儿)并不甚远,(我们)随便去(河滩)捎一块(石头)回来,哪一块(石头)也比它强。

括号内是经思维补充的内容,为此英译时也加了相应的形合手段,见下文括号内:

(We could) have used a chisel to break (the rock) up, (but no one) could be bothered to expend such a great deal of effort (over it); the riverbank was only a short distance (away), (and) any (old rock that we) brought back (from there) would have been easier to use than this one.

汉语少用形态,英语形态丰富。看英译,行为主体处处呈现,客体也不愿落下,如添加了 we, it, no one, the rock, old rock 等;逻辑关系十分明显,如添加了 but, and 等,连空间关系也如实设计,如 away, from there 等。汉语可断处皆续,较之于汉语源文,英译的确形态发达,长言回环,可是太密太实,失却了原作的灵性和鲜活。

5 话题词汇

5.1 翻译定义

(1) Translating consists in reproducing in the receptor language the closest natural equivalent of the source language message, first in terms of meaning and secondly in terms of style. (Eugene Nida & Charles R. Taber)

(2) Translating is rendering the meaning of a text into another language in the way the author intended the text. (Peter Newmark)

(3) Translation leads from a source-language text to a target-language text which is as close an equivalent as possible and presupposes an understanding of the content and style of the original. (Wilss)

(4) Translation is the replacement of textual material in one language by equivalent textual material in another language. (Catford)

(5) Give the meaning of sth. (said or written) in another language. (Oxford Advanced Learner's Dictionary of Current English with Chinese Translation, Revised Third Edition, 1984)

(6)翻译是用一种语言把另一种语言在内容与形式不可分割的统一中业已表达出来了的东西准确而完全地表达出来。(俄罗斯 费奥达罗夫)

(7)翻译是把一种语言的言语产物(话语),在保持内容不变的情况下改变为另一种语言的言语产物。(俄罗斯 巴尔胡达罗夫)

(8)翻译可以定义为是一种语言中介,通过它用译语创造出与原作在交际上等值的文本,而译文的交际等值表现为它在功能、内容和结构上与原作一致。(俄罗斯 科米沙罗夫)

(9)翻译是把一种语言(即源语)的信息用另一种语言(即译语)表达出来,使译文读者能得到原文作者所表达的思想,得到与原文读者大致相同的感受。(范仲英)

(10)翻译是把一种语言传达的信息用另一种语言传达出来,是使用不同语言的人进行交际,交流思想,达到互相了解的中介手段。(蔡毅)

(11)翻译:把已说出或写出的话的意思用另一种语言表达出来的活动。(《中国大百科全书·语言文字卷》1988 年)

(12)翻译是运用一种语言把另一种语言所表达的思维内容,准确而完整地重新表达出来的语言活动。(张培基等)

(13)翻译是译者将一种语言文字所蕴含的意思用另一种语言文字表述出来的文化活动。(王克非)

(14)翻译是把一种语言符号或信息编码表达的意义用另一种语言符号或信息编码表达出来的富有创造性的文化活动,它包括语内翻译、语际翻译和符际翻译。(曹明伦)

(15)翻译是以符号转换为手段,意义再生为任务的一项跨文化的交际活动。(许钧)

(16)翻译是文化符号系统之间进行的文化替换过程和结果。(王文华)

(17)翻译是译者将甲语文化信息转换成乙语文化信息并求得二者相似的思维活动和语际活动。(黄忠廉)

(18)翻译:把一种语言文字的意义用另一种语言文字表达出来(也指方言与民族共同语、方言与方言、古代语与现代语之间一种用另一种表达);把代表语言文字的符号或数码用语言文字表达出来。(《现代汉语词典》第5版)

(19)翻译(包括口译、笔译、同传与机译)是有文本参照的跨文化、跨语言的人类有目的的社会交际行为与活动。(杨自俭)

5.2 翻译理论

八备说 Eight Qualifications
案本 follow the source text closely
传神 lifelike
传统译论 traditional translation theories
达旨 paraphrase
得体 appropriateness
多元系统翻译标准 multi-system translation criteria
讹 e(deviation)
和谐说 theory of harmony
化境 Huajing (ultimate realm of transformation)
近似 approximation
似 similarity
三不易 three difficulties
三美 beautiful in sense, in sound, and in form
三似说 three likenesses
善译 perfect translation
舌人 interpreter
神似 alike in spirit; spiritual similarity
文与质 Wen vs. Zhi (refined and unhewn; literal quality and material quality)
五失本 five deviations from the original
信达切 faithfulness, expressiveness and closeness
信达雅 faithfulness, expressiveness and elegance
信与顺 faithfulness and fluentness
形似 alike in form; formal similarity
意似 alike in meaning; meaning similarity
科学翻译 science translation
科学翻译学 science translatology
译感 sense of translation
译师 translator; interpreter
中国翻译(研究) translation (studies) in China; Chinese translation (studies); Chinese-related translation (studies)
acceptability 可接受性
accuracy 准确
aesthetics of translation 翻译美学
applied translation studies 应用翻译学
appropriateness 得体
comprehension 理解
content 内容
conversing; conversion 转换
corpus-based translation studies 基于语料库的翻译研究
correspondence 对应
criteria of translation 翻译标准
descriptive translation studies 描写性翻译研究
direction of translation 翻译方向
dynamic equivalence 动态对等
equivalent effect 等效
equivalent translation 等值翻译
expression 表达
faithfulness 忠实
formal correspondence 形式对应
formal equivalence 形式对等
form 形式
functionalist translation theory 功能翻译理论
general translation studies 普通翻译学
hypotaxis 形合
interlanguage 中介语
knowledge of translation 翻译知识
levels of translation 翻译层次
linguistic translation 语言翻译
mental activity of translation 翻译心理活动
mental process of translating 翻译心理过程

models of translation 翻译模式
original language 原语
parataxis 意合
popular science translation 科普翻译
pragmatic translation 语用翻译
principles of translation 翻译原理
process of translation 翻译过程
pure translation studies 纯翻译学
receptor language 译语;目的语
receptor; receiver 读者;接受者
relevance translation theory 关联翻译理论
scientific and technological translation 科技翻译
shift 转换
Skopos Theory 目的论
source language 源语
source text 源文
special translation studies 特殊翻译学
style of translation 译风;翻译风格
style 风格
subject of translation 翻译主体
target language 译语;目标语
thoughts of translation 翻译思想
three principles of translation 翻译三原则
Tower of Babel 通天塔
transeme 译素
transformation process 转换过程
transformation 转换
translatability 可译性
translated literature 翻译文学
translating 翻译(行为)
translation criteria 翻译标准
translation criticism 翻译批评
translation culture 翻译文化
translation degree 翻译学位
translation equivalence 翻译对等
translation errors 翻译错误
translation experience 翻译经验
translation history 翻译史
translation language 翻译语言
translation major 翻译专业
translation on discourse level 语篇层翻译
translation on lexemic level 词层翻译
translation on phonemic level 词素层翻译
translation on phrase level 词组层翻译
translation on sentence level 句层翻译
translation on sentence-group level 语段层翻译
translation practice 翻译实践
translation psychology 翻译心理学
translation sociology 翻译社会学
translation studies 翻译研究
translation theory 翻译理论
translation thinking 翻译思维
translation unit 翻译单位
translation 译作;翻译(结果)
translatology 翻译学
translator; interpreter 译者
translator's competence 翻译能力
translatorial action 译者行为
universals of translation 翻译共性
untranslatability 不可译性
version 译本
views on translation 翻译观

5.3 翻译实践

编译 transediting; edited translation
变译 variety in translation; translation varieties; translation variation
参译 reference translation
阐译 explanatory translation
仿译 imitation-translation
分译 division; split translation
佛经翻译 Buddhistic translation
改译 modification plus translation; adaptation translation
汉译世界名著丛书 Library of Chinese Versions of World-noted Writings
汉译世界学术名著丛书 Library of Chinese Versions of World-noted Academic Writings
汉译西化 westernized translation; Europeanized translation
合译 combination translation
换译 exchange translation
减译 omission translation; reduction translation
零翻译 zero-translation

欧化 Europeanization
全译 full translation; complete translation
胜似 surpass
述评 review
死译 mechanical translation; awkward translation
缩译 abstract translation; condensed translation
相似 similarity
相似律 similarity law
洋泾浜 pidgin English
译场 workshops for translation
译评 translation and comment
译述 translation and report
译味 translating tastes
译写 translation and writing
译意 translating meaning
硬译 servile translation
摘译 selective translation
中式英语 Chinglish
转译 transfer
综述 summarized translation
abusive translation 滥译
auto translation 自译
back translation 回译
communicative translation 交际翻译
conference interpreting 会议传译
consecutive interpretation 交替传译
continual interpretation 连续翻译
domesticating translation 归化翻译
domestication 归化
drama translation 戏剧翻译
film and TV translation 影视翻译
foreignization 异化
foreignizing translation 异化翻译
formal translation 形译
free translation; liberal translation 意译
full equivalence 完全对应
interlingual translation 语际翻译
interpretation 口译
intersemiotic translation 符际翻译
intralingual translation 语内翻译
literal translation 直译
literary translation 文学翻译
mechanical translation 机械翻译
methods of translation 翻译方法
mistranslation 误译
on-line machine translation 网上机器翻译
oral interpretation 口译
paraphrase 释译
pedagogical translation 教学翻译
practical translation; applied translation; pragmatic translation 应用翻译
pragmatic approach 语用翻译法
prose translation 散文翻译
random translation 胡译;乱译
rewriting 改写
semantic translation 语义翻译
sight translation 视译
signed language translation 手语传译
simultaneous interpretation 同声传译
simultaneous interpreting 同声传译
software for translation 机译软件
specification 具体化
strategy of translation 翻译策略
total translation 完全/完整翻译
transcription 转写
transference 转移
transfer 转译
transformation 转换
translation copyright 翻译版权
translation course 翻译课
translation industry 翻译产业
translation of poetry 诗歌翻译
translation services 翻译服务
translation system 翻译系统
translation teaching 翻译教学
translation techniques 翻译技巧
translation test 翻译测试
translation textbook 翻译教材
translation tool 翻译工具
translation workshop 翻译工作坊
translationese syndrome 翻译征
translationese 翻译腔
translationism 翻译体
translator training; interpreter training 翻译培训
transliteration 音译
visual interpreting 视译

whispered interpreting 耳语传译
word-for-word translation 逐词译
written translation 笔译

5.4 缩略语

AAIT (美)亚特兰大口笔译工作者协会
AIIC 国际会议翻译协会
AITC 国际会议笔译协会
ALTF 法国文学翻译工作者协会
APETI 西班牙职业口笔译工作者协会
APT 职业翻译工作者协会
ASI 美国口译工作者协会
ASTI 瑞士口笔译工作者协会
ATA 美国翻译工作者协会
ATS 应用研究
CATTD (中国)翻译专业资格(水平)考试
CAT 机助翻译
CETA (美)汉英翻译协作组
C-E 汉英
CTIC 加拿大口笔译工作者理事会
DTS 描写翻译学
E-C 英汉
FIT 国际翻译工作者联合会
IAT (美)美洲国家翻译工作者协会
ISTA 印度科学翻译工作者协会
ITC (荷)国际翻译中心
MAT 机助翻译
MTI 翻译专业硕士(学位)
MT 机器翻译
NATIST 日本全国科技翻译协会
PTS 纯理论研究
SL 源语
ST 原文;原作;原语文本
TAPs 有声思维法
TA 翻译辅助
TC 翻译批评
TL 译语
TSC 日本翻译服务中心
TS 翻译研究
TT 译文;译作;译语文本
TT 译者培养

6 比读体悟

6.1 阿Q正传

The True Story of Ah Q

① 有一回,他似乎是姓赵,但第二日便模糊了,锣声镗镗的报到村里来,阿Q正喝了两碗黄酒,便手舞足蹈的说,这于他也很光彩,因为他和赵太爷原来是本家,细细的排起来他还比秀才长三辈呢。

① Once, he seemed to be named Zhao, but the next day there was some confusion about the matter again. This was after Mr. Zhao' son had passed the county examination and, to the sound of gongs, his success was announced in the village. Ah Q, who had just drunk two bowls of yellow wine, began to prance about declaring that this reflected credit on him too, since he belonged to the same clan as Mr. Zhao and by an exact reckoning was three generations senior to the successful candidate.

② 赵太爷愈看愈生气了,抢进几步说:"你敢胡说!我怎么会有你这样的本家?你姓赵么?"

② The more he looked at him, the angrier Mr. Zhao became. Advancing menacingly a few steps, he said, " How dare you talk such nonsense! How could I have such a relative as you? Is your surname Zhao?"

③ 阿Q并没有抗辩他确凿姓赵,只

③ Ah Q made no attempt to defend his right to the name

用手摸着左颊，和地保退出去了；外面又被地保训斥了一番，谢了地保二百文酒钱。知道的人都说阿Q太荒唐，自己去招打；此后便再没有人提起他的氏族来，所以我终于不知道阿Q究竟什么姓。

Zhao but rubbing his left cheek went out with the bailiff, once outside, he had to listen to another torrent of abuse. He then by way of atonement paid him two hundred cash. All who heard this said Ah Q was a great fool to ask for a beating like that. After this no further mention was made of Ah Q's ancestry, thus I still have no idea what his surname really was.

④ 他虽然多住未庄，然而也常常宿在别处，不能说是未庄人，即使说是"未庄人也"，也仍然是乖史法的。

④ Although he lived for the most part in Weizhuang, he often stayed in other places, so that it would be wrong to call him a native of Weizhuang. It would, in fact, amount to a distortion of history.

⑤ 我所聊以自慰的，是还有一个"阿"字非常正确，绝无附会假借的缺点，颇可以就正于通人。（鲁迅）

⑤ The only thing that consoles me is the fact that the character "Ah" is absolutely correct. This is definitely not the result of false analogy, and is well able to stand the test of scholarly criticism.（杨宪益、戴乃迭 译）

6.2《清华大学建校一百周年》

The Centenary Anniversary of Tsinghua University

清华大学始建于1911年，初期为清华学堂。在百年风雨历程中，清华的发展始终同国家的前途和民族的命运紧密相连，形成了"自强不息、厚德载物"的校训，"行胜于言"的校风，"严谨、勤奋、求实、创新"的学风和爱国奉献、追求卓越的光荣传统，培育出十七万名优秀人才，涌现出许多学术大师、兴国英才和治国栋梁，创造了大批高水平的研究成果。面向未来，清华大学按照综合性、研究型、开放型的办学定位，向着创建世界一流大学的奋斗目标不懈奋进，努力为中华民族的伟大复兴和人类文明的进步与发展作出更大的贡献。

Established in 1911, the institution was first called Tsinghua School. In the process of trials and hardships, the development of Tsinghua has been closely related to the future of China and the fate of the nation. The school motto of "Development of self in accordance with the celestial principle of consistency; Cultivation of amplitude in emulation of the earth's benevolent support of man and nature", the school style of "Action speaks louder than words", the study style of "Strict, diligent, practical, innovative" and the honorary tradition of patriotism, dedication, pursuit of excellence have been formed. 170 000 talents have been cultivated, a large number of academic masters, excellent talents and pillars who make the country prosperous have emerged in large numbers, and a huge quantity of high-level research achievements have been created. Facing the future, in accordance with the orientation to run the university in a comprehensive, research-oriented and open-style way, Tsinghua University makes unremitting efforts to reach the goal of becoming a world-class university, and make greater contributions to the great rejuvenation of the Chinese nation as well as the progress and development of human civilizations.

6.3 内容提要

Abstract

① 本书作者在整理缕析关学典籍的基础上，运用历史与逻辑相统一的原则和方法，着重探讨宋明理学思潮中关

① The author, on the basis of a through textual analysis of the literature of the Guan School, employs the principle and method of the unity of history ad logic. The focus of the study

学学派的形成、发展和终结的历史过程，主要剖析其领袖张载哲学的基本内容及其思辨逻辑，以求把握这一学派思想的显著特征及其与整个理学思潮发展的共同趋向。

is to present a critical inquiry into the formation, development and completion of the Guan School in Song-Ming Confucian thought. The main purpose is to investigate the basic content and the dialectic logic of the philosophy of Zhang Zai, the leader of the Guan School, for the sake of grasping the salient features of this particular school and the common tendencies of Song-Ming Confucian thought in general.

② 全书共分三部分。“总论”部分，辨析了关学思想的源流及其历史文化背景。“本论”部分，按照张载其学的逻辑进程，依次论证了张载确立“性与天道合一”的关学主题；张载追求“民物胞与”的大同理想和“孔颜乐处”的自由人格；张载以“天人合一”、“体用不二”的结构原则，构成了“气——道——性——心——诚”的哲学逻辑范畴体系。

② The book is divided into three parts. The prolegomenon sets forth the intellectual origins and the cultural and historical background of the thought of the Guan School. The main part of the book, according to the logical sequence of Zhang Zai's philosophy, demonstrates the following propositions: (1) the basic motif of the Guan School in Zhang Zai is thesis of "the unity of human nature and the way of Heaven", (2) Zhang Zai's quest for the ideal of the Great Harmony and for the free and easy personality as a result of "re-experiencing" the delight in life that Confucius and Yan Yuan had enjoyed, (3) Zhang Zai's construction of his categorical system, namely the philosophical logic of "vital force — the Way — human nature — mind-and-heart — sincerity", by the dual structural principles of "the unity of man and Heaven" and "the inseparability of substance and function".

③“附论”部分，考察了张载之后，北宋陷于“完颜之乱”、关学几乎“百年不闻学统”期间，以“道德性命之学”标宗的世俗化的全真道在关中崛然兴起，并炽传北方的思想动向，从这一侧面，展现出宋元整个中国传统思想走向“三教归一”的必然趋势；并把张载关学和整个宋时理学的基本精神，归总为对“天人合一”的理想人格的追求。至于元明以后作为宋时理学思潮的“关学”如何具体发展，作者留待《张载关学续论》一书中详论。(陈俊民)

③ The appendix discusses the emergence and rapid development of the this-worldly Taoist sect, the Complete Truth, with emphasis on "the Way, its power, nature and destiny", in the north in a period when the Northern Song was ruined by the Jurchens and the Guan School, for a hundred years, was not able to continue the transmission of its learning. From this angle, the book delineates the inevitable tendency of "Three Teachings in One" of the Song-Yuan intellectual developments. The author will study in detail the further growth of the Guan School in a sequel this book. (杜维明 译)

6.4 Hasty note

Dear Maria,

① This seems to be a busier week than usual after our 6 weeks away. It was nice of you to have a letter to greet me. Thank you, dear. May hasty note told you of my arrival.

② Last night I went to see your grandmother and dined with

匆匆留言

亲爱的玛丽亚：

① 我们分别六个星期了，这个星期似乎更忙一些。很高兴你能来信问候。谢谢你，亲爱的！匆忙中给你留言，希望告诉你我已到达。

② 昨晚，我去看探望了你奶奶，共

her. She is pretty well now and she told me she misses you very much. She hopes you'd better come back and have a short stay at home. Yet, I told her you are now very busy with your lessons. She told me to tell you that you must come back during Christmas holidays. Would that be possible?

进了晚餐。她现在身体不错。她说她很想你,希望你能回家住一阵子。不过,我跟她说你功课紧,她让我转告你圣诞节可要回家。你能回来吗?

③ No more now, dear Maria. Wish everything is well with you.

With love,

Mum

③ 亲爱的玛丽亚,就写到这儿。祝你一切顺心。

爱你的妈妈

(黄忠廉 译)

6.5 Luxury Hotel and Spa

豪华旅馆与温泉

① After a long day enjoying all that Three Castle Kingdom has to offer, a retreat to the elegantly Roman-themed Hotel and Spa is the perfect way to end the day. Whether guests are staying for a night or a week, they will never run out of things to do at this first class hotel resort. Set against the backdrop of a Roman palace and featuring amenities such as a 5 star restaurant, specialty shopping, themed dining, hiking trails and a world-class spa and fitness center, this one-of-a-kind resort is a "must do" for anyone visiting Three Castle Kingdom.

① 在三堡王国畅游一日后,回到风格高雅的古罗马式旅馆休闲,享受温泉水疗,不失为一日游乐的高潮。无论是小住一夜,或是逗留一周,这个一流的旅店区绝不会让游客兴致索然。这一休闲区以罗马宫殿为背景,设施配套齐全,有五星级餐厅、精品专卖商店、主题饮食饭店,还有供你健步的小道,高级的温泉水疗,一流的健身设施,任何一位来三堡王国游乐的人都应来此一游。

② For those looking for fun and adventure far beyond the wildest dreams of their imagination, you need not look further than Three Castle Kingdom — A Landmark Park. Whether guests are spending the day visiting the magnificent castle realms of the Theme Park, celebrating the night away at the Entertainment/Retail District, cooling off at the themed Water Park or relaxing at the magnificent Spa Resort, there's no limit to the world of discovery and adventure that awaits. With its wide variety of entertainment and leisure choices, this truly unique development offers choices for everyone and is certain to become the yardstick by which all others are measured.

② 假若游客想要冲破想象的极限,去寻欢乐,觅险境,绝不用舍近求远,由里程碑公司承担建造的三堡王国保你称心满意。游客白天可在主题公园历险,晚上能在零售休闲区娱乐,在主题水上公园嬉水乘凉,在温水浴池让身心为之一爽,新发现、新探险,惊喜接踵而来。想娱乐、要休闲,节目层出不穷,此园独步天下,游人各得其所。三堡王国为休闲娱乐业定下了看齐的标准。(叶子南 译)

6.6 Of Studies

谈读书

① Studies serve for delight, for ornament, and for ability. Their chief use for delight, is in privateness and retiring; for ornament, is in discourse; and for ability, is in the judgement and disposition of business. For expert men can execute, and perhaps judge of particulars, one by one; but the general counsels, and the plots and marshalling of affairs, come best from those that are learned. To spend too much time in studies is sloth; to use them

①读书足以怡情,足以傅彩,足以长才。其怡情也,最见于独处幽居之时;其傅彩也,最见于高谈阔论之中;其长才也,最见于处世判事之际。练达之士虽能分别处理细事或一一判别枝节,然纵观统筹、全局策划,则舍好学深思者莫属。读书费时过多易惰,

too much for ornament, is affectation; to make judgement wholly by their rules, is the humour of a scholar. They perfect nature, and are perfected by experience: for natural abilities are like natural plants, that need proyning by study; and studies themselves do give forth directions too much at large, except they be bounded in/by experience. Crafty men contemn studies, simple men admire them, and wise men use them; for they teach not their own use; but that is a wisdom without them, and above them, won by observation. Read not to contradict and confute; nor to believe and take for granted; not to find talk and discourse; but to weigh and consider. Some books are to be tasted, others to be swallowed, and some few to be chewed and digested; that is, some books are to be read only in parts; others to be read, but not curiously; and some few to be read wholly, and with diligence and attention. Some books also may be read by deputy, and extracts made of them by others; but that would be only in the less important arguments, and the meaner sort of books; else distilled books are, like common distilled waters, flashy things.

② Reading maketh a full man; conference a ready man; and writing an exact man. And therefore, if a man write little, he had need have a great memory; if he confer little, he had need have a present wit; and if he read little, he had need have much cunning, to seem to know that he doth not. Histories make men wise; poets witty; the mathematics subtile; natural philosophy deep; moral grave; logic and rhetoric able to contend. Abeunt studia in morse Nay there is no stand or impediment in the wit, but may be wrought out by fit studies: like as diseases of the body may have appropriate exercises. Bowling is good for the stone and reins; shooting for the lungs and breast; gentle walking for the stomach; riding for the head; and the like. So if a man's wit be wandering, let him study the mathematics; for in demonstrations, if his wit be called away never so little, he must begin again. If his wit be not apt to distinguish or find differences, let him study the schoolmen; for they are cymini sectores. If he be not apt to beat over matters, and to call up one thing to prove and illustrate another, let him study the lawyers'cases. So every defect of the mind may have a special receipt. (Sir Francis Bacon)

文采藻饰太盛则矫，全凭条文断事乃学究故态。读书补天然之不足，经验又补读书之不足，盖天生才干犹如自然花草，读书然后知如何修剪移接；而书中所示，如不以经验范之，则又大而无当。有一技之长者鄙读书，无知者羡读书，唯明知之士用读书，然书并不以用处告人，用书之智 不在书中，而在书外，全凭观察得之。读书时不可存心诘难作者，不可尽信书上所言，亦不可喉咙为寻章摘句，而应推敲细思。书有可浅尝者，有可吞食者，少数则须咀嚼消化。换言之，有只须读其部分者，有只须大体涉猎者，少数则须全读，读时须全神贯注，孜孜不倦。书亦可请人代读，取其所作摘要，但只限题材较次或价值不高者，否则书经提炼犹如水经蒸馏，淡而无味矣。

② 读书使人充实，讨论使人机智，笔记使人准确。因此不常做笔记者须记忆特强，不常讨论者须天生聪颖，不常读书者须欺世有术，始能无知而显有知。读史使人明智，读诗使人灵秀，数学使人周密，科学使人深刻，伦理学使人庄重，逻辑修辞之学使人善辩：凡有所学，皆成性格。人之才智但有碍，无不可读适当之书使之顺畅，一如身体百病，皆可借相宜之运动除之。滚球利睾肾，射箭利胸肺，慢步利肠胃，骑术利头脑，诸如此类。如智力不集中，可令读数学，盖演题须全神贯注，稍有分散即须重演；如不能辨异，可令读经院哲学，盖是辈皆吹毛求疵之人；如不善求同，不善以一物阐证另一物，可令读律师之案卷。如此头脑中凡有缺陷皆有特药可医。（王佐良 译）

6.7 推荐读物

(1)曹明伦，翻译之道：理论与实践，河北大学出版社 2007 年版。

(2)郭著章等，翻译名家研究，湖北教育出版社 1999 年版。

(3)黄忠廉等，译文观止，语文出版社 2009 年版。

(4)刘士聪,汉英英汉美文翻译与鉴赏(英汉对照),译林出版社2008年版。
(5)刘重德,英汉翻译例句词典,湖南文艺出版社1999年版。
(6)马红军,翻译批评散论,中国对外翻译出版公司2000年版。
(7)思果,译道探微,中国对外翻译出版公司2002年版。
(8)杨平编,名作精译(《中国翻译》英译汉选萃),青岛出版社2010年版。
(9)余光中,余光中谈翻译,中国对外翻译出版公司2002年版。
(10)袁锦翔,名家翻译研究与赏析,湖北教育出版社1990年版。

练习 7 课后练习

7.1 分析题

(1)试用英汉互译例子分析全译的定义。
(2)品读窍门,试用其一对英汉互译特点做拓展性探讨。
(3)试用你最欣赏的译文分析全译的艺术。

7.2 实训题

7.2.1 二马

她,真是她!在街那边走呢!他心里跳得快了,腿好象在裤子里直转圈。赶她!但是,跟她说什么呢?请她吃饭?现在已经三点了,那能还没吃午饭!请喝茶,太早!万一她有要紧事呢,耽误了她岂不……万一她不理我呢?……街上的人看我呢?万一她生了气,以后永不理我呢?都快赶上她了,他的勇气没有了。

7.2.2 **Remarks by US President Obama**

① The same can be said of the relationship between our two countries. Shanghai, of course, is a city that has great meaning in the history of the relationship between the United States and China. It was here, 37 years ago, that the Shanghai Communique opened the door to a new chapter of engagement between our governments and among our people.

② However, America's ties to this city — and to this country — stretch back further, to the earliest days of America ' s independence. In 1784, our founding father, George Washington, commissioned the Empress of China, a ship that set sail for these shores so that it could pursue trade with the Qing Dynasty. Washington wanted to see the ship carry the flag around the globe, and to forge new ties with nations like China. This is a common American impulse — the desire to reach for new horizons, and to forge new partnerships that are mutually beneficial.

7.3 思考题

(1)纵观古今中外有关翻译的比喻,谈谈你对翻译的认识。
(2)收集古今中外有关翻译的各种定义,并按一定范畴进行归类。

(3)翻译欣赏与翻译批评有何区别?
(4)查阅相关文献,了解给翻译下定义有哪些方式?
(5)设想一下,人类翻译是如何产生的?
(6)全译有何特征?在笔译和口译中分别如何体现?
(7)双向全译教程比单向全译教程有哪些优势和劣势?
(8)英译汉回译可以发现英语的什么特点?
(9)汉译英回译可以发现汉语的什么特点?
(10)“意一言多”如何反映可译性?
(11)“意一形多”如何反映全译的选择艺术?
(12)全译中形义矛盾是如何产生的?如何解决?
(13)英译汉如何体现趋简性?
(14)汉译英如何体现趋繁性?
(15)汉英互译的繁简问题与翻译腔有何关系?
(16)为什么不能小觑翻译技能的培养?
(17)什么是全译技能习得?如何习得?
(18)什么是全译技能学得?如何学得?

第2课 娱乐休闲

导 译

随着科技进步、经济发展,人类生活水平不断提高。伴随激烈竞争与高压工作,人们更加关注健康问题,关注生活的内容和质量。休闲娱乐是现代人生活内容之一,能放松精神、提供交流、缓减压力,具有重要意义。在美国大学里,休闲娱乐作为应用性课程,深受青睐。

译事广阔,既包含关乎全球发展的政经领域,也包含引领人类前进的科学技术,更包含知识百科的娱乐生活。娱乐休闲,就是因休而后闲,先娱而知乐,即休息时自娱之活动,可分为读书看报、视听欣赏、体育锻炼、美酒美食、访亲会友、消费购物、旅行游艺、数码网络等等。伴随我国经济腾飞,对外交往需求剧增,娱乐休闲是当前经济发展的重要支柱,是翻译需求量较大的热门领域,其中视听欣赏、美酒美食、消费购物、旅行游艺、数码网络分别涉及影视、饮食、商业、旅游、IT、交通等重要产业。

休闲娱乐多为生活之事,文风宜轻松幽默,不应过于学术;既要避免术语化,也不应平淡无奇。生活之事本应译之稍易,但各国民众乐之不同,好之有异,又为语言的转换增添障碍。因此,互译时既要把握语表相似,又要关注语义、语用的一致,看似容易,却陷阱颇多,唯有多辨多查,方可体会个中滋味。

1 课前练笔

1.1 金陵十三钗

① 张艺谋导演的最新电影《金陵十三钗》根据华人女作家严歌苓同名小说改编,并以南京大屠杀作为故事的背景和中心。贝尔饰演的殡葬师约翰·米勒去一家天主教堂

出席牧师的葬礼,日本人占领南京古城后,一群妓女和女学生躲入教堂避难。米勒为自己的艳遇窃喜,时常与其中会说英文的玉墨(倪妮饰演)调情谈笑。玉墨明白日本人不会攻击白人,所以要求米勒帮助她和同伴逃离南京,乔治也请求米勒保护那些无辜的女学生。

② 张艺谋颇具娱乐性地处理了这些奇怪个体之间的紧张关系,甚至展现了愤怒女学生和尤物宾客之间的激烈争吵。

1.2 Weekend in America

① In the United States Monday is the beginning of the workweek; it is the day most Americans like least. It is not surprising then that the day they like most is Saturday. Saturday is the end of the workweek; it is the beginning of the weekend.

② Life is different on the weekend; most Americans take care of their house, car or garden. They sleep later in the morning. They enjoy the feeling that the time seems to move more slowly. The week is for things you have to do; the weekend is for things you want to do. Some people may get in a car and go for a drive in the country. They like to take part in a sports activity outdoors. And on Saturday night they might go to a public eating place or a movie.

③ Automobile maker Henry Ford was the first major employer in the United States to establish a workweek of 5 days. He did that in 1926. Henry Ford thought that if the working people had more free time they would spend more money, something good for the economy. By 1940 it had become common for most Americans to work 8 hours a day, 5 days a week. Today the lives of most Americans are organized that way: 5 days of work or school followed by 2 days of rest. For many people Saturday night is the highpoint of the weekend and the week.

1.3 American Food

① What is "American food"? At first you might think the answer is easy as pie. To many people, American food means hamburgers, hotdogs, fried chicken and pizza. If you have a "sweet tooth", you might even think of apple-pie or chocolate chip cookies. It's true that Americans do eat those things. But are those the only kind of vittles you can find in America?

② Except for Thanksgiving turkey, it's hard to find a typically "American" food. The United States is a land of immigrants. So Americans eat food from many different countries. When people move to America, they bring their cooking styles with them. That's why you can find almost every kind of ethnic food in America. In some cases, Americans have adopted foods from other countries as favorites.

2 课前批评

2.1 亨氏西餐菜谱

大长今泡菜蟹肉比萨配青芥、辣蛋黄酱和海苔碎

步骤:1. 在比萨饼上涂抹比萨酱,然后放上洋葱、蟹柳、青椒、泡菜和芝士碎。2. 把比萨放入烤炉烘烤,至饼底焦黄松脆,芝士完全融化即可拿出。3. 把青芥与亨氏蛋黄酱混合,挤在比萨饼上。4. 撒上揉碎的海苔即可。

Kimchi and Crab Meat Pizza with Wasabi Mayonnaise and Crushed Seaweed

Cooking Method: 1. Spread pizza sauce on pizza dough, then put on onion, crab stick, green bell pepper, kimchi and cheese crush. 2. Bake the pizza till the dough brown and crispy. 3. Mix the wasabi and Heinz Mayonnaise and pour on top of the pizza. 4. Sprinkle crushed seaweed on the pizza.

烧烤牛肉串配菠萝茄汁饭

步骤:1. 把牛肉丁用亨氏烧烤酱腌 2 小时。2. 牛肉和迷你香肠串好后烤至牛肉熟。3. 炒米饭并放入玉米粒、红腰豆,用亨氏番茄沙司、盐、胡椒调味。4. 轻煎一下菠萝片放在米饭上,边上配烤好的牛肉香肠串,用新鲜牛至叶装饰。

BBQ Beef and Mini Sausage Skewer with Glazed Pineapple-tomato Rice

Cooking Method: 1. Marinate diced beef with Heinz BBQ sauce for 2 hours. 2. Skewer the beef and mini sausage, grill till beef cooked. 3. Saute rice with sweet corn and kidney bean, seasoning with tomato sauce, salt and pepper. 4. Fry pineapple and put on top of the rice. Serve with beef and sausage skewer and garnish with fresh oregano. (亨氏西餐菜谱实例)

2.2 WALL-E

Disney and Pixar join forces for this computer-animated tale about a wide-eyed robot that travels to the deepest reaches of outer space in search of a new-found friend. The year is 2700, and planet Earth has long been inhabitable. For hundreds of years, WALL-E has been taking out the trash, and collecting precious knick-knacks in order to stave off the boredom of his dreary routine. Little does WALL-E realize that he has recently stumbled onto a secret that could save planet Earth, and once again make the ravaged planet safe for all mankind. When highly advanced search robot EVE makes friends with WALL-E and realizes the value of

《机器人总动员》

由迪斯尼和皮克斯倾力打造的该电脑动画讲的是,一个大眼睛的机器人进入遥远的外太空搜寻新生物的故事。那是 2700 年,地球这个星球已经很长时间没人居住了。几百年以后,WALL-E 被派出去清理垃圾,除此之外,他还收集一些人造宝贝来打发日复一日不断重复的枯燥时光。小 WALL-E 意识到,他已经被一个能够拯救地球却再一次制造了对全人类的安全都

his remarkable discovery, she excitedly races back to let the humans know that there's hope for their home planet after all.

有威胁的秘密困惑着。当高科技搜索机器人 EVE 和 WALL-E 成为朋友时，她意识到了他的值得注意的发现。她兴奋地想飞回地球告诉人类：他们的星球还有希望。（花茶 译）

3 全译知识 翻译分类

翻译分类包括二分法和多分法。

3.1 二分法

二分法是非此即彼的分类法，以对象有无某一属性为标准，分出 A 与 B，A 与 B 构成一对范畴。如人工翻译简称"人译"，相应的是非人译，后者命名为机译，二者构成一对范畴。二分法可以多侧面地构建翻译类型系统，如：以翻译主体为准可分为人译与机译；以翻译的工具性为准可分为口译与笔译；以译作与原作的相似度为准可分为全译与变译；以翻译中形义的转化程度为准可分为直译与意译；以所译材料的情感性与实用度为准可分为文艺翻译与实用翻译；以方向性为准可分为外译与内译，内译指从外语译成母语的内向性翻译，外译指从母语译成外语的外向性翻译。

3.2 多分法

根据翻译的多个要素或特点进行分类，可形成多分法。实用翻译可分为社科翻译、科技翻译、经贸翻译、外事翻译等；变译可分为摘译、编译、译述、缩译、综述、述评、译评、改译、译写、阐译、参译、仿作等；文艺翻译可分为小说翻译、诗歌翻译、散文翻译、戏剧翻译、歌曲译配、影视译制等；口译可分为交传、接传和同传等。

4 全译窍门

4.1 影名画龙点睛

电影是现今影响力较大的休闲方式，一部好电影既有跌宕起伏的剧情，先进华丽的视效，更有画龙点睛的片名，因此译名的质量往往直接左右票房成绩。

从标准层看，电影译名应画龙点睛。步骤有三，内容、美感和吸引力，三者序不可逆，内容最重，兼顾美感，吸引力次之。第一，有内容，即影名表现影片信息，做到标题与内容统一，否则有故弄玄虚之嫌。如 True Lies，直译为《真实的谎言》贴切恰当，香港译本却为《魔鬼大帝》，实在匪夷所思。第二，有美感。电影是艺术，影名要蕴含艺术美。试比较 The Bridges of Madison County 的两个译名《廊桥遗梦》和《麦迪逊郡之桥》。其中，后者忠有余，而美不足；前者忠稍欠，但美充裕，留人遐想，也更符合影片的文艺性。第三，有吸引力。电影为观众而作，译名也应考虑观众效应，采用能吸引译语观众的词句。如因国人崇尚侠气，译者爱屋及乌，将诸如 Spider Man（《蜘蛛侠》）之类的英雄影片一律用"侠"字吊人胃口。

从操作层看，影名译法有四：直译、音译、意译和混合译。方法无谓好坏，唯达标准者最佳。直译最常见，如：Dances with Wolves（《与狼共舞》）。音译常译人名、地名，如 Harry Potter（《哈利波特》）。需要变通时用意译，如：Home Alone（《小鬼当家》）。大多数采用混合译，如：Waterloo Bridge（《魂断蓝桥》）。

从问题层看，译名切忌三点。第一，机械直译，如 First Wives Club（《发妻俱乐部》），被误译为《大老婆俱乐部》。第二，片面夸大，刺激露骨，如世界名片 The Shawshank Redemption（《肖申克的救赎》）被译作《刺激 1995》，丢尽身份。第三，文化偏颇，如《扬子江风云》，英译 Storm Over the Yangtze River，但"风云"与 storm 文化意义截然不同，有失偏颇。

4.2 菜名引人浮想

中华美食是世界三大菜系（中、法、土）之一，历史悠久，典故颇丰。中西食文化差异巨大，观念上，西餐重营养，中餐重感性。命名上，西餐菜名简单罗列，标出主、辅料及烹调方法，朴素实用；中餐菜名浪漫写意，蕴含民俗风情，追求引人浮想。语言差异加之巨大的文化差异，菜名翻译难上加难，常有笑话产生，如：口水鸡 slobbering chicken（流口水的鸡）、童子鸡 chicken without sexual life（没有性生活的鸡）、夫妻肺片 the couple's lung（夫妇二人的肺）等，面对此景逃之不及，何谈胃口？

从汉译角度看，中餐菜名考究，西餐汉译，应入乡随俗。从英译角度看，要传播中华饮食文化，菜名应尽量体现浪漫写意、引人联想之特点。实现引人浮想，步骤有三。第一，准确传达食谱内容，如：酸辣汤 hot & sour soup。第二，彰显审美效应，勾起食欲，如：hamburger 汉堡包。汉堡包是译界妙译，既有 ham 与"汉"的谐音，又有"包"（包子）的达意，其"堡"（城堡）字更给人巨大无比之感，实在诱惑十足。第三，揭示饮食文化的内涵，传播民族饮食文化和烹饪艺术，如：北京烤鸭 Beijing roast duck，东坡肉 Dongpo pork。

方法上，菜名翻译主要有三种方法。第一，直译，有四种情况：译口感，如酸辣白菜 sweet and sour Chinese cabbage；译做法，如：回锅肉 twice-cooked pork slices in brown sauce；译材料，如：椒盐排骨 spare ribs with pepper and salt；译地名人名，如：扬州炒饭 Yang-chow fried rice。第二，意译。对含有典故，从菜名无法分析材料、做法的，可意译，如：全家福 stewed assorted meat。第三，混合译。可用单一译法者少之又少，大多数译名实为多种译法的综合运用，如：夫妻肺片 pork lungs in chili sauce。

4.3 品牌彰显华贵

品牌翻译的艺术不仅限于双语转换，更在于彰显其经济价值。品牌翻译应彰显华贵，内涵有三：音韵美、意境美、简约美。

音韵美，指发音响亮、节奏分明、富有乐感，给人以听觉上美的享受，如 Coca-Cola（可口可乐）就是绝译，不但保留了英文音韵美，而且充分运用汉语双音和叠韵特点，不仅声音和谐悦耳，而且促人联想：清爽、快乐，可口亦可乐。意境美，指通过词汇的文化意境让人产生对美好事物向往的联想，如著名彩妆品牌：Lancôme 兰蔻，“兰蔻”既是音译，又让人联想到豆蔻年华的美丽少女，意境之美跃然纸上。简约美，指简洁明快，避免生僻，易于上口，便于记忆，如 Top of the Town 上品，国人自古有崇“上”之俗，“上品”仅以简单二字即传达了服饰品牌的高质量，体现了简约之美，给人以华贵之感。

4.4 娱乐消息抓人眼球

娱乐消息作为新生的新闻类型，以其轻松有趣的风格吸引了读者，成为现代人休闲娱乐的重要内容。面对海量资讯，译文能否抓住眼球尤为重要。娱乐消息要抓人眼球，方法有四：简洁明了、广用修辞、创造新词、雅俗共赏。

简洁明了意指多用精练短句。出于节约篇幅、提高阅读效率的实际需要，译者应采取一切手段使语言精练，如 Germany kill off England's golden generation. 德国绝杀英格兰“黄金一代”。译文无一费字，读来酣畅淋漓。广用修辞指运用双关、比喻、反讽、押韵、幽默、夸张等修辞手法提高标题趣味性，如 After election stuffing, Obama pardons turkey. 奥巴马感恩节前赦免火鸡。想想作为世上独一无二超级大国之总统，在白宫举行仪式“赦免”的不是战俘、囚犯，而是两只火鸡，确是别有风味。创造新词包括杜撰词及旧词新意，创造新词具有新鲜性、启发性、吸引力强等诸多优点。社会发展需要新的语言，新闻消息就是新词诞生的重要来源，它为语言补充血液，为时代注入新鲜气息，如 screenager（屏幕青少年），screenager 是杜撰新词，源于 screen（屏幕）和 teenager（青少年）的结合，新意十足，意为从小看电视、玩电脑长大的 80 后或 90 后一代。译文新词“屏幕青少年”乍看不解其意，再思可感其形象贴切，回想成长环境变化给孩子带来的巨大影响，对现实的担忧与对作者、译者的赞同交杂一起，不免惆怅。雅俗共赏可使娱乐消息雅俗共存，有幽默性、时尚性、亲切性等特点，如：I am not talking about the castles in the air, the donkey's carrot. 我并不是在谈论空中楼阁，叫大家望梅止渴。castles in the air 与“空中楼阁”对应，可直译；而 donkey's carrot 若直译为“驴的胡萝卜”未免让读者费解，意译“望梅止渴”通俗易懂，为读者熟悉，能够有效地抓住读者。

4.5 曲名传韵达意

音乐无国界，一直以来，人们似乎只陶醉于歌曲优美的旋律，对于曲名的翻译却不够重视，误译、拙译比比皆是。纵然尚无定论，但万变不离其宗，曲名翻译应达意传韵，这是曲译的根本要求。达意传韵，方法有四：音韵相近、传达曲意、追求典雅、简洁对仗。

首先，音韵相近。曲名是音乐语言，曲名翻译要从其音律、韵律和节律角度出发，尽可能使曲名融入歌曲旋律之中，使其具有可唱性，如奥斯卡金曲 Casablanca（《卡萨布兰卡》），电影《音乐之声》中的经典儿童歌曲 Do-Re-Mi（《多-来-咪》），都是尽量体现原语音韵的典型。其次，传达曲意。全译要求忠实，如果实在是囿于客观条件，可适当调整，但绝不能成胡译借口，直译需是首选，如：Lemon Tree（《柠檬树》），Hotel California（《加州旅馆》），River of Babylon（《巴比伦河》）。再次，追求典雅。翻译是艺术，不是简单依葫画瓢。典雅，既要高雅，又要有趣，不能只顾辞藻华丽，忽视读者共鸣，如 Five Hundred Miles 若直译《五百英里》便不似歌名，若译《归乡路漫漫》更符艺术特点。这五字，平仄调配，且具音乐重叠之美，朗朗上口。最后，简洁对仗，指借助词法、句法和修辞手段，以简明扼要、客观精辟的文字形式概括歌曲的主要内容，使读者能一览而知其大概，悟其主旨，如美国著名黑人女歌手 Whitney Huston 的 The Greatest Love of All 译成汉语可用两个字《至爱》，若译成《最伟大的爱》或《至高无上的爱》则稍显冗长，不够简练，破坏了传韵之美。

5 话题词汇

5.1 读书看报

跋 afterword
编者 editor
长篇小说 novel
党报 the Party paper
盗版 pirate
短篇小说 short story
扉页 flyleaf
封面 cover
《光明日报》Guangming Daily
画报 pictorial magazine
奖状 certificate of merit
经典著作 classic
科幻小说 science fiction
路透社 Reuter's News Agency
美联社 the Associated Press
年鉴 yearbook
前言 foreword
书评 book review
文集 collection of essays
文选 anthology
小报 tabloid
小人书 picture-book
新华社 Xinhua News Agency
序 preface
增刊 supplement
《中国日报》China Daily
中篇小说 novelette
16-mo 16 开本
32-mo 32 开本
64-mo 64 开本
annual 年刊
author 作者
back cover 封底
back number 过期杂志
bestseller 畅销书
book review 书评
cartoon, comics 漫画
circulation 发行量
column 栏
commentator 评论员
contents 目录
copyright 版权
cover girl 封面女郎
criticism 评论
daily 日报
deluxe edition 精装本
digest 文摘
editorial 社论
editor 编辑
exclusive news 独家新闻
extra 号外
fortnightly 半月刊
freelancer 自由撰稿人
front cover 封面
headline 标题
home news 国内新闻
hot news 最新新闻
library national 国家图书馆
media 媒体
monthly 月刊
news agency 新闻社
original edition 原版

paperback 平装本
periodical 期刊
press 出版社
printing 印刷
publication 出版
quarterly 季刊
revised edition 修订版
royalty 版税
scandal 丑闻
the first edition 初版
the front page 头版
the second edition 再版
weekly 周刊
world news 国际新闻

5.2 视听欣赏

壁画 mural painting
故事片 feature film
地方戏 regional opera
电子琴 electone
二胡 Erhu
粉笔画 chalk drawing
国画 Chinese painting
话剧 modern drama
纪录片 documentary film
交际舞 ballroom dance
京剧 Beijing opera
流行乐 pop music
伦理片 ethical film
民乐 folk music
默片 silent film
皮影戏 shadow show
书法 calligraphy
水墨画 ink and wash painting
素描 lineal drawing
文艺片 literary film
武侠片 swordsman film
扬琴 dulcimer
译制片 dubbed film
影片长度 footage
预告片 trailer
actor 男演员
actress 女演员
adaptation 改编
anthem 国歌
banned film 禁映影片
cast 阵容
choir 合奏;合唱
comedy 喜剧
conductor 乐队指挥
director 导演
distributor 发行人
double; stand-in 替身演员
duet 二重唱
extra; walker-on 临时演员
film festival 电影节
lyrics 歌词
montage 剪辑
movie star 电影明星
opera 歌剧
orchestra 乐队
premiere 首映式
produce 制片
properties 道具
quartette 四重唱
rhythm 节奏
scene 场景
shooting 摄制
slow motion 慢镜头
solo 独奏;独唱
sound effects 音响效果
special effects 特技
staff; stave 五线谱
star, lead 主角
studio 制片厂;摄影棚
tragedy 悲剧
trio 三重唱

5.3 访亲会友

出身 origin
代 generation
独生子 only child
队友 teammate
非婚生子 natural child
夫妇 couple
孤儿 orphan
后代 offspring
婚姻 marriage
继父 stepfather
继母 stepmother
朋友 pal
亲戚 relative
亲属 relative
情妇 mistress
室友 roommate
私生子(女) bastard child
团队 team
兄弟之情 brotherhood
血缘 blood relationship
养父母 foster parents
养子(女) adopted child
姻亲关系 affinity
游伴 playmate
友爱 fraternity
远表兄妹 distant cousin
岳父 father-in-law
岳母 mother-in-law
曾孙 great-grandson
曾孙女 great-granddaughter
acquaintance 熟人
buddy 好友
camping 宿营
colleague 同事
companion 伴侣
company 同伴
cooking 烹调
date 约会的异性
doorbell 门铃
drawing 画画
first interview 初次会面
greeting 寒暄问候
guest 客人
hiking 长途徒步旅行
hobby 业余爱好
host 主人
interests 兴趣爱好
jogging 慢跑
letter of introduction 介绍函
living room 客厅
mate 伴侣
on business 因公
play bridge 打桥牌
play cards 打扑克
play chess 下棋
reception room 接待室
swimming 游泳
take pictures 拍照
to knock at the door 敲门
to leave a message 留言
visiting hours 会客时间
writing fiction 写小说

5.4 消费购物

埃斯普利特 Esprit
艾格 Etam
百丽 Belle
报摊 newsstand
茶馆 teahouse
单价 unit price
鄂尔多斯 Erdos
服装店 clothes shop
集市 bazaar
价签 price tag
杰克琼斯 Jack&Jones
利郎 Lilanz
零售价 retail price
马克华菲 Mark Fairwhale

批发价 wholesale price
肉店 butcher's shop
水果摊 fruit stand
文具店 stationary shop
五金 hardware
洗衣店 laundry
小吃店 snack bar
眼镜店 optician's shop
药店 pharmacy
真维斯 Jeanswest
athletic equipment 体育用品
bracelet 镯子
brooch 胸针
buyer 买主;买方
cashier's desk 收银处
change 零钱
client; customer 顾客;客户
coin 硬币
consumer 消费者;用户
cosmetics 化妆用品
counter 柜台
dealer 经销商
detergent 洗衣粉
discount 打折
ear ring 耳环
fabrics 纺织品
fake 假的
fixed price 定价
free of charge 免费
genuine 真品
hair drier 吹风机
handbag 女手提包
hanger 衣挂
imitation 仿制品
jewelry, jewels 首饰;珠宝
knapsack 背包
lighter 打火机
lipstick 口红;唇膏
manufacturer 制造商
men's wear 男装
nail scissors 指甲剪
necklace 项链
note 纸币
ornaments 装饰品
pearl 珍珠
perfume 香水
razor 剃刀
retailer 零售商
salesman 售货员
sale 销售
shampoo 洗发香波
shelf 货架
shopping centre 商业中心区
show window 橱窗
sold out 售空
stall, stand 售货摊
suitcase 手提箱
to wrap up 包装
tooth brush 牙刷
tooth paste 牙膏
travelling bag 旅行包
trunk 大衣箱
underwear 内衣
wholesaler 批发商
women's wear 女装
zipper 拉链

5.5 数码网络

超级本 Ultrabook
第三代移动通信技术 3G
电子墨水 E Ink
耳机 headset
平板电脑 tablet
山寨 copycat
数码相机 digital camera
投影机 projector
网吧 net bar
网恋 cyber romance
网络出版 online publishing
网络管理员 network administrator
网络化 networking
网络经济 cyber economy
网络摄像机 webcam
网民 netizen

网上交易平台 online trading platform
网友 net friend
audio 音频
backup 备份
bandwidth 带宽
binary 二进制
bit 比特
broad band 宽带
bug 错误
byte 字节
click 点击鼠标
compatibility 兼容
copy 复制
courseware 课件
cut 剪切
database 数据库
driver 驱动程序或驱动器
e-mail 电子邮件
fiber optics 光纤
gateway 网关
hacker 黑客
hard disk 硬盘
hardware 硬件
image 图像
internet 互联网
keyboard 键盘
local area network 局域网
memory 储器;内存
modem 调制解调器
mouse 鼠标
multimedia 多媒体
M 兆
net; network 网络
operating system 操作系统
paste 粘贴
pixel 像素
printer 打印机
program 程序
resolution 分辨率
router 路由器
scanner 扫描仪
server 服务器
software 软件
T 太
video 视频
virus 病毒
wide area network 广域网
workstation 工作站

5.6 缩略语

AA 奥斯卡金像奖
AD 广告
AI 人工智能
ATM 自动提款机
BBC 英国广播电台
BBS 电子公告板
B2C 商家对顾客(电子商务模式之一)
BF 男朋友
BGM 背景音乐
BLOG 博客
CATV 有线电视
CBA 中国男子篮球职业联赛
CBD 中央商务区
CD 光盘
CPU 中央处理器
DISCO 迪斯科
DIY 自助
DJ 唱片骑士
DV 数字视频
EA 电子艺界游戏公司
E-Book 电子书
E-Commerce 电子商务
E-Learning 在线学习
EMS 特快专递
EQ 情商
GBA 新一代掌上游戏机
GB 任天堂手提游戏机
GF 女朋友
GPS 全球定位系统
HDTV 高清数字电视
IC 集成电路
ID 身份证
Intel 美国英特尔公司
ISO 国际标准化组织

IT 信息产业
LAN 局域网
LCD 液晶显示屏
MTV 音乐电视
NBA 美国男子篮球职业联赛
NB 笔记本型计算机
P2P 点对点下载技术
PC 计算机
PNP 即插即用
SFX 特技效果
TRK 音轨
USB 通用串行总线
VCR 录像机
VOA 美国之音
WAN 广域网
WWW 万维网
XM 圣诞节

体悟 6 比读体悟

6.1 西式幽默

① 学院请来一位洋教师。一天,洋教师出题,考查学生们用洋文作文的水准,题目极简单,随便议论议论校园内的一事一物,褒贬皆可。中国学生很灵,一挥而就,洋教师阅后,评出了最佳作文一篇,学生们听后大为不解,这种通篇说谎的文章怎么能被评为“最佳”?原来这篇作文是写学校食堂。写作文的学生来自郊区农村,人很老实,胆子又小,生怕得罪校方,便不顾真假,胡编乱造,竭力美化,唱赞歌。

② 洋教师说:“这文章写得当然好,而且绝妙无比,你们听……”“我们学校最美的地方,不是教室,不是操场,也不是校门口那个带喷水的小花坛,而是食堂。瞧,玻璃干净得几乎叫你看不到它的存在……”“如果你不小心在学校食堂跌了一跤,你会惊奇地发现你并没跌跤,因为你身上半点尘土也没留下;如果你长期在学校食堂里工作,恐怕你会把苍蝇是什么样子都忘了……”洋教师又停住,舌头“得”地弹一声,做一个怪脸说,“听呀,还要多幽默,我简直笑得念不下去了。”

Western Humor

① Our institute employed an English teacher. One day he set the students an essay to see how well they could write in English, the topic being "A Comment on Campus Life" — either complimentary or critical. That was simple. The Chinese students, quick at writing, finished it off at one go and turned it in in no time. Having gone through the students' essays the teacher picked one that he thought was the best. When he read it out to the students. They were perplexed. Of all the essays, why did he like this one better? Not a single word of it was true. The article was about the institute cafeteria and the author was a peaceable and timid student from a village in the outskirts. Taking care not to offend the institute authorities he had made up a high-sounding story in praise of the cafeteria, regardless of the realities.

② "This is certainly a good essay," he explained. "Absolutely matchless! Just listen..." He picked up the composition and began. "The most beautiful spot on campus is not the classroom building nor the sports-ground, nor the lawn with the fountain at the gate; the most beautiful spot on campus is our cafeteria. Look! The window-panes are so clean that you scarcely notice there is glass in them..." "If you were not careful enough," he continued, "and had a fall on the floor, you would be amazed to find that you had not fallen at all because you did not get a single particle of dust on your clothes. If you had been working in the cafeteria long enough, you would have forgotten what a fly looks like." He stopped, his tongue clicking rapidly to show admiration. Working up a funny expression on his face, he went on, "Listen, please! Do you think anyone else could have made it more humorous?" He laughed so heartily that he could hardly continue. (刘士聪 译)

6.2 元宵节的由来

The Origins of the Lantern Festival

① 元宵节是我国民间最隆重的节日之一，民间"正月十五闹元宵"，在我国已有悠久的历史。

① Falling on the fifteenth day of the first lunar month, the Lantern Festival is one of the grandest celebrations among the common people in China, and the custom of merry making on this night has a long history.

② 元宵节始于两千多年前的汉代。汉高祖刘邦死后，吕后篡权。吕后死后，汉文帝刘恒在周勃、陈平等人铲除诸吕势力后，登基做了皇帝。因为戡平诸吕的日子是正月十五日，所以，每逢这天晚上，汉文帝都要微服出宫，到街市上游玩，"与民同乐"，以示纪念。在古代，夜同宵，正月又称元月，于是，汉文帝就将正月十五定为元宵节，这一夜称作元宵，又称元夜、元夕。此说是否确凿还难有定论，但将正月十五看作一个祭祀天帝、祈求福佑的吉日，这倒是从汉朝开始的。

② The custom originated from the Han Dynasty (206 BC — AD 220) 2,000 years ago. After the death of Liu Bang, the first emperor of the Han Dynasty, Queen Lu usurped power. After her death, with the help of the ministers Zhou Bo and Chen Ping, Emperor Wen removed the supporters of the queen and ascended to the throne. For the reason that he got rid of Queen Lu's influence on the fifteenth day of the first lunar month, Emperor Wen would go out incognito on this day every year and stroll about the streets, amusing himself with the common people outside his palace. In ancient times, night was called xiao and the first lunar month was known as the yuan (meaning beginning or first in Chinese) month, so Emperor Wen set this night as yuanxiao, which was also named yuanye and yuanxi (both ye and xi mean "night"). Although there is not enough evidence to support this story, it is from the Han Dynasty that the date was regarded as the lucky time to worship the Heaven and pray for its blessings. (王善江 译)

6.3 Coffee Culture

咖啡文化

① Coffee has a history dating back to at least the 9th century. Originally discovered in Ethiopia, coffee beans were brought into the Middle East by Arab traders, spreading to Egypt, Yemen, Persia, Turkey, and North Africa by the 15th century. Muslim merchants eventually brought the beans to the thriving port city of Venice, where they sold them to wealthy Italian buyers. Soon, the Dutch began importing and growing coffee in places like Java and Ceylon, and the British East India Trading Company was popularizing the beverage in England. Coffee spread across Europe and even reached America.

① 咖啡的历史可以追溯到9世纪。最初埃塞俄比亚人发现了咖啡豆，阿拉伯商人将其带往中东地区，并在15世纪传播到埃及、也门、波斯、土耳其和北非。接着穆斯林商人把这些豆子带往繁荣的港口城市威尼斯，并将其卖给富有的意大利商人。很快，荷兰引进咖啡豆并在爪哇、锡兰等地开始种植。大不列颠东印度贸易公司将这种饮料在英国普及开来。经过这一系列的不断传播和发展，咖啡遍及欧洲，并最终来到美国。

② Where there has been coffee, there has been the coffee house. Coffee houses have traditionally served as centers of social

② 哪里有咖啡，哪里就有咖啡屋。咖啡馆自古以来就是供人休息、聊天、

interaction, places where people can come to relax, chat, and exchange ideas.

交流思想和社会交往的中心。

③ Although coffee houses today continue to serve their traditional purpose as lively social hubs in many communities, they have noticeably adapted to the times. It has become extremely common to see someone sitting at a Starbucks listening to music or surfing the web on his or her laptop. Coffee stores today also maintain fairly identifiable, yet unique aesthetic: wooden furniture and plush couches, paintings and murals drawn on walls, and soft-lighting combine to give coffee shops the cozy feeling of a home away from home.

③ 虽然如今的咖啡馆仍照传统在很多地方扮演社会活动中心的角色,但它也在与时俱进。在星巴克,常见人们用笔记本听歌、上网。至今咖啡馆仍然保持其清晰独特的审美品味:木制的家具、舒适的沙发、墙上的彩绘壁画、柔和的灯光,所有的一切,给咖啡馆营造了舒适安逸的氛围,仿佛置身于自己的另一个家中。

④ Coffee, it would seem, is more than just a drink. From early on after its inception, coffee has been tied closely with cultural trends and has been indicative of important periods in history. It was poured into the cups of the giants of the French Enlightenment as they changed the course of human thought, it was placed on the backs of Brazilian slaves in the era of Imperialism, it's fragrance was in the air as Beat poets like Kerouac and Ginsberg wrote of their alienation, and it is here now as the world continues to change in this era of technology and globalization. So the next time you enjoy your latte or your ice-cold caramel frappuccino, appreciate the fact that you are connected to countless numbers of people spanning many different cultures and eras through your love of that wondrous beverage: coffee.

④ 可以说,咖啡已不仅仅是一种饮料。自始至终,它都和文化发展紧密相连并成为历史重要时期的象征。咖啡在法国启蒙运动巨匠的杯中缓缓流动,正是他们改写了人类的思想进程;咖啡是帝国主义时代巴西奴隶肩上沉重的负担;咖啡在"垮掉派诗人"凯鲁亚克和金斯堡描写孤独寂寥的空气中肆意飘香。如今,它依旧在科技和全球化的时代里随着世界不断发展改变。因此下回,在享受热拿铁或冰卡布奇诺时,你可以想象,你正穿越文化和时空的界限与无数伟人进行思维的交流碰撞,因为你们共同热爱这美味的饮料:咖啡。(《双语时代》用例)

6.4 Companionship of books

与书为伴

① A man may usually be known by the books he reads as well as by the company he keeps; for there is a companionship of books as well as of men; and one should always live in the best company, whether it be of books or of men.

① 书如同人,都可成为伴侣;读其书,如同读其人;同样,观其朋友,也如同观其人。无论以书为友还是以人为伴,每个人都应有自己的知己。

② A good book may be among the best of friends. It is the same today that it always was, and it will never change. It is the most patient and cheerful of companions. It does not turn its back upon us in times of adversity or distress. It always receives us with the same kindness; amusing and instructing us in youth, and comforting and consoling us in age.

② 一本好书可以成为我们最好的朋友。昨天如此,今天亦如此,这一点亘古不变。书是我们最有耐心和最使人愉悦的朋友。无论身处逆境,还是遭遇苦难,它都不会背弃我们。它总是怀着善意接纳我们,年轻时,它给予我们快乐并指引我们;年老时,它给予我们心灵的慰藉并鼓励我们。

③ Men often discover their affinity to each other by the mutual love they have for a book just as two persons sometimes

③ 因为对一本书的热爱,我们发现彼此之间的亲密无间。书是更为真

discover a friend by the admiration which both entertain for a third. There is an old proverb, "Love me, love my dog." But there is more wisdom in this: "Love me, love my book." The book is a truer and higher bond of union. Men can think, feel, and sympathize with each other through their favorite author. They live in him together, and he in them.

实和高雅的联系纽带。人们通过自己最喜爱的作者,交流思想,产生心灵的共鸣。他们与作者同在,作者也与他们同在。

④ A good book is often the best urn of a life enshrining the best that life could think out; for the world of a man's life is, for the most part, but the world of his thoughts. Thus the best books are treasuries of good words, the golden thoughts, which, remembered and cherished, become our constant companions and comforters.

④ 一本好书往往是记载生命的最好的瓮,它蕴藏着生命中思想的瑰宝。因为思想占据了生活的大部分。因此,最好的书是言语之佳句,思想之瑰宝,最值得去怀念,去珍藏,是我们永远的伴侣和慰藉者。

⑤ Books possess an essence of immortality. They are by far the most lasting products of human effort. Temples and statues decay, but books survive. Time is of no account with great thoughts, which are as fresh today as when they first passed through their author's minds, ages ago. What was then said and thought still speaks to us as vividly as ever from the printed page. The only effect of time have been to sift out the bad products; for nothing in literature can long survive but what is really good.

⑤ 书是永恒不朽的。它是人类奋斗最为经久不衰的成果。庙宇和雕像可以被毁,而书却永存。无论何时,那些伟大的思想,都永远鲜活,如同首次涌上作者的心头。当时的言谈思想跃然纸上,依然向我们侃侃而谈。取其精华,去其糟粕,这是时间的唯一作用;因为只有真正优秀的东西,才能在文学中永存。

⑥ Books introduce us into the best society; they bring us into the presence of the greatest minds that have ever lived. We hear what they said and did; we see them as if they were really alive; we sympathize with them, enjoy with them, grieve with them; their experience becomes ours, and we feel as if we were in a measure actors with them in the scenes which they describe.

⑥ 书指引我们迈入最优秀的领域。它把我们带到历史上所有伟大人物面前。我们欣赏他们的言谈与举止;看到他们,如同看见一个鲜活的生命。我们与它产生共鸣,同享快乐,分担忧伤;我们经历它所遭遇的,如同演员在它描绘的舞台上演戏。(刘佩吉 译)

6.5 推荐读物

(1)英语沙龙

(2)浩瀚,娱乐休闲英语高频话题,水利水电出版社 2008 年版。

(3)李雪,娱乐休闲英语口语大全,机械工业出版社 2012 年版。

(4)www.rd.com

(5)www.hollywood.com

7 课后练习

7.1 分析题

(1)查阅资料讨论翻译的分类。

(2)品读窍门,试用其一分析某一译文精彩或不足之处。

(3)结合"比读体悟"内容,分析休闲娱乐翻译的轻松译笔。

7.2 实训题

7.2.1 歌词《因为爱情》

给你一张过去的CD,听听那时我们的爱情,
有时会突然忘了,我还在爱着你。
再唱不出那样的歌曲,听到都会红着脸躲避,
虽然会经常忘了,我依然爱着你。
因为爱情　不会轻易悲伤,所以一切都是幸福的模样。
因为爱情　简单的生长,依然随时可以为你疯狂。
因为爱情　怎么会有沧桑,所以我们还是年轻的模样。
因为爱情　在那个地方,依然还有人在那里游荡、人来人往。

7.2.2 Customs on Invitations on Britain

If you are invited to someone's home to have a meal it is usual to take some flowers or a box of chocolates. It is not usual to take a bottle of wine unless you know your host well. Although flowers and chocolates are quite acceptable it would be very nice if you could take something from your country. It is different if you are invited to a party, and it also depends on what kind of party it is. Many parties these days are " bring a bottle" parties. Unless your host is very rich then a bottle of wine is always welcome if it is a big party of say 30 or more people. Ask whether or not you should bring a bottle when you are invited if you aren't sure.

7.3 思考题

(1)影视作品名称汉译有何特点?

(2)中华美食英译有何规律?

(3)结合所译和比读材料,分析娱乐休闲文本的中枢翻译单位。

(4)请描写娱乐休闲文本的微观翻译过程?

(5)酒品汉译采用何种策略?

(6)娱乐休闲全译是否具有程式化特点?

(7)娱乐休闲文本中英文缩略语是否需要汉译?

(8)结合所译和比读材料分析直译与意译孰为娱乐休闲文本的主要策略?

(9)网络新词全译规律是什么?

(10)电子产品名称汉译有何特点?

(11)娱乐新闻汉译如何反映时代特点?

(12)休闲文本如何译出闲情?

第3课 医疗保健

导 译

“医疗”一词在近些年才出现，是为了与国际接轨而新生的字眼，之前大多使用“治疗”一词，如今“医疗”也包括“保健”的内容。

从广义上说，医学英语属于科学英语的范畴，它主要描述和讨论医学科学事实，提交医学研究成果，传授医学知识等，具有独特的词汇体系和语法特征，如词汇量大、一词多义、复合长句多、很少使用人称等特点。互译时，应遵循“忠实”与“通顺”这两个主要标准。而要达到这两个标准，译者必须具备一定的专业词汇，了解医学英语的句式特点以及相应的医学专业知识，辅之以必要的翻译技巧，并进行大量的实践。只有这样，才能在翻译时做到应对自如，使译文层次分明、文字准确、含义清楚。中医文本如何英译，如何处理英语医学文本的长句，如何区分并翻译各种进口药品名称，如何理解医学英语复杂的术语，本课提出了一些比较实用的解决方法。

练笔 1 课前练笔

1.1 亚健康

我们通常所说的“没病”，“身体挺好”这些概念，远远不是真正的健康的标准。为了引起人们对健康标准的重视，近年来，有些医学专家针对“没病就是健康”的传统观念提出了“亚健康”的概念。亚健康状态指的是，一个人的身体机能虽然没有明确的疾病表现，但是平时却缺乏活力，对外界的适应能力已有不同程度的减退。这就是一种不完全健康的表现。亚健康人群在生理上常表现为易感冒、易疲劳、易不适，这里所说的“不适”包括消化不良、睡眠不佳以及心理方面的不适，如自我控制能力下降，对外界事物反应过敏，内心平衡难以满足，情绪不稳定、容易波动等。

1.2 The No. 1 Health Problem in America

① The main impression growing out of twelve years on the faculty of a medical school is that the No. 1 health problem in the U. S. today, even more than AIDS or cancer, is that Americans don't know how to think about health and illness. Our reactions are formed on the terror level. We fear the worst, expect the worst, thus invite the worst. The result is that we are becoming a nation of weaklings and hypochondriacs, a self-medicating society incapable of distinguishing between casual, everyday symptoms and those that require professional attention.

② The most significant single statement about health to appear in the medical journals during the past decade is by Dr. Franz Ingelfinger, the late and former editor of the New England Journal of Medicine. Ingelfinger noted that almost all illnesses are self-limiting. That is, the human body is capable of handling them without outside intervention. The thrust of the article was that we need not feel we are helpless if disease tries to tear away at our bodies, and that we can have greater confidence in the reality of a healing system that is beautifully designed to meet most of its problems. And even when outside help is required, our own resources have something of value to offer in a combined strategy of treatment.

1.3 Aging

① Aging can be defined as the progressive deterioration, with the passage of time, of the structure and functions of a mature organism. This ultimately leads to the death of the organism. Either the progressive loss of function makes the organism less able to withstand infectious disease or, often, the failure of some vital organ precipitates the death of all the rest.

② What are the symptoms of aging? Decreased muscular strength, decreased lung capacity, decreased pumping of blood from the heart, decreased urine formation in the kidney, and decreased metabolic rate are just a few of the many body changes which occur with aging.

2 课前批评

2.1《中华人民共和国药品管理法》(节选)

第一条　为加强药品监督管理,保证药品质量,增进药品疗效,保障人体用药安全,维护人民身体健康和用药的合法权益,特制定本

Law of the People's Republic of China on the Administration of Drugs

Article 1 This law has been drawn up in order to strengthen drug control and administration, ensure the quality of drugs, enhance the efficacy of drugs, guarantee safe drug use and safeguard the physical

法。

health of the people.

第二条　国务院卫生行政部门主管全国药品监督管理工作。

Article 2　The State Council department responsible for health administration is the body in charge of national drug control and administration.

第三条　国家发展现代药和传统药,充分发挥其在预防、医疗和保健中的作用。

Article 3　The State develops both modern medicines and traditional medicines, and fully utilizes them in the prevention and treatment of disease, as well as in health care.

第四条　开办药品生产企业必须由所在省、自治区、直辖市药品生产经营主管部门审查同意,经所在省、自治区、直辖市卫生行政部门审核批准,并发给《药品生产企业许可证》。

(本章中引用的部分是1984年9月20日第六届全国人民代表大会常务委员会第七次会议通过的版本,该版本于2001年2月28日第九届全国人民代表大会常务委员会第二十次会议得到修正。)

Article 4 The establishment of a drug-producing enterprise must be examined and agreed to by the department in charge of drug production and handling in the province, autonomous region or municipality under the direct control of the Central Government in which the enterprise is located. It shall be subject to examination and approval by the department responsible for health administration in the province, autonomous region or municipality under the direct control of the Central Government, which shall issue the "Drug-Production Enterprise License".

2.2 Isoket

① For long-term and/or emergency treatment of angina pectoris.

② **Composition**: sosorbide dinitrate 20 mg per tablet, with prolonged action.

③ **Indications**: Angina pectoris, especially the so-called "effort angina"; prevention and subsequent treatment of myocardial infarction. Angina pectoris vasomotorica, a form induced by central nervous disorder, is not affected.

④ **Contra-indication**: Glaucoma.

⑤ **Dosage**: One tablet of Isoket retard to be taken with water and without chewing in the morning after breakfast, and one in the evening before retiring; this will protect the patient from attacks of angina pectoris during both the day and the night. If an attack does occur, half a tablet should be chewed and then swallowed, whereby an immediate action is produced.

硝酸异山梨酯

① 本品用于心绞痛长期治疗或急救使用。

② 成分:本品每片含硝酸异山梨酯20毫克,长效剂型。

③ 适应证:用于治疗心绞痛,尤其适用于"劳累性心绞痛";本品也适用于心肌梗死的预防与治疗;本品对由于中枢神经紊乱引起的心血舒缩性心绞痛不起作用。

④ 禁忌证:青光眼。

⑤ 用法与用量:每日早餐后与晚睡前服用,每次1片异舒吉控释片,以水吞服,无需咀嚼,可在白天与夜晚有效地避免心绞痛的发作。如心绞痛已发作,咀嚼并咽下本药品半片,症状可立即得到缓解。

⑥ Packings of 60 tablets ⑥ 包装:60 片/包
⑦ Made in Germany ⑦ 德国制造

3 全译知识 全译极似律

全译极似律即全译的内在规律,指译文与原文极度接近或相像的规律。

译作与原作不可能求"等",追求"等值"或"等效"只是理想,因受主体主观、客体客观、文化、思维、信息传播、社会历史等制约,全译只求与原作尽可能接近,达到极似。

极似分近似和胜似两层次。近似指译作模拟原作内容与形式的逼真程度。得原文近似在全译中随时可见,是全译的主体。胜似也是极似的内涵之一,即译作超过原作,遇上译语写作高手,译作文字超胜原作偶或发生。极似结构又可分为意似、形似和风格似。

3.1 意似

意似即内容的极似,是全译求极似的基础或起点。翻译旨在让译语读者了解原语文化。有时求得意似即达交际目的。如:

① It is better to present one image in a lifetime than to produce voluminous words.

【原译】:一生与其写书万卷,不如只呈现一个意象。

【试译】:与其终生著书万言,不如创造意象一个。

It is better X than Y 类句式常用来生成劝诫性警句,劝诫人们权衡轻重,具有一定的警醒作用。原文是浓缩结构,也是比况结构,明显地含有比较级的优胜比较;更是强调结构,因为使用了典型的强调句式"强调标记+结论项";汉译句式"与其 X,不如 Y"正好与之对应,"与其""不如"常置于前后两句句首,成对而立。原文的 X 与 Y 均用不定式短语进行比较,汉译的 X 与 Y 也多用动宾短语两相对照,因此原译的"一生"应移位"与其"之后,原译的"一个意象"应改为"意象一个",以与"万卷"对应。这一调整以及原译其他地方的修改旨在使译文与原文达至最大程度的意似。

3.2 形似

形似即形式的极似,是在意似的基础上尽量保持原文的宏观和微观结构,达到译文与原文形式的极似。形式是内容诸要素统一起来的结构或表现内容的方式,是阐述内容的,由结构、体裁、语言等因素构成的总和。形似并非硬搬原文形式因素,而是保留语序或用译语相应手段再现或复制原文某些特殊表达。如:

② An individual grape looks like a blood cell and research today shows that grapes are a wonderful heart and blood vitalizing food.

【原译】:每一颗葡萄看起来都像一个血液细胞,现代科学研究也都证明葡萄能极大增强心脏和血液的活力。

【试译】:每颗葡萄都像血细胞,当今研究表明葡萄是绝好的强心与活血食物。

除了 research 与 today 换译、vitalizing 语义上一分为二分别与 heart 和 blood 搭配外,其他词均为对译,整个句子以直译为主,与原文达至形似。

3.3 风格似

风格似即风格的极似。全译以意似为主，形似辅之，二者统一可得风格似。有意似无形似，难求风格似；风格似寓于形似之中，换言之，风格似要求基于意似追求形似。形似包括宏观结构的似和微观结构的似。宏观结构如结构、体裁等在全译中一般不会改变，所以风格似集中于语言层面的似，即微观结构的似。如：

③ Poetry is what gets lost in translation.

【原译】：诗歌是翻译中所失去的东西。

【改译】：诗者，译之所失也。

【试译】：诗即译中所失。

本例是美国诗人弗罗斯特的名言，poetry 在此多指诗性或诗意。原译传达了原文意义，达到了意似，但不简练。改译将 what gets lost 和 in translation 换译，整个句子是主谓对应，求得了意似；另外，用“者……也……”表判断，文体上比原文古雅，达意而不得体。试译意似兼形似，融上述二者之优长，尤其是“诗”与“失”首尾相应，给人印象更深，完成了名言化过程，也通俗易懂。

4 全译窍门

4.1 化繁为简

译文烦琐是比较突出的问题，如何化繁为简，现说两法。

第一，去掉可有可无的词。汉语有些词在上下文中意思明显，英译不必出现。如“教育事业”的“教育”本为事业，只译作 education 即可。又如：

① 肝主身之筋膜。

【原译】：The liver controls the tendons and membranes of the body.

【改译】：The liver controls the tendons.

② 人体是一个统一的有机体，它是由脏腑、组织和许多器官组成。

【原译】：The human body is a united organic wholeness. It is composed of solid organs and hollow organs, tissues and many organs.

【改译】：The human body is an organic entirety, composed of viscera, tissues and many other organs.

例①，“筋膜”可用 tendon 统而译之，membranes 可省；tendon 自然在人体内，of the body 也可省。例②，原译不必用 united，已含在 organic 里，用过去分词作状语，从而省略 it is；“脏腑”可直译为 viscera，solid organs 与 hollow organs 均可省去。再如：

③ 导致疾病的原因是多种多样的。The causes of diseases are various.

④ 饮食、劳动和休息，是人类生存和保持健康的必要条件。Food, work and rest are essential to human existence and health.

⑤ 血病的表现，一般分为出血、瘀血和血虚。Blood disorders are generally divided

into hemorrhage, blood stasis and hemopenia.

第二,用词代语,是简化译文的良方。汉译英时常用表示动作和状态的短语。其实,在很多情况下可用副词代替,不但表达准确,而且行文简练。如:

⑥ 津液有滋润和濡养人体组织器官的生理功能。

【原译】:The body fluid has the **physiological functions** of moisturizing and nourishing human tissues and organs.

【改译】:**Physiologically**, the body fluid moisturizes and nourishes all tissues and organs.

⑦ 在病理情况下,血液和津液之间也多相互影响。

【原译】:**Under pathological circumstances**, blood and body fluid often affect each other.

【改译】:**Pathologically**, blood and body fluid often affect each other.

4.2 追根溯源,明确词义

医学英语具有专业性强、词汇量大、结构复杂的特点,给医学翻译者造成了较大的障碍。许多词乍看犹如"当头棒喝",其实,若能对医学英语的构词规律有所了解,许多"高难"词均可不攻自破。现说两种比较特殊的构词方法。

希腊语、拉丁语的词素在医学英语中占有很大比例,蕴含着丰富的词根、词缀,通过组合可形成大量的描述复杂的医学现象与医学概念的词汇。如:cardio 意为"心,与心脏有关的",可派生出许多与之有关的词:cardiogram 心电图,cardiomyopathy 心肌病,cardiovascular 心血管的。

医学英语有大量的冠名术语,或纪念为医学事业作出贡献的科学家,由其姓名及发现或发明等构成;或根据希腊罗马神话神名冠名;或根据地名冠名;或源于文学作品等。通常采取"音译 + 意译"和意译方法,如:Meniere's syndrome 美尼尔氏综合征,Gram's method 革兰氏染色方法,Parkinson's syndrome 帕金森氏综合征,Achilles bursa 跟腱囊,narcissism 恋己癖,Tularemia 土拉病菌,Mediterranean anemia 地中海贫血,Andes disease 安第斯山地病。

4.3 巧译定语从句

医学英语除了词汇复杂外,也常用长句,定语从句的出现频率远远高于其他从句。定语从句汉译有两种方法:定语前置;断句,重复先行词或用代词代替先行词。还有一种较为实用的办法,即把定语从句译成其他关系从句。如:

⑧ The disease, which may occur at any age, is most frequent in early adult life. 此病虽可发生于任何年龄,但以年轻人最为常见。

⑨ The sick child who had been given the medicine soon fell asleep. 病孩服药后,很快就入睡了。

⑩ The most important symptom of tetanus is trismus, a painless spasm of the masseter muscles which causes difficulty in opening the mouth and masticating. 破伤风最重要的早期症状为牙关紧闭,即咀嚼肌无痛性痉挛,引起张口和咀嚼困难。

定语从句汉译时,文中与被修饰成分之间都构成了其他逻辑关系,读来自然,符合汉语表达习惯。

4.4 进口药品翻译策略

根据各国药典规定,药品名称包括化学名称、通用名称、商品名称以及习惯用名等。消费者最常接触的是药品的商品名。明确药品命名原理,采用适当译法,对药品的营销至关重要。

化学名称 即根据国际纯化学与应用化学联合会的命名规则,对某一特定化学结构的命名。汉译时采用中英文名对应的原则,如 3a,7p Dihydroxy-5p-Cholanoic acid 译为"3a, 7p 二羟基 5p 胆烷酸";2-Methyl-1-hexanol 译为"2－甲基－1－乙醇"。有时还应注意习惯的化学命名方式,如:sodium bicarbonate 译作"碳酸氢钠",而非"重碳酸钠";Adenosine Triphosphate 应译为"腺苷三磷酸",而非"三磷酸腺苷"。

通用名称 即药品的法定名称。药品使用通用名称,即同一处方或同一品种的药品使用相同的名称,有利于国家对药品的监督管理。汉译时应遵循以音译为主、意译为辅的原则。音译如:Nitrendipine 尼群地平,Rotundine 罗通定,Amcacin 阿米卡星,Bumetanide 布美他尼。意译如:Cholic Acid 胆酸,Tetracyline 四环素,Tryptophan 色氨酸,Xylitol 木糖醇。

商品名称 即药品生产厂商为树立品牌形象而编制的、具有类似商标性质的合法的名称,但不是唯一名称。不同企业的同一药品,通常具有不同的名称。生产企业为了给消费者留下深刻印象,更多采用创造词,如 Axid(消化性溃疡病药),Forane(麻醉药),都是英语中没有的词。正因其随意性,汉译方法较前两种更加灵活,但必须贯彻我国《药品商品名称命名原则》,同时具备以下几个标准:简洁新颖、好听好记、大众接受性,还应辅之以简朴美、音韵美和意境美。如抗真菌感染药物 Daktarin 译为"达克宁",看似平常,却达意悦耳。音译又如:Sigmart 喜格迈,Estracyt 艾去适,Fontien 复先安,Lantus 来得时。意译又如:Suprane 优宁,Crestor 可定,Minidiab 灭糖尿,Natulan 疗治癌,Uraly 消石素。有时还可采取音意合译,如:Neo-Octin 新握克丁,Medemycin 麦迪霉素。有时以音译为原则,选择谐音的汉字,既表音又表意,音意结合,如:Doriden 多睡丹,Webilin 胃必灵,Legalon 利肝隆。

5 话题词汇

5.1 医疗机构

病案室 record room
病理科 pathology department
病房 ward
创伤外科 traumatology department
儿科病房 pediatric ward
儿科重症室 pediatric intensive care unit
放射科 X-ray department
妇产科 obstetrics and gynecology department
供应室 supply-room
骨科 orthopedics department
挂号处 registration office
贵宾候诊室 VIP waiting room
候诊室 reception room
护理部 nursing department

护士办公室 nurse office
护士站 nursing station
矫形外科 orthopedic surgery department
精神病科 psychiatry department
蜡疗科 wax-therapy room
门诊部 out-patient department
门诊手术中心 outpatient surgical center
泌尿科 urology department
脑外科 thoracic surgery department
抢救室 resuscitation room
人流休息室 rest room for induced abortion
神经科 neurology department
神经外科 neurosurgery department
肾脏科 nephrology department
手术室 operation room
输液室 transfusion room
外科病房 surgical ward
外科治疗室 surgery therapeutic room
外科重症室 surgical intensive care unit
小儿科 pediatrics department
新生儿重症室 neonatal intensive care unit
血清实验室 serological laboratory
眼科 ophthalmology department
营养部 nutrition department
整形外科 plastic surgery
治疗室 therapeutic department
admitting office 住院处
anesthesiology department 麻醉科
audiometric room 测听室
bacteriological laboratory 细菌实验室
biochemical laboratory 生化实验室
blood bank 血库
cardiology department 心脏病科
central laboratory 中心实验室
clinical laboratory 临床实验室
color ultrasonic room 彩超室
consultation room 诊察室
consulting room 诊室
coronary care unit 心脏重症室
cystoscopy room 膀胱镜室
delivery room 分娩室
dental department 牙科
department of anus & intestine surgery 肛肠外科
department of cardiac surgery 心脏外科
department of cerebral surgery 胸外科
department of endocrinology 内分泌科
department of endoscope 内镜区
department of general surgery 普通外科
department of hepatobiliary surgery 肝胆外科
department of infectious diseases 传染病科
department of internal medicine 内科
department of physiotherapy 理疗科
department of plastic surgery 医学整形科
department of rheumatism 风湿科
department of surgery 外科
department of traditional Chinese medicine 中医科
department of venereology 性病专科
dermatology department 皮肤科
diet-preparation department 配膳室
disinfection-room 消毒室
dispensary; pharmacy 药房
doctor's office 医生办公室
dressing room 换药室
electrocardiogram room 心电图室
electroencephalogram room 脑电图室
electrotherapy room 电疗科
emergency observation room 急诊观察室
emergency operation room 急诊手术室
emergency room 急诊室
ENT(ear-nose-throat)department 耳鼻喉科
fetal monitor room 胎心监护室
fibrescope room 纤维镜室
gastroscope room 胃镜室
geriatrics department 老年病专科
heliotherapy room 光疗科
hematology department 血液科
hemodialysis room 血透室
hepatology department 肝病专科
hydrotherapy room 水疗科
induced abortion room 人工流产室
in-patient department 住院部
intensive care unit 重症室
isolation room 隔离室
labor room 待产室
laboratory of immunology 免疫室
medical intensive care unit 内科重症室

medical ward 内科病房

mortuary 太平间

5.2 医务人员

产科医师 obstetrician
儿科医师 pediatrician
放射科医师 radiologist
骨科医师 orthopedist
挂号员 registrar
护理部主任 head of the nursing department
护士长 head nurse
化验员 laboratory technician
矫形外科医师 plastic surgeon
泌尿外科医师 urologist surgeon
内科医师 physician
神经外科医师 neurosurgeon
实习护士 student nurse
实习医师 intern doctor
消毒员 sanitation worker
眼科医师 ophthalmologist
药剂医师 pharmacist
助产师 midwife

住院医师 resident doctor
专科医师 specialist
anaesthetist 麻醉科医师
assistant nurse 卫生员
assistant pharmacist 药剂医师
associate chief physician 副主任医师
attending doctor 主治医师
chief physician 主任医师
controller 总务科长
dentist 牙科医师
dermatologist 皮肤科医师
dietician 营养科医师
doctor for tuberculosis 结核科医师
E. N. T. doctors 耳鼻喉科医师
epidemiologist 流行病医师
general practitioner 全科医师
gynecologist 妇科医师

5.3 常见疾病

白内障 cataract
白血病 leukemia
鼻炎 rhinitis
肠炎 enteritis
低血糖 hypoglycemia
动脉硬化 arteriosclerosis
耳鸣 tinnitus
肝炎 hepatitis
高血压 hypertension
肩周炎 scapulohumeral periarthritis
颈椎病 cervical spondylosis
酒精中毒 alcoholic intoxication
阑尾炎 appendicitis
痢疾 dysentery
流感 influenza
疟疾 malaria
贫血 anemia
乳腺癌 cancer of breast
弱视 amblyopia

糖尿病 diabetes
色盲 color blindness
胃溃疡 gastric ulcer
胃炎 gastritis
心绞痛 angina pectoris
血友病 hemophilia
咽炎 pharyngitis
营养不良 malnutrition
早产 premature birth
支气管炎 bronchitis
中风 apoplexy
abortion 流产
acidosis 酸中毒
anaphylaxis 过敏症
angiitis 脉管炎
angioma 血管瘤
asthma 哮喘
carcinoma of esophagus 食管癌
arrhythmia 心律失常

cardiac failure 心力衰竭
cardiomyopathy 心肌病
cervicitis 宫颈炎
cirrhosis 肝硬化
dislocation of joint 关节脱位
dystocia 难产
gout 痛风
infertility 不育症
iron deficiency anemia 缺铁性贫血
measles 麻疹
myocardial infarction 心肌梗死
nephritis 肾炎
osteoporosis 骨质疏松症
pneumonia 肺炎
pneumothorax 气胸
prostatitis 前列腺炎
renal failure 肾(功能)衰竭
rheumatic fever 风湿病
scarlet fever 猩红热
septicemia 败血症
syphilis 梅毒
tachycardia 心动过速
tumour 肿瘤
typhoid 伤寒
cerebral thrombosis 脑血栓
cerebral hemorrhage 脑出血
concussion of brain 脑震荡
epilepsy 癫痫
meningitis 脑膜炎
migraine 偏头痛
neurasthenia 神经衰弱
neurosis 神经官能症
paranoid psychosis 偏执性精神病
Parkinson's disease 帕金森综合征
psychosis 精神病
schizophrenia 精神分裂症
tetanus 破伤风

5.4 常用中西医药物

阿托品 atropine
阿波霉素 albomycin
病毒灵 moroxydine
槟榔 areca
布洛芬 ibuprofen
杜冷丁 dolantin
复方干草合剂 brown mixture
复方阿司匹林 aspirin compound tablet
谷氨酸 glutamic acid
谷维素 oryzanol
红霉素 erythromycin
黄连素 berberine
甲硝唑 flagyl
降压灵 vertical
酵母片 yeast
利多卡因 lidocaine
痢特灵 furazolicone
利血平 reserpine
磷酸可待因 codeine phosphate
氯霉素 chloromycetin
麻黄素 ephedrine
脑复新 pyritinol hydrochloricde
扑尔敏 chlorpheniramine
扑热息痛 paracetamol
葡萄糖酸钙 calcium gluconate
庆大霉素 gentamycin
青霉素 penicillin
驱蛔灵 piperazine citrate
舒喘灵 salbutamol
索密痛 somedon
土霉素 terramycin
胃蛋白酶 pepsin
胃复康 benactyzine
先锋霉素 I cephtlothin
新诺明 sulfamethoxazole
小苏打 sodium bicarbonate
硝酸甘油 nitroglycerine
消心痛 isosorbide dinitrate
叶酸 folic acid
异博定 verapamil
Earthworm 地龙
East Asian Tree Fern Rhizome 狗脊
Elecampane Inula Root 土木香
Emblic Leafflower Fruit 余甘子

English Walnut Seed 胡桃仁
Entada Sten 榼藤子
Entadae Stem 过江龙
Ephedra Herb 麻黄
Epigeal Srephaia Root 地不容
Epimedium Herb 淫羊藿
Erect St. John'swort Herb 小连翘
Ergot 麦角
Eriocarpous Glochidion Leaf 漆大姑
Eucommia Bark 杜仲
European Grape Fruit 索索葡萄
European Hop Flower 啤酒花
European Verbena 马鞭草
European Waterhemlock Root 毒芹
False Chinese Swertia Herb 当药
Falsehellebore Root and Rhizome 藜芦
Falsesour Cherry 樱桃核
Fangchi Root 广防已
Feather Cockscomb Seed 青葙子
Fennel Fruit 小茴香
Fermented Soybean 淡豆豉
Fewflower Lysionotus Herb 石吊兰
Field Sowthistle Herb 苣荬菜
Fig 无花果
Figwort Root 玄参
FigwortflowerPicrorhizaRhizome 胡黄连
Filiform Cassytha Herb 无根藤
Fimbriae Orostachys 瓦松
Fineleaf Schizonepeta Herb 荆芥
Finger Citron 佛手
Fistular Onion Stalk 葱白
Fiveleaf Gynostemma Herb 绞股蓝
Flabelate Maiden-hair Herb 过坛龙
Flastem Milkvetch Seed 沙苑子
Flos Caryophyllata 丁香
Fluorite 紫石英
Forbes Wildginger Herb 杜衡
Forest Frog's Oviduct 蛤蟆油
Forrest Silkvine Stem or Root 黑骨头
Fortune Eupatorium Herb 佩兰
Fortune Firethorn Fruit 救兵粮
Fortune Loosestrife Herb 星宿菜
Fortune Meadowrue Herb 白蓬草
Fortune Paulownia Fruit; Royal Paulownia Fruit 泡桐果
Fortune Plumyew Twig and Leaf 三尖杉
Fortune Windmillpalm Petiole 棕榈
Fortune's Drynaria Rhizome 骨碎补
Fourstamen Stephania Root 粉防己;汉防己
Fragrant Eupatorium Herb 飞机草
Fragrant Plantainlily Herb 玉簪
Fragrant Sarcococca Herb 清香桂
Fragrant Solomonseal Rhizome 玉竹
Franchet Groundcherry Calyx and Fruit 锦灯笼
Frangrant Ainsliaea Herb 杏香兔耳风
Frankincense 乳香
Freshwater Sponge 紫梢花
Fringed Iris Herb 铁扁担
Fruticose Breyniae Leaf and Twig 黑面神

5.5 常用保健品

白藜芦醇 Resveratrol
二氧化硅 Silica
番茄红素 Lycopene
泛酸 Pantothenic Acid
红曲 Red Yeast Rice
L-赖氨酸 L-Lysine
硫辛酸 Lipoic
卵磷脂 Lecithin
纳豆激酶 Nattokinase
鲨鱼软骨 Shark Cartilage
水飞蓟 Milk Thistle (Silymarin)
褪激素(即脑白金)Melatonin
叶黄素 Lutein
孕酮 Progesterone
左旋肉碱 L-Carnitine
Alfalfa 紫花苜蓿
Aloe Vera 芦荟
Apple Cider Vinegar 苹果醋
Bilberry Products 越橘产品
Bone Health 骨骼保健
Borage 琉璃苣
Blueberry 蓝莓

Black Cherry 黑莓
Bee Products 蜂产品
Calcium/Magnesium 钙/镁
Calcium Citrate 柠檬酸钙
Coral Calcium 珊瑚钙(碳酸钙)
Chondroitin/Glucosamine 软骨素/葡糖胺(关节保健产品)
Chlorophyll 叶绿素
Coenzyme Q-10 辅酶 Q-10
Cod Liver Oil 鳕鱼肝油
Collagen 胶原蛋白
Creatine 肌酸
Curcumin 姜黄素
D-Ribose D-核糖
Evening Primrose Oil;GLA 月见草油;γ-亚麻酸
Fiber/Bran Supplements 膳食纤维/麸皮营养品
Fish Oils 鱼油
Flaxseed (Linseed) Oil 亚麻籽(胡麻)油
Garlic Supplements 大蒜补充剂
Ginkgo Biloba 银杏叶
Ginseng 人参
Glutamine 谷氨酰胺
Grape Seed;Grape Extract 葡萄籽;葡萄提取物
Inositol 肌醇
Krill Oil 磷虾油

5.6 缩略语

白细胞 WBC
不明原因发热 FUO
常规 rout.
低血压 LBP
恶心呕吐 N/V
放射治疗 RT
核磁共振 MRI
核糖核酸 RNA
后遗症 Seq.
甲型肝炎病毒 HAV
结核 TB
空腹血糖 FBS
门诊 OPC
皮下注射 Hypo
片剂 Tab.
人类免疫缺陷病毒 HIV
生理盐水 NS
生长素 GH
实习生 Int.
手术室 OR
AMB 救护车
ANA 麻醉
ANAL 镇痛药
ASA 阿司匹林
BBT 基础体温
BCG 卡介苗
BMR. 基础代谢
BP 血压
BS 血糖
Cal. 卡
Cap. 囊
CBC 血常规
CC. list 病危通知单
CDC 预产期
CNS 中枢神经系统
Co. 复方
Contra. 禁忌
DD 鉴别诊断
dept. 科
DNA 脱氧核糖核酸
DIW 葡萄糖液
ECG 心电图
ER. 急诊室
FFA 游离脂肪酸
HB 血红蛋白
HBV 乙型肝炎病毒
HR 心率
ICU 重症监护病房
MI 心梗
Neg. 阴性的

6 比读体悟

6.1 世纪病

① 人类跨入21世纪,我们将要迎接的是一个机会与挑战并存,风险与危机此起彼伏的时代。展望未来,我们的确来不得半点乐观,因为尽管我们在经济上、技术上取得越来越多的成就和进步,然而在生态上,我们却在遭受前所未有的失败:诸如土地沙漠化越来越严重,可供使用的淡水资源越来越匮乏,空气污染,酸雨以及食物中农药残留已经达到我们无法忍受的程度等——我们自己甚至都说不清是不是在生病。

② 世界各国的医学专家们多年来一直致力于构建一整套科学的有关人体健康的标准体系。当他们仔细地研究人体的每一部分怎样结构、怎样运转才能真正称为健康的同时,都不约而同地找到了人的身体健康与心理健康相互依存、相互制约的关系。因此从20世纪初开始,"各项检测指标都完全正常才是真正的健康"的标准已逐渐被世界各国所公认。20世纪50年代,世界卫生组织正式向全世界发布了权威的、科学的健康定义:"健康的概念是指一个人在精神、身体和社会交往三方面保持健康状态。"这期间日本人也提出了衡量健康的所谓"四快"标准,即吃得快,便得快,睡得快和说话快(思维敏捷)。

Disease of the Century

① At the threshold of the 21st century, we are going to embrace an age of chances and challenges, which is filled with risks and crises. Looking into the future, however, we can't afford to be optimistic. In spite of the prolific economic and technical achievements and advancements we have made, the ecological cost is unprecedented, as demonstrated by the increasingly severe desertification, shrinking supplies of fresh water, an unbearable scale of air pollution, acid rain and chemical residues in food etc. We cannot even tell whether we are sick.

② For years, the medical experts from all over the world have committed themselves to establishing a set of scientific criteria for health. When carefully studying how the structure and function of every part of the body contribute to real health, they arrive at the same conclusion that physical health and psychological health are interrelated and interdependent. Therefore, a new criterion of health that every checking index must be completely normal has been gradually adopted by the world since the beginning of the 20th century. In 1950s, World Health Organization (WHO) announced to the world an authoritative and scientific definition of health: "The concept of health is that one keeps healthy in energy, body and social communication." During the same period the Japanese proposed the so-called "Four Fast's" criterion for measuring health, namely, eat fast, digest fast, sleep fast and speak fast (a sign of smartness). (*方梦之用例*)

6.2 出境健康检疫申明卡

中华人民共和国出入境检验检疫

姓名:________
性别:☐ 男　☐ 女
出生日期:________
国籍(地区):________
护照/证件号码:________

Health Declaration Form on Exit

Entry-Exit Inspection and Quarantine of the P. R. China

Name: ________
Gender: ☐ Male　☐ Female
Date of Birth: ________
Nationality (Region): ________
Passport/ID Number: ________

离境时间:________

联系电话:家庭:________

办公:________

车(船)次/航班号:________

车厢(牌)号:________

座(铺)位号:________

目的地:________ 途径地区:______

1. 此前14天内您到过的国家和城市:________

2. 此后14天内的联系地址和联系电话:________

3. 如您有以下症状或疾病,请在项目前的方框(□)内划"√":

□ 发烧 □ 呼吸急促 □ 腹泻

□ 咳嗽 □ 呼吸困难

4. 过去14天内是否与传染性非典型肺炎患者或疑似患者有过密切接触?

□ 是 □ 否

我已阅知本申明卡所列事项,并保证以上申明内容正确属实。

日期 ________旅客签名 ________

填报须知:

1. 为了您和他人的健康,请如实逐项填报;

2. 如有隐瞒或虚假填报,将依据有关法律予以追究;

3. 如不提交此卡,检疫人员有权拒绝您出境。

4*. 体温测量________

*由检疫人员根据情况实施体温测量后填写。

Departure Time: ________

Phone Number: Home: ________

Office: ________

Vehicle (Ship)/Flight Number: ____

Carriage Number: ________

Seat (berth) Number: ________

Destination: ________ Via: ________

1. Please list the country(s) or city(s) you visited in the past 14 days: ________

2. Please give your address and phone number in the next 14 days: ________

3. Please mark the following items that fit you with a "√"

□ fever □ tachypnea □ diarrhea

□ cough □ dyspnea

4. Did you have a contact with any SARS case or suspected SARS case in the past 14 days?

□ Yes □ No

I have read through all the items listed in this form, and declare that all the information given in the form is true and correct.

Date: ______ Signature: ______

Notice:

1. For you and others' health, please fill this form in full and with accuracy.

2. You will be in accordance with the law if you hold back the truth or provide false information.

3. The quarantine inspector may deny the permission to exit if you do not submit the declaration form.

4*. Body Temperature ______ (for quarantine official only).

6.3 保健食品注册管理办法(试行)

第一章 总 则

第一条 为规范保健食品的注册行为,保证保健食品的质量,保障人体食用安全,根据《中华人民共和国食品卫生法》、《中华人民共和国行政许可法》,制定本办法。

Provisions for Health Food Registration (interim)

Chapter I General Provisions

Article 1 With a view to standardizing the registration of health food, guaranteeing the quality of health food, ensuring food safety for people's consumption, the Provisions are formulated in accordance with Food Hygiene Law of the People's Republic of China and Administrative Reconsideration

Law of the People's Republic of China.

第二条 本办法所称保健食品，是指声称具有特定保健功能或者以补充维生素、矿物质为目的的食品。即适宜于特定人群食用，具有调节机体功能，不以治疗疾病为目的，并且对人体不产生任何急性、亚急性或者慢性危害的食品。

Article 2 The health food mentioned in the Provisions refers to those foods which claim to have certain health function or aim at supplementing vitamins and minerals, namely, those foods which are used for certain group of people with the aim to adjust organic function instead of curing diseases and will not cause any acute, sub-acute or chronic damage to human body.

第三条 在中华人民共和国境内申请国产和进口保健食品注册，适用于本办法。

Article 3 The provisions apply to the registration of both domestic and imported health food in the territory of the People's Republic of China.

第四条 保健食品注册，是指国家食品药品监督管理局根据申请人的申请，依照法定程序、条件和要求，对申请注册的保健食品的安全性、有效性、质量可控性以及标签说明书内容进行系统评价和审查，并决定是否准予其注册的审批过程；包括对产品注册申请、变更申请和技术转让产品注册申请的审批。

Article 4 The registration of health food refers to the application and approval procedures of the State Food and Drug Administration to systematically assess and review the safety, effectiveness and quality control of the health food applying for registration, as well as their labels, package insert and other contents, and then determine whether to approve of the registration according to legal procedures, qualifications and requirements, depending on the application of the applicant. The procedures include the review and approval of registration application, application for alteration and registration application of technical transfer product.

6.4 AIDS Hitting African Farm Sector Hard

艾滋病重创非洲农业

① Once a largely urban problem, AIDS has moved to rural areas in developing countries, devastating thousands of farming communities and leaving impoverished survivors scarcely able to feed themselves. The disease is no longer a health problem alone, but is having a measurable impact on food production, household food security and rural people's ability to make a living.

① 以前，艾滋病主要是一个存在于城市中的问题，而现在艾滋病已经转向发展中国家的农村地区，摧毁了成千上万的农村社区，使穷困的幸存者们无以为生。这一疾病已不再是单纯的健康问题，而正在对食品生产、家用食品安全和农村人口谋生能力造成明显的冲击。

② The latest statistical evidence on sub-Saharan Africa — the worst-hit region — confirms the scale of the epidemic's impact on the countryside.

② 撒哈拉以南的非洲地区受艾滋病打击最重；最新的统计数字已证实这一流行病对农村地区造成的严重影响。

③ It is estimated that over half of the 28 million people living with HIV/AIDS in sub-Saharan Africa live in rural areas. In order lo estimate such figures, epidemiologists start with data taken from tests done on blood samples from pregnant women attending prenatal clinics. They then extrapolate the figures to estimate infection rates in larger areas. Recent findings point to two of the hardest-hit countries — Zimbabwe and Swaziland.

③ 据估计，撒哈拉以南非洲地区的2 800万艾滋病人或艾滋病病毒携带者中，有一半以上生活在农村地区。为了对这类数字进行评估，流行病学家们首先从参加产前检查的孕妇身上抽取血样进行化验，取得数据，然后推测出数字，对更广大地区的传染率进行

④ "This is a real wake-up call for government," says an expert on AIDS. "Policymakers are guided by evidence. Solid evidence is now coming in and will make governments understand how rural areas are actually more vulnerable to AIDS than urban areas."

⑤ Recent reports from other African countries show a similar pattern of rampant rural infection.

⑥ Poverty underlies the suffering and devastation behind these figures. The HIV/AIDS epidemic cannot be addressed without doing something about rural livelihoods: how people make their living, how they get enough food, what strategies they follow in order to survive.

推测。最近的研究结果表明,受传染最严重的国家是津巴布韦和斯威士兰。

④"这对各国政府来说是个真正的警报。"一位艾滋病专家说。"决策者们是跟着证据走的,现在已经有确凿的证据使各国政府明白,农村地区的确比城市更容易受到艾滋病的侵袭。"

⑤ 最近来自其他非洲国家的报告也表明农村地区的艾滋病传染十分猖獗。

⑥ 在这些数字背后,贫穷是人们遭受病痛折磨和打击的原因。农村人口如何谋生,如何获得足够的食物,采取什么样的办法维持生存——这些生计问题不解决,艾滋病的肆虐是得不到根治的。(陈德彰、申雨平等用例)

6.5 The Health of American Children

① Child mortality declined, too. In 2000, there were 18 deaths for every 100,000 children aged 5 to 14; a year later, 17 deaths for every 100,000 children in this age group. The infant mortality rate slightly increased. Seven of every 1,000 infants died before their first birthday in 2002, compared with a record low of 6.8 per 1,000 in 2001.

② Still, children are more likely to be overweight than they were before and child poverty has inched up after several years of decline.

③ The number of overweight children increased to 16 percent between 1999 and 2000, compared with from 11 percent in the early 1990s and 6 percent in the late 1970s.

④ That development "jeopardizes our children's future, making them vulnerable to chronic conditions such as diabetes and hypertension previously associated more with adults than with children," said Edward J. Sondik, director of the Center for Disease Control's National Center for Health Statistics.

⑤ The report said Mexican-American boys were at the highest risk, with 27 percent overweight followed by non-Hispanic girls at 23 percent.

美国儿童的健康问题

① 少年儿童死亡率也有所下降。2000年,年龄在5—14岁的儿童死亡率为18/100000,到2001年则下降为17/100000。但婴儿死亡率稍有上升。2002年,未满周岁儿童死亡率是7/1000,超过了2001年的历史最低点6.8/1000。

② 不过,少年儿童肥胖症较之以前有所增加,而且过去几年呈下降趋势的少年儿童贫困率开始抬头。

③ 少年儿童肥胖人数,从20世纪70年代末的6%和90年代初的11%,增加到1999年到2000年之间的16%。

④ 疾病控制中心下属的全国健康统计中心主任爱德华·J.桑迪克说,这种状况"会危及孩子们未来的发展,因为肥胖容易引发像糖尿病和高血压这样的慢性疾病,而以前这些疾病以成人患者居多"。

⑤ 报告显示,墨西哥裔男孩患肥胖症的比例最高,达到27%,其次是非西班牙裔女孩,达到23%。

⑥ The child obesity issue is a major cause for concern, a health expert said to reporters. "This is a trend that's been at work since 1980…and as a trend, it shows no sign of reversing," the expert said.

⑥ 一位健康专家对记者说,儿童肥胖问题应当引起人们的关注。这位专家说,“从 1980 年以来,这种情况早已成为一种趋势……而且现在并没有任何逆转的迹象”。(卢敏用例)

6.6 Aspirin

阿司匹林

Aspirin is unique. A little white pill is so versatile that it can relieve your headache, ease your aching limbs, lower your temperature and treat some of the deadliest human diseases. A roundup of evidence suggests that it helps prevent heart attacks, stroke, deep vein thrombosis, infertility, herpes and even some of the most devastating cancer, such as bowel, lung and breast. It is a list that continues to grow, which may help to explain why more than 25,000 scientific papers have been written on aspirin and why an estimated one trillion tablets have been consumed since the drug was first produced.

阿司匹林可是非同寻常。小小的白色药片,用途多样,既能减轻头痛、缓解四肢疼痛、降低体温,又能用来治疗人类某些致命的疾病。收集的一些证据表明,阿司匹林有助于防治心脏病发作、中风、深部静脉血栓形成、不育、疱疹,甚至还可以预防某些致命的癌症,如肠癌、肺癌、乳腺癌等。能用阿司匹林防治的疾病还在不断增加,而这也可以说明,为什么人们会写出两万五千多篇关于阿司匹林的科研论文,为什么自问世以来阿司匹林的服用量已经达到一万亿片。(陈德彰、申雨平等用例)

6.7 推荐读物

(1)陈再晋,最新英汉医学大辞典,世界图书出版公司 1999 年版。
(2)方梦之,科技翻译教程,上海外语教育出版社 2008 年版。
(3)贾德江等,医学英语读写译教程,中南大学出版社 2006 年版。
(4)琼·平卡姆,中式英语之鉴,外语教学与研究出版社 2000 年版。
(5)王燕,医学英语翻译与写作教程,重庆大学出版社 2008 年版。
(6)魏羽等,汉英科技翻译教程,西北工业大学出版社 2010 年版。
(7)魏志成,汉英比较翻译教程,清华大学出版社 2006 年版。
(8)叶子南,高级英汉翻译,清华大学出版社 2001 年版。
(9)张蓓,汉英时文翻译实践,清华大学出版社 2001 年版。
(10)赵增荣等,医学英语阅读与翻译,东南大学出版社 2001 年版。

7 课后练习

7.1 分析题

(1)试用所译和比读材料分析全译极似律。
(2)药品的命名有哪几种标准?其翻译原则是什么?

(3)在“比读体悟”这部分,你觉得自己译文与参考译文主要差距在哪儿?

7.2 实训题

7.2.1 同仁堂

中药是个大宝库。人们现在了解到化学药品的副作用和诊断、用药疗效上的变化,便要寻求更接近自然的药品,更注重自然药物。这为中药打入世界市场提供了一个良好的机会。同仁堂人的目标是:加强品质意识,推行品牌策略,研制更好、更多品种的药品,为世界人民服务。

7.2.2 Global Crisis, Global Action

① We, heads of State and Government and representatives of States and Governments, assembled at the United Nations, from 25 to 27 June 2001, for the twenty-sixth special session of the General Assembly, convened in accordance with resolution 55/13 of 3 November 2000, as a matter of urgency, to review and address the problem of HIV/AIDS in all its aspects, as well as to secure a global commitment to enhancing coordination and intensification of national, regional and international efforts to combat it in a comprehensive manner.

② Deeply concerned that the global HIV/AIDS epidemic, through its devastating scale and impact, constitutes a global emergency and one of the most formidable challenges to human life and dignity, as well as to the effective enjoyment of human rights, which undermines social and economic development throughout the world and affects all levels of society: national, community, family and individual.

7.3 思考题

(1)根据“话题词汇”总结传统中药名称翻译的规律。
(2)保健品的名称如何翻译才能吸引消费者?
(3)如何处理医学英语中定语从句的翻译。
(4)系统总结中医英语翻译的简化技巧。
(5)如何做好药品说明书的翻译?
(6)如何处理医学英语中修辞翻译?
(7)做好医学翻译应具备什么样的素质?
(8)如何应对医学术语的翻译?
(9)医学翻译的最大困难在哪里?如何去解决?
(10)试比较汉英药品说明书各一篇,试析其语篇翻译特点。
(11)中医英译时如何传播中国特有文化?
(12)医学英语的词法与句法及其翻译手段有哪些特点?

第4课 婚姻家庭

导 译

本课主要探讨三个方面话题的翻译问题：爱情、婚姻、家庭。爱情是婚姻的基础，家庭是构成社会的基本单位，因此三者实际上是密不可分的一个整体。

比较而言，关于爱情话题的文本通常具有较强的文学性，因此在翻译的过程中，对于译者的文学素养要求较高，要把原文中的韵味传达出来，做到"音美"、"意美"与"形美"。相对而言，大多数关于婚姻与家庭话题的文本的语言比较中性，介乎于科技文本与文学文本之间，在翻译的过程中要做到忠实、流畅、自然。因此一般的翻译技巧在这类话题文本的翻译中都可以找到用武之地。然而，由于中西文化的差异，译者在进行该类话题的翻译时，常常遇到一些具有中国特色的文化现象，比如中国文化中庞杂的亲属关系的英译，中国文化中特有的爱称的英译等都是摆在译者面前比较棘手的问题，在解决这类问题的过程中，译者应主要遵循"归化"与"异化"这两种原则，即究竟是以凸显中国文化为主，还是以译语读者的感受为前提，在不同的情境中，译者应灵活运用这两种方法。

1 课前练笔

1.1《我可能是天津人》片段

究竟家里姓什么？哪里人？不知道。我只知道自己的生日和乳名。生日是自己长大以后听家里大人说的，是农历十月十五酉时生人。所以我的乳名叫"酉"，北京人的习惯爱用儿化韵，前面加个小，后面加个"儿"，就叫"小酉儿"。

1.2 女人的"一样"和"不一样"

万事万物由方方面面组成,而那个"男女都一样"的口号,只是向女人提出要求,却没有相同的口号要求男人和女人做得一样:一样耐心持久地抚育孩子;一样任劳任怨地操持家务;一样尽心尽责地侍奉老人。仔细想想,"男女都一样"的口号曾鼓舞着许多妇女竭力地建树和男人一样的丰功伟绩,同时,女人却依然要做那些和男人不一样的事。

1.3 Of Love

It is a poor saying of Epicurus, Satis magnum alter alteri theatrum sumus; as if man, made for the contemplation of heaven, and all noble objects, should do nothing but kneel before a little idol, and make himself a subject, though not of the mouth (as beasts are), yet of the eye; which was given him for higher purposes.

It is a strange thing, to note the excess of this passion, and how it braves the nature, and value of things, by this; that the speaking in a perpetual hyperbole, is comely in nothing but in love. Neither is it merely in the phrase; for whereas it hath been well said, that the arch-flatterer, with whom all the petty flatterers have intelligence, is a man's self; certainly the lover is more. For there was never proud man thought so absurdly well of himself, as the lover doth of the person loved; and therefore it was well said, That it is impossible to love, and to be wise. Neither doth this weakness appear to others only, and not to the party loved; but to the loved most of all, except the love be reciprocal. For it is a true rule, that love is ever rewarded, either with the reciprocal, or with an inward and secret contempt.

1.4 Why We Should Have Children

In some societies people want children for what might be called familial reasons: to extend the family line or the family name, to propitiate the ancestors; to enable the proper functioning of religious rituals involving the family. Such reasons may seem thin in the modern, secularized society but they have been and are powerful indeed in other places.

In addition, one class of family reasons shares a border with the following category, namely, having children in order to maintain or improve a marriage: to hold the husband or occupy the wife; to repair or rejuvenate the marriage; to increase the number of children on the assumption that family happiness lies that way. The point is underlined by its converse: in some societies the failure to bear children (or males) is a threat to the marriage and a ready cause for divorce.

2 课前批评

2.1《谈结婚》节选

究竟是结婚的好呢,还是不结婚的好?这问题似乎同先有鸡呢还是先有鸡蛋一样,常常有人提起,而也常常没有人解决过的问题。照大体看来,想租房子的时候,是无眷莫问的,想做官的时候,又是朝里无裙莫做官的,想写文章的时候,是独身者不能写我的妻的,凡此种种似乎都是结婚的好。可是要想结婚,第一要有钱,第二要有闲,第三要有职,这潘驴……的五个条件,却也很不容易办到。更何况结婚之后,“儿子自己要来”。

A Chat about Marriage (Excerpt)

Marriage or no marriage, which is more desirable? That sounds like the chicken-and-egg question, which, though often discussed, remains a perpetual puzzle. Generally speaking, one who has no family dependents is not supposed to rent a house, one who has no petticoat influence in the government should refrain from becoming an official, an unmarried male writer is in no position to write about "my wife". All these seem to hint at the advantages of marriage. But, to get married, you need to have five prerequisites, namely, money, leisure, employment, good looks and potentness, of which all are not always available. What is more, after your marriage, your offspring will come to this world of themselves.

2.2 The American Middle-Class Families in Danger

During the past generation, the American middle-class family that once could count on hard work and fair play to keep itself financially secure had been transformed by economic risk and new realities. Now a pink slip, a bad diagnosis, or a disappearing spouse can reduce a family from solidly middle class to newly poor in a few months.

In just one generation, millions of mothers have gone to work, transforming basic family economics. Scholars, policymakers, and critics of all stripes have debated the social implications of these changes, but few have looked at the side effect: family risk has risen as well.

美国中产阶级家庭危机四伏

在上一代人中,美国中产阶级家庭原本依靠努力工作和公平竞争就能保持稳定的经济状况,如今因经济风险和新的现实状况而发生了变化。现在,一张解雇通知书,一个恶性诊断结果,或者配偶的离去,都可以使一个稳固的中产阶级家庭在几个月内成为新的贫困户。

仅仅大约一代人的时间里,数百万母亲出去工作,从而改变了基本的家庭经济状况。各行各业的学者、政策制定者以及批评家都在讨论这些变化的社会意义,但是很少有人看到其副作用:家庭风险也提高了。

3 全译知识 全译原则

全译中语用(语用价值)、语义(语里意义)、语形(语表形式)三者出现矛盾时,往往遵循语用优先、语义次之、语形第三的原则。

3.1 语用第一原则

全译的语用价值主要是反映原作风格。语用指语言的运用。语用学研究符号与使用者之间的关系,专门研究特定情景中特定话语意义的理解和表达,回答语言使用在上下文中有何交际价值的问题。语用成为首要原则。

一般情况下,译者必须在传达内容的前提下,在文体上尽量符合读者的需求,以求文通字顺,有可读性,采用规范的译语形式,避免翻译腔。从大处讲,全译要得原语文化之精华,融入译语文化,建起文化交流的桥梁。如:

① He hates her to the guts.

【原译】:他恨之入肠。

【试译】:他恨之入骨。

中西方取象不同,表明恨人恨到极点,汉语常说"恨之入骨"、"刻骨之恨"或"恨入骨髓",如冯梦龙《东周列国志》第十七回"蔡哀侯始知中了息侯之计,恨之入骨"。若有语境,原译完全可取,还为汉语吸收了新鲜表达。汉语表示程度之深,也可取"肠"的意象,常有人说"肠子都悔青了"。

3.2 语义第二原则

追求语用价值之后,就要追求语义即内容。语义是语形所承载的内容,包括词义、短语义、句义等。语义学研究符号与所指之间的关系,回答意义是按什么方法确定的问题。全译要力争如实地传达原作的内容,得作者之志。如:

② Some old people are oppressed by the fear of death.

【原译】:有些老年人因怕死而惶惶不安。

【试译】:有些老人因怕死而忧心忡忡。

原译中"惶惶不安"语义侧重于恐惧不安,程度超过原文。试译"忧心忡忡"则侧重于忧虑不安。原文的信息焦点在谓语,汉译在句末,符合汉语末尾焦点的要求,语用上也极似。

3.3 语形第三原则

传达语用和语义,要借用语表形式,它处于最弱的地位。语形是语表形式的简称,包括音形和字/词形及其音所构成的语流,或字/词所构成的文本。语形又以语法之句法为最,它研究符号与符号之间的关系,回答句子是按什么规则组成的问题。汉英互译形意互转,或取意舍形,或因意变形,或因意造形。如:

③ 知彼知己,百战不殆。You can fight a hundred battles without defeat if you know the enemy as well as yourself.

汉语多重隐含,含而不露,有意在言外之妙。原文缺形式连接手段,但内在的因果关系明晰可见,靠的是意合手段。英译时则要显化层次关系,先将前因后果关系颠倒过来,先译果,后说因,并加上表条件的连词 if。

形式第三原则,并非说形式不重要,而是说较之于语用和语义,一般情况下可以稍后考虑,或作出不同的形式选择。有时形式会重于内容。如某年冬,有盲人乞于纽约繁华大街,脖挂一牌,上书 Blind since childhood。有诗人路过,他向诗人乞讨,诗人说:"我也很穷,不过我可给你写个字。"当天乞丐受施不菲。后来,乞丐巧遇诗人,问他:"你到底为我写了什么?"诗人笑答:"Spring is coming, but I cannot see it."可见形式之妙,巧与不巧,不可小觑。

4 全译窍门

4.1 亲属关系英译

汉语的亲属称谓比英语复杂。要英语译称为读者所接受,可遵守以下原则:

遵守译语文化规范 汉语习用"排行称谓",如"大哥""二嫂""三弟"等,英语习用"姓名称谓"。互译时用译语中对应的称谓替代原语称谓,采用归化手法,以符合译语习惯,读来自然易懂。如:

① 爸爸,辛苦了!二姊,这是四妹和七弟么? How did you enjoy your journey, father? Fu-fang, is this Huei-fang? And Ah-Xuan?

遵守原语文化规范 为明确汉语的指称关系,反映人物关系,翻译时需在英语中选用恰当的称谓,采用异化手法翻译汉语亲属称谓语,需诠释亲属称谓的真实语义。如:

② 她从贫苦的姑家,又转到更贫苦的姨家。She had lived for a while with some impoverished paternal relatives, and then had been bundled of to some maternal relatives who were, if anything, even worse of.

汉语中姑姨亲属关系分明,而 aunt 包含姑姨在内的诸多女性长辈亲属,分别用 paternal relatives 和 maternal relatives 对应"姑"和"姨",以便英语读者了解中国文化。

4.2 爱称英译

爱称是常用在比较亲近的人之间,表示亲近、喜爱的一种称呼。汉语爱称通常有两种构成方式:第一,由乳名缩略再加"儿"、"子"等字构成;第二,用比较珍贵及重要的东西、特殊名词,甚至动物名称来称呼所喜爱的人,以示关系亲密。在英译汉语的爱称时,对第一种爱称构成方式常用音译法,而第二种爱称的翻译较为复杂,可遵守以下原则:

"my + 名词"的形式 一般来说,含喜爱、亲密之情的爱称为了表亲近关系,常用"my + 名词"的形式,以示友好、亲密。这时要避免表疏远或贬义时用的"you + 名词"的形式。如:

③ 贾母只得安慰他道:"好宝贝,你只管去,有我呢。他不敢委屈了你……" "Go,

my treasure," she urged him. "I won't let him be hard on you..."

异化及归化原则 根据不同的语境和翻译目的,需采取不同的翻译策略:若以传播中国古老文化为目的,更多采用异化翻译及直译法;若从英语为母语的读者的角度出发,则较多采用归化翻译及意译法。如:

④ 又向贾母道:"老祖宗,老菩萨,那里知道那佛经上说的利害……"

【译文Ⅰ】:She declared:" You don't know, Old Ancestress, all the solemn warnings there are in the Buddhist sutras about the sons born into noble families..."

【译文Ⅱ】:She turned to Grandmother Jia:" Bless you, my lucky lady! Bless you dearie! You don't know a half of the unseen harms and dangers the Scripture tells us of..."

译文Ⅰ以传递文化为主要目的,汉语"菩萨"本指人们崇拜的神灵,现比喻心肠仁慈的人,因此译为 Old Ancestress;译文Ⅱ却意译为 my lucky lady,顺应了语境,译文也使目标语读者更容易理解。

4.3 巧用介词

相对而言,英语介词和名词用得多,汉语动词用得多。英译时,汉语动词颇费心思。若能把汉语动词转为英语介词,即可迎刃而解,译文准确、简洁、晓畅,因为许多英语介词含有动作之义,如 across、against、by、down、in、into、on、over、past、up、toward 等。如:

⑤ 他们吃着粗茶淡饭,住着寒冷的窑洞,点着昏暗的油灯,长时间地工作。They worked long hours on meagre food, in cold caves, by dim lamps.

⑥ 这些人闹什么东西呢?闹名誉,闹地位,闹出风头。What are these people after? They are after fame and position and want to be in the limelight.

⑦ 政府正在开展一场反对铺张浪费的运动。The government is waging a campaign against waste and extravagance.

4.4 揣摩"万能动词"

英语"万能动词"的特点是搭配能力极强,用法十分丰富,不同语境下有不同的词义,翻译时,要根据具体的语境进行词义引申,尽量使其含义具体化。如下例中的 try 和 suffer。

⑧ Dobbin had been in the coffee-room for an hour or more. He had tried all the papers but could not read them. 杜宾在咖啡室少说也待了一个钟头。他翻遍了所有的报纸,可是什么也没看进去。

⑨ A scientist constantly tries to defeat his hypothesis, his theories, and his conclusion. 科学家经常设法否认自己的假设,推翻自己的理论,并放弃自己的结论。

⑩ Poetry suffers in translation — and the reader suffers with it. 诗歌经过翻译就要遭殃——诗歌遭殃,读者就要跟着受罪。

4.5 括号的妙用

英语惯用长句,汉译问题之一在于其从句、短语在译文中不便处置:放在有关词语之前,译文会佶屈聱牙,晦涩难懂;放在之后,句子又拖沓,结构松散。此时不妨采用"括号

翻译法”,即将难以处理的从句(或短语等)译在有关词语后,加上括号,便可使译文流畅简洁。如:

⑪ Additional social stresses may also occur because of the population explosion or problems arising from mass migration movements — themselves made relatively easy nowadays by modern means of transport. 由于人口激增与大规模的人口迁移活动(现代化交通方式的发展使得迁移活动变得相对容易)也可能造成新的社会压力。

⑫ I remember going to the British Museum one day to read up the treatment for some slight ailment of which I had a touch-hay fever, I fancy it was. 记得有一天我去大英博物馆,专门去查阅我曾患的小毛病(我想是苦草病)的治疗方法。

5 话题词汇

5.1 爱情

拜访 call on
宝贝 baby; honey; dear; darling; sweetie; dotey; sweetheart; heart
吃醋 to be jealous (usually of a rival in love); to wear yellow stockings
初恋 first love; puppy love
单身 bachelordom; bachelorhood
对某人念念不忘 get the hots for
房奴 house slaves
婚前性生活 premarital sex
旧情人 old flame
酷抠族 cool carl
灵魂伴侣 soul mate
裸婚 naked wedding
情敌 rival in love
情侣装 couples dress
情人眼里出西施 beauty is in the eyes of the lover
求爱 court; pursue a courtship; seek someone's love
认可 recognize
三角恋爱 the love triangle; the eternal triangle
闪电恋爱 whirlwind romance
闪电约会 speeddating
闪婚 flash marriage
闪居族 flash cohabitants
失恋 lose one's love; be crossed in love; be jilted
食草男 herbivore men
熟女 cougar
未婚先孕 premarital pregnancy
相爱 be in love; fall in love
一见钟情 fall in love at first sight
以貌取人 judge a person by his/her appearance; judge the book by its cover
蚁族 ant tribe
异地恋 long-distance relationship
缘分 predestined relationship; fate
宅男宅女 the stay-at-home type
钻石王老五 diamond bachelor
aspire after 渴望;追求
bachelor 单身汉
bachelor hall 单身住所
bachelorism 独身;独身者之怪癖
bachelorette 未婚女子
blind date 相亲
break up 分手
chick flick 文艺爱情片
cohabitation 同居
date (男女间的)约会;约会对象
egis 保护;维护
engagement 约会;婚约;诺言
Eros 爱神;愿望; 性爱
everlasting love 永恒的爱情

fancy sick 害相思病的
generosity 慷慨；宽宏；大方
inamorata 情人；情妇；姘妇
inamorato 情人；情夫；姘夫
inseparable love 如胶似漆的爱情
jealousy 妒忌
love letter 情书
love token 定情信物
lovelorn 失恋的；害相思病的
lover's vows 山盟海誓
lovey-dovey 情意绵绵的
mature 成熟
mutual attraction 相互吸引
one's own wishful thinking 一厢情愿
one-sided love 单相思
platonic love 精神恋爱；男女间的纯洁友谊
pull one's heartstrings 打动心弦
spinster 未婚妇女；老处女
tender 温柔的；软弱的
throw oneself at sb's feet 拜倒在某人的石榴裙下
tribute 殷勤；贡品；礼物；颂词
veracity 老实；诚实
whole-hearted love 全心全意的爱情
woo 求爱；追求；恳求
yearn 渴望；想念；怀念；向往
zest 强烈的兴趣；热情；热心

5.2 婚姻

白马王子 Prince Charming；Mr. Perfection
傍大款 find a sugar daddy
包办婚姻 arranged marriage；prearranged marriage
包养 pay for a mistress
大喜日子 a red letter day
登记结婚 wed in a civil ceremony
订婚 engage oneself to
订婚戒 engagement ring
夫兄弟婚 levirate marriage
贺礼 wedding gift
红双喜 double happiness
红丝带 red ribbon
婚礼晚会 wedding party
婚庆来宾 wedding guest
婚外恋 extramarital love；extramarital affair
婚姻 marriage；matrimony
婚姻财产制度 matrimonial property regime
婚姻介绍所 matrimonial agency
婚姻契约 marriage article；marriage contract
婚姻条例 marriage ordinance
婚姻制度 marriage system；matrimonial institution
嫁妆 trousseau；dowry
结婚一年（纸婚） paper wedding
结婚二年（棉婚） cotton wedding
结婚三年（皮婚） leather wedding
结婚四年（丝婚） silk wedding
结婚五年（木婚） wood wedding
结婚六年（铁婚） iron wedding
结婚七年（铜婚） copper wedding
结婚八年（青铜婚） bronze wedding
结婚九年（陶器婚） pottery wedding
结婚十年（锡婚） tin wedding
结婚十一年（钢婚） steel wedding
结婚十二年（麻婚） linen wedding
结婚十三年（花边婚） lace wedding
结婚十四年（象牙婚） ivory wedding
结婚十五年（水晶婚） crystal wedding
结婚二十年（瓷婚） china wedding
结婚二十五年（银婚） silver wedding
结婚三十年（珍珠婚） pearl wedding
结婚三十五年（珊瑚婚）coral wedding
结婚四十年（红宝石婚）ruby wedding
结婚四十五年（蓝宝石婚）sapphire wedding
结婚五十年（金婚） gold wedding
结婚五十五年（翡翠婚）emerald wedding
结婚六十年（钻石婚） diamond wedding
掠夺婚 marriage by capture；plundered marriage；
买卖婚 marriage by purchase；mercenary marriage；
媒人 match-maker；go-between
门当户对 be well-matched in social and economic status
门户不当的婚姻 left-hand marriage
聘礼 bride price
请帖 invitation card
提亲 marriage proposal
无效婚姻 invalid marriage；void marriage

新娘发型 bridal hairstyle
新娘化妆 bridal make-up
证婚人 witness of wedding
指定日期 appointed date
指明公职人员 designated public officer
auspicious day 黄道吉日
bigamy 重婚
bridal chamber 洞房;新房
bridegroom;groom 新郎
bridesmaid 伴娘
bride 新娘
child marriage 童养媳
concubinage 纳妾;非法同居;妾侍制度
contraceptives 避孕措施
couple-to-be 未婚夫妻
customary marriage 旧式婚姻
divorce by consent 协议离婚
divorce 离婚
early marriage 早婚
emcee 司仪;主持人
espousal 订婚; 婚礼; 拥护
ex-husband 前夫
ex-wife 前妻
family background 家境
family man 有家室的人
fiance(husband-to-be)未婚夫
fiancee(wife-to-be)未婚妻
free marriage 自由婚姻
freedom of marriage 婚姻自主
groomsman 伴郎
honeymoon 蜜月
in laws 姻亲
intended wife 未婚妻
late marriage 晚婚
leftover men 剩男
leftover women 剩女
legal marriage 合法婚姻
marital status 婚姻状况
marriage certificate 结婚证
marriage made in heaven 天生一对
marriageable age 可以结婚的年龄
matrilocal residence 从母居(已婚夫妇与女方亲戚共同居住)
mixed marriage 涉外婚姻;跨国婚姻
mixed-couple 异国夫妻;异(种)族夫妻
modern marriage 新式婚姻
monogamy 一夫一妻婚姻制度
Mr. Right 理想丈夫;如意郎君
newlywed 新婚夫妇
nuptial 婚礼的;结婚的;婚姻的
officiator 主婚人
other half 配偶
pastor 牧师
perfect match 郎才女貌
pre-nuptial 婚前的
propose for marriage 求婚
register office 结婚登记处
registrar 登记官
remarriage 再婚
say one's vows 立下婚誓
separation 分居
serial monogamy 系列一夫一妻制
shotgun marriage 奉子成婚
soul infidelity 精神出轨
spouse 配偶
suitor 求婚者
tie the nuptial knot 喜结良缘
trial marriage 试婚
usher 引宾员
validated marriage 认可婚姻
vows 婚誓
wedding anniversary 结婚周年纪念日
wedding card 喜帖
wedding ceremony 结婚典礼
wedding day 举行婚礼的日子
wedding dress 婚纱;结婚礼服
wedding feast 喜宴
wedding gown 结婚礼服
wedding march 婚礼进行曲
wedding night 花烛夜
wedding ring 婚姻戒指
wedding reception 婚宴
wedlock 结婚生活; 婚姻
well-matched couple 很般配的一对
willing divorce 自愿离婚

5.3 家庭

表兄弟 maternal male cousin
表姊妹 maternal female cousin
财产分割 partition; dismemberment of property
代位继承 representation; succession by subrogation
单独继承 single succession
第二顺序继承人 successor second in order
第一顺序继承人 successor first in order
非婚生子女 illegitimate child
夫妻分居 divorce from bed and board
夫妻共同财产 community property
共同继承 joint succession
姑夫 father's sister's husband; husband of paternal aunt; uncle
姑母 father's sister; paternal aunt
贵族出身 of noble birth
后代;后裔 offspring; descendant; progeny
婚后财产公证 notarization of postnuptial properties
婚生子女 children born in wedlock; legitimate child
婚姻登记 marriage registration
计划生育 family planning; planned parenthood
继承参与人 succession participant
继承法 inheritance law; law of succession
继承人 heir; successor
家庭的 household; domestic; familial
家庭主妇 housewife; housewives; materfamilias; domesticated wife
间接继承 indirect succession
连襟 husband of wife's sister
舅父;舅舅 mother's brother; maternal uncle
舅母;妗子 mother's brother's wife; maternal uncle's wife
拟制血亲 blood relations in fiction of law
旁系血亲 collateral descent; collateral relatives by blood
平民出身 of humble birth
全职妈妈 stay-at-home mom
涉外收养 adoption with foreign elements
收养法 adoption law
收养人 adoptive parent
收养协议 adoption agreement
送养人 person or institution placing out a child for adoption
堂兄弟 father's brother's sons; paternal male cousin
堂姊妹 father's brother's daughters; paternal female cousin
孝敬父母 be filial to one's parents
血缘 consanguinity; blood relationship
遗产 inheritance; estate; bequest; heritage; portion; legacy
遗产继承人 heir to property; inheritor
遗言 last will and testament
遗赠 bequest; legacy; devise
遗赠抚养协议 legacy-support agreement
遗赠继承 succession by devise
遗嘱继承 testate succession
直系血亲 lineal descent
自然继承 natural succession
祖先 ancestors; forebears; forefathers
adopt 收养
adopted daughter 养女
adopted son 养子
affinity 姻亲关系;嫡戚关系
alimony 赡养费
bastard 私生子
better half 配偶(妻子)
birth control 节育
blood 血;血统
boarding parents 寄养父母
branch 支;系
broken family 破碎家庭
brother-in-law 姐妹的丈夫
caste 社会地位
clan 氏族
conjugal relationship 夫妻关系
consolation money 抚慰金
custody 保管;监护;拘留;抚养权
daughter-in-law 儿媳妇
de facto marriage 事实婚姻
dependent 受扶养的人
descent 血统;遗传
divorce by agreement 协议离婚

divorce by litigation 诉讼离婚
extraction 家世
family tree 家谱
father-in-law 家翁;岳父
fetal education 胎教
filial 子女的
folks 亲人
foster child 养子;养女
foster father 养父
foster mother 养母
foster parent 养父母
generation 代
guardian 监护人
half- 同父异母;同母异父
hereditary succession 世袭继承
house-husband 家庭主夫;操持家务的丈夫
incompatibility 感情破裂
in-laws 姻亲
kin 同族亲戚
kindred 亲属
kinsmen by affinity 姻亲
kinsmen by blood 血亲
legal succession 法定继承
legatees 受遗赠人
life span 寿命
lineage 宗族;世系
maternal 母方的
mother-in-law 婆母;岳母
nephew 侄子;外甥
next of kin 近亲
niece 侄女;外甥女
only child 独生子女
origin 出身
orphan 孤儿
parental 父母亲的
parenting 养育
paternal 父系的
relative 亲戚;亲属
reproductive health 生殖健康
resumption of marriage 复婚
second cousin 第二代堂兄妹;第二代表兄妹
sibling 同胞兄妹
sister-in-law 夫或妻的姐妹
son-in-law 女婿
step father 继父
step mother 继母
step- 前夫(妻)的
stepbrother 异父(母)之兄弟
stepdaughter 继女
stepsister 异父(母)之姐妹
stepson 继子
stock 门第;血统
subsuccession 转继承
succession 继承
testator 遗嘱人
tribe 部族;部落
uncle 叔;伯;舅;姑父;姨父
unplanned pregnancy 意外怀孕
uxorious 疼爱妻子的;怕老婆的
visitation right 探视权
widow 寡妇
widower 鳏夫

5.4 缩略语

AA 制 Dutch treatment, to go Dutch
丁克族 DINK
妇权自保组织 WDO
妇协 WI
国际妇理会 ICW
国际家庭计协 IPPA
啃老族 NEET
乐活族 LOHAS
美国新家庭妇联 NHA
情商 EQ
全国妇理会 NCW
全国妇咨委 NWAC
中华全国妇联 ACWF
AAL 补充领养许可证
AFDC (美国)对有子女家庭补助计划
AM 包办婚姻
BMW (男士向女士的)求婚
CC 儿童护理
DCF 儿童和家庭部
EST 财产;遗产

FAMILY 爸爸妈妈我爱你们
FCC 爱华儿童家长协会
FF 朋友与家庭
FH 家庭史
FHI 国际家庭健康
FIS 家庭收入补贴
GF 女朋友
HB 家庭银行
HOMO 同性恋者
ILY 我爱你
LES 女同性恋者
LVG 恋爱游戏
LYL 非常爱你
MELO 通俗爱情剧
MPB 男人式的率直
NOW 全国妇女组织
PDA 公众示爱
POSSLQS 合用住所的异性伙伴
SP 无子女
SWAK 以吻封信
WYMM 愿意嫁给我吗
YOM 结婚年份

6 比读体悟

6.1《父亲》

①后来屋子被火烧掉了，他还想再做生意，把屋子重造起来。我安慰他说："三年后我自己就可积起钱造屋了，还是等一等吧。"他答应了。他给我留下许多造屋的材料，告诉我这样可以做什么，那样可以做什么。他死的前不久，还对我说：

②"早一点造起来吧，我可以给你监工。"

③但是他终于没有看见屋子重造起来就死了。他弥留的时候对我说，一切都满足了。但是我知道他倘能再活几年，我把屋子造起来，是他所最心愿的。我听到他弥留时的呻吟和叹息，我相信那不是病的痛苦呻吟和叹息。我知道他还想活几年，帮我造起屋子来。

④现在我自己已是几个孩子的父亲了。我爱孩子，但是我没有前一辈父亲的想法，帮孩子一直帮到老，帮到死还不足。我赞美前一辈父亲的美德，而自己却不能跟着他们的步伐走去。

⑤我觉得我的孩子累我，使我受到极大的束缚。我没有对他们的永久的计划，甚至连最短促的也没有。

Father

① It happened afterwards that the house was burned down. And he wanted to go back to his business in order to have the house rebuilt. I tried to console him, saying that there was no need for him to do it because in there years' time I myself would have laid by enough money for a new house. He agreed. Then he gave me a lot of building materials and told me what to do with them. Shortly before his death, he urged me.

② "You'd better get started right away so that I can watch to see that everything is done properly."

③ Unfortunately he didn't live long enough to see the new house. He told me on his deathbed that he had nothing to feel sorry about. But I knew he would be much happier if he could live a few more years just to see the new house put up. When I heard his dying groans and sighs, I believed they were caused not by physical pain, but by regret for not being able to live a few more years to help me with the new house.

④ Now I myself am a father of several children. Though I love my kids, I do not share the idea of father and people of his time that one can never do too much in his lifetime to help his children. Much as I admire father and people of his time for their moral excellence, I can never follow in their footsteps.

⑤ I think of my children as an encumbrance to me. I haven't worked out a long-term plan for them, nay, not even a short-term one.

⑥“倘使有人要,我愿意把他们送给人家!”我常常这样说,当我厌烦孩子的时候。

⑥ "I'd like to give away my kids to anyone who's willing to take them!" That's what I say whenever I am fed up with them.

⑦ 唉,和前一辈的做父亲的一比,我觉得我们这一辈生命力薄弱得可怜,我们二三十岁的人比不上六七十岁的前辈,他们虽然老的老死的死了,但是他们才是真正活着到现在到将来。

⑦ Alas, compared with father and people of his time, the present generation, I think, have pitifully low vitality. We in our twenties or thirties cannot compare with our elders in their sixties or seventies. Today they may be advanced in years or even no more, but they will, nevertheless, live forever and ever.

⑧ 而我们呢,虽然活着,却是早已死了。(鲁彦)

⑧ As for us, though still alive, we have long been dead. (张培基 译)

6.2《中华人民共和国婚姻法》(节选)

Marriage Law of the People's Republic of China (Excerpt)

第二章 结婚

第五条 结婚必须男女双方完全自愿,不许任何一方对他方加以强迫或任何第三者加以干涉。

第六条 结婚年龄,男不得早于二十二周岁,女不得早于二十周岁。晚婚晚育应予鼓励。

第七条 有下列情形之一的,禁止结婚:(一)直系血亲和三代以内的旁系血亲;(二)患有医学上认为不应当结婚的疾病。

第八条 要求结婚的男女双方必须亲自到婚姻登记机关进行结婚登记。符合本法规定的,予以登记,发给结婚证。取得结婚证,即确立夫妻关系。未办理结婚登记的,应当补办登记。

第九条 登记结婚后,根据男女双方约定,女方可以成为男方家庭的成员,男方可以成为女方家庭的成员。

第十条 有下列情形之一的,婚姻无效:(一)重婚的;(二)有禁止结婚的亲属关系的;(三)婚前患有医学上认为不

Chapter II Marriage

Article 5 Marriage must be based upon the complete willingness of both man and woman. Neither party may use compulsion on the other party and no third party may interfere.

Article 6 No marriage may be contracted before the man has reached 22 years of age and the woman 20 years of age. Late marriage and late childbirth shall be encouraged.

Article 7 No marriage may be contracted under any of the following circumstances: (1) if the man and the woman are lineal relatives by blood, or collateral relatives by blood up to the third degree of kinship; and (2) if the man or the woman is suffering from any disease, which is regarded by medical science as rendering a person unfit for marriage.

Article 8 Both the man and the woman desiring to contract a marriage shall register in person with the marriage registration office. If the proposed marriage is found to conform with the provisions of this Law, the couple shall be allowed to register and issued marriage certificates. The husband and wife relationship shall be established as soon as they acquire the marriage certificates. In the absence of the marriage registration, the man and the woman shall go through the procedures subsequently.

Article 9 After a marriage has been registered, the woman may become a member of the man's family or vice versa, depending on the agreed wishes of the two parties.

Article 10 Marriage shall be invalid under any of the following circumstances: (1) if one party commits bigamy; (2) if the man and the woman are relatives by blood up to the

应当结婚的疾病,婚后尚未治愈的;(四)未到法定婚龄的。

third degree of kinship; (3) if, before marriage, one party is suffering from a disease which is regarded by medical science as rendering a person unfit for marriage and, after marriage, a cure is not effected; and (4) if the legally marriageable age is not attained.

第十一条 因胁迫结婚的,受胁迫的一方可以向婚姻登记机关或人民法院请求撤销该婚姻。受胁迫的一方撤销婚姻的请求,应当自结婚登记之日起一年内提出。被非法限制人身自由的当事人请求撤销婚姻的,应当自恢复人身自由之日起一年内提出。

Article 11 In the case of a marriage made under coercion, the coerced party may make a request to the marriage registration office or the people's court for the dissolution of the marriage contract. Such a request shall be made within one year as of the marriage registration date. The party concerned whose personal freedom is curbed illegitimately shall make a request for dissolution of the marriage contract within one year as of the date on which his or her personal freedom is restored.

第十二条 无效或被撤销的婚姻,自始无效。当事人不具有夫妻的权利和义务。同居期间所得的财产,由当事人协议处理;协议不成时,由人民法院根据照顾无过错方的原则判决。

Article 12 Void or dissolved marriage shall be invalid from its inception. Neither party concerned shall have the rights and duties of husband or wife. The property acquired during their cohabitation shall be subject to disposition by mutual agreement. If they fail to reach an agreement, the people's court shall give a ruling on the principle of caring for the no-fault party.

6.3 On Going Home

① That I am trapped in this particular irrelevancy is never more apparent to me than when I am home. Paralyzed by the neurotic lassitude engendered by meeting one's past at every turn, around every corner, inside every cupboard, I go aimlessly from room to room. I decide to meet it head-on and clean out a drawer, and I spread the contents on the bed. A bathing suit I wore the summer I was seventeen. A letter of rejection from *The Nation*, an aerial photograph of the site for a shopping center my father did not build in 1954. Three teacups hand-painted with cabbage roses and signed "E. M.," my grandmother's initials. There is no final solution for letters of rejection from *The Nation* and teacups hand-painted in 1900. Nor is there any answer to snapshots of one's grandfather as a young man on skis, surveying around Donner Pass in the year 1910. I smooth out the snapshot and look into his face, and do and do not see my own. I close the drawer, and have another cup of coffee with my mother. We get along very well, veterans of a guerrilla war we never understood.

回家

① 这个不相干的问题困扰着我,在我返回老家后尤为明显。走过每个角落,打开每个食橱,转身驻足间,我一次次地面对过去,思绪不宁,及至疲乏不堪,我还是漫无目的地逐个房间走着。我决意正眼看去,清理出一个抽屉,把东西摊在床上。一件我十七岁那年夏天穿的泳衣;一封《民族周刊》的退稿信;一张从空中拍摄的选址照片,1954 年父亲曾打算在那里建购物中心;还有三只茶杯,上面有手绘的百叶蔷薇,并签有祖母名字的两个首字母“E. M.”。我不知道该如何处理 1900 年手绘的茶杯和《民族周刊》的退稿信,也不知道该如何处理祖父 1910 年的几张快照。照片里的祖父青春年少,踩着滑雪板,在察看唐纳山口。我抚平照片,注视着祖父的脸,依稀看到自己的影子,又似乎没有。我关上抽屉,陪母亲又喝了一杯咖啡。

我们现在相处得很好，就像打过游击战的老兵一样，真不明白过去为何有龃龉。

② Days pass. I see no one. I come to dread my husband's evening call, not only because he is full of news of what by now seems to me our remote life in Los Angeles, people he has seen, letters which require attention, but because he asks what I have been doing, suggests uneasily that I get out, drive to San Francisco or Berkeley. Instead I drive across the river to a family graveyard. It has been vandalized since my last visit and the monuments are broken, overturned in the dry grass. Because I once saw a rattlesnake in the grass I stay in the car and listen to a Country-and-Western station. Later I drive with my father to a ranch he has in the foothills. The man who runs his cattle on it asks us to the roundup, a week from Sunday, and although I know that I will be in Los Angeles I say, in the oblique way my family talks, that I will come. Once home I mention the broken monuments in the graveyard. My mother shrugs. (Joan Didion)

② 日子一天天过去，我没拜访任何人。我开始对丈夫晚间打来的电话感到害怕，不光是因为他老是跟我讲洛杉矶的情况，见到谁啦，哪些信件该回啦，等等，而洛杉矶的生活距离我似乎已遥远了啊！还因为他问我在做什么，有点拘束地建议我出去走走，开车去旧金山或伯克利。我却驾车去了河对岸的一块家族墓地。自我上次来过之后，墓地被破坏了，墓碑断裂，翻倒在枯草丛里。以前我曾在草丛里见到一条响尾蛇，所以这次我待在车上，收听乡村与西部音乐台的广播。后来我同父亲开车去了他在山麓小丘上的农场。为他放牛的人请我们下周日来看他赶拢牛群。尽管我明明知道那时我已回到洛杉矶了，但我还是以家里人绕弯子的方式说要来。一回到家里，我就提起了墓地里的断碑。母亲耸了耸肩。(《中国翻译》编辑部用例)

6.4 Marriage and Family

婚姻与家庭

① "Family" is of course an elastic word. But when British people say that their society is based on family life, they are thinking of "Family" in its narrow, peculiarly European sense of mother, father and children living together alone in their own house as an economic and social unit. Thus, every British marriage indicates the beginning of a new and independent family — hence the tremendous importance of marriage in British life. For both the man and the woman, marriage means leaving one's parents and starting one's own life. The man's first duty will then be to his wife, and the wife's to her husband. He will be entirely responsible for her financial support, and she for the running of the new home. Their children will be their common responsibility and theirs alone. Neither the wife's parents nor the husband's, nor their brothers or sisters, aunts or uncles, have any right to interfere with them — that are their own masters.

①“家”，当然是一个含义较灵活的词。但是当英国人在说社会是基于家庭生活之上时，他们就是从其狭义上考虑“家”的。这是欧洲人特有的观念，即父母和孩子住自己的房子，生活在一起，成为一个经济和社会的个体。这样，在英国每桩婚姻都标志着一种新的独立的家庭生活的开始。因此也可以说，婚姻是英国人生活中极为重要的一件事。婚姻对于男女双方来说都意味着要离开父母开始自己的生活。从此，男子的首要责任就是对妻子负责，妻子则对丈夫负责。丈夫要完全承担对妻子的经济支持，而妻子承担的是管理好这个新家的责任。养育孩子将完全是夫妻双方共同承担的责任。他们自己的事自己做主，双方

的父母都无权干涉;他们的兄弟、姐妹、婶姨、叔舅也都无权干涉。

② Readers of novels like Jane Austen's *Pride and Prejudice* will know that in former times marriage among wealthy families were arrangted by the girl's parents, that is, it was the parents' duty to find a suitable husband for their daughter, preferably a rich one, and by skillful encouragement to lead him eventually to ask their permission to marry her. Until that time, the girl was protected and maintained in the parents' home and the financial relief of getting rid of her could be seen in their giving the newly married pair a sum of money called a dowry. It is very different today. Most girls of today get a job when they leave school and become financially independent before their marriage. This has had two results. A girl chooses her own husband, and she gets no dowry.

② 读过简·奥斯汀的小说《傲慢与偏见》的读者就知道,在英国早期,富有家庭之间的婚姻是由女方父母安排的。也就是说,为女儿找一个合适的丈夫是父母的义务。父母们最希望的是,经过他们的巧妙安排,最终使富家子弟请求二老把女儿下嫁给他。在此之前,女方待字闺中,受到父母的保护。出嫁时得到的经济资助就是父母给新婚夫妇的一笔嫁妆钱。然而现在的情况已经完全改观。大多数女孩离开学校时会找份工作,这样在婚前就已经经济独立了。由此也带来两个结果:女孩自己选丈夫,而且无嫁妆可得。(陈德彰用例)

6.5 推荐读物

(1)包惠南,文化语境与语言翻译,中国对外翻译出版公司 2001 年版。
(2)刘宓庆,新编当代翻译理论,中国对外翻译出版公司 2005 年版。
(3)单其昌,汉英翻译技巧,外语教学与研究出版社 1990 年版。
(4)倜西等,英汉翻译手册,商务印书馆国际有限公司 2002 年版。
(5)田惠刚,中西人际称谓系统,外语教学与研究出版社 1998 年版。
(6)叶子南,高级英汉翻译理论与实践,清华大学出版社 2008 年版。
(7)张培基,英汉翻译教程,上海外语教育出版社 2009 年版。
(8)庄绎传,英汉翻译教程,外语教学与研究出版社 1999 年版。

7 课后练习

7.1 分析题

(1)试用所译和比读材料分析全译原则。
(2)试析 6.1《父亲》使用了哪些翻译窍门。
(3)试析汉英称谓翻译体现了哪些文化差异。

7.2 实训题

7.2.1 计划生育

计划生育取得的成就已为经济持续发展、人民生活水平的提高及全社会的进步创造了良好的环境。经专家计算,如果中国没有实行计划生育政策,而保持着 20 世纪 70 年代初的出生率，那么现在的人口将已超过15亿大关。计划生育给中国社会带来的直接影响是广泛而深远的，随着时间的推移，计划生育的利处对人们及后代的影响必将变得更为显著。

7.2.2 Marriage Across Nations

① The continual source of our strength was our mutual trust and respect.

② We wanted to avoid the mistake made by many couples of marrying for the wrong reasons, and only finding out ten, twenty, or thirty years later that they were incompatible, that they hardly took the time to know each other, that they overlooked serious personality conflicts in the expectation that marriage was an automatic way to make everything work out right. That point was emphasized by the fact that Gail's parents, after thirty-five years of marriage, were going through a bitter and painful divorce, which had destroyed Gail and for a time had a negative effect on our budding relationship.

7.3 思考题

(1)翻译爱情话题的文本时，应遵照什么原则？

(2)汉语称谓英译困难主要体现在什么方面？

(3)中国传统礼教如何影响汉英称谓翻译？

(4)试比较中西婚姻仪式差异，分析翻译中的文化转化问题。

(5)试析家庭幽默互译的困惑与方法。

(6)试析中西征婚文本的翻译。

(7)试析中西情书语篇的差别与转换艺术。

(8)试析英语爱情影视片名汉译的艺术。

(9)汉英翻译如何处理中国庞杂的亲属关系？

(10)较之于婚姻家庭语篇翻译，6.2 的翻译有何特点？

(11)汉语和英语中的爱称在构成方法上有何异同？

(12)家庭生活用语翻译如何注意生活气息的转达？

(13)试用归化观与异化观分析爱称翻译的差异。

第 5 课 历史文化

导 译

文化是有社会、语言、民族和地区属性的。每种文化都有自己独特的风格和内涵。翻译是一种“跨语言”、“跨文化”的活动，旨在使双方或者各方都能沟通，都能相互理解。在语言转换的同时，如何把中华民族的文化瑰宝用英语加以诠释而不失其独特品味、如何把蕴含着丰富而独特的文化底蕴的英语转换成带有“汉气”却不完全“汉化”的地道汉语。在处理文本中的历史文化因素时，要根据作者的意图、文本的类型、读者的需要、翻译的目的等来采取相应的“异化”或者“归化”翻译策略，归化译文有较高的可读性读起来通顺易懂读者群较为庞大，异化译文可以尽可能多的传递文化信息使读者体验异域表达与文化风味它们各有所长互相补充与完善。在翻译的实践过程也可采取直译、意译、直译加注释、音译加注释、套译等翻译方法。为了达到文化传通的目的，译者也要巧用汉语四字格，注意习语的翻译技巧以及灵活运用蕴含文化历史含义的专有名词的翻译方法。总之，翻译的真正归宿是通过语际转换再现原文文化，其实质是交流文化。

练笔 1 课前练笔

1.1 守岁

守岁的传统源自于一个有趣的民间故事。中国古代有一个叫做“年”的凶猛怪物，在除夕夜“年”会从地洞里出来吃人。因此在除夕夜，每家每户都会一起吃晚饭，晚饭以后没人敢睡觉，所有的家庭成员会坐在一起聊天互相壮胆。逐渐在除夕夜守岁的习惯形成了，因此在中国，庆祝春节也叫做过年。然而现在城市里很少有人以守岁来欢迎新年。

1.2 汉字

近些年,世界上学汉字的人多了起来,母语是拼音文字系统的人常常觉得汉字很难学。同时,不少人在学汉字的过程中体会了丰富的历史文化内容。以象形为基础的汉字,包含着中国人对世界的丰富体验,难怪西方有些诗人在接触汉字时,立即引起诗意的联想。

1.3 **Thanksgiving Day**

Thanksgiving was first celebrated in 1621, when Plymouth governor William Bradford invited neighboring Native Americans to join the Pilgrims for a three-day festival in gratitude for the successful harvest that followed a hard winter. The feast they sat down to had very little in common with today's celebration, however. It is quite likely that their feast consisted of fish, venison, corn and other vegetables. Today's traditional dinner of turkey, mashed potatoes, green bean casserole, cranberry sauce and pumpkin pie is mainly the result of a strong advertising campaign by turkey producers. Thanksgiving was proclaimed a national holiday by President Abraham Lincoln in 1863. Many Americans consider this to be only an American holiday although it is also celebrated in Canada and harvest festivals are held throughout the world.

1.4 **Monday**

Monday, the second day of the week, means literally "day of the moon". Here in Britain, it's generally the least popular of days because for most people it means a return to work or school after the weekend break. Often, this prospect is viewed with a lack of enthusiasm, a sad feeling that's sometimes referred to as "Monday morning blues". Sometimes the blues may be caused by too much weekend drinking; and formerly if workmen over-indulged and needed Monday as holiday, this was humorously known as "keeping St. Monday", as Monday was hoped to be a saint's day to be observed. Someone who can't afford to keep St. Monday is the housewife, for traditionally Monday was — and to some extent still is — "wash day", the proper day for doing the laundry. However, the day is not all blues and work. It has some redeeming features-that is, if you can believe folk rhymes, it's a good day on which to be born. "Monday's child is fair a face," says one traditional rhyme, while another promised optimistically that if you get married on Monday, you will be wealthy.

1.5 **How Names are Called in America**

People generally call each other by their first names much sooner in their acquaintance than people do in other walks of life. Taking that liberty too soon has closed many doors for the offender. Therefore, one must sense the proper moment to drop formal address and adopt subtle measures to prevent unwelcome intimate address. If you have been accepted wholeheartedly into a group, however important first names are in the world's eyes, it would be conspicuous for you to continue beyond a certain time to call them by their last names, such as Mr. Robinson and Mrs. Harvin. If an older woman enjoys having young people call her first name, she will ask you to do so — otherwise don't. In the business circle, many people think it demeaning to be called by the first name; it is best to use "Mr." or "Miss" with a business superior or an employer.

批评 2 课前批评

2.1 家

用拆字先生的办法,望文生义,家最初显然和猪圈有关,而家的发展,当然是让它越来越不像猪圈。不过,我并不喜欢那些一尘不染的家庭。清洁过了头,家反而不像家。家是给人住的,因此,我想一切都应该以让人不感到别扭为度。过分用心了,人便成了家的奴隶,整天替家当保姆,不值得。一个让人羡慕的家庭环境,所有的布置,都应该是以能促进家庭成员彼此之间的健康和谐为基本的前提。一个好的家居,要充满人情味,太干净、太讲究,人情味必打折扣。

Homes

Like people who divine fortunes by analyzing the component parts of a Chinese character, I'd conclude that a home at its very start was evidently associated with a pigsty. But with the gradual development of the human abode, a home dissociates itself farther and farther away from that place. On the other hand, I don't like a home that is kept spick-and-span. If overdone, a home ceases being a home. A home is a place for people to live in; therefore everything should be measured against the standard whether people feel at home in the home. Excessive attention to one's dwelling turns one into a slave in bondage to a material structure, and a round — the-clock housekeeper. It's hardly worth the while. The layout and ambience of an enviable home should be designed to guarantee the health of each and every family member and promote domestic harmony. An ideal home should be pervaded by human touch abridged.

(王恩冕用例)

2.2 George Washington

① George Washington was a stern administrator, deeply religious, a stickler for rules, and a strict military disciplinarian. Yet he was not a haughty aristocrat. Here are some facts which shed a more human light upon him.

① 乔治·华盛顿是一个严厉的行政官员,笃信宗教,坚持要求按规章制度办事,是一个一丝不苟的严格执行纪律的军事家。但他并非是一个高傲的贵族,这里有一些事实可以很好地

② For one thing, he took command of a ragged army of revolutionaries. This was an act of courage and moral conviction that flew directly in the face of tradition and of what might have appeared to be good common sense. Later, when Washington became president, he was able to hold together an explosive political situation. His calm wisdom and understanding helped him hammer out a model of sound administration for future chief executives to follow.

说明他是一个具有人情味的人。

② 首先,他敢于出任一直破破烂烂的革命军的司令。这是一个显示勇气和道义信念的行动。这一行动具有反传统精神,而且也违反了可能看来是一件十足常识的事。后来华盛顿出任总统时,他在一种富有爆炸性的政治局势面前做到了团结一致。他那种稳坐钓鱼台的明智态度和理智精神使他能够树立起一个健全政府的典范,供后来的总统们遵循。

③ Politics attracted him early in his career. He was member of the Virginia House of Burgesses and of the Continental Congress before he took command of the American Revolutionary Army. It is doubtful that the colonists could have endured the long, frustrating war without firm, ambience leadership of a man like George Washington. Whatever his personal feelings must have been, in defeat after defeat, Washington maintained his dignity.

③ 在其事业生涯中,他很早就被政治所吸引。在出任革命军统帅以前,他曾任弗吉尼亚州下议院议员和大陆会议代表。如果没有像华盛顿这样坚忍不拔的领导人,殖民地人民能否顶得住那一场旷日持久和屡遭挫败的战争,是难以预卜的。在一次又一次战败后,不管他内心有什么样的感受,他始终保持着他的尊严。(隋荣谊用例)

知识 3 全译知识 全译标准

全译标准取决于全译极似律,二者是外与内的关系。译者孜孜以求译作"极似"于原作,表现为三个维度,即意似、形似和风格似。意似是基本标准,形似是辅助标准,风格似才是最高标准。任何原作可从形式、意义和作用三个角度考察,语形、语义、语用构成语言的三个基本方面,所以全译可从语形极似、语义极似和语用极似三个方面考量。

3.1 语形极似

语形极似主要分为语音极似和语法极似。语音极似指译作在音响、韵律、节奏等方面与原作的极似。译者力求运用相似的译语语音手段反映原作的某些语音特色。语法极似指译作在词法、尤其是句法上与原作的极似。译者力求运用相似的译语语法手段反映原作的某些语法特色。如:

When one loves one's Art no service seems too hard.

【原译】:当你爱好你的艺术时,就觉得没有什么牺牲是难以忍受的。

【改译Ⅰ】:当你爱上了艺术,什么牺牲也能忍受。

【改译Ⅱ】:一旦你把艺术爱,什么奉献也不难。

【试译】:一旦你爱上艺术,没什么不可献出。

这是美国著名短篇小说家欧·亨利之名篇《爱的奉献》(A Service of Love)的开篇句,在情节的开始、发展、高潮和结局中重复四次,是小说的主旋律或基调。从语表形式看,原文12个音节,仿佛由两个诗行构成的一个诗句,从句六音节三音步,为扬抑格,主句也是六音节三音步,却是抑扬格,两句以Art和hard押尾韵。原译拖泥带水,毫无节奏可言。

3.2 语义极似

语义极似主要分为词/短语义极似和句义极似,词义是各级语义的基础。如上例,改译Ⅰ比原译简洁,语义基本极似,但少含蓄,节奏和押韵不符。改译Ⅱ用了否定形式,传达了含蓄之意,但语音美依旧没有传达。试译用双重否定"没有什么(不可)"译原文对全句的否定,语义达至极似。

例中service是古体用法,意为向爱人表忠心,献殷勤。改译Ⅰ选择"牺牲"义,太直率,不如"奉献"或"献出"含蓄,同时一石二鸟:既向爱人奉献爱情,又为爱情奉献对艺术的爱。用"你"译one,泛指任何人,符合小说开篇的语境,更拉近了读者与作者的距离。

3.3 语用极似

全译的语用就是原文的风格,全译语用极似即风格似,主要涉及修辞极似、语体极似和文化极似。风格极似除了辞格求极似外,还包括音、形、义三方面的同义选择,表达同一内容可用不同形式,所产生的效果和风格也会有所不同。如上例,试译用14个汉字对译原文12个音节,押尾韵,朗朗上口。后一句照译双重否定,再现了收敛式强调,同时用汉语顺口溜译原文顺口溜式谚语,传达了原文的语体色彩。

4 全译窍门

4.1 "不译"之译

汉译时,有时要去掉原文中可有可无的成分,采取减译法。被减现象多是英语语法需要而汉语不需的词语或语法范畴,旨在使译文更加流畅、更符合汉语习惯。有时英语必须写出的词,如代词、连词、冠词、介词等,译了反而会影响汉语的流畅性,或不符合汉语的表达习惯。如:

① Outside **it** was pitch dark and **it** was raining cats and dogs. 外面一团漆黑,大雨倾盆。

② **If** winter comes, can spring be far behind? 冬天来了,春天还会远吗?

③ Rumors had already spread **along** the streets and lanes. 流言蜚语传遍了大街小巷。

④ We must bring forward a new design **at the earliest possible date.** 我们必须尽快提出新设计。

⑤ He hopes that he may once again repeat, upon a greater scale than ever before, that process of destroying his enemies one by one by which he has so long thrived and prospered. 他希望能在比以往更大规模上再次逐个消灭敌人,他过去一直得心应手地运用这一战术。

例①省代词,例②省连接词,例③省介词,例④简化了介词短语,例⑤合并了概念。

4.2 巧用四字格

汉语拥有丰富的四字格,其含义深刻,构型短小,生命力旺盛,表现力强。四字格的典型是成语,因袭定型,词序固定,不能随意拆散或组合,有些则不是成语,结构松散,可据语境灵活组合。四字格运用得当,可令译文增色,锦上添花。

⑥ It was one clear and calm day in mid-January…那是一月里,一个天气晴朗、风平浪静的日子……

⑦ Gradually the river grows wider, the banks recede, the waters flows more quietly, and at the end, without any visible break, they became merged in the sea, and painlessly lose their individual being. 其后河面逐渐宽展,两岸相距愈远,水流也愈趋平缓,最后则流入大海,与海水浑然一体,看不出两者有任何界限,自然而然地结束其单独存在的那一段历程。

凡事有度,多用会走向反面。切忌滥用四字格,如一篇匈牙利小说谈到老祖母老了,译者可能觉得"老"字不雅,于是套用"人老珠黄",殊不知"人老珠黄"有年老色衰之意,用来形容操劳一生的老祖母,未免不伦不类。

4.3 注释之妙

语言间有常见的翻译技巧无法解决的文化差异,此时需要加注。通常在被注者右上角标以符号,如阿拉伯数字或"*",然后再自动生成脚注,写上所要注的内容。加注主要用来释文、解惑和补正,补充诸如词语内涵、背景知识、风土民俗、译者说明等,填补因文化差异造成的语义空缺,便于读者理解。

⑧ It was **Friday** and soon they'd go out and get drunk. 一到周五[①]他们就会出门喝得大醉。

4.4 正话反说

英汉语有相似的否定思维。但表达否定概念所使用的手段会有差异。任何时候都以否定译否定,译文有时不通顺,或者不符合译语习惯。如:

⑨ 她抱怨名单上没有她的名字。She complained about the **omission** of her name from the list.

---

① 周五为英国的发薪日。

⑩ 这些细菌要在温度达到 100 摄氏度时才会死亡。These bacteria **will not** die **until** the temperature reaches 100℃.

例⑨的"没有"译作了 omission,例⑩汉语的肯定式译成英语的否定式。

4.5 习语巧处理

英语习语包括俗语、谚语、俚语等,汉语习语广义上包括成语、俗语、歇后语、谚语、双关语、形象化语言等,其民族色彩甚为突出。习语的翻译原则是:传达原意,联系语境,灵活机动,防止死译硬译。

最方便的译法是套译法,双语的习语在形义以及色彩上相互吻合时,不妨直接套用。如:Like father like son. 有其父必有其子;Wall have ears. 隔墙有耳。Strike while the iron is hot. 趁热打铁。Misfortune might be a blessing in disguise. 塞翁失马,安知非福。

套译时,要避用民族特色太浓的习语,否则译文就会不伦不类,损及原意。如:

⑪ Many heads are better than one. 一人不及众人计。(不译"三个臭皮匠,顶个诸葛亮")

⑫ Never offer to teach fish to swim. 不要教鱼儿游泳。(不译"不要班门弄斧")

⑬ Even a worm will turn. 逼人入绝境,绵羊也反抗(不译"狗急跳墙")

有时还要当心"假朋友"。一些貌似有理据或合乎逻辑的习语极易导致译者相信自己直觉而疏于查考,望文生义,单从字面或比喻意义去联想,造成理解以至表达的错误。如:

⑭ There is no love lost between them.

【误译】:他们彼此恩爱,感情从未破裂。

【正译】:他们互相憎恨,毫无爱情可言。

4.6 专名宜"专"

就汉语人名地名英译而言,除历史原因和约定俗成外,还可用汉语拼音拼写,从"专名+通名"构成的专名为例,"太湖"之"太"是专名,"湖"是通名,先音译并与专名连用,再重复意译,将通名译为大写的地理或行政区划的名词,同时在整个专名前加上定冠词。如:太湖→the Taihu Lake,衡山→the Hengshan Mountain,渤海→the Bohai Sea,长江→the Changjiang River。

词汇 5 话题词汇

5.1 中国历史年表

北朝 the Northern Dynasties(386—581)
北齐 the Northern Qi Regime(550—577)
北宋 the Northern Song Dynasty(960—1127)
北魏 the Northern Wei Regime(386—534)
北周 the Northern Zhou Regime(557—581)
陈 the Chen Regime(557—589)
春秋 the Spring and Autumn Period(770—256B. C.)

东汉 the Eastern Han Dynasty(25—220)
东晋 the Eastern Jin Dynasty(317—420)
东魏 the Eastern Wei Regime(534—550)
东周 the Eastern Zhou Dynasty(770—256B. C.)
后汉 the Later Han Regime(947—950)
后晋 the Later Jin Regime(936—946)
后梁 the Later Liang Regime(907—923)
后唐 the Later Tang Regime(923—936)
后周 the Later Zhou Regime(951—960)
金 the Jin Dynasty(1115—1234)
梁 the Liang Regime(502—557)
辽 the Liao Dynasty(916—1125)
明 the Ming Dynasty(1368—1644)
南北朝 the Southern and Northern Dynasties(420—589)
南朝 the Southern Dynasties(420—589)
南宋 the Southern Song Dynasty(1127—1279)
齐 the Qi Regime(479—502)
秦 the Qin Dynasty(221—206 B. C.)
清 the Qing Dynasty(1644—1911)
三国 the Three Kingdoms(220—280)
商 the Shang Dynasty(16th c. —11th c. B. C.)
蜀 the Shu Kingdom(221—263)
宋 the Song Regime(420—479)
隋 the Sui Dynasty(581—618)
唐 the Tang Dynasty(618—907)
魏 the Wei Kingdom(220—265)
吴 the Wu Kingdom(222—280)
五代 the Five Dynasties(907—960)
西汉 the Western Han Dynasty (206 B. C.—24A. C.)
西晋 the Western Jin Dynasty(265—316)
西魏 the Western Wei Regime(535—556)
西夏 the Western Xia Dynasty(1038—1227)
西周 the Western Zhou Dynasty (11th c.—771B. C.)
夏 the Xia Dynasty(21st c. —16th c. B. C.)
元 the Yuan Dynasty(1271—1368)
战国 the Warring States Period(475—221B. C.)
中华民国 the Republic of China(1911—1949)
中华人民共和国 the People's Republic of China (founded in 1949)

5.2 中外传统节日

春节(阴历正月初一) Spring Festival (Chinese New Year)
端午节(阴历五月初五) Dragon Boat Festival
教师节(中国,9 月 10 日) Teacher's Day
元宵节(阴历正月十五日) Lantern Festival
中秋节(阴历八月十五日) Moon Festival
成人节(日本,1 月 15 日) Adults Day
敬老节(日本,9 月 15 日) Old People's Day
筷子节(日本,8 月 4 日) Chopsticks Day
男孩节(日本,5 月 5 日) Boy's Day
桃花节(日本女孩节,3 月 3 日) Peach Flower Festival (Doll's Festival)
枫糖节(加拿大,3—4 月) Maple Sugar Festival
父亲节(6 月的第三个星期日) Father's Day
复活节(春分月圆后第一个星期日) Easter
感恩节(美国,11 月最后一个星期四) Thanksgiving
古尔邦节(伊斯兰教,7 月下旬) Corban
鬼节(万圣节除夕,10 月 31 日夜) Halloween
国际儿童节(6 月 1 日) International Children's Day
国际妇女节(3 月 8 日) International Women's Day
国际劳动节(5 月 1 日) International Labour Day
狂欢节(巴西,二月中、下旬) Carnival
母亲节(5 月的第二个星期日) Mother's Day
情人节(2 月 14 日) St. Valentine's Day (Valentine's Day)
圣诞夜(12 月 24 日) Christmas Eve
圣帕特里克节(爱尔兰,3 月 17 日) St. Patrick's Day
宋干节(泰国新年 4 月 13 日) Songkran Festival Day
愚人节(4 月 1 日) April Fool's Day
元旦(1 月 1 日)New Year's Day
仲夏节(北欧 6 月) Mid-Summer Day

5.3 二十四节气

立春 the Beginning of Spring（1st solar term）Feb. 3,4, or 5

清明 Pure Brightness（5th solar term）Apr. 4,5 or 6

小寒 Lesser Cold（23rd solar term）Jan. 5,6 or 7

惊蛰 the Waking of Insects（3rd solar term）Mar. 5,6, or 7

立夏 the Beginning of Summer（7th solar term）May 5,6 or 7

芒种 Grain in Beard（9th solar term）Jun. 5,6 or 7

小暑 Lesser Heat（11th solar term）Jul. 6,7 or 8

大雪 Greater Snow（21st solar term）Dec. 6,7 or 8

立秋 the Beginning of Autumn（13th solar term）Aug. 7,8 or 9

白露 White Dew（15th solar term）Sep. 7,8 or 9

大寒 Greater Cold（24th solar term）Jan. 20 or 21

夏至 the Summer Solstice（10th solar term）Jun. 21 or 22

寒露 Cold Dew（17th solar term）Oct. 8 or 9

霜降 Frost's Descent（18th solar term）Oct. 23 or 24

立冬 the Beginning of Winter（19th solar term）Nov. 7 or 8

小雪 Lesser Snow（20th solar term）Nov. 22 or 23

雨水 Rain Water（2nd solar term）Feb. 18,19 or 20

谷雨 Grain Rain（6th solar term）Apr. 19,20 or 21

春分 the Spring Equinox（4th solar term）Mar. 20, 21 or 22

小满 Lesser Fullness of Grain（8th solar term）May 20,21 or 22

冬至 the Winter Solstice（22th solar term）Dec. 21, 22 or 23

大暑 Greater Heat（12th solar term）Jul. 22,23 or 24

处暑 the End of Heat（14th solar term）Aug. 22,23 or 24

秋分 the Autumn Equinox（16th solar term）Sep. 22,23 or 24

5.4 有典型文化内涵的动物习语

Bird

A bird in the hand is worth two in the bush. 双鸟在林,不如一鸟在手。

Birds of a feather flock together. 物以类聚,人以群分。

Fine feathers make fine birds. 人靠衣装,佛靠金装。

It's an ill bird that fouls its own nest. 家丑不可外扬。

Kill two birds with one stone. 一箭双雕。

The early bird catches the worm. 捷足先登;笨鸟先飞。

Fish

Fish begins to stink at the head. 上梁不正下梁歪。

Small fish in a big pond, big fish in a small pond. 小池塘里的大鱼,大池塘里的小鱼。(比喻某人是个小环境里面的大人物,或是大环境里面的小人物)

Teach fish to swim. 教鱼游泳。

The best fish smell when they are three days old. 久住招人嫌。

Horse

Don't ride the high horse. 勿摆架子。

I'm so hungry that I could eat a horse. 饥肠辘辘。

To lock the stable door after the horse is stolen. 亡羊补牢。

To put the cart before the horse. 本末倒置。

Cat

A fat cat. 有钱有势的人。

Like a cat on hot bricks. 像热锅上的蚂蚁。

The cat shuts its eyes when stealing cream. 掩耳盗铃。

When the cat is away, the mice will play. 山中无老虎,猴子称大王。

Dog

Barking dogs do not bite. 吠犬不咬人。

Dog doesn't eat dog. 同行不相妒。

Every dog has his day. 人人皆有得意时。

Fight dog, fight bear. 不获全胜不收兵。

He who has a mind to beat his dog will easily find a

stick. 欲加之罪,何患无辞。

Let sleeping dogs lie 不惹是生非。

Love me, love my dog. 爱屋及乌。

To help a lame dog over a stile. 雪中送炭。

Sheep

A lion in the way 拦路虎。

A wolf in sheep's clothing. 披着羊皮的狼。

A rat in a hole. 瓮中之鳖。

May as well be hanged for a sheep as a lamb. 一不做,二不休。

One swallow doesn't make a summer. 一燕不成夏。

Other Animals

The leopard can't change its sports. 本性难移。

To separate the sheep from the goats. 把好人与坏人分开。

To beard the lion in his den. 太岁头上动土。

5.5 缩略语

AMG 盟国军政府

AOH 爱尔兰古老秩序

AR 美国独立战争

BA 铜器时代

BC 公元前

BM 英国女王玛丽一世的别名

CB(中世纪妇女使用的)贞操带

CIGS 帝国总参谋

GCK 大韩帝国

ICBI 圣经勘误国际理事会

K. B. 英国古代最低级爵士

MA 中世纪

MRT 毛里塔尼亚

R. C. 罗马天主教

SK 高丽王国

TR 第三帝国

YM 基督教青年会

AI 英国爱尔兰人

ERP 欧洲复兴计划

BP 英国专利

CV (基督教《圣经》的)普通译本

AS 盎格鲁撒克逊人;盎格鲁撒克逊人的

AS 不擅社交的;非社交的;反社会的

IT 信息论

FP 联邦会议

CC 文化中心

CB (占卜用的)水晶球,玻璃球,预言未来的方法(乌托邦)

BT 准男爵

AR 评论年刊,年度综论

AR (尤指 1789 年法国大革命前的)社会及政治制度

CAS 中国科学院

OS 守旧派

KG 嘉德勋爵士

AL 美国联盟

MH 荣誉勋章

RH 殿下

SF 爱尔兰的新芬党

ARV 美国基督教《圣经》标准译本修订本

VISTA(美国)志愿服务队

AFDC(美国)对有子女家庭补助计划

CBE 最高级巴思爵士

myth 神话

vis. 子爵

QPM 女王公安勋章

6 比读体悟

6.1 郑和下西洋

Zheng He's Seven Voyages to the Western Seas

① 明朝前期,中国是世界上最先进、最发达的国家之一。为了显示中国富强,扩大明朝在海外各国的政治影响,加

① In the early Ming Dynasty, China was one of the most advanced and developed countries in the world. In order to display the national power and strengthen contacts with other

强与世界各国的联系，明成祖朱棣派郑和多次出使西洋(指文莱以西的东南亚和印度洋一带).

countries, Emperor Chengzu sent Zheng He, a senior general and eunuch, on his voyages to the Western Seas (Southeast Asia, west of Brunei and the Indian Ocean) on diplomatic missions.

② 郑和的船队满载着金银珠宝、丝绸、瓷器等中国特产，每到一个国家或地区，郑和都把这些东西当做明朝的礼物送给他们，表达了和他们友好交往的愿望。西洋各国非常友好地接待了郑和和他的船队，有些国家还派使者跟随他前来朝见中国皇帝。同时，郑和也从各国换回了珠宝、香料等特产。明成祖对郑和的成绩非常满意。郑和前后7次出使西洋，最远到达了非洲东海岸和红海沿岸。

② Zheng He fleets were loaded with large amounts of gold precious stones, porcelain and silk which were used as gifts to express goodwill. Some of the countries Zheng He visited also dispatched envoys bearing tribute to the Ming court on his ships. Meanwhile Zheng He exchanged with these countries special local products such as jewelry, spice and so on. Emperor Chengzu was satisfied with Zheng He's achievements. During the Seven voyages to the Western Seas, Zheng He sailed as far as the eastern coast of Africa and the Red Sea coast. (叶朗、朱良志 译)

6.2 孔子

Confucius

① 孔子名丘，字仲尼，公元前551年诞生在中国曲阜，卒于公元前479年。

① Confucius' given name is Qiu, also styled Zhongni. He was born in Qu Fu, China, 551 B.C..

② 孔子开创了中国历史上一个著名学派——儒学。他的思想核心是“仁”，表现形式是“礼”。孔子为宣扬自己的主张，周游列国，奔波一生。晚年删诗书，订礼乐，整理编撰了《春秋》、《诗》、《书》、《礼》、《乐》、《易》六部著作，流传至今，视为儒学经典。他首办私学，有弟子三千，其中贤人七十二。《论语》一书记录了他主要言论。

② Confucius founded Confucianism — the famous philosophical school in the history of China. The kernel of his thought is Ren(benevolence), its form of expression is Li(the Rites). Confucius travelled from one state to another preaching his doctrines until he was old. He spent his last years in compiling and editing. His works include Book of Spring and Autumn, Book of Odes, Book of History, Book of Rite, Book of Music and Book of Change. These six books regarded as the classical works of Confucianism have been handed down to the present time. He founded the first private school in Chinese history. He was the teacher of 3,000 disciples among whom 72 were Sages. His major sayings were written down in Lun Yu (The Analects), one of the Four Books.

③ 孔子生活在我国春秋(公元前770年—前476年)末年，晚年生活清贫，并无大名气，但卒后他的思想却惊人地影响中华民族两千五百多年。他的伦理道德学说对人们的意识形态产生过巨大影响，使中华民族凝聚一体，成为闻名于世的礼仪之邦。子曰:“三人行必有我师焉”，“己欲立而立人，己欲达而达人”，“学而不厌，诲人不倦”……他的至理名言至今仍闪烁着哲理的光芒。

③ Confucius lived in the late Spring and Autumn period (770—476 B.C.). In his last years he lived in relative poverty and no longer enjoyed great fame. But after his death, his thought continued to influence the Chinese people for over 2,500 years. His doctrine on morality and ethics has had a great effect on their ideology, strengthening the unity of the nation and making it known to the world for its courteous dealing and solemn rites. Confucius said, "Let there be three men walking together: from that number I should be sure to find my instructor." "To make accomplishment you must help other to be accomplished too." "Never be satiated with you knowledge and never be tired of teaching." …Today, these philosophical sayings are still shining brilliantly.

④ 在中华民族历史长河中,炎黄子孙为涌现出孔子这样一位杰出人物而感到自豪。伟大的思想家和教育家孔子的影响,目前已超出国界,为世界瞩目。愿通过对孔子更多了解和架起世界各国人民友谊及文化交流的桥梁,让世界充满仁爱、正义与和平。愿海内外炎黄子孙通过对孔子更好地了解和学术研究,激励起民族精神,开辟古为今用新途径,为振兴中华而加倍努力。

④ In the long span of the Chinese history, the descendants of the Yellow Emperor have been righteously proud of the existence of the outstanding Confucius. The influence of the great thinker and educator has now exceeded the national boundary and spread to other parts of the world. It is our earnest hope that through more understanding of Confucius and the bridge of friendship and cultural exchange, we can make the world filled with more love, justice and peace. We wish also that we offspring of the Yellow Emperor, either in China or abroad, through better understanding of Confucius and academic research, will be more inspired with nationalism, and find a new way of making the past serve the present, and redouble our efforts for the rejuvenation of China. (王岷源译)

6.3 The English Reserve and Politeness

To other Europeans, the best known quality of the British is "reserve". A reserved person is one who does not talk very much to strangers, does not show much emotion, and seldom gets excited. It is difficult to get to know a reserved person; he never tells you anything about himself, and you may work with him for years without ever knowing where he lives, how many children he has, and what his interests are. English people tend to be like that. If they are making a journey by bus, they will do their best to find an empty seat; if by train, an empty compartment. If they have to share the compartment with a stranger, they may travel many miles without starting a conversation. If a conversation does start, personal questions like "How old are you?" or even "What is your salary?" are not easily asked. Questions like "Where did you buy your watch?" or "What is your salary?" are almost impossible. Similarly, conversation in Britain is in general quiet and restrained and loud speech is considered ill-bred.

英国人的保守与礼貌

对于英国以外的欧洲人来说,英国人最显著的特点是"谨慎"。一个谨慎的人不太会和陌生人聊天,不会流露出太多的情感,并且很少会喜形于色。要了解一个谨慎的人并非易事;他从不随意谈及有关自己的任何事,也许与其共事了几年,却连他住在哪儿,有几个孩子,兴趣是什么都不知道。英国人通常有以下表现。如果乘坐公共汽车,他们会尽量找一个旁边没人的位子,如果坐火车他们通常找间单独的包厢,如果他们不得不与其他人共用一个包厢时,那么尽管车已经开出很久,他们也不会主动攀谈。即使是交谈,他们也不会轻易问像"您多大年纪?"或者"您叫什么名字?"这样的私人问题,他们也绝不会问"您的手表在哪里买的?"或"您的收入怎么样?"。英国人交谈的时候大都声音很轻,很有节制,大声说话会被人看做没有教养的表现。

6.4 The Palace of Westminster

The proper name for the Houses of Parliament is the Palace of Westminster and, in fact, there has been a royal palace on that site ever since the days of Edward the Confessor. The last king actually to live there was Henry VIII who left the Palace of Westminster after a bad fire in 1529. The Houses of Parliament are still a royal palace and were controlled by the Lord Great Chamberlain himself until 1965. There are records of a keeper of the palace since 1150, and he was paid 7d a day for the job from that day until 1884, when the position was abolished. And if you think that is funny, remember that even today all the M. P. s' cloakroom pegs have a little loop of red tape hanging from them — to hold their swords! The oldest part of the Houses of Parliament is Westminster Hall. Parts of this were built by William Rufus who succeeded William the Conqueror. But most of it was built by a famous architect called Henry Yevele between 1394 and 1399. When William Rufus first built Westminster Hall it was called the New Hall to stop it being confused with the Old Hall built by Edward the Confessor. From that day to this the courtyard in front of it has been known as "New Palace Yard."

西敏斯特宫

议会大厦的确切名称是西敏斯特宫,实际上自从撒克逊王爱德华以来,这个地方一直是一个皇宫。住在这个皇宫的最后一个国王是亨利八世,他在1952年一场大火之后迁出了西敏斯特宫。现在的议会大厦仍是一个皇宫。1965年以前一直由掌礼大臣本人亲自管理。这里保存着1150年以来的看守人记录,看守人每天可得7便士的报酬,这个职位一直到1884年才取消。如果你认为这一点很有趣的话,那么请你记住直到今天,各议员衣帽间的衣帽钉上还吊着红布袋做的小套环——供挂剑之用!议会大厦的最古老部分是西敏斯特大厅,它是由威廉一世的继承人威廉·鲁弗斯修建的,但大部分是由一名名叫亨利·耶维尔的著名建筑家于1394年至1399年之间建造的。威廉·鲁弗斯当初建造西敏斯特大厅时,把它称做新厅,以区别于撒克逊王爱德华建造的旧厅。此后,西敏斯特大厅前的庭院一直称做新宫院。(新梅林 译)

6.5 推荐读物

(1)李正中,王恩冕,大学英汉翻译教程,对外经济贸易大学出版社1992年版。
(2)辛华,英语姓名译名手册(修订本),商务印书馆1978年版。
(3)张培基等,英汉翻译教程,上海外语教育出版社1980年版。
(4)章思英,陈海燕,中国文化英语教程,外语教学与研究出版社2010年版。
(5)中国地名委员会,外国地名译名手册,商务印书馆1983年版。

7 课后练习

7.1 分析题

(1)试用所译和比读材料分析全译标准。
(2)试析英美文化差异汉译的不同处理。
(3)你赞成"释译"的方式吗?为什么?

7.2 实训题

7.2.1 指南针

在宋代,海外贸易非常发达。为了克服在海洋航行中的困难,到北宋末年,在航海上已经应用了指南针。南宋时还出现了将指南针安装在刻着度数和方位的圆盘上的罗盘针,使海上航行的人,在没有太阳的白天,没有月亮的夜晚,也能辨别方向。

7.2.2 American Food

" You are what you eat. " Nutrition experts often use this saying to promote better eating habits. What we put in our mouths does become a part of us. But we can look at this statement another way. What we eat reflects who we are — as people and as a culture. Do you want to understand another culture? Then you ought to find out about its food. Learning about American food can give us a real taste of American culture. What is " American food" ? At first you might think the answer is easy as pie. To many people, American food means hamburgers, hot dogs, fried chicken and pizza. If you have a " sweet tooth," you might even think of apple pie or chocolate chip cookies. It's true that Americans do eat those things. But are those the only kind of vittles you can find in America?

7.3 思考题

(1)请根据"名从主人"原则从语言文化角度探讨地名的翻译。
(2)请举例说明什么是"文化补偿"?
(3)请用典型的例子证明翻译中的"异化"与"归化"。
(4)有人认为"异化"与"归化"就是"直译"与"意译",你是否同意?
(5)翻译"文化负载词"的最大的难点是什么?
(6)有人认为中国的歇后语不可译,你是否同意?
(7)怎样在翻译中再现原文的交际功能?
(8)典型的文化现象回译时要注意什么?
(9)互译中如何再现原语民族的感情色彩?
(10)历史语境分析在互译中有什么作用?
(11)翻译历史事件如何小心惯性思维?
(12)互译中如何防范看似熟悉实则陌生的文化陷阱?
(13)如何翻译出原作的历史风格与时代风格?

第 6 课 旅游

导 译

旅游是一种集观光、娱乐、健身于一体的愉快而美好的活动。古往今来,旅游一直是人们增长知识、丰富阅历、强健体魄的美好追求。中国先哲提出了"观国之光"的思想,倡导"读万卷书,行万里路",游历名山大川,承天地之灵气,接山水之精华。20 世纪中期以来,现代旅游在全世界范围迅速兴起,旅游人数不断增加,旅游产业规模持续扩大,旅游经济地位显著提升,旅游活动成为各国人民交流文化、增进友谊、扩大交往的重要渠道,对人类生活和社会进步产生越来越广泛的影响。

旅游文本的翻译与旅游本身一样,具有吸引更多的译语读者前去参观游览的目的。中英文的旅游文本既有相似之处,又有不同之处,要根据各自的特点在翻译中进行调整。在正确传达原文文本信息内容的前提下,灵活运用音意兼顾、夸张、反复、变译等翻译技巧,点缀俗语、典故、诗词、楹联等文化现象,增强译文的可读性和感染力,满足旅游文本的信息性、情感性和指导性功能。

练笔 1 课前练笔

1.1 哈尔滨国际冰雪节

① 2012 年哈尔滨国际冰雪节从一月五日开幕,一直持续了三个月。它也毫无疑问成为了"中国冬之旅"的亮点和必行地。每年的这个时候,来自世界各地的艺术家们都会聚集在哈尔滨——这个位于中国北部,以冰雪著称的城市给人们带来一场由冰雪、焰火组成的视觉盛宴。这确实是一场名副其实的冰雪盛宴,成千上万吨的冰雪被艺术家们用他们的奇思妙想建造成了各种建筑物。这些同现实生活中的建筑物尺寸相仿的"冰屋"们绝对会让你震撼不已。除此之外,那些栩栩如生的冰雕也绝对能让你睁大眼球。

② 在“冰城”哈尔滨,你不仅可以看到各种美妙绝伦的冰雕,冰灯,还可去各大滑雪场滑雪。所以快来加入哈尔滨国际冰雪节吧!每逢一月开幕,不容错过的一月!

1.2 普陀山

普陀山属亚热带海洋性季风气候,夏无酷暑,冬无严寒,温和湿润,四季宜人。岛上植被丰茂,种类繁多,有“海盗植物园”之称。有引人注目的“千年樟”,树干周围有七米多,伟枝横空,苍劲挺拔,冠盖数亩,生机勃发。还有“普陀鹅耳枥”,虽貌不惊人,却属当世罕见珍木。此外,有野茶花和水仙花,特别是“普陀水仙”,为我国水仙三大名品之一。古树珍木,奇花异草,把名山普陀装点得更具迷人魅力。

1.3 Venice

① What images come to mind when you think of a trip to Venice? No doubt you imagine yourself taking a romantic gondola ride along narrow canals and under delicate bridges. Perhaps you picture the beautiful old buildings and famous works of art that have made the city one of Europe's leading tourist spots.

② Venice was built on more than 100 islands and has about 150 canals. The best-known of these, the Grand Canal, functions as the "main street" in the part of the city most popular with visitors. The canal winds through each of the six districts that comprise this historic city center before reaching Venice Lagoon.

③ One of these districts, San Marco, is home to many of Venice's main attractions, including St. Mark's Basilica. This spectacular church has five main arches and some extraordinary onion-shaped domes. It is decorated with priceless treasures, many of which were stolen from other countries when medieval Venice was a leading sea power.

1.4 St. Mark's Basilica

① St. Mark's Basilica stands at one end of St. Mark's Square. Napoleon called the square the "finest drawing room in Europe". Tourists have been going there for centuries to visit its celebrated café and get a taste of the party atmosphere.

② The best time to visit Venice is during the clear spring days of March and April. From June to August, the city is hot, sticky, and crowded with tourists. Autumn is quite pleasant, but winters are cold. Floods are common in November and December, presenting Venetians with one of their most difficult and ongoing problems.

③ It is well-known that Venice faces an uncertain future. The city is sinking into the sea, its historic buildings are falling to pieces, and the famous lagoon is badly polluted. Unless solutions are found soon for these complex problems, the "Queen of the Adriatic," as Venice is sometimes called, will not be able to sit on her watery throne for very much longer.

2 课前批评

2.1 雷峰夕照

雷峰塔建于吴越国时期(975年),吴越国王钱弘俶因为黄妃生得一子,对佛心生感激,所以建此塔以谢佛的恩德。塔初名"黄妃塔",是一座八面砖木结构楼阁式塔,塔心是砖砌的,塔檐、游廊、栏杆等为木结构。南宋以后,雷峰塔木构檐廊屡毁屡修。当时的《雷峰夕照》图中,斜阳的余晖照耀在塔身上,成了西湖边静穆的图画。明代嘉靖时雷峰塔被毁,仅存塔心。现塔于2000年在原址上重建,恢复雷峰夕照景观。

Leifeng Pagoda

Leifeng Pagoda can be traced back to 975 during the Kingdom of Wuyue, in which King Qian Hongchu was so happy to have his concubine give birth to a son that he erected a pagoda to express his gratitude to Buddha. This pagoda was an octagonal brick-and-wood structure of storied-pavilion type. The core part was built of bricks, but the eaves, veranda and railing were of a wooden structure. After the Southern Song Dynasty, the eaves and veranda were damaged and repaired repeatedly. In the painting Leifeng Pagoda in Evening Glow at that time, the pagoda was bathed in the sunset glow, forming a wonderful picture by the West Lake. It was destroyed in the mid 1500 during the Ming Dynasty, with the only brick core remaining. The new Leifeng Pagoda was re-constructed at the original site in 2000 to enhance the scenery of the lake.(彭萍用例,有修改)

2.2 龙舟节

(龙舟节)轻快的龙舟如银河流星,瑰丽的彩船似海市蜃楼,两岸那金碧辉煌的彩楼连成一片水晶宫,是仙境?是梦境?仰视彩鸽割飞,底眸漂灯留霓,烟火怒放,火树银花,灯舞回旋,千姿百态,气垫船腾起一江春潮,射击手点破满天彩球,跳伞健儿绽空中花蕾,抢鸭勇士谱水上凯歌。

The river is densely dotted with dragon-boats and decorated cruisers. Along the banks are buildings of Chinese style with flickering lights. Many interesting activities are waiting for you, such as fireworks, motorboats driving, shooting, and parachuting.(彭萍用例)

2.3 Toronto

With its colorful ethnic mix, rich history and

这里各民族水乳交融,文化

breathtaking architecture, Toronto offers non-stop adventures for the willing tourists. To get a sense of how big, various and magical Toronto is, the best place to start is the CN Tower, the tallest free-standing structure in the world. From this vantage point, visitors get a bird's-eye view of the city's striking skyline and unique geography.

多姿多彩,历史内涵丰富,建筑蔚为壮观,对迫不及待的游客来说,多伦多是个充满了冒险之旅的城市。要知道多伦多到底有多大,有多丰富多彩,有多少魔幻,理想的观赏点当属国家电视台。国家电视台是世界上最高的单体建筑,是俯瞰城市魅力轮廓和独特地理景观的理想之地。(彭萍用例)

知识 3 全译知识 全译过程

全译包括宏观过程和微观过程,宏观过程是全译活动涉及的一切行为,微观过程是全译活动本身,前者包含后者。

3.1 全译宏观过程

全译宏观过程可分为选、备、译、改、校五步。

选 即选材。全译宏观过程始于全译材料的委派或自选,前者是个人或机构委托或约请翻译的行为,后者是个人自由选择自由翻译的行为。

备 即准备。了解作者的经历、从业活动、从业背景、口笔语特点等;了解与所译相关的专业背景、基本原理、专门词汇等,预读相关书籍,备好必要的专业工具书等。

译 即全译。详见下述全译微观过程。

改 即修改。译不厌改,理解、转化和表达可能要反复多遍。翻译时,最好对棘手的问题作出标记,以便修改时重点解决,提高效率。修改过程是:比较译作与原作的内容,看是否失了原意;比较二者的形式,看有无必要再现形式特点,以显原作风格;单读译作,润色译文,看有无字不通文不顺,看有无更贴切的同义手段,以求更加符合译语表达习惯。

校 即校订。自译自校,有条件最好请人校对,自译者迷,旁观者清。请校之前,译者最好标出疑惑之处,以便他人知难而校,提高效率。校订者则最好采用全国统一规范的编校符号,以便译者修改或者文字输入。校订变动不大的稿子,可以直接输入排版;改动较大的稿子,则需誊正后交付输排,自己机上处理的译者可省去这一工序。

3.2 全译微观过程

全译微观过程指全译活动本身的语言-思维过程,包括理解、转化和表达。

理解 即原语理解,是以原语活动为主、思维转换为辅、兼涉译语内部言语表达的了解意义与风格的活动。理解是动态的,包括边听读边理解的过程,也包括重新听读重新理解的过程。理解是全译的基础和前奏。原作的表意因素包括句内因素和句外因素,前者包括语法、语义、语气等，后者指语境，包括交际对象、交际背景、交际场合、主体风格等。

转化 即语际转化，是以思维为主、语言为辅的黑箱活动，旨在转移原作的意义与风格。原作通过理解已获得信息内容，信息脱离原作形式，进入了译者的思维空间，以概念体系和形象体系而存在。在理解阶段，虽然有部分内容转换为思维形态，也有零星内容可用译语表达，但主体仍处于由原语转向思维的过程。只有到了转换阶段，才完全转为思维状态，同时以原语和译语并存。转换的对象，从大处看是文化信息，从小处看是原作内容和风格信息。

表达 即译语表达，是以译语活动为主、思维活动为辅、兼涉理解与表达、再现原作内容与风格的活动。在掌握原语所述的世界之后，按译语的语义规则和语法规则，从大脑词库中选取恰当的词语，将其有机地编排成内部言语，继而外化为语表形式，进入笔译之写的过程。往往是边看边转化边写，也可先心译再写。

4 全译窍门

4.1 音意兼顾译文化

许多旅游景点名音意双译一般都采用专名音译、通名意译的方法，涉及历史和传说中的人物时，尤其如此。音译加意译的方法，能达到音、意兼顾的双重效果，有助于游客了解中国文化。如：茅盾故居 Mao Dun's Former Residence；黄山 the Huangshan Mountain；太湖 the Taihu Lake；淮河 the Huaihe River；渤海 the Bohai Sea；豫园 the Yuyuan Garden；虎跑泉 the Tiger-pawed Spring；乾清宫 the Palace of Heavenly Purity；承德避暑山庄 the Chengde Summer Resort。有的富有中国文化特色的词须先音译，再意译释义紧随其后，如：佛跳墙 Fotiaoqiang（assorted meat and vegetables cooked in embers）；粽子 Zongzi, a pyramid shaped rice pudding wrapped in bamboo or reed leaves；秦始皇 Qin Shi-huang, the first emperor who united China in 221B. C.；观音 Guanyin（the Buddhist Goddess of Mercy）。

4.2 彰显效果

“夸张”就是在表述中故意言过其实，或夸大事实，或缩小事实，目的在于给读者留下深刻的印象。旅游文本的夸张通常属于“夸大事实”，可以渲染宣传的语气，起到彰显效果的作用。比较发现，汉语旅游材料多使用夸张，而英文少用。汉语行文讲究辞藻工整，纵横飘逸，重视酣畅淋漓的审美情趣，而英文更重简洁、严谨。因此，汉语旅游文本中的夸张手法英译汉时要适当删减，在保留原文实质信息的前提下，适当加以润色。

① 塔子山公园内九天楼鹤立鸡群，亭亭玉立，卓尔不凡；你看她层叠有致，舒张有度，俯仰自如，雍容大度，有如贵妇临轩；再看那雕梁画栋，飞檐垂瓴，花窗秀门，真似玉女笑面。Jiutian Pavilion, located in Tazishan Park, is a splendid pavilion with decorated eaves and tiles.

②（龙舟赛）演历史于古今，生传说于纷纭，珠联爱国情操、悲壮色彩，壁合神秘气氛、拼搏精神，动如摧枯拉朽、轰轰烈烈，势若排山倒海，可歌可泣。The Dragon-Boat Race, a most exciting group event, is held in memory of Qu Yuan, a patriotic statesman and poet in ancient China.

例①用了比喻和拟人，还运用了夸张，英译突出主要信息。例②原文可谓句句夸张，中文读者读后一定会激动不已，跃跃欲试，英译删减了夸张，用形容词 exciting 译出实质信息的同时稍加修饰，对"龙舟赛"的意义稍做解释。

4.3 反反复复

"反复"即重复使用某一词、某一短语、某一句等以强调和突出文字。加深读者的印象。英汉语旅游文本都常用这一技巧，汉语使用频率更高。一般说来，英语文本的反复可以直译，汉语的则要根据英语句法灵活处理，有时直译，多数要省译反复进行变通。如：

③These trains run **every** 20 minutes during the day and **every** hour in the evening until midnight. 白天每20分钟有一列火车开行，傍晚至午夜每小时均有一列火车开车。

④ Travel **in style** — dine **in style**. The MG Bahn is more than just a railway, and offers numerous **special** excursions in winter: fine food or going on a **special** outing all make the trip unforgettable. 优雅地旅行——优雅地用餐：马特宏圣哥达不仅仅是一条铁路，还有为游客提供的无数的冬季特别短途旅行项目：精美的食物或者特别的短途观光都会使您的旅行变得令人流连忘返。

⑤ 雾凇之美，美在壮观，美在奇绝。The beauty of rime lies in its spectacularity and uniqueness.

例③使用 every 两次，例④ 使用 in style 和 special 各两次，汉语如数译出，生动地再现了原文的语气。例⑤的汉语原文使用了反复，重复"美"，而英译未重复 beauty，若重复，会使英译冗长，反而起不到很好的宣传效果。

4.4 巧用辞格

修辞依据题旨情境，运用特定的手段修饰文辞，以加强语言表达的效果。旅游文本常用修辞手法，使语言表达更具吸引力，让读者获得更多的美感，从而激起游览兴趣。英汉语修辞手法基本相同，汉语修辞格的使用频率远高于英语。如：

⑥ Then came the twilight colors of sea and heaven, ... the winepink width of water merging into lawns of aquamarines, the sky a tender palette of pink and blue. 暮霭沉沉，海天一色，红浪翻涌，碧波横流，天空俨然是块柔和的调色板，粉蓝两色交相辉映。

⑦ 大桥两边的扇形斜拉索，颇似巨大的琴弦，在为那奔腾不息的黄浦江伴奏着豪迈雄壮的进行曲。The fan-shaped slanting cable-stays on both sides of the bridge seem to be the chords of a huge harp playing a heroic and majestic tune for the ceaselessly flowing water of the Huangpujiang River.

⑧ 长沙这座从远古走到现代的湖湘首邑，虽然历经数千年的风雨沧桑，仍不失古朴美丽的都市风采。Now Changsha, the capital city of Hunan Province, still shows its unsophisticated beauty after thousands of years' severe tests.

⑨ Where can you be greeted in 11 languages on Swiss National Day? In Interlaken of course! 瑞士国庆节期间在哪里可以收到11种语言的问候？当然是在因特拉肯！

例⑦，"颇似巨大的琴弦"属于明喻，用like和seem译出；"在……进行曲"属于暗喻，用了直译的手法，保留了原文的风格。例⑥，lawns of aquamarines 和 the sky a tender palette of pink and blue 为暗喻，前者译作"碧波横流"，颇具夸张，后者则译为明喻，使用喻词"俨然"。例⑧照译了拟人。例⑨照译了设问。

4.5 巧用变译

一般说来，英语旅游材料很少引经据典，汉语则相反，喜欢引经据典，尤其是引用古诗词。英译一般采用全译，但有时可以采用摘取式翻译、译述大意、压缩性翻译等变译。如：

⑩ 洞庭湖"衔远山，吞长江，浩浩荡荡，横无际涯。朝晖夕阴，气象万千"。Carrying the shadows of distant mountains in it and swallowing the Yangtze River, the vast and mighty Dongting Lake stretches afar. It is brilliant in the morning and gloomy at dusk, with its scenery abounding in changes.

⑪ 杭州因有美丽的西湖而成为闻名于世的风景旅游城市。北宋词人柳永在《望海潮》一词中写道："东南形胜，三吴都会，钱塘自古繁华。烟柳画桥，风帘翠幕，参差十万人家。云树绕堤沙。怒涛卷霜雪，天堑无涯。市列珠玑，户盈罗绮，竞豪奢。" Hangzhou is a world-known tourist city thanks to the beautiful West Lake and majestic waves in the Qiantangjiang River.

前一例引了范仲淹《岳阳楼记》的名句，译者只作了转述，并未全译。后一例，原文大部分引用了柳永的词，照直译出英语读者会感到不解和冗长，可以删除。

词汇 5 话题词汇

5.1 旅游业

一类社 China's Category A travel agency
二类社 China's Category B travel agency
三类社 China's Category C travel agency
地方旅游组织 local tourist organization
旅费 travelling expense
旅行 trip
旅行计划；节目 itinerary
旅游 travelling
旅游安排 tour arrangement
旅游报纸 travel press
旅游出版物 travel publication
旅游代号编码 tour code number
旅游地图 tourist map
旅游点 tourist spots
旅游活动 tourism activities
旅游记者 travel journalist
旅游界 tourism circles
旅游接待国 receiving country
旅游局 tourism administration
旅游俱乐部 touring club
旅游目的地 tourist destination
旅游目的国 tourist destination country

旅游团目录 tour catalog
旅游团陪同 tour escort / conductor / director
旅游委员会 tourist council
旅游路线 tour route
旅游协会 tourist association
旅游小册子 tour brochure
旅游业;旅游 tourism / travel industry / trade
旅游业务 tour operation / business
旅游指南 travel guide;guidebook
旅游周刊 tourist periodical
旅游组织 tourist organization
旅游专家 travel expert
区域旅游组织 regional tourist organization
全国旅游组织 national tourist organization
最低旅游价格 minimum tour price
backpacker 背包旅行者
guide practice 导游实践
internal tourism 境内旅游
international tourism 国际旅游
international guide 国际导游
local guide 地陪;地方导游
low/off season 淡季
multilingual guide 会多种语言的导游
national guide 全陪;全程导游
one-way trip 单程旅行
outbound tourism 出境游
outbound tourist 出境游客
peak season 旺季
professional (staff) 旅游专业人员
round-the-world trip 环球旅行
shoulder period/season 平季
sightseeing 游览
tour leader 领队;团长
tour talker 自动导游磁带机
touring 游览
tourist 游客

5.2 酒店住宿

一星级饭店 economy hotel(one-star hotel)
二星级饭店 some comfort hotel(two-star hotel)
三星级饭店 average hotel(three -star hotel)
四星级饭店 high comfort hotel(four -star hotel)
五星级饭店 deluxe hotel(five-star hotel)
饭店;酒店 hotel
酒店 tavern
廉价旅馆 budget hotel
旅馆;饭店 inn
马车店;大旅馆 caravansary
汽车饭店(旅店)motel(motor hotel)
青年招待所 youth hostel
小旅馆 lodge
招待所 hostel
big single room 大床房(一张双人大床)
combined type rooms 组合客房
double double 双人房(二张双人床)
double room 双人房(二张单人床)
honeymoon suite 蜜月套房
imperial suite 皇室套房
junior suite 简单套房
mini suite 小型套房
multi-functional room 多功能客房
on change 待清扫
penthouse suite 楼顶套房
presidential suite 总统套房
single room 单人房(一张单人床)
studio room 工作室型客房(设沙发床或躺椅)
suite deluxe 高级套房
triple room 三人房(三张单人床)
unmade room 未清扫房

5.3 中外名胜

白云观 the White Cloud Taoist Temple
半坡遗址 the Banpo Neolithic Village
北海公园 the Beihai Park
布达拉宫 the Potala Palace
长城 the Great Wall
长江三峡 the Three Gorges on the Yangtze River
承德避暑山庄 the Imperial Mountain Summer Resort in Chengde

大雁塔 the Big Wild Goose Pagoda
大运河 the Grand Canal
都江堰 the Dujiangyan Dam
甘露寺 the Sweet Dew Temple
革命历史博物馆 the Museum of Revolutionary History
桂林山水 Guilin Scenery with Hills and Waters
故宫博物院 the Palace Museum
鼓浪屿 the Gulangyu Islet
鼓楼 the Drum Tower
观音阁 the Goddess of Mercy Pavilion
国子监 the Imperial College
寒山寺 the Hanshan Temple
恒山 Mount Heng; the Hengshan Mountain
衡山 Mount Heng; the Hengshan Mountain
华清池 the Huaqing Hot Spring
华山 Mount Hua; the Huashan Mountain
黄果树瀑布 the Huangguoshu Falls
黄鹤楼 the Yellow Crane Tower
孔府 the Confucious Family Mansion
孔林 the Cemetery of Confucius
孔庙 the Confucius Temple
龙门石窟 the Longmen Stone Cave
庐山 the Lushan Mountain
毛主席纪念堂 Chairman Mao Zedong Memorial Hall
蓬莱水城 Penglai Water City
乾清宫 the Palace of Heavenly Purity
秦始皇兵马俑 Qin Terra-Cotta Warriors and Horses
人民大会堂 the Great Hall of the People
世界公园 the Beijing World Park
石林 the Stone Forest
嵩山 Mount Song; the Songshan Mountain
苏州园林 Suzhou Gardens
泰山 Mount Tai
台湾日月潭 the Sun and Moon Lake of Taiwan
天安门广场 the Tian'anmen Square
天池 the Heaven Pool
天坛 the Temple of Heaven
天下第一关 the First Pass Under Heaven
西湖 the West Lake
仙人洞 the Fairy Cave
颐和园 the Summer Palace
圆明园 the Ruins of Yuanmingyuan
岳阳楼 the Yueyang Tower
中华民族园 Chinese Ethnic Culture Park
中华世纪坛 China Century Altar
周口店北京猿人遗址 the Peking Man Site at Zhoukoudian
紫禁城 the Forbidden City
Acapulco, Mexico 墨西哥阿卡普尔科
Angkor Wat, Cambodia 柬埔寨吴哥窟
Arch of Triumph, France 法国凯旋门
Aswan High Dam, Egypt 印度阿斯旺水坝
Ayers Rock 艾尔斯巨石
Babylon, Iraq 伊拉克巴比伦遗迹
Bali, Indonesia 印度尼西亚巴厘岛
Bermuda 百慕大
Big Ben in London, England 英国伦敦大笨钟
Borobudur, Indonesia 印度尼西亚波罗浮屠
Buckingham Palace, England 白金汉宫
Cape of Good Hope, South Africa 南非好望角
Central Park, New York City, USA 美国纽约中央公园
Colosseum in Rome, Italy 意大利古罗马圆形剧场
Crocodile Farm, Thailand 泰国北榄鳄鱼湖
Cuzco, Mexico 墨西哥库斯科
Disneyland, California, USA 加利福尼亚迪斯尼乐园
Easter Island 复活节岛
Effiel Tower, France 法国埃菲尔铁塔
Elysee Palace, France 法国爱丽舍宫
Grand Canyon, Arizona, USA 美国亚利桑那州大峡谷
Great Barrier Reef 大堡礁
Hollywood, California, USA 美国加利福尼亚好莱坞
Honolulu, Hawaii, USA 美国夏威夷火奴鲁鲁
Hyde Park, England 英国海德公园
Kolner Dom, Koln, Germany 德国科隆大教堂
Las Vegas, Nevada, USA 美国内华达拉斯维加斯
Leaning Tower of Pisa, Italy 意大利比萨斜塔
London Tower Bridge, England 伦敦塔桥
Louvre, France 法国卢浮宫
Metropolitan Museum of Art, New York City, USA 纽约大都会艺术博物馆

Miami, Florida, USA 美国佛罗里达迈阿密
Monte Carlo, Monaco 摩洛哥蒙特卡罗
Mosque of St. Sophia in Istanbul (Constantinople), Turkey 土耳其圣索非亚教堂
Mount Cook 库克山
Mount Fuji, Japan 日本富士山
Nairobi National Park, Kenya 肯尼亚内罗毕国家公园
Niagara Falls, New York State, USA 美国尼亚加拉大瀑布
Notre Dame De Paris, France 法国巴黎圣母院
Panama Canal 巴拿马大运河
Parthenon, Greece 希腊巴台农神庙
Pattaya Beach, Thailand 泰国芭堤雅海滩
Pyramids, Egypt 埃及金字塔
Red Square in Moscow, Russia 莫斯科红场
the Sahara Desert 撒哈拉大沙漠
Sentosa, Singapore 新加坡圣淘沙
Statue of Liberty, New York City, USA 美国纽约自由女神像
Suez Canal, Egypt 印度苏伊士运河
Sydney Opera House, Australia 悉尼歌剧院
Taj Mahal, India 印度泰姬陵
the Himalayas 喜马拉雅山
the Mediterranean 地中海
the Nile, Egypt 埃及尼罗河
the White House, Washington DC., USA 美国华盛顿白宫
Times Square, New York City, USA 美国纽约时代广场
Venice, Italy 意大利威尼斯
Westminster Abbey, England 威斯敏斯特大教堂
World Trade Center, New York City, USA 美国纽约世界贸易中心
Yellowstone National Park, USA 美国黄石国家公园
Yosemite National Park, USA 美国尤塞米提国家公园

5.4 行业名言

安全可靠 safe and reliable
耳目一新 a new perspective
避暑胜地 summer resort
宾至如归 just be at home; feel at home
超乎想象 beyond your imagination
出土文物 unearthed cultural relics
东方独秀 like no other place in the orient
东方之珠 the oriental pearl
活力北京 kicking Beijing
景色如画 picturesque views
清洁舒适 clean and comfortable
全新感受 a novel experience
人迹罕至 the unbeaten track
食在广州 food in Guangzhou
天堂之旅 a trip to the paradise; explore the paradise
味在成都 delicacies in Chengdu
远离尘嚣 a true departure; an escape from the bustling
醉在贵州 intoxicated in Guizhou
a city in move 动感之都
adventure travel 探险之旅
ancient architectural complex 古建筑群
cultural visit 文化旅游
date trip 缘之旅
education visits 教育旅游
elder trip 夕阳之旅
excellent but not fancy 卓越不俗
female trip 女人旅游
fine views of London 伦敦美景
long established 久负盛名
national park 国家公园
photography trip 摄影之旅
the city of commoners 大众之城
the city of culture 文化之都
the city of elites 精英之都
the world city 世界之都

5.5 常用公示语

提供购物机会 Shopping offers
提供自助餐 Cafeteria available
预订座位 Reserved Seat
Admission charge £ 4 门票 4 镑
Admission is free 免票
Child reductions 儿童优惠
Concessions（票价）优惠
Do not touch the exhibits/objects 勿触摸展品/物品
Exhibition opening times 开馆时间
Flash photograph is not permitted 不准用闪光灯拍照
Forthcoming exhibitions 即将展出
No littering 勿乱扔废弃物
No smoking in this area 此处禁止吸烟
No smoking in this lift 电梯内禁止吸烟
Ticket office 售票处
Unemployed, disabled, students and children free 失业者,残疾人,学生和儿童免费
With access all day 全天开放

5.6 缩略语

太亚旅协 The Pacific Asia Travel Association（PATA）
国旅 China International Travel Sevice Head Office
青旅 China Cyts Tours Holding Co., Ltd.
中旅 China Travel Service Head Office
AP 美式计价（计算房租并包括每日三餐费用在内）
BP 百慕大计价（计算房租,包括美式早餐餐费）
CP 欧陆式计价（计算房租且包括欧陆式早餐餐费）
DR 豪华间
ER 经济间
EP 欧式计价（只计房租,不包括餐饮等费用）
ITX 游览包价旅游
MAP 修正美式计价（计算房租且包括两餐费/早餐,午餐,晚餐中选两餐）
PS 总统套房
SR 标准间
SS 套间
UR 高级套房
WTD 世界旅游日

6 比读体悟

6.1 桂林

Guilin

① 桂林是一个享有世界声誉的风景游览城市,也是一座具有悠久历史的文化名城。

① Guilin is a world-renowned tourist city as well as a cultural centre with a long history.

② 早在两千多年前,秦始皇开凿灵渠,沟通湘漓二江,桂林便成为“南连海域、北达中原”的南疆重镇。漫长的历史,孕育了灿烂的文化。从四五万年前的史前人类遗址,到明代靖江王陵的庞大古墓群;从历代迁客骚人的大量吟咏赞美桂林山水的诗文辞赋,到遍布桂林山壁洞穴的摩崖石刻、造像等,无一不与

② As early as 2,000 years ago, Emperor Qinshihuang had the Lingqu Canal built to link the Xiangjiang and Lijiang rivers, thus making Guilin an important city in the South connected to the Central Plain in the north and the sea in the south. A brilliant culture has developed over the long history. The relics of prehistoric mankind some 40,000 to 50,000 years ago, the large tumuli of Prince Jingjiang of the Ming Dynasty, the prose and poems in praise of the hills and rivers by poets and other

桂林的自然山水融为一体，使桂林山水增添了人文的异彩。

literary figures, the inscriptions and sculptures in the caves and on the cliffs all merge with the hills and rivers, add to the scenery a great humanistic splendor.

③ 桂林山水素以山青、水秀、洞奇、石美著称于世，享有“桂林山水甲天下”的美誉。在桂林方圆百余公里的范围内，奇峰林立，碧水萦回，“千峰环野力，一水抱城流”，“几程漓水曲，万点桂山尖”。此外，还有龙胜花坪原始森林，兴安灵渠古秦堤、海洋银杏林，资江漂流，龙胜，阳朔温泉等，构成了一个以桂林市为中心的庞大的辐射式大桂林风景区。

③ The scenery of Guilin, which is well-known for the green hills, limpid water, grotesque caves and fantastic stalagmites and stalactites, enjoys the reputation of " the best sight under Heaven. " Within 100 kilometers in circumference, grotesque peaks jut out around the city. The primeval forests, the ancient embankment, the gingko woods, the drift along the Zijiang River, and the hot springs from a large scenic area with Guilin as the centre.

④ 美丽的桂林山水，吸引着成千上万的中外游客。相信桂林将以更加娇美的姿态，更加优质的服务，热忱迎接前来光顾的中外游客。

④ Beautiful hills and rivers of Guilin are attracting hundreds of thousands of domestic and overseas tourists. We believe a more charming Guilin is always ready to provide her domestic and foreign friends with quality service. （彭萍用例）

6.2 台湾日月潭

The Sun and Moon Lake of Taiwan

① 台湾是祖国的第一大岛，由于地处亚热带，岛上林木青翠，景色秀丽，被世界许多国家称为“福摩萨”，这是葡萄牙语，意思是“美丽之岛”。就在这岛的中部。有居于“台湾八景”之首的岛上第一大湖——日月潭。

① Taiwan is the largest island of our country. Located in the Subtropic Zone, the island has beautiful scenes with fresh and green trees everywhere, so it is reputed as " Formosa" by many nations in the world, which means " a beautiful island" in Portuguese. It is in the middle part of this island where exists the largest lake on the island — Riyuetan (Sun and Moon Lake) — which ranks first in " Taiwan's Eight Scenes".

② 日月潭位于南投县中央的鱼池乡，在玉山之北，能高山之南。湖面海拔760米，是一个高山湖泊。湖周围35公里，面积100平方公里，深度平时约14米。湖滨树木蓊郁，苍翠欲滴，奇妙，幽绝的风韵，秀丽明媚的湖光水色，使万千人沉醉在它的怀抱中。湖中有一个孤岛——光华岛，也称珠子山，浮珠屿。

② It is situated in Yuchi Village in the center of Nantou County, north of Jade Mountain and south of Nenggao Mountain. It is an alpine lake of 35 kilometers in circumference and 100 square meters in area with its surface at an elevation of 760 meters. It is 14 meters in depth at ordinary times. It is surrounded by verdant trees on the lakeside and she intoxicates tens of thousands of people in her arms with her wonderful and dedicate charm and her radiant and enchanting scenery of lake water. There is an isolated island — Guanghua — in the lake, which is also known as Pearl Hill or Floating Pearl Islet.

③ 据台湾省通志说，当初因岛影倒照所致，以光华岛为界，潭水分丹碧二色。北半部称为前潭，水色丹，形如日轮，故名日潭，南半部称为后潭，水色碧，形似月弧，故名月潭，合称为日月潭。

③ According to the General Records of Taiwan Province, as a result of the inverted reflection of the island in the water, the lake water was divided into the two colors of red and green with Guanghua as the boundary. The northern half is called the front pool which looks like a round sun with the water in red, so it is known as the Sun Pool. The southern half is called the back pool which is crescent like a moon with the water in green, so it is known as the Moon Pool, both jointly called the Sun and Moon Lake.

④ 日月潭又名水里社，水里湖，龙湖……相传湖龄15 000年。在祖国各大名湖中，独具亚热带的秀丽，一风一雨无不蕴藏着大自然的美。潭水四时不竭，水极清纯，无垠的漫漫绿波，恍若明镜一面，青山倒映，幽艳，静艳。清晨，山中，潭上往往有薄如青纱的雾，山风一起，烟雾隐住了光华岛，而湖面更显得烟波浩渺了。若天色晴丽，湖上便有游船来往，有张网捕鱼的，有垂钓的……有可以划一独木孤舟浮泛湖面，真令人有"青山滴翠碧悠悠，湖光舫影泛中流"之感。日月潭水，碧波亮沏寒空，荡舟湖上，如浴在水晶宫中……

④ The Sun and Moon Lake is also known as "Shuilishe", "Shuili Lake", "Dragon Lake", etc. It has been said that the lake has an age of 15,000 years. It is the only one of all the major famous lakes of China that has the beauty of the Subtropics. All the winds and rains there contain the beauty of nature and the lake water is never drained in four seasons and quite clear and pure. The boundless expanse of green hills reflected in it. Early in the morning, there are often fine-gauze-like mists in the mountains and on the lake. When there comes a mountain wind, Guanghua Island is hidden amidst the mist and the lake looks much more misty in its wide expanse. If it clears up, there are pleasure-boats coming and going on the lake with some of the people spreading nets to catch fish and some angling on boat … You can also float on the lake in a dugout canoe, which will certainly give you a feeling of "verdant hills setting off against the green waves and the boat reflecting itself in the lake, floating on the middle stream". In the moonlit night, the bright light is shining onto the water of the lake and the green waves are brightening the cold sky. You will feel as if bathing in the Palace of Crystals if you are boating on the lake ...(吴扬才、吴扬满用例)

6.3 云南大观楼长联

上联为：五百里滇池，奔来眼底。披襟岸帻，喜茫茫空阔无边。看：东骧神骏，西翥灵仪，北走蜿蜒，南翔缟素。高人韵士，何妨选胜登临；趁蟹屿螺洲，梳裹就风鬟雾鬓，更苹天苇地，点缀些翠羽丹霞。莫孤负：四围香稻，万顷晴沙，九夏芙蓉，三春杨柳。

下联为：数千年往事，注到心头。把酒凌虚，叹滚滚英雄谁在？想：汉习楼船，唐标铁柱，宋挥玉斧，元跨革囊。伟烈丰功，费尽移山心力；尽珠帘画栋，卷不及暮雨朝云，便断碣残碑，都付与苍烟落照。只赢得：几杵疏钟，半江渔火，两行秋雁，一枕清霜。

白话译文：

The Daguan Pavilion Couplet

① 五百里浩瀚的滇池，在我的面前奔涌。敞开衣襟，推开冠戴，这一片茫茫无边的碧波真令人欣喜啊！请看：东方的金马山像神骏在奔驰，西岸的碧鸡山如凤凰在飞舞，北面的长虫山犹灵蛇在蠕动，南边的鹤山似白鹤在翱翔。诗人们！何不选择这个胜境，登上高楼欣赏一番呢？看那远处像螃蟹一样大的岛屿，像螺蛳一般小的沙洲，像少女梳理秀

① The Kunming Lake extending a hundred miles around rolls before my eyes. Wearing my hood high and throwing my chest out, how happy I am to see the vast expanse of water! Behold! The Golden Steed galloping in the east, the Green Phoenix flying in the west, the Long Snake serpentine in the north and the White Crane planning in the south. Brilliant talents may come to the height and enjoy the sight, visit the crab-like or shell-like islets which look like beauties with hair flowing in the air or veiled in the mist, where duckweed and

发般飘摇的垂柳,还有满目皆是的水草、芦苇,以及飞翔在其间有如翡翠一般的小鸟,天上灿烂的红霞,切莫辜负了:滇池四周飘香的金稻、明媚阳光下的万顷沙滩,夏季花红叶碧的芙蓉,春天青青的杨柳。

reed outspread as far as the sky dotted with green-feathered birds and rainbow-colored clouds. How can you not enjoy your fill of the fragrant paddy fields all around, sparkling fine sand far and near, slender lotus blooms in late summer and swaying willow trees in early spring!

② 几千年的历史,涌上我的心头。我举起酒杯对苍天顿生感慨,历史上曾经英雄滚滚如流水,而如今又有谁还存在呢? 试想:汉武帝为了开辟西南到印度一带的通途,在长安挖凿昆明湖,制造战船习水战;唐玄宗统一了南诏后,在弥渡立过铁柱以记功德;宁太祖在地图前挥起玉斧划大渡河为界;元世祖挥师南下,乘皮筏渡过金沙江统一了云南。这些丰功伟绩,真是费尽了移动大山的心力啊! 尽管也曾珠帘画栋,显赫一时。但是转眼间又改朝换代,如早晨的云,晚上的雨一般快。记功碑变成了断石残碑,在苍烟落日下倍感凄凉。到头来,只有几声幽怨的丧钟、半江暗淡的渔火、两行凄凉的秋雁、一枕清冷的寒霜,似乎在把从前来凭吊。

② The historical events passed thousands of years ago pour into my mind. Holding a cup of wine and facing immensity, I sigh, for how many heroes have passed away with rolling waves. Remember the warships maneuvered in ancient times, the iron pillar erected in the golden age, the frontier pacified with jade ax in the silver epoch and the leather rafts crossing the turbulent river in modern era. Valiant exploits have exhausted mountain-moving strength mental and physical, but pearly screens and painted beams last not longer than morning clouds and evening rain, and broken stone tablets and ruined monuments lie buried in the grizzling smoke and the sun's departing rays. What remains is only sparse bells ringing in cold hills, fishermen's lantern lights by riverside, two rows of wild geese flying in autumn sky and dreary dream of hoary winter frost. (许渊冲 译)

6.4 San Francisco　　漫步旧金山

① The best way to see this splendid city, where Spanish people were the first to make their homes, is to take one of the old cable cars which run along the nine main avenues. Fares are cheap; they have not risen, I'm told, for almost a hundred years.

① 要游览这座西班牙人最早在此落户的绚丽城市,最好的办法是乘坐旧式缆车。缆车穿越九条主大街,收费低廉,据说近百年来一直没涨过价。

② You leave the palm trees in the Union Square — the heart of San Francisco — and from the shop signs and the faces around you, you will notice that in the city live people from many nations — Austrians, Italians, Chinese and others — giving each part a special character. More Chinese live in China Town than in any other part of the world outside China. Here, with Chinese restaurants, Chinese post-boxes, and even odd telephone-boxes that look like pagodas, it is easy to feel you are in China itself.

② 联合广场是旧金山的中心。你从广场棕榈树下向外行,扫视店铺招牌和周围形形色色的面孔,就会注意到这座城市里居住着来自许多国家的人——奥地利人、意大利人、中国人等等——这就使每一地段呈现出迥然不同的特色。唐人街住着许多华人,其人数之众超过中国本土之外任何地方。这里有中国风味的餐馆、中国式邮筒,甚至还有奇异的电话亭,形如宝塔。凡此种种,不费想象就令你恍若置身中国境内了。

③ Fisherman's Wharf, a place all foreigners want to see, is at the end of the ride. In one of the gay little restaurants beside the harbor, as you enjoy the fresh Pacific seafood, you can admire the bright red paint of the Golden Gate Bridge in the harbor and watch the traffic crossing beneath the tall towers on its way to the pretty village of Tiberon.

③ 缆车的终点站是“渔民码头”，海外游客均一睹为快。在码头旁边一家装饰华丽的小饭馆里，你可以一边品尝太平洋的海鲜，一边欣赏海港里漆色鲜红的金门大桥，观看林立的高楼之下通往美丽村庄“蒂伯龙”的交通线上络绎不绝的车辆。(韩中华、王大伟用例)

6.5 Garden City Seville

花园城市塞维利亚

① If you are looking for beauty and culture, Seville is definitely the place to be. As the fourth largest city in Spain, Seville is a center for art and business. Just walking around the city is a treat for your eyes. This is because Seville is over 2,000 years old.

① 如果您正在寻找美丽的事物和文化，塞尔维亚绝对是个您该造访的地点。身为西班牙的第四大城，塞尔维亚是艺术与商业的中心。光是漫步在城市里就能为您带来一场视觉盛宴。这是因为塞尔维亚已有超过两千年的历史。

② The Cathedral of Seville is a fantastic sight and one of the largest Gothic churches ever. For an interesting mix of building styles throughout Seville's history, don't miss the Plaza de Espana.

② 塞尔维亚大教堂是一处令人惊艳的景点，同时也是有史以来最大的哥特式教堂之一。想要欣赏塞尔维亚各种不同时期的建筑风格汇集于一处，您可千万别错过西班牙广场。

③ If you are traveling during April, check out the Seville Fairs. There are daily parades and beautifully decorated tents all along the riverside. While you are there, try some local dishes and snacks. They can't be beat!

③ 如果您是在四月来此地旅游，不妨去塞尔维亚市集逛逛。那里每天都有游行，而且沿着河岸还有许多装饰精美的帐篷。当您在那里时，尝尝一些当地的菜肴与小吃吧。那滋味可是无与伦比的！

④ Seville also has some museums, and there is even one that is entirely about the flamenco arts. No matter what your reason for visiting Seville is, you will leave with a smile on your face.

④ 塞维利亚也有许多博物馆，甚至还有一间所展示的艺术品全都与佛朗明哥相关。不管您造访塞维利亚的原因为何，您都将带着微笑离开此地。(闫颖用例)

6.6 Caribbean Charm in Cartagena

卡塔赫纳的加勒比魅力

① The city's spectacular setting is a draw in itself. Protected by ancient stone walls that enclose its vibrant port, Cartagena is almost entirely surrounded by the Caribbean Sea. Pink, yellow and purple buildings line the cobblestone streets of the old city, faded after centuries under the powerful sun.

① 这座城市的壮丽风景本身就是一大吸引力。古城墙将这座充满活力的城市揽于怀中，四周几乎都是茫茫的加勒比海。古城中，鹅卵石铺设的街道旁排列着粉色、黄色和紫色的建筑。建筑的颜色在饱经了几个世纪的曝晒后已变得暗淡。

② Take a walk on the 16th-century walls of the old city. From there, the sea stretches as far as the eye can see. Relax and quench your thirst with some of the most coveted and exotic fruit juices in the world, like guanabana, lulo and nispero. The guanabana with a hint of milk added is a frothy delight.

② 在建于16世纪的古城墙上散个步吧。从那儿放眼远眺,茫茫大海无边无际。放松一下,喝点东西解解渴,来些世界上最令人垂涎的异域果汁,如红毛榴莲、奎东茄和枇杷。红毛榴莲汁中加一点牛奶就能产生泡沫,成为一杯令人喜爱的饮料。

③ If you want to explore beyond the city walls, arrange a boat ride at the harbor and watch the old city merge into the new as you pull away from the dock. Modern glass towers occupy a thin stretch of peninsula called Bocagrande. They appear to be built from the sea up to the sky and provide a sharp contrast to the adjacent old city.

③ 如果你想到城墙外去探索,可在港口乘船。当船只驶离码头后,您便会看见古城与新城连为一体。现代的玻璃大楼占据了博卡格兰德半岛的一狭长地区。它们看起来像是从海中耸立起来,直入云霄,与附近的古城形成了鲜明的对比。

④ Cartagena, the historic jewel of Colombia's Caribbean coast, is a secret that's getting out.

④ 卡塔赫纳,哥伦比亚加勒比海边的历史瑰宝,正向外人展示着它的神秘。(Shannan Adle 用例)

6.7 推荐读物

(1)《CITY 旅游》杂志,北京市旅游局。
(2)《旅行家》杂志,《旅行家》杂志社。
(3)《旅游》(TOURISM),旅游杂志社。
(4)《旅游休闲》杂志,海南省文化广电出版体育厅。
(5)《旅游学刊》,北京报刊发行局。
(6)《时尚旅游》杂志,中国旅游杂志社。
(7)《新旅行》(Voyage)杂志,财讯传媒集团。
(8)《中国旅游报》(China Tourism News),中国旅行游览事业管理总局。

练习 7 课后练习

7.1 分析题

(1)试用所译和比读材料分析全译过程。
(2)用比读语料,分析修辞在旅游文本翻译中的运用。
(3)用比读语料,分析导游词的词汇与语篇的翻译特点。

7.2 实训题

7.2.1 故宫

① 故宫旧城紫禁城,位于北京城的中心,为明、清两代的皇宫,是中国现存最大最完整的古代木结构建筑群。始建于明永乐四年(1406 年)历时 14 年才竣工。迄今已有 500

余年历史,有 24 位皇帝相继在此登基执政。

② 故宫建筑气势雄伟,豪华壮丽,是中国古建筑艺术的精华,其规格之巨和独具特色的建筑艺术享誉世界。在这里保存的大量珍贵文物、稀世绝宝,是研究明、清两代历史和历代艺术的重要物证。1925 年改名为故宫博物院,它是世界上最大的博物馆之一。1961 年被公布为全国重点文物保护单位。1987 年被联合国教科文组织列入“世界人类文化遗产”。新中国成立后人民政府拨巨款进行保护和修缮,现已成为久负盛名的旅游景观。

7.2.2 Grand Canyon

① From the depths of the canyon comes welling silence. Seldom can you hear the roar of the river. You can not catch the patter. Like applause, from the leaves of the cotton woods on the shelf — like plateau below you. For all sounds are swallowed in this gulf of spaces. "It makes one want to murmur." A woman once whispered to her companion. This silence is not the silence of death; rather, it is a presence. It is like a great piece of music. But music made of man works up to a climax and cease; the Grand Canyon is a climax, a chord echoing into eternity.

② Perhaps the most spectacular feature of the Canyon, its Redwall limestone cliff, stands about half way up the chasm and is practically vertical. Its average height is 550 feet — almost exactly that of the Washington Monument. Though it is actually gray-blue limestone, the surface of the cliff has been stained to a sunset hue by iron salts washing out of the rocks. Above the Redwall come alternating layers of red sandstone and shale 1,000 feet thick, then comes the nest pale-blue layers. The topmost layers are a yellowish limestone.

7.3 思考题

(1)旅游文本的翻译特点是什么?
(2)旅游文本翻译应遵循什么原则?
(3)旅游翻译工作者应具备哪些素质?
(4)旅游文本翻译策略有哪些?
(5)旅游文本的修辞翻译特点是什么?
(6)导游词特点及其翻译原则是什么?
(7)景点名称特点及其翻译原则是什么?
(8)旅游翻译中的文化因素有哪些?
(9)从跨文化交际视角如何看待旅游英语翻译的文化冲突?
(10)从跨文化交际视角如何看待旅游英语文本的典故和诗词翻译?
(11)从可接受性视角如何看待旅游文本翻译策略?
(12)从模糊语言视角如何看待旅游英语翻译?
(13)建立语料库,总结中英旅游导游词的翻译规律。
(14)考取导游证应注意哪些事项?

第7课 资源环保

导 译

随着科学技术的进步和经济的迅猛发展，人类对资源的过度开发和掠夺造成了严重的环境危机，引起了世界各国政府和人民群众的广泛关注。在此背景下，掌握资源与环保方面的知识变得十分重要，而掌握该领域的翻译技能则显得尤为重要。

全球在资源与环保方面的合作与交流越来越频繁，对翻译的需求也就越来越大。其中，淡水资源、土地沙漠化、气候变化(尤其是温室效应造成的全球变暖)、空气污染、化学污染、生物多样性、核能源等等都是全球关注的焦点，也是翻译的重点。与资源环保相关的文章多为议论文体，其中专有名词和术语很常见，如果缺乏这方面的词汇积累，在翻译的过程中就会遇到障碍。这就要求译者掌握社科类文章的翻译技能及全译知识。

在翻译中，语言的通顺与语言的文采同样重要。在资源环保题材文章的翻译中，对语言的逻辑性、专业性要求更高，这就要求译者既具有广博的社会科学知识，又要具有扎实的中英文基础，在译文语言条件许可时，在译文中既要保持原文的内容，又要保持原文的形式。在翻译资源环保材料时，除遵循应用翻译的一般规律与原则外，还要格外注意专有名词翻译要精准规范，这样翻译出的作品才会是专业的、地道的、同时又具有文采。

1 课前练笔

1.1 美国的风力发电

受20世纪70年代石油危机的影响，风力工业在美国曾兴旺一时。但是后来世界石油价格下跌了,研究可更新能源的资助也被减少。到20世纪80年代中期,风能作为一种大规模能源对美国的吸引力几乎荡然无存。

1.2 新水

想想看,一杯从阴沟和厕所里收来的(饮用)水?这也许是新加坡人很快就要面对的现实。一个国际专家小组宣称再生水——亦即所谓的“新水”是适于饮用的。公共事业委员会正在对这一发现进行评估,预计将在两个月后向政府提出建议。他们对新加坡一个实验工厂生产的再生水进行了两年的测试,结果表明再生水具有稳定的高品质,符合世界卫生组织的标准。

1.3 **Shipwrecks Endanger Environment**

Shipwrecks from the Second World War could cause catastrophic damage to the environment, scientists have warned. Oil spills from 1,080 ships on the Pacific floor could equate to the damage caused by the Exxon Valdez disaster in 1989. Researchers for the South Pacific Regional Environment Program believe the greatest dangers are from sunken oil tankers which will continue to corrode. After a typhoon two years ago the USS Mississinewa, a fuel tanker sunk by a Japanese human torpedo in 1944, suffered a ruptured hull. The Mississinewa, located at Ulithi Atoll near the Philippines, could still contain millions of liters of oil, as could another tanker, the USS Neosho, which lies near Australia's Great Barrier Reef and was sunk in 1942. Trevor Gilbert, who advised the Program, told *New Scientist* magazine: "With every year that passes, these vessels deteriorate more and the risk of significant oil release becomes more likely." Another adviser, Sefania Nawadra, said, "In tropical conditions, oil remains fluid even at depth. For example, the oil on the Mississinewa is as fluid as the day it came out of the refinery." The researchers, yet to receive funding for their work, have produced a map of the wrecks and hope governments will act on their work.

1.4 **Rat Plague**

Britain is facing a sharp rise in its rat population as growing numbers of people leave fast food scraps in the street, an environment group warned. Keep Britain Tidy said the rodents were abandoning their traditional haunts underground and were roaming the streets, enticed by discarded remnants of burgers, pizzas and crisps. "The rat population is on the rise and soon it will be as common to see a rodent on our street as it is to see a dog or a cat," said group Director, Sue Nelson. The practice of dumping fast food litter and scraps on the street rather than in the trash — with young men the worst offenders — was behind the rise. According to the National Rodent Survey in 2001, Britain's rat population has grown by nearly one quarter since 1998 and is now estimated at 60 million, two million more than the human population. On average a rat can give birth every 24—28 days and just a single pair of rats can produce a colony of 2,000 a year. Around 200 Britons a year contract Weil's

Disease — an infection which can lead to kidney or liver failure and eventually death and which is carried in rat's urine. To highlight the issue, Keep Britain Tidy launched a cinema advert entitled " How close do you want them to get?" The ad culminates in a shocking image of a young woman sleeping in a bed of rats — echoing the nightmare scenario from James Herbert's classic horror tale The Rats, in which mutant rodents begin to prey on humans.

2 课前批评

2.1 最佳居所

《田园生活》杂志将1309年以来历任诺森伯兰公爵的家乡阿尼克选为英国的最佳居住地点。在被问及是什么使这个8 000人的集镇如此不同凡响时,第12代诺森伯兰公爵说:“它就是一处美丽的居所。这里有绝佳的风景、美丽的海滩和上好的钓鱼场所,交通也不像伦敦那么糟糕。”壮丽的阿尼克城堡——哈利·波特电影中的霍格莫茨魔法学校就是它——也为它的获胜助了一臂之力。它还凭借低犯罪率、相宜的房价以及种类齐全的商铺击败了南方的对手。公爵说:“全国最好的二手书店有一个就在这里。”

The Best Place to Live

Country Life magazine chose Alnwick — home to the Dukes of Northumberland since 1309 the best place to live. " It's just a beautiful place to live in," the 12th Duke of Northumberland said when asked what made the market town, population 8,000, so special. " There is fantastic scenery, good beaches, great fishing and the traffic is not as bad as London. " The imposing presence of Alnwick castle — used as Hogwarts wizardry school in the Harry Potter films — also helped secure the town's victory. Alnwick also beat its southern rivals in its low crime rates, provision of affordable housing and a variety of local shops. " We've got one of the best second-hand bookshops in the country," said the Duke. (王琴译)

2.2 Population to Peak

Despite a growth burst that more than doubled the global human population over the past 50 years, a study released in *Nature* recently predicts it will peak at 9 billion by the year 2070 and then begin to decline. " People thought for many years that we would breed ourselves out of existence," says Warren Sanderson, a professor of economics and history at State University of New York and co-author of the study. " They thought we'd produce so many children, and there would be no

人口高峰

尽管过去50年的人口增长高峰使全球人口翻了两番还要多,最近发表在《自然》杂志上的一篇论文却预言全球人口将会在2070年达到90亿的峰值并开始下降。论文作者之一,纽约州立大学经济学及历史学教授沃伦·桑德森说:“长期以来的观念是人类会无节制地繁衍直至

standing room left on the planet. But now it seems our population will peak. And that's an optimistic message." The study is the first to pinpoint an end to the burgeoning population. The scientists estimate there is an 85 percent chance the species will taper to about 8.4 billion by the year 2100.

灭亡。人们认为我们会生出太多的孩子,以致这个星球上无立锥之地。但是现在看来人口会有一个上限,这是一个好消息。”这篇论文首次提出了人口膨胀的极限。科学家们估计有85%的可能到2100年全球人口会逐步减少到84亿。(陈伟 译)

知识 3 全译知识 全译策略

全译包括直译和意译两大策略。

3.1 直译

直译是传达原作意义、兼顾形式且为译语读者所接受的全译活动。重原文之义,兼原文之形,符合译语接受规范是直译有别于死译的特点。若译出原文的形与义,但妨碍译语读者接受,仍属无效之译。直译适用于思维与语言顺序同构的双语,典型的直译就是对译。如:

① 我要给你点颜色看看。

【译文Ⅰ】:I will give you some colours to see.

【译文Ⅱ】:I will give you a lesson.

② Though a translation may be like old wine in new bottles or a woman in man's clothing, the results can be both tasteful and alive.

【原译】:虽然一篇译文可以像置于新瓶中的老酒,或似身着男装的女子,但是,酒仍不失其甘醇,而女子仍风韵不减。

【试译】:译文好比老酒装新瓶,或者女扮男装,但酒不失醇,人不减韵。

例①要视语境而定,说话人果真要给对方看颜色,以便选用,译文Ⅰ没错,结构和语义基本一致。可见直译既可传达原文之内容,又要尽可能地保持原文的表达形式。例②,整体上看,两种译文都想力保原文的形式因素,尤其是前一句,基本上是词字对译。

3.2 意译

意译是传达原作意义不拘于形式的全译活动。传达原意是意译的显著特色。不拘于原作形式,多指不拘于语法形式,不受其束缚,形式服务于内容,常表现为对原作语言单位的增、减、转、换、分、合。

比如,同是例①,可能有人会理解为“我要教训你,让你知道我的厉害”。此时“颜色”已经失去本义,译成colours是徒劳的,正确译法是译文Ⅱ。又如例②总体上以直译为主,但含意译,全译七法试译就用了六法:前一句基本对译;Though虽居句首,也可译作“虽然……但是”,但成对使用过于虚化,试译选用一个转折关联词,置于译句后面,算是转译;in 由介词换译为动词"装"和"扮",由静换动;both 表明花开两朵,要各表一枝,tasteful 指物,alive 指人,导致后一句分译为两句,借此为 tasteful 添了"酒",为 alive 配了"人";results 在此抽象,与 both 与 and 一道均被减译;上述全译六法虽受全句直译趋势带动,但在有限范围内充分地改造了原文的形式,可谓是随心所欲不越矩。再看例:

③ In externals, they were two unobtrusive women; a perfectly secluded life gave them retiring manners and habits.

【原译】:从表面看,她们是两个毫不引人注目的姑娘,久处穷乡僻壤使她们养成了腼腆的态度和缄默的习惯。

【试译】:表面上看,她俩毫不引人注目;久居穷乡僻壤,生性腼腆,好缄默不语。

They, two women 合译为"她俩",既体现性别,又点明复数,判断句 they were two unobtrusive women 译作了描写句,系词被减;主语 a perfectly secluded life 被分离出来,由短语换译成了小句;retiring 有"腼腆;缄默"之意,分别与 manners 和 habits 搭配,原文也由一个小句分译为两个小句,小句换译为复句,与前面的译文共同构成更大的复句,整个译文由主语"她俩"引领,是典型的汉语流水句。

4 全译窍门

4.1 同义选择的艺术

任何语言都有语体之分,有高雅的、通俗的、粗野的,还有俚语、公文用语及术语等。文学作品中,作家通过不同的语体来刻画人物的性格特征,更是常用的方法。翻译时,必须审其雅俗,量其轻重,论其褒贬,即要注意同义词之间有不同的语体色彩、使用范围及程度:(1) 词义有轻重的不同;(2)词义有范围大小和侧重面的不同;(3)词义有感情色彩(如憎恶、蔑视、讽刺、诅咒、尊敬、亲昵等等)和语体色彩(如庄严、高雅、古朴、俚语、方言词语、公文用语、委婉词等等)的不同。只有这样,才能恰如其分地表达原文的精神。

全译主要解决语际意一言多的问题,全译经过理解、转换之后进入表达阶段。表达重在译语意一形多的同义选择,首先是语言同义选择,其次是言语同义选择,一般都经过原语意义与译语形式之间的表里反复互证,再经语用关照和文化统摄,最终确定恰当的译文。比如,"放弃"一词有 abandon, desert, forsake 等不同的词语选择:

① He abandoned all hopes of success. 他放弃了所有成功的希望。

② Don't desert me in the misfortune. 不要在逆境中放弃我。

前一例中 abandon 指彻底地、完全地放弃某种打算;后一例中 desert 指违背法律责任和义务,或自己的信仰和誓言的行为。

4.2 复数活译

英语复数不都译作"们",如 He had become a well-loved member of staff. 有人译为"他已成为深受人们爱戴的职员",可改为"他已成为受人爱戴的职员"。又如 Fans were milling around outside the hotel. 有人译成"追星族在酒店外徘徊。"有人偏要给"族"加

"们",纯属蛇足,"族"本指一类人。再如:

③ Flowers bloom all over the yard. 朵朵鲜花开满了庭院。

④ Newsmen went flying off to Mexico. 记者纷纷飞到墨西哥去了。

⑤ There were rows of houses which he had never seen before. 一排排的房子,都是他从来没见过的。

4.3 并列连词 and 活译

英语句法关系重形合,汉语句法结构多用意合。只有连词,才能充分体现英汉语形合与意合之别。英汉语形意转化,关键之一也在连词的处理。And 作为常用的并列连词,其前后两部分表示同时发生的动作,或同时存在的属性、特征等,可译为"又……又……"、"既……又……"、"一方面……,一方面……"、"而"等,如例⑧。有时 and 的前部分表原因或条件,后部分表结果,译为"因此"、"所以"、"从而"等,如例⑨。

⑥ The process of oxidation in human body gives off heat slowly and regularly. 人体内的氧化过程缓慢而又有规则地放出热量。

⑦ Sound is carried by air, and without air there can be no sound. 声音靠空气传播,因此没有空气也就没有声音。

And 的后部分有时具有让步意义,相当于 though,可译为"虽然",如例⑩。表同位关系,可译作"即"、"也是",如例⑪。有时连接两个原形动词,却表目的关系,如⑫。用在数字或数学概念中,表示相加,如例⑬。

⑧ Several disadvantages tend to limit the use of hydraulic controls and they do offer many distinct advantages. 液压控制虽有许多突出的优点,但也存在一些缺陷,使其应用范围受到限制。

⑨ When correcting, pay close attention to the seventh and last paragraph in the translation. 改稿时请密切注意译文的第七段,即最后一段。

⑩ Allow me to go and measure the pressure again. 请允许我去把压力再测一次。

⑪ Six and seven is thirteen. 六加七等于十三。

4.4 万用词 do 的译法

听不懂别人在讲什么时,你会说 Excuse me? 或 Pardon? 或 I'm sorry? 等。其实,美语中还有很多其他选择,比如 What's that? 和 Do what? do 的用法很丰富,译法也多样。如:

⑫ You can't do me like this. 你不能这样对我。

⑬ Everything will do. 任何东西都可以。

⑭ He is doing his master's in Madison. 他正在麦迪逊攻读硕士学位。

⑮ Let's do Rachel. 轮到雷切尔了。

⑯ We like to do our laundry on Sunday. 我们喜欢在星期天洗衣服。

do 的汉译极度情境化,显示了它的活力,如在 Let me help you do the dishes after dinner. 中是"洗"之意;在 Let's do sixty forty. 中是"分"之意;有人参加话剧表演想扮演王子,可以说 I want to do the Prince。再如:

⑰ Let's do three in this car and four in that car. 三个人坐这辆车,其他四个人坐那辆车。

⑱ I am willing to do the flags with other girls. 我愿意跟其他的女孩一起耍大旗。

5 话题词汇

5.1 机构

非政府组织 non-governmental organization
国际发展机构环境委员会 International Development Environment Committee
国际湖泊环境委员会 International Lake Environment Committee
国际环境局 International Environment Bureau
国家环境保护总局 State Environmental Protection Administration
环发大会首脑会议 Summit Session of UNCED
环境部 Department of the Environment
联合国环境规划署 United Nations Environment Programs
联合国环境与发展大会(环发大会) United Nations Conference on Environment and Development (UNCED)
欧洲自然保护资料中心 European Information Center for Nature Conservation
专业团体 professional society
Advisory Committee on Marine Pollution 海洋污染咨询委员会(海洋污染咨委会)
Advisory Group on Greenhouse Gases 致温室效应气体问题咨询小组
Commission for Atmospheric Sciences 大气科学委员会
Commission for Marine Meteorology 海洋气象学委员会
Committee for Climate Changes and the Ocean 气候变化和海洋委员会
Committee on Trade and Environment 贸易与环境委员会
Council on Environmental Quality 环境质量委员会
Drifting Buoy Co-operation Panel 漂流浮标站合作小组
European Environment Agency 欧洲环境机构
European Environmental Monitoring and Information Network 欧洲环境监测和资料网络
European Group on Ocean Stations 海洋观测站欧洲小组
Forest Stewardship Council 森林管理委员会
Scientific Committee on Problems of the Environment 环境问题科学委员会
State Environmental Protection Administration 国家环境保护总局
The U. S. Green Building Council 美国绿色建筑学会
United States Environment and Protection Agency 美国环境保护局
World Wide Fund for Nature (WWF) 世界大自然基金:世界野生生物基金会

5.2 环境

臭氧层 ozone layer
飞机发动机排放物 aircraft engine emission
飞机噪音 aircraft noise
工业废水 industrial effluents
工业排放物 industrial emissions
工业烟尘 industrial fumes
工业噪声 industrial noise
海洋环境 ocean circulation
海洋生态系统 marine ecosystem
环境事故 environmental accidents
环境风险评估 environmental risk assessment
环境核算 environmental accounting

环境审计 environmental auditing
环境影响 environmental impact
环境影响报告书 environmental impact statement
环境影响评价 environmental impact assessment
环境政策 environmental policy
环境指标 environmental indicators
空气污染物 air pollutants
绿化带 greenbelts
铅污染 lead contamination
全球变暖 global warming
森林砍伐 deforestation
沙漠化 desertification
生物多样性和保护区 biological diversity and protected areas
酸雨 acid rain
土壤侵蚀 soil erosion
土壤退化 soil degradation
温室效应 greenhouse effect
无机污染物 inorganic pollutants
沿海生态系统 coastal ecosystems
野生生物生境 wildlife habitats
benthic ecosystems 海底生态系统
coastal ecosystems 沿海生态系统
coastal environments 沿海环境
estuarine ecosystems 河口生态系统
freshwater degradation 淡水恶化
island ecosystems 岛屿生态系统
living marine resources 海洋生物资源
motor vehicle emissions 机动车辆排放物
municipal waste 城市废物
nitrogen oxides 氮氧化物
noise pollution 噪声污染
organic pollutants 有机物污染
persistent organic pollutants 难降解有机污染物
river pollution 河流污染

5.3 环境保护

保护区 protected areas
废物利用 waste use
辐射防护 radiation protection
辐射监测 radiation monitoring
国家保护区 national reserves
国家公园 national parks
海洋保护区 marine conservation areas
环境监测 environmental monitoring
基因资源保护 conservation of genetic resources
流域管理 watershed management
绿化带 greenbelts
森林保护 forest conservation
生物安全 biosafety
生物圈保护区 biosphere reserves
受保护的物种 protected species
水的再利用 water reuse
水资源保护 water resources conservation
水资源开发 water resources development
污染控制技术 pollution control technology
污染治理设备 pollution abatement equipment
野生生物保护 wildlife conservation
再造林 reafforestation
噪音治理 noise abatement
植被恢复 revegetation
植树造林 afforestation
crop protection 作物保护
Declaration of the Hague 海牙宣言
Declaration of the World Climate Conference 世界气候会议宣言
Declaration on the Human Environment 人类环境宣言
Declaration on the Protection of the Atmosphere 保护大气宣言
disposal at sea 海洋废物处理
Earth Day 地球日
environmental enhancement 改善环境
environmental renovation 环境复原
environmental restoration 环境修复
environmentally harmful 对环境有害的
environmentally safe 对环境安全的
low emission 低排放
marine resources conservation 海洋资源保护
noise monitoring 噪声监视
odor nuisance 恶臭公害
pollutant analysis 污染物分析
pollutant distribution 污染物分布

pollutant levels 污染物浓度
pollutant monitoring 污染物监测
pollution monitoring 污染监测
pollutant pathways 污染物路径
pollutant source identification 污染物来源鉴别
sustained, stable and coordinated development 持续、稳定、协调发展
urban heat island 城市热岛
waste recovery 废物回收

5.4 自然资源

波浪能 wave energy
潮汐能 tidal energy
风能 wind energy
海洋热能 thermal sea power
生物多样性和保护区 biological diversity and protected areas
太阳能 solar energy
铀 Uranium
catchment areas 集水区
deep sea deposits 深海矿藏
energy processes 能源过程
freshwater ecosystems 淡水生态系统
freshwater resources 淡水资源
mineral resources 矿产资源
non-renewable resources 不可再生资源
renewable resources 可再生资源
resource conservation 资源保护

5.5 物种

濒危动物物种 endangered animal species
濒危植物物种 endangered plant species
病毒 virus
哺乳动物 mammals
寄生生物 parasites
酵母 yeasts
灵长类 primates
陆地哺乳动物 land mammals
酶 enzymes
爬行动物 reptiles
微生物 microorganisms
无脊椎动物 invertebrates
细菌 bacteria
野生生物 wildlife
野生生物生境 wildlife habitats
移栖种 migratory species
原生生物 protozoa
杂草 weeds
真菌 fungi
植被 vegetation
adaptable species 适应性强的物种
algae 藻类
amphibians 两栖动物
animal behavior 动物习性
animal resources 动物资源
aquatic mammals 水生哺乳动物
aquatic microorganisms 水生微生物
aquatic plants 水生植物
arthropods 节肢动物
biological diversity 生物多样性
biological resources 生物资源
biosphere reserves 生物圈保护区
biotopes 群落生境
coral reefs 珊瑚礁
crustaceans 甲壳纲动物
demersal fish 底栖鱼
migratory species 迁徙物种
molluscs 软体动物
shellfish 贝壳类动物
terrestrial biological resources 陆地生物资源

5.6 自然遗产

大海岸 The High Coast
大峡谷 Grand Canyon
地貌景观 landscape
国家公园 National Park

溶洞 cave
文化景观 cultural landscape
自然景观 natural landscape
自然遗产 world natural heritage
biological evolution 生物演化
glacier 冰川
habitat 栖息地
natural areas 自然地带
natural sites 自然名胜

5.7 缩略语

API 空气污染指数
BACT 可得的最佳控制污染技术
dB 分贝
EER 能效比
EIA 环境影响评价
EIS 环境影响报告书
EMIS 环境管理信息系统
EMS 境管理系统
EMU 生态监测机构
GHG 温室气体
HSRP 危险废物减量计划
IEEP 国际环境教育方案
LEED 能源与环境设计的领先标准
MAB 人与生物圈计划
NPL 噪声污染级
PESHE 环境、安全、健康评估计划
POPs 持久性有机污染物
PPP 污染者付费原则
S/D 海水损害
TSP 总悬浮颗粒物
UNCED 联合国环境与发展大会
USTs 地下储槽
WCC 世界气候会议

6 比读体悟

6.1 中国城市化隐忧

Rise of the Chinese Megacity

① 描述中国城市化进程的文字，必定全是溢美之词。

① To write about urbanization in China is to traffic in superlatives.

② 中国经济过去三十年的持续增长主要集中在沿海地区，吸引数百万农民走出贫困山村，来到繁华的沿海地带。1992年以来，中国发生了一场人类史无前例的大迁徙，46座城市的人口突破百万大关，全国这一规模的城市共计102个。

② Three decades of sustained economic growth, concentrated along the booming coast, had lured millions from the impoverished Chinese countryside. This great migration — unprecedented in human history — has put 46 Chinese cities over the one million mark since 1992, out of a national total of 102.

③ 中国耗尽了世界上几乎一半的钢铁和水泥，大量重型施工设备也转战于中国的建筑工地上。塔式起重机就是一个例子，它现在已经成为中国市区随处可见的标志。

③ Nearly half the world's steel and cement is devoured there, and much of the world's heavy construction equipment has relocated to the People's Republic. Tower canes, for example, have become the ubiquitous symbol of urban China.

④ 但对于地球来说，这些都不是好兆头。具有讽刺意味的是，此时，西方世界已着手恢复地球环境的原有秩序，真

④ None of this bodes well for planet Earth. How ironic that, just as the West has begun to get its environmental house in order — finally taking serious action to reduce its carbon

正采取行动减少碳足迹、阻止全球变暖、摆脱对石油的依赖，而数以百万的中国人却正期盼铺张的生活方式和物质享乐，将人类置于环境面临崩溃的境地。

footprint, combat global warming, and end its oil addiction — here come the millions of China, wanting the very lifestyle and material amenities that have put us on the verge of environmental collapse. (朱小玲 译)

6.2 为什么通常在沙漠和北极地区发现石油？

Why Is Oil Usually Found in Deserts and Arctic Areas?

① 因为板块构造运动——地球表层各大板块随时间漂移，大部分石油和天然气田才最终停留在它们今天所在之地。河流三角洲和近海大陆架也都储有石油和天然气。

① Most oil and gas fields have ended up where they are because of plate tectonics — the shifting over time of large plates on the surface of the earth. River deltas and continental margins offshore also hold reserves.

② 石油和天然气大多是产生自缺氧环境中迅速被掩埋的死去的微生物，那种环境氧气奇缺致使它们无法分解。这种缺氧条件使那些死去的微生物保持它们的氢碳键——产生矿物燃料的一种必要成分。新近演化成的大洋盆地，由板块构造（运动）和大陆断裂（变形）形成，正好为迅速将微生物埋葬在缺氧水域提供了合适环境。河流携带着丰富的有机残骸注入了这些盆地。因为这些盆地已使水循环范围缩小，它们也具有比开阔的大洋更低的氧气含量。

② Oil and gas result mostly from dead microorganisms buried quickly in anoxic environments, where oxygen is so scarce that they do not decompose. This lack of oxygen enables them to maintain their hydrogen-carbon bonds, a necessary ingredient for the production of fossil fuels. Newly developing ocean basins, formed by plate tectonics and continental rifting (deformation), provide just the right conditions for rapid burial in anoxic waters. Rivers fill these basins with sediments carrying abundant organic remains. Because the basins have constricted water circulation, they also have lower oxygen levels than the open ocean.

③ 板块构造运动也起着创造一个使有机物缓慢转化成石油和天然气的"压力锅"的作用。这个过程通常要经历好几百万年，从而给石油和天然气沉积物以时间随板块运动迁移到地球各处。因为这些碳氢化合物比水要轻得多，最后，它们在浮力作用下竭力上升到地球表层。断裂或板块之间碰撞以及其他地壳构造力可以将它们锁定在地下存储库里。我们把这些存储库称为石油和天然气田。

③ Plate tectonics is also responsible for creating the "pressure cooker" that slowly matures the organic into oil and gas. This process usually takes millions of years, giving the oil and gas deposits time to migrate around the globe on the back of plate movements. Because these hydrocarbons are much more buoyant than water, they eventually force their way to the surface. Alternatively, rifting, collisions between landmasses, and other tectonic forces can free the mature oil and gas from deep within sedimentary basins and then trap these organic fluids in reservoirs before they escape to the earth's surface. We know these reservoirs as oil and gas fields. (邓建生 译)

6.3 技术使变废为宝充满希望

Technologies Promise to Turn Garbage into Gold

① 一些公司声称，他们的新技术能"迅速处理"旧电脑、香蕉皮、报废轮胎和其他废物，而不是把它们抛入废物填埋场。

① Instead of tossing old computer, banana peels, used tires and other garbage into a hole in the ground, companies claim their new technologies can "zap" trash away.

② 这可能听起来像科幻小说，然而，

② It may sound like science fiction, but a range of

一系列设备正逐渐流行起来，这些设备利用高温及（在某些情况下）高压把废物分解成固体和产生能量的气体——没有或只有极少的排放物。

devices are catching on that use intense heat and, in some cases, pressure to break garbage down into solids and energy producing gases — with little or no emissions.

③ 例如，美国康涅狄格州威尔顿的Startech公司和首都华盛顿的Solena集团在缺氧的容器中用炽热的等离子体把废物烘烤到3万度——是太阳温度的三倍。

③ For instance, Startech Corp. in Wilton, Conn., and the Solena Group in Washington, D. C., use molten hot plasma to scorch garbage in an oxygen-starved container to 30,000 degree — or three times as hot as the sun.

④ 宾夕法尼亚州费城的另一家公司——改变世界技术公司——把废物和水结合，用极高温和极高压使水和废物的混合物分解成煤气、轻油、重油和固态碳。煤气用来燃烧，水被排出，轻油、重油和碳作为能源销售。

④ Another firm, Changing World Technologies of Philadelphia, Pa., combines waste with water and applies extreme heat and pressure to separate the mixture into gas, light oil, heavy oil and solid carbon. The gas is burned, the water is drained and the oils and carbon are sold as energy sources.（王宏平 译）

6.4 **Hunter or Killer**?

For more than a century, scientists have debated what killed off the big animals in Australia and the Americas. Two new studies place the blame squarely on ancient human hunters equipped with fire, spears and an appetite for meat. The studies, appearing in the journal *Science*, conclude that after early humans migrated into Australia and the Americas, the heavy-weight animals of these new continents were driven to extinction within a few thousand years. In the Americas, 73 percent of the large plant-eaters, along with the saber-toothed cat, were done within 1,200 years after humans migrated to the continents about 13,600 years ago. In Australia, researchers precisely dated bone specimens of elephant-sized marsupials, giant snakes, huge lizards and other extinct animals. They found that the wildlife disappeared within 10,000 years after humans arrived at the down-under continent. An expert said the dating is significant because some researchers have blamed the extinctions on extended droughts that occurred later. But she noted that the animals had withstood climate changes previously; so it is unlikely they all would have succumbed to natural forces. Also, disease is improbable since so many different species of reptiles, birds and mammals disappeared at about the same time. Diseases are unlikely to affect all species the same way.

猎手还是杀手？

一个多世纪以来，科学家们一直在争论是什么造成了澳洲和美洲大型动物的灭绝。根据两项新的研究，这一罪责无疑应该由以火和矛武装起来的、喜欢吃肉的古人类猎手来承担。发表在《科学》杂志上的研究成果表明，在早期人类移居到澳洲和美洲以后，这两块新大陆上的大型动物即在数千年内被赶尽杀绝。人类在大约13 600年前移居到美洲，以后1 200年内美洲大陆上73%的大型食草动物就和剑齿虎一同灭绝。在澳洲，研究者们精确测定了体大如象的有袋类动物，巨蛇，巨蜥，以及其他一些已灭绝动物标本的年代。他们发现这些动物都是在人类到达澳洲后10 000年之内消失的。一位专家说，这次年代测定具有重要意义，因为有些研究者把动物灭绝归咎于发生较晚的长期干旱。她强调说这些动物以前就曾经经受住了气候变化的考验，因为他们不可能全都被自然的力量打垮。疾病之说也不能成立。因为有那么多不同种类的爬行动物，鸟类和哺乳动物几乎在同

时灭绝,而疾病不大可能给所有物种造成同样的影响。(张楠 译)

6.5 There is Hope

The effects of environmental damage continue to the present, for example, algae now choking and killing many coral reefs in the Caribbean can be traced to the slaughter more than 3,000 years ago of the green sea turtle and other animals that grazed on the sea plant. "There has been a longtime belief that everything was fine until the…Europeans showed up," said Karen Bjorndal, a zoology professor at the University of Florida. "Now we have discovered that the start of the environmental problem (in the sea) go way back before that." Based on the combined research of 19 scientists on four continents, the study shows that careless and excessive harvesting of food from the sea as early as 10,000 years ago caused changes in the ecosystems and made the environment more easily damaged by the wholesale exploitation of modern man. However, Bjorndal believes some of the environmental loss can be recovered with new programs to protect sea life and control fishing. Many of the depleted animals are not extinct and could be brought back to restore almost balance, "One of our main messages is that there is hope." she said.

还有希望

环境破坏的恶果延续至今,例如:如今的海藻正在窒息并杀死加勒比海的许多珊瑚礁,原因则可追溯到3 000多年前对绿海龟以及其他海藻为食的动物的屠杀。佛罗里达大学的动物学教授卡伦·比约恩代说:“长期以来有一种观念,就是一切都好,直到……欧洲人出现。现在我们发现(海洋)环境问题在这之前就已经开始了。”以四大洲19位科学家的联合研究结果为基础,论文指出早在1万年前,从海洋中任意地过度取食就已经导致了生态系统的变化,使环境更易遭受现代人大规模开发的破坏。不过,比约恩代仍然认为某些环境破坏可以通过保护海洋生物以及控制捕捞的新举措得到恢复。许多被捕猎殆尽的动物尚未灭绝,人类能使他们回到海洋生态系统中,重建失去的生态平衡。他说:“我们的主要观点之一就是:还有希望。”(白立明 译)

6.6 World's Biggest Rat Hunt

New Zealand conservation officials have dropped 120 tons of bait and a team of 20 rat hunters onto a remote sub-Antarctic island in what they say is the largest rodent eradication project the world has ever seen. They aim to wipe out up to 200,000 Norway rats probably introduced to Campbell Island, 438 miles south of New Zealand's South Island, by 19th century whalers and sealers. The $1.1 million kill is designed to restore the 11,300 hectare island to its natural state and allow the return of a flightless teal duck and a species of wading bird found only on the island. The Department of Conservation said it would be two years before it knew if rats had gone from the island — reported to have the highest concentration of rats in the world — but already most of the bait had been carried to burrows by hungry rats. New Zealand has had success in eliminating rats from smaller islands, including Kapiti Island near Wellington, which is now a bird sanctuary.

世界最大的灭鼠行动

新西兰环保官员在一个边远的亚南极区岛屿上投下了120吨毒饵并派出了由20人组成的灭鼠队。据称这是世界有史以来规模最大的一次灭鼠行动。他们的目标是将新西兰南岛南部438英里处坎贝尔岛上多达20万只的挪威鼠斩尽杀绝。这些挪威鼠可能是被19世纪的捕鲸者和捕海豹者带到岛上的。耗资110万美元的这次屠杀旨在使11 300公顷的坎贝尔岛恢复其自然状态,并使岛上特有的一种不能飞的短颈野鸭及一种涉禽得以重返家园。环保部宣称要到两年以后才能知道老鼠是否已从坎贝尔岛绝迹——据说该岛是世界上老鼠密度最

Norway rats are prodigious breeders, with females capable of producing up to seven litters of a dozen pups each year. The gestation period is just 22 days, and females mate when they are as young as three months old.

高的地方——不过大部分毒饵已经被饥饿的老鼠搬进了地穴。新西兰曾在较小的岛屿上灭鼠成功,比如惠灵顿附近的卡比提岛,那里现在是鸟类天堂。挪威鼠繁殖力惊人,雌鼠从三月大时就开始交配,妊娠期仅22天,一胎产仔12只,每年可产仔7次之多。(阎晓玲 译)

6.7 推荐读物

(1)姜维焕,英语科普阅读(1),西安交通大学出版社2000年版。
(2)郭继荣等,英语科普阅读(2),西安交通大学出版社2000年版。
(3)李庆明等,英语科普阅读(3),西安交通大学出版社2000年版。
(4)陈乃芳等,宇宙、环境与生命,外语教学与研究出版社2001年版。
(5)于苏俊,环境科学专业英语,西安交通大学出版社2005年版。
(6)(英)Tony Juniper,拯救地球,化学工业出版社2010年版。

练习 7 课后练习

7.1 分析题

(1)试用所译和比读材料分析全译策略。
(2)试析动物概念的翻译特点。
(3)试析大众报刊翻译的语篇特点。

7.2 实训题

7.2.1 全球变暖

沿海城市淹没、农田干裂、洋流紊乱、热带疾病蔓延、冰山消融——人为因素引起的温室效应将会带来无尽的灾难。美国国家科学院在2005年时宣称——如果地球的气候发生具有深远影响的变化,那么全球经济就可能遭受广泛的破坏,其破坏力只有第二次世界大战可与之相比。

7.2.2 A Survey on Change to Seasons

The coming of the spring in Britain may come quietly this year due to dwindling numbers of cuckoos, conservationists said. The Woodland Trust said numbers of the grey birds, beloved by Britons for announcing the end of winter with their distinctive cooing, has fallen by up to 60 percent since the 1970s. Amid fears cuckoos are falling victims to an ever more unsettled climate and aggressive modern farming methods, the charity asked Britons to go on alert for the noisy birds. "Every one is needed to listen out for the first cuckoo they hear." The Trust said in a statement. "Even if you usually hear the cuckoo, but don't hear one this year, please let us know." Infamous for their habit of laying eggs in other birds' nests — a hen cuckoo can swap another bird's egg with her own in just 15 seconds — the birds have always held a special place in British hearts as harbingers of spring.

7.3 思考题

(1)如何避免望文生义的翻译陷阱?

(2)翻译成语俗语,应注意哪些方面?

(4)查阅相关文献,了解广告有哪些翻译方式?

(5)分析全部翻译与部分翻译的共同之处及各自特点。

(6)顺译与逆译有何特征?在笔译和口译中分别如何体现?

(7)翻译时,如何注意翻译的流畅性?

(8)翻译时,怎样做到逆向思维?

(9)怎样翻译人称委婉语?

(10)在翻译中,如何把动物形象转换成人的形象?

(11)试析比喻直译或意译有何缘由。

(12)分析汉英互译中词汇空缺现象产生的原因。

第8课 新闻媒体

导译

新闻文本记叙全世界每天发生的各类事件，内容兼容并包、无所不及，政治经济、科学技术、文化教育、风土人情、宗教信仰等面面俱到。新闻语篇信息内容多样，信息功能也各不相同，其文体的复杂性不言自明。

新闻翻译就是用另一种语言对原文中的信息进行发掘、加工和再次传播的过程。新闻文本具有自身的词汇、语法、修辞和语篇特征，新闻文本翻译，由于不同的翻译目的和时效性要求，必然变译与全译平分秋色。但本课将只探讨新闻文本的语体特色及全译策略。新闻翻译要求译者甄别信息、补充背景、方便受众、重组结构，并注重褒贬处理、虚实对译、修辞再现、委婉处理，同时关注新闻翻译中的意识形态问题。

1 课前练笔

1.1 林书豪——追逐梦想，寻找喜悦

① 在职业篮球球员当中，林书豪的背景跟大多数人不同。他毕业于哈佛大学，该校出身的NBA球员寥寥可数，而且他是唯一一位美籍华裔的NBA球员。但是看他在球场上的表现，会觉得他毫无疑问属于那里。他的动作迅速优雅，展现出多年来坚持不懈的练习，其动力来自于对于篮球的热爱。

② 林书豪对篮球的喜爱其实源于台湾。他父亲在台湾时开始看篮球比赛，后来移居美国，对于该项运动的兴趣有增无减。他把这份对篮球的热爱传给儿子，带领当时五岁的他认识篮球比赛。书豪的童年时期有很多时光都以打篮球为乐，并且向父亲和哥哥学艺。

③ 但是家人教的不止是篮球。在球赛之后，父母讨论的不只是他的分数，还包括他对于其他球员的行为。这让书豪知道，品行比打得好重要。这一课他至今还铭记在心。

1.2 Surge in Winter Weddings

① Brides are increasingly shunning summer weddings and getting married during winter instead to cut costs amid the economic gloom, figures suggest. Register office data shows that thousands more people are tying the knot between October and March than in previous years, to save money on hosting receptions. Companies offering wedding services are also reporting booming business as couples take advantage of prices thousands of pounds cheaper than during the peak summer months.

② The trend is even said to be having an impact on wedding attire, with more designers offering coats, shawls and different colored dresses from the traditional white and ivory gowns bought by most brides.

1.3 The U. S. Strategic Outreach to the Asia Pacific Region

① Secretary of State Hillary Clinton says the U. S. strategic outreach to the Asia Pacific region will be a top priority as Washington transitions away from a decade of military efforts in Iraq and Afghanistan. Clinton told a gathering of U. S. diplomats in Washington on Tuesday the future of Asia will continue to be vital to U. S. interests, saying a government-wide effort is being made to develop new relationships there.

② In her wide ranging speech at the Global Chiefs of Mission conference, Clinton outlined her priorities for American diplomatic efforts over the next year. She said U. S. diplomats will continue to focus on sustainable development programs around the world, help build a transparent and fair global economic system, and promote democracy in the Middle East and other developing areas.

2 课前批评

2.1 中国股市将对外资进一步开放

① 中国将为境外机构投资中国股市开放更多渠道。此举旨在支撑股价，并在经济放缓之际帮助抵消资本流出。

② 中国证监会上周五晚宣布，境外持有的人民币可用于购买境内股票。外界期待已久的这项改革，对于推动人民币国际化十分关键。

③ 中国媒体还报道称，政府正

China Opens Door Wider to Foreign Investors

① China will open more channels for foreign institutions to invest in its stock markets, a move aimed at supporting share prices and helping to counter capital outflows as the economy slows.

② The Chinese Securities Regulator announced late on Friday that RMB held offshore could be used to buy equities within China, a long-awaited reform that is critical to promoting more international use of the Chinese currency.

③ Local media also reported that the government

准备显著提高合格境外机构投资者的股票份额，让这些机构能够向近乎封闭的中国股市投资。

was preparing to expand significantly the number of quotas that allow foreign institutions to invest in China's closely guarded markets.

④ 境外基金在中国扮演的角色微不足道，仅占股市总市值的大约1%。新的开放措施不太可能改变这一局面，至少在初期将是如此。但综合来看，此类措施突显北京方面有意逐渐放开资本管制，让更多机构资金注入类似赌场的中国股市。

④ Foreign funds play a tiny role in China, accounting for just about 1 per cent of total market value, and the new openings are unlikely to change that, at least initially. But together they underline Beijing's desire to liberalize capital controls gradually and to bring more institutional money into markets that often resemble casinos.

2.2 Hong Kong Airport Plans to Add IMAX Theater

① In Hong Kong for a long layover? Travelers to and from the city will soon have access to the world's largest airport entertainment option to help pass the time.

② UA Cinemas recently said that it would be opening an IMAX theater in Hong Kong International Airport in the second quarter of 2012. The cinema will be located in a new 'entertainment zone' in Terminal 2.

③ On Feb. 14, the airport ranked No. 4 in the 2011 Airport Service Quality Awards produced by Airports Council International, falling behind airports in Seoul, Singapore ('arguably the world's most fabulous airport,' according to Middle Seat columnist Scott McCartney) and Beijing. The council's annual rankings are based on passenger-satisfaction surveys and are considered one of the air-travel industry's most prestigious accolades.

④ The Hong Kong airport's new movieplex will seat up to 358 and have a screen that is 45 feet high and 75 feet wide, making it the largest of Hong Kong's three IMAX theaters. It will show both 2-D and 3-D movies. While its impact on passenger satisfaction remains to be seen, it will be the first airport IMAX theater in the

香港国际机场拟建IMAX影院

① 不得不滞留香港候机？很快，出入香港的旅客们就能够选择全球最“巨型”的机场娱乐方式来打发时间了。

② 娱艺院线近日表示，今年第二季度将在香港国际机场开设一家IMAX影院。该影院将入驻香港国际机场2号航站楼一处新开辟的“娱乐区域”。

③ 在2月14日国际机场协会宣布的2011年度机场服务质量奖获奖名单中，香港国际机场排名第四，紧随首尔、新加坡和北京机场之后。其中，新加坡的樟宜机场被《华尔街日报》“首席座位”专栏作家斯科特·麦卡尼称赞为“全球最佳机场”。国际机场协会的年度排名是根据乘客满意度调查得出的，被视为航空业最具权威的嘉奖。

④ 香港国际机场拟开设的新影院最多可容纳358位观众，其银幕宽75英尺（约22.9米）、高45英尺（约13.7米），在香港三家IMAX影院中尺寸最大。该影院将播放2D和3D电影。

world. 虽然此举能否提升乘客的满意度还有待观察,但其“全球首家机场IMAX影院”的头衔看来已是板上钉钉了。

3 全译知识 全译单位

全译单位即全译所运用的单位,是全译中意义相对完整能自由理解、转化和表达的思维单位和语言/言语单位。全译单位有多种,使用程度不一。全译单位包括音位、词素、词、短语、小句、复句、句群、段、章/节、篇/书,基本单位则是词、短语、小句、复句、句群。小句相当于简单句、复句的分句,小句占据全译基本单位的中枢。

3.1 词

词与小句的翻译关系:词的翻译受控于小句;词可与小句互换。

除专名外,词一般是入句定义定形。原语词一旦进入译语,外延会有变化,或扩或缩,在形态发达的语言里,会引起相应的形态变化;原语中内涵丰富的词,有时要用译语小句表达,原语小句有时可用译语词表达。如:

① 她正在上海巡回访问,听取群众的意见。She is on her listening tour of Shanghai.

汉语为复句,后小句可与前小句的“巡回访问”构成“听取意见的巡回访问”,与listening tour 相似,汉语小句浓缩为英语的词。

3.2 短语

短语与小句的翻译关系:短语翻译从属于小句;短语可与小句互换。

短语的语义,随小句而定;短语的结构,随小句而建。短语与小句互换,指双语间短语有时译作小句,或小句译作短语。如:

② When things aren't going well, he'll just beat it. 情况不妙他就躲避。

③ As satellites cannot fly without carriers, China has achieved remarkable progress in rocket technology too, enabling the country to squeeze into the competitive world launching market. 没有运载火箭就不能发卫星,中国的火箭技术也取得了长足进步,已跻身于竞争激烈的世界发射市场。

例②前一小句译作了汉语短语,作汉译的时间状语。例③,分词短语“enabling...”表明技术进步的结果,enabling the country to squeeze into 完全可以译成“跻身于”,行为上与前面的施事“中国”保持一致,由原文的短语译成了汉语的小句,只是小句的主语承前定语省略,构成了汉语的流水句。

3.3 小句

小句是全译的中枢单位,在词、短语、小句、复句、句群等全译基本单位中,理解时小句可瞻前顾后,转换时它可中介周转,表达时它可左顾右盼。全译围绕它而展开。如例

①、例②和例③的小句译为词和短语，例④、例⑤的原语小句与译语小句的互换，或与复句和句群互换。

3.4 复句

复句与小句的翻译关系：复句翻译依赖于小句；复句可与小句互换。

复句翻译依赖于小句，指复句不能直接翻译，须由一个个小句的翻译来完成，离开了小句翻译，也就无所谓复句翻译，因为复句由小句与小句联结而成。在全译中，复句可压缩为小句，小句可扩展为复句。如：

④ We must therefore conclude that when the distance between the molecules is very small, there are forces of repulsion and that these forces increase rapidly as the distance between the molecules decreases.

【原译】：因此我们必须断定：当分子之间距离很小时，就产生排斥力，并且这种排斥力随着分子之间距离的减小而迅速增大。

【试译】：因此我们必须得出结论：分子间距离很小时会产生排斥力，随着距离减小，排斥力会迅速增大。

原文主句带有两个由 that 引导的宾语从句，宾语从句又各自套有由 when 和 as 引导的从句，四个从句即四个小句。原译与试译均依赖于小句，保留了原文的句法结构，反映了原文的内涵。

3.5 句群

句群与小句的翻译关系：句群翻译寄托于小句；句群可与小句互换。

句群是成群的句，有三种构建模式：小句＋小句；小句＋复句；复句＋复句。因复句可分为多个小句，句群翻译寄托于小句，表明它既可由一个个小句直接翻译而成，更有可能托付于复句，通过复句翻译来完成。同是依赖于小句翻译，句群与小句的关系要远于复句，换言之，句群翻译或要经过复句翻译中转。据翻译的需要，小句可扩为句群，句群也可缩为小句。如：

⑤ To have discarded, as I believe, all usual frailties, to have become incapable of envy, ambition, malice, the desire to score off my neighbour, to enjoy this purification even as I enjoy the clean voluptuousness of the warm breeze on my skin and the cool support of the water. 我自信已抛弃一切通病，不再嫉妒，不再野心勃勃，不再心怀叵测，不再有欺压邻里的欲念。和风拂面，凉水浮身，清洁沁脾。此时此刻，享受到了净化的快乐。

原文是由三个不定式短语构成的修辞单部句，精炼，鲜明，生动，情感强烈，汉译分作三个句子表达，展示了英语小句扩充为汉语句群的过程。

窍门 4 全译窍门

4.1 标题译美

新闻标题位于版面上最引人注目的位置，具有画龙点睛的作用。英美新闻标题以新颖独特、生动形象、短小精悍见长,能够浓缩主题、彰显内涵,已经形成具有特定语篇建构意义的标题话语。首先,新闻标题翻译要求简明而要、重点突出,在狭小的篇幅中最大化地呈现信息,通常采用省略手段。如:

① Billion-Dollar Boomers, Babies 亿万富翁与新生代

② Microsoft: Busted 微软公司惨遭打击

其次,频繁运用缩略语。为缩短版面,扩大信息量,为读者提供精确完整的信息。如:

③ BRICS Will Work Together More 金砖国家将继续广泛合作

④ OECD Urges ECB to Be Ready 经合组织敦促欧洲央行行动

⑤ 购买中国新股需谨慎 Cautionary Tale: China's IPOs

⑥ 全国政协主席在京接见归国留学生 CPPCC Head Meets Returned Overseas Students in Beijing

再次,巧妙地使用明喻、暗喻、头韵、双关、仿拟、对照等修辞手段。标题翻译时,通常很难保留原有的修辞效果,可用其他修辞手段弥补,或放弃修辞以求信息的准确传递。如:

⑦ A Vow to Zip His Lips(夸张)誓将守口如瓶

⑧ Liberty: Mother of Invention(典故)自由是发明之母

⑨ Middle East: A Cradle of Terrer(比喻)中东——恐怖主义的摇篮

⑩ After the Boom, Everything is Gloom(尾韵)繁荣好景不再,萧条接踵而来

⑪ Looking Back to Look Ahead(对照)回首往昔,展望未来

⑫ Soccer Kicks off with Violence(双关)足球开踢,拳打脚踢

4.2 导语重构

新闻导语经典结构是倒金字塔,源于美国南北战争和电报的运用。为避免电报线路中断,致使新闻没有结尾无法刊发,人们逐步使用倒金字塔结构,即把最重要的结果写在最前面,再按照事实的重要性把五个 W(who, what, when, where, why)依次写下去,所以又称结论性导语或概括性导语,其优点是,一句话概括整个新闻事件,但它显得冗长、死板,不够简洁生动,且千篇一律、公式化。译者面对这类较长的复杂单句,通常是将原句切分为较具可读性的多个小句,然后按照事件的事件顺序或逻辑顺序重新组构。如:

⑬ Peter White, 40, of 13 Roseland Gardens, a passenger in a taxi that toppled off a Warwickshire highway cliff on January 2, filed a \$3,000,000 damage suit in a superior court yesterday against the driver, Jonathan Sawdy, 41, of Derby, driving at a " wanton and reckless rate of speed" under the influence of intoxicants. 彼得·怀特,40 岁,家住玫瑰园路 13 号,1 月 2 日乘坐一辆出租车翻下华威克郡公路悬崖。昨天于高级法院起诉出租车司机要求 300 万美元的损失赔偿。司机约翰逊·索迪,41 岁,达比人,由于喝了酒,驾车速度疯狂而冒险。

4.3 虚实对译

外交新闻常见“闪烁其词”,意即言不由衷、故意自由滥用一些表达。翻译时应据语

境处理，该虚则虚，该实则实。如：

⑭ In a secret case in Australia over "Spycatcher", former British civil service head Sir Robert Armstrong admitted he had previously been economical with the truth. 在澳大利亚秘密调查间谍案件中，前英国内政部长罗伯特·阿姆斯特朗承认之前一直对事实保持谨慎态度。

⑮ The Australian Government has softened its hardline attitude in the domestic air pilots' dispute, signaling that it is prepared to help get it back before the Industrial Relations Commission. 澳大利亚政府对国内飞行员罢工事件的态度已有所软化，这一迹象表明政府有意将问题交回劳资关系委员会解决。

例⑭中 economical with the truth 意为“隐瞒真相”，此处采用了弱陈的修辞方式，表明了言者的态度。例⑮的画线部分分别直译为“国内民航飞行员争端”和“工业关系委员会”，未能传出原文真意。若加注解，译文会冗长，译文有所取舍，译出了原文内涵。

4.4 褒贬处理

新闻文本经常出现看似中性、不带情感、但翻译时可褒可贬的词汇，如 ambition 或译“雄心”，或译“野心”。译者要树立公正客观的翻译观，同时也应具有政治敏感性。如：

⑯ Santander Sets Its Sights on Britain 桑德坦银行觊觎英国；桑德坦银行关注英国

有些词语并不存在明显或强烈的政治含义，但其情感意义需关注。如 die 可译为“逝世、仙逝、辞世、过世、去世、牺牲”，甚至是“死去、死掉、一命呜呼、去见上帝、去见马克思”。再如：to attribute to 归功于、归因于、归咎于；to be allied to 结盟、联合、勾结；to be killed 被杀、遇害、遇难、罹难、牺牲；to blame 责备、指责、责难；to put down 镇压、制止、平定；leader 领袖、领导人、头目；lover 恋人、情人、爱侣、情妇；news 消息、风声、噩耗。

4.5 文以载道

新闻媒体是国家政府的喉舌，涉及各国的利益，因此是各国利用意识形态手段建构自己和他国形象的重要宣传机器。翻译过程中的需要把握意识形态的支配作用。

中国现行的“对外开放政策”规范的译法是 opening-up policy，而美国媒体的译名却是 the open door policy，让读者联想起鸦片战争后，美国为同其他列强争夺中国殖民利益而提出的一项臭名昭著的侵略政策。很显然，译者采取的是一种蔑视和诋毁的态度。“中国大陆”常被译为 Mainland China，给人感觉是还有另外一个中国，显然是台独思想的操控。正确的译名应为 the Chinese Mainland，或 the mainland of China，或 China's mainland。

词汇 5 话题词汇

5.1 媒体术语

国际新闻 world news | 国内新闻 home news

地方新闻 local news
政治新闻 political news
经济新闻 economic news
科技新闻 technological news
文化新闻 cultural news
体育新闻 sports news
暴力与犯罪新闻 violence and crime news
灾难新闻 disaster news
天气新闻 weather news
娱乐 entertainment
特写 feature story
深度报道 enterprise copy
社论 editorial
讣告 obituary
独家新闻 exclusive
小道消息 grapevine
社会轶闻 affair
报纸中缝广告 gutter position
硬新闻 hard news
软新闻 soft news
倒金字塔结构 inverted pyramid
媒体形象 media image
要闻 top news
招聘广告 want ad
周刊 newsweekly
舆论监督 watchdog
新闻综述 wrap-up
ABC(accuracy, brevity and clarity)准确;简洁;明晰
accredited journalist 特派记者
agony column 私事广告栏
anchor booth 新闻节目主持人播音室
anecdotal lead 轶事导语
apocryphal story 假新闻
audience survey 受众调研
authoritative source 权威人士
back alley news 小道消息
briefing 信息发布会
bureau 新闻机构的办事处
commercial 商业广告
communication media 传播媒介
dope story 内幕消息
ethics of journalism 新闻道德
frequency 频率
frontpage 头版
news conference 记者招待会
news commentary 新闻评论
network time 联播时间
openness 透明度
press office 新闻处
reprint 转载
snap shot 抓拍镜头
topliner 头条新闻人物
analysts 分析家
authoritative sources 权威人士
diplomatic sources 外交人士
educational circles 教育界
experts 专家
financial quarters 金融界方面
Foreign Ministry spokesman 外交部发言人
government official 政府官员
government statement 政府声明
highly-placed sources 高层消息灵通人士
judicial circles 司法界
in-group source 圈内人士
military sources 军方人士
observers 观察家
official sources 官方人士
police sources 警方人士
quarters/circles 方面;阶层
reliable sources 消息可靠人士
spokesman 发言人
the quarters concerned 有关方面
unconfirmed report 未经证实的消息
unimpeachable sources 消息可靠人士
well-informed sources 消息灵通人士
well-placed sources 重要消息灵通人士
witnesses 证人;目击者

5.2 地名昵称

Big Apple (大苹果)纽约
Beantown(豆城)波士顿

Hub of the Universe(宇宙中心)波士顿市
City of Angels(天使之城)洛杉矶
Crescent City(新月城)新奥尔良
Dice City(赌城)拉斯维加斯
Film Capital of the World(世界影都)好莱坞
Land of Lincoln(林肯之乡)伊利诺伊州
Mother of Presidents(总统之母)弗吉尼亚州
Empire State(帝国州)纽约州
City by the Golden Gate(金门城)旧金山市
Windy City(风之城)芝加哥市
Golden State(黄金州)加利福尼亚州
Foggy Bottom(美国国务院所在地)美国政府
Pentagon(五角大楼)美国国防部
Motor City(汽车城)底特律
Fleet Street(舰队街) 英国新闻界
Elysee(爱丽舍宫) 法国政府
Buckingham Palace(白金汉宫)英国皇室
No. 10 Downing Street(唐宁街 10 号)英国政府
Horn of Africa(非洲之角)索马里和埃塞俄比亚
Zhongnanhai(中南海)中国政府

5.3 新词互译

housingwise 就住房问题看
curriculumwise 在课程方面
perestroika 组织机构调整
microtransaction 小笔交易
eco-consciousness 生态意识
post-feminism 后女权运动
biodiesel 生物燃料
cyber culture 网络文化
bridge job 退休前的过渡工作
bright flight 中小学生外流
cult of celebrity 名人崇拜
Afro-pean 欧化的非洲人
digicam 数码照相机
Prozac 抗沮丧剂
hotsy-potatsy 市场行销高手
cyberspace 网络空间
prenup 婚前财产协议
baby boom 生育高峰
Beat Generation 垮掉的一代
couch potato 沙发土豆(爱看电视的人)
mouse potato 电脑迷
Fifth Avenue 第五大道
Harlem 哈雷姆黑人区
Marijuana 大麻
Gallup polls 盖洛普民意测验
Ku Klux Klan 三 K 党
soap operas 肥皂剧
teleconference 可视会议
e-commerce 电子商务
e-mall 虚拟商场
virtual reality 虚拟现实
hypertext 超文本
multi-meida 多媒体
web browser 网络浏览器
hacker 黑客
suicide bombing 自杀性爆炸
botel 汽艇游客旅馆
workfare 工作福利
helipad 直升机起降场
sitcom 情景喜剧
beatnik 颓废一代
peacenik 和平分子
anti-inflation 反通货膨胀
antiestablishment 反政府
antiart 非主流艺术
antimusic 非正统音乐
multitasking 同时从事多项工作的能力
crunch 危机;困境
scenario 行动方案
fro-jo 冻酸奶
gene therapy 基因疗法
genebank 基因库
anamania 日本动画片迷
bonkbuster 色情小说
blockbuster 电影大片
quality time 与孩子谈话时间
talk show 脱口秀
pickup 皮卡车
bungee-jumping 蹦极
eco-audit 环保监测
假唱 lip-sync a prerecorded song
女强人 a strong woman

网络杂志 webzine
网民 netizen
网上购物 on-line shopping
电子商务 e-commerce
网络精英 netpreneur
早恋 puppy love
痞子文学 punk literature
托儿 shill
菜篮子工程 non-staple food project
大龄青年 single youth above normal matrimonial age
小金库 unauthorized cash reserves
减负 lighten the burden on students
打假 crack down on counterfeiters

5.4 中外媒体

AFP：Agence Francaise de Presse 法新社
AP：Associated Press 美联社
DPA：Deutsche Presse Agentur 德新社
KYODO：Kyodo News Agency 共同社
MENA：Middle East News Agency 中东社
ITA-TASS 俄通社－塔斯社
UPI：United Press International 合众国际社
Xinhua News Agency 新华社
ABC：American Broadcasting Company 美国广播公司
BBC：British Broadcasting Company 英国广播公司
CBS：Columbia Broadcasting System（美）哥伦比亚广播公司
CNN：Cable News Network（美）有线电视新闻网
NBC：National Broadcasting Company（美）全国广播公司
VOA：Voice of America 美国之音
CRI：China Radio International 中国国际广播
CCTV：International 中国中央电视台国际频道

5.5 报刊译名

美国
USA Today 今日美国报
Wall Street Journal 华尔街日报
New York Times 纽约时报
Los Angeles Times 洛杉矶时报
Washington Post 华盛敦邮报
Chicago Tribune 芝加哥论坛报
New York Post 纽约邮报
Philadelphia Inquirer 费城问讯报
Houston Chronicle 休斯敦纪事报
Detroit Free Press 底特律自由新闻报
Dallas Morning News 达拉斯晨报
Time 时代周刊
Newsweek 新闻周刊
Reader's Digest 读者文摘
Fortune 财富杂志
American Economic Review 美国经济评论
Playboy 花花公子
英国
The Times 泰晤士报
Sunday Times 星期日泰晤士报
Daily Telegraph 每日电讯报
Guardian 卫报
Observer 观察家报
Daily Mail 每日邮报
Mirror 镜报
The Sun 太阳报
The Independent 独立报
中国
21 世纪报 21st Century
南华早报 South China Morning Post
人民日报 People's Daily
中国日报 China Daily
加拿大
Toronto Star 多伦多之星
Ottawa Citizen 渥太华市民报
Montreal Gazette 蒙特利尔报
Vancouver Sun 温哥华太阳报

5.6 特色复合词组

cancer-causing drug 治癌药物
oil-producing country 产油国
peace-keeping force 维和部队
policy-making body 决策机构
far-reaching significance 深远意义
high-ranking official 高级官员
long-standing issue 由来已久的问题
wide-spreading AIDS 到处蔓延的艾滋病
poverty-stricken area 贫困地区
deep-rooted social problems 根深蒂固的社会问题
foreign-owned enterprise 外资企业
export-oriented economy 外向型经济
long-faced job loser 愁眉苦脸的失业者
quick-frozen food 速冻食品
dimly-lit room 光线昏暗的房间
highly-sophisticated technology 尖端技术
richly-paid job 薪水丰厚的工作
inflation-proof deposit 保值储蓄
interest-free loan 无息贷款
labor-intensive enterprise 劳动力密集型企业
vehicle-free promenade 步行街
arms-reduction talks 裁军谈判
labor-management conflict 劳资冲突
supply-demand imbalance 供求失调
year-end report 年终报告
fair-trade agreement 互惠贸易协定
long-range nuclear missile 远程核导弹
long-term, low-interest loan 长期低息贷款
top-level talk 最高层会谈
100-metre dash 百米赛跑
one-man government 独裁政府
one-way street 单向道
21-gun salute 21 响礼炮
dusk-to-dawn curfew 彻夜宵禁
face-to-face talk 会晤;面晤
ground-to-air missile 地对空导弹
good-to-excellent care 无微不至的关怀
middle-of-the-road policy 中立政策
on-the-job training 在职培训;岗位培训
on-the-spot interview 现场采访
hand-to-mouth pay 温饱工资
touch-and-go affair 一触即发的局势
One-country-two-system policy 一国两制的政策
be-kind-to-animal campaign 保护动物运动

5.7 缩略语

BBS 电子公告板
CAAC 中国民航总局
NASA 美国国家航天总署
CPC 中国共产党
NPC 全国人民代表大会
CPPCC 中国人民政治协商会议
CIA 中央情报局
FBI 联邦调查局
GI 美国兵
GMT 格林尼治时间
IMF 国际货币基金组织
IP 因特网传输协议
ISP 因特网服务商
OPEC 石油输出国组织
UNESCO 联合国教科文组织
UNICEF 联合国(国际)儿童基金会
WHO 世界卫生组织
WTO 世界贸易组织
ADB 亚洲开发银行
FGF 世界财富论坛
GNP 国民生产总值
GDP 国内生产总值
BIS 国际结算银行
WTO 世界贸易组织

6 比读体悟

6.1 透视"穿越剧"爆红背后的秘密

The Eye-Catching Time Travel TV Series

① 作为世界最为智慧的物理学家之一,斯蒂芬 o 霍金曾说过:"我对时间非常痴迷。"

① Stephen Hawking, one of the world's smartest physicists, once said: "I'm obsessed by time."

② 我们中的很多人亦是如此,因为"穿越剧"的走红已经证实了这一点。

② Many of us are, and the popularity of time travel TV series has just proved that.

③ 随着去年《宫》和《步步惊心》接连获得令人赞叹的收视率之后,《宫 2》于今年 1 月 20 日开播,引来无数"穿越迷"的追捧。

③ After Palace and Startling by Each Step achieved startling ratings last year, Palace 2 aired on January 20, attracting time travel fans back to TV.

④《步步惊心》制片人蔡艺侬认为,"穿越剧"将古代和现代连接起来,为观众提供了更多的想象空间。

④ Time travel series connect both today and the past, thus offering room for imagination, said Cai Yinong, the producer of Startling by Each Step.

英雄主义情节

Dream of Heroism

⑤ 丰富的想象力使得青年人能够有机会实现那些现实中难以企及的梦想。

⑤ Imagination creates a chance for the young to fulfill a dream that's hard to achieve in reality.

⑥ 从上世纪 90 年代末开始,有关男主角穿越回古代的小说作品盛行于市,《寻秦记》便是当时最火的一部。

⑥ Starting from late 1990s, novels about men traveling back to the past prevailed, with A Step Into the Past as the most popular example.

⑦ 在这些故事中,男主角运用现代的记忆和智慧干成了许多大事。此类作品通常讲述的是"英雄梦成真"的故事,此外还伴随着令人艳羡的恋情。

⑦ In these stories, the male protagonists accomplish great things with their modern skills and wisdom. It's usually a "dream of heroism come true", along with enviable romances.

⑧ 2001 年,电视剧《寻秦记》获得的巨大成功使得电视剧制作公司纷纷收购类似"穿越"题材剧本。就在去年,"穿越剧"达到了鼎盛时期。

⑧ The big success of the TV series adapted from A Step Into the Past in 2001 has inspired TV production companies to buy up similar time travel tales. Last year saw their popularity peak.

文化怀旧

Cultural Nostalgia

⑨ 去年 12 月,由上海大学和上海社会科学院联合推出的一份调查报告问及:"如果穿越到过去,最你想回到哪个朝代?"

⑨ "Which dynasty would you like to live in if you could travel to the past?" asked a survey jointly launched by Shanghai University and Shanghai Social Sciences Association last December.

⑩ 在 2 543 名受访者中,有 60% 的

⑩ About 60 percent of the 2,543 respondents chose the

人选择唐朝，另外两个热门选项分别是清朝和春秋战国时期。

Tang Dynasty, while the Qing Dynasty, and the Spring and Autumn and Warring States periods were the other top two destinations.

⑪ 上海大学教授欧阳光明在该活动的新闻发布会上表示："该调查结果反映出人们对美好时代的定义：即经济文化繁荣昌盛，社会安定，官场公正廉洁，对外开放不闭塞。"

⑪ Ouyang Guangming, professor at Shanghai University, said at the press release: "The survey result reflects people's definition of the good days: prosperous economy and culture, steady society, fair and uncorrupted politics, and opening up to the outside world."

⑫ 人们普遍存在一种"穿越"情结。伍迪·艾伦的新作《午夜巴黎》已经被提名角逐2012年奥斯卡最佳影片，最佳导演，最佳原创剧本和最佳艺术指导等奖项。该片一大亮点就在于现代与文化怀旧的对抗。

⑫ The love for time traveling is universal. Woody Allen's latest movie Midnight in Paris, which has been nominated for Best Picture, Directing, Original Screenplay and Art Direction for the 2012 Academy Awards, features modernity versus cultural nostalgia.

⑬《纽约时报》评论道："过去的日子似乎比当下更生动，更充实……过去的美好时光一直诱惑着我们，因为时光不能倒流，无论我们多么希望也无法回到过去。"

⑬ "The past seems so much more vivid, more substantial, than the present... The good old days are so alluring because we were not around, however much we wish we were," The New York Times commented.

6.2 京剧将纳入义务教育课程

Peking Opera: A New Music Course for Schools

①《智斗》、《包龙图打坐在开封府》等经典京剧唱段将正式进入中小学课堂。据从北京市教委获悉，教育部今年将在全国10个省、市、自治区试点在音乐课程中增加京剧内容。北京作为参与试点的地区，从新学期起将在20所中小学试点开设京剧课。

① Classical Peking Opera arias such as Outwitting the Enemy and Bao Longtu Presides over a Court Trial will be officially made part of the music program of China's primary and middle schools. According to sources of Beijing Education Commission, the Ministry of Education has decided to make Peking Opera a music course in primary and middle schools as starting from this year in ten provinces, municipalities and autonomous regions. Beijing as one of these areas designated for the pilot program, will start from the forthcoming new semester offering Peking Opera courses in twenty primary and middle schools.

② 市教委体美处副处长王军介绍，为传承民族优秀文化，教育部对九年制义务教育阶段音乐课程标准进行了修订，增加了有关京剧的教学内容，并在10个省市区各选20所中小学进行试点。目前，15首京剧教学曲目已经确定，根据不同年级确定不同的教学唱段。教材编写和光盘研制工作也已启动。

② Wang Jun, Deputy Section Head in charge of fine arts and physical education under Beijing Education Commission, revealed that the Ministry of Education had revised the standards of the music course in the nine-year compulsory education system by adding in Peking Opera, with the view of inheriting and enhancing the quintessence of national culture. Twenty primary and middle schools each have been chosen as pioneers in ten provinces, municipalities and autonomous regions for trying out the pilot program. Up to now the fifteen arias for teaching purposes have been decided on and each will be taught to students by the grade. The compiling of the textbooks and making of DVD haven also got started. (卢敏用例)

6.3 Global Warming Could Make Humans Shorter

科学家称全球变暖将使人类变矮

① Global warming could make humans shorter, warn scientists who claim to have found evidence that it caused the world's first horses to shrunk nearly 50 million years ago.

① 科学家警告说,全球变暖可能会使人类变矮。科学家宣称已经找到证据:近5 000万年前全球变暖就曾让世界上最早的马个头变小。

② In fact, a team from the universities of Florida and Nebraska says it has found a link between the Earth heating up and the size of mammals — horses, in this case, the last time the world heated up.

② 事实上,来自佛罗里达州和内布拉斯加州的大学的一支研究团队称,他们已经找到地球变暖和哺乳动物个头之间的联系。这一案例中马变矮的现象是上一次全球变暖时发生的。

③ The scientists used fossils to follow the evolution of horses from their earliest appearance 56 million years ago.

③ 科学家用化石来追溯马从5 600万年前诞生至今的进化历程。

④ As temperatures went up their size went down, and vice versa; at one point they were as small as a house cat, said Dr Jonathan Bloch, curator of the Florida Museum of Natural History, was quoted by the *Daily Mail* as saying.

④ 随着气温的上升,马的个头变小,反之马的个头就变大。《每日邮报》援引佛罗里达自然历史博物馆馆长乔纳森·布洛赫博士的话说,它们曾一度像家猫那么小。

⑤ The scientists say that the current warming could have the same effect on mammals — and could even make humans smaller.

⑤ 科学家称,当前的全球变暖可能也会对哺乳动物产生同样的影响,甚至可能会让人类的个子也变小。

⑥ "Horses started out small, about the size of a small dog like a miniature schnauzer. What's surprising is that after they first appeared, they then became even smaller and then dramatically increased in size, and that exactly corresponds to the global warming event, followed by cooling.

⑥ "马最初的个头很小,和一只小狗的个头差不多,大约也就像一只迷你型雪纳瑞犬那么大。令人惊讶的是,在马诞生后过了一段时间,它们的个子变得更小,之后个头又显著变大,而这些变化与全球变暖和变冷正好是相对应的。"

⑦ "It had been known that mammals were small during that time and that it was warm, but we hadn't understood that temperature specifically was driving the evolution of body size," Dr Bloch said in the *Science* journal.

⑦ "我们已经知道哺乳动物在那个时期个头较小,而那个时期气候也较暖,但我们还未意识到正是温度驱动着身体大小的进化。"布洛赫博士在《科学》杂志中写道。

6.4 Android No Longer a Free Agent

安卓不再提供免费午餐

① So much for Google's new patent power.

① 谷歌新的专利力量不过如此。

② A key reason for the search giant's $12.5 billion deal for

② 搜索巨头谷歌斥资125亿美元

Motorola Mobility was to get hold of the latter's huge intellectual-property portfolio. The idea was to protect mobile-device makers using Google's Android mobile operating system from the likes of Microsoft, Apple, Oracle and others claiming that Android violates their intellectual property.

收购摩托罗拉移动通信的一个主要原因是希望获得后者数量众多的知识产权。谷歌的想法是想保护使用谷歌安卓操作系统的移动设备生产商不受微软、苹果、甲骨文等宣称安卓侵犯了其知识产权的公司的“骚扰”。

③ But it didn't stop Samsung from striking a deal Wednesday to pay royalties on its Android devices to Microsoft. That appears to resolve patent claims Microsoft has against Samsung's Android devices.

③ 但这却没能阻止三星周三与微软达成协议，为所生产的安卓移动设备向微软支付版权费。这看起来是为平息微软向三星生产的安卓移动设备提出的侵权指控。

④ That is bad news for Google's mobile strategy as it means Android is no longer free. Google gives away the operating system to device makers because it wants the widest possible distribution. With 48% market share, Android took the top spot among smart phone operating systems globally in the second quarter, estimates Strategy Analytics. The hope is that will drive more mobile searches and give Google an advantage in delivering future mobile services.

④ 这对谷歌的移动战略来说是个坏消息，因为这意味着安卓不再是免费的了。谷歌免费向设备生产商提供安卓操作系统，因为它希望安卓能够尽可能广泛地安装使用。据名为战略分析的市场研究机构估计，今年二季度，安卓以48%的市场份额成为全球智能手机操作系统的领头羊。谷歌希望这能推动更多的移动搜索，使谷歌今后推出移动服务时占有优势。

⑤ But now that the top two Android device makers, Samsung and HTC, are paying royalties to Microsoft, it becomes harder for others to get away without paying — and potentially easier for Apple and others to extract their own pound of flesh. In addition, it narrows the effective price gap with operating systems like Microsoft's Windows Phone.

⑤ 不过，鉴于两大安卓设备生产商三星和宏达都开始向微软支付版权费，其他公司将更难以享受免费系统，进而可能使苹果等公司面临的竞争压力减少。此外，这还缩小了安卓与微软视窗电话等操作系统之间的实际价格差距。

6.5 Working Against Holiday Blues

摆脱节后忧虑症

① Below are some suggested steps to get rid of your post winter festive season holiday blues.

① 下面这些步骤会帮助你摆脱你的节后忧虑症。

②1. Expect some letdown. The holiday season is both joyful and stressful at once. There is family to get along with, gifts to buy and return, people to visit, activities to throw yourself into, plenty of festive food to eat, sales to rush to, and parties to plan and attend. Topped off with the excitement of New Year's Eve, your adrenaline has probably been pumping a lot of the time during the New Year's period. Returning to the usual routine and probably quieter workplace than normal can dampen your spirits just by the absence of exciting things to do and look forward to.

② 1. 了解节后会有段时间心情低落。节假日期间总是愉快与压力并存。走亲访友、交换礼物、拜访熟人、参加活动、节日大餐、打折血拼、还有数不尽的派对……尤其是年三十儿的晚上。恐怕你的肾上腺素在整个春假期间都一直处于兴奋状态吧？所以一回到相对安静的日常工作状态，没了激动人心的事情去期待，你自然会觉

Expecting to feel a little low is a way of telling yourself that this is a normal feeling and that it will soon pass once the routine re-establishes itself.

得有点失落。了解节后自己的心情会受到影响,告诉自己这是一种正常的感受。这段时间很快就会随着日常生活的继续而过去的。

③ 2. Expect to enjoy the year ahead. Trying to keep a positive frame of mind and planning for interesting and fulfilling events throughout the year is a good way to calm your current blues. Think ahead to the changing seasons and the sorts of things you'd like to be doing as the year moves on, and the sorts of activities and events you'd like to be a part of. Doing something about the things you'd like to happen is the first step and once you're immersed in planning and doing, you'll be too busy to fret.

③ 2. 期待新的这一年。另一个驱赶忧虑心情的办法,就是保持一个积极的心态,好好计划新一年的各种活动。想想未来的变化和你想要在这一年做的事儿,或是想要参与的任何活动。为想做的事情计划并打算是第一步,而一旦当你开始忙碌地计划起来,你就不会有时间忧虑啦。

6.6 推荐读物

(1)曾庆丰,实用电讯新闻翻译教程,暨南大学出版社 1999 年版。
(2)贾卉,意识形态与美国《新闻周刊》涉华词语的翻译,上海翻译 2008 年第 2 期。
(3)刘其中,新闻翻译教程,中国人民大学出版社 2004 年版。
(4)王恩冕,如何翻译英语报刊经济文章,对外经济贸易大学出版社 2005 年版。
(5)常玉田,经贸汉译英教程,对外经济贸易大学出版社 2002 年版。
(6)冯庆华,实用翻译教程,上海外语教育出版社 2002 年版。
(7)许明武,新闻英语与翻译,中国对外翻译出版公司 2003 年版。
(8)周学艺,英美报刊导读,北京大学出版社 2003 年版。
(9)陈明瑶、卢彩虹,新闻英语语体与翻译研究,国防工业出版社 2006 年版。
(10)张健,新闻英语文体与范文评析,上海外语教育出版社 2004 年版。

7 课后练习

7.1 分析题

(1)试用所译和比读材料分析全译单位。
(2)新闻语篇中意识形态是如何起到操控作用的?
(3)试用你最欣赏的译文,分析新闻语篇全译的策略。

7.2 实训题

7.2.1 中国文化的商务内涵

西方商人受"中国热"的驱使,认为中国需要国外技术,因而便匆忙带着各种各样的工艺方案冲进了中国市场。有人成功有人失败。失败的一个重要原因是他们没有足够重视人民中国的国情:中国政府是最大的"老板",国有企业依据政府工作的优先权、政策和计划从事经营。

7.2.2 Radioactive Traces Found in Japan Baby Formula

① In the latest radiation food scare to hit Japan, the country's largest maker of baby formula said it found radioactive cesium in cans on store shelves.

② Although the measured amount falls well below the level the government has declared hazardous, the discovery lengthens the list of foods affected by the nuclear accident, and is the first in a product targeted at the age group considered most vulnerable to the effects of radioactivity.

③ But experts and a growing network of concerned parents have increasingly questioned whether the government's existing standards are safe enough for babies, considered to be much more sensitive to radiation exposure. The latest revelation is likely to stoke fears among consumers already on edge about the safety of the nation's food supply since the March 11 Fukushima Daiichi nuclear accident, following reports over the summer of beef contamination and, more recently, some instances of tainted rice.

7.3 思考题

(1)新闻翻译应把握哪些原则?

(2)新闻领域的全译与变译的区别?

(3)新闻标题的翻译方法有哪些?

(4)导语翻译的策略有哪些?

(5)新闻导语翻译应注意哪些语境问题?

(6)中英文的新闻评论有何语篇差异?互译如何处理?

(7)新闻评论翻译应注意哪些问题?

(8)汉英新闻翻译时应采取何种外宣策略?

(9)新闻翻译涉及哪些伦理范畴?

(10)媒体新词对中国语言有哪些影响?

(11)大陆和港澳台地区新闻翻译的理念和策略有何差异?

(12)从提高国家软实力角度如何看待汉英新闻翻译中的异化策略?

(13)从历时和共时角度分析西方新闻媒体对中国国家形象的建构。

第 9 课 国际贸易

导 译

随着世界经济一体化进程的加快,国际间有型与无型产品的流通也日趋频繁。这种世界各个国家或地区间的产品流通被称为国际贸易。它是各国在国际分工的基础上相互联系的主要形式,反应了世界各国在经济上的相互依赖关系。国际贸易的一般流程为:客户询盘、报价磋商、签立订单、支付、包装、装船、报关、准备单据、交单收汇等。

国际贸易词汇包含大量的专业术语,因此,对国际贸易英汉互译时,要熟练地掌握国际贸易方面的知识,同时根据其用词特点,更要注意翻译的严谨与正规。这主要体现在以下几个方面:商务合同英语用词缜密,如若条款表述不清,则容易导致纠纷。因此,多使用限定词来明确双方的利益,从而保障双方各自的权力、约束其履行各自的义务;信用证文体具有强有力的法律约束力,因此,文本中多见书面语和古体词,某些语气词也频繁出现;商务书信遣词造句独成一体,沟通过程中形成了一些内容清晰、表达准确的套用语,套语的使用可以减少沟通中的障碍;商务谈判中,为改善谈判气氛和双方的信任度,多使用礼貌语言而增加谈判成功的机会。因此,翻译时可巧用套语,留意礼貌语气,看清数字,区分精确与模糊。

1 课前练笔

1.1 建立贸易关系

① 敬启者:

② 我们很高兴从贵方当地商会获悉贵公司有意购买中国丝绸女衬衫。

③ 现奉告，我公司是中国丝绸服装的主要出口商之一，专营此类商品已有20多年。中国丝绸服装以其质地精良、设计独特和工艺精湛而闻名，在美洲和东欧销路很好。

④ 为使贵方大致了解我产品，现附上我公司所经营的各种产品的目录，上面标明详细规格和包装方法。请告知我们贵方感兴趣的商品。一旦受到具体询盘，即刻报价。

⑤ 希望我们能在平等互利的基础上建立贸易关系。我们可以预见我方产品在贵方市场上的良好前景。

⑥ 盼速复。

1.2 产品定价

① 定价策略多种多样，以下是确立价格时应该考虑的因素：

② 1. 应充分了解国际市场行情，确定有关同类产品竞争价格的所有市场数据并加以分析。同时考虑某一特定市场的政策及规定。

③ 2. 在国际市场价格水平基础上，可根据出口商品的具体目的或进口商的要求调整价格。

④ 3. 由于国际市场可能因供求格局的改变而上下波动，必须注意市场供求关系的变化和市场价格涨落的趋势。

⑤ 4. 出口价格应采用适当的价格增长幅度。高价格增长额并不意味着高利润。

⑥ 5. 合同商品的质量、数量、运费、交货地点及条件也将影响出口价格的制定。

1.3 Import and Export

Every country has to import the articles and commodities it does not itself produce, and it has to earn foreign exchange to pay for them. It does this by exporting its own manufactured articles and surplus raw materials. Thus the import and export trades are two sides of the same coin, and both can have beneficial effects on the home market. Imports create competition for home-produced goods; exporting gives a manufacturer a larger market for his products, so helping to reduce the unit cost. In each case the effect is to keep prices in the home market down.

1.4 Multinationals Add Millions of Workers Abroad, Cut at Home

① U. S.-based multinational corporations added 1.5 million workers to their payrolls in Asia and the Pacific region during the 2000s, and 477,500 workers in Latin America, while cutting payrolls at home by 864,000, the Commerce Department reported.

② The faster growth abroad was concentrated in emerging markets, such as China, Brazil, India and Eastern Europe, according to economists Kevin Barefoot and Raymond Mataloni, of the U. S. Commerce Department.

③ "Judging by the destination of sales by affiliates in those countries," the economists wrote in a recent survey, "the goal of the U. S. multinational corporations expanded production was to primarily sell to local customers rather than to reduce their labor costs for goods and services destined for sale in the U. S., Western Europe and other high-income countries."

1.5 International Technological Transfer

① The major flow of technology has been among firms in the industrialized countries. The growth has several reasons. The developing countries have become increasingly aware of the role of technology in fostering economic development and the ability to compete in international production.

② The transnational enterprises (TNEs) play a central role in the transfer of technology and the rate of technological diffusion. The greater part of the technology transferred among firms in the industrial market economies involves advanced systems of TNEs. The dominant channel of transfer include licenses, patents, and sale of technological know-how, and direct investment. Firms in the industrialized countries increasingly use a combination of these channels to gain new technological expertise.

③ Meanwhile, the politics of economic cooperation between the Western market economies and the Eastern, centralized economies that has prevailed for the past two decades has provided opportunities for trade between these two groups, and along with the trade has come the transfer of technology. In addition, the rapid expansion of trade between the industrialized economies and the developing countries, and the increased flow of foreign direct investment to the developing countries, have also provided channels for the transfer of technology needed by these countries for industrialization and development.

批评 2 课前批评

2.1 北京朝阳国际商务节

① 北京朝阳国际商务节是北京市重要的经贸活动之一，是以推进国际经济发展与企业文化交流为宗旨的传统区域性国际商务盛会。

② 几年来，北京朝阳国际商务节实现了让世界了解中国、让世界关注北京的目标，成为各界全面了解北京市及朝阳区投资环境、考察合作项目以及广泛接触合作伙伴的大型商务活动，并以主题鲜明、活动

Introduction to Beijing Chaoyang International Business Festival

① As one of the important economic and trading activities in Beijing, the Beijing Chaoyang International Business Festival is an international event in the district with the theme to promote the international economic development and enterprise cultural exchange.

② Beijing Chaoyang International Business Festival has become a window to China and to Beijing in particular in recent years. Through the events, people of all trades and professions come to know the investment environment of Beijing and Chaoyang District, find projects of cooperation, and establish

丰富、成效显著、国际性强等特点形成了自己独特的品牌。

contacts with their partners. The event is characterized by its clear themes, colorful activities, good results, and active international involvement.

③本着"国际化、专业化、市场化"的原则,第四届北京朝阳国际商务节将向世界充分展现一个充满蓬勃商务活力、无限投资潜力和具有高度国际竞争力的商务中心区新形象。

③ Following the internationalized, professional, and market-oriented principle, the 4th BCIBF will show the whole world a new image of the Beijing CBD, which is internationally competitive, attractive to investors, and bustling with commercial activities.

2.2 A Query about Merging of Enterprises

对企业兼并的质疑

There's no question that the big are getting bigger and more powerful. Multinational corporations accounted for less than 20% of international trade in 1982. Today the figure is more than 25% and growing rapidly. International affiliates account for a fast-growing segment of production in economies that open up and welcome foreign investment. In Argentina, for instance, after the reforms of the early 1990s, multinationals went from 43% to almost 70% of the industrial production of the 200 largest firms. This phenomenon has created serious concerns over the role of smaller economic firms, of national businessmen and over the ultimate stability of the world economy.

无疑,大企业正在变得更大、更强。1982 年,跨国公司在国际贸易中只占不到 20% 的份额。而如今,这个数字超过了 25%,并且还在迅速上升。在那些对外开放并鼓励外资的国家中,国际分公司在国民生产中成为一个快速增长的部门。例如,在阿根廷,经过 20 世纪 90 年代初的改革之后,跨国公司在 200 家大型企业的工业生产中从 43% 增加到几乎 70%。这个现象引起了人们对小型企业、民族商人以及世界经济的最终稳定性的严重忧虑。

3 全译知识 对译

对译即典型的直译,概括地讲,是逐字/词翻译,是原语单位与译语单位依次对出、词义逐一对应、交际价值对等的全译方法。

对译要求翻译单位逐项对应,对译多在小句之内,也见于其外。词典中词目与短语的翻译多属对译。总体上看,对译在全译中当用则用,对译不成,则采用全译其他六法。对译虽说存在,但要慎用,更应与其他六法巧妙配用。对译的概率排序大致是:词对译 > 短语对译 > 小句对译 > 复句对译 > 句群对译。

3.1 词对译

词对译,指译语词与原语词的对应替换。词对译是对译的主体,也是最常用最重要

的译法,有时几乎是移字过纸,词典中的词目释义很多就是词对译,翻译中以实词对译为主。如:

① 形合 hypotaxis 意合 parataxis 手指 finger

② morning paper 晨报 begin to ask a question 开始提问

例①均为词对译,例②中的每个实词均为对译,所构成的短语也是对译。

3.2 短语对译

短语对译,指译语短语与原语短语的对应替换。短语对译基于词对译,词与词容易对应,但词与词的组配会受到许多规则管约,加之不同语言的短语组配各有各的特定要求,所以短语对译比词对译要少一些。短语对译既含词词对译,如例②是基于词对译且词序不变的短语对译;也含短语整体对译。如:

③ 沏茶 make tea;杂粮 mixed cropping

④ prostrate at the feet of sb. 拜倒在某人的脚下

例③是词与短语均对应的翻译;例④整体对应,局部也大体对译,只是 sb. 向前转译了。

3.3 小句对译

小句对译,指译语小句与原语小句的对应替换。小句对译基于短语对译,更基于词对译,短语本身加上语气有时可以成句,但并非所有的短语加语气都能成句,所以小句对译比短语对译又少许多。包括小句整体的对译,也包括由词词对译构成的小句对译。如:

⑤ We call this God's Amazing Pharmacy... 我们称之为上帝的神药……

⑥ He knew your father's traditional obligations to the traveler, and in them he trusted.

【原译】:你们的祖先一向善待游客,他明了这点,而且深信不疑。

【试译】:他知道令尊一向善待游客,对此深信不疑。

两例算是绝对。前一例,We call this God's Amazing Pharmacy 与"我们称之为上帝的神药"词词对译,进而是短语与短语对译,最终构成了英语小句与汉语小句的对译。后一例,试译的两个小句均是一一对译,原译将 He knew 转译,虽然意义明了,但不简洁。

3.4 复句对译

复句对译,指译语复句与原语复句的对应替换。复句对译基于小句、语和词的对译,难度更大,使用频率更少。如:

⑦ They called Jos "old Buck", and invaded his dinner-table, and laughed and drank for long hours there.

【原译】:他们管乔斯叫"老家伙",占住了他的饭桌子嘻嘻哈哈地喝酒,一坐就是好半天。

【试译】:他们叫乔斯"老家伙",占了他的餐桌,有笑有吃的,一待就是好半天。

⑧ When he returned he lit his pipe, smoked thoughtfully and finally spoke. 他回来后点起烟斗,抽着烟,深思着,末了说道……

例⑦试译除了原文最后的短语 for long hours there 外，前面短语中的实词个个对译为汉语，各词所构成的短语也个个对应，滴水不漏。例⑧基本上也是复句对译，除实词承前省略外，只减译了几个虚词，并不损意。

3.5 句群对译

句群对译，指译语句群与原语句群的对应替换。句群对译基于复句、小句、短语和词的对译，难度最大，使用频率最少。如：

⑧ A sliced carrot looks like the human eye. The pupil, iris and radiating lines look just like the human eye. 切片的胡萝卜看似人的眼睛。瞳孔、虹膜和放射线酷似人的眼睛。

原文两个小句构成了句群，其实词个个对译为汉语，而虚词有时可以忽略不计，各词所构成的短语也个个对应，几乎天衣无缝。

4 全译窍门

4.1 译出语气词的生命

语气词 will，would，shall，should，must 等在商务文体中出现频率很高。其中，will 是一般将来时，语气比 shall 要弱，可用来译"将"、"要"、"会"等。如：

① 真正的包装艺术是把货物摆放成良好的、紧凑的形状，并在颠簸的旅途中会保持原状。The real art of packing is to get the contents into a nice, compact shape that **will** stay in perfect condition during the roughest journey.

would 在 would like to 和 would you please 结构中可以缓和指示和命令的语气，以示礼貌，分别用来译"想要""请"等。如：

② 我想邀请贵方参加本周举行的出口商品交易会。I **would like to** invite you to attend Export Commodities Fair this week.

③ 请贵公司在接收到新产品时告知我方。**Would you please** inform us when you receive the new products?

信用证的法律约束性强，开证行处于绝对的优势，其强制性语气常用特定词语表达：must、should、shall，三个词语气由强而弱。谈及开证行自己的责任时语气明显弱化，常用 shall；对受益人提出要求时，常用 should，偶用 must。如：

④ 货运单据上都应有信用证号。L/C No. **should** appear on all shipping documents.

⑤ 我行将贷记你方在上海总行的账户。We **shall** credit your Shanghai head office account.

4.2 巧用套语

商务信函遣词造句、语篇格式等方面自有特色：讲究体谅原则，内容清晰、完整、具体，表达简洁，用词正确，措辞礼貌；往往形成一些套话，互译时要学会使用。如：

信头套语　(My) Dear Mr./Mrs./Miss/Sir(s)（我）尊敬的……先生/……女

士/……小姐/先生(dear 切忌译作“亲爱的”);We have received/**are pleased to** receive/**have pleasure of** receiving your letter of...……来函收悉/……来函已收讫;We thank you for your letter of . . . and have much pleasure in replying to your various questions as follows 感谢贵方……月……日的来信,很愉快地答复各种问题如下;In response/ reply to your letter of ...谨复……来函。

信中套语 We should be pleased to let you have samples. 欣然奉上我方产品样品。We have pleasures in sending you our list which presents full information about our various products. 欣然奉上我方提供的各类产品详细情况清单。We are pleased to inform you that .../ We have pleasure in informing you that.../ Please allow us to call your attention to.../ We think it advisable to inform you that... 特此奉告……In reply to your letter of .../ I have to inform you that (of) .../ Answering your letter of ...I would say that...特回复贵公司某月某日函……We regret to inform you that (of) .../ It is with great regret that we.../ We are sorry to inform you.../ I express my sorrow for announcing you that...非常遗憾,我们奉告您关于……;We are very (indeed, much) sorry to hear that.../To our deep regret, we were informed that...得悉……我们甚为遗憾;We thank you much for your inquiry of.../ We are much obliged by your inquiry dated.../ Thanks for your inquiry of...我方对于贵方来函询……价,深表谢意;As stated below .../As indicated overleaf ... 如下所记……Attached you will find.../ Sent with this.../As shown in the enclosed documents...如附件所述……

信尾套语 Best wishes 祝好(此致敬礼);My best regards 谨致问候;Yours sincerely/ truly/ faithfully 敬上(谨上);We look forward to receiving your early reply./ We should appreciate an early reply./Your prompt reply would be greatly appreciated. 我们盼望尽快收到回复。敬候佳音 We are awaiting/ waiting for/ looking forward to your favorable reply. 关于……一事,盼惠复一音。We hope to hear/ Will you please let us hear from you about/concerning…

4.3 商务谈判礼貌译

为追求效果最大化,谈判翻译讲究礼貌有时能事半功倍。

多用请求 祈使句语气比较生硬,而请求句式更为婉转,以“请”字引出的句式多由may、can、Would you please…和 Could you …引导。如:

⑥ 请您尽快将贵公司最新产品目录和价目表发送至我方。**Would you please** send us your latest catalogue and price-list as soon as possible?

运用虚拟 虚拟句式本身就表达含蓄婉转,不会难为对方。如:

⑦ 买方要求卖方两个月内发货。The buyer **demands** that the seller **should** ship the goods with two months.

⑧ 如贵方将交货日期提前至1月中旬,我方将不胜感激。We **should be** grateful if you advance delivery to the middle of January.

语气缓和 商务谈判各有立场,若直接否定对方,谈判可能陷持。要弱化语气,则用缓和性词语:It seems that...,I'm afraid that...,I wish(hope)...,I think it advisable to...等。

如：

⑨ 我方恐怕不能接受贵方报盘。I'm afraid that I can't accept your offer.

⑩ 我理解你，但我们不能保证立即装货。I understand you but we can't guarantee a prompt shipment.

4.4 合同"有限"翻译

商务合同具有法律效力，其中责任、时间、数量等常用有限定作用的结构明确具体的范围，译时要倍加小心。如：

⑪ 甲方和乙方签订了本合约。This contract is made by and between Party A and Party B.

⑫ 自3月10日起，卖方已无权接受任何订单。The seller shall be unauthorized to accept any order **on and after** March 10.

例⑫中双介词 on and after 指包括当天在内的以后日期，也可用 inclusive，including 和 included，上句的时间可改为 on March 10 (inclusive)或 on and including March 10。为避免不必要的麻烦，如涂改等，英译金额要在所译数字之后以大写形式重写数字，用括号括起。在大写前加 SAY，意为"大写"，在数字后加 ONLY，意为"整"。如：

⑬ 如卖方违约，买方有权按合同规定接受8 500元的赔偿。If the seller breaks the contract. the buyer is entitled to accept The indemnity of CNY 8,500 (**SAY** EIGHT THOUSAND AND FIVE HUNDRED CHINESE YUAN **ONLY**).

4.5 信用证英译动转静

信用证中有关装运时间、装运港、目的港、单位人数等英译时，常省略系动词和助动词，不会引起歧义。如例⑭、⑮和⑯省略系动词 be，例⑰和⑱省略助动词 should be。

⑭ T. T. reimbursement (is) not acceptable. 我们不接受电汇偿付。

⑮ Latest date of shipment: March 14th, 2011. 最迟装运期是2011年3月14日。

⑯ Packing list in three fold. 装箱单一式三份。

⑰ All shipping documents (should be) to be sent direct to the opening office by registered airmail. 所有装运单据应以航空挂号信的形式直接寄至开证行。

⑱ Each document to be dated (should) not (be) later than B/L date. 所有单据的出单日期应不晚于提单日期。

5 话题词汇

5.1 交易磋商与订约

初级的 primary
董事会 board of directors
分销商 distributor
工业品 industrial goods
国外订货单 indent
加工 process

交易 transaction
经营 operation
企业 enterprise
企业家 entrepreneur
期满 expiration
认购 subscribe
实体 entity
实现 realize
双边的 bilateral
通知 inform
违反 breach
协作 collaboration
样品 sample
中间人 middleman
制成品 finished goods
执行 perform
租赁 lease
acceptance 承兑
accordingly 按照(合约)办事
approve 审批
anticipate 预期
bid 递盘
binding 有约束力的
break 终止
cable reply 电复
capacity 能力
claused 有附加条款的
countersign 会签
come into effect 生效
confirmation 确认
contract 合同
counter offer 还盘
default 违约
duplicate 副本
enclosure 随信附件
entitle 有权
favourable 优惠的
firm offer 实盘
franchise 特约经销
further 促进
immediately 立即地
inquiry 询盘
interpretation 解释
investigation 调查
lapse 失效
liability 责任
licensor 许可方
market 行情
multilateral 多边的
negotiation 磋商
offer 发盘
offeree 受盘人
offerer 发盘人
open 有效地
originals 原本
partner 合伙人
postpone 推迟
practice 惯例
project 项目
promotion 推销
prompt 即刻的
prospect 机会
provisions 规定
push 推销
purchase 购买
reach 达成
renew 续签
reply 回复
representative 代表
revise 修改
revoke 撤回
said 上述的
satisfy 履行(契约)
say 比如说
side (一方)当事人
signature 签名
source 厂商
stipulate 订立
standard 标准
subject 受限的
substitute 代替物
terminate 撤销
terms and conditions 条款
valid 有效的

5.2 支付

储户 depositor
费用 charges
分期付款 installment
估价 evaluation
坏账 bad debt
汇兑 transfer
回扣 rebate
金额 amount
会计 accountant
零售 retail
(物价)猛增 soar
批发 wholesale
日常开支 overhead
讨价还价 bargain
提取 withdraw
退款 refund
现时的 current
销售额 sales
押金 margin
余额 balance
预算 budget
运费 freight
优惠的 preferential
赞助人 sponsor
指数 index
中国元 Chinese Yuan
资产 asset
advance 预付款
available 可支付的
back 偿付
benefit 补助金
beneficiary 受益人
blank 空白的
cash in advance 预付现金
cash with order 订货付款
check 支票
collection 托收
confirming bank 保兑银行
commission 佣金
correspondent bank 代理行
currency 货币
deferred payment 延期支付
dishonor 拒付
discount 贴现
draft 汇票
draw 出票
dues 应付款费用
duty 关税
endorse 背书
extra 额外费用
face value 票面价值
figure 估计
finance 供资金给
floor 低价
hard (市价)坚挺
honored 兑付
insolvency 无偿还能力
jack 提高(价格)
lend 贷款
liquid 短期的
loss 亏损
maturity 到期
means 收入
on demand 见票即付
opinion 评价
option 购买权
par 票面价值
post 缴存
premium 津贴
presentation 提示
principal 委托人
proceeds 收入
quotation 报价
recession 衰退
recourse 追索
remittance 汇付
remitter 汇款人
sacrifice 亏本出售
security 保证金
short 空头地
slump (物价)暴跌
soft 疲软的

spot 现付的
sound 资金充实的
surcharge 附加费
surplus 盈金;顺差
tender 投标
tenor 期限
tie-up 冻结
toll 服务费;运费
traffic 交易量
translation 换算
turnover 营业额
variable 可变的
wharfage 码头费

5.3 包装标记

编号 reference
标牌 label
玻璃制品 glassware
防水的 waterproof
规格 specification
集装箱 container
净重 net weight
唛头 mark
毛重 gross weight
泡沫 foam
皮重 tare
恰当的 appropriate
设计 design
体积 volume
完整的 intact
箱 case
易燃的 inflammable
易碎的 fragile
硬纸板 cardboard
邮包 parcel
整批的 bulk
直立的 upright
中性 neutral
adhesive tape 胶带
appearance 外观
apparently 表面地
bales off 散包
barrel 桶
blister packing 起泡包装
block 块
bundle 捆
business 商号
canvas 帆布
capacity 容积
carton 纸箱
cask 木桶
code 代码
consignor 发货人
crate 板条箱
crush 压挤
customary 习惯性的
dump 投掷
explosive 爆炸性物品
film 薄膜
flat 平的
goodwill 商誉
hazardous 危险的
immediate packing 直接包装
improper 不当的
indicative 指示性的
make 型号
machinery 机构
merchandise 商品
moisture 潮湿
nude 裸的
plastic 塑料的
regular 正规的
reminder 催单
sack 麻袋
saw dust 木屑
seaworthy 适于航运的
skin packing 吸塑包装
stuffing 填充的
tag 标签
tight 密封的
wax paper 蜡纸
waybill 运单
wooden 木质的

wrapper 包装纸

5.4 货运单证

保单 guarantee
报表 account
报关手续 entry
报文 message
备用的 stand-by
表格 sheet
撤销 reversal
单据 document
订单 order
发票 invoice
见票 sight
开立(信用证等)establish
目录 catalogue
请求 request
申请 application
收据 receipt
提单 bill of lading
通知单 note
通知书 advice
许可 permit
许可证 license
原产地证书 certificate of origin
acknowledge 确认
amendment 更改
anticipatory 预期的
authorization 授权
bank statement 银行水单
clean bill 光票
damage 损害
declaration 申报
distribution 分发
divisible 可分割的
evidence 凭证
export drawback 出口退税单
extended 扩展的
information 信息
inspection certificate 检验单
list 单
manifest 清单
master 主要的
meet 执行(订单)
minimum 最小的
origin 原产地
paper 流通票据
performance 性能
plan 图
promissory 约定支付的
quality certificate 品质检验证书
recognition 确认
related 有关的
registry 登记
response 回复
revocable 可撤销的
revolving 可循环的
seeing 鉴于
send 发运(货物)
statement 清单
statistical 统计的
supply 货源
transferable 可转让的
triplicate 一式三份
title 契据
unconfirmed 不保兑的
universal 通用的
usance 远期
valuation 估价单
weight memo 重量单

5.5 装船交货

承运人 carrier
储备 store
船;飞机 vessel
船次 sailing
存货 inventory
代理 agent

到货 arrival
发运 dispatch
挂靠港 port of call
海关 customs
航线 route
交货 delivery
码头 yard
目的地 destination
说明 instruction
托运 shipping
物品 article
有效期 life
运送 forward
中转站 terminal
装货 load
准时的 punctual
actual 实际的
alongside 船边
approaching 接近的
assemble 装配
assistance 协助
assure 使……确信
backlog 积压而未交付的订货
call at 停泊
charter 租船
combined 联合的
commencement 开始
conference 会议
confront 面临
congestion 拥挤
constructive 推定的
convey 传达
deck 甲板
definite 确切的
departure 发货
designate 设定
duly 定期的
effect 实现
entertain 接受(订货等)
free on truck 卡车上交货
frontier 边境
full 装满的
handle 搬运
hasten 加快
lay day (货物)装卸日期
lighter 驳船
line (航运,航空)公司
liner 轮班
mention 提及
named 指定的
observe 遵守
on board 在船(或车、飞机)上
optional port 选择港
partial 分批的
particular 细节
preparation 准备
prohibit 禁止
rush 紧急的
scheduled 预订的
shipping space 舱位
shipment 装运;装船
sort 分类
speed 加速
station 站点
tanker 游轮
terms 条件
timely 及时地
touch 短暂停靠
tramp 不定期船
transit 运输
tranship 转运
unload 卸货
urgent 迫切的
voyage 定程
warehouse 仓库

5.6 商检、索赔与仲裁

剥夺 deprive
补偿 compensation
裁定 award
承担 bear
处罚 penalty
磋商 consultation

道歉 apologize
过期的 overdue
监督 supervision
检验 inspection
劣等的 inferior
赔偿 remedy
强加 impose
上诉 appeal
审核 review
疏忽 negligence
索赔 claim
维持 maintain
效力 effectiveness
义务 obligation
遭受 sustain
争议 dispute
证实 verify
制裁 sanction
administration 管理
amicable 友善的
arbitration 仲裁
appreciate 感激
arise 发生
arrange 安排
as per 按照
assert 断言
circumstance 情况
complain 抱怨
comply 遵照
concerned 与……有关
conciliation 调解
consequence 后果
contact 联系
deadline 最后期限
decline 谢绝
deduct 从……中扣除
disqualification 不合格
embargo 禁运
estimate 估计
exempt 豁免
exercise one's right 行使某人的权力
fundamental 基本的
force majeure 不可抗力
hang 悬而未决
hear 审讯
innocent 清白的
inconvenience 不便
incur 招致
institution 机构
intentional 故意的
leave 委托
lodge 提出
missing 遗失的
prejudice 侵害
red 负债
recovery 复原
reinspection 复检
release 发出
render 给予
replace 取代
resort 诉诸
retain 保留
rule 作出裁决
settle 解决
severely 严重地
shortage 短缺
spoil 变坏
square（账目）情节的
submit 提交
sue 控告
survey report 检验报告
tribunal 法庭
unexpected 意想不到的
work out 有预期结果

5.7 缩略语

本地收货费用 ORC
报关单 C/D
出口申报书 E/D
立即生效 s. i. r
码头操作费 THC
特快专递 EMS
中国商品检验局 CCIB
中国国际贸易促进会 CCPIT

中国外贸运输公司 CNFTTC
最惠国待遇 MFN
A. V. 从价
B/E 汇票
CFR 成本加运费
CIF 到岸价
C. I. O. 订货时付款
C. O. D. 交货付款
CPT 运费付至目的地
C. T. D. 联合运输单据
CTG 国币贸易理事会
C. W. O. 随订单付现
CY 集装箱
D/C 跟单信用证
D/D 即期汇票
DDP 完税后交货
DDU 未完税交货
DEQ 目的港码头交货
DES 目的港船上交货
D. P. V. 完税价格
EEC 欧洲经济共同体
EFTA 欧洲自由贸易联盟
EXW 工厂交货价
EXQ 码头交货价
FCA 货交承运人
F. C. L. 整箱货
F. I. O. S. 传方不负担装卸及积载费用
F. O. B. 离岸价
F. O. Q. 码头交货价
F. O. I 免息
GATT 关贸总协定
ICC 国际商会
I/L 进口许可证
IMF 国际货币基金组织
L/G 担保书
LCL 拼箱货
M. I. O. 多式联运
P. O. D. 付款交货
S/N 装运通知单
T/T 电汇
UNCTAD 联合国贸易与发展会议
W/T 重量

6 比读体悟

6.1 开立信用证

① 兹开立第456号不可撤销的信用证,受益人纽约ABC公司,开证人中国进出口公司上海分公司,最高金额56 000美元,溢交或短交货物金额以5%为限。

② 本信用证凭受益人开具以我行为付款人按发票金额100%计算无追索权的即期汇票用款,该汇票一式两份,并须附有下列装运单据:

③ 全套清洁无疵,“货已装船”,“运费预付”,空白抬头,空白背书的海运提单,并须注明“通知目的港中国对外贸易运输公司”。

④ 发票一式五份,注明合同号码。

Open an L/C

① We open an irrevocable Letter of Credit No. 456 in favor of ABC Company, New York for account of: China National Import & Export Corporation, Shanghai to the extent of: $56,000 (U. S. Dollars Fifty-Six Thousand only), and 5% more or less is allowed.

② This credit is available by beneficiary's draft (s), drawn on us, in duplicate, without recourse, on sight, for 100% of the invoice value, and accompanied by the following shipping documents:

③ A full set of clean "on board", "freight prepaid" Ocean Bills of Lading, made out to order and unendorsed, marked: "Notify China National Foreign Trade Transportation Corporation, at the port of destination."

④ Invoice in quintuplicate copies, indicating the Contract numbers.

⑤ 重量单/装箱单一式两份，载明每箱毛重和净重。

⑤ Weight Memo/Packing List in duplicate, indicating gross and net weights of each package.

⑥ 制造商出品的品质，数量/重量证明书一式三份。

⑥ Certificates of Quality, Quantity/Weight in 3 Copies issued by the manufacturers.

⑦ 请将本证通知受益人为荷，

⑦ Please advise the beneficiary of the terms of credit.

⑧ 感谢贵方的协助。

⑧ We thank you for your assistance in the matter.（陈准民、陈建平 译）

6.2 发盘

Offer

① 除非首先发盘，否则就不可能有接受，也就达不成协议。《联合国国际货物销售合同公约》明确规定，“向一个或一个以上特定的人提出订立合同的建议，如果十分确定并且表明发盘人在得到接受时承受约束的旨意，即构成发盘”。发盘是卖方向买方提出，以期签订合同。换句话说，它是指卖方向买方提出的交易条款（包括数量、价格、装运时间、付款方式等），即询问买方是否愿意按照此条款与买方达成交易。简单来说，发盘是询问是否订立合同的表示。因此，发盘必须包含合同的基本条款，否则就达不成具体、明确的要求。但在实践中，发盘可能不会明确规定，一旦被接受发盘人即受其约束。

① There can be no acceptance, and therefore no agreement, unless there was an offer in the first place. According to United Nations Convention on Contracts for Sales of Goods, a proposal for concluding a contract addressed to one or more specific persons constitutes an offer if its is sufficiently specific and indicates the intention of the offeror to be bound in case of acceptance. An offer is a proposal made by sellers to buyers in order to enter into a contract. In other words, it refers to trading terms (including quantity, price, time of shipment, terms of payment, etc.) put forward by offerors to offerees, on which the offerors are willing to conclude business with the offerees. In brief, an offer is an expression to enter into a contract. Therefore an offer must contain the essential terms of the contract. Otherwise the requirement to the concrete and definite may not be satisfied. In practice, however, an offer may not expressly stipulate that once it is accepted the offeror will be bound.

② 一旦接受发盘，就必须表明订立合同的意旨。首先它必须能够被接受（不包含任何不可能的条件），其次发盘的内容必须十分完整（不需要额外的信息进行解释）。发盘不是广告。发盘也不同于发盘邀请。发盘邀请可能包括报价、拍卖公告、招股说明书、商业广告、邀请招标广告。

② An offer to contract must be made with the intention to create, if accepted, a legal relationship. It must be capable of being accepted (not containing any impossible conditions), must also be complete (not requiring more information to define the offer), and not merely announcement, prospectus, commercial advertisements and tender notices.（耿静先 译）

6.3 Packing of Commodity

产品包装

① Packing, in business practice, is one of the most important problems which confront the merchants engaged in foreign trade. It needs more care in export trade than domestic trade. The real art of packing is to get the contents into a nice, compact shape that will stay in perfect condition with nothing missing during the roughest journey. Every buyer expects that his

① 按照商业惯例，包装是从事国际贸易的商人所要面临最重要的问题之一。出口贸易中的包装必须必国内贸易中的包装更为仔细。真正的包装艺术是把货物摆放成良好的、紧凑的形状，并能在颠簸的旅途中保持原状，

goods will reach him in perfect condition. Nothing is more infuriating to a buyer than to find his goods damaged or part missing on arrival. It has been estimated that as much as 70% of all cargo loss could be prevented by proper packaging and marking. Hence, in this respect, suitable packing is of great necessity and importance.

不丢失。买方都希望货物完整无缺地到达他的手中,如果货物到达时,买方发现货物受损或部分丢失,这是最让他恼火的。据估计,大约70%的货物损失可以通过恰当的包装和标记得以预防。所以,适当的包装是非常必要和重要的。

② Packing can be divided into transport packing (also called outer packing) and sales packing (also called inner packing). A third kind of packing, neutral packing is also often used in international trade.

② 根据包装材料和包装方法,包装可分为运输包装(又称外包装)和销售包装(内包装)。另一种包装,中性包装,也经常在国际贸易中使用。

③ Transport packing is mainly to keep the goods safe and sound during transportation. It must not only be solid enough to prevent the packed goods from any damages, but also be pilferage-proof, easy to store, convenient to load and unload.

③ 运输包装的主要目的是保护货物在运输过程中的安全。它必须非常坚硬使货物免受损坏,还必须能防盗,易于储存和装卸。

④ Sales packing is not only adopted as a form of protection to reduce the risk of goods being damaged in transit and prevent pilferage, but mainly with the purpose of promoting sales. It is now universally recognized as a decisive aid in selling household consuming goods.

④ 销售包装又称内包装、小包装或直接包装。它除了保护商品免受损坏和防盗以外,主要起促销的作用。现在,作为一种非常重要的辅助手段,它广泛应用于家庭消费品的销售。

⑤ Neutral packing is a kind of packing without carrying the name and address of the manufacturer, the origin of the country, the trade mark and brand on both outer and inner packages. The purpose of using neutral packing by exporters is to break down the tariff and non-tariff barriers of some countries or regions, or meet the special demand of the transaction (such as entrepot). It may also help the manufacturers in exporting countries to increase the competitiveness of their products, expand the exports and market profitably in the importing countries.

⑤ 中性包装是一种既不标明生产国、产生的地名和名称,也不表明商标和牌子的包装。出口商采用中性包装的目的是打破某些进口国家和地区的关税和非关税壁垒,或适应交易的特殊需要(如转口销售)。它还能帮助生产厂商提高产品的竞争能力,对进口国扩大出口并赚取外汇。(熊伟译)

6.4 Trade Barriers

贸易壁垒

① For one reason or another, all countries impose trade barriers on certain goods crossing their borders. Some trade barriers are directly related to exports. For example, the United States permits strategic military materials to be shipped abroad only after government permission has been obtained. Most trade barriers, however, are designed to restrict imports. Two of the most common barriers are quotas and tariffs.

① 所有的国家由于不同的原因对通过边境的某些商品都设有贸易壁垒。有一些贸易是直接和出口有关的。例如:在美国,只有在获得了政府的准许后,才允许将战略军事物资运往国外。然而,大多数贸易壁垒是用来限制进口的。配额和关税是两种最常见的进口壁垒。

Quotas

配额

② A quota is a quantitative restriction that is expressed in

② 配额是用物质的数量或价值

terms of either physical quantity or value. For example, a quota that states no more than 50,000 Class A widgets may be imported from Europe each year is a restriction stated in terms of physical quantity. Meanwhile, a quota that restricts importation of a certain type of Japanese glassware to no more than $ 1 million worth a year is stated in terms of value.

表示的数量限制。例如,对从欧洲进口的A级小器具每年不超过50 000套的配额是一种以物质数量表示的限制。同时,对某一种日本玻璃器皿的进口不超过100万美元的限制是一种以价值表示的配额。

Tariffs

③ A tariff is a duty or fee levied on goods being imported into the country. These tariffs can be of two types: revenue or protective. A revenue tariff is designed to raise money for the government. These tariffs are usually low. A protective tariff is designed to discourage foreign businesses from shipping certain goods into the country. The basic reason for a protective tariff is to keep out goods that will undersell products made in the home country. For this reason, protective tariffs are often very high, thereby forcing the foreign business to raise its prices to cover the tariff.

④ Tariff duties are of three types: specific, ad valorem, and compound. Specific duties are levied at the rate of so much per unit or pound. Ad valorem duties are levied on the basis of the product's value. Compound duties are a combination of specific and ad valorem duties.

关税

③ 关税是对进口到一个国家的商品所征收的税额和费用。这类关税可有两种:岁收关税和保护关税。岁收关税是用来为政府筹集钱款。这种关税一般较低。保护性关税是用来阻碍外国企业将某种商品运进一个国家。征收保护性关税的基本目的是不让可能以低于本国制造产品的价格出售的商品进口。由于这个原因,保护性关税常常很高,从而迫使外国企业提高其价格以偿付关税。

④ 海关关税有三类:从量税、从价税和混合税。从量税是按每单位或每磅产品征收一定的税;从价税按产品的价值征收;混合税由从量税和从价税共同组成。(冯祥春、孙春丽 译)

6.5 Bill of Lading

① A bill of lading is, firstly, a contract between the shipper and the shipping company; secondly, a receipt for the consignment; and thirdly, a document of title. A bill of lading doesn't only contain a full description of the consignment-numbers and weights and marks of packages-but a lot of information as well. It quotes the name of the shipper and the carrying vessel, the ports of shipment and destination, the freight rate, the name of the consignee, and the date of shipment, which is very important from a contractual point of view.

② It may also contain a number of other clauses. Some bills of lading are marked "freight paid", when a shipper is selling CIF or CFR, others may allow transshipment, which means that the cargo may be transferred from one ship to another at some intermediate port. It is often important to a shipper that his bill of lading should be "clean" rather than "dirty", that is, that the shipping company should not have made any qualifications about the quantity or condition of the cargo actually shipped.

提单

① 提单首先是发货人与轮船公司之间的一种合同;其次,是收到货物的收据;第三,是所有权的一种单证。提单不只包含货物的详细说明——数量、重量和箱包的唛头——它还包含许多其他情况。提单提供了发货人的姓名、装运港及目的港、运费率、收货人姓名以及装运日期,从合同的观点来看,装运日期极为重要。

② 提单也可能包含许多其他条款。在发货人按CIF或CFR条款出售货物时,提单上注明"运费已付"。有些提单准许转船,转船的意思是货物可在一些中间港从一艘船转到另一艘船上。对发货人来说,有一点常常也很重要,那就是提单应该是"清洁"的,而不是"不清洁"的;也就是说,轮船公

司对实际装运的货物,对其数量及情况,不应注有任何条件。

③ According to whether the goods are loaded or not, the Bills of Lading can be classified into shipped B/L (the goods have already been loaded on board the carrying vessel bound for the port of destination) and received B/L (an evidence given by the ship owner that the goods have been received for shipment but have not yet been actually loaded on a particular ship).

③ 依据货物是否装船,提单可分为装运提单(货物已装上开往目的港的运输船只)和备运提单(船方签发的表明货已收到,但还没有实际装上船的证明)。

④ On the basis of the fact whether the Bills of hading can be transferable, the Bills can be classified into straight Bill and order Bill. In straight Bill, the name of the consignee is definitely written. This person alone is entitled to take delivery of goods. This kind of B/L can not be transferred because it has lost the function of document of title to the goods. Ordinary banks are unwilling to advance the payment for it. In order B/L, the name of the consignee is not written. The consignee is designated according to the order of the shipper or the opening bank.

④ 根据提单是否可以流通,提单可分为记名提单和指示提单。在记名提单里收货人的姓名必须明确地写出,只有该收货人才有权提取货物。这种提单不能转让,因为它已失去作为货物所有权凭证的功能。一般银行不愿为其垫款。在指示提单上不填写收货人姓名,收货人由托运人或开证行的指令决定。

⑤ There are also direct bill of lading, transshipment bill of lading, clean bill and unclean bill.

⑤ 提单还可分为直运提单、转船提单、清洁提单和不清洁提单等。(熊伟 译)

6.6 推荐读物

(1)冯祥春等,国际经贸英语文章精选,对外经济贸易大学出版社 2010 年版。

(2)黄锡光等,国际贸易实务(双语),复旦大学出版社 2007 年版。

(3)万树玉,英美最新国际经贸文选,新华出版社 2003 年版。

(4) http://cn.wsj.com/gb/bilingual.asp

(5) http://www.ftchinese.com/channel/english.html

练习 7 课后练习

7.1 分析题

(1)试用所译和比读材料分析对译及其特点。

(2)举例说明全译方法在信用证文体英译汉时的运用。

(3)总结并归纳产品包装英译汉时的增译现象。

7.2 实训题

7.2.1 询盘

邀请发盘通常是国际贸易谈判所涉及的四个步骤中的第一步,进出口商均可利用邀请发盘来开始可能的交易。通过这一步骤,出口商可以向进口商就某个交易提出有条件的建议,进口商也可获得某笔交易的某些条件。这也称作询盘(询价)。在国际贸易中,潜在的客户也常常会就贸易条件发出询盘。这些询盘可能通过传真、电子邮件、电话或信件等方式发来。即使无法立即报价,也应该及时告知询价人,以显示自己的工作效率与诚意。每一个询盘都是一个销售机会,一个可能带来长期合作关系的机会。询价通常包括品名、品质、型号、欲购数量和交货期等。经验丰富的出口商此时会对询价人的资信状况、财力和对方国家的进口壁垒等作一些调查,然后据此作出相应的决定是否做这笔生意。

7.2.2 **Major Provisions**

① FORCE MAJEURE: In case where the Seller fails to ship a part or the whole of the goods within the time of shipment contracted owing to any cause or causes due to force majeure, the part or the whole not yet shipped, as the case may be, shall be cancelled without any obligation on the part of the Seller, provided a proper evidence is furnished by the Seller to the Buyer.

② ARBITRATION: Any disputes arising from the contract and in the performance thereof shall be settled by way of amicable negotiation. In case where no amicable settlement can be reached between the Buyer and the Seller, the matter at issue shall be submitted to arbitration to be held in the defendant's country. If the defendant is the Seller, arbitration shall be held in Beijing at China International Economic and Trade Arbitration Commission in accordance with its Rules of Arbitration. The award made by the said Commission shall be final and binding on both the Buyer and the Seller.

7.3 思考题

(1)比较外贸信函中的中英差异及互译特点。
(2)试析商务谈判用语特点及翻译。
(3)行业惯例对国际货代词语翻译有何影响?
(4)商务合同中被动语态的语用意义及翻译。
(5)国际商务合同英译时应注意哪些问题?
(6)结合全译方法,分析外贸函电缩略语的翻译方法。
(7)举例分析信用证语篇中一词多义的翻译策略。
(8)英语信用证条款翻译应注意哪些问题?
(9)合同汉译英时如何对常用同义词进行选择?
(10)海运提单术语有何特点?过期提单和可转让提单的英译?

第10课 商品广告

导 译

广告,广义上包括公益性宣传广告和商业行为的广告,狭义上是指以营利为目的的商业行为的广告,通常指商品广告,是向潜在的消费群体介绍商品,激发其兴趣,从而促其购买的一种手段。按广告目标领域分,有消费者广告、服务业广告、产业广告等。按广告传播媒体分,有电影广告、电台广告、报纸广告、杂志广告、互联网广告、邮件广告、户外广告等。按广告内容来划分,有食品广告、服装广告、药品广告、汽车广告、教育广告、招聘广告、房屋租赁广告等。

一则完整的商品广告由标题、正文和落款组成。标题吸引消费者注意,具有诱导性、独特性和简明性。正文包括开头、主体和结尾。开头,是承接标题,转入主体的过渡。主体要介绍商品名称、规格、性能、特点、用途、价格、企业经营范围、服务内容等。结尾要简短有力,与广告标题相呼应。落款要写明生产单位、销售单位名称、地址、电话、邮编等。

商品广告翻译具有商品广告创作的所有特点,顺应市场规律,突出产品,吸引消费者是第一准则。其次,商品广告翻译必须符合商家的营销战略。此外,商业广告翻译用于商业宣传,必须符合宣传范围内的有关法律和法规。最后,商品广告的宣传对象是消费者,商品广告翻译也应以消费者为中心,一切从打动消费者的消费欲望出发。译者应充分研究宣传对象的心理,考虑产品销售对象的语言习惯、文化积淀与心理定势,以投其所好,供其所需。

1 课前练笔

1.1 榕山宾馆

① 位于福州市中心的榕山宾馆,环境优美,交通便利,装潢典雅,设施豪华,是理想的商旅之家。

② 宾馆拥有豪华套房300多间,环境清洁、幽静。6个装饰精美的餐厅提供各式中西美味,服务周到,气氛舒适。全套休闲健身设施,使您白日驰骋商场的紧张神经得以放松并享受锻炼的乐趣。

③ 宾馆拥有现代化商务中心。先进的通讯设施和多功能会议厅,使您即使远离办公室,也能事半功倍。

④ 不管您的事业遍及何处,宾馆提供的国际电脑网络服务将使您与世界相连接。

1.2 北京市百货大楼

① 北京市百货大楼坐落在闻名遐迩的王府井商业步行街中心地段,1955年9月开业,是新中国历史上第一家由国家投资兴建的大型百货零售店,曾是北京商品最齐全的商店。

② 1999年,北京市百货大楼装修改造后,引进国内外知名品牌提升商品品位,同时向社会推出十满意承诺:"一团火"精神使您满意;礼貌待客,用规范的礼貌用语使您满意;购买商品数量使您满意;价格公道、计量准确使您满意;方便购物使您满意;特殊服务使您满意;执行《消费者权益保护法》使您满意;管理系统使您满意;商品售后服务使您满意;顾客投诉解决使您满意。

1.3 Rolex Oyster

① Somewhere in the world — in dense jungle, or basking desert, or polar wasteland — an explorer could even now be navigating by dead reckoning. For this task, an absolutely reliable time-piece is essential.

② Ever since its introduction in 1926, the Rolex Oyster has been the choice of explorers and adventures. The virtual indestructibility of the Oyster case and utter reliability of the movement it contains have ensured that countless oysters have accompanied their wearers into history books. Yet the Rolex Oysters that have voyaged to the ends of the earth and depths of ocean are in every respect the same watches that you will find in any official Rolex jeweler.

③ Every single Rolex Oyster that leaves Geneva is capable of accompanying its owner wherever he or she cares to venture.

④ Where in the world will you be taking yours?

1.4 Tomorrow Will Be a Reflection of Tonight

① Nighttime is a special time, a time of rest and renewal. Your body begins to relax to unwind from the activity of the day and slip into the softer rhythm of the night. It is when your body turns the energy needed for the smiles and laughter of the day into the magical replenishment of the night. This is the time your skin needs special care.

② Night of Olay is a special night care cream, created to make the most of the magic of the night. It is greaseless and remarkably light to touch, a sheer pleasure on your skin, allowing it to breathe naturally while it absorbs this special nighttime nourishment.

③ Hour after quiet hour all through the night. Night of Olay enhances your skin's own natural renewal by bathing it in continuous moisture, easing tiny dry wrinkle lines and encouraging the regeneration of softer younger looking skin.

④ Night of Olay tonight will be reflected in your youthful radiance tomorrow.

1.5 The Showplace that Goes Places

① There are two fundamental reasons for buying any motor home: drivability and livability.

② A GMC Motorhome is designed to supply both in abundance.

③ Consider GMC's front-wheel drive. It means there is no driveshaft running from the front to the rear. This allows for a low center of gravity, thereby contributing to a stable ride.

④ And in the rear, the wheels are arranged in tandem, one behind the other, rather than side by side.

⑤ This arrangement offers several advantages:

⑥ First, when combined with GMC's air suspension system, it helps to make for a smooth and stable ride. Second, it allows the use of six brakes rather than four, one at each wheel. And third, it provides impressive room inside. Because when the rear wheels are in tandem, they intrude less on interior space.

⑦ Then there's the livability factor. A GMC is not only pleasant to look at. It's a pleasure to live in, as well.

⑧ The interior is orderly and efficient.

⑨ The galley has all the conveniences you could want, including a room 7-cubic-foot refrigerator with freezer. An efficient and convenient range. And a stainless steel sink with double bowl.

⑩ And as you can see, the seating area is a joy to behold. With a choice of beautifully coordinated colors, fabrics and floor plans.

2 课前批评

2.1 乐陵金丝小枣

乐陵金丝小枣位于全国三大产区之首,因其体型小、色红、核小、皮薄、肉质丰满,以优异的品质和丰富的营养闻名于世。本品含有果胶、维生素、蛋白质、脂肪,丰富的铁、钙、磷和维生素A、维生素P等营养物质,增热补血、滋肝健脾、益气养肾、润肤延寿,营养丰富,是历史悠久、中外驰名的高级补品。

Leling Small Sweet Dates

Leling Small Sweet Dates are of the best quality in china's three big date-growing areas. They are well-known for their small bodies, tiny pits, thin skin, rich pulp, good quality and rich nutrients. The dates contain various nutritious elements such as pectin vitamins, protein and fat and are rich in ferrum, calcium, phosphorus and vitamin AP. They serve to improve your health by enriching the blood to promote the production of heat, nourishing the liver and invigorating the spleen, supplementing qi and the kidney, to prolong your life. It is a high-grade tonic with a long history, well-known both at home and abroad. (李明用例)

2.2 Cholesterol Has Natural Enemies

① In the battle against cholesterol, it seems man has a natural ally.

② Deep-sea, cold-water fish contain special oil called omega-3. An oil that recent studies indicate help control cholesterol.

③ Now Squibb brings you omega-3 in a dietary supplement.

④ Introducing Proto-chol.

⑤ A natural oil from only Deep-sea, cold-water fish rich in omega-3, and it's concentrated in an easy-to-swallow sealed gel cap, so there is no fishy taste or smell.

⑥ Of course, Proto-chol should be part of a complete cholesterol control program, which includes regular exercise, food low in saturated fats and regular

胆固醇的天然克星

① 在与胆固醇的抗争中,人类似乎有个天然的盟友。

② 深海冷水鱼类体内含有一种称为欧米茄-3的特别油脂,经最新科学研究表明,这种油脂有助于抑制胆固醇。

③ 斯贵博公司现奉献给您含有欧米茄-3的营养补充食品。

④ 隆重推出降胆固醇油。

⑤ 这种油脂仅取之于含有丰富的深海冷水鱼类,浓缩后置于便于吞服的密封胶内,故无鱼腥味。

⑥ 当然,服用降胆固醇油只是抑制胆固醇整个方案的一部分,还需经常锻炼,食用低脂肪

medical checkups.	食品,定期到医院检查。
⑦ So start your cholesterol control program today.	⑦ 劝君采取行动,早日降低胆固醇。
⑧ Cholesterol is an enemy you should fight everyday.	⑧ 胆固醇是您必须每日与之斗争的顽敌。
E. R. Squibb & Sons, Inc.	斯贵博父子公司(陈新 译)

知识 3 全译知识 增译

增译,即增加式全译,指根据语用和语义的需要增加必要的语言单位的全译方法。增译的原则是:增形不增意,即语形上增加了语言单位,但语义上未作任何添加。增译的单位有词、短语和小句,按使用频率排列,词增译最多,短语增译次之,小句增译最少。

3.1 词增译

词增译,指根据语用和语义的需要在译文中增加原文没有的词的增译方法。词增译首先表现在增加译语特有的某些词类,如英语无量词,而汉语量词丰富,汉译时须添恰当的量词。词增译其次表现在增加原文中无其形却含其义的词语,如汉译有时必须根据具体的逻辑关系增加相应关联词;英译有时要增加英语连词等。如:

① Each art has its own medium: the painter his pigments, the musician his sounds, and the writer, words. 凡艺术皆有工具,画家用颜料,音乐家用声音,作家呢,则用词语。

② The sentence was passed. The child must go from her — to others — to forget her. Her heart and her treasure — her joy, hope, love, worship — her God, almost! 判决书下达了:孩子得离开她,跟别人,会忘掉她。孩子是她的心肝宝贝,她的快乐希望,她的所爱所拜,差点没成她的上帝!

例①,原文的后几个分句承前省略了谓语 has,译文添上;原文在 the writer 后略作停顿,在对译的同时增译了语气词"呢",显示原文的生命气息。例②是情急下的语言,添加"孩子是",以保证汉译成句,后面添加几个"她的",以构成排比,产生急促的语势。

3.2 短语增译

短语增译,指根据语用和语义的需要在译文中增加原文所无的短语的增译方法。英译汉时,有时增加单个词语难以准确达意,需要增加短语。短语增译以词增译为基础,频率略低于词增译。如:

③ They stood and stared at each other, pale as culprits. 他们站着你看我我看你,面如死灰,像一对犯人。

短语 pale as culprits 内涵丰富,pale 本来就蕴含"脸色",译者赋其形象,揭示其蕴含,无意中就增译了短语,但意义没有旁逸斜出。

3.3 小句增译

小句增译,指根据语用和语义的需要在译文中增加原文所无的小句的增译方法。将原语词或短语扩充为译语小句，或所增的小句内涵蕴于原文，不加有时会导致译语不易理解。小句增译的频率低于短语增译。如：

④ During the gold-rush days Great Grandma had made the long westward trek to California to live with an uncle, only to discover he had been murdered for his gold while she was on her way. 淘金热那会儿，曾祖母千里投奔她加利福尼亚的叔叔，到了之后，才得知就在赶来的途中叔叔因为黄金而遇害了。

⑤ I began to ask a question, but Lyonya put his fingers to his lips. 我刚要提问，雷昂亚就拿手伸近嘴唇，要我别吱声。

例④，据原文，"千里投亲"与"得知亲人遇害"认知上有间隔；据逻辑，指她到加州之后，了解到亲人遇害，所以增译小句"到了之后"，才可将上下文连接起来，保证思维的连贯性。例⑤，原作有关体语的描述有时需要用解释、改换等进行处理，以利译语读者理解。

窍门 4 全译窍门

4.1 译出生动

受广告费用和读者注意力等因素影响，广告篇幅一般不长，因此广告语言必须简洁生动。一般说来，中文广告较文雅，喜用四字结构，简洁明了，以求达到音韵和谐、增强说服力和感染力的效果，而且四字成语搭配灵活，言简意赅，体现了汉语流水句的特点。如：

① 衣食住行，有龙则灵。

【译文Ⅰ】：Your everyday life is very busy, Our LongCard can make it easy.

【译文Ⅱ】：Long Card makes your busy life easy.

② Fresh up with Seven-up 君饮七喜，倍添神气

例①是建行龙卡的广告，译文Ⅰ有些冗拖，拘泥形式；译文Ⅱ显得简洁，busy 和 easy 句内押韵，富有创意，读来上口。例②是七喜饮料的广告，充分地反映了英语用单音节词以求简洁的特点，朗朗上口，便于识记。

英文广告常杜撰新词怪词，以突出产品的新、奇、特，满足消费者的追潮心理。如例③中，TWOGETHER 合 together 和 two 于一体，情趣横生，汉译却无法炮制。

③ TWOGETHER

The ultimate all-inclusive one price sunkissed holiday.

【译文】：两人共度一个阳光灿烂的假日，一切费用均包括在单人价格之内。

4.2 音意兼济

最为理想的商标翻译应当既贴近原始商标的发音，又能体现商品的特征、符合目标受众的接受心理。异国情调浓郁，表意明确，易于联想和记忆，音意兼济，有利于诱发消费者联想，加深对商品的印象，会起到意想不到的宣传效果。

Coca-Cola 的汉译"可口可乐"算是典范。上世纪 20 年代,可口可乐已在上海生产,初译为"蝌蝌啃蜡",其接受状况可想而知。于是可口可乐专门负责海外业务的出口公司公开悬赏征求译名。时在英国的上海教授蒋彝,以"可口可乐"四字捧走了奖金。佳译不凡,不但音似,还更有寓意,透射出产品给消费者的感受:好喝、清爽、快乐、可口亦可乐、让消费者胃口十足,"挡不住的感觉"油然而生。

再如,德国名车 BMW 是 Bavarian Motor Works(巴伐利亚汽车制造厂)的缩写,无文化含义,意译则太长,移植 BMW,则不合习惯。仿作"宝马","马"存其车的喻义,"宝"则含稀有珍贵之意,二字巧合,性能卓越的名车便铭刻脑际。

4.3 善用褒义词

商品广告常用含有褒义色彩的评价性形容词,倾向于美化所述商品,富于感情色彩和渲染力,旨在增强描述性和吸引力,为广告语增添了魅力。据调查,简单而最常用且富于感情色彩和表达力的形容词有:new, good/better/best, free, fresh, delicious, full, sure, clean, wonderful, special, crisp, fine, big, great, real, easy, bright, extra, safe, rich。如:

④ Give a Seiko to all, and to all a good time. 精工表走时准确,戴表人心情愉悦。

"走时准确"是对任何手表的基本要求,Seiko 却异乎寻常,还能令戴表人"心情愉悦"。有时,商品广告还通过比较来抬高自己。虽不直接贬低别人,却常用形容词比较级来修饰与突出自己的商品。有些形容词还以最高级的形式出现,以增强购买者的信心。如:

⑤ There's never been a better *Time*. 从未有过的好《时代》。

⑥ Minolta, finest to put you finest. 第一流的美能达,第一流的你。

4.4 套用名诗谚语

古今中外的名诗佳句,历来深受各国人民喜爱,有些甚至家喻户晓,妇孺皆知,千古传诵。而谚语大都短小精悍,寓意深刻,经久不衰。汉语广告英译时,如能巧用名诗谚语,塑造产品形象,定能增强广告的感染力,使读者倍感亲切,百闻不厌,从而有助于销售。如:

⑦ 城乡路万千,路路有航天。East, west, Hangtian is best.

英国诗人 George Orwell 的诗句 East, west, home is best. 已成乡恋佳句,常当谚语引用。本例中商标"航天"代替了 home,原文的对偶和押韵手法在译文短短的五个词中得以重现。读英译,读者不禁联想:无论天南海北,无论城市乡村,只要乘上航天牌汽车出游,眺望窗外变幻无穷的优美景色,享受车内豪华舒适的环境,定能心旷神怡,流连忘返。又如:

⑧ 百闻不如一尝。Tasting is believing.

这是浙江省粮油食品进出口股份有限公司的广告。原文显然套用了"百闻不如一见",而英译也套用了谚语 Seeing is believing. 所不同的是,汉谚改了最后一字,英谚改了头一个词,新鲜活泼,殊途同归。

4.5 巧设问句

商品广告常用反问句、设问句和一般疑问句,旨在引起注意,激起共鸣,引发思考,加深印象，从而诱导消费行动。据统计，广告英语每30句就有一个疑问句，特别是在广告标题中，疑问句显然比陈述句更能吸引人的注意力，因为疑问句能引起好奇与思考。如伊卡璐脍炙人口的广告语 Does she? Or doesn't she?（她染发了？还是没染？）翻译疑问句一般采用直译，即按原文疑问句类型译出。如：

⑪ 想和我一样漂亮吗？请用"诗芬"吧。Want to be beautiful as I? Please use Sifone.

⑫ The Economist?

Isn't that a peculiar name for a journal that also discusses America, Britain, Europe, science & technology, world politics, books plus arts, current affair…along with business, finance and economics?

【译文】:《经济学家》?

这不是一家杂志的专用名称吗？它讨论美国、英国、欧洲、科学技术和世界政治、书籍、艺术、时事……还有商业、财政和经济。

5 话题词汇

5.1 食品

粮食制品 cereal product
酶 enzyme
配方 formula
配料 ingredient
配料表 list of ingredients
软包装 flexible package
食品包装材料 packaging material for food
食品包装容器 food container
食品产品合格证 food product qualification
食品加工 food processing
食品添加剂 food additive
食品营养强化剂 food enrichment
食品制造 food manufacturing
食品质量监督 food quality supervision
食品资源 food resource
硬包装 rigid package
原料 raw material
主料 major ingredient (material)
acid treatment 酸处理
amino acid 氨基酸
animal protein 动物蛋白
aseptic packaging (aseptic packing) 无菌包装
baking 烘焙
biologic contamination 生物性污染
brewing 酿造
browning 褐变
calorie 热量
carbohydrate 碳水化合物
chemical contamination 化学性污染
cold storage 冷藏
commercial sterilization 商业无菌
condiment (seasoning) 调味品
crude fiber 粗纤维
curing preservation (preserved by curing process) 腌制保藏
dairy product 乳制品
dehydration 脱水
dietary fiber 膳食纤维
disinfection 消毒
drying preservation (preserved by dehydration; drying process) 干制保藏
drying 干燥
edible oil and fat 食用油脂
extrusion (puffing) 膨化
fatty acid 脂肪酸
fermentation 发酵

food contamination 食品污染
food poisoning 食物中毒
heavy metal 重金属
inoculation 接种
liposoluble vitamin (fat soluble vitamin)脂溶性维生素
mashing 打浆
meat product 肉制品
mineral matter 矿物质
mould 霉变
non-alcoholic drink(soft drink)无酒精饮料
nutrient 营养素
pasteurization 巴氏消毒
pastry 糕点
pressing 压榨
quick-freezing 速冻
rancidity 酸败
refining 精制
refreshment (refreshing)保鲜
residue of pesticide 农药残留
smoking 熏制
softening 软化
spoilage 腐败
starch-based product 淀粉制品
sterilization 灭菌
sugar 糖食
trace element 微量元素
vacuum packing 真空包装
vegetable protein food 植物蛋白食品
vegetable protein 植物蛋白
vitamin 维生素
water soluble vitamin 水溶性维生素

5.2 化妆品

彩妆 cosmetics
唇彩 lip gloss;lip color
唇线笔 lip liner
发胶 styling gel
粉饼 pressed powder
粉底 foundation (compact, stick)
粉扑 powder puffs
粉刷 cosmetic brush; face brush
海绵扑 sponge puffs
护发素 hair conditioner
护肤 skin care
护肤霜 moisturizers and creams
保湿 moisturizer
护手霜 hand lotion;moisturizer
睫毛夹 lash curler
紧肤水 firming lotion
焗油膏 conditioning hairdressing;hairdressing gel; treatment
卷发器 rollers; perm rollers
冷烫水 perm; perming formula
眉笔 brow pencil
眉粉 brow powder
眉刷 brow brush
面膜 facial mask;masque
摩丝 mousse
磨砂膏 facial scrub
沐浴露 body wash
去死皮 exfoliating scrub
染发 hair color
日霜 day cream
润肤露 body lotion;moisturizer
散粉 loose powder
晚霜 night cream
洗发水 shampoo
洗面奶 facial cleanser;face wash(foaming, milky, cream)
卸装乳 makeup removing lotion
卸装水 makeup remover
眼膜 eye mask
眼线液(眼线笔)liquid eye liner; eye liner
眼影刷 eye shadow
指甲油 nail polish
口红刷 lip brush
胭脂扫 blush brush
转笔刀 pencil sharpener
电动剃毛器 electric shaver-for women
纸巾 facial tissue
吸油纸 oil-absorbing sheets
化妆棉 cotton pads
化妆包 cosmetic bag

after sun 晒后用品
alcohol-free 无酒精
anti-抗;防
anti-wrinkle 抗老防皱
balancing 平衡酸碱
blusher 腮红
combination 混合性皮肤
dry 干性皮肤
essence 精华液
eye gel 眼胶;眼霜
foam 泡沫
gentle 温和的
hydra-保湿用
lip care 护唇用
lipstick 口红;唇膏
long lasting 持久性
loose power 蜜粉
lotion 水;露
milk 乳
oil-control 抑制油脂
peeling 敷面剥落式面膜
remover 去除;卸妆
revitalize 活化
scrub 磨砂式去角质
sensitive 敏感性皮肤
spot 青春痘用
waterproof 防水
white-美白用

5.3 电器

安培 ampere
冰箱 refrigerator
排气机 air exhauster
排气扇 smoke exhauster
磁带 tape recorder
电灯泡 bulb
电动剃须刀 electric shaver
电饭锅 electric cooker
电风扇 electric fan
电烤箱 electronic oven
电暖气 electric heater
电视机 television
电熨斗 electric iron
豆浆机 soya-bean milk grinder; soya-bean milking
计算器 electric calculator
搅拌机 food blender
净水器 filter purifier
扩音机 loud-speaker
录音机 dictaphone; dictating machine
麦克风 microphone
煤气炉 household gas stove
暖脚器 electric foot warmer
日光灯 fluorescent lamp
收音机 radio
图像变形 anamorphic
电动吸尘器 electric vacuum cleaner
消毒碗柜 disinfection cabinet
消声室 anechoic chamber
音响爱好者 audiophile
饮水机 water dispenser
有源超低音音箱 active subwoofer
榨汁机 juice extractor;juicer
真空管 tube
功放接收机 a/v receiver
前置放大器;调谐器 a/v preamplifier;turner
air conditioning 空调
application software 应用软件
assembly language 汇编语言
broiler 烘烤机
can opener 开罐头刀
compactor 捣碎器
compiler 编译器
defroster 除霜装置
device programmer 设备编程器
dicer 切块机
dishwasher 洗碗机
dry cell 干电池
dryer 干衣机
eggbeater 打蛋器
embedded system 嵌入式系统
emulator 仿真器
fan 风扇
flash memory 闪存
flashlight 手电筒

freezer 冷冻箱
furnace 壁炉
general-purpose computer 通用计算机
host 主机
humidifier 湿度调节器
instruction pointer 指令指针
iron 熨斗
kernel 内核
linker 连接程序
memory space 内存空间
microwave oven 微波炉
monitor 监视器
mutual exclusion 互斥现象
object code 目标代码
oven 烤箱/炉
percolator 过滤器
physical address 物理地址
range hood 抽油烟机
rotisserie 电转烤肉架
stove 炉子
tap 电线搭接处
toaster 烤面包机
vacuum cleaner 吸尘器

5.4 汽车

爆震 detonation
避震器 shock absorber
刹车系统 brake system
刹车油 brake fluid
超速传动 overdrive
齿轮润滑油 gear lubricant
传动系统 drive line system
点火开关 Ignition switch
电动汽油泵 electric fuel pump
电瓶水 battery acid
电子燃料喷射 electronic fuel-injection system
垫片 gasket
调整器 regulator
碟式刹车 disc brakes
动力转向 power steering
飞轮 flywheel
风扇皮带 fan belt
钢板弹簧 leaf spring
钢圈 wheel rim
共振器 resonator
内胎 tire tube
排气量 displacement
排气系统 exhaust system
偏滑测试 side slip tester
平稳杆 stabilizer bar
汽缸体 cylinder block
汽油表 fuel level indicator
前悬吊 front suspension
曲轴箱 crankcase
牵引力控制系统 traction control system
燃烧室 combustion chamber
散热器 radiator
水泵 water pump
水套 water jackets
速率表 speedometer drive
悬吊系统 suspension system
压力水箱盖 pressure cap
压缩机 compressor
氧气感知器 oxygen sensor
引擎 engine
引擎系统 automotive engine
轴距 wheel base
主轴承 main bearing
驻车刹车系统 parking brake system
转向拉杆 steering linkages
自动水平控制装置 automatic level control
automatic transmission 自动排档变速箱
clutch system 离合器
condenser 冷凝器
connecting rod 连杆
cooling system 冷却系统
drum brakes 鼓式刹车
flywheel 飞轮
gear lubricant 齿轮润滑油
heat-control valve 热控制阀
load-carrying 承载负荷的;承载的;承重的
long base car 长轴距轿车
luggage carrier 行李箱;行李架

luggage carrying capacity (luggage capacity)行包承载能力;行李容量
main bearing 主轴承
manual transmission 手排档变速箱
microprocessor controlled car 微机控制轿车(一般指微机控制点火、喷油、变速的轿车)
multicylinder car 多缸发动机汽车
Nissan Bluebird 日产蓝鸟轿车
oil pan 油底壳
oil pressure gauge 机油压力表
oil pump 机油泵
Piston 活塞
posh car 最漂亮的轿车(【英】俚),豪华轿车
power steering 动力转向
rear suspension 后悬吊
refrigerant oil 冷冻油
remoulded car 改造的汽车;改装的汽车; 改型汽车
safety car 安全汽车(指碰撞时,乘员不致遭受重大伤害的轿车,目前处于试验阶段)
scraped car 报废汽车, 废车
screen buffer 屏幕缓冲
slip Joint 滑动接头
spark Plug 火星塞
spark Test 火花测试
speedometer drive 速率表
steering gear 轮向齿轮
steering system 转向系统
thermostat 节温器
tire size 轮胎尺寸
tubeless tires 无内胎轮胎
vibration damper 减震器
wheel balance 轮胎平衡

5.5 缩略语

3D 三维
ABS 防锁死刹车系统
ADI 人体每日允许摄入量
AE 大气雾化效果
AFC 高级画面捕获
AFDO 食品与药品官员协会
AR 自动恢复
AV 音频和视频
BIOS 基本输入;输出系统
BOS 刹车优先系统
CEA 消费者电子协会
CFCs 氯氟碳
CG 计算机生成图像
City Safety 城市安全系统
CNT 碳微管
COAST 条状缓存
CPU 中央处理器
CSE 可分配空间
CV 定电压
DIC 数字图像控制
DOD 放电深度
DOT 动态超频技术
DPP 直接打印协议
DVD-R 可记录 DVD 盘
EBD 制动力分配
ESP 电子稳定程序
GMP 良好操作规范
GPU 图形处理器
GRAS 公认安全的
HACCP 危害分析和关键控制点(食品安全管理体系代名词)
HDC 陡坡缓降系统
HDMI 高清晰度多媒体接口
HTPC 家庭影院个人电脑
HT 超级传输
ICH 输入/输出控制中心
IC 集成电路
INTIN 中断输入
IPS 平面开关
IPTV 网络电视
IRD 集成接收解码器
IR 红外线
KDC 就地装配的汽车
LACF 低酸罐头及酸化食品
LCD 液晶显示屏
LCL 零担的(货运)
LED 光学二极管
LMOs 改性活生物体

LP 长时间播放
LSI 大规模集成电路
MCT 内存控制器
MEDMED 皮肤最低致红剂量
MIA 肉类检查法
MPV 多用途汽车
MRL 最大残余限量
MT 兆传输率
NC 降噪
NMHC 不含甲烷的碳氢化合物(排放)
NOP 非操作指令
NR 违规记录
OCV 开路电压
PC 聚碳酸酯
PMO 巴氏消毒牛奶条例
PRP 前提方案
PSB 预紧式安全带
RTE 即食的
SE 沙门氏菌
SOPs 标准操作规程
SPF 防晒倍数;防晒系数
SRS 安全气囊
SSM 安全支持性措施
SSO 卫生标准操作程序
STB 机顶盒
SUV 运动型多用途车
UBHC(发动机中)未燃尽的碳氢化合物
UVA 表示长波紫外线
UVB 表示中波紫外线
WOC 车重

6 比读体悟

6.1 唐三彩

Tri-colored Pottery of the Tang Dynasty

① 唐三彩是中国古代陶瓷艺术中的一颗灿烂的明珠。由于它出现于唐代,又多用黄、绿、赭三种釉色,故名唐三彩。

① Tri-colored pottery, which is known as a splendid pearl in the art of ancient Chinese ceramics, originated in the Tang Dynasty. It is mainly a three-colored glaze: yellow, green and brown, hence the name " tri-colored pottery of the Tang Dynasty".

② 西安作为唐代的都城,周围出土了大量的唐三彩器物,被誉为唐三彩的故乡。

② Xi'an was the capital of the Tang Dynasty. It is also the hometown of tri-colored pottery. Large numbers of these pottery wares have been unearthed from around the city.

③ 唐三彩制品造型雄浑简练,生动传神;釉色相互溶渗,绚丽多彩。在唐代不但为达官贵人所珍爱,还远涉重洋,被运往日本、伊朗、埃及、意大利等国。

③ The shapes of tri-colored pottery articles are bold, vivid and life-like, and the glazed colors are mutually-permeated, multifarious, gorgeous and fully expressive. They were treasured even at that time by the Tang people, and were shipped to Japan, Iran, Egypt, Italy and other countries across the ocean.

④ 陕西继承唐代传统,恢复唐三彩的制作已有几十年的历史,拥有造型、配釉、烧窑等方面经验丰富的艺人,所制产品受到国内外人士的称赞。凡到陕西的游客,莫不以能得到一件唐三彩制品而为快事。将唐三彩陈设案头,能使室内洋溢出古香古色的东方艺术情趣。唐三

④ The traditional way of making tri-colored pottery has been carried on in Shaanxi. The manufacture of these wares was resumed decades ago. Now the province boasts many artists and artisans with rich experience in modeling, glazing and baking. The products are spoken of highly by people both at home and abroad. All visitors to Shaanxi think it is a pleasure to have tri-colored potteries. If you put them on the

彩还可以作为高雅而珍贵的礼品用来馈赠亲友。

desk in your room, the room will be filled with the charm of antique oriental art. They are also elegant and valuable presents for your friends and relatives. (李运兴 译)

6.2 联想电脑

① 新联想是一家极富创新性的国际化的科技公司，由联想及原IBM个人电脑事业部组成。作为全球个人电脑市场的领导企业，联想从事开发、制造并销售最可靠的、安全易用的技术产品及优质专业的服务，帮助全球客户和合作伙伴取得成功。我们成功的基础是让客户实现他们的目标：工作高效、生活丰富多彩。

② 我们的公司

联想的总部设在纽约的Purchase，同时在中国北京和美国北卡罗来纳州的罗利设立两个主要运营中心，通过联想自己的销售机构、联想业务合作伙伴以及与IBM的联盟，新联想的销售网络遍及全世界。联想在全球有19 000多名员工。研发中心分布在中国的北京、深圳、厦门、成都和上海，日本的东京以及美国北卡罗莱纳州的罗利。

③ 我们的价值观

联想公司及员工郑重承诺，以下四个核心价值观是我们一切工作的基础：

成就客户——致力于客户的满意与成功；

创业创新——追求速度和效率，专注于对客户和公司有影响的创新；

精准求实——基于事实的决策与业务管理；

诚信正直——建立信任与负责任的人际关系。

Lenovo

① The new Lenovo is an internationalized hi-tech corporation full of creativity, made up with the Lenovo and the original IBM personal computer division. As the leading enterprise of PC market in the world, Lenovo is committed to development, manufacture and sale of the most reliable, safe and user-friendly state-of-art products and quality professional service, helping global clients and business partners achieve success. The basis of our success is to help clients attain to their aim: efficient work, rich and colorful life.

② Our Corporation

The headquarters of Lenovo is established at Purchase of New York, simultaneously two major operational centers are set up in Beijing, China and Raleigh, North Carolina, the US. Through our own sale networks, business partners and the merge with IBM, the sale networks of new Lenovo reach every corner of the world. Across the world there are 19,000 staff of Lenovo. Our research and development centers are distributed in Beijing, Shenzhen, Xiamen, Chengdu and Shanghai of China, Tokyo of Japan and Raleigh, North Carolina of the US.

③ Our values

The corporation and our staff are sincerely committed to the promise that the following four values are the basis of our work.

Guaranteeing the achievement of our clients — be committed to the satisfaction and success of our clients.

Committed to enterprise and creativity — be in pursuit of speed and efficiency, concentrating on innovations that will influence both clients and the corporation.

Striving for precision, accuracy and realism — decisions and business management based on facts.

Devoted to good faith and honesty — establishment of trustworthy and responsible interpersonal relationship. (伍锋译)

6.3 MAXIMUS AIR CARGO

① MAXIMUS AIR CARGO with its headquarters in the UAE's capital Abu Dhabi is the largest all cargo airline in the

航空货运公司

① MAXIMUS 航空货运公司(MAXIMUS AIR CARGO)总部位于

UAE and premier operator of outsized cargo aircraft in the Middle East.

阿拉伯联合酋长国的首付阿布扎比，是阿拉伯联合酋长国最大的全类型货运公司，也是中东特大型货物航空运输业务的主要经营者。

② By operating a fully owned fleet now comprising AN-124-100 Ruslan, Airbus A300-600RF, Ilyushin IL-76TD Candid and the recently added Lockheed L-382 Hercules cargo aircraft, MAXIMUS AIR CARGO not only has the ideal aircraft for just about any air cargo requirement, it has also rapidly gained a strong reputation for its 'first-class-approach' to the regions air cargo charter market.

② 凭借由安－124－100 Ruslan，空客 A300－600RF、伊尔 IL－76TD Candid 以及最近新增的洛克希德 L－382 大力神运输机所组成的自有机队，MAXIMUS 航空货运公司不仅拥有可满足任何航空货运要求的飞机，还因其“一流的运输手段”而迅速在地区性航空货运租赁市场上赢得了卓著的声誉。

③ MAXIMUS AIR CARGO being granted an Air Operators Certificate (AOC) and a civilian Certificate of Airworthiness in accordance with CAR-OPS by the UAE's General Civil Aviation Authority (GCAA), the company is fully adhering to the stringent UAE Civil Aviation Authority standards, comparable to JAR OPS-1.

③ MAXIMUS 航空货运公司已经获得了航空运营人证书（AOC）和阿拉伯联合酋长国民用航空管理总局（GCAA）根据 CAR-OPS 颁发的民用适航证。公司完全遵守阿拉伯联合酋长国民用航空管理标准，该标准相当于严格的 JAR OPS-1 标准。

④ Established in 2005, the company with its qualified and highly skilled 106 member strong workforce is focusing on superior customer care when managing air transport requirements and logistics solutions to Royalty, governments, multinationals, humanitarian & relief organizations alike. With a belief that superior customer service and outstanding reliability is what the market demands, MAXIMUS' philosophy is rooted in offering its customers responsive, most practical & cost effective solutions, which combine a personal approach with innovative customer service.

④ 自 2005 年成立以来，公司及其 106 名技术熟练的员工始终致力于为王室、政府、跨国公司、人道主义和救灾机构等组织提供一流的服务，满足他们的航空运输要求，为他们提供物流解决方案，将个性化建议与创新性客户服务完美结合。

⑤ Looking forward, MAXIMUS AIR CARGO's plans are firmly aimed at adding further all cargo aircraft to its fleet and expanding its portfolio in the aviation support service area in the near future.

⑤ 展望未来，MAXIMUS 航空货运公司将坚持不懈地致力于扩展运输机队，并将于近期增加在航空支持服务领域的投资。（彭萍 译）

6.4 Ugly is Only Skin-deep

其貌不扬

① It may not be much to look at. But beneath that humble exterior beats an air-cooled engine. It won't boil over and ruin your piston rings. It won't freeze over and ruin your life. It's in the back of the car for better traction in snow and sand. And it will give you about 29 miles to a gallon of gas.

① “大众”或许不中看，但在简陋的外表下跳动的却是一台心脏部件——气冷式发动机。它不会因沸溢而毁坏活塞环，也不会因结冰而误了您的事。它位于车的后部，以增大雪

地沙土上行驶的牵引力。每行驶 29 英里,仅耗汽油 1 加仑。

② After a while you get to like so much about the VW, you even get to like what it looks like.

② 稍待你喜爱上“大众”,你甚至对其丑貌也会情有独钟。

③ You find that there's enough legroom for almost anybody's legs. Enough headroom for almost anybody's head. With a hat on it. Snugfitting bucket seats. Doors that close so well you can hardly close them. They are so airtight, it is better to open the window a crack first.

③ 你会发现其足够的伸腿空间,再长的腿也得以舒展;绰绰有余的头部空间,再高的个子戴上帽子也可昂首挺胸;凹背单人座椅,舒适贴身;关闭得再好不过的车门是如此密不透风,你最好先把车窗留条缝。

④ Those plain, unglamorous wheels are each suspended independently. So when a bump makes one wheel bounce, the bounce does not make the other wheel bump. It is things like that you pay the \$1,585 for, when you buy a VW. The ugliness doesn't add a thing to the cost of the car.

④ 其朴实无华、不显魅力的车轮各自独立悬挂。当颠簸使一轮跳起时,弹跳不会涉及其他车轮。只要支付 1 585 美元,那样的尤物就归您了。其丑陋的外表丝毫不增添你购车的费用。

⑤ That's the beauty of it.

⑤ 这就是“大众”之美!(方梦之用例)

6.5 推荐读物

(1)安亚平,中国名牌产品商标词译名分析及翻译方法,上海科技翻译 2004 年版。

(2)胡晓云,世界广告经典案例,高等教育出版社 2004 年版。

(3)戚云方,广告与广告英语,浙江大学出版社 2003 年版。

(4)Hatim, Basil. Communication Across Cultures. Shanghai Foreign Language Education Press, 2001.

(5)Muller, Barbarn. International Advertising: Communication Across Culture. Dongbei University of Finance and Economics Press, 1998.

练习 7 课后练习

7.1 分析题

(1)试用所译和比读材料分析增译及其特点。

(2)任选一则中国名牌商品广告英译,试析译文有无硬译死译现象。

(3)试用比读材料分析广告翻译的文学性。

7.2 实训题

7.2.1 蜜三刀

本厂生产的“云龙山”牌蜜三刀,是传统名点,驰名南北。相传北宋时期,徐州太守苏东坡得宝刀一把,在青石上连砍三刀,留下三条刀印,蜜三刀故而得名。1983 年荣获商业部优质产品称号。

该厂还生产奶油饼干、烤蛋糕等,均被评为商业部优秀产品。

7.2.2 The Man in the HATHAWAY Shirt

① American men are beginning to realize that it is ridiculous to buy good suits and then spoil the effect by wearing an ordinary, mass-produced shirt. Hence the growing popularity of HATHAWAY shirts, which are in a class by themselves.

② HATHAWAY shirts wear infinitely longer — a matter of years. They make you look younger and more distinguished, because of the subtle way HATHAWAY cut collars. The whole shirt is tailored more generously, and is therefore more comfortable. The tails are longer, and stay in your trousers. The buttons are mother-of-pearl. Even the stitching has an ante-bellum elegance about it.

③ Above all, HATHAWAY make their shirts of remarkable fabrics, collected from the four corners of the earth-Viyella and Aertex from England, woolen taffeta from Scotland, Sea Island cotton from West Indies, hand-woven madras from India, broadcloth from Manchester, linen batiste from Paris, hand-blocked silks from England, exclusive cottons from the best weavers in America. You will get a great deal of quiet satisfaction out of wearing shirts which are in such impeccable taste.

④ HATHAWAY shirts are made by a small company of dedicated craftsmen in the little town of Waterville, Maine. They have been at it, man and boy, for one hundred and twenty-years.

7.3 思考题

(1)广告的分类有哪些?翻译规律有何不同?

(2)一般书面广告语的构成要素是什么?

(3)分析广告句法及其翻译有何特点。

(4)广告标题翻译有何规律?

(5)广告口号翻译有何规律?

(6)如何体现广告翻译的音美和意美?

(7)广告直译的条件是什么?

(8)怎样处理广告翻译中的文化差异?

(9)英语广告中省略句汉译如何处理?

(10)如何在汉英广告翻译中套用英语名句?

(11)如何处理广告翻译中的修辞?

(12)英语广告汉译新词如何处理?

(13)比较四字格在广告与其他文体中的译法差异。

第 11 课 交通通信

导 译

交通通信事业的发展,促进了商品流通与信息传递,加速了城市化进程,改变了我们的生活方式和思维方式,推进了经济与社会的发展。

交通分为交通运输和邮电两个方面。交通运输的任务是输送旅客和货物,有五种运输方式:铁路、公路、水路、航空、管道。交通运输业正逐渐转向更为专业化的物流业。邮政旨在传递信件和包裹;电信旨在传送语言、符号和图像。

根据我国交通运输部、铁道部和工业与信息化部的“十二五”规划,预计下列领域将成为我国“十二五”规划时期的翻译重点:1. 交通运输领域:现代信息技术在交通运输领域的集成应用、交通基础设施、运输装备;高能效、低能耗、低排放交通运输行业的发展模式,交通应急反应体系的建立和高速铁路等。2. 通信领域:3G 业务、移动互联网业务、互联网接入服务、移动电子商务及增值业务等;互联网、传输、无线、核心网、接入网、IT 支撑等方面的新技术、网络与信息安全等。

交通通信英语,作为科技英语的一个分支,同样具有词义多、长句多、被动句多、词性转换多、非谓语动词多、专业性强等特点,这些特点都是由交通电信英语文献的内容所决定的。因此,交通通信翻译必须遵循科技翻译的方法和技巧。

练笔 1 课前练笔

1.1 移动电话

① 在一定程度上多亏了无线网络的发展,电话正在与个人电脑和电视融合起来。不

久之后，配有高分辨率显示屏的轻巧手机便可以与卫星连接。人们可以随时随地通话，收发电子邮件或者参加视像电话会议。这种手机也许还会吸收电脑的许多主要功能。移动通信工具有望带来一些互联网所能提供的新服务，如股票交易、购物及预订戏票和飞机票。

② 电信革命已在全球范围内展开。不久之后，用一台装置就可以收到几乎任何形式的电子通信信号。最有可能的是一部三合一手机。在家里它可以用作无绳电话，在路上用作移动电话，在办公室里用作内部通话装置。有些专家甚至认为移动视像电话将超过电视，成为主要的视频信息来源。

1.2 Two Train Derailed

① Two train derailments at the weekend cut Sydney's rail links with Melbourne and the NSW North Coast. Almost 500 metres of track on the Sydney-Melbourne line was ripped up late on Saturday when 11 waggons of a goods train jumped the rails near Benalla, in northern Victoria.

② Salvage work was hampered yesterday by the swampy surrounds, and work to repair the track was expected to continue today.

③ Early yesterday morning, nine waggons of a goods train were derailed on the main NSW North Coast line near Grafton. Breakdown crews were called to clear the track, which was still closed late yesterday.

1.3 IPhone 4S Sales Hits Record 4m on Launch

① Apple has sold a record 4m of its latest incarnation of the iPhone in its first three days on sale in spite of criticism that the new product was a more limited technological leap forward than its predecessors.

② Analysts had expected the company, based in Cupertino, California, to sell between 2m and 4m of the iPhone 4S in the initial rush, compared with 1.7m of the iPhone 4 in three days after its release in the summer of 2010.

③ The iPhone 4 was greeted with more enthusiasm by critics than the 4S, which has a similar exterior but faster processors, improved camera and a voice-recognition program called Siri.

④ The technology improvements were more modest than many expected and the device was not introduced by the widely admired Steve Jobs, who was gravely ill and died the day after other executives showed off the phone.

⑤ The more muted buzz around the debut concerned investors because the iPhone now accounts for nearly half of Apple's revenue, and indeed some queues at Apple stores were shorter this year.

⑥ But the early sales received a boost from a number of factors.

⑦ The phones were available on the top three US carriers, instead of AT&T alone; they were in two more countries than the iPhone 4 at launch, Canada and Australia; and the three-day launch weekend ran from Friday through Sunday, instead of Thursday through Saturday, allowing more time for in-store shopping.

批评 2 课前批评

2.1 中国公路建设

① 中国目前已经建成1.9万公里公路。自1990年以来,中国每年都要新增3 700公里公路。到2020年公路网将连接中国所有主要城市。中国公路总里程将仅次于美国,达到55 000公里。

② 高速公路网将带来深远的影响。城市带将形成;人们的生活方式将会发生变化;枢纽城市的经济增长率将迅速上升,因为便利的交通条件将吸引更多的投资者。

③ 在公路建设中,中国也很重视支线公路建设,因为支线公路可以使小城镇充分利用附近干线公路建设带来的发展机遇。

The Highway Construction in China

① Up to now, China has built 19,000 km of highways. Since 1990, some 3,700 km of high-ways have been added each year. By 2020, highway networks will connect all major Chinese cities, and the total length of China's highways will be 55,000 km, second only to that of the United States.

② The impact of highway networks will be huge. Urban belts will emerge; people's lifestyles will change; and the economic growth rate of interchange cities will surge, as the convenient transportation facilities will attract more investors.

③ During its highway construction, China pays great attention to the building of feeder roads, as they can help smaller towns make full use of the development opportunities brought about by the construction of nearby trunk highways. (卢敏用例)

2.2 The Wind Tunnel

The wind tunnel studies have helped make many aerodynamic improvements in automobiles. Today many cars have hoods that slope to act as wedge against the wind. Windshields are also better designed to cut down on wind resistance. Social games are installed under the front section of the car to reduce the flow, or movement of air under the ear. Other improvements include retractable head lamps and smaller radiator grilles. Some designers have stopped using radiator grilles altogether. Others want to eliminate mud flaps, rain gutters, and even side trim to reduce air turbulence.

风洞

风洞的研究已经使汽车在减少风阻方面取得了很大的改进。当今,很多汽车的引擎盖都是弧线型的,以减少风阻。为了减少风阻,汽车的挡风玻璃设计得更加先进。汽车的前部下面安装了特制的条带以降低汽车底部的空气流动。其他一些改进包括可伸缩的大灯和减少散热格栅。一些设计师不再使用冷却器格栅;另外一些设计师为了减少风阻,打算取消挡泥板、导雨槽,甚至是汽车

两侧的导流条。（翟天利用例）

3 全译知识 减译

减译，即删减式全译，指根据语用和语义的需要删减原文语言单位的全译方法。减译的原则是：减形不减意，即语形上看似省去了若干语言单位，实际意义未减。减译的单位包括词、短语和小句，词减译最多，短语减译次之，句子减译最少。

3.1 词减译

词减译，指根据语用和语义的需要删减原语词的减译方法。首先减虚词，如冠词、连词、介词等；其次减某些实词，最常见的是代词。词减译主要是因了语言形式的差异，有时也因同义冗余而减。如：

① The Japanese build their traditional houses on boats when land becomes too expensive.

【原译】：由于土地变得十分昂贵，日本人就在船上建起了他们传统的住房。

【试译】：土地越来越贵，日本人就把传统的住房建在船上。

原文的时间从句转换为原因从句，汉语的表原因更多靠前因后果的逻辑顺序，不必用关联词，所以省去 when。代词 their 因语境省略。

3.2 短语减译

短语减译，指根据语用和语义的需要删减原语短语的减译方法。词减译是短语减译的必要条件，减短语必然导致减词。因此，短语减译比词减译的难度稍大，频率稍低。短语减译主要是同义现象存在，或因双语语义蕴涵不一，原语中要明说的，译语则可以隐含。如：

② A blood test showed that the level of a fatty substance called cholesterol in his blood was very high. 验血表明，他血液中的胆固醇含量很高。

③ The fist manned landing on the moon surface was achieved by American astronauts on July 20, 1969. 1969 年 7 月 20 日美国宇航员首次登月。

例②减去了同义短语 a fatty substance called；例③将原文信息重组，依靠语境，manned 因后面的 American astronauts 而省，was achieved 因 landing 而省，surface 也因 landing on the moon 的汉语意思“登月”而省，登月自然是登上月球的表面。

3.3 小句减译

小句减译，指根据语用和语义的需要删减原语小句的减译方法。任何语言，尤其是汉语，都追求意合，注重以简驭繁，力图以精短的形式承载更多信息。互译时，要视情况而省略原文的某些小句或将其压缩为短语，进而将原语复句简化为译语小句，以求言简意赅。如：

④ Part-time waitress applicants who had worked at a job would receive preference over those who have not. 应聘业余女招待,有工作经验者优先。

例④中两类应聘者对比的逻辑关系十分明确,小句 who have not 在汉译中隐去,被"优先"隐含或挤兑。优先的潜台词就是无工作经验者靠后,已是不言而喻,译出反成蛇足;汉译删减了被比对象,译文的逻辑关系相当明了。

4 全译窍门

4.1 "交通"辨译

"交通"一词误译常见。交通是各种运输和邮政电信事业的总称。交通的客体包括人、货物和信息三类,即交通运输是包括人和物的实体位移以及虚拟的信息共享。

说到"交通",首先会想到 transportation,它与"运输"含义相似,仅指依赖五种运输工具实现人与物的被动位移,或指交通工具或机关。如:road and rail transportation 公路及铁路运输;public transportation 公共交通工具;public transportation company 公交公司。英语表"交通"义的另一个词是 traffic,它侧重于"往来于街道的车辆",或交通量,如:traffic accident 交通事故,车祸;an increase in passenger traffic 客运量的增加。还有 transport,多指交通或交通系统。

"交通"真正相应的英语词是 communication。前缀 com-既表"共有"义,又表"共享"义。如:public communication 公共传播;communications between the West and the East 中西方交流;communications satellite 通信卫星。人类早期信息传递与货运是一体化的,正如有了丝绸之路,才会促进东西文化交流。而进入工业社会,电磁技术用于信息传递,从电报到互联网,完成了信息通过编码以光速传递的过程。由此,交通运输概念分离出了通信行业,从 communication 分出了 telecommunication(电信,通讯)。所以,communication 涵盖了交通运输和邮电通信二者,"交通银行"从 1908 年起就译作 Bank of Communications。

中国"交通部"实为中华人民共和国交通运输部,负责水路、公路和交通建设,不负责民航、铁路、邮政和电信。所以,"交通部"官方译为 Ministry of Transport of the People's Republic of China。我国五所"交大"中的"交通"均用汉语拼音 Jiao Tong、Jiao tong 或 Chiao Tung,其内涵已近古籍之义,无法用 communications 涵盖。此外,还有一些专业术语有其他译法,如:交通警察 point constable 或 pointsman,交通工具 vehicle,交通高峰 rush hour,交通补贴译为 travel allowance,交通指挥台 police stand。

4.2 数字特殊之译

英语有许多表示特殊数量概念的英语前缀,从 1~10 约有 30 个,掌握特殊数量概念的英语前缀或单词,并准确翻译特殊数量概念词至关重要。

表"一":mono-, unit-, un-,如:unary 一元关系;monolithic component 单片部件;unidirectional conductor 单向导体。表示"二":bi-, di-, dual-和 dua,如:binary 二进制;dichromatic cable 双色电缆;dual frequency diversity 双频分集。表示"三":trio-, tri-和

tertiary-,如:triode 三极管:trio test 三重组检验;tertiary group 三次群。表示"四": quad-, quadri-, quadr-, tetr-, tetra-, 如: quaternary 四进制; quadriphase loop 四相环; quadruple register 四路寄存器; tetrode transistor 晶体四极管;tetrapolar 四极的。表示"五":quint-, quin-和 qui-,如:quinary 五进制;qui-binary code 五二码;quintic curve 五次曲线。表示"六":sex-, se-, hexa-, 如: se-六进制; sextet 六位字节; decima 十六进制。表示"七": septe-,hepta-,如:septenary 七进制;heptahedron 七面体;heptago 七边形。表示"八":octo-或 oct-,如:octonary 八进制;octet 八比特组。表示"九":noven-, non-,如:novenary 九进制;nonagon 九边形。表示"十":deca-,如:decatron 十进管。

表百、千、百万及以上特殊概念数字的前缀有 hecto-百;kilo-千、mega-兆或 gig-吉、tera-太,如:hectowatt 百瓦,hectometer wave 百米波;kilopackets 千分组,kilovoltmeter 千伏表;mega cycle 兆周,megohm mete 兆欧表;gigacycle 吉周,gigohm 吉欧;teraohm 太欧,teracycle 太周。

4.3 模糊之译

模糊的翻译可按下列步骤进行:仔细分析相关知识背景,充分考虑语境因素,翻译时要符合译语逻辑性,可采用对译、换译等。如:

① Firstly, a terminal area is a very dynamic environment requiring almost continuous monitoring by human controllers, and aircraft resequencing may take place, under certain circumstances, at any time. 首先,机场周围的环境是不断变化的,需要管制员近乎不间断的监测,在特定的情况下,随时都有可能需要重新安排飞机起落。

② Road bed is the subgrade on which are laid the ballast, ties and rails. There are two types of it… cut and fill. It should be firm, well drained and of adequate dimensions. 路基就是上面铺着道砟,轨枕和钢轨的底基。路基有两种类型,即路堑和路堤。路基坚固,排水性好,并有足够的面积和厚度。

③ Dr. John Smith made a thousand and one explanations of this strange phenomenon of nature. 约翰·史密斯博士对这种奇怪的自然现象的解释多极了。

例①中,terminal area 为模糊范畴,可指候机楼,也可指候机楼周边地区,可以模糊对译模糊。例②以精确换译模糊,dimensions 在此有三维含义,可将其内涵"体积"和"大小"具体化,或将其外延"面积"扩大,这样含义就十分清晰了。例③以模糊换译精确,a thousand and one 是确切词语,把精确的表达方式意译成了模糊词语"多极了"。

4.4 译贵简,洁为美

任何语言都会要求以最少的文字传递最大的信息。应用翻译作品也讲究对称美、流畅美、逻辑美、完整美,精练美和修辞美,表现在词汇层,也表现在句法层。在词汇层,汉译英时以词代语,如以 metal surface 代 the surface of metal;以 steel bar 代 the bar made of steel;以 power cable 代 the cable for conducting electrical power。使用复合词,如 database 数据库, rail-car 动车, blastoff 溅落。缩略词,如 communication satellite 缩为 comsat, magnetic levitation 缩为 maglev, advanced passenger train 缩为 APT。用术语代替日常用语,如用 radiate 代 spread out in all directions from the center,用 reassemble 代 put the component parts together again。

句法层，以短语代替从句或句子，简化句型结构，使之简洁明了，如：

⑤ Maglev floats in the air, supported by the force of the immensely powerful magnets. Instead of rolling on rails, it actually flies, using magnets for propulsion. Unhindered by any friction except wind resistance, the maglev can attain speeds unheard of in ordinary land travel. 磁浮列车是悬浮在空气中的，由超强磁铁的磁力支持着。它不是在钢轨上滚动，实际上是利用磁铁做推动力在飞行。由于除风力外，没有任何其他的摩擦阻力，磁浮列车能达到普通地面行驶车辆闻所未闻的高速度。

4.5 合成词巧译

合成词和意义由各组成部分的合成，常用翻译技巧有：

换译 按汉语习惯适当转移有关组成部分，含有 free、less、loss、let、based、upper、in、resistance 或 resistant 等。如：scale-free network 无尺度网络，noise free channel 无噪信道，certificateless signature 无证书签名，packet loss 丢包，wavelet transform 小波变换，knowledge-based system 基于知识系统，identity-based signature 基于身份的签名，upper-frequency limit 频率上限，inband distortion 带内信号失真，forgery resistance 防伪造性，collision-resistant material 抗碰撞材料。

增译 增加虽无其词而有其义的部分，使译名清楚，如：adaptive algorithm 自适应算法。

减译 省略原合成词中某些虚词，减形不减意，常见的是减译介词 to，如：signal-to-noise ratio 信噪比。

零译 保留原合成词中的部分英文或拉丁文，如：Mac OS X operating system Mac OS X 操作系统。

缩略 把原合成词中的某部分词组译成其缩写形式，一般是取首字母，如把原文的是英语 High-Fidelity 缩写译成 Hi-Fi。

词汇 5 话题词汇

5.1 公路

车道封闭 Lane Closed
车辆慢行 Slow Down
车辆绕行 Detour
此路不通 Dead End
单行交通 One-Way Traffic
道路封闭 Road Closed
道路或车道变窄 Road/ Lane Narrows
道路交通信息 Traffic Information
道路两侧变窄 Road Narrows on Both Sides
道路施工 Road Work Ahead
道路右侧变窄 Road Narrows on Right
道路左侧变窄 Road Narrows on Left
陡坡减速 Steep Incline-Slow Down
多雾路段 Foggy Area
方向引导 Direction Sign
禁鸣喇叭 No Horn
禁止超越线 No Passing
落石 Falling Rocks
前方弯道 Bend Ahead
事故多发点 Accident Area

双向交通 Two-Way Traffic
Accident Hazardous Location 易肇祸路段
Automatic Vehicle Identification 自动车辆辨识
No U-turn 不准回转;请勿回转
Zebra Lines 斑马线
Speed Reduction Marking 减速标线
Real-Time Bus Information System 公车动态信息系统
accident 肇事;事故;意外事件
accident (crash) severity 事故严重性
accident analysis 事故分析;意外分析;肇事分析
accident assessment 事故鉴定
accident casualties 事故伤亡
accident investigation 事故调查
accident involvement rate 肇事牵连率
accident liability assessment 事故责任鉴定
brake reaction time 刹车反应时间;制动反应时间
bus route inquiring system 公车路线查询系统
bypass highway 绕越公路
bypass road 外环道
curb parking 路边停车(场)
curb ramp 缘石坡道
guardrail 护栏
intoxicated driving 酒后驾车
speed limit control 速限控制
speed parameter 速度参数

5.2 铁路

磁浮铁路 magnetic levitation railway; maglev
单轨铁路;独轨铁路 monorail; monorail railway
地下铁道;地铁 subway; metro; underground railway
电气化铁路;电力铁路 electrified railway; electric railway
干线 trunk line; main line
干线铁路 main line railway; trunk railway
高架铁路 elevatd railway
高速铁路 high speed railway
轨距 rail gauge
轻轨铁路 light railway; light rail
区间 section
市郊铁路 suburban railway
铁路等级 railway classification
铁路专用线 railway special line
窄轨铁路 narrow-gage railway
支线 branch line
(electric) platform truck 站台车
arrival time-table 到站时刻表
barrier 栅栏门
carriage; coach; car 车厢
departure time-table 发车时刻表
inquiry office, information desk 问讯处
service desk 服务台
junction 枢纽站
left-luggage office 行李暂存处
luggage barrow 行李推车
open wagon;(railway) wagon;(railway) truck 敞车
ordinary seat 硬席
pantry 餐车食品室
passenger station 客车站
platform bridge 天桥
platform ticket 站台票
platform tunnel 站台地道
platform 站台
platform-ticket 验票口
rack, baggage rack 行李架
railway station 车站
station hall 车站大厅
dining car; restaurant car; diner 餐车
ticket office; booking office 售票处
ticket-collector; gateman 收票员
time-table 时刻表
waiting room 候车室

5.3 水路

船舱 hold
船厂 dockyard;shipyard
船的栏杆 ship's rail
船东 ship-owner

船籍 ship's registry
船码头 quay;dock
船首 bow
船梯 ladder
船尾 stern
船坞 dock;boatyard
船舷 ship's side
甲板 deck
救生筏 life raft
救援艇 rescue boat
首楼甲板 forecastle deck
卸货重量 landing weight
压舱 ballasting
载货甲板 cargo deck
住舱甲板 accommodation deck
装运重量 shipping weight
boat 船;艇
dredger 挖泥船
ferry, ferryboat 渡船;渡轮
fishing boat 渔船
freighter 货船
launch 艇
lifeboat 救生艇
lighter 驳船
liner, ocean liner 远洋班轮
mainmast 主桅
mast 桅
merchant ship 商船
mizzenmast 后桅
motorboat 摩托艇
oars 桨;橹
outboard 尾部装有马达的小艇
paddle steamer; paddle boat 明轮船
passenger boat 客船
patrol boat 巡逻艇
submarine 潜水艇
tiller 舵杆
vessel 巡逻艇;缉私艇
water line 吃水线

5.4 物流

班机运输 scheduled Airline
包机运输 chartered Carrier
船的栏杆 ship's rail
电动托盘搬运车 electric pallet trucks
电动托盘堆垛车 electric pallet stacks
分拣 sorting
共同配送 joint distribution
供应链 supply chain
航空快递 air express
航空运单 air waybill
集货 goods collection
集中托运 consolidation
集装箱运输 container transport
集装运输 containerized transport
计费重量 chargeable weight
甲板 deck
梁式起重机 beam cranes
流通加工 distribution processing
配送中心 distribution center
前移式叉车 reach fork lift trucks
桥式起重机 overhead travelling cranes
轻货 low density cargo
甩挂运输 rop and pull transport
物流中心 logistics center
卸货重量 landing weight
悬臂起重机 cantilever cranes
压舱 ballasting
直达运输 through transport
中转运输 transfer transport
重货 high density cargo
additional charge 额外费用
anchor 锚
ballast 压舱物
beam 船辐(船的宽度)
berth, bunk 舱位

5.5 邮政

包裹吊牌 parcel tag
包裹附单 dispatch note

包裹营业台 parcel counter
包裹邮件 parcel post
包装纸 brown paper; parcel paper
本地邮件 local mail
本国大宗包裹 domestic mail in bulk
本国邮件 domestic mail
本人不在 addressee absent
本人拒收 refused by addressee
船运邮件 sea mail
国际包裹五联单 bill in five parts for international postal parcels
信筒 pillar box
住宅楼房信报箱 private letter box for multi-storey and high-rise block of flats
by air mail 航空邮寄
acknowledgement of receipt 回执
air mail; airmail 航空邮件
cash on deliver 货到付款
circular (letter) 通知
collection 收信
consignee (包裹)收件人
correspondence 通信
covering letter 附信
date stamp (加盖)日期邮戳
date 日期
diplomatic pouch, diplomatic bag 外交邮袋
exchange of letters 书信往来
exemption from postal charges 邮资总付
express delivery letter, special delivery letter 快递信件
extra postage 附加邮资
franking, stamping 邮资
heading 台头
letter box 信箱 (美: mailbox)
letterhead 印在专用印笺上头的单位名称,地址等
mail sorter 信件分类装置
mailbag 邮袋
money order 汇票
postal order 汇单
parcel 邮包,包裹
payee (汇单)收款人
please forward 请转发
postage paid 邮资已付
postal district 邮区
postcard 明信片
postmark 邮戳
post-office box 邮政信箱
postscript(P. S.) 附笔;后记
printed matter 印刷品
registered letter 挂号信
sorting table 分拣台
sub-post office 邮政支局 (美: branch post office)

5.6 电信

待机模式 standby mode
短信 short message; text message
对讲机 Walkie-Talkie
高保真 high fidelity(常简写为 hi-fi)
呼出通话 outgoing call
呼叫转移 call divert
近来的呼叫 recent call
快速拨号 speed dial
蓝牙 bluetooth
漫游 roaming
全球定位系统 GPS (Global Positioning System)
全球通 Gotone
全球移动通信系统 GSM (Global System For Mobile Communications)
任意键应答 any key answer
手机充值 cellular phone replenishing/recharging
手机入网费 initiation charges for mobile phone; mobile access fee
手机实名制 mobile phone identification policy
手机用户 mobile phone user; subscriber
双向收费 two-way charging scheme
移动梦网 Monternet
语音拨号 voice dial
语音提示 voice prompt
自动重拨 automatic redial
CDMA cellular system 码分多址蜂窝系统
electromagnetic pollution 电磁污染
electromagnetic screen 电磁屏蔽装置
general packet radio service 宽频移动数据服务
process 进程

proxy server 代理服务器
proxy 代理
remote boot 远程引导
remote control 远程控制
route 路线
router 路由器
script 脚本
search engine 搜索引擎
subdirectory 子目录
subnet mask 子网掩码
subnet 子网
thread 线程
throughput 吞吐量
wireless application protocol 无线应用通信标准协议

5.7 缩略语

超文本标记语言 HTML
超文本传送协议 HTTP
传输控制协议/网际协议 TCP/IP
第三代 3-G
点到点协议 PPP
个人手提移动电话系统 PHS
简单网络管理协议 SNMP
简单邮件传送协议 SMTP
局域网 LAN
三维 3-D
数码摄像机 DV
网际控制报文协议 ICMP
网络新闻传送协议 NNTP
文件传送协议 FTP
无线保真 Wi-Fi
液晶显示 LCD
远程登录 Telnet
A. B. S. 美国船级社
AASHTO 美国州公路与运输官员协会
ACI 美国混凝土学会;美国混凝土研究会
ASCE 美国土木工程师协会
ARTBA 美国公路与运输承造人协会
CDMA 码多分址
FHWA 美国联邦公路总署
GPRS 通用分组无线业务
GPS 全球定位系统
GRT 注册(容积)总吨
GSM 全球移动通信系统
IACS 国际船级社协会
IATA 国际航空运输协会
ICAO 国际民用航空组织
IMDG 国际海上危险品货物规则(国际危规)
IMO 国际海事组织
ITE 美国交通工程师学会
MMS 多媒体信息服务
NRT 注册(容积)净吨
PAS 个人接入系统
SIM 客户身份识别卡
SMS 短信服务
TPL 第三方物流
WAP 无线应用协
WLAN 无线局域网

体悟 6 比读体悟

6.1 互联网

Internet

国际互联网最初是为美国国防部建立的一个试验性网络,现在涵盖了世界范围内的2 000多万台计算机,估计每年还要增加50万台。它提供电子邮件、数以千计的简报式新闻以及各种数据库服

Internet, originally established as an experimental network for the U. S. Defense Department, now spans more than 20 million computers worldwide, with an estimated 500, 000 increase every year. It offers electronic mail, thousands of bulletin board-type news-groups and a variety of database

务。你可以用电子邮件把问候语与电视图像、声音、数据等压缩在一起。更重要的是,它通过大信息量的数据交换促进人们之间的合作。人们已经进行了在互联网现场传输声音和图像的实验。互联网的庞大规模使它有望成为信息高速公路的主干线。但为了支持越来越多的用户和多媒体应用,必须增加频带宽度,这是信息高速公路的核心技术问题。

services. The electronic mail allows you to encapsulate your greetings with video images and sound as well as date. More importantly, it enhances collaborative working through and information-rich exchange of data. Experiments on transmitting live audio and video over the Internet have also been conducted. The sheer size of the Internet makes it a candidate for the backbone of the Information Superhighway. But in order to support the growing number of users and the multimedia applications, the available bandwidth will have to increase dramatically, which is the technical problem at the core of the Information Superhighway. (王志奎用例)

6.2 载人飞船

The Manned Spaceship

① 2003年10月16日,中国第一架载人宇宙飞船安全返回地面。这标志着中国成为继美国和苏联之后第三个成功将人类送上太空的国家。对于中国来说,这是在航天科技上的巨大突破。

① The safe return of China's first manned spaceship on October 16, 2003 has made China the third country in the world that has successfully sent man into space following the United States and the former Soviet Union. For China, this has been a huge breakthrough in space technology.

② 与无人飞船相比,载人飞船因有人类直接参与而在技术上有一些特殊要求,包括:

② Unlike the unmanned spaceship, the manned spaceship, which involves direct participation of human beings, must meet some special technological requirements.

③ 1. 环境控制

③ 1. Environmental control

宇航员生活和工作的舱段要求严格密封,并采取环境控制措施,其主要作用是调节舱内和太空服内的温度、湿度和压力,吸收人体新陈代谢产物,控制舱内有害物质,提供氧气、通风、用水并处理废物。

The modules where the astronauts work or live must be tightly sealed and implement an environmental control program to regulate the temperature, humidity and pressure in the modules and the spacesuits, absorb the end products of metabolism, handle harmful matters in the modules and provide oxygen, ventilation and water while disposing of the waste.

④ 2. 应急救生

④ 2. Emergency lifesaving

载人飞船须配备各种救生装置,在各个飞行阶段可以采用各种不同的应急救生手段。

The manned spaceship must be equipped with a variety of emergency equipment so that different emergency lifesaving measures can be adopted at different stages of spaceflight accordingly.

⑤ 3. 人工控制

⑤ 3. Manual control

由人参与操纵和控制飞船,可提高系统的可靠性,处理预料不到的紧急情况。为此载人飞船都设有手动控制装置和各种设备,以便于宇航员工作。

Human involvement in the operation and control of the spaceship can increase the reliability of the system and help handle unpredictable emergencies; therefore, the manned spaceship is equipped with manual control devices and various apparatuses to make the job more convenient for the astronauts.

⑥ 4. 安全返回

⑥ 4. Safe return

为确保宇航员安全返回,除了通过隔热层和舱内温度调节进行严格的温度

To ensure the safe return of the astronauts, in addition to the strict temperature control by means of the thermal-protective

控制，返回过程中的过载程度也必须控制在人的耐受范围内，同时，较高的落点精度也很重要。

coating and temperature regulation in the modules, the force of overloading during the landing process must also be restricted within man's endurance capacity. Meanwhile, high precision of landing is also very important.

⑦ 5. 高可靠性

⑦ 5. High reliability

载人飞船的各系统和设备均要进行可靠性设计，关键部件采用备份系统，飞船须在严格的环境条件下进行地面测试和模拟飞行试验，以排除隐患。飞船的设计还要保证宇航员能对有故障的设备进行必要的维修和置换。

All the systems and equipment of the manned spaceship must undergo reliability design, and the key units must have backup systems. The spaceship must pass ground test and simulated flight test under strict control of environments so as to avoid hidden perils. The design of the spaceship must also allow the astronauts to carry out maintenance and replacement in case of equipment failure.

⑧ 从长远的观点看，人类进入外层空间，向宇宙的深度和广度进军是历史的必然。"载人航天技术的发展及其实际应用，对国家的政治、军事、经济和科技等均有重要的影响.

⑧ From a long-term point of view, it is a historical inevitability for man to venture into the outer space and explore the universe in depth and in width. The development and application of manned spaceflight technology will have great influence on a country's politics, military affairs, economy and science and technology.（张春柏用例）

6.3 What's Logistics?

物流是什么？

① The Definition of Logistics

The Council of Logistics Management defines logistics as follows:

Logistics is that part of the supply chain process that plans, implements, and controls the efficient, effective flow and storage of goods, services, and related information from the point of origin to the point of consumption in order to meet customers' requirements.

① 物流的定义

物流管理协会将物流定义如下：

物流——是供应链流程的一部分，计划、实施并控制货物、服务和相关信息从生产端到消费端之间高效率、高产出的流通和储存，以满足顾客的要求。

② Note that this includes inbound, outbound, internal, and external movements, and return of materials for environmental purposes.

② 注意此定义包括向内的、向外的、内部的和外部的活动，还包括出于环保目的的材料回收。

③ So logistics can be broadly defined as the time related positioning of resources, ensuring that materials, people, operational capacity, and information are in the right place at the right time in the right quantity and at the right quality and cost.

③ 因此，物流可以广义地定义为资源合适定位所及的全过程，确保原料、人力、生产能力和信息能够在需要的时间以正确的数量、良好的质量和适当的成本到达准确的地点。（张晓云用例）

6.4 Electric Traction

电力牵引

① It is generally held that the most efficient method of railway operation, and ultimately the most economical, given a reasonably cheap electricity supply, is with electricity as the

① 一般认为，如果能得到合理的廉价电源，以电能为动力便是铁路运输最有效的、归根结底也是最经济的

motive power. The electric locomotive is not dependent, like its steam counterpart, on the competence of driving and firing or the quality of the fuel burned. On the other hand, the speeds that will be possible with any given load are completely predictable and apart from signal or permanent way checks, or other delay — producing casualties, exact observance of schedule times can be guaranteed within narrow limits. With such accurate timetable observance trains can be operated with shorter turnaround times at terminals, which means that more intensive use can be made of rolling stock than is generally possible with steam power.

方式。电力机车并不像蒸汽机车那样,它不依靠驱动和点火能力或所用燃料的质量。此外,电力机车在装载任何一定负荷时,其可能行驶的速度完全可以预测,除了信号和线路检查或者严重生产事故引起的晚点之外,能够严格遵守行车时间。由于能准确地按列车时刻表行车,列车在各车站的周转时间缩短了,因此,电力牵引与蒸汽牵引比较,前者更能充分利用机车车辆。

② In suburban areas the rapid acceleration afforded by electric motors from rest and in recovery from speed restrictions makes it possible to work trains with very frequent stops at higher speeds and a closer headway than with steam locomotives. Multiple — unit working, which brings the motors of two or more sets of passenger stock, or two or more locomotives, under the control of one motorman in the leading driving cabin, would be impossible with steam, for each steam locomotive must be manned by its own driver and fireman. Moreover, except on the fastest and heaviest passenger and freight duties, on which it is advisable to have a second man at the head end to assist in the observation of signals and, if necessary, to attend to the electrical equipment, the equivalent of the steam locomotive fireman is unnecessary; thus the great majority of electric trains have a driver only, which makes for considerable economies in staffing.

② 在郊区,电力机车由于电动机启动后能迅速加速,并能从限制速度迅速恢复到正常速度,所以与蒸汽机车比较,在频繁停站的情况下,行车速度较高,而且连发列车的间隔距离较短。当使用带电机的多节车组的列车时,两组或多组客车的电机或是两台或多台机车,均由在驾驶室的一个司机来控制操作,而蒸汽机车则不可能如此,因为每个蒸汽机车必须由自己的驾驶员和司炉工操作。此外,只有在速度最快,载重量最大的客、货车上,电力机车上才需要有第二个人帮助观察信号,并在需要时,照应一下电气设备,除此之外,并不需要有如蒸汽机车的司炉工。因此,大多数电气列车只有一个驾驶员,这就节省了相当多的人力。(卢敏用例)

6.5 Container Ships

集装箱船

① This most popular of unitized vessels has grown from simple port container ships to large super container liners of 53,000 dwt and 2,800 container capacity. Ships of up to 31—32 knot speed are available now. The rapid expansion of container shipping has resulted in the creation of shipping and terminal over-capacity on dense trade routes (Atlantic and Pacific). Secondary trade routes are new converting to containerization with many first and second generation ships diverted to these routes after being displaced from the highly competitive dense trade routes.

① 最流行的单元化船只已从简单的港口集装箱船发展为具有5.3万吨载重量2 800个集装箱装载能力的大型超级集装箱班船。现在,船速已高达31—32km(mile/h)。集装箱装运的快速扩展,已导致大西洋和太平洋密集贸易航线上货运和集散港的超载。中级贸易航线上目前也正转向集装箱化。其中有从高度竞争的密集贸易航线上撤换下来的第一代和第二代船只。

② Future container ships will continue to increase in size though not in speed. We expect future transoceanic container ships to have capacities of 3,000—4,000 container equivalents and speeds of 25—26 knots. The major change will be in the hull form with multi-hulled (catamaran, trimaran) ships increasingly popular. Such vessels will probably not handle individual containers but transfer containers in container block of 8—64 containers by strong back gantry lift or horizontal warehouse ship type conveyor transfer.

② 将来的集装箱船,虽然速度不会增长,但规模将继续增加。希望将来横渡大洋的集装箱船,具有相当于3 000—4 000个集装箱的能力、速度达25—26节。主要的变化将是在船体上,多体(双体,三体)船将日益流行,这样的船可能不是处理单个的集装箱,而是将8—64个集装箱装入一个集装体中。由强基底的龙门吊吊装。或由仓库船型的输送设备水平转运。

③ Trailer ships are the most volume and stability limited vessels of all commercial cargo ships. Because they cover a narrow range of size, the use of constant ratios is reasonable for this ship type. Ro/Ros have a low L/D (length to depth ratio) because they need large hull depth due to the addition of the half carriage.

③ 滚动式拖运架装卸货船是所有商业货船中容积和稳定性受最大限制的船舶。因为船只大小变化不大,这种船的各种比率可取为常数。由于增加了船体拖运架,要求船体加深,滚装船的长深比(L/D)不大。

④ Other than slightly greater depth and beam, a Ro/Ro has similar dimensions to a container ship of comparable deadweight.

④ 除了船深、船宽稍大以外,滚装船和与其载重量相近的集装箱船相比,尺寸接近。(朱梅心用例)

6.6 推荐读物

(1)朱梅心,港口及航道工程专业英语,人民交通出版社出版1995年版。
(2)张晓云,物流英语,北京大学出版社2007年版。
(3)翟天利,科技英语阅读与翻译实用教程,新时代出版社2003年版。
(4)翁凤翔,国际航运专业英语,对外经济贸易大学出版社2008年版。
(5)刘鼎铭,集装箱化与现代物流辞典,东华大学出版社2003年版。
(6)胡树威,英汉汉英海事物流经贸常用语词典,大连海事大学出版社2005年版。
(7)陈焕江,徐双应,交通运输专业英语,机械工业出版社2002年版。
(8)严稽文,电信英语,人民邮电出版社2006年版。
(9)张黎新,周晶,王霖霖,地铁实用英语,外语教学与研究出版社2006年版。
(10)闵丽平,城市轨道交通专业英语,中国铁道出版社2006年版。

练习 7 课后练习

7.1 分析题

(1)试用所译和比读材料分析减译及其特点。
(2)任选《参考消息》一篇交通通信译文,分析其翻译的美感。
(3)品读窍门,探讨通信英语数字翻译的其他特点。

7.2 实训题

7.2.1 交通事故

俗语说:“十次事故九次快”,所以要“宁停三分,不抢一秒”。心急地赶时间、争强好胜、寻找刺激是产生超速行驶的心理特征。超速行驶不仅会使避免撞车更加困难,而且会使撞车的可能性和严重性增大。车速越高,方向的操纵性越差,一旦遇到紧急情况,很难控制车辆的速度和方向。因此,相关部门要更广泛地应用高科技手段如电子眼来捕捉超速驾驶者。

7.2.2 Speed Kills Phone Batteries

① Days after buying his Samsung Electronics Co. Galaxy Nexus smartphone from Verizon Wireless, David Jacobs found himself switching off the fourth-generation broadband connection that had drawn him to the $300 device in the first place.

② "I love everything about the phone, but with 4G on, it just sucks down the battery," said the 25-year-old Mr. Jacobs, who lives in Los Angeles and works in digital advertising. "It's very frustrating. Why can't I get a phone to last a whole day?"

③ Mr. Jacobs is among the rising number of 4G smartphone users who are discovering their speedy broadband service also zips through battery life. The main culprit is spotty 4G service — even in the nation's largest cities — which requires the phones to search constantly for a signal, draining their batteries.

④ Fourth-generation service is just starting to take hold, but complaints about battery life could slow the push by wireless carriers to convert customers to the higher-speed networks. Smartphone makers, however, are working on ways to respond to the new power demands.

7.3 思考题

(1)交通通信术语翻译的特点有哪些?

(2)交通通信术语翻译的策略有哪些?

(3)试论音译法在交通通信术语翻译中的应用。

(4)试比较科技翻译与文学翻译的美感的不同体现。

(5)交通通信英语的不同修辞有哪些翻译技巧?

(6)交通公示语的英译有何语篇特点?

(7)交通公示语的英译容易犯哪些错误?原因是什么?

(8)科技翻译中动名词误译的原因是什么?如何解决?

(9)如何利用逻辑解决翻译中语法无法解决歧义问题?

(10)试分析模糊性翻译与准确翻译的平衡点。

(11)试析实用翻译的流畅美和修辞美?

第 12 课 工农业

导 译

“工农业”指的是工业和农业。农业为第一产业,包括农、林、牧、渔等各行业。工业为第二产业,包括采掘、制造、自来水、电力、蒸汽、热水、煤气和建筑等各行业。随着国际交流的日益深入和频繁,工农业英语也越来越受到重视。工农业英语语言特点鲜明,词汇上多由词缀法构词、合成法复合词,缩略词很多,较多的专业术语词汇;句法上大量采用名词化结构,多为长句和复杂句式,较多的被动句式、否定句式;文体风格上具有逻辑严密、分类精细、客观性强、指令明确等总体特征。

工农业英语翻译属于应用翻译的领域。翻译这类文本的专业词汇时,由于其意义比较专一、稳定,可采用直译、意译、音译、形译、直译加注和补译等翻译方法,同时要掌握较多的专业词根词缀、专业术语和标准的翻译;翻译工农业英语的复杂长句时,要进行必要的词序、语序和语态的转换、拆分长难句、增词和减词、变被动为主动等调整,以达到用简洁明了的语言忠实地再现原文的内容。总之,总体上要做到逻辑层次清楚、措辞精确严谨、语言通顺自然、术语地道规范。

工农业英语翻译在当前的翻译市场中占有很大的份额。只有扎实的语言功底、熟悉工农业基本常识和严谨认真的精神,才能把该领域的翻译工作做好。

1 课前练笔

1.1 中国食品安全问题

① 最近袭击中国的一系列食品安全丑闻,引起了对监管措施进行改革的呼吁。第三

届中国食品安全论坛期间，与会者决心实施更加严格的执法，确保中国的食品安全问题。

② 买还是不买，这是许多人现在要考虑的问题。随着中国陆续出现的问题，食品安全恐慌的风波引起新一轮的担忧。顾客告诉我们，他们希望违反食品安全的问题以更加有效和更加及时的方式得以解决。

③ 污染食品丑闻已经引起全国的关注。因此，有关部门更加严格地实施法律和规章来解决涉及每个人健康的国家食品安全问题是很急迫的。

1.2 Car Retarder

One of the latest railroad inventions is a machine that will do the work of car riders in a freight yard. A " car retarder" it is called. It is a machine operated by compressed air which reaches above the rails of the classification tracks and pressing against the sides of the turning car wheels, checks or retards the speed of the car so that it will come to a stop at the proper place.

1.3 Vegetable Factory

① Vegetables are a vital part of our diet. The vegetables and cooking methods used may vary widely from country to country and from region to region, but vegetables form a part of the everyday diet of just about everyone on the planet.

② Actually growing vegetables, though, is no easy task. The soil must be tilled and seeds sown, and the farmer must tend the crops, watering and fertilizing, guarding against weeds and pests, while waiting for harvest time. A natural disaster such as drought or flood can kill off the whole crop before can be harvest. Cultivating vegetables under natural conditions is a job requiring steady and strenuous labor.

1.4 Edible Films Made from Diary, Bio-fuel Byproducts

A method developed by Agricultural Research Service (ARS) scientists uses by-products — not only from dairy processing, but also from biofuel production — to create biodegradable protective films. The scientists used carbon dioxide as an environmentally friendly solvent to isolate dairy proteins from milk, instead of harsh chemicals or acids that can be difficult to dispose of. Carbon dioxide (CO_2) is another byproduct of the glucose fermentation that is used to make ethanol. Using CO_2 makes the edible film more water-resistant and biodegradable. The resulting food coatings are glossy, transparent and completely edible. Like conventional food packaging, edible films can extend the shelf life of many foods, protect products from damage, prevent exposure to moisture and oxygen and improve appearance.

2 课前批评

2.1 农业、畜牧业和食品工业中的科技

近年来,对于分子生物学、植物遗传学、生物化学以及相关领域的前沿研究,中国政府给予了高度的优先权,这样能够增加农作物和牲畜产量。未来的几十年,科技肯定是中国食品保障的重要因素之一。中国人口必然增长,经济会持续发展,而在庄稼用地和水资源方面受到严重制约,因此,除了实现农业现代化,别无它法。

Science and Technology in Agriculture, Livestock Production, and Food Industry

In recent years the Chinese government has also given high priority to advanced research in molecular biology, plant genetics, biotechnology, and related fields, which is aimed at increasing crop yields and livestock productivity. Science and technology will certainly be among the key factors in China's food security during the next few decades. With China's inevitable population growth, its likely economic development, and its serious constraints in cropland and water, the country has no other choice than to modernize its agricultural sector.

2.2 Biomimicry: Why the World is Full of Intelligent Designs

① We humans like to think we're pretty good at design and technology — but we often forget that Mother Nature had a head start of 3.6 billion years. Now, the way that geckoes climb walls, or hummingbirds hover, is at the centre of a burgeoning industry: biomimicry, the science of "reverse-engineering" clever ideas from the natural world.

② Such efforts are, in a way, nothing new. Joseph Paxton's designs for the Crystal Palace that housed the Great Exhibition of 1851 were based, in part, on his observations of the structure of giant water lilies. George de Mestral, a Swiss engineer, came up with the concept of Velcro after observing the way burdock seeds clung to his clothes and the fur of his dog.

③ Yet as we become more and more concerned about the environmental impact of our behavior,

仿生学:世上的聪明设计何其多

① 我们人类乐于认为自己精于设计和技术——但我们常常忘记,大自然领先了我们足足360万年。现在,壁虎爬墙或是蜂鸟在空中的悬停正处于快速发展的产业的核心,这一产业就是仿生学,即对自然界的奇思妙想"施以逆向工程"的科学。

② 这些做法从某种程度上讲一点都不新奇。约瑟夫·帕克斯顿为1851年万国博览会设计的"水晶宫",部分构思便是基于对王莲结构的观察。瑞士工程师乔治·德·梅斯特拉尔则是在观察到牛蒡子粘在他衣服上及其宠物狗皮毛上的方式以后,设计出了维可牢尼龙粘扣。

biomimicry is becoming fashionable.

3 全译知识 转译

转译,即转移式全译,指根据语用和语义的需要转移原文语言单位的全译方法。转译通常在语法层面上进行,是应语用和语义的需要而进行的语形变化,转译的原则是:移形不易意,即形式上发生转移,而意义力求不变。转移涉及词、短语和句子,按频率,词转译最多,短语转译其次,句子转译最少。

3.1 词转译

词转译,指根据语用和语义的需要转移原语词的转译方法。词转译主要取决于语义搭配或词在全句中的交际作用。如:

① 当时我10岁,母亲34岁。I was ten and mother was thirty-four by then.

② It is not a sensation I could expect anyone except Laura to understand. 反正这种感觉,除了劳拉我不希望任何人了解。

例①,"当时"是旧信息,修饰整个复句,两人的年龄才是新信息,汉译将这一时间状语转至整个复句末尾。例②,原文否定词 not 否定客观事物 sensation,汉译则否定了主观意愿"希望(expect)",否定中心转移了,更符合汉语主观表态的认知心理。

3.2 短语转译

短语转译,指根据语用和语义的需要转移原文短语的转译方法。短语转译主要是表达同样的语用和语义而变动原语短语的位置,以适应译语语形的要求。如:

③ The undersea world is well-known as a source of natural beauty and a stimulus to human fantasy. The importance of oceanography as a key to the understanding of our planet is seldom as well appreciated. 海底世界是自然美的源泉和人类幻想的动力,这是人所共知的。而海洋学是考察地球的钥匙,其重要性就认识不足了。

④ I have never had much of an eye for noticing the clothes of women. 对女人的穿着,我向来不太关注,也没鉴赏力。

例③,原文前一小句的信息焦点是 is well-known,后一小句的是 is seldom appreciated,汉译体现了两句信息焦点对比,为此后一句的 importance 只好转至其内容之后,以求整个原文在汉语中的语用等值;此外,is well-known 转至句末,单独成为小句,表达了原文的信息焦点,同时也保证其前后内容构成了思维上一个完整的判断,译成汉语也成小句。例④,原文的话题是女人的穿着,信息中心是 had much of any eye,汉译时可移至句末,因此 for 引导的介词短语译作原文的状语,是旧信息,译时被前置,整个译文语用极似。

3.3 小句转译

小句转译,指根据语用和语义的需要转移原文小句的转译方法。小句不长时,有时可以按译语表达需要予以转移。如：

⑤ 如果我能够，我要写下我的悔恨和悲哀，为子君，为自己。I want, if I can, to describe my remorse and grief for Tzechun's sake as well as for my own.

本例为鲁迅《伤逝》的开篇句，句末两个状语突破常位而置于殊位，突出了悲情主题。译得更成功的是将原文的前一小句转移插入后一小句之中，有意松散后一小句英译的结构，衬托出一种低缓忧伤的主调。又如例⑤中因 I can note 所观察的对象太多太长，汉译时有必要先陈述所观察的对象，再交代主人公的观察行为，这样 I can note 汉译就后移了。

3.4 复句转译

复句转译，指根据语用和语义的需要转移原文复句的转译方法。复句因其较长而较少转译。如：

⑥ I can observe her without her knowing, and this gives me pleasure; for it is as in a moving picture that I can note the grace of her gestures, whether she raises a glass of wine to her lips or turns with a remark to one of her neighbours or takes a cigarette from her case with those slender fingers. 我能在她毫无察觉的情况下打量她。如同看电影里，不论是举杯果酒到唇边，或是侧头与邻座谈话，还是纤手从烟盒里夹烟，她那优雅的动作，我都能看得真切。真叫人赏心悦目。

原文为复句，小句 this gives me pleasure 是信息中心，其后 for 所引导的内容旨在解释原因，但原因过长，内含强调句型、同位语从句等，既可理解为译者将因果关系换置，用复句表达的原因转译至前，也可以理解为将短短的小句表达的结果转译至后，以符合汉语句末焦点信息的要求。

窍门 4 全译窍门

4.1 数字巧译

工农业英语文献中经常有表示数量的词语出现，尽管两种语言多用阿拉伯数字表示数量，但注意的是，汉语和英语在数量词语的表达方法上又有所不同，例如英语中没有“万、亿”的概念等，在翻译过程中，要做到正确的理解原文，谨慎地进行转换。英语中没有量词，在汉译时，需要根据实际情况增加量词。要求译者有较好的汉语词汇知识。此外，对于倍数的表达和翻译，也是工农业翻译的难点，因为英语表示倍数及其增减多种多样，汉译时要注意以下几点：

hundreds, thousands, millions, lots, scores, decades 等词后面加 of，分别翻译成：数百、成千、几百万、许多、几打、几十年。

① These bones tell us that many thousands of years ago the world was inhabited by certain mammals. 这些骨头表明，在数千年前，地球上就出现了哺乳动物。

数字前加 about、some、nearly、approximately、more or less、or so 翻译为大约、一些、接

近、~左右、~上下。

② Development costs have been estimated at approximately 100 million dollars. 据估算,研制经费大约为1亿美元。

数字前加 more than、over、above、up to 等词翻译为超过、以上、多;less than、under、below 翻译为不足、以下、不到。

4.2 倍数的翻译

1. "……数字(或倍数)+ 比较级 + than……"数字或倍数多半是净增减的数(或倍数)。如:

(1) A is two/ twice more than B. A 比 B 多 2 倍。

(2) A is two/ twice less than B. A 比 B 少 2/A 是 B 的 1/3。

(3) A is five times longer than B. A 比 B 长 5 倍。

This sort of membrane is twice thinner than ordinary paper. 这种薄膜比普通纸张要薄一半(即是普通纸厚度的1/2)。

2. "……倍数 + as + 形容词或副词 + as + ……"实际上增加 n - 1 倍或减少到 1/n。

(1) A is twice as long as B. A 的长度是 B 的两倍(或译:A 比 B 长一倍)。

(2) A is ten times as light as B. A(比 B 轻)是 B 重的 1/10。

The oxygen atom is nearly l6 times as heavy as the hydrogen atom. 氧原子的重量约为氢原子的16倍。(氧原子比氢原子重了约15倍)。

3. "……as + 形容词(如 high, many, much 等)+ as + 具体数字",(高,多)达……(具体数字)。

The temperature is as high as 500℃. 温度高达500℃。

4. A is as much (many, fast, large, long) again as B 相当于 A is twice as much (large, long) as B. 表示净增加倍,A 比 B 多(大,长……)1 倍,或 A is half as much (large, 1ong) again as B. A 比 B 多(大,长……)一半(即 A 是 B 的一倍半)。

The wheel turns as fast again as that one. 这个轮转动比那个快一倍。

5. "…… + by/to + 数字或倍数……"有比较级出现或有表示减少意义的动词或分词出现时,by 后表示的都净增减的数或净增加的倍数。to 后表示增加到(减少到)某个数字。但是,表示增减意义的谓语加 by a factor of + n,则表示增加 n - 1 倍或减小(n - 1)/n。

The production of integrated circuits has been increased by twice /to three times as compared with last year. 集成电路的产量比去年增加了两倍。

The equipment reduced the error probability by a factor of 5. 该设备误差概率降低了4/5。

6. 由一些数词组成的词组:a fifty-fifty basis, on a half and half basis(平均地;在对开分的基础上);in halves(两半) ten to one(十之八九,很有可能)。

The current flows through T1 and T2 on a fifty-fifty basis. 电流平均流过 T1 和 T2。

The current has been split in halves. 电流分成两半。

4.3 音形兼备译术语

语言转换过程中，尤其在工农业英文中，新事物层出不穷，新发现、新科技日新月异，音译与形译使用很多，丰富了译入语表达形式。

音译法 是翻译工农业英语专业名词的一种常用方法。工农业英语中某些由专有名词构成的术语、单位名称、新型材料的名称等，在翻译时都可采用音译法，如某些计量单位：Ohm 欧姆；Calorie 卡路里；Ampere 安培；Volt 伏特；Joule 焦耳。再如某些科技发明及材料名称及人名：radar 雷达；laser 莱塞（激光）；sonar 声呐；pump 泵（浦）；engine 引擎（发动机）；nylon 尼龙；Archimedes 阿基米德；Bernoulli 伯努利；Euler 欧拉。

形译法 指对于英语中用以描述某种事物外形的词汇，在译为汉语时，同样借助具体形象的翻译方法。有的选用近似这种字母形状翻译，如 I-bar 工字铁，T-beam 丁字梁，V-belt 三角皮带；有的保留原字母不译，以字母表达形状，如 A-frame A 形架，O-ring O 形环，T-joint T 形接头；有的保留原字母不译，以字母代表一种概念，如，Q-antenna Q 天线，X-ray X 射线。

4.4 常用词根词缀翻译

在工农业英语的翻译中，涉及很多专业词汇，这些词汇罕见生僻，是翻译中的难点和重点。因此，掌握大量的专业的词缀和词根的意义，可以在较短的时间内掌握更多的工农业专业术语，对于我们翻译工农业英语资料有很大的益处。此外，了解一些词根词缀在工农业英语中的特殊意义，可以提高翻译的准确性。

常用术语前缀

actin-光线；射线；辐射	arthro-关节	derm-皮；皮肤	petr-；petro-岩石；含石油的
aer-高空；航空；气体	blasto-芽；胚胎	dextro-右；右旋	phil-；philo-爱好；嗜好
algo 疼痛	calor-热	diplo-双；复	phon-声音；音调
alti-高；高度	cardi-；cardio 心；心脏	dynam-力；动力	pleo-多
amin-；amino-氨基	celio-；coelio-腹部	electr-电	pneumat-空气；气体
angio-血管；脉管	chemico-；chemo-化学	hepat-肝脏	pneumo-肺
antho-花	cosm-宇宙；世界	hist-体素；组织	pol-；polar-轴、极、偏振
anthropo-人；人类	dermat-外壳	peri-周围的	
arterio-动脉			

常用词根

-dent-牙齿	-hydr-水	-medi-治愈	-press-力
-equ-相等的	-ject-抛掷	-mis-发送	-rect-直；正
-flect-弯曲	-junct-结合	-opt-视觉	-spire-呼吸
-fract-断折	-lum-光	-pend-挂	-vent-风
-fuse-倾倒	-luna-月亮	-port-搬运	-vert-转向
-gene-生育	-magni-大		

常用术语后缀

-be 微小生物	-dynia 痛	-grade 度；级；步行方式	-hedron 面体
-blast 芽；胚胎；细胞	-gony 发生	-graphy 记录法	-lite 岩石；矿物
-dermia 皮肤病症	-gon 角形	-graph 书写；记录仪器	-lysis 分解

-meter 仪器
-ode 物;级管
-pathy 疾病
-ped 足
-phobia 恐惧
-phone 语言;电话
-scope 观察仪器
-sphere 层;圈
-stat 仪器
-therapy 疗法
-toxin 毒素
-trophy 营养
-vore 以……为食

5 话题词汇

5.1 工业

半成品 semi-finished products
采矿工业 mining industry
操作方法 working technique; method of operation
草根工业 grassroots industry
产品设计 design of products
朝阳产业 sunrise industry
成品 finished products
驰名商标 well-known trademark
出资方式 means of contributing investment
传统产品 traditional products
电力工业 power industry
电子工业 electronics industry
豆腐渣工程 jerry-built projects
独家代理 sole agency; exclusive agent
独家经营;专营权 exclusive right
纺织工业 textile industry
飞机制造工业 aircraft industry
服务业 service industry
服装工业 clothing industry
改进技术规程 improve the technological process
钢铁工业 iron and steel industry
高附加值的深加工 intensive processing with high added value
隔离开关 isolating switch
工程绘图 engineering drawing
工业基地 industrial base
工业控制一体化 integrated industrial control
工业停滞 industrial stagnation
工业园区 industrial park
工业增加值 industrial added value
国有企业 state-owned enterprise
合营期限 contractual term of a joint venture
合作方式 methods of cooperation
黑色金属工业 ferrous industry
后备工业 supporting industry
化学工业 chemical industry
机械制造业 machine-building industry
基础工业 basic industry
技术、智力、资本密集型 technology-, knowledge- or capital-intensive
技术转让 technology transfer
建筑工业 building industry
纠正行业不正之风 rectify malpractice in various trades
劳动密集型 labor-intensive
龙头产品 flagship product
配套工程 auxiliary/supporting project
配套资金 supporting funds
批量生产 mass production
企业所得税 corporate income tax
拳头产品 highly competitive product
人才市场 human resources market
生产力 productive forces
生产资料 capital goods
市场疲软 a market slump
乡镇企业 township enterprises
知识产权 intellectual property
滞销货 unsalable product
elaborately transformed manufactures 精加工
electrical machinery factory 电机厂
floor area 建筑面积
go through the formalities 办手续
government assignment 政府划拨
grant or transfer 出让或转让

highly processed goods 深加工产品
industrial cluster 产业集群
industrial optimization 产业优化
lead-edge technologies 领先技术
location classification 地段等级
manufacturing expenses 制造费用
metallurgical industry 冶金产业
pillar industry 支柱产业
planning approval 规划许可
project approval 项目许可
structural readjustment 结构调整
subsidies and grants 津贴和拨款
surplus capacity 生产能力过剩
water conservancy project 水利工程

5.2 农业

保护耕地 protect arable land
播种面积 sown area
"菜篮子"工程 the Vegetable Basket Project
餐饮业 catering trade
产业化扶贫 reduce poverty through industrial development
复种 multiple cropping
改良土壤 soil improvement
耕地保护制度 system for protecting arable land
旱地 arid/non-irrigated land
集约/粗放型农业 intensive/extensive agriculture
减免农业税 reduce and exempt the agricultural tax
减轻农民负担 lighten the burden on the peasants
开垦荒地 reclaim wasteland
粮食安全 food security
粮食储备 grain reserves
粮食品种 grain varieties
粮食直补 direct subsidies to grain producers
粮食综合生产能力 overall grain production capacity
粮食作物 cereal crops
绿色革命 Green Revolution
绿色食品 green food
绿色证书 green certificate
奶制品 dairy product
农村综合改革 comprehensive reforms in rural areas
农林牧副渔全面发展 all-round development of/in farming, forestry, animal, sideline production and fishery
农贸市场 farm produce market
农民工 rural migrant workers
农民专业合作社 specialized farmer cooperatives
农田水利化 bring land under irrigation
农田水利建设 construction of water conservancy works
农业基础设施 agricultural infrastructure
农业技术 agricultural technology
农业科技投入 spend on agricultural science and technology
农用物资 farm inputs
三农 agriculture, rural areas and farmers
社会主义新农村 Socialist New Countryside
水产业 aquatic products industry; fishery
水稻田 paddy field
水利设施 water conservancy facilities
特色现代农业 modern agriculture with distinctive local features
梯田 terraced field
土壤肥力 soil fertility
脱贫 shake off poverty
沃地 fertile land
消费信贷 consumer credit
小城镇建设 development of small towns
兴修水利 undertake water conservancy projects
畜牧业 animal husbandry
议价粮 grain sold at a negotiated price
油料作物 oil-bearing crops
有机肥 organic fertilizer
agricultural and sideline products 农副产品
agricultural commodities 农产品
agro-food systems 农业粮食系统
artificial diet 加工的食物
biological agents 生物因子
biological control 生物控制
capture-based aquaculture 基于捕捞的水产养殖
cereal importers 谷物进口国
chemical contaminants 化学污染物
chemical herbicides 化学除草剂

chromosomal manipulation 染色体控制
conservation agriculture 保护性农业
counter-season vegetables 反季节蔬菜
cover crops 覆盖作物
crop and livestock productivity 作物和家畜的生产率
crop failures 作物歉收
crop rotation 作物轮种
crossbreeding 杂交育种
disease and pest problems 病虫害
diversified food production 多样化粮食生产
extension systems 推广系统
farming techniques 耕作技术
farm subsidy 农产品补贴
fodder crops 饲料作物
food chain 食物链
food crisis and implementation of
food processing, preservation and storage technologies 粮食加工、保存和储藏技术
food quality and safety 食品质量与安全
food security 食品安全
organic agriculture 生态农业
organic farming 有机耕作
persistent drought 持续干旱
pollution-free vegetables 无公害蔬菜
soil biota 土壤生物
soil erosion 土壤侵蚀
soil improvement 土壤改良
soil micro-organisms 土壤微生物
soil nutrient balancing 土壤养分平衡
subsidize food 补贴粮食
weed control 控制杂草

5.3 林业

absorb dioxide and produce oxygen 吸收二氧化碳，放出氧气
afforested areas 绿化区域(面积)
afforested project 造林工程
air seeding 空播
awful weather 气候恶劣
ban forest 禁伐林
be surrounded by thick trees 被密林环绕
be worn away by wind and sandstorms 被沙尘暴吞食
botanical garden 植物园
breed new varieties of trees 培育树木新品种
by artificial seeding 人工播种
by poor management 由于管理不善
clouds of dust 尘土遮天
combat forest fires 防火林
concede the land to forestry 退耕还林
conserve water and soil 水土保持
curb the sand 防治风沙
develop forestry 发展林业
dry climate 干旱的气候
due to a deteriorating ecological environment 由于生态环境恶化
enclose the hills for natural forestation 封山育林
forest development 林业发展
forest farm/lands 林场/地
forest fires 森林火灾
forest resources 森林资源
forests for timber 木材林
form thick forests 形成密林
greening campaign 绿化运动
grow saplings 培育树苗
halt desertification 防止沙化
large stretches of forests 大片森林
natural forests 自然林
natural grassland 天然草原
newly afforested area 新绿地区
non-forested area 无林区
on either side of the river 两岸植树
prevent water loss and soil erosion 防治水土流失
protect forests 护林
provide fodder and fuel 提供饲料与燃料
provide shelter belts for farmland 保护农田
regulate climate 调节气候
sand breaks 防沙林
seedling/tree nursery 苗圃
select fine seed strains 选良种
shifting dunes and sand 移动的沙丘与沙子
shifting sand burying crops 移动的沙子埋掉庄稼
soil erosion 土壤流失

strengthen the management of forests 加强森林管理
survival rate 成活率
tea grove 茶林/山
the advance of sand 沙丘的推进
the amount of tree and grass coverage increased 植被面积增加了
the consumption of timber 木材消耗
the forest cover rate;the tree cover 森林覆盖率
the grassland diminishes 草原变少
The Ministry of Forestry 林业部
the national afforest drive 全国绿化运动
the national compulsory tree-planting activities 全国义务植树活动
the national tree-planting festival 全国植树节
timber resources 木材资源
tree-planting date 植树日
trees of economic value 经济林
turn back the advancing of desert 阻止沙丘前进
turn the country green 绿化祖国

5.4 缩略语

AC 交流电
AC 沥青混凝土
BSA 农业科学学士
BW 堆焊
CE 土木工程师
CEE 土木与环境工程
CF 粗纤维
CI 费用指数
CW 冷压焊,冷焊
DBL 双
DC 直流电
DR 钻进
EE 粗脂肪
FA 工厂自动化
HV 高(电)压
ICE 内燃机
IE 工业工程师
IZ 工业区
ME 机械工程师
ME 机械工程
MFD 制造的
NE 净能
OD 外径
PI 精密仪表
RC 钢筋混凝土
RWD 后轮驱动
SFA 国家林业局
SPL 样衣
TI 技术检查
UC 在建筑中
vet. 兽医
xf 超细的,特细的
XL 超大,特大号

体悟 6 比读体悟

6.1 巩固和加强农业基础地位

Consolidating and strengthening the position of agriculture as the foundation of the economy

① 坚持把"三农"工作放在重中之重,在工业化、城镇化深入发展中同步推进农业现代化,巩固和发展农业农村好形势。

① We will steadfastly make agriculture, rural areas, and farmers the top priority of the government's work; carry out agricultural modernization while deepening industrialization and urbanization; and consolidate and build upon the favorable situation in agriculture and rural areas.

② 确保农产品供给,多渠道增加农

② We will ensure an adequate supply of agricultural

民收入。要把保障粮食安全作为首要目标,毫不放松地抓好农业生产。稳定粮食种植面积,支持优势产区生产棉花、油料、糖料等大宗产品。大力发展畜牧业、渔业、林业。切实抓好新一轮"菜篮子"工程建设,大中城市郊区要有基本的菜地面积和生鲜食品供给能力。强化农业科技支撑,发展壮大农作物种业,大规模开展高产创建。继续实施粮食最低收购价政策,今年小麦最低收购价每50公斤提高5到7元,水稻最低收购价每50公斤提高9到23元。大力发展农村非农产业,壮大县域经济,提高农民职业技能和创业、创收能力,促进农民就地就近转移就业。提高扶贫标准,加大扶贫开发力度。

products and increase farmers' incomes through multiple channels. We will make safeguarding food security our primary goal, and work tirelessly to increase agricultural production. We will keep the area planted in grain crops stable, and support the growing of cotton, oilseed and sugar crops in the most suitable areas. We will energetically develop the animal husbandry, fishery, and forestry sectors. We will effectively carry out the new round of the "vegetable basket" program and ensure that suburbs of large and medium-sized cities have a basic area for growing vegetables and a basic ability to supply fresh produce for urban residents. We will get science and technology to better support agriculture, develop and expand the crop seed industry, and launch large-scale efforts to increase agricultural production. We will continue to implement the policy of minimum grain purchase prices, raise the floor price for wheat by 5 to 7 yuan per 50 kg and increase the floor price for rice by 9 to 23 yuan per 50 kg this year. We will energetically develop nonagricultural industries in rural areas, strengthen county economies, improve farmers' vocational skills and their ability to start their own businesses and increase their incomes, and encourage them to find nonagricultural employment in their hometowns or nearby areas. We will raise the poverty line, and intensify our efforts to alleviate poverty through development.

③ 大兴水利,全面加强农业农村基础设施建设。重点加强农田水利建设、中小河流治理、小型水库和病险水闸除险加固以及山洪地质灾害防治。完善排灌设施,发展节水灌溉,加固河流堤岸,搞好清淤疏浚,消除水库隐患,扩大防洪库容。通过几年努力,全面提高防汛抗旱、防灾减灾能力。大力推进农村土地开发整理,大规模建设旱涝保收高标准农田,加快全国新增千亿斤粮食生产能力建设。加强农村水电路气房建设,大力改善农村生产生活条件,努力为农民建设美好家园。

③ We will put great effort into water conservancy, and comprehensively strengthen agricultural and rural infrastructure. We will focus on developing more irrigation and water conservancy projects, harnessing small and medium-sized rivers, reinforcing small reservoirs and faulty and dangerous sluices, and preventing and responding to geological disasters from mountain torrents. We will improve irrigation and drainage facilities, develop water-saving irrigation, reinforce river embankments, clear away silt and dredge waterways, eliminate hidden dangers in reservoirs, and increase their storage capacity to prevent floods. Through several years of hard work, we will comprehensively improve our ability to prevent floods, control droughts, and prevent and mitigate natural disasters. We will vigorously develop and improve rural land, develop arable land that meets high drought and flood resistance standards on a large scale, and accelerate our work to increase the country's grain production capacity by 50 million tons. We will intensify work on projects to provide running water and electricity to rural homes, build and improve roads, exploit methane and construct rural housing, and energetically improve rural working and living conditions, so that farmers can live in a nice environment.

6.2 浦东新兴工业区

Pudong Modern Industries

① 站在上海的外滩,倚浦江东望,只见昔日那片旧棚简屋、苇塘阡陌的浦东大地,到处是气魄非凡的摩天大楼。如今,浦东光楼已成了上海的一大旅游景观。但是,高楼大厦并非浦东的全部。更令人振奋的是技术先进、装备精良、工业产值高达上海四分之一的新兴工业区的崛起。

① Standing on the famous Bund of Shanghai and looking eastward across the Huangpu River, one cannot but see clusters of magnificent high – rise buildings in Pudong, which used to be largely a rural area scattered with dilapidated old houses, fields of weeds, poodles and pools. Viewing skyscrapers in Pudong has become a tourist attraction for visitors in Shanghai. But high-rise buildings are not all that Pudong has. What is more inspiring is the emergence of modern industries that make use of advanced technology, state-of-the-art equipment and the industrial output valued more than a quarter of that of the Greater Shanghai.

② 近年来,浦东的整体工业快速发展,出现了六大支柱产业,即以生产"别克"轿车的上海通用汽车合资企业为领袖的汽车产业,以生产超大规模集成电路的中日合资企业为龙头的电子信息产业,以生产不锈钢的中德合资企业为骨干的钢铁产业,以中德、中美合资企业为主体的石油化工及精细化工产业,以中日合资企业为代表的家用电器产业,以上海医药工业与一批世界著名医药企业联手发展起来的生物医药产业。

② The last few years have seen a rapid upgrading of Pudong's industrial sector as a whole, best captured by the emergence of six pillar industries: the automaking industry headed by Shanghai General Motors joint venture manufacturing Buick cars, the electronics-information industry led by a Sino-Japanese joint venture producing super large-scale integrated circuits, the steel-making industry with a Sino-German joint venture as its backbone producing stainless steel sheet, the petrochemical and fine chemical industry centering around Sino-German and Sino-US joint ventures, the home electrical appliances industry represented by Sino-Japanese joint ventures, and the bioengineering and pharmaceutical industry developed jointly by local pharmaceutical manufacturers and a number of world-renowned pharmaceutical enterprises.

③ 美国通用汽车公司、德国巴斯夫公司、日立电器公司等一批跨国公司的高级职员在谈到他们总部的投资意图时无不坦陈,外方看中的是浦东在其全球战略中的地域优势、良好的投资环境和企业素质。在短短的几年里,伴随着这么多世界一流企业的投资项目,当今世界最富生命力和带动力的一些关键产业迅速落户到浦东,跨国公司的全球销售服务网络也延伸到中国。这是全球范围市场竞争的延伸。

③ When senior representatives of General Motors of the United States, BSF of Germany and Hitachi Electric of Japan talked about their investment in Pudong, they all pointed to Pudong's geographical advantage, good investment environment and the high quality of local enterprises as Pudong's attractions for their respective firms in their global strategy. In just a few years, along with the launch of investment projects by transnationals, so many world's first class and most dynamic and vital industries have steeled in Pudong. At the same time, the global sales and after-sales service network of the investing transnationals have extended to China. This is an extension of global market competitions.

④目前在浦东的前200家强强联姻企业中,具有自我设计和开发能力的虽然不多,但中方大约有200名副总经理、1 000名部门经理、3 000名高中级工程技术人员、30 000名熟练工人正在一边干,一边学。这是支撑浦东产业高地的人才基础。这些企业和人才,正以其产业关联性和协作关系,最终带动长江流域乃至全国数千家企业,面向国内、国际两个市场,进行一体化生产和销售,使浦东成为溶中国现代产业于世界经济主流的龙头和纽带。

④ Currently, among Pudong's 200 biggest joint ventures, not many have independent designing and developing capabilities. However, on the Chinese side, about 200 deputy managing directors, 1,000 division managers, 3,000 senior and intermediate-level engineers and technologists and 30,000 skilled workers have been learning on the job. This is the talent resource foundation for sustaining Pudong's industrial leading position. These enterprises and talents, through production-related association and cooperation, are expected to boost thousands of enterprises in the Yangtze River Valley, as well as in other parts of the country, engaging in integrated production and sales for both domestic and international markets. By doing so, Pudong will function as a leader and bridge to integrate China's modern industry with the mainstream of the world's economy.

6.3 What's Next for Nuclear Power?

核电将何去何从?

① To most of us, nuclear is an all-or-nothing word. Nuclear war is unthinkable. Nuclear weapons must never be used. Nuclear power plants must be perfectly safe. Nuclear meltdown is the end of the world. "Going nuclear" means you've hit the fatal button, and there's no turning back.

①我们无法使核电免于灾难。但我们能让它更安全。对于绝大多数人来说,核是一个非此即彼寓意极端的词。核战争是无法想象的。核武器必须永远禁用。核电站必须绝对安全。核反应堆核心熔毁的灾难就是世界末日。"发展核"就意味着你按下了致命的按钮,没有回头路了。

② The crisis in Japan is teaching us that this isn't true. Nuclear safety, like nuclear doom, is never certain. Too many things can go wrong. And then, just when catastrophe seems inevitable, things can go right. Our challenge in managing the current crisis, and in preparing for the next one, is to broaden our options. We can't anticipate or prevent every scenario. But we can give ourselves a fighting chance.

②日本的核危机让我们知道并非如此。核安全,如同核末日一样,都不是绝对的。有太多的事情可能出错。而接下来,就在灾难似乎无法避免的时候,事情又可以向着正确的方向发展。在处理眼下的危机以及为下一次危机做好准备的过程中,我们面临的挑战是要增加我们的选择。我们无法预料或者阻止每一次事故的发生。但我们可以让自己有抗争的机会。

③ Nuclear industry likes to think failure isn't an option. It builds power plant according to a principle called "defense in depth." Under this principle, as articulated by the Nuclear Energy Agency, "consecutive and independent levels of protection would all have to fail" before harm could happen. But the levels of protection at Fukushima weren't really independent. They were all

③核行业不喜欢考虑失败的可能。他们根据所谓"纵深防御"的原则来修建核电站。按核能机构的表述,依据该原则,只有当"连续且互相独立的各级保护全部失灵"后才会出现损害。但福岛的各级保护并不是真正相

taken out by the same chain of events. The quake triggered the tsunami, knocking out the diesel generators. The cooling system's power failure led to explosions that knocked out the cooling system's conduits. The overhead reactors produced hydrogen explosions that blew off the roofs of the reactor buildings, exposing spent-fuel pools to the atmosphere. (Slate, Mar. 16, 2011)

互独立。它们都被同一串事件摧毁。地震引发了海啸,摧毁了柴油发电机。冷却系统的断电导致爆炸,破坏了冷却系统的管道。过热的反应堆产生了氢气爆炸,掀掉了反应堆建筑的顶部,使乏燃料池暴露在空气中。(徐嘉文译)

6.4 Buildings with Minds of Their Own

有头脑的建筑物

① What if architects could build living systems rather than static buildings — dynamic structures that modify their internal and external forms in response to changes in their environment? This provocative idea is making waves in the field of architecture. Houses, for example, might shrink in the winter to reduce surface area and volume, thus cutting heating costs. They could cover themselves to escape the heat of the summer sun or shake snow off the roof in winter. Skyscrapers could alter their aerodynamic profiles, swaying slightly to distribute increased loads during hurricanes. Office buildings could reconfigure themselves to improve ventilation.

① 要是建筑师能创造出活的而非静止不动的建筑物——这些动态结构可根据环境变化而改变其内部和外部形态——会是怎样的情形呢?这个大胆的设想正冲击着建筑学领域。比方说,房子冬季可以缩小,以减少面积和容积,从而降低取暖费用。这种房子能遮蔽自己,以躲避夏日的骄阳,或者在冬天抖落房顶的积雪。摩天大楼遇到飓风时可进行小幅度摇摆以改变自身空气动力外形,分散增加的负荷。写字楼可以改换自身的外形,以改善通风条件。

② Such "responsive architecture" would depend on two sorts of technology: control systems capable of deciding what to do, and structural components able to change the building's shape as required. Architects have been working to improve the control systems in buildings for many years, but shape-shifting technology is at a much earlier stage of development.

② 这种"敏感建筑"将依赖于两种技术:能决定要进行何种操作的控制系统,以及能根据需要改变建筑形状的结构组件。多年来建筑师们一直致力于改进建筑物的控制系统,但是变形技术却处于发展的早期阶段。

③ One approach being pursued by researchers is to imitate nature. Many natural constructions, including spiders' webs and cell membranes, are "tensegrity systems" — robust structures made up of many interconnected elements which can be manipulated to change shape without losing their structural integrity. "These structures can bend and twist, but no element in the structure bends and twists," says Robert Skelton of the Structural Systems and Control Laboratory at the University of California in San Diego. "It's the architecture of life."

③ 研究者们所采用的一个方法就是模仿大自然。包括蜘蛛网和细胞膜在内的很多自然构造都是"张拉整体结构"——这种坚实的结构由很多互相联系的元素构成,可通过操纵来改变形状,却不会失去结构的整体性。"这些结构可以弯曲变形,"加州大学圣迭戈分校结构系统和控制实验室的罗伯特·斯凯尔顿如是说。"这是生命建筑学。"

④ While Dr. Skelton is working on solving the engineering equations associated with tensegrity systems, Tristan Destree Sterk at the Office for Robotic Architectural Media & the Bureau for Responsive Architecture, an architectural practice based in

④ 当斯凯尔顿博士在研究如何解决与张拉整体系统相关的工程学方程之时,加拿大温哥华的一个建筑实践团体"自动化建筑媒体办公室与敏

Vancouver, Canada, has begun to construct prototypes of shape-changing " building envelopes" based on tensegrity structures. Lightweight skeletal frameworks, composed of rods and wires and controlled by pneumatic " muscles", serve as the walls of a building; adjusting their configuration changes the building's shape. Mr. Sterk is also developing the " brain" needed to control such a building based on information from internal and external sensors. (*The Economist Nov.* 30, 2006)

感建筑局”的特里斯坦·德艾斯特雷·施特克以开始建造基于拉张整体结构原理的会变形的“建造封套”模型。由杆子和电线组成并受风动“肌肉”控制的轻质框架被用作建筑的墙体;调整其结构就能改变建筑物形状。施特克先生也在开发基于内外传感器所发信息控制这种建筑物所需的“大脑”。(武军 译)

6.5 推荐读物

(1)方梦之,英语科技文体:范式与翻译,国防工业出版社2011年版。

(2)李维颐,科技翻译工作手册,天津科学技术出版社1986年版。

(3)清华大学《英汉技术词典》编写委员会,英汉技术词典,国防工业出版社1978年版。

(4)王爱君,科技英语阅读与翻译教程,新时代出版社2004年版。

(5)王知津,新编英汉科技缩略语大辞典,科学技术文献出版社1995年版。

(6)吴光华,英汉科技大辞典,上海交通大学出版社1998年版。

(7)谢小苑,科技英语翻译技巧与实践,国防工业出版社2008年版。

(8)英语文摘,英语世界等杂志。

7 课后练习

7.1 分析题

(1)试用所译和比读材料分析转译及其特点。

(2)试用本课的比读材料分析工农业英语的句式翻译特点。

(3)品读翻译窍门了解工业英语的全译策略。

7.2 实训题

7.2.1 政府工作报告

深化农村改革,增强农村发展活力。坚持和完善农村基本经营制度,健全覆盖耕地、林地、草原等家庭承包经营制度。有序推进农村土地管理制度改革。探索建立耕地保护补偿机制。继续推进农村综合改革。解决13亿中国人的吃饭问题始终是头等大事,任何时候都不能掉以轻心。我们有信心也有能力办好这件大事。

7.2.2 An international seed bank is being set up in the Arctic

① If catastrophe were to befall humanity — be it plague, nuclear war or an asteroid striking the Earth — what provision could be made for the survivors? This week work began on a project to re-establish agriculture should such a calamity occur. On a remote Arctic island, a vault is being dug to house the seeds of up to 3m different crops, as part of plans to protect food supplies across the world.

② The Svalbard International Seed Vault, as the facility is called, will cost the Norwegian government, which is paying for it, about $3m. Eventually it will contain samples of every known crop variety that can be grown from seed, from the tropics to the highest latitudes.

7.3 思考题

(1) 探析音译法在工农业术语翻译中的应用。
(2) 归纳工农业英语中否定句的种类和汉译方法。
(3) 归纳工农业缩略语的特点及翻译方法。
(4) 试用功能翻译理论分析工农业翻译的方法。
(5) 试析形译法在工农业英语翻译之中的应用。
(6) 分析工农业英语中非限定动词的应用和翻译方法。
(7) 工农业英语翻译中词义引申有哪些类别?
(8) 试从美学角度分析工农业英语翻译策略。
(9) 举例说明工农业英语翻译中的虚实互化现象的应用有哪些?
(10) 公式的翻译方法有哪些?
(11) 工农业翻译中零翻译的使用有哪些?
(12) 分析工农业英语中名词结构的翻译方法有哪些?
(13) 分析科技论文图表翻译的技巧。

第 13 课 企事业单位

导 译

企事业单位中的企业单位通常指从事生产、运输、贸易等经济活动的部门，如公司、工厂、矿山、铁路等；事业单位通常指将国家为了社会公益目的，由国家机关举办或者其他组织利用国有资产举办的，从事教科文卫等活动的社会服务组织，如学校、医院、科研院所、体育机构、新闻出版等。两种单位类型都包含单位简介、名称、职称头衔等信息，也是翻译中不可或缺的内容。因此，企事业单位全译的重点在于名称、职称头衔和单位简介。

汉语企事业单位的名称概括性强，表意较笼统，便于搭配；而英语企事业单位名称强调简明性、逻辑性、紧凑性和客观性，词汇搭配要求较严。英汉双语搭配及用词上的区分是企事业单位简介全译的难点。此外，充分认识到中外企业文化和价值观的差异也十分必要。国内单位通过简介展示形象，意在获得读者的信赖；英语单位简介则以读者为目标，更强调单位与读者之间的利益关系，所以汉语单位简介表达宽泛笼统，英语简介表达丰富精细，这是翻译时应考虑的问题。

练笔 1 课前练笔

1.1 上海宇宙礼品工业有限公司

① 本公司创立于 1995 年，是一家外商独资企业，专业从事玩具礼品相关产品的开发、生产及出口销售。随着业务的不断扩大，竭诚欢迎专业人士加入我们的行列。

② 外贸业务助理

③ 大学以上学历，英语、外贸等相关专业，一年以上国际贸易经验，勤奋好学，有独立工作能力。

④ 机械工程师

⑤ 大学以上学历,机械制造专业,掌握自动化电脑设计,英语流利,至少具有机械设计两年经验,熟悉塑料和电器制造。

⑥ 船务

⑦ 大学国际贸易或相关专业学位,精通英语,三年进出口贸易和船务经验,熟悉海关条例。

⑧ 地址:上海虹中路639号 邮编201103

⑨ 电子邮箱:hr@cosmos-gift. com

1.2 Risk of Investment

① A: Well, I'm thinking of establishing a food joint venture of big scale.

② B: That's great. We have so many favorable conditions for you to invest in China.

③ A: Yes, China is a big country with a large population, rich resources and a comparatively low level of wages and salaries. However, the problem is that we're still doubtful of investment in China.

④ B: Let me put your mind at ease. The way I see it, a joint venture means, primary, less taxation and more benefits for the investors.

⑤ A: That sounds good.

⑥ B: Well, a joint venture means preferred treatment for the investors. A joint venture pays less income tax or even no income tax at all under certain conditions in the first five profit making years.

⑦ A: Profit-making years? You mean the years of production?

⑧ B: No. I mean the years when you make a profit. What's more, all lawful rights and interests of foreign investors are protected by Chinese law.

1.3 Aloha Freight Forwarders

① Aloha Freight Forwarders handles in excess of 300 shipments per day between Hawaii and the Mainland. We handle all types and sizes of shipments, from small packages to full container loads. We have the expertise to handle specialized cargo such as hazardous materials and over-sized equipment on flat beds. Ocean departures from Los Angeles to the Islands are twice per week. Departures from Honolulu to Los Angeles are weekly.

② Freight received in Los Angeles by Friday afternoon will sail to all Islands early Saturday morning directly from Oalu by the following Friday. The neighbor islands are delivered by the following Tuesday or Wednesday.

③ We can pickup or receive multiple shipments from multiple shippers and perform detailed consolidations, and if required, load the freight in sequence per instructions. We will also perform distribution to multiple consignees of shipper loaded containers. We currently perform consolidation for numerous customers and are very familiar with the unique requirements for this type of service.

④ Our ocean charges are usually based on the cube or dimensions of the freight. As a customer, you should have those measurements or the cubic feet before we can give you an estimate. There are several ways to obtain a rate estimate. You can call our office with the dimensions, origin, and destination, and we will be glad to give you a quote.

批评 2 课前批评

2.1 清华大学 Tsinghua University

清华大学是中国著名的高等学府，是中国培养高级科学技术人才和发展科学技术的重要基地之一。清华大学创建于1911年，前身清华学堂是一所留美预备学校。辛亥革命后更名为清华学校，1925年开始办大学部，1928年更名为国立清华大学。抗日战争爆发后，清华大学南迁长沙，后迁至昆明，与北京大学、南开大学联合组成国立西南联合大学。1952年进行院系调整，清华大学成为一所多学科性工业大学，重点为国家培养工程技术人才，被誉为"红色工程师的摇篮"。

Tsinghua University, one of the renowned institutions of higher learning in China, is an important base both for bringing up senior professionals of science and technology in China and for promoting the progress of Chinese science and technology. Founded in 1911, it started as Tsinghua Xuetang, a school preparing students for studies in the US. After the 1911 Revolution, it was renamed Tsinghua School and then enrolled its first college students in 1925. In 1928, the school was renamed National Tsinghua University. During the Anti-Japanese War, the university moved south to Changsha, and then to Kunming, where it became part of Southwest Associated University by merging with Beijing University and Nankai University. In the nationwide reorganization of institutions of higher learning in 1952, Tsinghua University became a university of engineering with multiple disciplines, focusing on training qualified engineering personnel, and thus it was reputed as " the Cradle of Red Engineers". (许建平 译)

2.2 Company of Baby Products 婴儿用品公司

① Eddie: Our company is a specialized manufacturer and supplier of baby products. It was founded in 1978. We have been engaged in baby products for 30 years.

② Nathan: I think I have come to the right place.

③ Eddie: What line of business are you in ?

① 埃迪：我们公司是婴儿用品的专业生产厂家和供应商。创建于1978年。我们经营婴儿用品有30多年了。

② 纳森：看来我来对了。

③ 埃迪：贵公司主要经营什

么?

④ Nathan: We mainly deal in import and export trade. We handle only brand name goods and trade marked goods.

④ 纳森:我们主要做进出口贸易。只经营名牌产品和有注册商标的产品。

⑤ Eddie: Do you handle baby products?

⑤ 埃迪:贵公司经营婴儿用品吗?

⑥ Nathan: Yes. But we are quite new in the line of baby products.

⑥ 纳森:是的。但是我们做婴儿用品这行不久。

⑦ Eddie: We are an authorized exporter of baby products.

⑦ 埃迪:我们是经政府批准的婴儿用品出口公司。

⑧ Nathan: Do you have any business connections in America?

⑧ 纳森:贵公司在美国是否有业务联系?

⑨ Eddie: Yes. We have three distributors and two agencies in Atlanta and Boston.

⑨ 埃迪:有。在亚特兰大和波士顿有三个分销商和两个代理机构。

⑩ Nathan: Our company is based in New York. I wonder if you are interested in doing business with us.

纳森:⑩ 我们的公司设在纽约。不知贵公司是否有兴趣与我们建立贸易关系。(杨智敏、陈红锐 译)

知识 3 全译知识 换译

换译,即交换式全译,指根据语用和语义的需要交换原语单位的全译方法。换译旨在准确传达原文语义、追求译文通顺流畅,不仅符合译语的语法规范和表达习惯,而且与原文达到最大限度的相似,易于为读者理解和接受。换译的原则是:换形不换意,即形式交换,而意义力求不变。换译单位有词、短语、小句和复句。

3.1 词的换译

词的换译,指根据语用和语义的需要交换原语词的换译方法。常见的有词类换译,成分换译,词换译作短语和小句,词与词前后位置的换译,等等。如:

① 我们常常坐在海滩上,把脚趾插进沉重而潮湿的沙里,看又大又慢、有绿有白的碎浪滚滚而来,脑子里尽在遐想。It had become a custom with us to sit on the beach and dig our toes into the wet heavy sand and then watch the big blue and white slowmoving waves crash into shore while our minds wandered off to some wild and fanciful thoughts.

"常常"换译作了英语小句 It had become a custom,显得更书面化;原文的主语"我们"因"常常"的变故而换作了英语的宾格 us,做了 with 的介词宾语,成分有变;为把表性质的形容词"大、绿、白"集中放在表临时特征的形容词"慢"之前共同修饰"浪",英译对"慢"与"绿"的前后顺序做了互换,以符合英语表达。

3.2 短语换译

短语换译，指根据语用和语义的需要交换原语短语的换译方法。常见的有动静换译，短语与词、小句、复句、句群的换译，等等。如：

② A little of everything and nothing at all. 凡事都浅尝辄止，终将一事无成。

③ It is the coldest day, they say, since 1812, but the people have stood in the streets all night. 据说这是自1812年以来最冷的一天，但人们已在街上站了整整一夜。

例②是英谚，简洁明了，汉译要将其意合换作形合，由两个短语换译作了两个小句。例③插入语 they say 与 It is the coldest day 是第一次换译，时间状语 since 1812 与 is the coldest day 是第二次换译，have stood 与 in the streets 是第三次换译。

3.3 小句换译

小句换译，指根据语用和语义的需要交换原语小句的换译方法。常见的有主被换译，肯否换译，小句与词、短语、复句、句群的换译，陈述、疑问、祈使、感叹四类句型换译，等等。如：

④ 我母亲和我都是耽于梦想的人。My mother and I liked to dream a lot.

⑤ How my friends would laugh if they knew I had come to this!

【原译】：倘若朋友们了解到我如此大的变化，一定会觉得好笑。

【试译】：倘若朋友们知道我已成了这个样子，还不知要怎样取笑我呢！

例④原为判断句，对"我"母子俩作出性质判断，属于静句，英译则处理为描写，属于动句，句型发生了更换。例⑤原译未译出虚拟语气（would laugh）表推测的感情色彩，试译用肯否正反换译（"还不知……呢！"）再现了推测的语用功能。又如：

⑥ Bile is introduced into the duodenum by the bile duct. 胆汁是通过胆道进入十二指肠的。

⑦ Friction can be reduced and the life of the machine prolonged by lubrication. 润滑能减少摩擦，延长机器寿命。

英语被动句的使用率高于汉语，汉语被动句不常见，除用有标被动句外，还用"挨、把、给、叫、让、由、加以、经过、获得、受到、为……所、予以、遭到（受）"等，英语被动句更可换译为汉语的主动句、判断句、无主句、中动句等，以走出被动局面。例⑥译作了判断句，例⑦译作了主动句。

3.4 复句换译

复句换译，指根据语用和语义的需要交换原语复句的换译方法。常见的有复句类型的换译，复句中各小句前后顺序换译，复句与短语、小句、句群的换译，等等。如：

⑧ 买车，车丢了；省钱，钱丢了；自己的一切努力只为别人来欺侮！He lost the rickshaw he had bought, lost the money he had saved. All his efforts ended up in his being bullied and humiliated.

⑨ Not that she had money. She never had money. 并不是她有钱，她从来就未曾富过。

例⑧，原文为多重复句，英译将前面的二重复句如实译出，将最后的小句独立成句，使得原文复句译成了句群。例⑨由句群与复句的换译，语序没变，但译文的单位层次与原文相比有了变化。

4 全译窍门

4.1 “公司”何其多

汉语“公司”较为笼统，一般英译为 company 和 corporation。如：中国国际贸易展览公司 China International Trade Exhibition Company，中国工艺进出口公司 China National Arts Crafts IM/EX Corporation。英语讲求精确性和综合性，firm、house、business、concern、combine、partnership、complex、group、establishment、venture、conglomerate、multinational、transnational、lines、agency、office、system、stores、services、exchange、center 等均表不同性质的“公司”。

Line 通常指轮船、航空、航运等公司，如 Atlantic Container Line 大西洋集装箱海运公司。Agency 通常指代理行性质的公司，如 China Ocean Shipping Agency 中国外轮代理公司。Stores 通常指百货公司，如 Great Universal Stores 大世界百货公司。Associates 指联合公司，如 British Nuclear Associates 英国核子联合公司。System 通常指广播、航空等公司，如 Malaysian Airline System Bhd. 马来西亚航空公司。Office 多与 Head，Branch 连用表示总公司和分公司，如 3M China Limited Guangzhou Branch Office 3M 中国有限公司广州分公司。Services 通常指服务公司，如 Africa-New Zealand Service 非洲—新西兰服务公司。Exchange 和 Center 也可表示公司，如 American Manufacturers Foreign Credit Insurance Exchange 美国制造商出口信用保险公司，Binks（Shanghai）Engineering Exhibition Center，Ltd. 宾克斯(上海)涂装工程设备展示有限公司。

4.2 “厂”家如林

汉语概念概括性强，表意较笼统，搭配较容易，而英语词义精准，搭配较严格。“厂”的翻译即是典型例证。汉译英如：半导体器械厂 Semiconductor Apparatus Plant，保温瓶厂 Thermos Flask Factory，化工厂 Chemical Works，炼油厂 Oil Refinery，毛纺织厂 Woolen Mill，船舶修理厂 Ship Repair Yard，啤酒厂 Beer Brewery。

英译汉通常要根据英语“厂”的性质和具体环境选取相应的词。通常情况下 factory 译作“厂”，如：Transistor Factory 晶体管厂，Insecticide Factory 农药厂，Pottery and Porcelain Factory 陶瓷厂。Plant 和 works 有时也译作“厂”，如：Auto Repair and Assembly Plant 汽车修配厂，Artificial Fiber Plant 人造纤维厂，Milk Processing Plant 乳品加工厂，Automobile Works 汽车制造厂，Foundry Works 铸造厂，Steel Works 炼钢厂等。Mill 也可指某一性质的工厂，如：Timber Mill 木材厂，Woolen Sweater Mill 羊毛衫厂，Printing and Dyeing Mill 印染厂。

4.3 称谓头衔译如其分

汉语在概括词前加上表区别特征的词可以构成新词。汉译英方面，如“工程师、经理、教练”前面加上表区别特征的“总”字，可以形成像“总工程师、总经理、总教练”，英译时则每个词都用新词表述，三者分别译成 chief engineer，general manager 和 head coach。

由于汉语表达较为模糊，为词语搭配创造了有利条件，vice president，deputy manager 和 associate professor 可分别译作“副总裁、副经理、副教授”。汉语“副”字具有很强的搭配能力，意思虽较模糊笼统，分别加在“总裁、经理、教授”之前构成新词。

4.4 单位简介的译法

单位简介即对单位作简单介绍，涉及企事业单位的性质、规模、投资、产品、服务、工作、企业文化、企业特点等。简介翻译属于信息型翻译，具有广告的特征，旨在对外宣传，重在传达信息的真实性，注重接受者的反应。具体来说，应关注中国企业价值观和语言风格的差异。

汉语单位简介较注重企业的价值层面，着重展示企业形象，突出企业至上，给读者树立强大可靠的形象，以获得消费者信赖。而英语集中展示产品的消费价值，即企业与消费者的利益关系，强调简明性、逻辑性、紧凑性和客观性，大量使用专业词汇。

汉语四字排比表达企业产品的特点、服务的质量、单位性质等。英译时则要再处理，既要达原文之寓意，又不失英语之地道。如：造型美观 beautiful appearance model，质量上乘 super quality，设计新颖 stylish design，服务周到 courteous service，收费合理 reasonable prices。

反过来，英译汉可充分利用汉语的四字格，以求寓意简明，工整上口。如：win a world-wide reputation 誉满全球，enjoy a high reputation at home and abroad 享誉中外，have a long historical standing 历史悠久，have a reliable reputation 信誉可靠。

5 话题词汇

5.1 单位名称

保安服务公司 Security Service Company
点子公司 Consultancy Company
电冰箱有限公司 Refrigerator Co., Ltd.
电风扇工业公司 Electric Fan Industry Company
电子技术开发公司 Electronic Technology Development Co.
电子器材公司 Electronic Equipment & Materials Corporation
对外服务公司 Foreign Service Company
对外经济发展公司 Foreign Economic Development Company
对外贸易公司 Foreign Trade Company
饭店集团有限公司 Hotel Group Ltd.
房产投资有限公司 Realty & Investment Company Ltd.
房地产开发公司 Real Estate Development Company
纺织企业集团 Textile Enterprise Group
服务公司 Service Company
钢铁公司 Iron and Steel Company
工程承包有限公司 Project Contracting Co., Ltd.
工艺美术品公司 Arts and Crafts Corporation
广告公司 Advertising Company
国货有限公司 China Products Company Ltd.
国际贸易展览公司 International Trade Exhibition Company
海外电信公司 Overseas Telcos
化纤工业集团公司 Chemical Fiber Industry Group
计算机集团公司 Computers Group Co.

技贸公司 Technology and Trade Co., Ltd.
建筑工程公司 Construction Engineering Co.
建筑设计合资公司 Building Design Joint Venture Corporation
进出口公司 Import & Export Co.
旅游公司 Travel Corporation
毛纺织有限公司 Woolen Textile Co., Ltd.
贸易有限公司 Trading Company Ltd.
能源开发公司 Energy Development Corporation
农贸公司 Agricultural Materials Company
气象服务公司 Meteorological Service Company
汽车企业集团 Automobile Enterprise Group
时装有限公司 Fashion Company Ltd.
实业集团公司 Industrial Group Corporation
水产品有限公司 Aquatic Products Company Ltd.
私人廉价航空公司 private budget airline
私人直接投资公司 private equity firm
塑料制品有限公司 Plastics Products Co., Ltd.
物业服务公司 realty service enterprise
物业管理公司 realty management enterprise
物业开发公司 property developer
系统工程公司 System Engineering Corporation
希望工程小学 Project Hope Primary School
饮料有限公司 Beverage Company Ltd.
针织有限公司 Knitting Company Ltd.
证券公司 Securities Company
制衣实业公司 Garments Industrial Company
咨询公司 Consulting Company
academy of design 设计学院
academy of fine arts 美术学院
AT&T 美国电话电报公司
brain center 神经医学中心
Britannia Airways 大不列颠航空公司
cancer control and prevention center 癌症防治中心
cerebral vascular clinic 脑血管中心
Chemical Engineering Consulting Corporation 化工工程咨询公司
children's hospital 儿童医院
China Eastern 中国东方航空公司
college of agriculture 农学院
college of science and engineering 理工科大学
comprehensive university 综合性大学
conservatory of music 音乐学院
Continuing Education School 成人教育学院
Delta Airlines 达美航空公司
drug store 药店
Electrical Machinery Manufacturing Company 电力机械制造公司
Feed Technological Development Group 饲料技术开发集团
General Electric 通用电气公司
General Oil Company 石油总公司
health center for women and children 妇幼保健院
health evaluation center 健康检查中心
Household Electrical Appliances Co., Ltd. 家用电器有限公司
hyperbaric oxygen therapy center 高压氧治疗中心
institute of traditional Chinese medicine 中医院
Instrument and Equipment Company 仪器设备公司
International Advertising and Exposition Co., Ltd. 国际广告展览有限公司
International Commercial Service Company 国际商业服务公司
International Container Co., Ltd. 国际集装箱有限公司
International Economic & Technological Cooperation Corporation 国际经济技术合作公司
International Economic Development Corporation 国际经济开发公司
International Engineering Group 国际工程集团
International Investment Company Ltd. 国际投资有限公司
International Information Processing Co., Ltd. 国际信息处理有限公司
International Leasing Company 国际租赁公司
International Scientific and Technological Consulting Corporation 国际科技咨询公司
key university 重点大学
maternity hospital 产科医院
medical cosmetic center 医学美容中心
medical school 医学院
mental hospital 精神病院
New Building Materials Supply Company 新型建筑材料供应公司
Non-Governmental Transport Information Center 民

办交通信息中心
parenting school 育儿学校
pet clinic 宠物医院
physical education college 体育学院
plastic surgery hospital 整形外科医院
Plastics and Leather Industrial Company 塑料皮革工业公司
Procter & Gamble 宝洁公司
private institutions of higher learning 民办高校
polyclinic 综合医院
quarantine station 防疫站
rest home 休养所
Royal Dutch Shell 英荷壳牌集团
sanatorium 疗养院
school for the aged 老年大学
secondary specialized (technical) school for adults 成人中等专科学校
stomatological hospital 口腔医院
teachers' college 师范学院
teachers' college for vocational studies 教师进修学院
Technical Development and Consultancy Co. 技术开发咨询公司
Telephonic Technology Development Service Co. 电话技术开发服务公司
Telecommunications Development Co. 电信开发公司
tuberculosis hospital 结核病医院
tumor hospital 肿瘤医院
United Securities Co. Ltd. 联合证券有限公司
Wal-Mart Stores 沃尔玛公司
weight reducing 肥胖防治中心

5.2 职位职称

办公室副主任 deputy director of office
办公室主任 director of office
部门经理 section manager
财务经理 fund manager
财务主管 controller
采购员 purchaser
测试工程师 test engineer
常务理事 managing director
出口经理 export manager
董事长 chairman of the board
副总经理 vice general manager
高级会计师 senior accountant
高级经济师 senior economist
高级软件工程师 senior software engineer
公关部经理 PR manager
技术支持经理 technical support manager
技术文员 technical assistant
进口经理 import manager
经纪人 broker
科长 section chief
科员 clerk
领班 captain
品质经理 QA manager
软件工程师 software engineer
首席执行官 chief executive officer
售货员 sales clerk
售后服务主管 customer service supervisor
售后服务专员 customer service executive
推销员 salesperson
外汇部核算员 F. X. settlement clerk
外汇部职员 F. X. clerk
网站营运经理 web operations supervisor
维护工程师 maintenance engineer
文书打字兼秘书 clerk typist & secretary
文字处理操作员 word processing operator
销售部经理 sales manager
销售代表 sales representative
行政董事 managing director
营业部经理 business manager
执行董事 executive director
执行副总裁 executive vice-president
执行主席 executive chairman
主任 chairman; director
主席团执行主席 executive chairman of the presidium
助理经理 assistant manager
总裁 president
总工程师 chief engineer
总经理 general manager
总经理秘书 general manager's secretary

总经理助理 general manager's assistant
academician 院士
assistant engineer 助理工程师
assistant experiment engineer 助理实验师
assistant doctor 医士
assistant lecturer 助理讲师
assistant pharmacist 药士
associate professor 副教授
associate research fellow 副研究员
associate senior doctor 副主任医师
chief engineer 总工程师
chief executive officer 首席执行官
chief secretary 主任秘书
class adviser 班主任
dean of college 学院院长
dean of general affairs 总务长
dean of studies 教务主任
dean of the faculty 系主任
dentist-in-charge 牙科主治医师
deputy secretary-general 副秘书长
deputy dean 副院长
director of research institute 研究所所长
director of the hospital 院长
division chairman 学部主任
doctor 医师
ESL teacher 第二外语教师
exchange scholar 交换学者
executive chairman 执行主席
experiment engineer 实验师
general manager 总经理
gynecologist-in-charge 妇科主治医师
head coach 总教练
headmaster of primary school 小学校长
head nurse 护士长
head of the department of medical administration 医务部主任
honorary president 名誉校长
honorary professor 名誉教授
instructor 讲师
laboratory technician 实验员
managing director 常务理事
nurse 护士
nurse-in-charge 主管护士
nurse practitioner 护师
nutritionist 营养学家
oculist-in-charge 眼科主治医师
pharmacist 药师
pharmacist-in-charge 主管药师
pharmaceutical sales representative 医药代表
physician-in-charge 内科主治医师
physical therapist 理疗师
physician 主治医师
president of university 大学校长
principal of secondary school 中学校长
professor 教授
professor of medicine 讲课主任医师
professor of nursing 主管护师
professor of pediatrics 儿科主任医师
professor of pharmacy 主任医师
professor of treatment 医疗主任医师
research associate 助理研究员
secretary-general 总干事
senior engineer 高级工程师
senior experiment engineer 高级实验师
senior lecturer 高级讲师
stenographer 速记员
surgeon-in-charge 外科主治医师
teacher of special grade 特级教师
technical designer 技术设计员
therapist 临床医学家
trustee of board of trustees 校董事会董事
tutor 家教

5.3 单位简介

仓储企业 storeroom enterprise
房地产企业 real-estate enterprise
分公司 branch office
分权式组织结构 holding company structure
高科技工业园区 high-tech industrial park
公司地址 company address
公司名称 company name
工业企业 industrial enterprises
工业区 industrial zone
工厂位置 factory location

国有企业 state-owned enterprise
集权式组织结构 gnitary structure
集团公司 group
计算机服务及软件企业 computer services and software enterprise
建筑业企业 building industry
交通运输业企业 transportation
金融企业 finance enterprise
竞争力优势 competitive edge
竞争能力 competitive power
居民服务企业 resident service enterprise
跨国公司 multinational corporation
合资企业 joint venture
联营公司 affiliated company
零售业企业 retail business
民营企业 private enterprise
农林牧渔 farm; wilds; forage grass, fishing
批发业 sales in bulk
商号 firm
商务及科技服务企业 business and technical service enterprise
外资企业 foreign-funded enterprise
文体、娱乐企业 cultural entertainment enterprise
信息传输企业 information transaction enterprise
邮政业企业 postal service
展示 presentation
制造商 manufacturer
住宿和餐馆业企业 hotel and restaurant
子公司 subsidiary company
总公司 headquarters, head office
租赁企业 loans enterprise
Advertising Dept. 广告部
Customer Service Dept. 客服部
Engineering Dept. 工程部
Equipment Dept. 设备部
Financial Dept. 财务部
General Affairs Dept. 总务部
Human Resources Dept. 人力资源部
Import and Export Dept. 进出口部
Marketing Dept. 销售部
Management Information System 资讯部
Manufacturing Dept. 制造部
Material Dept. 资材部
Personnel Dept. 人事部
Planning Dept. 企划部
Product Development Dept. 产品开发部
Public Relations Dept. 公共关系部
Purchasing Dept. 采购部
Quality Assurance Dept. 品保部
Research and Development Dept. 研发部
Sales Dept. 营业部
affiliated organization 分支机构
business agency 管理机构
business failure 企业倒闭
business goodwill 企业信誉
business mortality 企业倒闭率
close corporation 封闭型公司
combination law 企业联营法
company incorporated 注册公司
company image 公司形象
corporate bond dividend 公司债券红利
corporate charter 公司执照
corporate entity 法人实体
corporate seal 公司印章
corporation income tax 公司所得税
corporation law 公司法
corporate regulations 公司章程
corporate combination 公司合并
corporate juridical person 法人
debt-laden company 债台高筑公司
dummy corporation 虚拟公司
employee involvement 员工参与
entrepreneur 企业家
entrepreneurial mentality 企业家精神
entrepreneurial organization 经营的组织
entrepreneurship 企业家身份
family business 家族企业
foreign branch office 国外办事处
foreign direct investment 国外直接投资
foreign-affiliated company 外资公司
incorporated business 法人企业
incorporation 组成公司
incorporator 公司创办人
labor-intensive enterprise 劳动密集型企业
limited company(股份)有限公司
limited liability company 有限责任公司

limited liability partnership 有限责任合伙公司
listed enterprise 上市企业
partnership 合伙企业
private financial institution 民间金融机构
publicly-held corporation 公开招股公司
publicly-traded company 公开上市公司
small and medium-sized firm 中小企业
start-up company 新办公司
sole proprietor company 独资公司
subordinate unit 下属单位
teamwork 团队合作
unlimited liability company 无限责任公司
unsound corporation 财产上有问题的公司
visionary company 理想的公司
well-handled business 管理良好的企业

5.4 缩略语

非营利 NFP
非上市有限公司 PLC
分公司 BO
工厂 FTY
国际投资公司 IIB
国有企业 SOE
公司 Co.
股份公司 Jnt. stk
股份有限公司 Incor.
合资公司 JV
经营单位 BU
控制的外国公司 CFC
跨国公司 MNE
企业 Cpr.
私人有限公司 PLC
私营企业 POEs
外商独资企业 WOFE
外商投资企业 FIE
有限公司 Co., Ltd.
中小企业 SME
Atty. 代理人
AVP 协理
CBO 商务长
C. Eng. 特准执业工程师
CEO 首席执行官
CFA 特许财务分析师
CFO 首席财务官
CMA 注册管理会计师
COO 首席运营官
CPA 注册会计师
CTO 首席技术官
D. Eng. 工学博士
Dept. 部门
Dir. 董事
Dlr. 经营商
DRI 负责人
ENG 工程部
GM 总经理
HRD 人资部
Matl. 资材部
MBA 工商管理硕士
MFG 制造部
Mgr. 经理
MIS 资讯部
Pres. 董事长
Ptnr. 股东
Pur. 采购部
QA 品保部
R&D 研发部
VP 副总裁

体悟 6 比读体悟

6.1 福信公司

Fuxin Company

① 福建福信一珍生物工程有限公

① Fujian Fuxin Yizhen Biological Engineering Company

司是由福建省洪山企业集团公司与香港福信投资有限公司合资兴办的高科技企业，注册资本2000万元人民币。公司生产基地位于国家级科技园区洪山公园内。公司拥有雄厚的技术力量，大、中专以上的技术、管理人才占员工总数的百分之三十以上，并与国内多家科研机构建立了紧密型的合作关系。于若木等著名的营养学家、生物学家、医学专家受聘担任公司的高级顾问。

Limited is a high-tech joint venture of Fujian Hongshan Enterprise Group Company and Hong Kong Fuxin Investment Company Limited, with registered capital of 20 million RMB. The manufacturing base locates in the Hongshan Park — a state-level sci-technical park. The company is strong in technical resources, and more than 30% of its staff are technical and management talents with educational background above polytechnic school or college. Meanwhile, the company has established close cooperative relationships with many domestic research institutions. Many well-known nutritionists (such as Yu Ruomu), biologists and medical experts are invited as company's senior consultants.

② 公司环境优美，设备先进，拥有中国第一条年产30吨核酸花粉合剂的现代化生产线。第二、第三条生产线亦将陆续建成。

② The company is in beautiful surroundings. It boasts of China's first modern streamline with a yearly output of 30 Ton nucleic pollen mixtures. The second and third streamline is about to accomplish.

③ 公司以"惟公有福，惟诚有信"的福信企业精神和"团结、拼搏、务实、创新、奉献"的洪山集团企业精神为动力，锐意进取，蒸蒸日上。

③ Treasuring the spirit of honesty, unity, realism, innovation and sacrifice, the company is advancing with vigor and enthusiasm and will become more and more prosperous. (吴中东、宫玉波 译)

6.2 大学聘约合同

Contract of Employment of a University

① 南方师范大学外语系(聘方)聘请帕特里奇先生(受聘方)为外语系英语教师。双方本着友好合作的精神，同意签订并遵守本合同。

① The Foreign Languages Department of the South Normal University (the engaging party) has engaged Mr. Partridge (the engaged party) as a teacher of English. The two parties in the spirit of friendship and cooperation have entered into an Agreement to sign and to comply with the present contract.

② 1. 聘期定为一年，自2002年9月1日到职之日起至2003年9月1日止。

② 1. The term of service is one year, that is, from Sept. 1, 2002, the first day of the term of office, to Sept. 1, 2003, the last day of the term of office.

③ 2. 受聘方的工作任务，经双方协商确定如下：

③ 2. By mutual consultation the work of the engaged party is decided as follows:

④ (1) 担任英语师资、研究生、进修生的培训工作；

④ (1) Training teachers of English, graduate students and students taking refresher courses;

⑤ (2) 从事高年级英语教学，指导学生开展英语课外活动；

⑤ (2) Conducting senior English classes and advising students on extra-curricular activities in the language;

⑥ (3) 编写英语教材和补充读物，以及进行英语录音等工作；

⑥ (3) Compiling English textbooks and supplementary teaching materials, and undertaking tape recordings and other work connected with the language;

⑦ (4) 每周工作量为：18 ~ 20 课时。

⑦ (4) Having from 18 up to 22 teaching periods a week;

⑧ 3. 受聘方的工作时间为每周5天,每天8小时。受聘方按照中国政府的法定节假日放假,并按学校规定的寒暑假放假。

⑧ 3. The engaged party works five days a week, eight hours a day. The engaged party will have holidays as legally prescribed by the Chinese Government. The vacation is fixed according to the school calendar.

⑨ 4. 聘方每月支付给受聘方工资人民币2 800元,并为受聘方提供各种待遇。

⑨ 4. The engaging party pays the engaged party a monthly salary of two thousand eight hundred Yuan (Chinese currency) and provides him with various benefits.

⑩ 5. 受聘方在离境、过境或入境时,必须遵守中国政府有关外国人居住、工资福利及旅行等一系列管理规定,并遵守聘方的工作制度。

⑩ 5. The engaged party must observe the regulations of the Chinese Government concerning residence, wages and benefits, and travel for foreigners when entering, leaving and passing through the territory of the country, and must follow the working system of the engaging party.

⑪ 聘方欢迎受聘方在工作中提出意见,并酌情采纳。受聘方遵守聘方的工作制度。

⑪ The engaging party welcomes any suggestions put forward by the engaged party and will take them into consideration so far as circumstances permit. The engaged party will observe the decisions of the engaging party and will do his work in the spirit of active cooperation to accomplish the tasks assigned.

⑫ 6. 双方均不得无故解除合同。聘方如果要求中途解除合同,则除按照待遇条件承担受聘方的有关费用外,须给受聘方增发一个月的工资补偿金,并于一个月内安排受聘方及其家属回国。如果受聘方中途提出辞职,聘方自同意之日起即停发工资,受聘方不再享受各种待遇条件。受聘方及其家属回国的一切费用均由本人自理。

⑫ 6. Neither party shall, without sufficient cause or reason, cancel the contract. If the engaging party finds it imperative to terminate the contract, then, in addition to bearing the corresponding expenses for wages and benefit, it must pay the engaged party one month's extra salary as compensation allowance, and arrange for him and his family to go back to their own country within a month. If the engaged party submits his resignation in the course of his service, the engaging party will stop paying him salary from the day when his resignation is approved by the engaging party, and the engaged party will no longer enjoy the wages and benefits provided. When leaving China, the engaged party and his family will have to pay for expenses.

⑬ 7. 本合同自受聘方到职之日起生效,聘期满,即自行失效。如一方要求延长聘期,必须在合同期满前向对方提出,经双方协商确定后,可另行签约延长聘期合同。

⑬ 7. The present contract comes into effect on the first day of the term of service herein stipulated and ceases to be effective at its expiration. If either party wishes to renew the contract, the other party shall be notified before it expires. Upon agreement by both parties through consultation, a new contract may be signed.

⑭ 8. 本合同在执行中如有争议,由双方协商解决。

⑭ 8. Should any matter which is not provided for in this contract arise during the course of its performance, it should be settled through consultation by the two parties.

⑮ 9. 本合同用中文和英文两种文字写成。两种文字具有同等效力。

⑮ 9. The present contract is done in Chinese and English, both versions being equally valid. (石定乐、蔡蔚 译)

6.3 Citigroup, Inc.

Citigroup, Inc. was founded in 1812 and is based in New York. Citigroup, Inc., together with its subsidiaries, provides a range of financial products and services to consumer and corporate customers in the United States and internationally. The company's Global Consumer Group segment offers various banking, lending, insurance, and investment products and services through its branches, automated teller machines (ATMs), and automated lending machines (ALMs), the Internet, telephone, and mail. As of December 31,2007, this segment operated through a network of 8,527 branches, approximately 20,000 ATMs, and 530 ALMs. Its Markets and Banking segment offers a range of trading, investment banking, and commercial lending products and services, such as securities and banking, and transaction services to companies, governments, and institutions. The company's Global Wealth Management segment provides investment advice, financial planning, and brokerage services to affluent individuals, companies, and non-profits organizations; personalized wealth management services for high-net-worth clients; and research to individuals and institutions. Its Alternative Investments segment manages products across five asset classes, such as private equity, hedge funds, real estate, structured products, and managed futures. The company also originates and services prime residential mortgage loans.

花旗集团有限公司

花旗集团有限公司创建于1812年,总部设在美国纽约。该集团及其子公司向美国和世界消费者以及公司消费者提供各种金融产品和服务。公司的全球消费者部通过分行、自动取款机、互联网、电话和邮寄的方式,出售各种银行业、出租、保险、投资产品与服务。2007年12月31日该部门通过8 527个分行、大约20 000台自动取款机和530台自动贷款机进行运营。市场和银行部提供一系列的贸易、银行投资、商业借贷产品和服务,如:有价证券、银行业务、对公司、政府和机构的交易服务。公司的全球理财部向资金丰富的个人、公司和非营利性机构提供投资建议、金融理财和经纪服务;个性化高端客户理财服务;进行个人和机构调研。公司的另类投资部管理五个资产级别的产品,如:私人资产、投机性投资公司、不动产、结构性金融产品、未来规划。公司还创办了首个个人抵押贷款业务。(何琳译)

6.4 Incentive Plans Linked to Organizational Objectives

① Over the years, organizations have implemented incentive plans for a variety of reasons: high labor costs, competitive product markets, slow technological advances, and high potential for production bottlenecks. While these reasons are still cited, contemporary arguments for incentive plans focus on pay-for-performance and link compensation rewards to organizational goals. By meshing compensation and organizational objectives, managers believe that employees will assume "ownership" of their jobs, thereby improving their effort and overall job performance. Incentives are designed to encourage employees to put out more effort to complete their job tasks — effort they might not be motivated to expend under hourly and/or seniority-based compensation systems. Financial incentives are therefore offered to improve or maintain high levels of productivity and quality.

与组织目标相关的激励措施

① 多年以来,企业实施激励措施出于各种理由:高昂的劳动成本、产品市场的竞争、技术进步缓慢以及潜在的巨大生产瓶颈。尽管这些理由仍然被提起,但目前关于激励措施的争论主要集中在两方面:一是按工作表现领取报酬,二是薪金回报与企业目标挂钩。经理们认为,薪金与企业目标挂钩可使员工能努力保住对工作的“所有权”,从而使其工作更加努力,提高整体工作绩效。出台激励措施是为了让员工付出更大努力,以完成各自的工作任务。在以计时或以资历领取报酬的体制下,员工则不会付出同样

的努力。因此,物质奖励就是为了保持生产率和生产质量的高水平,或将该水平进一步提高。

② Do incentive plans work? Various studies have demonstrated a measurable relationship between incentive plans and improved organizational performance. In a survey of organizations with more than 500 employees, conducted by the New York Stock Exchange, 70 percent of organizations with gain sharing programs stated that those programs improved productivity. In the area of manufacturing, productivity will often improve by as much as 20 percent after the adoption of incentive plans. Improvements, however, are not limited to goods-producing industries. Service organizations, not-for-profit, and government agencies also show productivity gains when incentives are linked to organizational goals.

② 激励措施能发挥作用吗？各类研究表明,激励措施与提高组织绩效之间存在着一种可计量的关系。纽约股票交易所对员工超过500人的企业做过一项调查,该调查显示,推行利润分享的企业中有70%认为,利润分享措施提高了生产率。在制造业,采用激励措施后,生产率通常提高20%。当然,生产率的提高不仅限于产品制造业。当激励措施与组织目标挂钩时,在各类服务企业、非营利机构和政府机构中,效率也同样得到提高。

③ However, incentive plans have not always led to organizational improvement. First, incentive plans sometimes fail to satisfy employee needs. Second, management may have failed to give adequate attention to the design and implementation of the plan. Furthermore, the success of an incentive plan will depend on the environment that exists within an organization. A plan is more likely to work in an organization where morale is high, employees believe they are being treated fairly, and there is harmony between employees and management.

③ 但是,激励措施并非总是能够提高企业绩效。首先,激励措施有时不能满足员工的需求。其次,管理人员对激励措施的设计与实施未能给予足够的重视。除此之外,激励措施的成功还有赖于企业的氛围。在士气高昂、机制公允、员工与管理者关系和谐的企业,激励措施更有可能产生积极的效果。(卢敏 译)

6.5 推荐读物

(1)莫爱屏,话语与翻译,武汉大学出版社2010年版。

(2)钱歌川,翻译的技巧,世界图书出版公司北京公司2011年版。

(3)戎林海,翻译问题探微,东南大学出版社2010年版。

(4)邵志洪,英汉对比翻译导论,华东理工大学出版社2010年版。

(5)唐义均,汉英翻译技巧示例,外文出版社2011年版。

(6)Anderson, F. E. & Ma, Yingxin & Tarling, N., The English Language and the Asian Student,山东大学出版社2009年版。

(7)Martin, J. R., Matthiessen C., & Painter, C., Deploying Functional Grammar,商务印书馆2010年版。

(8)Martin, J. R., Discourse Semantics,上海交通大学出版社2010年版。

(9)Redman, S., English Vocabulary in Use (Intermediate Edition),外语教学与研究出版社,剑桥大学出版社2001年版。

(10)Whaley, L. J., Introduction to Typology: The Unity and Diversity of Language,世界图书出版公司北京公司2009年版。

7 课后练习

7.1 分析题

(1)试用所译和比读材料分析换译及其特点。
(2)试析《与组织目标相关的激励措施》汉译运用四字格的艺术。
(3)试用《花旗集团有限公司》来分析单位简介的翻译。

7.2 实训题

7.2.1 北京工美集团

北京工美集团是以生产工艺美术品为主,融科技、生产、经营、教育、出版于一体的多元化经济联合体。集团拥有工商企业50余家,合资企业21家,驻外贸易机构1个,开展"三来一补"业务。特殊工艺、地毯、抽纱共有50多种产品获国际和国家大奖,自营进出口商品60大类上万个品种花色,销往全世界130多个国家和地区。

7.2.2 Fashion Industry

No one can claim that the fashion industry contributes anything really important to society. Fashion designers are rarely concerned with vital things like warmth, comfort and durability. They are only interested in outward appearance and they take advantage of the fact that women will put up with any amount of discomfort, providing they look right. There can hardly be a man who hasn't at some time smiled at the sight of a woman shivering in a thin dress on a wintry day, or delicately picking her way through deep snow in high-heeled shoes.

7.3 思考题

(1)试论企业的类型特点及其英译特点。
(2)faculty 和 department 都可以翻译为"系",有什么区别?
(3)请考察企事业单位各种头衔英译的文化内涵。
(4)请考察中国高校名称英译的文化内涵。
(5)航空航运方面的公司名称怎么译?
(6)简述英语企事业单位简介的特点和汉译技巧。
(7)简述汉语企事业单位简介的特点和英译技巧。
(8)简述汉语学校简介的特点和英译技巧。
(9)简述英语学校简介的特点和汉译技巧。
(10)简述企业单位名称翻译的注意事项。
(11)简述事业单位名称翻译的注意事项。
(12)企事业单位简介翻译的共性有哪些?
(13)企事业单位简介翻译的差异有哪些?

第 14 课 经管

导 译

经管(经济和管理),属于经济学范畴,涉及企业一般管理、市场营销、生产与运作、国际商务、会计、财务管理、金融银行业、电子商务、组织行为领域、科学管理,管理经济学等领域的内容。

经管英语涉及范围广,各种文章的风格和语法特点差异很大。文本类型可分为两类。一类偏重于学术,包括学术论文、专著、研究报告等,其语言一般风格严谨,逻辑性强,因此语句较长,结构较复杂。另一类面向实践,包括面向实践的管理教材、管理手册、商务文件、信函、报告等。实践性强的管理专业英语有时也称为商务英语,其特点是简明扼要,结构短小,专业性较强。

鉴于经管英语的文本和词汇特征,经管翻译要采用一般和特殊相结合的方法。经管英语属于专门用途英语,汉译时首先要遵循专门用途英语文本的翻译规则和要求,同时更要考虑经管英语独特的语言特征。英译时要特别注意专业术语的使用。正确使用专业词汇,能使文章和商务文件所描述的内容更准确、内涵更丰富,便于同行业人员沟通,同时,也能体现译者的专业水平。

1 课前练笔

1.1 企业运营中的职业分配

个人必须通过分配职业这样一种方式来达成两种目的。首先,劳动者必须被安排到他最具有效率的岗位上。其次,应该给每人安排最适当的工作。人的一生大部分时间都用于工作。如果一个人能选择他最喜欢的工作,那么,他的一生就会更美好。

1.2 管理层和员工的关系

在西方,员工会议通常是一个交流知识和信息、提出建议和意见以改进公司状况的时机。在中国的公司,我参加的第一次员工会议是由公司的首席技术官主持的,我惊讶地发现,只有首席技术官一个人在会上发言,而且长达1个小时之久。等他讲完话,所有人好像都没有异议,然后会议就结束了,我根本没有机会提出我事先准备的想法和建议。

1.3 **We're Still a Healthy Company**

① I think there are a lot of management style differences — a lot of ways to manage — but if you don't create an open environment you will fail. If you sat through one of my management meetings you wouldn't know who was the boss. Sometimes the youngest kids know the most because they're actually using the credit cards and systems. It's an environment where brains are used to win in the marketplace, to help the customer, to figure things out, to share, to get to the next level. They're not used to justify bad decisions, to politicize an issue, to get yourself promoted.

② I believed I should pay for performance, but I don't think performance is a simple thing. If you're running a business, you have to do marketing well, hiring well, training people well. You've got to do your ops well, your systems well. You've got to invest in new branches and new sales and new traders. It's the whole package. In a lot of business you can get a lot of profit, but you've taken on too much risk and you've not invested enough for the future. You see that happening all the time.

1.4 **Nestle: Good Product, Good Life**

① Nestle is one of the world's most decentralized companies. By delegating decision-making as close as possible to local markets, Nestle has a significant competitive advantage in terms of swift response to local market needs.

② Nestle is a decentralized organization where responsibility for operating decisions is delegated to local units, which have a high degree of autonomy concerning pricing, distribution, marketing, etc. This resulted in heavy price competition in several key segments of the food and beverage market. Nestle's goal is to build a superior market position in each of these niches. Nestle uses local brands in a wide range of local markets and focuses on trying to optimize ingredients and processing technology to local conditions. That is why, the company needs to be flexible and able to adapt rapidly to local demand and cultural differences.

③ Nestle claims that it can reduce risks and concentrate its marketing resources by narrowing its initial market focus to just a few strategic brands.

批评 2 课前批评

2.1 智者的眼睛

① 某电视台请一位商界奇才做嘉宾主持,大家非常希望能听他谈谈成功之路。但他只是淡淡一笑,说:"还是出个题考考你们吧。某地发现了一个金矿,人们一窝蜂地涌上去,然而一条大河挡住了必经之路。如果是你,会怎么办?"

② 有人说"绕道走",也有人说"游过去"。商界奇才含笑不语,最后他说:"为什么非得去淘金,为什么不可以买一条船开展营运?"大家愕然。商界奇才说:"那样的情况,就是'宰'得渡客只剩下一条短裤,他们也会心甘情愿的,因为前面有金矿啊!"

③ 干他人不想干的,做他人不曾做的,这就是成功之道。困境在智者眼中,往往意味着一个潜在的机遇!

How a Wise Man Sees It

① A man recognized as a genius in business circles was invited as a guest of honor to a TV interview. Everybody was eager to hear a success story from him. He, however, only said with a slight smile, "Won't it be better for me to ask you for advice on a certain problem?" Here is the problem he raised:

People all rushed to the place where a gold mine had recently been discovered, but they were blocked by a river flowing across the only way to it. What would you do if you were among them?

② "Make a roundabout way." someone suggested. "Swim across." said another. The genius smiled without a word. Eventually he gave his view: "Why not do something else instead of rushing to the mine? How about buying a boat to do some ferrying?" The audience was shocked. He explained calmly: "The man could extort money from the passengers to the greatest extent. They were willing to pay because there was gold on the other bank"

③ Do what the others would not like to do or do something never attempted before by others — that is the key to success. A straitened circumstance, in the eyes of a wise man, often means a potential chance for success. (陈文伯 译)

2.2 Converting the Masses: Starbucks in China

Sell coffee to China's tea drinkers. Starbucks' solution is to select high-profile locations on the busiest street, where stores are sure to seduce the see-and-be-seen set. As Starbucks launches an aggressive expansion in China, a coffee frontier steeped in nearly 5,000 years of tea. The goal: to build hip hang-outs that tap into a

星巴克强力吸引中国消费者

向中国的饮茶人兜售咖啡,星巴克的招数是选择繁华街道的黄金地段,在那儿咖啡店一定会吸引那些爱凑热闹的人。随着星巴克在中国开拓市场的强劲势头,具有近五千年历史的中

new taste for China's emerging middle class. The company is counting on selecting such high-visibility, high-traffic café locations that they market themselves. Its main advertising medium is the store itself. People don't go there for the coffee but to present themselves as modern Chinese in a public setting.

国茶文化就渗透了来自咖啡王国的浓香。目标是把星巴克建成时尚的常去的场所,吸引中国新兴中产阶级品尝新的口味。星巴克公司依靠选择那种显眼的、交通发达的咖啡店店址来做自我宣传;星巴克最主要的宣传媒介是咖啡店本身。人们光顾星巴克并不为了喝咖啡,而是为了在公共场合有机会表明自己是时尚的中国人。

知识 3 全译知识 分译

分译,即拆分式全译,指根据语用和语义的需要将原语单位拆成若干、译成相应的译语单位的全译方法。分译的原则是:分形不损意。分译不仅限于把原语单位简单地切分,还包括把原语词语或小句剥离出来,甚或从不同地方把若干个单位提取出来,独立组成相应的译语单位。分译单位有词、短语、小句、复句和句群。按频率,小句分译最多,短语分译较多,词分译和复句分译较少,句群分译最少。

3.1 词分译

词分译,指根据语用和语义的需要原语词从原文中分离出来升为译语短语或小句的分译方法。原语词照样译出,或搭配不当,或别扭拗口,这时需考虑整个句意,将其从句中分出,译成短语或小句。能分译的多为起修饰作用的副词和形容词,动词和名词也偶可分译。如:

① I was admittedly shy.

【原译】:我是以腼腆胆怯著称的。

【试译】:我是有名的害羞,谁都知道。

原句属口语语体,admittedly 可译为"大家都知道"、"人人明白"等;而译作"以……著称",属书面用语,比较正式及庄重,不妨将其独立,译成小句"谁都知道",还以口语特色。

3.2 短语分译

短语分译,指根据语用和语义的需要原语短语从原文中分离出来升为译语小句或复句的分译方法。英语常将短语用作修饰语,而汉语善用小句,汉译时可先将短语从句中分出,还原成各种从句,译作相应的汉语小句。可分译的短语有:分词短语、不定式短语、介词短语等。如:

② All is silent. The coffin is closed and carried slowly down the stairway, through the corridors, and out into the windswept streets. Outside, a sea of faces. Fluttering red banners against a background of snow. 万籁俱寂。灵柩合上了,被缓慢地抬下楼梯,通过走廊,抬到那寒风凛冽的大街上。外面人山人海,白雪皑皑,红旗飘展。

③ After friendly consultations conducted in accordance with the principles of equality and mutual benefit, the Parties have agreed to enter into a distributorship relationship in accordance with Applicable Laws and the provisions of this Contract. 双方本着平等互利原则,经友好协商,依照有关法律,同意按照本合同条款,建立经销关系。

例②,“外面人山人海,白雪皑皑,红旗飘展”比译成“外面人山人海,迎风飘动的红旗,映衬着白雪”音响效果要好得多,突出了单部句激昂的情调。例③,译文将原文介词短语拆开,改写为几个小句,译文更简练明了,更符合汉语读者的心理预期。

3.3 小句分译

小句分译,指根据语用和语义的需要原语词从原文中分离出来升为译语复句甚至句群的分译方法。小句若含有表示动作或性质概念的动词性名词、形容词或非谓语动词,按其逻辑关系可以译成小句。小句分译以词分译和短语分译为基础,小句自然也就分解扩充为复句甚至句群。如:

④ Either Party may terminate the contract in case of failure on the other Party to fulfill or perform any of its obligations here under and in the event that such failure remains remedied sixty days after the service of a written notice as described in Article X below by the non-defaulting Party to the other Party specifying the failure in question and requiring it to be remedied. 如果一方未完成或未履行合同规定的义务,且未按照下述第 X 条之规定在另一方向其书面通知其违约行为并令其改正后的六十天内仍未予以改正,另一方则可终止本合同。

原文的介词短语、分词后置短语、宾语从句等拆分开来,译文层次更加分明,行文更加晓畅,易于理解。若按原文的结构译出,则十分夹缠。

3.4 复句分译

复句分译,指根据语用和语义的需要原语复句拆分译作小句、形成更复杂的复句或句群的分译方法。枝繁叶茂的英语复句可分译为由层层推进的若干汉语小句组成的复句或句群。如:

⑤ Over the last 30 years, social scientists have conducted more than 1,000 studies of how we react to beautiful and not-so-beautiful people.

【原译】:最近 30 年来,社会科学家进行了 1 000 多项我们如何对漂亮的人和相貌平平的人反应的研究。

【试译】:近 30 年来,社会科学家进行了千余项研究,探讨人们对相貌平平者和俊俏者的反应。

studies 与其后内容呈引导与揭示关系,由于所揭示内容非常丰富,汉译虽说同样用小句译出,但与 studies 的关系必须分开叙说,不然会产生原译式大肚子句,有翻译腔倾向。

4 全译窍门

4.1 意随境迁

没有语境就没有翻译。词义有可能随着特定语境的变化而变化。中国的经管词汇运用中可能改变原产于西方的经济学术语的含义,以适合中国国情,反映中国经济特色。如"商品经济"最初译为 a commodity economy,令许多外国人不得要领,后来改为 market economy,与英语使用规范相适用,信息传达才通畅。原作中还有一些作者个人用语,一般词典查不到,只能根据上下文把握其意,根据中文习惯选择恰当的词语表达。如例①中 E-economy 意即 electronic economy。

① The E-economy was truly born when the average consumer could easily and securely conduct online transactions such as buying and selling stock. 电子经济是伴随着普通消费者能够轻松并安全地进行在线交易而正式诞生,如买进和卖出股票。

4.2 随科择译

遇到共享词,不要急于翻译,需结合上下文语境和专业背景,确定正确的译文。所谓共享词,即经管英语词汇与其他专门用途英语共用的词汇,但词义相差悬殊,因此不能望文生义,胡乱猜测。如 share 在金融指"股票",在经管指"市场份额、市场占有率";channel 在经管中专指市场中介渠道,而非"海峡、沟渠"。又如,"这太贵了。你宰人!"中的"宰人"不是 kill people,从经管专业角度看是"向顾客索取高价",可译为:You are overcharging!

4.3 缩略有道

缩略词一般由专业术语缩写而成。汉译时,众所周知、约定俗成的概念或术语,可采取略译,甚至直接引用,如 GIF,GDP,WTO,GNP 等。汉译英时,汉语经管词汇在文中第一次出现,可直接译成相对应的英语缩略词,并在括号中标明全称;该词汇在文中再出现时,则只需译其缩略词,不必用全称。如"客户关系管理"在语篇中首次出现时译为 CRM (Customer Relationship Management),下次则使用 CRM。

4.4 雅俗有别

行话是商业交易和特殊活动的一种非正式语言,不是该领域的专家或熟手难以听懂。如:

② 投资者想在股票降价时获得利润,便可以从证券商那里借股票来卖空。The investor can make a shot sale by means of selling stocks from the stockbroker to make profits when the prices are brought down.

例②中"卖空"(shot sale)是股票交易市场的行话。行话翻译得当,可能新颖时髦,生动诙谐，形象有力，翻译不当容易给人轻佻的感觉，或者使人觉得怪诞可笑，不伦不类。与经管类文章有关的行话很多，如：bust 降职，降级；pro 专业人员，jawbone 施加压力，lowdown 内幕真相，脱手 sell it，钱 green，促销 hype。

4.5 释到佳处

中国市场经济中出现的新政策、新现象，用几个字概括出来，言简意赅，便于接受。但是，这些词语英译时，应按中国人的视角译。有时，仅用直译或意译，不能准确达意，需要在术语前后加以解释，以便准确地表达原意。如“两保一挂”直译为 double guarantee and one link，之后加注释 the guarantee to submit due taxes to the state and to complete technological renovations approved by the state, and the linkage of total wages with economic benefits（保证实现应向国家上缴的税利，保证完成国家批准的技术改造项目，以及工资总额同经济效益挂钩）。

5 话题词汇

5.1 管理经济学

产品质量 quality of products
定量目标 quantitative objective
定性目标 qualitative objective
多种经营 diversification
个人利益 personal interest
个人责任 personal responsibility
工作效率 work efficiency
股票期权 stock option
顾客服务 customer service
管理方格图 managerial grid
管理决策 managerial decision
管理职能 managerial function
集体目标 group objective
检验记录 inspection record
紧缩政策 retrenchment strategy
经济体系 economic system
考绩制度 merit system
科学管理 scientific management
可考核目标 verifiable objective
应付账 accounts payable
控制手段 control device
劳资纠纷 labor dispute
利益冲突 conflict of interests
目标管理 management by objectives
内部环境 internal environment
派生政策 derivative policy
批准程序 approval procedure
评价工具 appraisal tool
强化理论 reinforcement theory
缺勤率 absenteeism
人际关系 human relation
人力投入 human input
人员流动 turnover
商业道德 business ethics
社会责任 public responsibility
生产能力 capacity to produce
授权 delegation of authority
特许经营 franchise
投入原则 the commitment principle
投资回报 return on investment
外部环境 external environment
误工记录 record of labor-hours lost
现代经营管理 modern operational management
销售量 sales volume
行为科学 behavior science
行政管理能力 administrative ability

应变策略 consistency strategy
有竞争力的价格 competitive price
增长目标 growth goal
专利产品 proprietary product
追随 followership
资本货物 capital goods
自我实现 self-actualization
自主权 autonomy
activity ratio 活动比率
agile manufacturing 敏捷制造
appreciation of currency 货币升值
artifacts 人工环境
assessment center 评价中心
balance sheet 资产负债表
behavioral decision model 行为决策模型
behavior modification 行为修正
bill of materials 物料清单
boundary-spanning roles 跨界角色
bounded rationality 有限理性
brand competition 品牌竞争
business portfolio matrix 商业资产组合矩阵
business strategy 商业策略
channel management 渠道管理
capital budgeting 投资预算
cash cows 摇钱树
certified public accountant 注册会计师
chain of command 指挥链
charismatic authority 魅力权威模式
classical perspective 古典管理理论
closed system 封闭系统
code of ethics 伦理规范
commercial loans 商业贷款
competitive advantage 竞争优势
consumer behavior 消费者行为
contingency perspective 权变观
contingency planning 随即计划
corporate social responsibility 公司社会责任
corporate strategy 公司战略
cost leadership strategy 成本领先战略
current ratios 流动比率
debt ratios 负债比率
decision tree 决策树(体系)
differentiated marketing 有区别的营销手段
differentiation strategy 差异化战略
directive leadership 指示领导
discount rate 贴现率
dividend 股息
downward communication 下行沟通
dumping 倾销
durable goods 耐用品
dynamic network 动态网络
economic feasibility 经济可行性
employee-centered work redesign 员工工作再设计
empowering employees 职工授权
empowerment 权力下放
escalation of commitment 递增效忠
esteem needs 尊重的需要
ethical behavior 道德表现
ethical dilemma 伦理困境
expected value 预期价值
external communication 外部环境
external customer 外部顾客
external forces 外部力量
feedback controls 反馈控制
feed forward controls 前馈控制
financial statements 财务报表
flattening organization 扁平化组织
focus strategy 集中战略
force-field analysis 立场分析
foreign direct investment 海外直接投资
foreign exchange exposure 外汇风险
functional structure 职能式战略
GE matrix 职能式结构
generic strategies 一般性策略
globalization of economy 经济全球化
global strategy 全球化战略
grand strategy 主战略
grapevine 藤状网络式沟通
groupthink 群体思想
halo-and-horn effect 月晕效应
hybrid layout 混合式布置
income statement 损益表
industrial engineering 工业工程
inflation 通货膨胀
informal groups 非正式群体
informational roles 信息角色

instrumental values 工具价值
integrating mechanisms 结合机制
interdependence 互相依赖
internal customer 内部顾客
international invitation to tender 国际招标
interpersonal roles 人际交往能力
job description 岗位描述
job rotation 岗位轮换
job satisfaction 工作满意度
job-shop production system 职务专业化
just-in-time purchasing 及时采购
labor-management relations 劳工管理关系
lateral communication 横向沟通
law of requisite variety 必要多样性定律
learning organizations 学习型组织
line of credit 信用额度
line personnel 线形人事管理
liquidation 资产变现
liquidity ratios 流动率
liquidity risk 变现风险
locus of control 控制点
locus of decision making 局域网
long-term liabilities 长期债务
management by exception 例外管理
market positioning 市场定位
market segmentation 市场细分
master production schedule 总生产进度表
matrix structure 矩阵结构
maturity value 到期值
mechanistic systems 机械式组织
multi-domestic strategy 多国本土化战略
national income 国家收入
need for achievement 成就需要
negative reinforcement 消极强化
net present value 净现值
non-programmed decision 非程序化决策
non-tariff barriers 非关税壁垒
nonverbal communication 非语言沟通
objectives function 目标函数
operational feasibility 造作可行性
operational plan 作业计划
organic（clan）control 有机控制
organic system 有机系统
organization 组织安排
organizational commitment 组织承诺
organizational culture 组织文化
owner's equity 所有者权益
participative management 参与管理
path-goal model 途径—目标模型
payoff table 决定(因素)表;结算表;成果表
performance appraisal 绩效考评
pooled interdependence 共有相互依存
positive reinforcement 正强化
process management 过程管理
product life cycle 产品生命周期
profitable organization 营利组织
profit maximization 利润最大化
protected class 受保护一类
quality control 质量控制
rate of return 回报率
rational-legal authority 法理权威模式
reciprocal interdependence 交互性的互赖性
referent power 指示权力
relationship marketing 关系营销
relationship orientation 关系导向
rented goods 租赁商品
revenue 收入
reward power 奖励权力
scalar principle 等级原则
schedules of reinforcement 强化时间表
scientific management 科学管理
selective perception 选择性理解
self managed teams 自我管理型团队
self-oriented roles 自我取向角色
sequential interdependence 顺序式互赖
services differentiation 服务差异化
short-term financing 短期融资
single-use plans 一次性计划
social context 社会关联性
span of control 控制幅度;管理幅度
special-purpose team 特殊目标小组
staff personnel management 员工人事管理
stakeholders 利益相关者
survey feedback 调查反馈
tangible costs 可收回成本
tariff classification 关税税则分类

task orientation 任务导向型
technical feasibility 技术可行性
telecommuting 远程办公
terminal values 终极价值
the exclusive agency 独家代理
traditional authority 传统权威模式
transformation process 变革过程
turbulent environments 动荡环境
unity of command 统一指挥
upward communication 上行沟通
utility approach 功利主义观
variable-ratio schedule 变动比率增时制
video conference 视频会议
warehouse layout 仓库布局
working capital 流动资金
work motivation 工作激励手段
written communication 笔头交流

5.2 领导模式

变革型领导 transformational leaders
参与型领导 participative leadership
超凡魅力的领导 charismatic leader
成就取向型领导 achievement-oriented leadership
高－高型领导者 high-high leader
基层管理者 first-line managers
民主式领导 democratic leader
事务型领导者 transactional leaders
远景领导者 visionary leadership
支持型领导 supportive leadership
执行性领导 transactional leadership
职能管理者 functional manager
指导型领导 instrumental leadership
中层管理者 middle managers
专制式领导 autocratic leader
自由放任式领导 free-rein leader

5.3 管理方法

ABC classification ABC 分类法
activity-based costing 业务量成本法;作业成本法
backflush 倒冲法
behavioral approach 行为法
breakeven analysis 盈亏平衡分析
contingency approaches 随即制宜法
delphi technique 魔鬼提倡法
dialectical inquiry 辩证探求法
direct-deduct inventory transaction processing 直接增减库存法
fixed-interval schedule 定时给奖
fixed-ratio schedule 定比给奖
human rights approach 人权方法
lot for lot 按需订货法
motivational techniques 激励方法
partial schedule of reinforcement 间断性奖励
pre-deduct inventory transaction processing 前减库存处理法
strategic decision-making matrix 战略决策矩阵
the cooperative social systems approach 协作社会系统法
the contingency approach 随机制宜法
the decision theory approach 决策理论法
the empirical approach 经验法
the interpersonal behavior approach 人际行为法
the managerial roles approach 管理任务法
the mathematical approach 数学法
the operational approach 经营法
the social-technical systems approach 社会技术系统法
the systems approach 系统法
vendor scheduling 采购计划法

5.4 工资

工资标准 pay rate
工资存根 pay stub
工资支票 pay check
工资周期 pay period
计件工资 piece wage
加薪 raise

奖金 bonus
净工资 net pay
扣除费用 deductions
时薪 wage
薪水 salary
佣金 commission
直接存入银行 direct deposit
总额 gross

5.5 职务

部门经理 Branch Manager
操作经理 Operations Manager
产品经理 Product Manager
房地产经理 Property Manager
服务经理 Service Manager
副总裁 Vice-President
副总裁助理 Assistant Vice-President
管理顾问 Management Consultant
管理员 Controller(General)
国际监管 Controller(International)
进出口经理 Import/Export Manager
库存管理经理 Inventory Control Manager
零售店经理 Retail Store Manager
区域经理 Regional Manager
商店经理助理 Assistant Store Manager
生产经理 Production Manager
食品服务经理 Food Service Manager
市场行政总监 Executive Marketing Director
售买经理 Vending Manager
土地担保协调员 Field Assurance Coordinator
项目经理 Project Manager
运营总监 Director of Operations
制造业经理 Manufacturing Manager
总经理 General Manager

5.6 新经济词汇

暗箱操作 black box work
财政、信贷双紧方针 the principles of tightening finance and credit
产品国产化 production indigenization
产业政策 industrial policy
厂长(经理)负责制 factory director (manager) responsibility system
承包经营责任制 contract management responsibility system
吃大锅饭 eating from the " same big public pot"
戴帽下达 allocation with a cap
浮动工资制 floating wage system
国家经济命脉 lifeblood of the national economy
红包 red packet
宏观调控体系 macro economic adjustment and control system
火炬计划 torch program
技术密集型产业 technology intensive industry
剪刀差 scissors difference
交钥匙工程 turn-key project
经济杠杆 economic lever
经济特区 special economic zones
摸着石头过河 crossing the river by feeling the stones
拳头产品 hit products; competitive products
软着陆 soft landing
三角债 triangle debt; chains of debt
上不封顶,下不保底 practice of imposing no ceiling or bottom limit
社会主义市场经济 socialist market economy
双轨制价格 two-track price system
铁饭碗 iron rice bowl
下海 engage in business
乡镇企业 township and village enterprises
小金库 little exchequer; little money locker
再就业工程 re-employment program
专项基金 special fund
资金密集型产业 funds intensive industry

5.7 缩略词

供应链管理 SCM
归属需要 nAff

会计信息系统 AIS
价值工程 VE
进料质量管理 IQC
经济订货批量 EOQ
经营杠杆系数 DOL
可签约 ATP
客户抱怨比 CPM
客户关系管理 CRM
企业资产管理 EAM
情景领导理论 SLT
全面质量管理 TQM
实时管理 JIT
物料清单 BOM
线性规划 LP
信息管理系统 MIS
主管决策系统 EIS
组织公民行为 OCB
ACRS 快速成本回收制度
AQL 可接受质量水平
BARS 行为定位评分法
BI 商业智能
CFO 财务总裁
COO 首席运营官
CRP 能力需求计划
CTO 首席技术官
DRP 分销资源计划
DSS 决策制定系统
EAPs 员工辅助项目顾问
EFT 电子资金转换
ELS 经济批量
ERP 企业资源规划
FQC 成品质量管理
HRISs 人力资源信息系统
IPQC 制程质量管理
JCM 职务特征模型
KM 知识管理
MBO 目标管理责任制
MBWA 走动式管理
MPS 主生产计划
nAch 成就需要
nPow 权力需要
OB 组织行为
OD 组织发展
PERT 计划评核术
SDLC 发展周期系统
TPM 全面生产管理
ZBB 零基预算

6 比读体悟

6.1 如何让你的员工不仅是为钱而战?

① 奖金和股票期权往往能提高业绩。但是,它们也会导致不道德行为,加剧人员流动,引起嫉妒和不满。在 20 世纪 70 年代中后期和 80 年代,有一种管理思想开始出现,该观点认为企业领导的主要任务是最大限度地提升股东利益。这种观点具体到公司环境就变成了对于员工进行基于业绩的经济激励。人们似乎认为:只要激励得当,人们就会努力地提高业绩,从而提升公司的业绩。

The Problem with Financial Incentives — and What to Do about It

① Bonuses and stock options often improve performance. But they can also lead to unethical behavior, fuel turnover and foster envy and discontent. Starting in the mid to late 1970s and 1980s, the view emerged in management thinking that the primary role of corporate leadership was to maximize the interests of shareholders. This broader perspective translated at lower levels of organizations into an emphasis on rewarding employees with financial incentives contingent upon performance. The thinking seemed to be: Get the incentives right, and people will be motivated to perform better, resulting in better performance for the firm.

② 然而,批评者指出,许多高层管理人员由于短期业绩而赢得丰厚报酬,但最终却给公司带来灾难,高管的天价薪酬引起了媒体和公众哗然,可即便如此,这样的薪酬体系仍然在继续。《华尔街日报》在三月中旬报道称美国50家大公司的总裁去年的奖金涨幅超过30%,这是经济衰退以来的最高幅度。

② And despite the bad press and public uproar that big payouts generated in the wake of the financial crisis — when critics pointed out that many top executives had been heavily rewarded for short-term performances that ultimately proved disastrous — the system marches on. CEO bonuses at 50 big US companies rose more than 30% last year, a gain not seen since before the recession, The *Wall Street Journal* reported in mid-March.

③ 必须明确,我们不是建议公司放弃经济激励。事实上,有证据表明这些奖励可以激发更好的业绩和生产率。但这些收益是有代价的。我们关注的是经济激励产生了意想不到的后果。经济激励对不道德的行为、嫉妒和员工流动、以及员工对于工作的内在兴趣有什么影响?我们可以采取什么措施来减轻其负面影响?

③ To be clear, we are not suggesting that companies abandon financial incentives. Indeed, there is a wealth of evidence that these incentives can motivate higher levels of performance and productivity. But these gains come at a cost. Our concern is about the unintended consequences of financial incentives. What do they mean for unethical behavior, jealousy and turnover, and intrinsic interest in the work? And what measures can be taken to lessen their negative impact?

6.2 工商企业成功之道

每一个成功的工商企业都是建立在一些卓越的意识之上的,即懂得审时度势,抓住机遇,承担责任,并不乏幽默感。但这一切都没有比对市场了解的能力更为重要。高级管理人员的一个非常重要的本事是能很自然地设身处地地为客户着想,并从他们那里获得真知灼见。他们利用这种能力来指导技术、产品和售后服务,乃至公司战略计划的各个方面。比尔·盖茨之类的成功者就曾把这种本事带进他们各自创立的企业中。没有这种能力,他们的事业或许只是昙花一现,至少没有今天这样成功。但是许多高层经理,特别是工业公司的高层经理,把与顾客接触看成销售和市场营销人员的事。即便他们确实也认为市场是公司的重心,但随着公司的发展,他们中在多数人也只与消费者保持十分有限的接触而已。他们判断和把握市场,依赖于下属送来的报告,即二手、三手的材料。

Key to Success in Businesses

Every successful business is built on superior senses — of timing, opportunity, responsibility and not infrequently humor. None however is more critical than the ability to sense the market. A senior executive's instinctive capacity to empathize with and gain insights from customers is the single most important skill he or she can use to direct technologies product and service offerings indeed all elements of a company's strategic posture. People like Bill Gates brought this ability to the enterprises they founded. Without it their ventures might have been short-lived or at least far less successful. But many top-level managers, particularly those at industrial companies, consider customer contact the bailiwick of sales and marketing staff. And even if they do believe that market focus is a priority most retain only limited contact with consumers as their organizations grow relying instead on subordinates' reports-second or third hand information-to define and sense the market for them.

6.3 战略管理

① 战略管理是企业为了实现其长

Strategic management

① Strategic management is the art, science and craft of

期目标而制定、执行和评估跨部门决策的艺术、科学和工艺。它是理清公司使命、远景和目标，以项目和行动计划等常用形式来发展为既定目标而设计的政策和计划，并分配资源以执行政策与计划，项目与行动计划的过程。战略管理的目的是有效协调和整合企业内各职能部门的活动，以实现企业的长期组织目标。平衡记分卡是常用的管理工具，用以衡量企业整体绩效以及明确进度。

formulating, implementing and evaluating cross-functional decisions that will enable an organization to achieve its long-term objectives. It is the process of specifying the organization's mission, vision and objective, developing policies and plans, often in terms of projects and programs, which are designed to achieve these objectives, and then allocating resources to implement the policies and plans, projects and programs. Strategic management seeks to coordinate and integrate the activities of the various functional areas of a business in order to achieve long-term organizational objectives. A balanced scorecard is often used to evaluate the overall performance of the business and its progress toward objectives.

② 战略管理是最高级别的管理活动。首席执行官经董事会的授权和同意对组织的战略进行规划、加工和指引。然后，该战略在组织的最高领导团队或者高管的监督下执行。战略管理能为组织的发展掌舵，它也是一门类似于“组织学”的学科。在商业管理领域，对组织和大环境之间的“战略协同”，或者“战略一致性”的谈论是很有效的。所谓一致性，指的是组织的行为与管理层的期望一致，而管理层的期望与市场和大环境一致。

② Strategic management is the highest level of managerial activity. Strategies are typically planned, crafted or guided by the Chief Executive Officer, approved or authorized by the Board of Directors, and then implemented under the supervision of the organization's top management team or senior executives. Strategic management provides overall direction to the enterprise and is closely related to the field of Organization Studies. In the field of business administration it is useful to talk about " strategic alignment" between the organization and its environment or " strategic consistency". There is strategic consistency when the actions of an organization are consistent with the expectations of management, and these in turn are with the market and the context. (赵军峰用例)

6.4 Focus on the Emotions

情感战略

① Apple has a branding strategy that focuses on the emotions. The Apple brand personality is about lifestyle; imagination; liberty regained; innovation; passion; hopes, dreams and aspirations; and power-to-the-people through technology. The Apple brand is not just intimate with its customers, it's loved. The preference for Apple products, for instance, not only kept the company alive for much of the 1990's but it even enable the company to sustain pricing that is at a premium to its competitors.

① 苹果公司品牌战略的重点是构建与客户的感情联系。苹果的品牌个性即与生活方式、想象力、重获自由、创新、激情、希望、梦想和科技对人们的影响力等因素密切相关。苹果品牌与客户的联系不能简单地用“亲密”来描述，而应该用“爱”来形容。消费者对于苹果产品的偏爱不仅使其挺过了20世纪90年代的生存危机，而且使竞争对手望尘莫及。

② Apple fully understands that all aspects of the customer experience are important and that all brand touch-points must reinforce the Apple brand. Apple is expanding and improving its distribution capabilities by opening its own retail stores in key cities around the world in up-market, quality shopping venues. It

② 苹果十分了解让客户全方位体验的重要性，力求所有的品牌触摸点都能增强其品牌的力量。苹果通过在全球各大主要城市开设高档零售商店来提升其分销能力。同时，还与许

has entered into strategic alliances with other companies to sell Apple's products and services.

多公司建立战略伙伴关系以销售其产品和服务。(成应翠、蒋佳池用例)

6.5 Why Middle Managers May Be the Most Important People in Your Company

为什么中层管理者可能是公司最重要人员

① Wharton management professor Ethan Mollick has a message for knowledge-based companies: Pay closer attention to your middle managers. They may have a greater impact on company performance than almost any other part of the organization. In other words, says Mollick," The often overlooked and sometimes-maligned middle managers matter. They are not interchangeable parts in an organization." His view upends the long-held belief that performance differences between firms are due mainly to organizational factors — such as business strategy, management systems and HR practices — rather than to differences among employees.

① 沃顿商学院管理学教授莫里克对以知识为基础的公司给予一句忠告:请重视公司的中层管理人员,因为和其他部门或人员相比,他们对公司运营有着更大的影响。换句话说,莫里克表示,“人们常常忽视甚至不屑于关注中层管理人员,事实上他们有着非常重要的作用”。在公司里,他们的位置不可替代。长久以来,人们认为,公司彼此之间运营状况之所以不同,主要是由不同的公司因素导致,例如商业战略、管理体系、人力资源实践等等,而不是因为雇佣人员的不同导致。莫里克的观点改变了这种思维模式。

② The importance of individual skills and characteristics can be especially significant when measuring firm performance in industries and fields that value innovation, like computer games, software, consulting, biotech and marketing, according to Mollick, who recently completed a paper on this topic titled, "People and Process: Suits and Innovators: Individuals and Firm Performance." It is in these knowledge-intensive industries where variation in the abilities of middle managers - the "suits" he refers to in his paper — has a " particularly large impact on firm performance, much larger than that of individuals who are assigned innovative roles," he says.

② 莫里克认为,在一些重视创新的领域,例如计算机游戏产业、软件产业、咨询行业、生物技术部门和市场营销部门,个人技能与特点尤其重要。莫里克日前撰写了一篇题为《人员和流程:循规者和创新者以及个人与企业绩效》的研究报告。上述知识密集型产业,中层管理人员的能力至关重要,和从事创新和开发的员工相比,他们对公司运营有着更大的影响。在研究报告里,他把这些中层管理者称为“循规者”。

③ The influence these suits exert, he suggests, stems from their key role in project management, including such tasks as resource allocation and supervision of deadlines — responsibilities often perceived as the bureaucratic, more routine and less glamorous side of the business. Middle managers also can play a key role in fostering innovative and creative environments.

③ 他认为,这些“循规者”在项目管理中发挥了关键性作用,因而拥有很大的影响力。他们的任务包括资源分配、监督工作是否按时完成等等。这些常被认为是公司行政层面的责任,常规性的工作,并没有十足吸引力。但是,在帮助公司营造创新氛围方面,中层管理人员发挥着关键的作用。

6.6 推荐读物

(1)成应翠等,品商战淘英语,科学出版社 2010 年版。
(2)陈文伯,译艺:英汉双向笔译,群言出版社 2008 年版。
(3)林梅,深度对话:全球财经领袖访谈录,中国宇航出版社 2011 年版。
(4)石春祯,石春祯英语阅读理解 220 篇,新华出版社 2008 年版。
(5)田华实等,用英语说中国・经济,上海科学普及出版社 2009 年版。
(6)叶乃沂,新编经济管理专业英语,西南交通大学出版社 2002 年版。
(7)赵军峰,商务口译,外语教学与研究出版社 2009 年版。
(8)http://www.chinadaily.com.cn/
(9)http://wenku.baidu.com/view/d08247d180eb6294dd886c97.html

练习 7 课后练习

7.1 分析题

(1)试用所译和比读材料分析分译及其特点。
(2)试用意随境迁方法,分析比读材料中经管术语的含义。
(3)结合比读材料,找出文中用到的全译方法。

7.2 实训题

7.2.1 连锁经营

1995 年,国家正式提出了把发展连锁经营作为带有方向性的一项流通体制改革。政府的强力推动与企业市场化内在发展需要相结合,我国连锁业快速步入成长期,每年以约 4%左右的速度扩张,仅用 10 年就基本完成了欧美历经百年的零售业革命,连锁经营的领域也由最初的零售行业开始向服务业拓展,超市、便利店、各类品牌专卖店、专业连锁店等作为新的购物形式,已受到消费者的普遍认同,并日益深入百姓生活。

7.2.2 How to Provide Macroeconomic Stability

Economics has many substantive areas of knowledge where there is agreement but also contains areas of controversy. That's inescapable. You're much better off knowing what the controversies are, what the issues are and what the arguments are on both sides than you are operating in a vacuum or in ignorance. Economics is a very difficult subject. I've compared it to trying to learn how to repair a car when the engine is running. The economy is always changing, our knowledge of it is very incomplete, and our ability to predict it is not impressive. Nevertheless, I think in the end good economic policy research makes a very big difference to the welfare of the average person.

7.3 思考题

(1)business 与 operation 在经管翻译中如何区分含义?

(2)举例说明经管英语中比喻的运用。
(3)收集中国当下流行的新经济词汇,考察其英译特点。
(4)如何把握经管翻译中雅俗的分寸?
(5)试析新经济词汇的汉译策略。
(6)试析新经济词汇的英译策略。
(7)经管翻译的原则是什么?
(8)经管英语中职务类词汇翻译有何特点?
(9)如何把握和理解共享词在经管翻译中的含义?
(10)试析商务信函的语篇变化特点。
(11)举例说明经管英语中行话翻译的特点。
(12)试比较两类经管英语文本的翻译差异。
(13)结合意随境迁翻译策略,分析文化在经管英语翻译中的作用。

第 15 课 政治外交

导 译

政治与外交文本翻译是极其严肃认真的任务。政治与外交文本的内容大多涉及国家的方针、政策;国家领导人的对外的政治态度;涉及国家主权和领土完整;关系国家的政治、安全、经济、军事利益;关系地区乃至世界形势的稳定等重大问题。此类文本的翻译政策性强,敏感度高。不仅要使所译文字再现我们国家的方针政策,还要使译入语读者能够正确没有偏差地理解我们党和国家的这些方针政策。

准确把握政治与外交文本的文体特征,是做好这类文本翻译工作的一个重要前提。政治与外交文本既具有一般文本的共性文体特征,又有其自身所拥有的结构严密紧凑、语言明晰精炼、措词精准讲究、论证严肃理性等鲜明特点,这就要求译者必须根据其特点进行翻译。翻译时不仅要字斟句酌以保持原文本语言的严谨正式、练达深邃;语气的严肃庄重、雄浑有力。更要使译文达到原文所要实现的目的、预期的效果及功能。

政治与外交文本因其涉及的内容非常广泛,几乎涉及人类社会政治、经济、科技、军事、文化、外交等所有领域、所有方面。任何一个国家都有一些特有的、具有独特含义的用语,即文化负载词,这些词语是因各国的历史传统、政治制度、发展模式、意识形态、价值观念、生活方式等不同而产生的。因此,译者需要很强的综合知识能力。

1 课前练笔

1.1 发展中欧关系符合双方利益

第六届中国－欧盟领导人峰会于星期四在北京举行,会议表明中国和欧盟之间的关系正在健康地发展。此次会晤是今年年初新一届中国领导人执政以来双方的首次会面,也是继中国于10月13日首次发表与欧盟关系文件和欧盟于9月10日批准与中国关系新战略之后,双方领导人的首次峰会。

1.2 第六轮六方会谈团长会新闻公报

2007年7月18日至20日,第六轮六方会谈团长会在北京举行。会议回顾了第六轮六方会谈第一阶段会议以来的工作和进展,对各方为推进六方会谈进程所作出建设性努力表示满意,对各方就增进相互信任和改善相互关系进行富有成效的双边磋商和协调表示欢迎。各方为实现半岛无核化,实现有关国家关系正常化,实现东北亚地区持久和平与稳定,在相互尊重、平等协商的气氛中,就六方会谈下一阶段工作进行了坦诚务实的讨论,达成框架共识。

1.3 President Reagan's White House Staff

President Reagan's White House staff is divided into three parts: the upstairs part headed by the pragmatic James Baker, the downstairs part headed by the conservative William Clark, and the backstairs part patrolled by their assistants, who tell the press about the differences between upstairs and downstairs.

1.4 China's Rise

① Americans and others around the globe can feel the effects of China's voracious appetite for the resources and the enormous output of its factories, staffed by an endless stream of migrants who toil for $2 a day churning out low-cost goods, undercutting foreign competitors and upending the low-end global workforce.

② The World has never seen a nation as big as China rise as fast as China has in the past 20 years. Its ascent, like those of the United States, Germany and Japan before it, is challenging more established powers. Its continued progress depends on harmony with these and other nations.

批评 2 课前批评

2.1 心雄万夫的美国女性

美国是女人大显身手之地。她们目前已经拥有该国大约百分之八十五的财富,而且不日即将囊括全部。离婚堪称进财致富之道,手续简便,容易忘却。心雄万夫的女性,往往尽情恣意重演此技,巧

Ambitious American Females

American is the land of opportunities for women. Already they own about eight-five percent of the wealth of the nation. Soon they will have it all. Divorce has become a lucrative process, simple to arrange and easy to forget; and ambitious females can repeat it as often as they please and parlay their

取豪夺，直至获利激增，高达天文数字。丈夫去世，随之而来的报偿也颇为可观。因此一些夫人太太更愿寄望于此。她们知道，等待有限，总不会遥遥无期，劳瘁痒疾与高血压用不了多久就必定叫那可怜鬼一命呜呼。

winnings to astronomical figures. The husband's death also brings satisfactory rewards and some ladies prefer to relay upon this method. They know that the waiting period will not be unduly protracted, for overwork and hypertension are bound to get the poor devil before long, and he will die at his desk. (连淑能用例)

2.2 Why the Americans Are So Restless

① Americans cleave to the things of this world as if assured that they will never die, and yet are in such a rush to snatch any that come within their reach, as if expecting to stop living before they have relished them. They clutch everything but hold nothing fast, and so lose grip as they hurry after some new delight.

② An American will build a house in which to pass his old age and sell it before the roof is on; he will plant a garden and rent it just as the trees are coming into bearing; he will clear a field and leave others to reap the harvest; he will take up a profession and leave it, settle in one place and soon go off elsewhere with his changing desires. If his private business allows him a moment's relaxation, he will plunge at once into the whirlpool of politics. Then, if at the end of a year crammed with work he has a little spare leisure, his restless curiosity goes with him traveling up and down the vast territories of the United States. Thus he will travel five hundred miles in a few days as a distraction from his happiness.

不安稳的美国人

① 美国人固守人世间的财产，好像深信自己永远不会死亡，可一旦享乐近在咫尺，却又迫不及待地伸手攫取，仿佛是要抢在临终之前及时行乐。他们什么都抓在手里，却又什么都抓不紧。在匆匆追求新欢的过程中往往丢了旧爱。

② 美国人会为安度晚年去兴建一幢房子，却又会在还没架上房梁时就把它卖掉；他会在花园里植树栽花，却又会在花园快要结果收获时把它租给别人；他会开垦出农田，却又让他人收获成果；他会热衷于一门专业，却又马上将其放弃；他会在某处安家落户，却又会情移念转另寻安身之地。如果在处理个人私事之余仍有片刻闲暇，美国人会一头栽进政治纷争的漩涡中。年终之际，忙碌了整整一年的美国人一旦稍有空闲，便会怀着一颗永不安分的好奇之心纵横于辽阔的美国大地。他会在短短数日内驰骋500英里，尽情享受这种快乐的消遣。(许建平用例)

知识 3 全译知识 合译

合译,即整合式全译,指根据语用和语义的需要将原语单位合并或融合的全译方法。合译的原则是:合形不损意。合译可保证译文更加严谨、简洁、紧凑,但是求简而不能陋简。合译单位有词、短语、小句、复句和句群,按频率,小句合译最多,短语合译较多,复句合译较少,句群合译最少。

3.1 短语合译

短语合译,指根据语用和语义的需要原语短语缩合为译语词的合译方法。合译包括组合式和融合式,前者是原语的几个单位重新组织合并为一个整体,仍可见到原有的单位;后者是原语几个单位或一个单位合为更小的一个整体,难以分出原有的单位。如:

① After the two coolers the water is separated from the air, which passed the drying zone of the dryer, leaving it with only a small amount of residual humidity.

【原译】:经两只冷却器之后,水与空气分离,接着空气通过干燥区;离开干燥器时,空气中只有少量残余水分。

【试译】:经过两只冷却器,水气分离,空气通过干燥区的干燥器,仅剩少量水分。

句中的 water from the air 缩合为"水气",似词非词,受"空气"后管控,才知不是词,显得简练;有 passed the drying zone of the dryer 在先,leaving it 可蕴涵其中,不细辨不易察觉,用"通过"即可概括;有"空气"在主导,水分自然指含在其中。

3.2 小句合译

小句合译,指根据语用和语义的需要原语小句缩合为译语词或短语的合译方法,即原语小句表达的内容可用译语一个词或短语表达,是简洁译文的良方。不少词语在一定的语境下可取代宾语、定语、让步、条件等从句,这是一种言简意赅的意合句。如:

② Since he is a beggar, he must not be a chooser.

【原译】:(既然)(他是)要饭的,就必不会挑肥拣瘦。

【试译】:要饭就不得挑拣。

③ If we compress a gas, it becomes hotter.

【原译】:如果压缩空气,气体就热起来。

【试译】:空气压缩会变热。

例②相当于将原文改造为 Beggars must not be choosers,用名词 choosers 去代替判断句 he is a chooser。例③,科技文体表示一般规律时句中的 we 可以不译;原文可以压缩,用汉语的连动句简洁达意。

3.3 复句合译

复句合译,指根据语用和语义的需要原语复句缩合为译语短语或小句的合译方法。英语中从句套从句,结构关系错综复杂,汉语则简句见长,层次分明,环环相扣。汉译时,可充分运用汉语的特殊句式,如把字句、被字句、连动句、兼语句、判断句、存现句等,压缩各种英语从句,化繁为简,化零为整。如:

④ He marked the date on the calendar that he kept in his backpack: "June, 5, 1971."

【原译】:他背包里有本日历,在"1971年6月5日"上面他画了个记号。

【试译】:他在背包里的日历上将"1971年6月5日"做了记号。

⑤ There is no month in the whole year, in which nature wears a more beautiful appearance than in the month of August! 四时之美,八月为最!

例④,原文为复句,汉译将从句 he kept in his backpack 压缩为短语,做了汉译的定语,表明日历之所在,这样整个复句因原有分句压缩为短语而合译为汉语小句。例⑤是典型的删英语之繁就汉语之简,由高度形合转向高度意合,原文的关系代词、连接性虚词等几乎消融,潜入汉译,而信息量未损。类似的汉译在钱钟书《管锥编》中最明显。

3.4 句群合译

句群合译,指根据语用和语义的需要原语句群缩合为译语短语、小句或复句的合译方法,原语几个句子语形上虽相对独立,但语义上结合紧密,可据译语表达之需两两融合,组成新的小句或复句,使得译文结构更紧凑,意义更连贯。这种译法多见于英译汉。如:

⑥ Their bodies were never recovered. That was the dreadful part of it. 糟糕的是连尸体也未找到。

⑦ We have received your order. It is booked and we are processing it. 已接受贵方订单,现在执行中。

例⑥由句群合译为小句:前一句 bodies 是旧知,never recovered 是新知;后一句 that 是旧知,指代前一句的全部信息,dreadful part 是新知,也是全文的信息中心。因两句新旧知交合,可以合成,取新知(糟糕)在前、旧知在后(尸体未找到)的句式,这一倒序式(前旧后新为正序式)将话题或主题性前置,以传递最重要的信息为宗旨,译文语义重心在句首,修辞上与原文极似。例⑦由句群合译为复句:We 在交际语境中因双方往来可知各自所完成的行为而省去交际者;原文频换主语,代词复用,对汉语是个挑战,汉译将 booked 与 processing 合译为"执行",it 承前句宾语省略,恰似行云如流水。

4 全译窍门

4.1 结构紧凑避松散

政治外交文本属于论述文体,其议论说明极为理性,句段构建十分严谨慎重,充分体现其内部联系和逻辑关系,因此,译者要具有相当的心智。翻译前可先分析原文是以演绎法还是归纳法展开,据此,译者可考虑译文段落安排,使观点清晰展现,达到层次分明、递进有序的效果。一般来说,原文在论说过程中有意识地将观点、主张做前后或主次排列是一种常态,很多时候只要顺着原文译下去即可。

政治外交文本凸显严密性，句子结构紧凑，环环相扣。此类文本在句子转化层面可将结构紧凑、环环相扣的句子适当拆解。在守住原文逻辑脉络的前提下，抓住句子的内在逻辑，调整原有的句序，按译语结构顺序，即可将原文清楚地表达出来，忌拖泥带水。

4.2 侧重异化避晦涩

政治外交文本，如报告、文件、公务信函等，基本属于信息型，其核心是真实性，即以客观信息为翻译转换的重心，作者则处于隐身地位。翻译中应注重信息和客观事实的真实传递。政治性文本明确表明观点、态度、立场；相对应的译文也必须立场坚定，旗帜鲜明；注重措辞的严谨性和用词的政治含义。

外交文本翻译侧重于异化，即以传递原文内容与形式为主要目标。如例①中 money talks 若归化，可译作"有钱能使鬼推磨"；若要将原文形式原汁原味地传达给译语读者，则要采用异化策略，译成西方资本主义社会所炫耀的"金钱万能论"。

① The Chinese people are wiser than to believe what Westerners call money talks. 中国人非常聪明，绝不会相信西方人所鼓吹的金钱万能论。

4.3 把握分寸词委婉

政治外交涉及国家的政策方针、重要决策或重大利益，其语言严谨、精炼、准确，翻译要在忠实于原文的前提下，精准地传递信息。不过，它还有委婉、含蓄、灵活的一面，这就需要翻译时讲究措辞，或委婉、或含蓄、或模糊，力求有分寸感。如：

② Democratic Party leaders met in Washington yesterday to begin the post-mortem on their three successive presidential election defeat. 民主党领导人昨天聚会华盛顿，开始仔细查找该党连续三次总统竞选失利的原因。

句中的 begin the post-mortem 若译为"对尸体进行检验或者解剖以查明死因"，不但不通，无法达意，还叫人不知所云。若据上下文译成"仔细查找"，不仅措辞委婉，语义也合乎情理。

4.4 特色新词要新译

将中国推介给世界是外宣翻译的重任。其中，中国特色词汇英译是比较突出的现象。中国文化特色词语英译时应注意语言和文化的差异，要特别慎重，中国文化特色词语英译要反复推敲，特别要考虑译文的接受效果。一般而言，英译中国文化特色词采用音译、音译加解释、直译、直译加解释、阐释等方法。如：

③ 黑车 unlicensed taxis

④ 春运 the peak transportation period during China's lunar new year holidays

⑤ 春晚 Spring Festival Eve Entertainment Party

例③的"黑"并非颜色，而指"非法运行的"，意译为 unlicensed。例④英语中无对应词，只能采用释译。例⑤"春晚"是"春节联欢晚会"的缩略形式，按其全称译出。

⑥ "三个代表" Three Represents (to represent the development need of advanced forces of production, to represent the forward direction of advanced culture and to represent the fundamental interests of the broad masses)

⑦"三通"Three direct links of trade, mail, and air and shipping services across the Taiwan Strait

上述词语只有知晓当代中国社会的人才能理解,否则,Three Represents,three direct links 将不知所指,因而有必要加入阐释中国社会文化背景的词语。例⑧则是汉语中典型的同义重复,形成特有的对仗。英译时要删繁就简,用明快地道的英语表达,不一定照原文一一对译。

⑧ 聚精会神搞建设,一心一意谋发展 concentrate on development

5 话题词汇

5.1 组织机构

办公厅 the General Office
财政委员会 the Financial and Economic Affairs Committee
法规备案审查室 the Office for Recording and Examining Laws
法律委员会 the Law Committee
法制工作委员会 the Legislative Affairs Commission
法制室 the Legal Office
国家法室 the Office for State Law
华侨委员会 the Overseas Chinese Affairs Committee
环境与资源保护委员会 the Environmental and Resources Protection Committee
机关党委 the Party Committee of the Organizations
机关服务中心 the Service Center of the Organizations
机关工会 the Trade Union of the Organizations
机关纪委 Discipline Inspection Commission of the Organizations
经济法室 the Office for Economic Law
离退休干部局 the Retired Officials Affairs Bureau
联络局 the Liaison Bureau
秘书局 the Bureau of Secretaries
民法会 the Office for Civil Law
民族委员会 the Ethnic Affairs Committee
农业与农村委员会 the Agricultural and Rural Affairs Committee
全国人大常委会委员长会议 the Chairmen's Council of the Standing Committee of the National People's Congress
全国人民代表大会 the National People's Congress of China
全国人民代表大会常务委员会 the Standing Committee of the National People's Congress
人民大会堂管理局 the Administrative Bureau for the Great Hall of the People
外事局 the Bureau of Foreign Affairs
外事委员会 the Foreign Affairs Committee
新闻局 the News (Information) Bureau
信访局 of Public Voice Bureau
刑法会 the Office for Criminal Law
行政法室 the Office for Administrative Law
研究室 the Research Office
预算工作委员会 the Budget Committee, the Budget Affairs Commission
Chinese Academy of Social Sciences 中国社会科学院
Development Research Centre of the State Council 国务院发展研究中心
General Administration of Customs of the People's Republic of China 中华人民共和国海关总署
General Administration of Press and Publication; National Copyright Administration 国家新闻出版总署
Hong Kong and Macao Affairs Office of State Council 国务院港澳事务办公室
Information Office of the State Council 国务院新闻

办公室

Legislative Affairs Office of the State council, P. R. China 国务院法制办公室

Ministry of Agriculture of the People's Republic of China 中华人民共和国农业部

Ministry of Civil Affairs of the People's Republic of China 中华人民共和国民政部

Ministry of Commerce of the People's Republic of China 中华人民共和国商务部

Ministry of Communications of the People's Republic of China 中华人民共和国交通部

Ministry of Construction of the People's Republic of China 中华人民共和国建设部

Ministry of Education of the People's Republic of China 中华人民共和国教育部

Ministry of Finance of the People's Republic of China 中华人民共和国财政部

Ministry of Foreign Affairs of the People's Republic of China 中华人民共和国外交部

Ministry of Justice of the People's Republic of China 中华人民共和国司法部

Ministry of Human and Social Security of the People's Republic of China 中华人民共和国人力资源与社会保障部

Ministry of Land and Resources of the People's Republic of China 中华人民共和国国土资源部

Ministry of National Defense of the People's Republic of China 中华人民共和国国防部

Ministry of Public Security of the People's Republic of China 中华人民共和国公安部

Ministry of State Security of the People's Republic of China 中华人民共和国国家安全部

Ministry of Supervision of the People's Republic of China 中华人民共和国监察部

National Development and Reform Commission of the People's Republic of China 中华人民共和国国家发展和改革委员会

National School of Administration 国家行政学院

National Tourism Administration 国家旅游局

Office of the Leading Group for Western Region Development of the State Council 国务院西部开发领导小组办公室

Overseas Chinese Affairs Office of the State Council; Office of Overseas Chinese Affairs 国务院侨务办公室

Special Administrative Region Basic Law Committee 香港特别行政区基本法委员会

State Administration (Bureau) of Foreign Experts Affair 国家外国专家局

State Administration for Religious Affairs P. R. C. 国家宗教事务局

State Administration of Cultural Heritage (under the Ministry of Culture) 国家文物局(隶属文化部)

State Ethnic Affairs Commission of the People's Republic of China 中华人民共和国国家民族事务委员会

State Intellectual Property Office (SIPO) 国家知识产权局

State-owned Assets Supervision and Administration Commission of the State Council 国务院国有资产监督管理委员会

Taiwan Affairs Office of the State Council 国务院台湾事务办公室

the Macao Special Administrative Region Basic Law Committee; the Committee for the Basic Law of the Macao Special Administrative Region 澳门特别行政区基本法委员会

Xinhua News Agency 新华通讯社

5.2 会议、公约、宪章

保障措施协定 Agreement on Safeguards

东盟国家议会组织 the ASEAN Inter-Parliamentary Organization

关于战时保护平民之日内瓦公约 Geneva Convention Relative to the Protection of Civilian Persons in Time of War

国际货币基金协定 Agreement of the International Monetary Fund

海员遣返公约 Convention Concerning the Repatriation of Seamen

和平解决国际争端公约 Convention for Peaceful Settlement of International Conflicts

建立海关合作理事会公约 Convention Establishing a Customs Cooperation Council

建立世界知识产权组织公约 Convention Establishing the World Intellectual Organization
联合国特权与豁免公约 Convention on the Privileges and Immunities of the United Nations
联合国宪章 Charter of United Nations
男女同工同酬公约 Convention Concerning Equal Remuneration for Men and Women Workers for Work of Equal Value
欧洲议会 European Parliament
太平洋岛国论坛议会大会 Parliamentary Assembly of the Pacific Islands Forum
维也纳领事关系公约 Vienna Convention on Consular Relations
维也纳条约法公约 Vienna Convention on the Law of Treaty
维也纳外交关系公约 Vienna Convention on Diplomatic Relations
亚欧年轻议员会议 the Asia Europe Young Parliamentarians Meeting
亚太议员环境与发展大会 the Asia-Pacific Parliamentary Conference on Environment and Development
亚洲议会和平协会执行理事会 the Conference of the Executive Council of the Association of Asian Parliaments for Peace
亚洲议员人口与发展会议 the Asia Forum of Parliamentarians on Population and Development
制定最低工资确定办法公约 Convention Concerning the Creation of Minimum Wage Fixing Machinery
专门机构特权与豁免公约 Convention on the Privileges and Immunities of the Specialized
Articles of Agreement of the International Development association 国际开发协会协定
Articles of Agreement of the Charter of the Asian and Pacific Development Centre 亚洲和太平洋发展中心章程
Convention Establishing the World Intellectual Organization 建立世界知识产权组织公约
Convention on the Elimination of All Forms of Discrimination Against Women 消除对妇女一切形式歧视公约
Convention on the Prevention and Punishment of the Crime of Genocide 防止及惩治灭绝种族罪公约
Convention on the Rights of the Child 联合国儿童权利公约
Convention on the Settlement of Investment Disputes Between States and Nationals of Other States 关于解决国家与他国国民之间的投资争端的公约
Convention Relating to the Status of Refugees 关于难民地位的公约
International Convention for the Safety of Life at Sea 国际海上人命安全公约
International Convention on Economic, Social and Cultural Rights 经济、社会及文化权利国际公约
International Convention on the Elimination of All Forms of Racial Discrimination 消除一切形式种族歧视国际公约
Protocol on the Accession of the People's Republic of China 中华人民共和国加入议定书

5.3 职务与职衔

参事 Counselor
党组书记 Secretary Of The Party Leadership Group
发言人 Spokesman
副处长 Deputy Director
副局长;副局级主任 Deputy Director-General
副社长 Deputy Director
副委员长 Vice-Chairman (Chairperson)
副主任科员 Senior Staff Member
顾问 Adviser
局长;正局级主任 Director-General of a Bureau (Department)
科长 section chief
科员 staff member
全国人民代表大会常务委员会委员长 Chairman (Chairperson) of The Standing Committee of The National People's Congress (NPC)
社长 Director
省委书记 Secretary of The Provincial Committee of The CPC
特派员 Commissioner

县委常委 The Stand Committee Member of CPC County Committee
县委书记 Secretary of The CPC County Committee
巡视员 Inspector
中央候补委员 Alternate Member of The CPC Central
中央委员 Member of The CPC Central Committee
（专委会）主任委员 Chairman (of a Special Committee)
Committee of The National Committee of The CPPCC 政协全国委员会
Member of The Standing Committee 常委会
Member 委员
Vice-Chairman 副主席
Member of The Judicial Committee 审判委员会委员
President 院长
Vice President 副院长
Deputy Procurator-General 副检察长
Member of The Procuratorial Committee 检查委员会委员
Procurator-General 检察长
Procurator 检察员
Administrator 署长
Auditor-General 审计长
Assistant Minister 部长助理
Minister 主任
Secretary-General 秘书长
State Councilor 国务委员
Vice Secretary-General 副秘书长
Deputy Director-General 副厅长
Deputy Director-General 副主任
Director-General of a Department 厅长
Director-General of The General Office 办公厅主任
Director-General 司长
Deputy Director-General 副司长
Deputy Director of a Division 副处长
Deputy Section Chief 副科长
Director of a Division 处长
Chief Executive of The County 县长
Chief Executive of The-District Government 区长
Commissioner of The Prefecture 地区专员
Deputy Division Chief 副处长
Director of The General Office 办公厅主任
Division Chief 处长
Executive Vice Governor 常务副省长
Governor 省长

5.4 中国特色词汇

安居工程 Comfortable Housing Project
长远利益 long-term interests
城镇居民最低生活保障 a minimum standard of living for city residents
多边外交 multilateral diplomacy
反对霸权主义 oppose hegemony
反对强权政治 oppose power politics
反对形式主义 oppose formalism
反对一切形式的恐怖主义 oppose terrorism in all guises
防洪工程 flood-prevention project
扶贫工程 Anti-Poverty Project
海外侨胞 overseas Chinese and their relatives
宏观调控 macro-regulation and control
互不干涉内政 mutual non-interference into each other's international affairs
互不侵犯 mutual non-aggression
互利合作，共同繁荣 mutually beneficial cooperation and common prosperity
互相尊重主权和领土完整 mutual respect for sovereignty and territorial integrity
基层监督 grass-roots supervision
基层群众 ordinary workers
价格听证会 public price hearings
坚持和谐发展 maintain social harmony during development
交流互访 mutual exchange and visit
扩大内需，刺激消费 expand domestic demand and consumption
扩大中等收入者比重 raise the proportion of the middle-income group
农业综合改革 overall rural reforms
区域发展总体战略 overall strategy for regional development

社会生产力 overall production capacity
素质教育 competence-oriented education
缩小贫富差距 narrow the gap between the rich and poor
维护国家独立、主权和领土完整 maintain (preserve) national independence, sovereignty and territorial integrity
维护社会安定和谐 maintain/safeguard social stability and harmony
维护社会秩序 maintain public order
温饱工程 Decent-Life Project
物质文明 material civilization
西部大开发 Go-West Campaign
希望工程 Project Hope
一个中心,两个基本点 one focus, two basic points
执政为民的宗旨 our obligation to run the government for the people
a basic cost of living allowance system 最低生活保障制度
a basic political system of China 基本政治制度
act on the principle of democratic centralism 实行民主集中制的原则
adhere to reforms and opening to the outside world 坚持改革开放
adhere to the basic socialist economic system 坚持社会主义基本经济制度
adhere to the four cardinal principles 坚持四项基本原则
advocate development of cross-straits relations 主张发展两岸关系
be in line with conditions in China 符合中国国情
brain drain;brain flow 人才流动
build a socialist country under the rule of law 建设社会主义法治国家
govern the country according to law 依法治国
government authority at the country and township levels, the grass-roots organs of the state power 基层政权
government's work style 政风建设
improve public administration 加强社会管理
improve the ability to implement policies 增强执行力
improve the government's ability to perform its duties and strengthen public trust 提高政府执行力和公信力
improve the government's style of work 加强政风建设
improve the legal system 健全法制
improve the oversight mechanism 健全监督机制
improve the people's physical fitness 增强人民体质
improve the people's well being 改善民生
improve the performance of the central government 加强中央政权建设
improve the socialist legal system 推动健全社会主义法治
income distribution 收入分配
increase in real terms 实际增长
increase mutual understanding 增进了解
increase the proportion of 提高比重比例
increase understanding of the legal system 增强法制观念
reform and opening-up 改革开放
Taiwan authorities 台湾当局
Taiwan compatriots 台湾同胞
Taiwan is an inalienable part of the Chinese territory 台湾是中国领土不可分割的一部分
The Five Principles of Peaceful Coexistence 和平共处五项原则

5.5 缩略语

朝核 North Korean nuclear issue
反恐 counter-terrorism
个税 individual income tax
公关 public relation
国企 state-operated enterprise
军演 military exercises
社保 social security
世博会 World Exhibition or Exposition
特区 Special Administrative Region
外长 Minister of Foreign Affairs
AP 美联社
APEC 亚太经济合作组织
CBD 中央商务区
CIA 美国中情局

FBI 美国联邦调查局
FDA 美国食品药物管理局
GDP 国内生产总值
IMP 进口
INT 国际的
IOS 国际标准化组织
IP 国际协议
IRC 国际红十字会
LAN 局域网
NAACP 全国黑人权益促进会,即黑人为了增进权益的最大机构
NASA 美国航天太空总署
NATO 北大西洋公约组织
PNIR 永久正常贸易关系
UNESCO 联合国教育科学文化组织
UPU 万国邮政联盟
USDA 美国农业部
USIS 美国新闻处
WHO 世界卫生组织
WTO 世界贸易组织

体悟 6 比读体悟

6.1 第七届亚欧外长会议主席声明

Chairman's Statement of the Seventh ASEM Foreign Ministers' Meeting

外长们同意,在实现千年发展目标和约翰内斯堡行动纲领有关目标方面,亚洲和欧洲具有相当大的对话与合作空间。这在本次外长会议上得到充分印证。亚洲已通过贸易投资促进可持续增长,从而实现经济发展,他们强调南南合作的重要性,这既需要新型捐助国的参与,也需要传统捐助国的继续支持。鉴此,外长们对2005年4月印尼亚非峰会的成果表示欢迎。他们还强调2005年联合国首脑会议应为实现千年发展目标注入新的动力。他们重申致力于成功结束世界贸易组织多哈发展议程,强调2005年12月香港部长级会议以平衡方式取得更大结果的重要性。

The Ministers shared the view that in achieving the MDGs and the goals contained in the Johannesburg Plan of Implementation, there is a considerable scope for further dialogue and cooperation between Asia and Europe successfully demonstrated by this meeting, In the light of the successful economic development in Asia through self-sustained growth led by trade and investment, they underlined the importance of South-South cooperation involving emerging donor countries, along with continued support by traditional donors. In this regard, the Ministers welcomed the outcome of the Asia-Africa Summit held in Indonesia April 2005. The importance of the 2005 UN Summit meeting providing renewed impetus to the process of achieving the MDGs was also stressed. They reiterated their commitment to a successful conclusion of the Doha Development Agenda of the WTO, and stressed the importance of well-balanced and ambitious results of the Hong Kong Ministerial Conference in December 2005.(姜秋霞用例)

6.2 中国对当前国际形势的看法

China's View on Current International Situation

① 当前,国际局势正在发生深刻的变化。和平与发展仍是当今时代的主题。世界多极化和经济全球化在曲折中继续发展。总体和平、局部战争,总体缓和、局部紧张,总体稳定、局部动荡,将是

① Currently, the international situation is undergoing complex and deep changes. Peace and development remain the main themes of the present times. World multi-polarization and economic globalization continue their development in zigzags. For a period of time in the future, the basic posture of the

今后一个时期国际局势的基本态势。

international situation will be overall peace and localized war, overall easing and localized tension, overall stability and localized turbulence.

② 人类的和平与发展仍面临着不容忽视的挑战。不公正、不合理的国际政治、经济旧秩序尚未根本改变,局部的战乱、紧张、动荡此起彼伏,南北差距进一步拉大。恐怖主义等非传统安全问题更加突出,全球安全面临的不确定因素增多。

② Peace and development of mankind are still faced with challenges that brook no neglect. The unfair and irrational old international political and economic order has not been fundamentally changed. Localized wars, tension and turbulence rise one after another. The gap between the South and the North has widened. Non-traditional security problems such as terrorism have become more salient and the uncertainties confronting global security have been on the increase.

③ 面对新的挑战,各国应超越传统观念,顺应时代潮流,加强交流合作,密切相互协调。应当积极推动世界多极化和国际关系民主化,努力建立适应各国发展水平和要求的国际经济新秩序,改革不合理的国际金融和贸易体制,保障所有国家特别是发展中国家平等发展的权利。应当充分尊重各国文明发展的多样性,各种文明和各种发展道路应和谐共存,在竞争比较中取长补短,在求同存异中共同进步。

③ Faced with the new challenges, all the countries should surmount the traditional concepts, go along with the tide of the times, enhance exchanges and cooperation and strengthen their mutual coordination. They should actively boost world multi-polarization and democratization of international relations and strive to establish a new international economic order adapted to the development levels and demands of various countries. They should reform the irrational international financial and trade system to safeguard the right to equal development of all the countries, particularly the developing countries. The diversity of the development of civilizations of various countries should be respected. The various civilizations and diverse roads to development should coexist harmoniously, draw on others' strong points to make up one's own weak ones in competition and comparison and make common progress through seeking common ground and shelving differences

④ 中国愿同各国加强协调与合作,为建立公正、合理的国际政治、经济新秩序,为实现一个持久和平与普遍繁荣的世界做出积极地努力。

④ China is ready, together with other countries, to enhance coordination and cooperation and exert active efforts to establish a fair and rational new international political and economic order and achieve lasting peace and universal prosperity in the world. (张春柏用例)

6.3 亚洲政党国际会议

The International Conference of Asian Political Parties

亚洲政党国际会议是亚洲各国政党顺应和平发展的时代潮流、适应亚洲区域合作迅猛发展的势头、寻求扩大政党和国际交流与合作的重要创举。已成为亚洲各主权国家合法政党交流政治理念、寻求政治共识、增进理解与信任的重要论坛,成为发挥政党独特作用、促进区

The International Conference of Asian Political Parties (ICAPP) is a great undertaking in which the region's political parties adjust to contemporary trends such as peace and development, adapt to the rapid development of regional cooperation and expand international exchanges and cooperation. The ICAPP has become an important forum where legal political parties of sovereign Asian countries can exchange

域合作与共同发展的新渠道与新机制。本届亚洲政党国际会议为亚洲各国政党的国际交往注入了新的活力。与会各国政党领导人和代表，就地区安全与多边合作、经济增长与社会进步、政党建设与国家发展三个议题进行了深入探讨与交流。

ideas, seek political consensus and increase understanding and trust. It has also become a new channel and new mechanism through which political parties can play a unique role in promoting regional cooperation and mutual development. The leaders and representatives of the Asian political parties at this conference have carried out extensive discussion and exchanges of ideas on the three topics of regional security and multilateral cooperation, economic development and social progress, as well as party building and national development. (梅德明用例)

6.4 Richard Milhous Nixon's Speech in Visit to China

尼克松1972年访华讲话

① On behalf of all your American guests, I wish to thank you for the incomparable hospitality for which the Chinese people are justly famous throughout the world. I particularly want to pay tribute, not only to those who prepared the magnificent dinner, but also to those who have provided the splendid music. Never have I heard American music played better in a foreign land.

① 我谨代表你们的所有美国客人向你们表示感谢，感谢你们的无可比拟的盛情款待。中国人民以这种盛情款待而闻名世界。我不仅要特别赞扬那些准备了这次盛大晚宴的人，而且还要赞扬那些给我们演奏这样美好音乐的人。我在外国从来没有听到过演奏得这么好的美国音乐。

② Mr. Prime Minister, I wish to thank you for your very gracious and eloquent remarks. At this very moment, through the wonder of telecommunications, more people are seeing and hearing what we say than an any other such occasion in the whole history of the world. Yet, what we say here will not be long remembered. What we do here can change the world.

② 总理先生，我要感谢你的非常盛情和雄辩的讲话。就在这个时刻，通过电讯的奇迹，看到和听到我们讲话的人比在整个世界历史上任何其他的场合都要多。不过，我们在这里讲的话，人们不会长久记住。我们在这里所做的事却能改变世界。

③ As you said in your toast, the Chinese people are a great people, American people are a great people. If our two peoples are enemies the future of this world we share together is dark indeed. But if we can find common ground to work together, the chance for world peace is immeasurably increased.

③ 正如你在祝酒时所讲的那样，中国人民是伟大的人民，美国人民是伟大的人民。如果我们两国人民是敌人的话，那么我们共同居住的这个世界的前途的确是黑暗的。但是，如果我们能够找到进行合作的共同点，那么实现世界和平的机会就无可估量地大大增加。

④ In the spirit of frankness which I hope will characterize our talks this week, let us recognize at the outset these points: We have at times in the past been enemies. We have great differences today. What bring us together is that we have common interests which transcend those differences. As we discuss our differences, neither of us will compromise our principles. But while we cannot close the gulf between us, we can try to bridge it so that we may

④ 我希望我们这个星期的会谈将是坦率的。本着这种坦率的精神，让我们一开始就认识到这样几点：过去的一些时期我们曾是敌人。今天我们仍有巨大的分歧。使我们走到一起的，是我们有超过这些分歧的共同利益。在我们讨论我们分歧的时候，我

be able to talk across it.

们哪一方都不会在我们的原则上妥协。但是,虽然我们不能弥合我们之间的鸿沟,我们却能够设法搭一座桥梁,以便我们能够越过它进行会谈。(魏志成用例)

6.5 The U. S-Europe Divide

President Bush is making a noble effort to pull together the fraying alliance, but the fact is Europeans and Americans no longer share a common view of the world. On the all-important question of power — the utility of power, the morality of the world — they have parted ways. Europeans believe they are moving beyond power into a self-contained world of laws and rules and transnational negotiation and cooperation. Europe itself has entered a post-historical paradise, the realization of Immanuel Kant's "Perpetual Peace". The United States, meanwhile, remains mired in history, exercising power in the anarchic Hobbesian world where international rules are unreliable and where security and the promotion of a liberal order still depend on the possession and use of military might. This is why, on major strategic and international questions today, Americans are from Mars and Europeans are from Venus: They agree on little and understand one another less and less.

欧美的分歧

布什总统正竭力将摩擦不断的联盟扯到一起,然而事实上欧美已经不再拥有共同的世界观。在至关重要的权利问题上,如对权利的使用及权利的道义性的看法上,他们已经分道扬镳。欧洲人坚信,他们已经超越权利的境界,进入一个依靠法制、谈判与合作的完备的世界。欧洲已步入后历史时代的天堂,实现了以马内利·康德所说的“永久的和平”。而与此同时,美国依然陷入历史的困境中,在无政府主义的霍布斯哲学的世界里施展着权力,因为在这个世界上国际准则并不可靠,还需要用军事力量去维护安全和自由秩序。所以在当今重大战略和国际问题上美国与欧洲的立场相去甚远。他们少有共识,双方越来越缺乏理解。(张春柏用例)

6.6 Unparalleled Cultural Diversity of China

China is providing the fascination in the 21st century. Since the Second World War, countries like Britain and Germany have had major achievements and minor problems, while Southeast Asia has had major problems and minor achievements. China, though, is experiencing both major achievements and major problems. I do believe the tough line on population control has been a great contribution to humanity on an international level. Now the questions is whether China can harness its great economic power — but I'm positive that China will become a superpower like the United States in the future. Europe also appears to have an exciting future before it — its cultural diversity is unparalleled.

中国文化多样性举世无双

中国是21世纪最富吸引力的国家。自从第二次世界大战以来,英国和德国这样的国家取得了大成就,遇到了小问题;东南亚遇到了大问题,取得了小成就;而中国既取得了大成就,也面临大问题。我确实相信,中国在人口控制方面采取的强硬路线在国际上为人类做出了重大贡献。现在的问题是中国能否驾驭其巨大的经济力量,但我本人相信,中国将来一定会成为像美国那样的超级大国。欧洲的未来也显得令人振奋——其文化多样性举世无双。(梅德明用例)

6.7 推荐读物

(1)陈海庆,布局谋篇:英汉篇章互译技巧,大连理工大学出版社2009年版。
(2)陈宏薇,高级汉英翻译,外语教学与研究出版社2009年版。
(3)陈新,英汉文体翻译教程,北京大学出版社2002年版。
(4)许明武,新闻英语与翻译,中国对外翻译出版公司2003年版。
(5)何刚强,翻译理论与技巧,外语教学与研究出版社2009年版。
(6)姜秋霞,外事笔译,外语教学与研究出版社2009年版。
(7)刘宓庆,文体与翻译,中国对外翻译出版公司1998年版。

练习 7 课后练习

7.1 分析题

(1)试用所译和比读材料分析合译及其特点。
(2)结合窍门与比读材料,试析政论文本的翻译特点。
(3)选择经典的政治外交英汉对照文本,分析其翻译技巧。

7.2 实训题

7.2.1 未来十五年的主要奋斗目标

在推进改革和发展的同时,社会主义精神文明和民主法制建设要取得显著进展,实现社会全面进步。这个奋斗目标,展现了20世纪末、21世纪初我国现代化建设的美好前景,表达了中华民族自立自强的雄心壮志。实现了这个目标,我国社会生产力、综合国力和人民生活水平都将再上一个大台阶,社会经济面貌将发生历史性的巨大变化,为21世纪中叶基本实现现代化,奠定坚实的基础。这个目标是宏伟的,经过努力也是一定能够实现的。

7.2.2 The Proliferation of Nuclear

I do think a world war is less likely for the present, although I worry about the proliferation of nuclear weapons at one end and lethal small arms at the other. It is terrifying the way that power is increasingly disseminated to small, completely ruthless groups like terrorists, drug traffickers and local warlords. The great imponderable is that some nut could create a nuclear explosion. Or that some essentially local conflict could escalate out of control. You cannot isolate instability: it gets exported. Another worry stems from the huge economic imbalances in a world where the richest 20% have 86% of global GDP, and the 20 poorest countries only 1%.

7.3 思考题

(1)政治外交翻译如何再现原文风格?

(2)政治外交翻译中多义的词汇如何确定其义?
(3)政治外交翻译如何把握情感的分寸?
(4)译文如何在宏观上再现原文政治性?
(5)如何考虑政治外交翻译中的敏感性?
(6)译文词句之间可作哪些微调?
(7)译文如何做到语用极似?
(8)译文如何做到语义相对极似?
(9)如何翻译文化负载词和特色词?
(10)外交翻译常用哪些模糊语言手段?
(11)外交辞令有什么样的翻译规律?
(12)如何区分政治翻译与翻译中的政治?

第 16 课 科学技术

导 译

科学与技术是两个不同的概念，既有明确的区别又有紧密的联系，通常合称“科学技术”。广义地看，科技是自然科学、社会科学和工程技术的总和。狭义的科技指自然科学和工程技术，不包含社会科学。

从语言功能角度把各种传递科技信息的语篇划归为实用文体，即科技语体，它泛指一切话题为科学和技术的书面语和口语，语域层次多，范围广。相应的翻译属于实用翻译，翻译要再现原文的风格，就科技翻译而论，一般要求选词准确，符合专业性，句子结构严谨，逻辑严谨，语言简洁。所以译者除了要有良好的科技专业知识外，还要了解科技英语与普通英语文体的差异，掌握一些科技文体的语言结构特色与篇章要求。

科技文体作为一种独立的文体形式，有其自身的特点：多数科技文章使用无人称句；语气正式；陈述客观准确；语言规范；文体质朴；逻辑性强；专业术语性强。了解这七个显著特点将有助于英汉科技翻译。

练笔 1 课前练笔

1.1 高层建筑

在本世纪初期，二十层左右的建筑群一排排面对面地拔地而起，相互之间仅由昏暗而狭窄的街道隔开，形成了“都市峡谷”。人们主要关心的是，如何把最大量的人口安置在最小的面积上，而由此造成的拥挤状态和它对于人们以及对于作为一个相互作用的有机体的城市的影响，就不是房屋设计考虑范围内的事情了。

1.2 火箭与燃料

单级火箭不能产生足够的动力把卫星送到应该达到的位置,因此就需要多级火箭,即三级或四级火箭。在多级火箭内,第一级火箭推送整个箭体脱离地面,上升一定的高度。然后,当一级火箭内的燃料或氧化剂用完之后,就与箭体脱离,同时二级火箭进行点火。当二级火箭燃料烧完后,也同样自行脱落,此时三级火箭点火。

1.3 **Automotive Night Vision**

① Driving becomes more difficult after sunset. Not only is visibility generally reduced, but an even more serious challenge on unlighted roads are the headlamps of approaching vehicles, which can dazzle a driver's eyes. Night-vision systems can help drivers navigate in the dark, but to be of real help, they must be able to see both in the light and in the dark. They also must produce natural-looking images of the road, which is usually populated with animate and inanimate objects.

② Night-vision systems were introduced into the automotive market in the 2000 model year. The Cadillac Deville that year used a thermal camera that was sensitive to the long-wave infrared part of the electro-magnetic spectrum along with a display that projected a virtual image of the road scene using the windshield.

③ Although this system excelled at detecting warm objects, such as pedestrians and animals, the image contrast was generally poorer for cool, inanimate objects, such as lane markings, signs and reflective road markings. Also, because automobile, windshields are not transmitting-wave infrared radiation, the camera had to be mounted on the outside of the vehicle, exposing it to the weather and, potentially, to damage from front-end collisions and road debris.

1.4 **What is Nanotechnology**?

Nanotechnology is the design, characterization, production, and application of structures, devices, and systems by controlling the shape and size at the nanometer scale. A nanometer is one billionth of a meter. For comparison, a single human hair is about 80,000 nm wide, a red blood cell is approximately 7,000 nm wide and a water molecule is almost 0.3 nm across. The nanoscale generally is defined in nanotechnology to be from 100 nm down to the size of atoms (approximately 0.2 nm). Understanding and controlling matter at the nanoscale interests researchers in the sciences, medicine, agriculture, and industry because a material's properties at the nanoscale can be very different from those at a larger scale. As reports of new discoveries and applications for nanotechnology emerged, governmental, industrial, and public stakeholders recognized the need to develop a standard nanotechnology terminology to facilitate communication among the various communities.

2 课前批评

2.1 现代控制理论

近年来现代控制理论和大系统理论已经在各个工程技术领域内得到了广泛的应用,并取得了一系列显著成就。在电力拖动直流调速系统的设计中人们也采用了线形二次状态反馈理论设计系统的最优控制律以克服经典频域设计法的某些不足。但线形二次状态反馈法计算复杂,工程实际应用不方便。故本文提出一种简化的二次状态反馈法来设计直流调速系统。该方法兼具频域设计法和线形二次状态反馈法的优点。文中示例表明,采用这种方法设计的直流调速系统具有良好的稳定性与鲁棒性。

Modern Control Theory

Modern Control Theory and Large Scale System Theory have been widely applied in all engineering fields and many amazing achievements have been obtained recently. And in designing electrical drive d. c. speed control system, the optimum feedback control law of the design system of linear quadratic state feedback theory has been used to overcome some limitations of classical frequency domain design method. However, the computation of linear quadratic state feedback design method is complicated and it is not easy to put into practice. To overcome these defects, this paper intends to propose a simplified linear quadratic state feedback design method for d. c. speed control system. The new method possesses the advantages of both frequency domain design method and linear quadratic state feedback design method. The illustrative example presented in section 4 of this paper shows that d. c. speed control system designed by this method is stable and robust. (杨寿康用例)

2.2 The Age of Automation

"Automation" has been, and still is, a greatly misused word, but its proper meaning, and therefore its implications, is gradually becoming better understood. Perhaps I could attempt an explanation, if not a definition, by saying that it is a concept through which a machine-system is caused to operate with maximum efficiency by means of adequate measurement, observation, and control of its behaviour. It involves a detailed and continuous knowledge of the functioning of the system, so that the best corrective actions can be applied immediately they become necessary.

自动化时代

自动化一直是、现在仍然是一个被许多人误用的词,但是它本身固有的意义以及它在许多方面的含义正逐渐为人们所理解。也许我下面的话可以作为自动化这个词的说明,即使不算个定义的话:自动化就是对机器系统的工作状态进行适当测量、观察和控制,使之以最高的效率运转这样一个概念。自动化要求不断地详细了解机器的运行,

Automation in this true sense is brought to full fruition only through a thorough exploitation of its three major elements, communication, computation, and control—the three "Cs". I believe there is a great need to make sure that some, at any rate, of the implications to our society of three "Cs" in combination are recognized and understood.	一旦必要时可以立即采取最佳的改正措施。从自动化这种真正的含义来看,只有在充分利用它的三个主要因素,即通讯、计算和控制之后,才能完全实现。因此,我认为很有必要使大家认识和了解到这种通讯、计算和控制三结合对我们社会的意义,至少是某些方面的意义。(杨寿康用例)

3 全译知识 科技全译

科技一般与文艺相对,多指自然科学与工程技术,其实还应包括人文社会科学。

3.1 人文社科全译

人文社会科学一般指研究人文社会现象的科学,包括政治学、经济学、法学、史学、美学、文艺学、心理学、伦理学、语言学、翻译学等,其文体特点是用词端庄,论证严谨,结构繁复。总之,重理也重情,或理中带情。如:

① It would be a pity for a man who handed down hundreds of wise decision from the bench to be remembered only for the one unwise decision he made in Congress. 一个在法院作过数百次英明裁决的人,却因国会上一次愚蠢的决定而背千古骂名,那才真是遗憾呢!

原文的 wise decision, unwise decision, be remembered 等及其汉译的"英明裁决"、"愚蠢的决定"和"千古骂名"等都带有明显的褒贬色彩;原文不长,但较复杂,汉译也在"人"前摆长龙,也为骂名列长因,结构繁复;原文首句发感慨,汉译移后,"那"、"才"、"真"、"呢"足以传达原文丰沛的情感。又如:

② Could any spectacle, for instance, be more grimly whimsical than that of gunners using science to shatter man's bodies while close at hand surgeons use it to restore them? 譬如,一边是炮手用科学把人体炸得粉碎,一边是外科医生就近用科学重新缝合。难道还有什么能比这更冷酷无情、更荒谬绝伦的吗?

与上例一样,英语喜欢先摆观点或作出评价,再说所评之事,这是英语思维的特点。汉语则相反,先摆事实,再说道理。况且原文为问句,汉语的问句一般不能太长,过长气转不及,所以汉译破长为短,但气势不减,一个"难道"平地峰起,grimly whimsical 后一词本意为"古怪",因前一词而增生语境义,二者分译,更显层次,情感逐浪升高。

3.2 科学技术全译

自然科学和工程技术,可简称"科学技术"或"科技",研究自然界各种物质和现象及其利用与改造中积累下来的经验和知识。其文体特点是专业词汇多、句法关系严密、重逻辑避情感；其翻译重内容而轻形式，即为了传达内容可对形式做任何程度的转化。如：

③ Hydraulic turbines may be grouped in two general classes: the impulse type which utilizes the kinetic energy of a high-velocity jet which acts upon only a small part of the circumference at any instant, and a reaction type which develops power from the combined action of pressure and velocity of the water that completely fills thinner and water passages.

【原译】：水轮机可分为两大类：一类是冲击式，它利用一股高速射流的动能瞬时作用于轮周的一小部分来进行工作；另一类是反作用式，它将水全部充满叶轮和水道，利用水压和水速的共同作用产生动力。

【试译】：水轮机可分两大类：一是冲击式，即利用高速射流的动能瞬间冲击轮周边缘；一是反作用式，即用水充满叶轮和水道，借水压和水速的双重作用产生动力。

本例中轮机和流体力学的术语频频出现，除了普通物理学知识外，还得了解更专的专业知识。另外，科技文体讲分类，常用定语从句揭示各类的内涵，多为解释说明性质，一般分译出来。本例的两种分类带有定语从句，显得更为复杂，而汉译不能如此繁复，必须跳出原文的枝蔓，可添加"一类是"、"另一类是"等语词，因为科技翻译自有其美，美在言简意赅，能在流畅之余追求点节奏，则更好。

窍门 4 全译窍门

4.1 科学尚简

科学尚简，要求以最少的文字符号准确地表达、传递最大的信息量。因此，语言精练、结构紧凑就成了科技语言的突出特征。科技文献汉译英应考虑这一特征。如：

① 这些机器很容易拆卸，并在检查后重新装配好。

【译文Ⅰ】：These machines can easily be taken to pieces and put together again after they have been looked at.

【译文Ⅱ】：These machines can easily be dismantled and reassembled after being examined.

译文Ⅱ使用了专业词 dismantled, reassembled，更准确、更精练地表达了原义。可见简洁明晰是科技文体的特点之一和最基本要求之一；英译汉也要简短精练，一目了然，都应力求避免烦琐、冗赘和重复。如以下例②译文Ⅰ欠佳，译文Ⅱ简洁明了。

② It is forbidden to dismantle it without permission so as to avoid any damage to its parts.

【译文Ⅰ】：为了避免损坏设备的零件，未经许可不得拆卸该设备。

【译文Ⅱ】：严禁乱拆，以免损坏该设备的零件。

4.2 善译图表题名

图(figure)表(table)有其特殊功能，能把语言文字难以说清的内容简明地呈现出来。图表题名应具有"自明性"，即只看图、图题和图例，不阅读正文即可理解图意；图表题名应简短确切。这一标准和英文图表题名的要求基本一致:图表题名应具有自明性,即读者只需要根据图表就能确定研究对象、研究过程,不需要参考文中的其他内容就能阐释图表的意义;其次,图表题名应足够详细和精确。因此,图表的中文题名和英文题名几乎具有一一对应的

关系,英译时就应将汉语题名准确译出。如例③中“修正”与“简化”的-ed 分词叠放,容易产生歧义;例④中“计算结果”重复翻译。

③ 图 4 修正的简化超级网络

【原译】: Fig. 4 Modified simplified super-network

【改译】: Figure 4 Simplified super-network after modification

④ 表 2 不同 Φ 下的计算结果与静载下计算结果对比

【原译】: Tab. 2 Contrasts between calculated results under static loads and calculated results under different φ

【改译】: Table 2 Contrast of calculated results from static loads and different φ

4.3 破解长龙

长句是科技英语的一大特点。英语句长的原因很多,但根本原因是语言结构层次多而复杂:句中并列成分多,各种短语、修饰语多,并列分句或各种从句多。汉译时,首先要弄通英语原句结构,理清关系,抓住核心,再按汉语的表达方式与习惯译出,力求既能正确表达内容,又不拘泥原文形式。所以抓住句子各部分的语序极为重要。如果英语长句按照时间顺序或逻辑关系排列,且与汉语表达方法基本一致时,便可按照原文的顺序翻译。如:

⑥ However, (Ⅰ) even if prediction becomes possible, people (Ⅱ) who live in areas (Ⅲ) where earthquakes are a common occurrence (Ⅳ) will still have to do their best to prevent disasters by building structures (Ⅴ) that are resistant to ground movement and (Ⅵ) by being personally prepared.

本例是由一个主句、三个定语从句和一个让步状语从句组成。其句法关系依次是:Ⅰ是 even if 引导的让步状语从句;Ⅱ是定语从句,修饰主句的主语 people;Ⅲ是 where 引导的定语从句,修饰 areas;Ⅳ是主句(其中主句的主语 people 被两个定语从句隔开);Ⅴ是第三个定语从句修饰 building structures;需要注意的是,主句中的两个 by 引导的状语短语被 that 引导的定语从句隔开了。翻译时采用顺译法,这一点可以从以上例句所表明的序号清楚地看到。

【译文】:然而,即使可以预测,居住在地震频发区的人们还是应尽力预防灾难,办法是建造能够抗震的房屋,同时做好个人准备。

4.4 逻辑释疑

科技文章具有逻辑性强,各种成分之间、句子之间均有密切的逻辑联系。科技文章常有些令人费解、甚至误解的句子,所以逻辑分析在科技翻译中有排难解惑之用。如:

⑦ The pressure of increasing population leads to the vertical growth of cities with the result that people are forced to adjust themselves to congestion in order to maintain these relatively artificial land values. 人口增长的压力造成城市向高空发展，从而人为地提高地价，其结果是人们被迫适应城市的拥挤状况，住进了高楼。

本句看似费解：人们为什么要被迫适应拥挤以维持人为的地价？实为误解，以为 in order to maintain…修饰前面从句的谓语 are forced to adjust…这不符合逻辑。根据逻辑分析，这个不定式短语应修饰 lead，即前面主句的谓语。

4.5 静词动译

英语有些名词一般情况下是静态的，如 knowledge（learning, that which is known），但在某些搭配中获得了动态性质，汉译时要转向动态。如：

⑧ Automation involves a detailed and continuous knowledge of the functioning of the system, so that the best corrective actions can be applied immediately they become necessary. 自动化要求不断详细了解（机器）系统的操作，以便必要时，立即采取最佳校正措施。

例⑧中，knowledge 前有 continuous，后有 the functioning of the system，其动态性跃然纸上，意为“了解”。

5 话题词汇

5.1 自然科学

二恶英 dioxin
严重急性呼吸综合征 Severe Acute Respiratory Syndromes（SARS）
分子遗传学 molecular genetics
干扰素 interferon
干细胞 stem cells
超导体 superconductor
横坐标 abscissa
基础研究 basic research
基因疫苗 gene vaccine
基因诊断 gene diagnosis
基因治疗 gene therapy
机载激光测深 airborne laser sounding
机载遥感器 airborne sensor
加常数 addition constant
降水概率 precipitation probability
降水量 precipitation
空间站 space station
量子纠缠 quantum entanglement
模拟地图 analog map
贫铀弹 depleted uranium bomb
平差值 adjusted value
千年生态系统评估 millennium ecosystem assessment
色盲片 achromatic film
摄影基线 air base
生命体征 vital signs
生物防治 biological control
生物入侵 biological invasion
生物信息学 bioinformatics
实用地图学 applied cartography
酸雨 acid rain
太阳风暴 solar storm
太阳能 solar energy
炭疽 anthrax
唐氏综合征 Downs syndrome
体细胞遗传学 somatic genetics
通信卫星 communication satellite
微积分 calculus
温室效应 greenhouse effect

西尼罗河病毒 West Nile virus
像差 aberration
像场角 angular field of view
消冰作用 ablation
冰川消融区 ablation area of glacier
异常 abnormal
医学遗传学 medical genetics
遗传筛选 genetic screening
营养免疫 nutrition immunology
应用研究 application research
有机(生化)纳米材料 organic (biochemical) nanomaterial
远程医学 telemedicine
载人航天 manned space flight
植物全息图像 plant holographic images
主动式遥感 active remote sensing
转基因动物 transgenic animal
转基因食品 genetically modified food
准晶 quasicrystal
自主计算 autonomic computing
admissible error 容许误差
algae 海藻
amino acids 氨基酸
annealing 退火
antenna 天线
antivirus 抗病毒
argument 变元,自变量
artery 动脉
astronomer 天文学家
astronomical object 星球;星体
bacterium 细菌
botany 植物学
catalyst 催化剂
caterpillar 蠋
chlorophyll 叶绿素
coefficient 系数
comet 彗星
composite reaction 复合反应
conductance 电导
constant 常量
coral 珊瑚
cosmos 宇宙
critical temperature 临界温度
crystal pattern 晶体结构
default 默认值
derivative 导数
differential 微分
distortion 畸变
electrolytic cell 电解池
elongation 伸长度
emphysema 肺气肿
enzyme 酶
erosion 侵蚀
eruption 爆发;喷发
excess pressure 附加压力
fossil 化石
function library 函数库
fungus 菌类
geologist 地质学家
glacier 冰川
gland 腺体
grasshopper 蚱蜢
gravitational force 万有引力
half time period 半衰期
herbicide 除草剂
hibernate 冬眠
hormone 荷尔蒙
ice sheet 冰原
intermetallic compound 金属间化合物
intermolecular force 分子间力
intestine 肠
irreversible process 不可逆过程
kinetic equations 动力学方程
landlocked area 内陆
larvae 幼虫
lattice constant 晶格常数
lichen 地衣
magnetic dipole 磁偶极子
machinability 加工性能
mammal 哺乳类动物
Mars 火星
matrix 矩阵
meteor 流星;大气现象
meteorology 气象学
meteorologist 气象学家
micron 微米(百万分之一米)

molten lava 岩浆
moss 藓类(植物)
nectar 花蜜
negative pole 负极
null value 空值
observatory 天文台
open system 敞开系统
opposite span 相反旋转
organism 有机物
pancreas 胰腺
phase rule 相律
photosynthesis 光合作用
planet 行星
pollen 花粉
primate 灵长动物
protein 蛋白质
rapid 急流
reptile 爬行动物
saturated vapor 饱和蒸汽
scale 鳞片
sedimentation 沉降
seismic activity 地震活动性
solar system 太阳系
square centimeter 平方厘米
standard electromotive force 标准电动势
surface process control 表面过程控制
variable 变量
vein 静脉
yield 产率
yield strength 屈服强度

5.2 工程技术

半导体材料 semiconductor material
变压器 transformer
并行工程 concurrent engineering
博客 blog; blogger
插槽 slot
插座 socket
参数 parameter
超级链接 hyperlink
充值卡 rechargeable card
处理器 processor
传感器 sensor
磁悬浮列车 magnetic suspension train
存取 access
代用燃料 alternative fuel
带宽 bandwidth
电感器 inductor
电容器 capacitor
电抗 reactance
电路 circuit
电流 current
电压 voltage
电子货币 e-cash
电阻 resistance
动漫 comic and animation
孵化器 incubator
高新技术 high technology; hi-tech
公差;容差 tolerance
共享软件 shareware
光纤通信 optical fiber communication
轨道交通 rail transport
黑客 hacker
回路;环路 loop
活动桌面 active desktop
机顶盒 set-top box
基因工程 genetic engineering
监视器 monitor
金属玻璃 metallic glasses
可视图文 visual pictures and literature
蓝牙技术 bluetooth
垃圾邮件 spasm/junk mails
浏览器 browser
漫游 roaming; surf; browse
敏捷制造 agile manufacturing
免费软件 freeware
纳米 nanometer
纳米材料 nano-material
纳米粒子 nano-particle
纳米技术 nano-technology
内联网 intranet
能源监控 energy audit
平台 platform
千年虫 millennium bug

轻轨 light rail（vehicles）；LRV
燃料电池 fuel cell
杀毒软件 virus-killer
生态灭绝 ecocide
生物芯片 biochip
视频点播 video-on-demand
数字地球 digital earth
数字显示器 digital display
外联网 extranet
网吧 internet bar
网虫 netter；internet geek
网格计算 grid computing
网络 network
网络电脑 network computer
网络数据库 network database
网络综合征 Net Synthesis
网民 netizen；net citizen；cyber citizen
网上新手 newbie
网页 webpage
网友 net friend；cyber pal
网站 website，web site
相量 phasor
信息高速公路 information superhighway
信息家电 info-electrical appliance
虚拟人 visual human
虚拟现实技术 virtual reality technology
遥感 remote sensing
液晶 liquid crystal
仪表 meter
移动计算 mobile computing
域名 domain name
远程登录 telnet
元件，分量 component
指针 pointer
智能卡 smart card
主页 homepage
组织培养技术 tissue culture technology
子弹头列车 bullet train
access time 存取时间
algorithm 算法
alternator 交流发电机
ambient temperature 环境温度
applications package 应用程序包
armature 电枢
array 数组
backup 备份
bar-code reader 条形码阅读机
batch processing 批处理
buffer 缓冲区
bug 故障；（程序）错误
built-in 内置的
cache 高速缓冲存储器
channel 信道，通道
chip 芯片；晶片
code 编写代码
cognitive modelling system 认知模型系统
compatibility 兼容性
configuration file 配置文件
data entry 数据输入
demodulate 解调
diagram 简图；曲线图
dialogue box 对话框
digital signal processor 数字信号处理
dimension 维
data processing 数据处理
debug 调试
electron tube 电子管
emulate 仿真；模仿
entry 登录项；输入项
fiber optics 光纤
flowchart 流程图
flux 通量
frequency converter 频率转换器
gear 齿轮
graphical interface 图形界面
harmonics 谐波
hybrid 混合物；杂种
hypermedia 超媒体
hypertext 超级文本
immunity 抗扰度（力）
impedance 阻抗
impulse response 冲击响应
index 下标
infrared transmitter/receiver 红外线发射机/接收机
initialization 初始化

integrated circuit 集成电路
interactive video 交互视频
laptop 手提电脑
local area network 局域网
magnetic core 磁芯
magnetic drum 磁鼓
manual 手册
menu system 菜单系统
menu bar 菜单条
microcode 微代码
microprocessor 微处理器
network architecture 网络体系结构
network interface 网络接口
network operating system 网络操作系统
network topology 网络布局;网络结构
node 结点
non-interactive 非交互式的
overflow 溢出
palmtop 掌上电脑
parallel port 并行口
parity 奇偶性
partition 划分
photoelectric 光电的
pixel 像素
plot 绘图;描绘
port 端口;出入口
power-factor 功率因子
priority 优先级
protected mode 保护模式
protocol 规约;协议
pull-down menu 下拉菜单
potentiometer 电位器
programmer 程序员
prompt 提示;提示符
prototype 原型;样机
punched card 穿孔卡片
radiation 辐射
rating 额定值;标称值
real-time scheduling 实时调度
reboot 重新启动
rectifier 整流器
replicate 复制
resolution 精度;分辨率
retrieval 检索
sampling 采样
screen buffer 屏幕缓冲区
screen interface 屏幕界面
serial port 串行口
server 服务器
shrink-wrapped product 压缩打包产品
Silicon Valley 硅谷
software engineering 软件工程
solid-state memory 固态内存
speech processing 语音处理
spike 尖峰信号
string 字符串
synchronous orbit satellite 同步轨道卫星
synchronized mode 同步模式
telecommunication 远程通信
template 样板,模板
thermionic valve 热离子管;热阴电子管
time domain 时域
transfer function 传输函数;转移函数
transfer rate 传输速率
transistor 晶体管
tuned circuit 调谐电路
twisted-pair cable 双扭线电缆
upgrade 升级
user interface 用户界面
vacuum tube 真空管
virtual memory 虚拟内存
video adapter 视频适配器
wide area network 广域网
write-protect 写保护

5.3 缩略语

安全电子交易协议 SET
不间断电源系统 UPS
电子布告栏 BBS
调制解调器 Modem
动态链接库 DLL
多媒体短信服务 MMS
广域信息服务系统 WAIS
全球定位系统 GPS

全球通 GSM
数字电视 DTV
通讯协议 TCP/IP
万维网 WWW
文本短信服务 SMS
文件传送协议 FTP
液晶显示器 LCD
邮局协议 POP
域名管理系统 DNS
中国强制认证 CCC
转基因生物 GMO
AIDS 艾滋病
ATM 异步传输模式
BAS 建筑设备自动化系统
CEO 首席执行官
DAT 数字音频磁带
DBA 数据库管理员
DBMS 数据库管理系统
DDB 分布式数据库
DNA 数字自然音影技术
DVB 数字视频广播
DVD 多功能数码光盘
EVD 增强型多媒体盘片系统
FMT 柔性制造技术
GMO 转基因生物
IGBT 绝缘栅双极晶体管
ISO 国际标准化组织
ISS 国际空间站
LSI 大规模集成
MEMS 微机电系统
MTBF 平均无故障工作时间
OLE 对象连接与嵌入
OCR 光学字符识别
PCR 聚合酶链反应
RISC 精简指令集计算
rms 均方根
SET 安全电子交易协议
SQL 结构化查询语言
STB 机顶盒
STM 同步传输模式
WAP 移动上网
WHO 世界卫生组织
WYSIWYG 所见即所得

6 比读体悟

6.1 什么是建模?

① 首先需要认识到,学习怎样应用数学和学习数学是很不一样的。成功地应用数学的技巧与理解概念、证明定理或解方程的技巧是大有区别的。因此,本书肯定是与某一数学分支的教材不同。书中没有那么多理论,只有几个指导原则。但这并不是说数学建模是门很简单的学科。难点不是在于学习和理解涉及的数学知识,而在于明白如何运用。许多例子都说明,非常简单的数学知识可以用以解决很难的问题,当然,一般来说,问题的复杂程度也要求所用数学知识的难度。

What Is Modeling?

① It is important to realize at the outset that learning to apply mathematics is a very different activity from learning mathematics. The skills needed to be successful in applying mathematics are quite different from those needed to understand concepts, to prove theorems or to solve equations. For this reason, this book is bound to appear different from a text dealing with a particular branch of mathematics. There is no theory to learn and there are only a few guiding principles. This is not to suggest, however, that mathematical modeling is an easy subject. The difficulty is not in learning and understanding the mathematics involved but in seeing where and how to apply it. There are many examples of very simple mathematics giving useful solutions to very difficult problems, although generally speaking the complexity of the problem and of the required mathematical treatment go hand in hand.

② 专业建模人员需要面对各种各样的现实问题,他们的主要任务就是把每个实际问题转化成数学问题。这就是建模的本质。建模过程可能包括为弄清问题而进行的讨论、确定问题中涉及的参数、估计、近似以及提出采取的步骤等,这都需要花费金钱和时间。

② Professional modelers have to deal with a variety of real problems, and their main task is to translate each problem into a mathematical forms. This is the essence of modeling, and it can involve discussions to clarify the problem, identification of problem variables, estimation, approximation and advocation of courses of action that may cost money and time.

③ 能源行业有许多可以说明如何建模的例子。显然,水、电、气、油的流动以及根据随时变化的需要对之进行合理配置的问题都需要用数学方法来解决。提供能源的危险性,特别是在利用核能的今天,也都是用统计或数学模型来分析的。

③ The power industry provides many examples of how mathematical modeling is used. Problems of flow of water, electricity, gas and oil, and the necessity to match provision of these with varying demand, clearly lend themselves to mathematical treatment. The risk aspects of power provision, much publicized these days in connection with nuclear power, are also analyzed by use of statistical and mathematical models.

(马新英用例)

6.2 磁悬浮列车

Magnetically Levitating Trains

① 车速超过每小时 240 公里(150 英里)的高速地面运输技术基本上可以分为两类:

① High-speed ground transportation (HSGT) technologies with vehicle speeds exceeding 150 mph can be divided into two basic categories:

② 高速铁路系统——最高速度每小时 240—320 公里(150—200 英里),跟传统的铁路一样,钢轮在钢轨上打转;该系统能借改进铁路路基和车厢而提速。

② High-speed rail (HSR) systems, with top speeds between 150 and 200 mph, use steel wheels on steel rails, as with traditional railroads, but can achieve higher speeds because of the design of both the rail bed and cars.

③ 高速磁悬浮系统——最高速度每小时 400—480 公里(250—300 英里),利用安装在车体或导轨上强大的磁铁产生吸力或斥力,将列车升起,悬浮在轨道上,并推动列车前进。磁悬浮列车可以喻为飞行的列车或制导的飞机。

③ High-speed magnetic levitation (MAGLEV) systems, with top speeds between 250 and 300 mph, use forces of attraction or repulsion from powerful magnets placed in either the vehicle or the guideway beneath it both to lift the vehicle above the guideway and to propel it forward. A MAGLEV vehicle can be likened to a flying train or a guided aircraft.

④ 如果跟公路运输和空中运输有效地结合起来,那么高速地面运输技术,特别是磁悬浮列车,对今后解决交通拥堵将起重要作用。

④ If linked effectively with highways and air service, HSGT technologies — particularly MAGLEV — could have a significant impact on congestion in the future.

⑤ 将高速铁路技术与磁浮技术相比较,看来首选后者。虽然新一代高速铁路已达每小时约 298 公里(186 英里)的商业运行速度,但再要提速,将面临许多工程问题。这说明发展铁路技术的空间已经有限。反之,磁悬浮技术方兴未艾,它将随着工程技术的进展而大有进

⑤ When comparing HSR with MAGLEV technologies, MAGLEV appears to be the technology of choice. Though the new generation of HSR technology can reach commercial speeds of up to 186 mph, additional increases in speed pose great engineering problems, suggesting that rail transportation is a mature technology. MAGLEV technology, on the other hand, is in its infancy and will improve substantially with

展。

additional engineering.

⑥ 跟高速铁路不同，磁悬浮列车在导轨和列车之间没有物理接触，因此磨损少、噪声小、可靠性好，容易保养。乘坐磁悬浮列车跟乘坐在平稳气流中飞行的航班同样舒适，爬坡和车身内倾转弯都不必骤然减速，因此线路占地（通过居民区）比铁路少。而且，磁悬浮列车跟高速电气列车一样，都靠电运行，沿线不排放烟尘。

⑥ In contrast to HSR, MAGLEV systems involve no physical contact between the guideway and the vehicle, which means less wear, less maintenance, less noise, and greater reliability. MAGLEV rides are as comfortable as those on airliners flying in nonturbulent air. MAGLEV trains can climb grades and curves without substantially reducing speed, thus permitting lines that are less intrusive on existing communities than rail lines. And, as with electric HSR, there are no emissions along the guideway because MAGLEV runs on electricity.

⑦ 虽然磁悬浮系统的基建费用比高速铁路系统高，但是运行费用大致相当，它以高速吸引乘客，总收入更高。

⑦ Though the capital costs of a MAGLEV system are somewhat higher than those of an HSR system, operating costs are about the same, and with MAGLEV's higher speeds it can attract more riders and produce more revenues.（方梦之用例）

6.3 Space Station Program Faces EVA, Weight and Power Problems

空间站计划面临太空舱外活动、重量和能源问题

① NASA has revealed that the current design for Space Station Freedom is over-weight, drawing too much power and requires an unacceptable amount of Extravehicular Activity (EVA) to maintain it. However, the space agency claims these problems are to be expected during the design phase of any major space project. These latest problems to hit Freedom are a further embarrassment for NASA during a difficult period.

① 美国国家航空和宇航局（NASA）透露自由号空间站目前的设计超重，要消耗太多的能量，需要难以接受的太空舱外活动量（EVA）来维护它。然而宇航局声称这些问题在任何大型空间项目的设计阶段就要预料到。自由号遇到的这些问题对于处于困难时期的宇航局又是一个更大的难堪。

② The Freedom Space Station is currently in "Phase C", a design stage which will lead to a final configuration. In 1992 the Critical Design Review would "freeze" the design of station and manufacture of space station hardware will begin.

② 自由号空间站目前处于第三个阶段，即设计阶段，关系到最后的组装。在 1992 年关键设计评审部门会冻结空间站的设计，然后启动空间站硬件制造工作。

③ However, recent studies have thrown the current design of the space station into question. Some members of Congress are calling for the station to be redesigned or for its cancellation.

③ 然而，最近的研究工作对空间站目前的设计提出质疑。一些国会议员要求重新设计空间站或取消设计。（黄峻峰 译）

6.4 Solar Energy Closes in on Cost-Effective Electricity

太阳能发电成本正大幅度降低

① Advances in manufacturing methods for several photovoltaic (PV) technologies are lowering the cost of making commercial photovoltaic modules. New records in PV cell

① 几种光电技术制造方法的进步正在降低商业生产光电池模块的成本。制造光电池的效率再创新纪录。

efficiency are also being reported. Photovoltaic modules themselves must be low-cost relative to the amount of energy they produce. In fact, manufacturing advances have reduced the cost of photovoltaic modules by nearly one third among major US manufacturers, just as many manufacturers in commercial production are scaling up their output. But laboratory work alone will not lead to cost-effective solar-generated electricity.

相对于其产生的大量能量，光电模块本身必须是低成本的。事实上，正当商业生产中的许多制造商大比例地增加产量时，制造工艺上的进步已经使美国主要制造商的光电模块的成本降低了近三分之一。但是，实验室工作本身并不会导致低成本的太阳能发电。

② There are few global solutions for manufacturing because PV cells can be made in a variety of ways. They can also be made with several types of materials, although all PV cells are basically large-area p-n junction photodiodes. This article focuses on common problems in commercial production, as well as manufacturing techniques of each type of cell.

② 由于光电池的制造方法有很多，所以在制造方面没有全面的解决办法。尽管所有光电池基本上都是些大面积的 p-n 节光电二极管，但是其制作材料可以是多种多样的。本文重点关注在商业生产中存在的普遍问题以及不同种类的电池的制造技术。

③ The Photovoltaic Manufacturing Technology Project (PVMaT) is a cost-sharing arrangement between the US government and industry that has been aiding both commercial and precommercial PV companies with manufacturing issues. PVMaT is funded by the Department of Energy and run by the National Renewable Energy Laboratory (NREL).

③ 光电制造技术工程项目(PVMaT)是由美国政府和企业共同投资的计划项目，专门帮助进行商业生产和预商业生产的公司解决制造方面的问题。该项目由能源部拨款，并由国家再生能源实验室（NREL）执行。（黄峻峰 译）

6.5 The Role of Mathematics and Mathematical Analysis

数学和数学分析

① An important feature of the application of mathematics to other sciences is that it enables us to make scientific predictions, that is to draw, on the basis of logic and with the aid of mathematical methods, correct conclusions whose agreement with reality is then confirmed by experience, experiment and practice. Here we confine ourselves to two remarkable examples illustrating what has been said.

① 数学应用于其他学科的一个重要特点是它使我们能够做出科学的推测，即用数学手段逻辑地推导出正确的结论，其真实性由经验、实验和实践证实。下面我们举两个典型例子来说明。

② As is known, the modern science of aviation was created by the famous Russian scientist Professor N. E. Zhukovsky (1847—1921). He derived by means of mathematical methods certain formulas and laws which enabled him to predict the possibility of aerobatics and, in particular, of looping the loop. Soon the loop was in fact performed by the Russian pilot, captain P. N. Nesterov. The possibility of looping the loop was thus discovered mathematically before it was realized physically!

② 众所周知，现代航空学是由著名的俄罗斯科学家茹科夫斯基(N. E. Zhukovsky)教授创立的。他用数学手段推导出一些公式和定律，据此来预测航空表演的可能性，特别是他预测出了翻筋斗的可能性。之后不久即由俄罗斯飞行员耐斯特洛夫（P. N. Nesterov)上尉做到。因此，我们说翻筋头表演是先从数学上预测了可能性之后才在实践中实现的。

③ Here is another example. J. Leverrier, a French astronomer, studied planetary motion in the solar system. When applying the laws of classical mechanics expressed in the form of some known functional relationships he discovered a discrepancy between the theoretical results and real observation. Then he found that the discrepancy can be eliminated if the existence of an unknown planet possessing a certain mass and moving in a certain orbit is assumed. Soon this new planet (Neptune) was in fact found (in 1846) exactly at the time moment and position predicted by Leverrier who thus discovered a new heavenly body by means of calculations made on a piece of paper at his desk! Nowadays astronomical predictions are taken for granted but they are only possible because the techniques of mathematics and mathematical analysis are based on our knowledge of objective law of reality. (Edwards Charless Henry)

③ 再举一例。法国天文学家莱沃瑞尔(J. Leverrier)研究太阳系中天体运动。他在运用某些以函数关系表达的经典机械学定律时发现理论结果与实际观察结果有差异。进而发现这一差异可以通过假设存在一个有一定质量并沿一定轨道运行的星体而消除。不久之后(1846 年)真的在莱沃瑞尔预言的时间和位置发现了一个新的星体(海王星)。因此,我们说莱沃瑞尔是在他书桌的演草纸上通过计算发现了一个新天体!现在人们对天文学上的预言习以为常了,但这正是因为数学和数学分析的技巧是以我们对现实世界客观规律的认识为基础的。(马新英用例)

6.6 推荐读物

(1)方梦之,英语科技文体:范式与翻译,国防工业出版社 2011 年版。
(2)范武邱,科技翻译能力拓展研究,国防工业出版社 2011 年版。
(3)冯志杰,汉英科技翻译指要,中国对外翻译出版公司 1998 年版。
(4)何刚强,笔译理论与技巧,外语教学与研究出版社 2009 年版。
(5)赵萱,郑仰成,科技英语翻译,外语教学与研究出版社 2006 年版。
(6)www. popscichina. com
(7)www. scichina. com
(8)www. stdaily. com

练习 7 课后练习

7.1 分析题

(1)试用所译和比读材料分析科技翻译。
(2)试用话语分析的方法翻译科技文章。
(3)用你最熟悉材料分析科技翻译的一般特点。

7.2 实训题

7.2.1 太阳能电池

太阳能电池可以把一种形式的能量(太阳能)转化为另一种形式(电能)。在太阳能电池里,被称为光子的光粒子使电子移动。把两种材料放在一起,一种载有电子,倾向于释放电子;另一种已有一些被放出,倾向于吸引电子。当光子打中两种材料的连接部时,电子越过连接部,形成产生电流所需的空穴。一束光由许多光子组成,可以移动许多电子。

7.2.2 **Virtual Reality Technology**

As a technology developed on the basis of computer graphics, robotics, mechanics, cybernetics and other sciences, virtual reality technology aims to build an artificial environment where people can perform various real-time activities, such as driving, operating and designing in a "natural" way. It has two main features: immersion, which provides the "participants" with a sense of being personally on the scene; and interactivity, which enables the "participants" to observe and handle virtual objects in a familiar and comfortable way. This future technology started from the mid 1980s and has found wide application in military training & manoeuvre, medicine, education, engineering design and other fields.

7.3 思考题

(1)科技翻译应注重形似还是神似?
(2)科技翻译与文学翻译有何区别? 标准有何异同?
(3)科技翻译如何运用语言学理论分析科技文章?
(4)逻辑分析对科技翻译有哪些作用?
(5)如何提高科技翻译质量? 有哪些重要手段?
(6)如何从英汉对比角度正确翻译科技英语长句?
(7)信息论对科技英语复杂结构汉译有何帮助?
(8)科技翻译采用直译法有何优缺点?
(9)科技英译如何达到准确且简洁?
(10)科技英译哪些情况下需要采用分译法?
(11)科技英译采用合句法有哪些优点?
(12)翻译科技文摘时应注意哪些问题?
(13)术语翻译的基本要求是什么? 汉译时如何体现?
(14)体裁分析对科技翻译有何帮助?
(15)就科技英语的特点和用途而言科技翻译的标准有哪些?
(16)做好科技翻译译者应具备哪些基本素质?

第17课 法律

导 译

作为翻译对象的法律，主要指法律文件，法律文件类别繁多，具体包括法律、法规、条约、国际公约、国际惯例、涉外经济合同、司法文书等等。法律翻译就其翻译目的的不同，可以是仅供参考的法律翻译，这类译文仅服务于基本的跨语言、跨文化交际，本身不像原文具有法律效力；也可以是为原法律文件提供具有相同司法效用的译本文件，即译文本身也是（准）法律文件，具有（准）法律效力。本课所探讨的法律翻译属于后者。

综合权衡法律文件的权威性及法律译文的（拟）同等功效性，法律文件的翻译多半是全译，即理想的法律文件译本无论从语言表达形式层面还是文本预期功能（司法效力）层面都应该尽可能“全”地接近原文本。当译文的形式与功能发生“冲突”之际，便是全译七法的“用武”之时。具体而言，法律翻译应以对译为主，最大限度地兼顾形式与功能的统一，同时适度地辅之以增译、减译、转译、换译、分译、合译，有度地“牺牲”形式以调和形式与功能间的矛盾。一言以蔽之，法律翻译当力求兼顾语言表达形式及预期司法效力两方面，如欲兼顾而不可得，适度调整形式以适功能。

1 课前练笔

1.1《中华人民共和国法官职业道德基本准则》（节选）

第一条 为加强法官职业道德建设，保证法官正确履行法律赋予的职责，根据《中华人民共和国法官法》和其他相关规定，制定本准则。

第二条 法官职业道德的核心是公正、廉洁、为民。基本要求是忠诚司法事业、保证司法公正、确保司法廉洁、坚持司法为民、维护司法形象。

第三条 法官应当自觉遵守法官职业道德,在本职工作和业外活动中严格要求自己,维护人民法院形象和司法公信力。

第四条 牢固树立社会主义法治理念,忠于党、忠于国家、忠于人民、忠于法律,做中国特色社会主义事业建设者和捍卫者。

1.2 Universal Copyright Convention

Article I

Each Contracting State undertakes to provide for the adequate and effective protection of the rights of authors and other copyright proprietors in literary, scientific and artistic works, including writings, musical, dramatic and cinematographic works, and paintings, engravings and sculpture.

Article II

1. Published works of nationals of any Contracting State and works first published in that State shall enjoy in each other Contracting State the same protection as that other State accords to works of its nationals first published in its own territory, as well as the protection specially granted by this Convention.

2. Unpublished works of nationals of each Contracting State shall enjoy in each other Contracting State the same protection as that other State accords to unpublished works of its nationals first published in its own territory, as well as the protection specially granted by this Convention.

3. For the purpose of this convention any contracting state may, by domestic legislation, assimilate to its own nationals any person domiciled in that state.

1.3 How are Illinois' Appellate and Supreme Courts Organized

① The Illinois Appellate Court is the first court of appeal for all criminal cases except those involving death penalty (which are automatically appealed directly from the Circuit Court to the Illinois Supreme Court) and those criminal appeals in which an applicable federal or state statute has been held invalid. Either the defense or prosecution may appeal rulings of the trial court. However, because the law protects a defendant from being tried twice for the same crime, the prosecution cannot appeal a not-guilty verdict.

② The main function of both the Appellate and Supreme Courts in Illinois is to ensure that the trial court correctly interprets the law in a given case. For example, the defense may argue before the Appellate Court that unconstitutionally obtained evidence was admitted by the trial court. The Appellate Court can take one of several actions on such an appeal. It can deny the petition of appeal outright. Or, if the court decides the appeal has merit, it can affirm, reverse, modify or vacate the original decision, or it can remand the case back to the lower court for reconsideration. In the latter instance, the Appellate Court may order a new trial but specify the questionable evidence that had been introduced in the first trial be held inadmissible in the new trial. Under certain limited circumstances, decisions of the Appellate Court can be appealed to the Illinois Supreme Court, the highest court in the state.

2 课前批评

2.1《中华人民共和国戒严法》(节选)

第二条 在发生严重危及国家的统一、安全或者社会公共安全的动乱、暴乱或者严重骚乱,不采取非常措施不足以维护社会秩序、保护人民的生命和财产安全的紧急状态时,国家可以决定实行戒严。

第三条 全国或者个别省、自治区、直辖市的戒严,由国务院提请全国人民代表大会常务委员会决定;中华人民共和国主席根据全国人民代表大会常务委员会的决定,发布戒严令。省、自治区、直辖市的范围内部分地区的戒严,由国务院决定,国务院总理发布戒严令。

Martial Law

① Article 2 The State may decide to apply martial law when such state of emergency as unrest, rebellion or grave riot occurs which seriously endangers unification and security of the State or public security and under which public order cannot be maintained and safety of people's lives and property cannot be ensured unless extraordinary measures are taken.

② Article 3 When it is necessary to impose martial law in the country as a whole or in an individual province, autonomous region or municipality directly under the Central Government, the matter shall be submitted by the State Council to the Standing Committee of the National People's Congress for decision; the President of the People's Republic of China shall, in accordance with the decision made by the Standing Committee of the National People's Congress, proclaim the order of martial law. When it is necessary to impose martial law in part(s) of a province, autonomous region or municipality directly under the Central Government, the matter shall be decided on by the State Council, and the Premier of the State Council shall proclaim the order of martial law.

2.2 What is Law?

There have been and will continue to be different definitions of law. Aristotle saw law as a rule of conduct. Cicero contended that law was the agreement of reason and nature, the distinction between the just

何谓法?

现在已经有,而且今后还会有很多关于法的不同定义。亚里士多德视法为行为的准则。西塞罗主张法是自然与理性的

and the unjust. The British jurist Sir William Blackstone described law as " a rule of civil conduct prescribed by the supreme power in a state, commanding what is right, and prohibiting what is wrong. " In America, the eminent jurist Oliver Wendell Holmes, Jr., contended that law was a set of rules that allowed one to predict how a court would resolve a particular dispute: " the prophecies of what the courts will do in fact, and nothing more pretentious, are what I mean by law. "

统一,是正义与非正义之间的界限。英国法学家布莱克斯通将法描述为“国家最高权力规定的市民行动准则,它规定正确的事,禁止做违法的事”。在美国,杰出的法学家奥利弗·温德尔·霍姆斯主张,法是允许人们去预测法院将如何解决某一特定纠纷的一整套准则:“是对法院在事实上将如何处理的预测,而绝非其他更虚饰的东西,便是我所谓的法”。(杨俊峰用例)

3 全译知识 翻译腔

翻译腔指囿于接近原文形式亏于交际效果的译文风格。腔是一种说话腔调,多含贬义,如学生腔,公文腔等。有的翻译腔面目可憎,但久而久之,可浸入汉语。

3.1 翻译腔种种

翻译腔让人习非成是,会侵害译者对译语的敏感,阻隔译文交际功能的实现。翻译腔有多种,如:的的不休;当当不止;因为所以;被被被动;你我他它;怪腔怪调;梗塞不畅;拗口晦涩;夹缠不清。

试比较翻译腔与地道汉语:认为只有自己最了不起——唯我独尊;他睡在他的背上——他仰着;一年的末尾——年终;离开同伴而过孤独的生活——离群索居;尽可能快地——尽快;警察的人数不够——警力不够;重视古代,轻视现代——厚古薄今;头向下脚向上地竖着——倒立;传达情意——传情;冒着生死的危险——出生入死;调拨并发给——拨付。

3.2 翻译腔的缺点

译语膨化 这种膨化有时极不显眼,译句看似无问题,但总觉得不对劲。究其因,过多保留了原作松散的形式而不予提炼,导致译语形式繁复而信息含量小,好像得了多语症。如:

① Writers cannot bear the fact that poet John Keats died at 26, and only half playfully judge their own lives as failures when they pass that year.

【原译】:作家们无法忍受这一事实:约翰·济慈二十六岁时就死了,于是就几乎半开玩笑地评判他们自己的一生是个失败,这时,他们才刚刚过了这一年。

【试译】:诗人约翰·济慈26岁早逝,作家们为之惋惜;一到这个年龄,就戏称自己一无所成。

原文说作家们不能接受事实,实为济慈英年早逝而惋惜;"几乎半开玩笑地评判"实为"戏称"。凡此种种,表明译者汉语思维不简练,不善于概念化,即不善于概括。

译语虚化 英语多用代词、虚词,尤其是连词,容易造成"当当不止"、被动较多、常见你我他它等现象,伴生不自然、不通畅之感,阅读的愉悦会受到干扰。如:

② I was so impressed by these words that I used them later for a Christmas card.

【原译】:我为这些话所深深感动,后来我就把它们写在圣诞贺卡上。

【试译】:这番话太感人了,我后来写入了圣诞贺卡。

③ I was in the middle before I knew that I had begun.

【原译】:等我发觉我自己开始爱上你的时候,我已经走了一半路了。

【改译】:我是到了不能自拔的时候,才发现爱上了你。

【试译】:等我发现爱上你的时候,已是欲罢不能。

例②,原文虚词、代词等照单译出,原译显得虚胖,试译去掉被动形态,减少代词的翻译,舍去了介词,译得更实更简洁。例③选自英国简·奥斯丁的《傲慢与偏见》,原译把 in the middle 译成了"走了一半路",过直了;改译理解了原文内涵,借用了汉语中的成语"不能自拔",避免了洋腔洋调;试译则直意兼顾,避用"(当)……的时候",用"欲罢不能"译 in the middle,更能显出深陷爱河、人在爱途的心态。

译语晦涩 受原文形式影响,译文思维不清。译者有时会下意识地随原语结构而去,沉溺其中不能自拔,以致译文不连贯不清晰,使读者迷惑不解。译得不明白,根本的原因还是理解不清,思维不清,或拙于译语表达。如:

④ The study found that non-smoking wives of men who smoke cigarettes face a much greater than normal danger of developing lung cancer. The more cigarettes smoked by the husband, the greater the threat faced by his non-smoking wife.

【原译】:这项研究表明抽烟男子的不抽烟妻子罹患肺癌的危险比一般人大得多,丈夫抽烟越多,其不抽烟的妻子面临的威胁越大。

【试译】:研究表明,丈夫抽烟而妻子不抽,妻子患肺癌的危险大得多。丈夫抽得越多,妻子威胁越大。

non-smoking wives of men who smoke cigarettes 译作"抽烟男子的不抽烟妻子"还真是准确,可是入句之后交际价值不足,它实际上包含两个判断:丈夫抽烟,妻子不抽烟,按其实际逻辑关系表达,才可跳出原文的形式羁绊。另外,将丈夫抽烟移前,妻子不抽置后,正好与下一句的思维顺序相对应,形成一种内在节奏,更有利于消除晦涩。

译语夹缠 译者有时困于原语长句,也仿之摆长龙,结果是唠唠叨叨,缠夹不清。如:

⑤ But Russia and China, both with veto powers in the Council and backed by India, South Africa and Brazil, have vehemently opposed the idea of slapping U. N. sanctions on Damascus, which Western diplomats say would be the logical next step.

【原译】:但拥有否决权并得到印度、南非、巴西支持的俄罗斯与中国强烈反对联合国对大马士革进行制裁这一主张。西方外交官说,联合国制裁对叙利亚而言是可想而知的下一步。

【试译】:俄罗斯与中国都有否决权,得到了印度、南非、巴西的支持,强烈反对联合国制裁大马士革。尽管西方外交官认为制裁是必然的。

这是某报译自路透社 2011 年 8 月 11 日的报道。“强烈反对”之前的施事和之后的受事太长，未将 the idea of 及其内涵分清，结果译出“这一主张”显得啰唆。原译未借语境之力承前省略被制裁者，汉译用词也不凝练，试译一分为三，采用了汉语典型的流水句。

4 全译窍门

4.1 律法条名凝练施“译”

律法条名的翻译不可小觑。首先，相对于整个法律文本来说它在内容上具有极强的提纲挈领作用，它清晰地折射出该部律法的“司法等级”（法、条例、办法等）、“制定方”（国家、省、地方等）、“适用领域”（环保、外企管理、知识产权等）等核心信息。鉴于法律文本的司法权威性与严肃性，译文作为具有对等法律效用的法律文本或“准”法律文本必须要完整、准确、清晰地再现上述必要信息，这是翻译律法条名的刚性要求。

其次，无论是汉语还是英语，律法条名在表达形式上具备一些共性特征，如表现为偏正短语，成分间修饰关系清晰无歧义，用词用字尽量简短凝练等。有鉴于此，律法条名英译的重难点便是如何协调内容较大与形式较简的矛盾，即如何在凝练而不损害“内容”的前提下，让瘦身后的译文得以匹配简约的文字表达形式。一般说来，英译时应尽量在做到清晰表意的前提下不使用介词（about, in 等）或准介词（involving, governing 等）；必用介词时，尽量只用 on 或 of 等介词，为了避免语义修饰关系模糊尽量只使用一次，最多两次。如：

① 文物保护法

【原译】:Law on the Protection of Cultural Relics

【改译】:Cultural Relics Protection Law

② 涉外经济合同法

【原译】:Law on Economic Contracts Involving Foreign Interest

【改译】:Foreign-related Economic Contracts Law

4.2 法律口号释译并举

英译法律口号有两大难点。第一，无论何种性质的（政治的、广告的、法律的等等）口号性语言，均有较强的“吁请”功能，而英语表达该功能一般用祈使句。第二，嵌藏于汉语法律口号中的行为对象（如“整治”什么，“开展”什么）往往在内容上具有较强的文化特异性，跨语言传意时解释不足难使外国读者理解，字面直译往往因原语言文化环境的缺失而导致在译入语读者看来有明显的语义缺损。翻译法律口号要求：第一，宏观上译出吁请功能；第二，微观上要阐明口号所涉及的特定对象，如何通过信息增补等明晰化手段以补偿“时移境迁”所带来的语义缺失，从而努力实现跨语言、跨文化交流的最佳效果。如：

③ 继续开展“扫黄”,“打非”的斗争。

【原译】:We should continue to eliminate pornography and to fight the illegal.

【改译】:We should continue to eliminate pornography and other illegal publications.

④ 深入开展“严打”斗争和专项整治。

【原译】:Enforce the law strictly and launch special campaigns.

【改译】:We cracked down on all criminal activities and launched special campaigns to fight the crime and social evils that the people detest.

4.3 目的条款译之有道

“目的”条款为多数法律文献所共有,系指“为了……根据……(特)制定本法/本条例/本细则”等,常列为法律文件的首条,开宗明义指明立法依据,行文上似有“套路”可循:(1)字面上看似列举了若干个依据,深层里却隐藏着“因果”、“递进”等逻辑内涵,对此译者必须明白其中深义。(2)汉语目的条款行文程式有定,冗词频现,同语反复,结构冗长,而英译必须清晰简约,切忌机械复制。(3)目的条款的典型三部分“为了”、“根据”、“制定”几个核心词的常用对应词为 in order to, for the purpose of, with a view to, in accordance with, pursuant to, formulate, enact 等,英译者可酌情选用。如:

⑤ 为了加强外债管理,确保本市借用外债的规模适度,债务结构合理,资金投向符合国民经济和社会发展的需求,对外维护国家信誉,根据国家有关规定,制定本规定。

These provisions are formulated in accordance with the pertinent provisions of the People's Republic of China with a view to strengthening the control of foreign loans so as to ensure that foreign loans contracted by Shanghai Municipality will be appropriate and based on careful and rational planning and that they will be used to satisfy the needs of national economy and social development, thus upholding the good reputation of the People's Republic of China.

4.4 译名精确统一至上

法律文献英译,为维护同一概念、内涵或事物在法律上始终同一,以免引起歧义,词语(尤其是概念性或归纳性名词)一经选定,就必须前后统一。如果一味为了文采而变换用词,模糊了所指,牺牲了法律语言的精严性,其结果必是失大于得。以《上海市涉外经济法规规章汇编》为例,其英译多次实词性重复,译文都或多或少地走样,甚至是失真。如下例中原文同一页的“方针”却英译为 principle 和 policy 两个词,有损法律的精确性。

⑥ 根据对外开放的方针……

【译文】:According to the principle of opening to the outside world...

⑦ 根据党和国家对外开放的方针……

【译文】:...in line with the opening policy of the Party and the state...

4.5 从“长”计“译”

与汉语相比,英语法律文本的句法结构有两个特点,一是密,成分结构衔接紧密,频繁使用介词、关系代词、关系副词等形合手段,以加强语言的有形连接,形意结合,以形显意，与法律文本严谨的措辞风格相得益彰；二是长，条款作为法律文献的基本信息单位，信息承载量普遍较大，特别青睐长句，长句中各类从属结构交替使用，充分体现了英语长句的特征。而上述特征均为汉语的短板，汉译法律文献时不免要在句法形式上适度理性地向原文靠拢，以相对的译文长句对原文的绝对长句，从“长”计“译”。如：

⑧ Neither House, during the session of Congress, shall, without the Consent of the other, adjourn for more than three days, nor to any other place than that in which the two Houses shall be sitting.

【译文】：在国会开会期，任何一院若未经另一院同意不得休会三日以上，也不得迁移到两院举行集会以外的其他任何地点。

4.6 短长相济

法律文本中频繁使用的复合长句，集中体现了英语“从属结构”（subordinations）在表现形式上的多样性，这里重点关注其中一类，即状语性（“地”式）从属结构。状语是动词性表达结构的修饰成分，由于英语“先天”层面曲折变化（inflections）形式欠发达，直接导致语言成分间的形式逻辑联系，要极大程度地依赖位置上的“就近”原则，来弥补语义关联欠清晰、易生歧义的不足。具体表现在法律文本中状语与动词的关系上，有两点非常突出，一是为了“拉近”状语与动词的距离，短状语经常以插入语（通常是短语而不是从句）的形式出现在主句谓语动词的近旁；二是长状语多以从句的形式出现在主句前面，其信息含量之大，又使得译者不得不适度偏离“从‘长’计‘译’”原则，借助“分译”、“移位”等辅助手段，避开汉语形式逻辑欠严整的“短板”，以“多”（小句相对多）补“长”，以“灵”（成分位置相对灵活）济“刚”，与“从‘长’计‘译’”原则互补短长，形成“合力”。请看下例：

⑨ If, at any time during the execution of the Contract, either of the Parties to the Contract is prevented from executing the Contract by cases of Force Majeure such as war, serious fire, flood, typhoon and earthquake, etc, the time for execution of the Contract shall be extended for a period equal to the effect of those causes.

【原译】：如果合同双方在合同期的任何时候任何一方受到诸如战争、严重火灾、洪水、台风、地震等不可抗力事件的影响而不能执行合同时，履行合同的期限应延长至相当于事件所影响的时间。

【改译】：如果在合同期的任何时候，合同双方的任何一方受到诸如战争、严重火灾、洪水、台风、地震等不可抗力事件的影响而不能执行合同时，履行合同的期限应予以延长，延长的期限应相当于事件所影响的时间。

5 话题词汇

5.1 通用词汇

办法 measures

补充规定 supplementary provisions

法 law
法典 code
分则 specific provisions
附则 supplementary provisions
管理条例;规定 administrative regulations
规定 provisions
规范 specifications
(基本)准则 code
基本法 basic law
决定 decision
命令 decree
批复(official) reply
(实施)细则(detailed) rules
试行办法 trial measures
条例 regulations
通告 announcement
通则 general rules
通知 circular
统一规则 uniform rules
协议 agreement
序言 preamble
暂行办法 interim measures
暂行条例 provisional regulations; interim regulations
暂行通则 interim general rules
章程 articles of association
准则 criteria
总则 general provisions
act 法;法案
additional protocol 附件议定书
agreement 协定
amendments 修正案
annex 附件
article 款
bill 议案
chapter 章
charter 宪章
constitution 章程
convention 公约
covenant 合同;契约
draft 草案
international convention 国际公约
interpretation 解释
introduction 引言;导言
item 目;项
miscellaneous provisions 其他规定
ordinance 法令;条例
paragraph 段;节
part 编;部
preliminary provision 绪则;初步条款
protocol 议定书;草约
resolution 决议
scheme 计划;协议
section 条
statute 规约;规范
subparagraph 分段;分节
subsection 分款;分项
treaty 条约
understanding 谅解
warrant 令状

5.2 机关

地方人民代表大会 Local People's Congress
法院 court of law;law court;court of justice
分庭;派出法庭 branch court
高级人民法院 Higher People's Courts
海事法院 Maritime Courts
基层人民法院 Grassroots People's Courts
检察机关 procuratorial organ
检察院 procuratorate
军事人民法院 People's Military Courts
立案庭 case listing division of the court
立法机关 legislature
民事审判庭 civil division of the court
全国人民代表大会 National People's Congress (NPC)
人民审判庭 People's Tribunals
省人民代表大会 Provincial People's Congress
司法机关 judiciary;judicature
铁路运输法院 Railway Transportation Courts
刑事审判庭 criminal division of the court
行政审判庭 administrative division of the court
中级人民法院 Intermediate People's Courts
最高人民法院 Supreme People's Court

最高人民检察院 Supreme People's Procuratorate
assembly 大会;议会
congress 国会
Coroners' Courts(英)验尸官法院
County Courts(英)郡法院(民事)
County or Municipal Court(美)初审法院
Court of Appeal (Civil Division)(英)上诉法院(民事庭)
Court of Appeal (Criminal Division)(英)上诉法院(刑事庭)
Court of Records(美)保存记录的法院;正规法院
Courts Martial(英)军事法庭
Crown Courts(英)刑事法院
Department of Justice(美)司法部
Equity Court(英)衡平法院
General Assembly(国际组织的)大会
High Court (Chancery Division)(英)高等法院(大法官庭)
High Court (Family Division)(英)高等法院(家事庭)
High Court (Queen's Bench Division)(英)高等法院(王座庭)
High Court(英)高等法院(民事)
House of Commons(英国议会)下议院
House of Lords(英国议会)上议院
House of Representatives 众议院
International Court of Justice(联合国)国际法院
Magistrate's Courts(英)地方法院(刑事)
parliament 议会
Privy Council(英)枢密院
Senate(美、法等国)参议院
Small Claims Court(美)小额求偿法院(一种无记录法院)
State Supreme Court(美)州最高法院
Superior Court of Appellate Division(美)州上诉法院
The Restrictive Practice Court(英)反垄断法院
The Tribunals Service(英)专业法庭
US Circuit Court(美)联邦巡回法院
US District Court(美)联邦地区法院
US Supreme Court(美)联邦最高法院
Youth Courts(英)青少年法院(刑事)

5.3 司法人员

法官 judge
法官助理 assistant judge
法院院长 president of the court
检察长 chief procurator
检察官 prosecutor
人民陪审员 people's assessor
审判长 chief adjudicator
审判法官 adjudicator
审判委员会 adjudication committee of the court
司法警察;法警 judicial police
最高人民检察院检察长 attorney general of the Supreme People's Procuratorate
bailiff 法警
bench and bar 法官和律师
bench 法官(总称);法庭;法官席
chancellor(英)司法官;(美)大法官
chief justice 首席法官;法院院长
director of public prosecutions(美)检察官
juror 陪审员
jury 陪审团
justice 法官;推事
justice of the peace 治安官
magistrate 地方法官;司法行政官
prosecuting attorney(美)检察官
public procurator 检察官;公诉官
recorder(英)(市)首席法官
solicitor 法务官

5.4 民法刑法

并科原则 doctrine of cumulating punishments
不要式民事法律行为 informal civil legal act
不要因民事法律行为 non-causative civil legal act
惩罚与教育相结合原则 principle of combining punishment with education
从民事法律行为 accessory civil legal act

单方民事法律行为 unilateral civil legal act
多方民事法律行为 joint act civil legal act
法人 legal person
犯意表示 expression for a crime
犯罪 crime; commit a crime
犯罪动机 criminal motive
犯罪对象 target of a crime
犯罪构成 constitution of a crime
犯罪既遂 completion of a crime
犯罪客体 object of a crime
犯罪目的 criminal intent; criminal purpose
犯罪未遂 attempted crime
犯罪形态 criminal pattern
犯罪预备 a crime in preparation; preparation for a crime
犯罪中断 suspension of a crime
犯罪中止 abandonment/discontinuance of a crime
犯罪主体 subject of a crime
附期限民事法律行为 civil legal act with term
附条件民事法律行为 conditional civil legal act
公民 citizen
故意犯罪 intentional crime; willful crime
过失犯罪 negligent crime
户籍 census register
监护 guardianship
结果犯 consequential offence
结果加重犯 aggregated consequential offence
可撤销民事行为 revocable civil act
量刑 criterion for sentencing; sentencing criterion
量刑幅度 extent for discretionary action of sentencing
民法法律规范 norm of civil law
民法法系 civil law system
民法基本原则 fundamental principles of civil law
民法通则 general principles of the civil law
民事法律行为 civil legal act
民事权利能力 the capacity for civil rights
民事权益 civil rights and interests
民事行为 civil act
民事责任承担方式 methods of bearing civil liability
诺成性民事法律行为 consental civil legal act
平等主体 civil subjects with equal status
权利本位 standard of right
社会本位 standard of society
涉外民事关系 civil relations with foreign elements
生前民事法律行为 civil legal act before death
实践性民事法律行为 practical civil legal act
双方民事法律行为 bilateral civil legal act
死后民事法律行为 civil legal act after death
危险犯 potential damage offence
无偿民事法律行为 civil legal act without consideration; civil legal act without award
刑罚 penalty; punishment
刑事责任 criminal liability/responsibility
刑事责任能力 criminal responsibility; capacity for criminal responsibility
刑事责任年龄 age for criminal responsibility
刑事侦查 criminal detection
行为犯 behavioral offence
要式民事法律行为 formal civil legal act
要因民事法律行为 causative civil legal act
有偿民事法律行为 civil legal act with consideration
主民事法律行为 principle civil legal act
准民事法律行为 quasi-civil legal act
自然人 natural person
罪刑法定原则 principle of a legally prescribed punishment for a specified crime
罪刑相适应原则 principle of suiting punishment to crime
罪责自负原则 principle of bearing responsibility solely for one's own crime
acquittal 宣告无罪
adjudication 审判;裁判
aggravating circumstances 加重情节
alibi 不再犯罪现场
arraignment 传讯
bail 保释
clemency 豁免;宽恕
closing argument 总结陈述;终结辩论
complaint 刑事控告书
concurrent sentence 合并判决
confinement 监禁;关押
contempt of court 藐视法庭
conviction 定罪

corpus delicti 犯罪事实
custody 羁押;拘禁;监禁
decriminalization 非刑事化
delinquency 青少年违法行为
diminished capacity 责任减等
due process 正当程序
element (of a crime) 犯罪要件
felony 重罪
forfeiture 剥夺;没收
good time 缩减的刑期
guilty plea 认罪答辩
guilty verdict 有罪判决
inchoate offense 未完成犯罪
interrogation 讯问
justification 正当理由
M'Naghten rule 麦纳顿规则
mandatory sentence 强制判决
mens rea 犯罪意图
Miranda rights 米兰达权利
Miranda warnings 米兰达警告
misdemeanor 轻罪
parole 假释
peremptory challenge 无因回避
probation 缓刑
recidivism 累犯
stare decisis 遵循先例
suspended sentence 暂缓监禁
trial de novo 重新审判
Wharton's Rule 沃顿原则
writ of certiorari 调卷令状
Year and a Day Rule 满一年原则(如受害者满一年未死亡,不得以杀人罪起诉被告)

5.5 司法程序

被告 defendant;the accused
被拘留者 detainee
驳回控告 dismiss the charge
传唤 summons
传票 citation
打官司 go to court
定某人有罪 convict somebody (of a crime)
对……有管辖权 have jurisdiction on/over
翻供 revoke verbal evidence
管辖权 jurisdiction
和解 settlement
扣留;扣押 detain
扣押某人财产 levy on somebody's property
立案 case listing
免除某人的债务 release somebody from his debt
判决;裁定 verdict
判决;宣告某人无罪 acquit somebody
上诉 appeal
上诉人 appellant
上诉书 instrument of appeal
申诉;申请 petition
审判 trial;try
释放 set free;release
受理 take cognizance of
提起刑事诉讼 file an indictment
听证 hear;hearing
庭外和解 outside court settlement
为(某人)辩护 defend;plead;argue for
伪证 perjury
向法院起诉 file a complaint with the court
向某人送达传票 serve somebody with a summons
休庭 recess
原告 plaintiff;accuser
证词;证明 testimony
证据 evidence
证明无罪 testify to somebody's innocence
证人 witness
作不利于某人的证明 testify against somebody
作对某人有利的证明 testify on behalf of somebody
作证 testify
a writ of attachment 扣押令;拘留状
a writ of error 再审令
a writ of execution 执行令
adjourn 休庭
adjudicate 判决;裁决
adversarial 对抗式;辩论式(审判)
affirm 确认;维持原判
appellate court 上诉法院
appellate jurisdiction 上诉管辖权

arrest warrant 逮捕令
attorney 代理人;律师
award 判决给予;仲裁裁决
barrister(美)大律师;出席高等法院的律师
bear false witness against 作对(某人)不利的伪证
beyond reasonable doubt 不存在合理的怀疑(刑事审判)
bring a lawsuit against 起诉(某人)
burden of proof 证明责任;举证责任
certiorari 调卷;提审
complaint(民事)诉状
docket 摘要记入;立案
examine 审问
fair preponderance of evidence 根据证据的比重或相对优势作出判决(民事审判)
garnishment 扣押(为诉讼等目的由第三方扣押债务人的财产)
hand down 作出判决
in custody 扣留
indict 指控
inquisitorial 询问式(审判)
interrogate 讯问
justify doing something 证明做…是有法律依据的
justify 证明……是正当的;为……辩护
legal counsel 法律顾问;律师
lien holder 财产留置人
lien 留置权;留置物
litigant 诉讼当事人
litigation 诉讼
lodge a complaint against 起诉(某人)
on balance of probabilities 依据证据的可能性大小作出判决(民事审判)
overrule 驳回;废除
plead guilty;not guilty 认罪,不认罪
pleadings(书面)诉讼请求
procurator 诉讼代理人
reconcile 调和;调解
reject an appeal 驳回上诉
remand 发回重申
retain 聘请(律师)
retrial 重审
reverse a judgment 撤销原判
review 审查
search warrant 搜查令
solicitor 事务律师;诉状律师
swear a witness 让证人宣誓
swear 宣誓;发誓
take the witness stand 出席作证
writ 传票;令状

5.6 缩略语

打非 eliminate illegal publications
打拐 crack down on women and children abduction
打私 crack down on smuggling
法工委 Legislative Affairs Work Committee
高法 Supreme People's Court of the PRC
高检 Supreme People's Procuratorate of the PRC
两打 crack down on grave criminal and economic offenses
民诉 civil action;civil case
民刑纠纷 civil and criminal disputes
扫黄 eliminate pornography
刑一庭 No. 1 Criminal Court of the People's Court
AFFT 口供;宣誓书;誓言
ARB 仲裁
AR 行政规章
BB 保释保证书
BL 出庭律师(英国)
CA 民政事务
CBR 实例推理
CFR 美国联邦法规
CSA《管制物品法》
DA 地区检察官
DN 引渡条款
Europol 欧洲警察办公室
F/O 交付给…… 以……为受益人
INTERPOL 国际刑(事)警(察)组织
J. S. 英国债务传票
MPC《模范刑法典》
N. A. 不适用
N. P. 公证人
OA 法定受让人
PJ 首席裁判官

qcd 放弃权利行为
RCP 民事诉讼规则
repr 代理人
RICO《反勒索及受贿组织法》
ROR 具结释放
SA 斯特拉斯堡协定
UCR《统一犯罪汇编》
VOM 被害人－犯罪人调解模式
VORP 被害人－犯罪人和解模式
YAR 约翰安特卫普规则(共同海损理算规则)

6 比读体悟

6.1 司法改革与人权保护

Judicial Reform and Protection of Human Rights

① 依法治国是中国政府的基本治国方略。十三年来,全国各级人大和政府,在加快立法进程,建立中国特色社会主义法律体系的同时,高度重视严格执法和公正司法,使司法中的人权得到有效保障。

① Running the country in accordance with the law is a strategy of fundamental importance for management of state affairs by the Chinese Government. In accelerating the process of law making and striving to build a complete legal system with Chinese characteristics, the Chinese Government has over the past thirteen years attached great importance to law enforcement in strict accordance with the law. Judicial protection of human rights has been effectively ensured as a result.

② 1989 年以来,随着中国改革开放和现代化建设的发展,经济、政治、社会生活出现了许多新情况,公安、司法部门依法严厉打击各种严重犯罪,保证了国家财产的安全,为广大人民群众创建了安全的生产生活环境。公安、司法部门始终把杀人、抢劫、强奸、爆炸、绑架、盗窃等严重影响人民群众安全的多发性犯罪作为打击重点。近年来,又把称霸一方、欺压群众、作恶多端的黑恶势力犯罪作为重中之重,实施严厉打击。2001 年就审理此类案件 350 件,1 953 人。同时,严厉打击暴力恐怖犯罪,对恐怖势力、宗教极端势力和民族分裂势力组织、策划的爆炸、杀人、纵火等犯罪活动,坚决依法予以打击。批捕起诉了一批利用"法轮功"等邪教组织破坏法律实施、危害社会治安的犯罪分子,保护了人民的安全。

② Along with further development of China's reform and opening up and modernization drive since 1989, there have emerged numerous new circumstances in the country ' s economic, political and social life. In response, public security and judicial departments have, in accordance with the law, dealt severe blows on crimes and this has effectively ensured safety of state property and people's lives and property. To create a safe environment for production and living, these departments have concentrated on cracking down on crimes that seriously endanger people ' s safety and frequently occur, including homicide, robbery, rape, explosion, kidnapping and larceny. In the last years, the crackdown has been targeted, in particular, against crimes committed by Mafia — like gangs, those local bullies who ride roughshod over the people. In 2001 alone, 350 such cases were tried, involving 1,953 offenders. Meanwhile, severe blows have been dealt upon crimes of violence and terrorism. Resolute actions have been taken in accordance with the law to fight crimes of explosion, homicide and arson organized and planned by groups of terror, religious extremism and national separatism. A group of criminal offenders have been arrested and prosecuted for sabotaging the implementation of law and undermining social security by making use of Falun Gong and other cults. (冯伟年用例)

6.2 中华人民共和国香港特别行政区基本法(节选)

The Basic Law of Hong Kong Special Administrative Region of The People's Republic of China

第一章 总 则

第一条 香港特别行政区是中华人民共和国不可分离的部分。

第二条 全国人民代表大会授权香港特别行政区依照本法的规定实行高度自治,享有行政管理权、立法权、独立的司法权和终审权。

第三条 香港特别行政区的行政机关和立法机关由香港永久性居民依照本法有关规定组成。

第四条 香港特别行政区依法保障香港特别行政区居民和其他人的权利和自由。

第五条 香港特别行政区不实行社会主义制度和政策,保持原有的资本主义制度和生活方式,五十年不变。

第六条 香港特别行政区依法保护私有财产权。

第七条 香港特别行政区境内的土地和自然资源属于国家所有,由香港特别行政区政府负责管理、使用、开发、出租或批给个人、法人或团体使用或开发,其收入全归香港特别行政区政府支配。

第八条 香港原有法律,即普通法、衡平法、条例、附属立法和习惯法,除同本法相抵触或经香港特别行政区的立法机关作出修改者外,予以保留。

Chapter I General Principles

Article 1 The Hong Kong Special Administrative Region is an inalienable part of the People's Republic of China.

Article 2 The National People's Congress authorizes the Hong Kong Special Administrative Region to exercise a high degree of autonomy and enjoy executive, legislative and independent judicial power, including that of final adjudication, in accordance with the provisions of this Law.

Article 3 The executive authorities and legislature of the Hong Kong Special Administrative Region shall be composed of permanent residents of Hong Kong in accordance with the relevant provisions of this Law.

Article 4 The Hong Kong Special Administrative Region shall safeguard the rights and freedoms of the residents of the Hong Kong Special Administrative Region and of other persons in the Region in accordance with law.

Article 5 The socialist system and policies shall not be practiced in the Hong Kong Special Administrative Region, and the previous capitalist system and way of life shall remain unchanged for 50 years.

Article 6 The Hong Kong Special Administrative Region shall protect the right of private ownership of property in accordance with law.

Article 7 The land and natural resources within the Hong Kong Special Administrative Region shall be State property. The Government of the Hong Kong Special Administrative Region shall be responsible for their management, use and development and for their lease or grant to individuals, legal persons or organizations for use or development. The revenues derived therefrom shall be exclusively at the disposal of the government of the Region.

Article 8 The laws previously in force in Hong Kong, that is, the common law, rules of equity, ordinances, subordinate legislation and customary law shall be maintained, except for any that contravene this Law, and subject to any amendment by the legislature of the Hong Kong Special Administrative

第九条 香港特别行政区的行政机关、立法机关和司法机关，除使用中文外，还可使用英文，英文也是正式语文。

第十条 香港特别行政区除悬挂中华人民共和国国旗和国徽外，还可使用香港特别行政区区旗和区徽。香港特别行政区的区旗是五星花蕊的紫荆花红旗。香港特别行政区的区徽，中间是五星花蕊的紫荆花，周围写有"中华人民共和国香港特别行政区"和英文"香港"。

Region.

Article 9 In addition to the Chinese language, English may also be used as an official language by the executive authorities, legislature and judiciary of the Hong Kong Special Administrative Region.

Article 10 Apart from displaying the national flag and national emblem of the People's Republic of China, the Hong Kong Special Administrative Region may also use a regional flag and regional emblem. The regional flag of the Hong Kong Special Administrative Region is a red flag with a bauhinia highlighted by five star-tipped stamens. The regional emblem of the Hong Kong Special Administrative Region is a bauhinia in the centre highlighted by five star-tipped stamens and encircled by the words "Hong Kong Special Administrative Region of the People's Republic of China" in Chinese and "HONG KONG" in English.

6.3 Two Types of Juries

① There are two types of juries. The first, the petit jury, is used in both civil and criminal cases. In civil cases its task is generally to determine liability to pay money damages; in criminal cases its task is to determine punishable guilty, and it usually does so with a minimum of criticism. There its position as a bulwark of liberty, a protector against executive oppression, and a mode of lessening the rigors of too strict legislation is secure. In England, where the use of the civil jury has been greatly reduced by legislation, the criminal jury remains in its traditional form. It is a noteworthy fact, however, that the jury is not now and has never been required to be used in equity cases.

② The second type of jury is the grand jury. It differs from the trial or petit jury in that it does not decide questions of guilt or innocence. Its function is accusatory. When a possible offender is brought before a magistrate, and the magistrate believes there is suspicion of guilt, the matter is presented to the grand jury for investigation. If the grand jury finds enough evidence to warrant a trial, it will issue a true bill of indictment and the case will proceed. If the evidence is insufficient, the case will be dismissed. On occasion, the grand jury is charged with a special

两种陪审团

① 陪审团分两种。第一种，即小陪审团，民事和刑事案件都适用。在民事案件中，小陪审团的任务一般是确定支付赔偿金的责任；在刑事案件中，其任务是确定应予处罚的罪责。而且，一般在完成这一任务时，它极少受到批评。在刑事案件中，小陪审团的地位极其稳固，因为它是自由的堡垒，是公民不受行政压迫的保障，也是缓和过于苛求的立法的一种方式。在英国，由于立法使民事陪审团的使用大为减少，刑事陪审团却原封不动地保存了下来。但是值得注意的是，在衡平法案件中，从古到今都是不要求使用陪审团的。

② 第二种陪审团是大陪审团。其不同于审理事实的陪审团即小陪审团之处，在于它不对有罪还是无罪作出决定。大陪审团的职能是起诉。一个可能被认为犯罪的罪犯被送交地方基层司法官而该基层司法官又认为其确有犯罪嫌疑，则此案归大陪审团侦查。大陪审团如果发现充分证据足以进行审理，就颁发准予起诉书，案件也就开

commission to investigate specific types of possible criminal activity among the general population or among governmental officials, and such investigations may also result in indictments. The grand jury has been abolished in England and in approximately one-half of our states. Its existence, however, is guaranteed by the Constitution in federal cases.

始了。如证据不足,则案件不予受理。有时候,则责成大陪审团担任侦查一般群众或政府官员中间有特种犯罪嫌疑活动的特殊任务。这种侦查也会导致起诉。大陪审团在英国全国和美国的约半数州内已经被废除了。但是美国联邦宪法保障了联邦案件中大陪审团的继续存在。(周玲用例)

6.4 The Constitution of the United States of America

美利坚合众国宪法

Article I

① Section 1. All legislative Powers herein granted shall be vested in a Congress of the United States, which shall consist of a Senate and House of Representatives.

② Section 1. The House of Representatives shall be composed of Members chosen every second Year by the People of the several States, and the Electors in each State shall have the Qualifications requisite for Electors of the most numerous Branch of the State Legislature.

③ No Person shall be a Representative who shall not have attained to the Age of twenty five years, and been seven Years a Citizen of the United States, and who shall not, when elected, be an inhabitant of that State in which he shall be chosen.

④ Representatives and direct Taxes shall be apportioned among the several States which may be included within this Union, according to their respective Numbers, which shall be determined by adding to the whole Number of free Persons, including those bound to Service for a Term of Years, and excluding Indians not taxed, three fifths of all other Persons. The actual enumeration shall be made within three Years after the first Meeting of the Congress of the United States, and within every subsequent Term of ten Years, in such Manner as they shall by law direct. The number of Representatives shall not exceed one for every thirty thousand, but each State shall have at least one Representative; and until such enumeration shall be made, the State of New Hampshire shall be entitled to choose three, Massachusetts eight, Rhode Island and Providence Plantations one, Connecticut five, New York six, New Jersey four, Pennsylvania eight, Delaware one, Maryland six, Virginia ten, North Carolina five, South Carolina five, and Georgia three.

第一条

① 第一款 本宪法授予的全部立法权,应属于由参议院和众议院组成的合众国国会。

② 第二款 众议院应由各选举州的人民每两年选举产生的众议院组成。每个州的选举人须具备该州州议会人数最多一院(州众议员)选举人所必需的资格。

③ 凡年龄不满二十五岁,成为合众国公民不满七年,若在一州当选时,不是该州居民者,不得担任众议员。

④ 众议员名额和直接税税额,在本联邦所包括的选举州中,按照其各自人口比例进行分配。各州人口数,按自由人总数加上其他所有人口的五分之三予以确定。自由人总数包括必须服一定年限劳役的人,但不包括未被征税的印第安人。人口的实际统计在合众国国会第一次会议后三年内以及此后每十年内,依法律规定的方式进行。每三万人选出的众议员人数不得超过一名,但每州至少须有一名众议院;在进行上述人口统计以前,新罕布什尔州有权选出三名,麻萨诸塞州八名,罗德岛州和普罗维登斯一名,康涅狄格州五名,纽约州六名,新泽西州四名,宾夕法尼亚州八名,特拉华州一名,马里兰州六名,弗吉尼亚州十名,北卡罗来纳州五名,南卡罗来纳州五名,佐治亚州三名。

⑤ When vacancies happen in the Representation from any State, the Executive Authority thereof shall issue Writs of Election to fill such Vacancies.

⑤ 任何一州代表出现缺额时，该州行政当局应发布选举令，选出众议员填补该空缺。

⑥ The House of Representatives shall choose their Speaker and other Officers; and shall have the sole Power of Impeachment.

⑥ 众议院应选举本院议长和其他官员，唯众议院具有弹劾权。（傅伟良用例）

6.5 推荐读物

（1）陈忠诚，法窗译话，中国对外翻译出版公司 1992 年版。

（2）陈忠诚，法苑译谭，中国法治出版社 2000 年版。

（3）傅伟良，法律英语翻译，石油工业出版社 2010 年版。

（4）陆文慧，法律翻译从实践出发，法律出版社 2004 年版。

（5）潘维大，刘文琦，英美法导读，法律出版社 2000 年版。

（6）周玲，如何翻译英语法律文献，对外经济贸易大学出版社 2006 年版。

练习 7 课后练习

7.1 分析题

（1）收集翻译语料，试析其中的翻译腔。

（2）任选比读体悟中的一篇材料，分析其全译方法。

（3）以 2.1 为例，试析全译之“全”的重要性。

7.2 实训题

7.2.1 法官职业化

法官职业化取得重大进展，从 2002 年开始，法院一律从通过国家司法考试取得任职资格的人员中择优录用法官。2002 年 3 月，全国有 36 万人参加了首次国家司法考试，为司法公正提供了人才支持。审判长、独立审判员选任制度已在全国普遍推行，一批具有较高素质的优秀法官担任审判长，主持合议庭庭审活动，由合议庭依照法定职责对案件进行裁判，提高了办案质量和效率。

7.2.2 Miranda Warning

You've probably heard it lots of times on TV crime shows: " You have the right to remain silent. Anything you say can and will be used against you in a court of law. You have the right to speak to an attorney, and to have an attorney present during any questioning. If you cannot afford a lawyer, one will be provided for you at government expense. " That is the Miranda Warning, named after a famous case involving a suspect named Miranda. All of the statements in the warning are true; however, it is not necessary for a police officer to recite the magic words in order to arrest.

7.3 思考题

(1)法律文本有哪些特有的文体特征,对翻译有何启示?
(2)哪些全译方法对翻译目的条款行之有效?
(3)如何译出法律文本的司法权威性?
(4)如何翻译法律文本中频现的近义性表达法?
(5)如何翻译法律文本的长状语?
(6)翻译法律文本中的从句时常作哪些调整?
(7)英汉法律互译中句子如何避"短"扬"长"?
(8)法律翻译如何做到"形""意"兼顾?
(9)法律条文的标题在表意和行文方面有哪些特点?常用哪些翻译方法?
(10)法律宣传口号用词简练,言简意邃,翻译时要特别注意什么?
(11)哪些全译方法在法律翻译中使用频率较高?

第 18 课 教育

导 译

education 源于拉丁文 educate，本义为“引出”或“导出”，具有内发之意，强调教育旨在把自然人所固有的或潜在的素质，自内而外引发出来，以成为现实的发展状态。“教，上所施，下所效也”；“育，养子使作善也”。中国传统教育观强调“效”和“善”，西方教育观则关注自由、个性和发展。

凡能增进知识，传授技能，改变思想，升华精神及涉及学校教育之文本，均可纳入教育翻译之列。谈及全译，结合文本类型及教育的本体功能，教育翻译属信息型和诱导型文本，应纳入实用翻译之范畴故应以传递信息为重，同时虑及传递效果。信息上保证内容传递的准确、真实和有效，诱导功能上以求唤起读者的体验和行动。译者唯有感应交际意图，揣摩文本功能，以译语文化为导向，兼顾诱导、感化受众，使读者沉浸在母语般的译文中，译文方能既喜闻乐见而又雅俗共赏，切勿苛求文本对等，而生搬硬套，啰唆冗长。

爱因斯坦有言：“什么是教育？当你把受过的教育都忘记了，剩下的就是教育。”不妨套用：什么是译能？当你把翻译的痕迹都消融了，剩下的便是翻译能力。

练笔 1 课前练笔

1.1 高等学府“阴盛阳衰”

南开大学今年招收的女生人数超过男生，在该校男女同校办学的几十余年历史中尚属首次。女大学生的增长显示了政府为保障教育公平所做的努力，也折射出社会观念的变迁:在过去,很多家庭受“重男轻女”思想的影响,女孩求学机会偏低。

1.2 中华人民共和国教育概况

① 中国具有五千年悠久的历史,自古就有尊师重教的传统。古代中国教育不仅为中华文明的传承和发展发挥了巨大作用,而且为世界文明的发展作出了巨大贡献。

② 近代中国教育总体上发展缓慢。1949 年 10 月 1 日,中华人民共和国成立,中国教育事业从此进入了一个完全崭新的发展阶段,全面推进素质教育,培养富有创新精神和实践能力的新一代。

1.3 **Primary Education in Australia**

Australia attaches great importance to education. In all six states except Tasmania, for children aged 6—15, school attendance is compulsory. Most children in Australia study in government schools where they enjoy free tuition at primary and secondary levels. Some children, however, are educated in non-government schools, including Catholic schools.

1.4 **Graduate School: University of Maryland**

① Candidates for admission must meet the minimum requirements set by the Graduate School, which normally requires Graduate Record Examinations scores for admission to graduate programs. The Graduate School uses GRE scores as part of the data on which it bases its admission decisions. The score, however, are never the sole criteria for admission. Applicants whose native language is not English must take the Test of English as a Foreign Language.

② The Graduate School requires official transcripts for all prior undergraduate and graduate study. Some programs may require additional evidence of ability to succeed. Such evidence may include a portfolio, an interview, or documentation of prior work experience.

1.5 **The Ivy League School: Excellence in Education**

① Harvard is not the only great school in the U. S., of course. A small industry has grown up around the ranking of the best tertiary schools, and year after year, seven schools dominate most of these Top Twenty or Top Fifty lists. Harvard is nearly always at or close to the top, joined frequently by Yale (in Connecticut), Princeton (in New Jersey), Dartmouth (in New Hampshire), Cornell (in New York State), Columbia (in New York City), the University of Pennsylvania, and Brown (in Rhode Island). These eight private universities are collectively referred to as the Ivy League schools.

② Why the name? Ivy is a vine. As these eight universities are old (the youngest among them, Cornell, was founded in 1853), ivy has had plenty of time to decorate the outsides of the more historic buildings on these campuses. Though there is an association called the Ivy League, it refers to the above schools' participation in an American football athletic conference rather than to any academic alliance.

2 课前批评

2.1 早期性教育冲破牢笼

Early Sex Education Breaks Down Barriers

① 据2001年起就在成都开展试点的青少年性健康教育专家胡萍介绍，近10年间，中国少年儿童的青春期已大大提前，早期性教育因此日趋迫切。

① Early-age sex education has become increasingly necessary in China, as adolescence has started arriving earlier over the last decade, said Hu Ping, a sex educator in Chengdu city since 2001.

② 今天的孩子越来越多地接触到与"性"相关的符号。街头广告牌上的性感女郎，超市收银台前和糖果摆在一起的安全套，电视里的男女亲热场面，还有互联网上散播的一切。

② Kids have more convenient access to sex-related things today. There are sexy models in street advertisements, condoms placed next to candies in supermarkets, intimate pictures on TV and all over the Internet.

③ 学校应当与家长一起担当起性健康教育的重任。家长们背景不同，带来的教育也会参差不齐。对于有些家长来说，给孩子讲授性健康知识没准会适得其反，但是学校就能给每个孩子都提供很好的教育。

③ Schools should share the burden of sex education with parents. Parents have different backgrounds, which can lead to an uneven education. It might actually be worse for some of them to teach their children about sex, while schools can provide good education for every child.

2.2 Preventive Parenting

预防性育儿法

① Behavioral scientists find that only 60% of babies have easy temperaments from birth. Most of the rest are placed in the so-called difficult category.

① 行为科学家们发现，只有60%的婴儿生来就性格随和。其余大多数的婴儿被划归为所谓的"困难"类别。

② The best way to keep a difficult baby from becoming an impossible child is to practice preventive parenting — something some parents do naturally.

② 防止"困难"婴儿变成无药可救的孩子的最好办法是实施预防性育儿法——有些父母自然地在这么做。

③ When a baby is resistant to novelty, parents must finesse how they present new things. Well before the first day of pre-school, parents can begin slowly exposing the child to the idea: go for a drive to the school one day, return for a walk around the halls the

③ 当婴儿对新生事物有抵触情绪时，父母必须巧妙地调整给孩子展示新事物的方式。早在孩子第一天上幼儿园之前，父母就可以开始让他慢慢了解这

next. Give the child lead time.

个新事物:某一天开车去幼儿园,另一天回家时绕幼儿园的教学楼走一圈。让孩子先有段学前适应时间。(隋荣谊用例)

3 全译知识 全译批评

全译批评,指依据全译标准对全译及其相关方面进行分析与评价的活动。全译批评主要考察译文对原文的极似程度,包括微观批评和宏观批评。微观批评主要涉及全译语言层面微观过程的批评,也可称为译内评论;宏观批评主要涉及基于微观过程而延伸至文化层面的批评,也可称为译外批评。

3.1 译内批评

译内评论是微观批评,指从语表形式、语里意义和语用价值三个角度对全译活动及其成品进行批评。三个角度是任何全译批评的抓手和落脚点。

语表形式批评 即对语表形式的批评。交际价值、语里意义全靠形式承载,所以结构、题材、体裁等宏观形式可成为评价对象,语音、词汇、语法、语篇等更是考察译文与原文是否求得了极似效果的重点。如:

① In the evening she wears soft rich colors, dark red, olive green, midnight blue, always of the most supple flowing texture.

【原译】:而在夜晚她却穿着柔和的,色彩浓艳的诸如暗盘色,橄榄绿,深蓝色之类质地柔软的衣服。

【试译】:夜晚她总穿暗红色、橄榄绿或深蓝色的衣裳,色彩浓艳柔和,质地柔软光滑。

例①中原译漏译了 always, most 和 flowing 三词,还犯了汉译偏正结构“的的不休”的毛病。译者未理清原文的层次,原文以 colors 代衣,用 dark red、olive green、midnight blue 做 colors 的同位语,而 always of the most supple flowing texture 则第二次修饰 colors,所以译者完全按照原作思路逐层译出了。

语里意义批评 是全译批评的主体。语表形式批评之后,进而从语里意义上去把握,考量译文是否反映了原文内容,是否足额地传达了原文的所有意思,具体而言,包括词义、短语义和句义。如:

② The stars seemed little cuts in the black cover, through which a bright beyond was seen.

【原译】:星星像黑锅盖上的小窟窿,透过小窟窿可以看见外面的光。

【试译】:星星宛如黑幕上的小隙,从中透出外面的光。

③ You may think you're the world's greatest speaker, but if the auditorium's sound system is singing static — well, forget it.

【原译】:你可能认为自己是世界上最伟大的演讲大师,但如果观众席上效果不好——那么就请忘掉这点不悦,请继续你的演讲吧。

【试译】:你可能自认为是世上最伟大的演说家,一旦礼堂音响系统发生静电干扰,那你就别做梦啦。

例②,cover 多义,可指盖子、幕、覆盖物、掩蔽物、床罩等,入句可以定义,星夜闪烁,背景是夜幕,而编织成的幕,会有许多细小的缝隙,既可理解为星星如同夜幕上的透出光的缝隙,也可理解为因缝隙而透见外面的光;同时,cut 理解为"缝隙",一则显出星星的高远,二则其四射的光形如星光。例③,it 颇为棘手,it 入句,在此无确切意义,也可指前言所说的自我认识,forget(about) it,并非简单的"忘记这一点",而是"休想,不可能"。

语用价值批评 考察译文的整体效果。对形式和内容进行批评后,最后要上升到整体的高度,从语用价值考察是否达到了交际目的,译文是否得体,修辞是否切当,文化交流是否有隔,译语读者是否能接受。如:

④ If a home is happy, it cannot fit too close. 家庭幸福,房窄何妨?

⑤ I don't think you are right.

【原译】:我以为你是不对的。

【试译】:我不以为你是对的。

例④,cannot…too 为收敛式强调,语义为"无论怎样也不为过",出语含蓄;将双重否定译为反诘句,语表不同,修辞效果却相似。例⑤常常将否定词转译至 right 之前,所得的原译语气太直,原文的交际价值反而不等值,试译的语气比较婉转,词序句型也完全一致,达到了语用极似。

3.2 译外批评

译外评论是宏观批评,指从语言对比、思维转换和文化交流三个角度对全译活动及其成品进行批评。与译内批评具有对应关系和延伸关系。

语言对比批评 同语表形式相对,且是它的延伸,是用得最多的译外批评。这一批评对比全译中双语语表形式,包括交叉批评和平行批评。

交叉批评,主要指甲语言通过翻译活动对乙语言产生的影响。如五四以来汉译作品中偏正结构使用"的"字最佳用量研究表明,一般情况下汉译作品无论定语有多长,偏正结构中"的"字使用数不得超过三两个正常,一个最好。再如汉译作品中关联词用得较本土作品要多,副词作状语语用"地"字较多,等等。平行批评主要指双语语言系统的对比,主要从语音、词汇、语法、篇章结构等层面对比说明全译的正误及其理据,大部分语言层面的批评属于此类。比如,译者词汇贫乏,译文好比患了贫血症,干瘪乏味,毫无生气;语法欧化,形式化较多,一读便知道非地道汉语。如:

⑥ Most Americans remember Mark Twain as the father of Huck Finn's idyllic cruise through eternal boyhood and Tom Sawyer's endless summer of freedom and adventure. 大多数美国人都记得马克·吐温是描写哈克·芬恩那不朽童年、诗情画意般的漂游以及汤姆·索亚那漫漫仲夏、逍遥自在的历险的作者。

Father 之前有 17 个词,译成长长的定语限定"作者",通常看来,有"的的不休"之嫌,但就本例来说,长长的限定有一种语势,旨在突出马克·吐温是两部名著的作者,饱含赞赏之情,不仅形式相当,更达修辞极似。

思维转换批评 同语里意义相对,且是它的延伸,是有待发掘的译外批评。这一批评对比全译中的两种思维，分析其中的思维转换模式，考察译者对形象思维和抽象思维以及二者所构成的直觉思维的转换是否成功。如：

⑦ A brewer's wife may drink of a ton.

【原译】：近水楼台先得月。

【改译】：酿酒人的妻子不愁酒。

【试译】：酿酒人妻先得酒。

⑧ I tried to teach the lessons I had prepared, but was met with a sea of guarded faces.

【原译】：我准备教我备好的课，可是，却见到了海洋般的警戒着的脸。

【试译】：我正要讲课，却见一张张脸满是戒备。

例⑦，原译为套用，但失原文形象，让汉文化少了些鲜色；改译达意，作为俗语还可提炼；试译结合原译与改译之优点，套用原译七言结构的思维模式，装入原作的内容，为汉语的"近水楼台先得月"增添了同义俗语。例⑧，原文意象 sea 照译未完成思维转换，"准备教我备好的课"未进行思维压缩，可以去掉原文的冗余信息 I had prepared。

文化交流批评 同语用价值相对，且是它的延伸，是现在越来越受到关注的译外批评。这一批评对比全译所涉及的两种文化，分析文化交流的过程及其成果，考察译者的文化交流是否成功。

立于跨文化的角度，可以从政治、经济、历史、宗教等角度评论翻译成功与否。如：

⑨ Rats desert a falling house.

【原译】：树倒猢狲散。

【改译】：屋倒鼠搬家。

⑩ Each day that I escape death, each day of suffering that helps to free me from earthly cares, I make a new little paper bird and add it to the others.

【原译】：每天当我从死亡线上挣脱出来，我每多活一天，多遭一天罪，也就距脱离尘世苦海的日子近了一天，我就叠上一只小小的纸鸟，把它跟其他纸鸟粘贴在一起。

【试译】：每天当我挣脱了死亡线，每天当病痛的折磨帮我摆脱尘世的牵挂，我就折一只小纸鸟，和其他纸鸟摆在一起。

例⑨，原译为套译，采用了归化的文化策略。如果原语文化并不难懂，又能为译语输入新鲜表达，不妨异化：思维模式仿用译语结构，采用原语的文化意象，如改译就极其形象，且不失生动，是通过翻译成功吸收异域文化的范例。例⑩，原文的宗教背景是佛教：磨难有助于人摆脱尘世的苦恼，于人有益，因此主人公所持的是乐观情绪。而原译反映的是活着就是遭罪、早死就是快活的悲观思想，与原文宗教观相左。

4 全译窍门

4.1 篇名标记译有别

英汉语书名和文名不同，英语书名用斜体，文名用正常字体加引号。汉语则不加区分，一律用"《》"，英汉互译时要加小心。如：

① I have read quite a number of Henry James's works, such as *The Portrait of a Lady*, *The Golden Bowl*, *The American and The Art of Fiction*. 我读过亨利·詹姆斯的好多作品，如《贵妇的肖像》、《金碗》、《美国人》和《小说艺术》。

4.2 研究员研究不同

中国现行的专业技术职称，几乎都会区分高级、副高级、中级和初级等。“研究员”应译成 researcher 还是 professor？要看是否能体现它在中国职称系统中的等级和内涵。英语的 researcher 并未体现职称等级，中国的研究员更具有学术内涵。

中国研究员系统、图书资料系统、档案系统和文物博物系统都设有研究员，笼统翻译成 professor 会造成混淆，翻译应体现其研究领域，比如图书资料研究馆员应译为 professor of library science，档案研究馆员应译成 professor of archive science，文物博物研究馆员应译成 professor of relics and museology，以体现国际性，也考虑“等级”和“内涵”。

4.3 主语灵活隐现

主语是句子的灵魂所在，恰当地确定主语，可使译文内涵清晰，体现作者的用意，亦能规避中西思维差异而导致的误译。反之，句子松散乏力，甚至会误导读者。如：

② 中国在过去的二十年中发生了翻天覆地的变化。The last two decades has witnessed earth-shaking changes in China.

③ 厨房里少了一条鱼，主人发誓要一查到底，揪出偷鱼的贼。Finding a fish in kitchen was lost, the host swore to find out the thief who stole the fish.

④ 共同的利益把我们两个伟大的国家联系在一起。What holds our two great nations together is the cement of common interests.

例②，译文确定 the last two decades 作主语，地道流畅，同样强调了原文“二十年”时间界限。例③选定 the host 作主语，将其作为 find 的逻辑主语，凸显了句子的表意重心。例④，主语选择突破思维定势，译文富有灵魂。

4.4 there 比“那儿”要远

there 除用作副词表方向外，还常用作感叹词，表“得意、鼓励、同情、悲哀、不耐烦、失望、安慰、挑衅”等，译为“哟”、“瞧”、“好啦”与“得啦”等，不可简单译成“那儿”。

⑤ There now! 你看！

⑥ There! Do you feel better now? 怎么样，你好些了吗？

⑦ There, there. Stop crying. 好了，好了，别哭了。

⑧ There, there, you said too much. 得啦，得啦，你说的太多了。

⑨ There, I've filled it up again. 瞧，我又把它灌满了。

⑩ There, what's that? 哟，那是什么？

例⑤中 there 显示所说的话是对的，其他几例则随语境译出了不同的情感。不过，there 即使用作副词也寓意丰富，用以引起注意，加强语气等，如例⑪比“她来了”更为传神。

⑪ There she is. 瞧，她来了。

4.5 “婉约否定”:英语婉约之道

英语否定常借 not, no, never, hardly 等否定词和 dis-, not-, un-, in-, none-, -less 等否定词缀来完成。有时形式肯定而实际否定,称之为“婉约否定”,汉译时要变肯定为否定。如:

⑫ If ever I heard the like. 我从来没有听到过这种说法。

⑬ He is more dead than alive. 与其说他活着,不如说他死了。

⑭ He is far from being honest. 他决非诚实之人。

⑮ This case is not as you represent, far from it! 这事完全不同你说的,完全不同。

⑯ Your request is beyond my power. 你的请求我办不到。

例⑫,虚拟语气句有时省略主语,用 if 引导假设条件句来表达否定意义。例⑬,互为反义的形容词和副词采用-er + than 或 more + 原级 + than 形式比较表达否定意义时,不可直译,否则影响表达效果,甚至可能违背原意。例⑭, far from + 动名词结构表示否定意义,可译成“远非……”、“绝不……”。有时, far from + 其他成分作为独立单句置于句末,以加重主句的语气,汉译时要译出否定义,如例⑮。有时译作否定句意义会更加简明,但语用上会有差别,如例⑯若译成“你的请求超出了我的能力”就更委婉。

4.6 怎一个“好”字了得

well 是常见词,蕴含意义丰富,处理得当,译文会更加灵动;反之,则黯然失色,甚至无法达到翻译主旨。well 除用作副词表程度外,还常用作感叹词,表示“快慰、让步、期望、讥讽、解释、责备、犹豫”等,译为“好吧”“不过”“好啦”“嗯”等,不可简单译成“好”。如:

⑰ Well, I didn't think to see you here! 哎呀,没想到会在这儿见到你!

⑱ Well, perhaps that's true. 嗯,也许那是真的。

⑲ Well, you shouldn't get angry about such a trifle. 嗳,你不应该为这么一点小事生气。

⑳ Well, who was it? 那么,那是谁呢?

㉑ Well, then? 嗯!后来怎么啦?

例⑰表示惊异、怀疑。例⑱表示同意、让步。例⑲表示规劝、责备。例⑳引入新的话题。例㉑表示无可奈何。

词汇 5 话题词汇

5.1 教育体制

教育理学硕士 master of Science in Education
教育文学硕士 master of Arts in Teaching
教育学博士 doctor of Education
理学硕士 master of Science
艺术硕士 master of Fine Arts
academic activities 学术活动

board expenses 伙食费
Certificate of Attendance 肄业证书
Certificate of Completion 结业证书
Certificate of Graduation 毕业证书
compulsory education 义务教育
confer 授予(学位)
distance education 远程教育
education 学历
food allowance 伙食补助
general education 普遍教育
graduate student 研究生
higher education 高等教育
key disciplinary areas 重点学科
pedagogical education 师范教育
preschool education 学前教育
primary education 初等教育
prize fellow 奖学金获得者
rewards 奖励
scholarship 奖学金
self-taught examination 自学考试
subject 学科
talent 人才
the length of education 学制
universal education 普及教育
versatile talents 复合型人才
vocational and technical education 职业技术教育

5.2 职称职务

副研究馆员(档案系列) associate professor of archive science
副研究员(研究系列)associate professor (of)
高级教师(中小学)senior teacher
馆员(档案系列)archivist
管理员(档案系列)file clerk
实验师(实验系列)experimentalist
实验室主任 laboratory chief
实验员 laboratory technician
训练部部长(军校)chief of the training branch
研究馆员(档案系列)professor of archive science
研究生指导教师 research supervisor
研究实习员(研究系列)research assistant
研究员(研究系列)professor
院务部部长(军校)chief of the logistic Branch
政委(军校)political commissary
政治部主任(军校)chief of the political branch
助理馆员(档案系列)assistant archivist
助理讲师 assistant lecturer
助理研究员(研究系列)research associate
acting president(大学)代理校长
associate professor 副教授
bachelor 学士
chairman(系)主任
commissary in charge of entertainment 文娱委员
commissary in charge of organization 组织委员
commissary in charge of physical labor 劳动委员
commissary in charge of publicity 宣传委员
commissary in charge of sports 体育委员
commissary in charge of studie 学习委员
dean of studies 教务长
guest professor 客座教授
head of the teaching and research 教研室主任
head teacher 班主任
headmaster(小学)校长
honorary professor 名誉教授
league branch secretary 团支部书记
lecturer 讲师
lifetime professor 终身教授
party branch secretary 党支部书记
post doctorate 博士后
supervisor 论文导师
vice-chairman 副主任
vice-monitor 副班长

5.3 教育机构

表演系 Acting Department
材料工程系 Department of Materials Engineering
材料科学系 Department of Materials Science
地理系 Department of Geography
地球物理系 Department of Geophysics
地质系 Department of Geology

电机工程系 Department of Electrical Engineering
电子系 Department of Electronics
工程物理系 Department of Engineering Physics
工业设计系 Department of Industrial Design
海洋学系 Department of Oceanography
化学系 Department of Chemistry
环境工程学系 Department of Environmental Engineering
机械工程系 Department of Mechanical Engineering
建筑工程系 Department of Architectural Engineering
聋哑学校 school of deaf-mutes
汽车工程系 Department of Automobile Engineering
畜牧系 Department of Animal Husbandry
boarding school 寄宿学校
center for post-doctoral studies 博士后科研流动站
conservatory of music 音乐学院
Department of Accounting 会计系
Department of Atomic Energy 原子能系
Department of Higher Education of the Ministry of Education 教育部高等教育司
Department of International Economics 国际经济系
Department of International Relations 国际关系系
Department of Literature 文学系
Department of Medicine 医学系
Department of Pharmacy 药学系
Department of Philosophy 哲学系
Department of Political Science 政治系
Department of Vocational and Adult Education 职业教育与成人教育司
educational policy 教育方针
exam-dominated education 应试教育
junior middle school 初中
key middle school 重点中学
literacy class 扫盲班
Ministry of Education 教育部
normal university 师范大学
quality-oriented education 素质教育
specialized secondary school 中专学校
State Education Commission 国家教育委员会
technical school 技校
the Academic Degrees Appraisal Committee under the State Council 国务院学位委员会
the Academic Council of the Chinese Academy of Sciences 中国科学院学术委员会
university of liberal arts 文科大学
university of science and engineering 理工科大学

5.4 专业课程

材料力学 Mechanics of Materials
财务会计 Financial Accounting
单片机原理 Principle of Single Chip Computer
电子商务 Electronic Commerce
法理学 Nomology
海商法 Law of Maritime Commerce
函数分析 Functional Analysis
宏微观经济学 Macro Micro Economics
化工原理 Principles of Chemical Industry
环境工程 Environmental Engineering
货币银行学 Currency Banking
机械原理 Principle of Mechanics
机械制图 Mechanical Graphing
基因诊断 Gene Diagnosis
基因治疗 Gene Therapy
Advanced Mathematics 高等数学
Algebra 代数学
Anesthesia 麻醉学
Applied Chemistry 应用化学
Artificial Intelligence 人工智能
basic course 基础课
Calculus 微积分
Computer Practice 上机操作
Extension Courses 函授课程
elective/optional course 选修课
Enterprise Management 企业管理
Graduation Practice 毕业实习
Graduation Thesis 毕业论文
Graduation Thesis 毕业设计
Linear Algebra 线性代数
major 主修
Material Chemistry 材料化学
Military Theory 军事理论
minor 副修;辅修

Moral Education 德育
Office Automatization 办公自动化
open class 公开课
Political Economics 政治经济学
Principle of Marxism
马克思主义原理
compulsory course 必修课
Science of Auditing 审计学
specialized course 专业课
Statistics 统计原理

5.5 课堂教学

百分制 100-mark system
补考 make-up examination
成绩单 school report
过程目标 enabling objective
结果目标 terminal objective
军校学员 cadet
课程表 school timetable
录取 enroll
三学期制 the trimester system
双语教育 bilingual education
文盲 illiterate
五分制 the 5-grade marking system
校训 University/School Motto
形成性测试 formative assessment
修业年限 period of schooling
学分制 credit system
学习成绩 academic record; school record
abroad student 留学生
academic year 学年
assessment 评估
auditor 旁听生(美)
bilingual 双语的
boarder 寄宿生
commoner 自费生
day-student 走读生
diphthong 双元音
educational system 学制
government-supported student 公费生
grade examination papers 阅卷
graduate student 研究生(美)
guest student 旁听生(英)
heuristic method 启发式
intern 实习生
language proficiency 语言水平
marks 分数
morphology 词法
prize fellow 奖学金生
returned student 回国留学生
semester 学期(美)
term 学期(英)
undergraduate 大学(肄业)生
evaluation 评价

5.6 缩略语

标准英语 SE
高级经理工商管理硕士 EMBA
工商管理博士 D. B. A.
管理专业研究生入学考试 GMAT
国际音标 IPA
美国传统音标体系 AHD
美国教育考试服务中心 ETS
全国公共英语等级考试 PETS
硕士研究生入学资格考试 GRE
托福 TOEFL
文学博士 D. A.
英语口语考试(美国)TSE
英语专业考试 TEM
远程语言教学 CALT
职业英语考试 TOPE
EAP 学术英语
EISE 教育信息服务处
FLT 外语教学
GCSE 普通中等教育证书
HBS 哈佛大学商学院
IB 国际高中毕业考试
ISC 私立学校委员会
LC 合作学习
OET 职业英语测试

QT 快速测试
RAE 科研水平评估
SAM 学校行政及管理
SST 奖学金选拔考试
TAE 教学质量评估
TESL 作为第二种语言的英语教学
UFT (美国)教师联合会

6 比读体悟

6.1 兴趣是最好的老师

① 对孩子的个性培养是非常重要的,做父母的不要强迫孩子做不想做的事。现在的父母望子成龙,总是为孩子设计出一条光明大道,他们常根据自己的喜好规定孩子应该做什么,不该做什么,而这些规定常常并非孩子自己的意愿,很多有特定才能的孩子在父母的设计下反而一无所成。

② 我也曾想让儿子去当一个艺术家,比如我让他学画画,但儿子不喜欢,儿子喜欢数学,甚至到了痴迷程度,有时解出一道难题就欣喜若狂。我尊重儿子的选择,支持儿子上奥校,参加各种数学活动。儿子参加过不少数学竞赛,在北京及至全国的数学竞赛中都拿过名次。儿子与数学有缘,小学毕业后,考上了101 中学实验数学班,中学毕业直接上了清华大学数学系,大学毕业后又去美国学习统计学。俗话说:"兴趣是最好的老师。"儿子的兴趣成就了他的事业。

Interest Is the Best Tutor

① To foster the children's personality is important. On no account should we parents force our children to do what they don't want to do. Parents of today, in their ardent desire to see their children amount to something, tend to impose what they believe is the right course on their children. They decide the dos and don'ts for their children regardless of their feelings. Many gifted children end up getting nowhere simply because of parental manipulation.

② For a time I had wanted my son to become an artist, I had asked him to learn how to paint, but this was not to my son's liking. He loved mathematics with a passion that bordered on religion, and he went into raptures whenever he solved a difficult problem. Respecting my son's choice, I sent him to an Olympic mathematics school and took him to all sorts of activities related to mathematics. He had attended many mathematics competitions at national and municipal levels, and came away with many top awards. It seemed he was predestined to learn mathematics. After graduating from primary school, he was admitted to an experimental mathematics class of Beijing No. 101 Middle School. He went straight on to the Mathematics Department of Tsinghua University upon graduation from middle school. Immediately after finishing college in China, he went to the United States to pursue statistical science. "Interest is the best tutor," as the saying goes. My son's childhood interest precisely set the stage for his promising future. (张光明用例)

6.2 为师之道

① 我想,教师要给学生的,是一把开启知识宝库的钥匙,而不是把学生的脑子变成一个容器。教师的工作是启发学生,通过自己的思考、实践、实验去求得

Teaching English to Millions of Students

① I should say teacher's vital role is teaching in such a way as to provide students with a key to the treasure house of knowledge, not to turn their brains into mere receptacles. Teachers' work is primarily to prompt students to think for

知识,鼓励他们大胆提出问题和不同意见。经过研讨,得出自己的结论,而不是由教师包办代替。

themselves, help them to practice, to experiment in order to get hold of knowledge. More importantly, teachers should encourage their students to come up with contradictory opinions at academic discussions, to thrash out problems for themselves, and to draw conclusions of their own. It is not by any manner of means a teacher's monopoly.

② 我喜欢那些爱提"怪"问题的学生。提不出问题的,不能算是好学生。

② I favor those students who surprise me with "awkward" or embarrassing questions. I've no affection for numb ones.

③ 其实,学习就是一个不断出错误和改正错误的过程。年轻人要学,我们自己也要学。一句话,教育是要使人从无知变成有知,从愚昧变成聪明,从野蛮变成文明,而不是相反。

③ In point of truth, learning is a process of making and correcting errors. Young people ought to learn ceaselessly, we elders ought to do the same. In a word, education orientates a person from ignorance to intelligence, from stupidity to wisdom, from barbarity to civility. Never the other way round.

④ 就说这流行音乐吧,我就不如年轻人懂得多。我有个习惯,自己不懂的东西,绝不轻易反对,而是努力去学懂它。

④ Take pop music for example. Younger people know more about it than I do. But I have a way with me: I don't hastily oppose what I don't know. Instead, I'll try to learn about it.

⑤ 你看吧,大街上姑娘们大声谈笑,我行我素;小伙子也穿红戴绿。中国人胆子大起来了,不那么缩头缩脑了。你还能拿年轻人头发长短,裤脚大小来衡量谁是好学生谁是坏学生吗?

⑤ Look at those young girls in the street talking and laughing loudly, freely, obliviously of you. And young boys swagger in red and green. This generation of Chinese seems to be bolder than the older generation -- not timid and retreating. How could you any longer judge young scholars to be good or not so good by their long or short hairs, or by their larger or smaller trouser legs?

⑥ 现在,我们需要知识,我们需要教育,我们需要现代化。

⑥ Today, we need knowledge, we need education, we need modernization.

⑦ 我们到底需要培养什么样的大学生?我们今后能在色彩纷繁、瞬息万变的当今世界站住脚吗?看来,首先要启发学生的学习兴趣和主动性,培养他们自学的能力。

⑦ What, after all, is the kind of college students that we want and bring up and out? The way we teach now, can they go out into the world and gain a footing in the kaleidoscopic and twinklingly volatile society? In my view, we should first of all try to induce the young people's study interest and initiative, and help them cultivate the ability to be self-taught. (张光明用例)

6.3 大学生品质

The Qualities of University Students

① 人的品质,由四方面来展现:道德的、健康的、文化的和专业的。

① A person's qualities are displayed in four aspects: morals, health, culture and skill.

② 大学生,作为国家公民,应该培养自己遵守公民基本道德规范。其中最要紧的,我认为是诚信守法,尊重他人,关心社会。道德品质并非与生俱来,要靠

② As citizens, students should cultivate in themselves moral standards of respect for their fellow-citizens. In my opinion, the most important of such standards are a sincere respect for the law, respect for other people and concern for

接受教育,要靠理性的力量,更靠大学生本人的身体力行。古人云,勿以恶小而为之,勿以善小而不为。既然当大学生,就应该下决心用几年时间把自己锻炼成为一个道德高尚的人。

society. Moral quality is not inborn; you must rely on education and the strength of rationality, but most of all on your own exertions. An ancient saying goes: " Do you think any vice trivial, and so practise it; do not think any virtue trivial, and so neglect it. " And so, as university students, we must make a decision that over the next few years we will mold ourselves into person with high moral character.

③ 现代意义的健康品质,已经不仅仅局限于身体,它还包括心理,更包括对社会环境的适应,能够与别人共同相处、和谐生活。在我们的生活中,有竞争就要分出成败,作选择就会有所得失。心理的不健康无非就是忧成败、患得失。既然当大学生,就应该树立正确的世界观、人生观,做到我们中国人说的仁者不忧,勇者不惧。

③ In the modern sense, the quality of health is not confined to physical well-being; it also encompasses psychological well-being, but even more so does it include adapting to the social environment and living in harmony with other people. In our lives we encounter competition, which involves success and failure. When we make choices, sometimes we gain and sometimes we lose. If we were not psychologically healthy, we may worry about success or failure, gain and loss. So we university students must set up a correct world view and view of life, and become, as we Chinese say, " benevolent and unworried, bold and unafraid. "

④ 文化品质是指一个人接受继承人类文明成果的广度和深度。几千年来,人类科学的、技术的、哲学的、文学的、艺术的成就浩如烟海,在现在的这样的一个知识时代,最糟糕的、带有侮辱性的称谓,莫过于“没有文化”。既然当大学生,就应该如饥似渴汲取文化营养,充实自己的人生。

④ The quality of culture involves inheriting the fruits of human civilization in breadth and in depth. For thousands of years, mankind has created achievements as vast as the oceans in the fields of science, technology, philosophy, literature and art. In our present era of knowledge, there is nothing more deplorable and shameful than to be labeled " uncultured". And so, as university students, we must absorb cultural nutrition as if we were hungry and thirsty for it, to enrich our life.

⑤ 专业品质常常是人们用以求职谋生的。农业时代,中国人说“荒年饿不死手艺人”,到工业时代,就有了“学会数理化,走遍天下都不怕”的说法,现在大家追求学历,选择专业,大多就是希望掌握专门的学问和技能。

⑤ The quality of skill is often used simply to find a job and make a living. When China was in the agricultural era, it used to be said that " an artisan does not starve even in a lean year. " In the industrial age, it is said that " someone who has mastered sciences will have no fear of unemployment. " Nowadays, everybody is pursuing an educational qualification and choosing a profession, and most of them hope to grasp a special branch of learning or skill.

6.4 Raising Children

美式教养观

① The job of raising children is a tough one. Children don't come with an instruction manual. And each child is different. So parents sometimes pull their hair out in frustration, not knowing what to do. But in raising children — as in all of life — what we do is influenced by our culture. Naturally then, American parents teach their children basic American values.

① 养育孩子是件伤脑筋的差事,孩子们并不是生下来就附有说明书的,而每个孩子又都不尽相同,所以有时候父母们无奈地拽自己的头发,不知该怎么办。然而以教养孩子而言,就像生活中所有的事一样,我们的行

为都受文化的影响，因此，美国父母很自然地会教导他们的孩子基本的美国价值观。

② To Americans, the goal of parents is to help children stand on their own two feet. From infancy, each child may get his or her own room. As children grow, they gain more freedom to make their own choices. Teenagers choose their own forms of entertainment, as well as the friends to share them with. When they reach young adulthood, they choose their own careers and marriage partners. Of course, many young adults still seek their parents' advice and approval for the choices they make. But once they "leave the nest" at around 18 to 21 years old, they want to be on their own, not "tied to their mother's apron strings."

② 对美国人而言，教养的目标在于帮助孩子们自力更生。从婴幼儿期开始，每一个孩子都可能拥有自己的房间；随着孩子的成长，他们有更多机会自己作决定；青少年们选择自己喜欢的娱乐方式，以及跟什么样的朋友一起玩；当他们进入了青年期之后，他们选择自己的事业和结婚伴侣。当然，很多的年轻人在作选择时，还是会寻求父母的忠告和赞同，但是当他们一旦在十八到二十一岁左右"离了巢"之后，就希望能够独立，不再是个离不开妈妈的孩子了。

③ The relationship between parents and children in America is very informal. American parents try to treat their children as individuals — not as extensions of themselves. They allow them to fulfill their own dreams. Americans praise and encourage their children to give them the confidence to succeed. When children become adults, their relationship with their parents becomes more like a friendship among equals. But contrary to popular belief, most adult Americans don't make their parents pay for room and board when they come to visit. Even as adults, they respect and honor their parents.

③ 在美国，亲子之间的关系不是那么的严肃，美国父母们试着将孩子视为个体，而不是他们自我的延伸。他们允许孩子去实现自己的梦想。美国人会赞美并鼓励孩子以给予他们成功的信心。当孩子长大成人之后，亲子之间的关系会更像地位平等的朋友，可是与大家一向所以为的恰好相反，当父母来访时，大部分的美国成年人并不会要求父母付食宿费，因为就算已经成年，他们还是很敬重父母的。

④ Most young couples with children struggle with the issue of childcare. Mothers have traditionally stayed home with their children. In recent years, though, a growing trend is to put preschoolers in a day care center so Mom can work. Many Americans have strong feelings about which type of arrangement is best. Some argue that attending a day care center can be a positive experience for children. Others insist that mothers are the best caregivers for children. A number of women are now leaving the work force to become full-time homemakers.

④ 大部分有孩子的年轻夫妻们都为了养育孩子的问题而大伤脑筋。传统上，母亲们会和孩子待在家里。但是近几年来，把孩子放在幼儿园而让妈妈去工作的趋势渐长。对于哪一种安排才是最好的，许多美国人都有自己强烈的主张，有些人认为进幼儿园对孩子而言是很正面的经历，另一群人则坚持母亲是照顾孩子的最佳人选，许多的妇女现在也离开工作市场成为全职的家庭主妇。

⑤ Being a parent is a tall order. It takes patience, love, wisdom, courage and a good sense of humor to raise children (and not lose your sanity). Some people are just deciding not to have children at all, since they're not sure it's worth it. But raising children means training the next generation and preserving our

⑤ 担任亲职是必须付出极大代价的，教养孩子需要付出耐心、爱心、智能、勇气以及高度的幽默感（同时不失去你明智的判断力）。有些人根本不生孩子，因为他们不确定这样的付

culture. What could be worthy more than that?

出值不值得，但是养育孩子意味着训练下一代并且保留我们的文化，又有什么会比这更有价值呢？（彭蒙惠用例）

6.5 A Liberal Education

开明教育

① Education is the instruction of the intellect in the laws of Nature, under which name I include not merely things and their forces, but men and their ways; and the fashioning of the affections and of the will into an earnest and loving desire to move in harmony with those laws. For me, education means neither more nor less than this. Anything which professes to call itself education must be tried by this standard, and if it fails to stand the test, I will not call it education, whatever may be the force of authority, or of numbers, upon the other side.

① 教育就是用自然法则去指导头脑，归之于这一法则的不仅仅是万事万物以及它们的影响，还包括人类和他们的行为；教育就是要将情感和意志塑造成一种按照这些法则去行事的真诚而又热烈的愿望。对我而言，这便是教育最确切的含义。任何自称为教育的东西都必须用此标准来检验。凡经不起这种检验的我都不承认其为教育，无论对方权位多高，人数多重。

② It is important to remember that, in strictness, there is no such thing as an uneducated man. Take an extreme case. Suppose that an adult man, in the full vigour of his faculties, could be suddenly placed in the world, as Adam is said to have been, and then left to do as he best might. How long would he be left uneducated? Not five minutes. Nature would begin to teach him, through the eye, the ear, the touch, the properties of objects. Pain and pleasure would be at his elbow telling him to do this and avoid that; and by slow degrees the man would receive an education which, if narrow, would be thorough, real, and adequate to his circumstances, though there would be no extras and very few accomplishments.

② 有一点必须记住：从严格意义上说，无知者是不存在的。不妨举一个极端的例子。假设把一个生理机能已得到充分发育的成人突然投到这个世界上来，像传说中的亚当那样，然后由着他去行动。他无知的状态会持续多久呢？不会超过五分钟。大自然会通过他的视觉、听觉以及触觉来教会他认识物体的属性。疼痛感和愉悦感也会随时告诉他该做什么，或不该做什么。渐渐地他就获得了一种教育，这种教育即使有限，即使谈不上是任何非凡技艺的传授，但它却是彻底的，真实的，足以使他应付周围的各种环境。

③ To every one of us the world was once as fresh and new as to Adam. And then, long before we were susceptible of any other modes of instruction, Nature took us in hand, and every minute of waking life brought its educational influence, shaping our actions into rough accordance with Nature's laws, so that we might not be ended untimely by too gross disobedience. And Nature is still continuing her patient education of us in that great university, the universe, of which we are all members — Nature having no Test-Acts.

③ 在我们每个人的眼里，这个世界曾经是那么的新鲜和陌生，犹如它在亚当的眼里一样。然后，当其他形式的教育还未曾对我们产生影响时，自然就已经搀扶起我们，每分钟都在对日益觉醒的生命施以教育的影响，调整我们的行为，同自然法则大体上保持一致，使我们不至于因严重的违背而夭折。自然不断地在宇宙这包罗万象的学府里对我们进行着富有耐心

的教育，我们都是这所学府里的学员——自然是没有测试令的。

④ The object of what we commonly call education — that education in which man intervenes and which I shall distinguish as artificial education — is to make good these defects in Nature's methods; to prepare the child to receive Nature's education, neither incapably nor ignorantly, nor with willful disobedience; and to understand the preliminary symptoms of her displeasure, without waiting for the box on the ear. In short, all artificial education ought to be an anticipation of natural education. And a liberal education is an artificial education which has not only prepared a man to escape the great evils of disobedience to natural laws, but has trained him to appreciate and to seize upon the rewards, which Nature scatters with as free a hand as her penalties.

④ 我们通常所说的教育——即介入了人为因素的那种教育，我把它称作认为教育加以区别——旨在弥补自然教育者教育方法中的不足之处；旨在帮助孩子们做好接受自然教育的准备，免得他们对自然教育一筹莫展或懵然无知，更不至于有意违抗；它还旨在使我们领悟到自然教育者不悦的先兆，而不至于等着吃耳光。总之，一切认为教育都应该是自然教育的准备。而开明教育就是这样一种认为教育，它不仅使人类避免犯下违背自然法则的弥天大罪，而且还培养他们识别并抓住自然赐予他们奖赏的能力。自然在赐予奖赏和施以惩罚时是同样慷慨大度的。

⑤ That man, I think, has had a liberal education who has been so trained in youth that his body is the ready servant of his will, and does with ease and pleasure all the work that, as a mechanism, it is capable of; whose mind is stored with a knowledge of the great and fundamental truths of Nature and of the laws of her operations; one who, no stunted ascetic, is full of life and fire, but whose passions are trained to come to heel by a vigorous will, the servant of a tender conscience.

⑤ 我以为，一个受过开明教育的人从小就应该受到这样的训练，他的躯体已成为他意志的忠实奴仆，它能轻松愉悦地从事一切他的生理机能所能承受的工作；他的头脑里贮存着最伟大最根本的真理：那就是自然和它的运动法则；他不是一个发育不全的禁欲主义者，而是充满了活力和热情的，但他的情感已经学会由强有力的意志来制约，完全服从于敏感的良心。

⑥ Such a one and no other, I conceive, has had a liberal education; for he is, as completely as a man can be, in harmony with Nature. He will make the best of her, and she of him. They will get on together rarely; she as his ever beneficent mother; he as her mouthpiece, her conscious self, her minister and interpreter.

⑥ 我认为，唯有这样的人才是受过开明教育的；因为作为一个人，他已经彻底地和自然水乳交融。他能充分地利用自然，自然也能同样地利用他。他们的相处将达到尽善尽美的境界——自然是使他们受益不尽的母亲；而他则是自然有意识的化身，是它的代言者、执行者和诠释者。（杨自伍译）

6.6 推荐读物

(1)单其昌，汉英翻译技巧，外语教学与研究出版社 1990 年版。

(2)许建平，英汉互译实践与技巧，清华大学出版社 2000 年版。

(3)Nida, E. A., The Theory and Practice of Translation，上海外语教育出版社 2004，，

年版。

(4) Gentzler, E., Contemporary Translation Theories,上海外语教育出版社2004年版。

7 课后练习

7.1 分析题

(1)试用所译和比读材料进行全译批评。

(2)试析大学课程名称的翻译特点。

(3)试析大学专业名称的翻译特点。

7.2 实训题

7.2.1 我们培育讲求实效的梦想家

① 七十多年来,香港理工大学及其前身培育了约三十万名毕业生。他们在不同行业大展所长,当中不乏业界领袖,为香港、中国内地及全世界的社会和经济发展作出重要贡献。

② 我们称理大学生为"讲求实效的梦想家"——他们善于质疑辨析、有良好的沟通能力、懂得创意解难,而且在各领域扮演重伦理的领袖角色。他们积极贡献世界、勇于挑战现实、创造美好未来。

7.2.2 U. S. -China Friendship Volunteers Program

① The U. S. -China Friendship Volunteers program is an inter-governmental cooperative program between China and the U. S. The two sides reached an agreement in principle in 1988 on the sending of Peace Corps volunteers by the U. S. to teach in China. On June 29th, 1998, the Chinese Ministry of Education (MOE) and its U. S. counterpart signed in Beijing the Agreement Between the Government of the Unite States of America and the Government of the People's Republic of China Concerning the United States Volunteer Program in China.

② The program is coordinated by the Chinese Ministry of Foreign Affairs, administered by the MOE, and implemented by the China Educational Association for International Exchange (CEAIE). According to the Agreement, U. S. volunteers mainly teach Basic English and courses related to environmental protection in the host colleges in four Western provinces (or Municipality) of Sichuan, Chongqing (Municipality), Guizhou and Gansu.

7.3 思考题

(1)请从产权归属角度讨论"民办大学"的英译?

(2)如何翻译具有中国特色的学校奖惩制度?

(3)如何避免翻译国外教育体制时的文化信息误译?

(4)中国各种高校名称英译中的文化问题。

(5)文本用途与翻译策略之间有何互动关系?
(6)翻译教学与教学翻译之间有何区别与联系?
(7)中英文校训翻译的异同点何在?
(8)如何运用“同义反译”增强表达色彩?
(9)试论英汉互译中标点符号的转换问题。
(10)翻译述要在译者培养中的运用。
(11)翻译理论学习的语境化研究。
(12)试论翻译能力评价的维度。
(13)双语平行语料库对翻译教学有何作用?

第19课 文学

导 译

文学常指包含情感、虚构和想象等综合因素的语言艺术行为和作品，如诗歌、小说、戏剧、散文等。文学的想象性、审美性、创造性、抒情性是它与非文学(科学和日常语言)的显著区别，不同体裁表现程度也不尽相同，小说对音韵、格律等语言形式的关注就不如诗歌和散文，后两者对语言描写的内容(人物、情节、环境等)的重视远不如小说。

从内容上讲，文学翻译是对文学作品的语言形式、艺术手法、情节内容、形象意境等的再现；从语言特征上讲，文学翻译作品的语言也应具有想象性、审美性、创造性、抒情性，或如高山流水，或如小溪潺潺，或如松涛阵阵，或如杨柳拂风；或深沉，或明快，或简洁，或含蓄，或讽刺，或幽默。每篇都可谓字字珠玑，句句夺目，就如一个大观园，徜徉其中，让你目不暇接，让你流连忘返。文学翻译与文学创作一样，也是语言的艺术，要求译文忠实于原作，且具同样的艺术感染力。文学翻译是带着镣铐跳舞，是一种特殊的艺术活动，一种再创造。其创造过程力求谐其韵、达其义、构其形、传其情、显其象、化其境。

1 课前练笔

1.1 军嫂

那天，霞姐给学生教王维的《九月九日忆山东兄弟》，当她念到"独在异乡为异客，每逢佳节倍思亲"时泪水悄悄地滑落了，这时窗外邮递员扬起了手中的信，霞姐接过信，心却在怦怦地跳。一下课，霞姐跑回宿舍，关上了门。霞姐出来时脸若桃花，学生就说老师好漂亮。

一放学，霞姐直奔我家，她公布了一个爆炸性的消息，哥准备春节回家过年。我们全家沉浸在喜悦中……随着春节的临近，霞姐每天在我家都是幸福地忙着，忙着准备年货，忙着洗被子和衣服……但随着春节的临近，还是没见哥回来。大年三十，飘起了雪。霞姐站在村口直到深夜，她成了一个雪人。

1.2 浮生六记

是夜送亲城外，返已漏三下，腹饥索饵，婢妪以枣脯进，余嫌其甜。芸暗牵余袖，随至其室，见藏有暖粥并小菜焉。余欣然举箸，忽闻芸堂兄玉衡呼曰："淑妹速来！"芸急闭门曰："已疲乏，将卧矣。"玉衡挤身而入，见余将吃粥，乃笑睨芸曰："顷我索粥，汝曰，'尽矣'，乃藏此专待汝婿耶？"芸大窘，避去，上下哗笑之。余亦负气，挈老仆先归。自吃粥被嘲，再往，芸即避匿，余知其恐贻人笑也。

1.3 Duty

— By Ellen S. Hooper

I slept and dreamed that life was Beauty.
I woke and found that life was Duty.
Was then thy dream a shadowy lie?
Toil on, sad heart, courageously.
And thou shalt find thy dream to be
A noonday light and truth to thee.

1.4 Glories of the Storm

It begins when a feeling of stillness creeps into my consciousness. Everything has suddenly gone quiet. Birds do not chirp. Leaves do not rustle. Insects do not sing.

The air that has been hot all day becomes heavy. It hangs over the trees, presses the heads of the flowers to the ground, sits on my shoulders. With a vague feeling of uneasiness I move to the window. There, in the west, lies the answer — cloud has piled on cloud to form a ridge of mammoth white towers, rearing against blue sky.

Their piercing whiteness is of brief duration. Soon the marshmallow rims flatten to anvil tops, and the clouds reveal their darker nature. They impose themselves before the late-afternoon sun, and the day darkens early. Then a gust of wind whips the dust along the road, chill warning of what is to come.

2 课前批评

2.1 桃花源记

晋太元中，武陵人捕鱼为业。

At the Source of Peach Blossom Creek

In the reign of Taiyuan of the Jin Dynasty, there

缘溪行,忘路之远近。忽逢桃花林。夹岸数百步,中无杂树,芳草鲜美,落英缤纷。渔人甚异之。复前行,欲穷其林。

林尽水源,便得一山。山有小口,仿佛若有光;便舍船,从口入。初极狭,才通人。复行数十步,豁然开朗。土地平旷,屋舍俨然,有良田、美池、桑竹之属。阡陌交通,鸡犬相闻。其中往来种作,男女衣著,悉如外人。黄发垂髫,并怡然自乐。(陶渊明)

was a man of Wuling who was a fisherman by trade. One day he was fishing up a stream in his boat, heedless of how far he had gone, when suddenly he came upon a forest of peach trees. On either bank for several hundred yards there were no other kinds of tree. The fragrant grass was beautiful to look at, all patterned with fallen blossoms. The fisherman was extremely surprised and went on further, determined to get to the end of this wood. At the end of the wood he found the source of the stream and, at the foot of a cliff, there was a small cave in which there seemed to be a faint light. He left his boat and went into the mouth of the cave. At first it was very narrow, only wide enough for a man, but after forty or fifty yards he suddenly found himself in the open. The place he had come to was level and spacious. There were houses and cottages arranged in a planned order; there were fine fields and beautiful pools; there were mulberry trees, bamboo groves, and many other kinds of trees as well. There were raised pathways round the fields; and he heard the fowls crowing and dogs barking. Going to and fro in all this, and busied in working and planting, were people, both men and women. Their dress was not unlike that of people outside, and all of them, whether old people with white hair or children with their hair tied in a knot, were happy and content with themselves. (林戴 译)

2.2 The First Snow

The first snow came. How beautiful it was, falling so silently all day long, all night long, on the mountains, on the meadows, on the roofs of the living, on the graves of the dead! All white save the river, that marked its course by a winding black line across the landscape; and the leafless trees, that against the leaden sky now revealed more fully the wonderful beauty and intricacies of their branches. What silence, too, came with the snow, and what seclusion! Every sound was muffled; every noise changed to something soft and

初雪

初雪飘零。多么美啊!它整日整夜那么静静地飘着,落在山岭上,落在草地上,落在世人的屋顶上,落在死者的坟墓上!在一片白茫茫之中,只有河流在美丽的画面上划出一道曲曲弯弯的黑线;还有那叶儿落净的树木,映衬着铅灰色的天空,此刻更显得枝丫交错,姿态万千。初雪飘落时,何等的幽静!一切声

musical. No more tramping hoofs, no more rattling wheels! Only the chiming of sleigh-bells, beating as swift and merrily as the hearts of children. (Henry Longfellow)

响都趋沉寂,一切噪音都化作柔和的音乐。再也听不见马蹄哒哒,再也听不见车轮辚辚!唯有雪橇的铃铛,奏出和谐的乐声,那明快欢乐的节拍犹如孩子们心房的搏动。(范钜清 译)

知识 3 全译知识 文学译味

文学是以语言文字为工具形象地反映客观现实的艺术,通常分为诗歌、散文、小说、戏剧等四种体裁。其特点是用词最丰富,手段最繁复,情感最充沛,风格最多样。总之是重情不重理,或寓理于情。所以,文学翻译除了传达内容之外,尤其讲究形式美的传达,以求最终传达原作的风格或意味,其中以诗歌翻译为最。要译出文学的味道,选择同义表达手段时,就要力求准确、鲜明、生动和流畅。

3.1 准确

所谓准确,即能恰如其分地用语言描写人事风物的状态,表达作者的思想感情。翻译讲究炼字,要把用字炼到异乎寻常的地步,使其产生不平常的效果,产生奇妙的艺术魅力。如:

① Almost all men have been taught to call life a passage and themselves the travellers.

【原译】:几乎无人不晓浮生如过路,人呢,不过是个过客。

【试译】:几乎人人受过这样的教诲:浮生如路人似客。

原译将 have been taught 译作"晓",过于中性,"晓"可能是主动获知,也可能是被动告知,而原文具有告诫意味,所以试译"受过……教诲"比较恰当;加之"这样的"指代,更明确了前后的逻辑关系。life 本为"生命"或"一生",入句产生语境意义,尤其是因 passage 而添"短暂虚幻"之意,对人生有了消极的看法,译作"浮生"极其准确。人人受诲的话语最易成为格言,所以应考虑格言化;其中 call 即 regard as,具有暗喻功能,译作"若"、"如"、"似",虽转暗喻为明喻,却更便于揭示原作内涵;因"浮生如路"四字格的作用,themselves the travellers 也压缩成了"人似客",最终构成了七言,可进入汉语格言。

3.2 鲜明

所谓鲜明,即语言能明朗而突出地表现人事风物的个性特征和本质特点。文学创作忌熟,熟即俗,优秀的作品叫以其独特的个性与众不同,先给人以陌生感,再产生难忘的印象。如:

② How amused every one would be if they know what really happened. 如果大家知道事情真相,准得把人笑死。

amuse 前加上 How 构成感叹句,语气极度增强,How 仅译作"多么",不够味道,也不够准确,译作"把人笑死",恰如其分。

3.3 生动

所谓生动，即译语的运用要新鲜活泼，绘声绘色，活灵活现地表现人物形象和生活图景，让读者如临其境，如见其人，如闻其声，译文传达思想而不失生命气息。如：

③ Some fishing boats were becalmed just in front of us. Their shadows slept, or almost slept, upon that water, a gentle quivering alone showing that it was not complete sleep, or if sleep, that it was sleep with dreams. 渔舟三五，横泊眼前，樯影倒映水面，仿佛睡去，偶尔微颤，似又未尝深眠，恍若惊梦。

译文深受古文影响，干净明快，生动有韵。“渔舟三五，横泊眼前”仿佛拈起原文的意象，完全按汉语的意境构筑语篇；“slept, or almost slept”译作“仿佛睡去”，“倒映水面”又将 upon that water 译得动了起来；“it was not complete sleep, or if sleep”凝练为“似又未尝深眠”，译 that it was sleep with dreams 为“恍若惊梦”，解释“未深眠”的原因。

3.4 流畅

受外语的影响，译文流畅成了问题。所谓流畅，即文字要求不生造词语，语从己出；运笔自如，行云流水。运笔之妙，存乎于心，要多译多改。译文不仅要落得了笔，还要念得上口。如：

④ The church was surrounded by yew trees which seemed almost coeval with itself. 教堂四周有紫杉环抱，几乎一样古老。

⑤ He read until his guests arrived.

【原译】：他阅读直到他的客人到了。

【试译】：客人到了，他才放下阅读。

例④避用了被动句，用汉语“有”字句表明了事物的存在，汉译后一句省去了主语，承前省略紫杉和教堂，如行云流水；例⑤，原译受 until 的词典注释“直到……才”影响的影响而欧化，试译不拘于形式，按事件发生的时间顺序或者行为的因果关系布局，符合事理，也便符合汉语语法，更具可读性。

4 全译窍门

4.1 谐其韵

文学翻译首先要善于感知语言的音韵美（语音的和谐美），即原文通过精心运用元音、辅音、音节以及词语与句子结构的重复等手段，使文字具有一定的韵律、节奏等音韵效果。最为典型的范例是对诗词歌赋的翻译。英语音韵之美主要归功于头韵、腹韵、尾韵和拟声词的运用，而双声叠韵是汉语旨在强化音韵美的构词方式。音韵美，在很多情况下宛如魔术师，能为整句、甚至整段文字添上美的光泽。因而，翻译时应当力求“谐其韵”。谐，即仿，充分发挥译语特点，再现原作的音韵效果。如：

① Change is part of life and the making of character, hon. When things happen that you do not like, you have two choices: You get bitter or better. 变化是生活的一部分,也塑造了人的意志品德,亲爱的,当你不喜欢的事情发生了,你有两种选择:要么痛苦不堪、要么痛快达观。

读罢本例谁都会拍案叫绝,抑或过目不忘! bitter/better 是关键因素,二者构成头韵和尾韵,视听觉相拥,音形美携手。作为英语强项的头韵却是汉语的弱项,译者驭字能力不俗,巧译为"痛苦不堪/痛快达观",可谓神来之笔,尽显原文音韵效果。

② 寻寻觅觅,冷冷清清,凄凄惨惨戚戚。

【译文Ⅰ】:I look for what I miss;/ I know not what it is./ I feel so sad, so dreary, / so lonely, without cheer.

【译文Ⅱ】:So dim, so dark,/So dense, so dull,/So damp, so dank, so dead!

原词七对叠声词简约而生动地刻画了词人愁寂孤苦的心理,创造出奇妙的音韵效果。相比之下,译文Ⅰ明显不足,破坏了原文叠词之美。译文Ⅱ胜出一筹,连用了七个 so 和七个以 d 字母开头的形容词,一气呵成,词趣洋溢,音韵迭出。

4.2 达其义

达其义,即要忠实通顺地再现原文的意义,美文要显其美,俏句要显其俏,丽词要显其丽。学好翻译,能翻善译,必须持严谨的科学态度,一个介词,一个短语,一个句子都马虎不得。要达其义,就要斟酌再三、反复揣摩,找出精当、贴切、符合语境的表达法。如:

③ On the wings of hope, of love, of joy, Miss Meadows sped back to the music hall, up the aisle, up the steps, over to the piano. 美多斯小姐仿佛插上了希望的翅膀,爱情的翅膀,欢乐的翅膀,一路飞奔回到音乐厅,她穿过通道,跃上台阶,三步并作两步走到钢琴前。

英语介词发达,汉语稍逊,英译汉时常用词类转换法将英语介词译成汉语动词。本例 up 如何措词,颇费斟酌。据 up 与 the steps 的搭配,译者从 up 的多个义项中选用"跃上",可谓达义,能体现所描述的欢快气氛,感情色彩方面最切合上下文。

④ 北国的槐树,也是一种能使人联想起秋来的点缀。

【译文Ⅰ】:The scholar-trees in North China are also an attraction that calls to mind the advent of autumn.

【译文Ⅱ】:Locust trees in the North, as a decorative embellishment of nature, also associate us with autumn.

例中"联想起秋来"非等闲之笔,是点题之句。译文Ⅱ中 also associate us with autumn 译笔轻飘,未能触及原句的深层。译文Ⅰ用了源自古法语的名词 advent,相较小词 coming 或 arrival,此大词含义更加厚重,寓意更趋多元,译句因之生辉,更加准确,充分传递了原文之言简意赅。

4.3 构其形

构其形,即再现形象,是文学翻译的核心。文学翻译力求入乎其中、出乎其外,在感知原作形象美的基础上,充分发挥译语优势,用艺术性语言构建原作形象。如:

⑤ One day she was pink and flawless; another pale and tragical. When she was pink she was felling less than when pale; her more perfect beauty accorded with her less elevated mood; her more intense mood with her less perfect beauty. 今天光艳照人,白玉无瑕;明天却又沮丧苍白,满面苍凉。鲜艳往往出自于无忧;而苍白,却总是由于多愁。胸中没了思虑她便美丽无瑕,一旦烦愁涌起,便又容色憔悴。

原文多处省略主、谓语,叙述节奏轻盈流畅,如诗般赞美苔丝的纯洁美丽。汉译保留省略,简洁明快,精准措辞,活灵活现地重构了苔丝的肖像美,形象美在原文之上。

⑥ 二人正说着,只见湘云走来,笑道:"爱哥哥,林姐姐,你们天天一处玩,我好容易来了,也不理我一理儿。"黛玉笑道:"偏是咬舌子爱说话,连个二哥哥也叫不来,只是'爱'哥哥的。回来赶围棋儿,又该你闹'幺爱三四五'了。"Just then Xiang-yun burst in on them and reproved them smilingly for abandoning her: "Couthin Bao, Couthin Lin: you can thee each other every day, It'th not often I get a chanthe to come here; yet now I have come, you both ignore me!" Dai-yu burst out laughing: "Lisper doesn't seem to make you any less talkative! Listen to you: 'Couthin!' 'Couthin!' Presently, when you're playing Racing Go, you'll be all 'thicktheth' and 'theventh'!"

原文湘云说话咬舌,"二""爱"不分。黛玉口不饶人,打趣湘云。英国翻译家霍克斯巧译"爱哥哥"为"宝表哥","幺爱三四五"为"六七"。生动形象地重构了人物特点,人物形象呼之欲出。

4.4 传其情

文学是含情的文字,文学作品是"情书",没有七情六欲,就没有文学。可见,情感是文学最重要的标志。文学翻译最根本的任务就是传其情,或情感移植。如:

⑦ I'm p-paralyzed with happiness. 我高兴得瘫……瘫掉了。

⑧ 我的孩子们!我憧憬于你们的生活,每天不止一次。My dear children! How often I am enchanted with visualizing your future life, more than one time a day!

例⑦,p-paralyzed 是黛西初遇尼克时的结巴语,译文叠用"瘫"字,照之结巴,再塑了黛西激动、喜悦之情。例⑧,译者按字面直译,保留了原句尾的强调,符合句尾重心原则,传递了作者对未来的欣喜、急切和期盼之情。

⑨ 正盼望着,只见一个老嬷嬷出来。宝玉如得了珍宝,便赶上来拉他说道:"快进去告诉:老爷要打我呢!快去,快去!要紧,要紧!"宝玉一则急了,说话不明白,二则老婆子偏生又聋,竟不曾听见是什么话,把"要紧"二字,只听作"跳井"二字,便笑道:"跳井叫他跳去,二爷怕什么?"Then suddenly, in answer to his prayers, an old woman appeared — a darling, precious treasure of an old woman (or so she seemed at that moment) — and he dashed forward and clung to her beseechingly. "Quickly!" he said. "Go and tell them that Sir Zheng is going to beat me. Quickly! Quickly! Go and tell. GO AND TELL." Partly because agitation had made him incoherent and partly because, as ill luck would have it, the old woman was deaf, almost everything he said had escaped her except for the "Go and tell", which she misheard as "in the well". She smiled at him reassuringly. "Let her jump in the well then, young master. Don't you worry your pretty head about it!"

原文是宝玉挨打的一个插曲。据情节,恰逢金钏儿跳井而死,曹雪芹巧用飞白,让老婆子误听"要紧"为"跳井",将宝玉急于向贾母求援的焦急心情烘托了出来;霍克斯用 go and tell 与 in the well 读音上近似来曲传原文之妙。

4.5 显其象

文学意象是文学作品中被作家心灵化了的物象，是主观情趣与客观物象有机结合的艺术审美形态，是具体化了的感觉。在文学翻译中，译者必须对原文意象凝神观照，把“我”的性情外射到原作意象之中，体会并玩味原作中的意象之美，使主客交融，然后用贴切的译语显其象，重显与原作相同的意象，达到文辞相应，再现原作之美。以本课 1.4 Glories of the Storm 为例，原文形象逼真地描述了暴风雨来临前自然事物的情、形、状的变化，拟人手法创造了三个意象：空气的欺压之势（它笼罩树木，逼迫花卉垂向地面，并坐压在我的双肩）；云层阴暗的本色（它们强行遮住西斜的红日，使天色早早地黑了下来）；劲风的狂躁暴虐（抽打着道路，激起尘土飞扬）。译者欣赏意象，领会意象，运用自己的经验，充分发挥想象力，在译文中显其象，补白了原文含义模糊的地方，将其审美感受自然传入译文。又如：

⑩ 春蚕到死丝方尽，蜡炬成灰泪始干。The silkworm till its death spins silk from love-sick heart; /The candle burned to ashes has no tears to shed.

原文极具意象之美，“春蚕的丝、蜡烛的泪”能引发人们无限的联想，产生象外之象。每个读者都会生成属于自己的意象。翻译家许渊冲领悟了原文意象之美，将“丝”译成 silk，把“思”译成 love-sick，而 sick 与 silk 音似形近，音美兼形美，重显了原作意象之美。

4.6 化其境

意境与意象密切相关，意象重在意与象融合，意境重在意、象与境的融合。意境将意象与“境”相融，植入更具艺术弥漫性的时空，其基本特点是情景交融，虚实相生，具有较强的审美冲击力，使读者如临其境，感同身受。意境出于又高于意象，可意会不可言传。为了更好地传达原文意境，译者务必提高自身的审美能力和文学再创造能力，把握两种语言的语言差异和文化差异，巧妙运用模糊语言来传递意境，体现出意境的核心内容——模糊美，即含蓄美、朦胧美，如：

⑪ Some fishing boats were becalmed just in front of us. Their shadows slept, or almost slept, upon that water, a gentle quivering alone showing that it was not complete sleep, or if sleep, that it was sleep with dreams.

【译文Ⅰ】：在我们面前停泊了几条渔船，它们的影子在水面上睡着了，或者说是几乎睡着了，一个轻微的颤动，说明影子没有完全睡着，假如说是睡着了，那么，也是一边在睡，一边在做梦。

【译文Ⅱ】：渔舟三五，横泊眼前，樯影倒映水面，仿佛睡去，偶尔微颤，似又未尝深眠，恍若惊梦。

英语原文叙事条理清晰，写景逻辑分明。译文Ⅰ忠实有余，意境全无，译笔苍白、枯涩、乏味。译文Ⅱ则跳出原文的束缚，得其意，化其境，充分发挥汉语诗意语言优势，立足于对原文意境的渲染与再创造，译笔文采斐然，意境迭出。

⑫ 余冬日往视，但见衰柳寒烟，一水茫茫而已。I went there, however, on a winter day and saw only a stretch of cold water against some sparse willow trees and a frosty sky.

原句有“意”（衰、寒、茫茫），有“境”（冬日、柳、烟、水），情景交融，深邃幽远，让人充满联想和感触。林语堂之译切合原文，也传情景，但由于英语没有汉语那么多产生朦胧美的词，无法完全再现和传递原文特有的意境。

5 话题词汇

5.1 文学原理

Aestheticism 唯美主义
Affective Fallacy 情感谬误
Archetypal Criticism 原型批评
Atmosphere;Mood;Ambience 作品基调
Augustan Age 奥古斯都文学盛世
Beat Writers 垮掉派作家
Decadence 颓废主义
Deconstruction 解构主义
didactic literature 教诲文学
dissociation of sensibility 思想与感受的分裂
Enlightenment 启蒙运动
Expressionism 表现主义
flat character 干瘪的人物形象
hermeneutic 释义学
imagism 意象主义
imitation 模仿
impressionistic criticism 印象主义文学批评
intentional fallacy 意图谬误
involvement 感情介入
judicial criticism 分析批评
literature of sensibility 主情文学
literature of the absurd 荒诞派文学
mimetic criticism 模仿式文学批评
modernism 现代主义
Narratology 叙事学
naturalism 自然主义
neoclassic 新古典主义
phenomenology 现象学
Platonic Love 柏拉图式爱恋
postmodernism 后现代主义
practical criticism 实用文学批评
pragmatic criticism 实用主义文学批评
prosody; metrics 韵律学
reader-response criticism 读者反映批评
Reception Theory 接受理论
rhetorical criticism 修辞学批评
round character 丰满的人物形象
sentimentalism 感伤主义
sociology of literature 文学社会学
stock response 定型反应
stream of consciousness 意识流
Structuralist Criticism 结构主义批评
Surrealism 超现实主义
Symbolist Movement 象征主义运动
the anxiety of influence 怕受影响的阅读心理
theoretical criticism 理论化文学批评
textual criticism 文本批评

5.2 创作方法

报告文学 reportage
悲喜剧 tragicomedy
长篇小说 saga (river) novel
视觉韵 eye-rhyme
田园诗;田园散文 idyll
图形诗 pattern poem
五行打油诗 limerick
戏剧大纲 scenario
小小说 short short story
选集 anthology
演出用具 properties
轶事 anecdote
应景诗 occasional poems
游记 book of travels

韵文 verse
中篇小说 long short story
主题 theme
alliteration 头韵
allusion 典故
allegory 寓言
anadiplosis 顶真
anagram 析字
analogy 类比
anastrophe 倒装
antagonist 对立角色
anticlimax 突降法
antithesis 对比;对偶
antonomasia 借代
archaism 仿古
argot 黑话
aside 旁白
assonance 元韵(谐音)
aureate style; euphuism 绚丽体
bathos 递降;突降
bombast 浮夸之辞
bowdlerize 作品删节
burlesque 滑稽讽刺作品
cacophony;dissonance 非谐音
carpe diem 及时行乐
Chivalric Romance;Medieval Romance 骑士传奇;中世纪传奇
chronicle 编年史
chronicle plays 编年历史剧
classical allusion 典故
climax 递升
colloquialism 惯用语
comedy of humours 性格喜剧
comedy of manners 风俗喜剧
comic relief 戏剧性缓解
commedia dell'arte 即兴喜剧
concrete poetry 具象诗
confessional poetry 自白诗
consonance 辅韵
courtly love 骑士恋
covert narrator 隐性叙述者
curt style 简洁文体
dirge 挽歌
dramatic monologue 戏剧独白诗
dramatized narrator 戏剧化叙述者
dumb show 默剧
elegy 哀歌
ellipsis 省略
empathy 移情
epigram 警句诗;铭辞
epiphany 顿悟
epithalamion 喜歌
epopee 叙事诗
equivoque 文字游戏
euphemism 讳饰(委婉语)
euphony 谐音
euphuism 尤弗伊斯体;夸饰文体
exposition 交代(情节)
fabliau 寓言诗
farce 闹剧;滑稽剧
folklore 民间传说
gothic novel 哥特小说
grand style 庄重文体
graveyard poets 墓畔诗人
heroic couplet 英雄双韵体
heroic drama 英雄剧
imagery 意象
high comedy 风雅喜剧
high style 高雅文体
hyperbole 夸张
iambic pentameter 五步抑扬格
incantation 咒语
interlude 插剧
intrigue 错综情节
jargon 行话
light verse 轻松诗;谐趣诗
masque 假面歌舞剧
melodrama 情节剧
metaphor 暗喻(隐喻)
metonymy 转喻
mind style 心理风格
miracle plays 奇迹剧
misinterpretation 别解
morality plays 道德剧
motif 题旨
mystery story 怪诞小说

omniscient narrator 全知叙述者
omniscient point of view 全知视点
onomatopoeia 拟声
overt narrator 显性叙述者
oxymoron 精警(矛盾修辞法)
palindrome (chiasmus)回文
pantomime 哑剧
parallelism 排比
parody 仿拟;滑稽模仿
pastoral elegy 牧人哀歌
pastoral 牧歌
periodic sentence 尾重句;圆周句
periphrasis 折绕
persona 第一人称
plain style 朴素体
poetic diction 诗意辞藻
poetic license 诗的破格
problem play 问题剧
prolepsis 预期叙述
prose poem 散文诗
protagonist 主人公
psycho-narration 心理叙述
purple patch 华丽辞藻
quaesitio 连问
refrain 叠句
reiterative 叠字
rhetorical question 修辞疑问句
roman a clef 影射小说
romantic comedy 爱情喜剧
rules of rhyming 韵律
satiric comedy 讽刺喜剧
simile 明喻
soliloquy 独白
style of language varieties 语体风格
stock characters 定型人物
stock situations 定型情景
synaesthesia 联觉;通感
tautology 同义反复
Three Unities 三一律
transferred epithet 移就
translation of figures of speech 辞格翻译
two-part allegorical saying 歇后语
varieties in language 语言变体
vulgarities 粗俗语
whodunit 推理小说
zeugma 拈连

5.3 名家名篇

《阿Q正传》The True Story of Ah Q
《楚辞》The Songs of Chu
《春秋》The Spring and Autumn Annals
《大学》The Great Learning
《道德经》Tao Te Ching
《窦娥冤》The Injustice to Dou E
《封神演义》Canonization of the Gods
《官场现形记》Exposure of the Official World
《鬼谷子》Kuei Ku-tzu
《韩非子》Hanfeizi
《汉书》History of the Han Dynasty
《红楼梦》The Story of the Stone
《后汉书》Book of the Later Han
《淮南子》Huainanzi
《金瓶梅》The Golden Lotus
《警世通言》Stories to Warn Men
《老子》Lao Tzu
《礼记》The Book of Rites
《聊斋志异》Strange Stories from a Lonely Studio
《吕氏春秋》Lv Spring and Autumn
《论语》The Analects of Confucius
《骆驼祥子》The Rickshaw Boy
《孟子》Mencius
《墨子》Mo Tzu
《荀子》Hsun Tzu
《牡丹亭》The Peony Pavilion
《儒林外史 》The Scholars
《三国演义》 Three Kingdoms
《三国志》Records of Three Kingdoms
《三言二拍》San Yan Er Pai
《山海经》 The Classic of Mountains and Rivers
《尚书》The Book of History
《诗经》The Odes/ The Book of Songs
《史记》Records of the Historian
《世说新语》A New Account of the Tales of the World

《世说新语》New Anecdotes of Social Talk
《水浒传》Water Margin
《隋唐演义》Romance of the Sui-Tang Empires
《孙子兵法》The Art of War
《唐诗三百首》Three Hundred Tang Poems
《围城》Fortress Besieged
《文心雕龙》Dragon Carving and the Literary Mind
《西厢记》The Western Chamber
《西游记》The Journey to the West
《醒世恒言》Stories to Awaken Men
《徐霞客游记》Xu Xiake's Travels
《喻世明言》Stories to Enlightenment
《战国策》War Policy
《中庸》The Doctrine of the Mean
《周易》/《易经》The Book of Changes
《庄子》Chuang Tse
《资治通鉴》History as a Mirror
《子夜》Midnight
An American Tragedy《美国悲剧》/Theodore Dreiser 西奥多·德莱塞
Beloved《深爱》/ Song of Solomon《所罗门之歌》/ Toni Morrison 托妮·莫里森
Brave New World《勇敢新世界》/Aldous Huxley 奥尔德斯·赫胥黎
Camille《茶花女》/Alexandre Dumas fils 小仲马
Catch-22《第 22 条军规》/Joseph Heller 约瑟夫·海勒
Das Kapital《资本论》/Karl Marx 卡尔·马克思
Democracy in America《论美国的民主》/Alexis de Tocqueville 亚历西斯·托克维尔
Detstvo Gorkogo《童年》/V Lyudyakh《在人间》/ Maxim Gorky 马克西姆·高尔基
Faust《浮士德》/Johann Wolfgang von Goethe 约翰·沃尔夫冈·冯·歌德
For Whom the Bell Tolls《丧钟为谁而鸣》/ The Sun Also Rises《太阳照常升起》/ The Old Man And The Sea《老人与海》/ Ernest Hemingway 欧内斯特·海明威
Frankenstein《弗兰克斯坦》/Mary Wollstonecraft Shelley 玛丽·沃斯通克拉夫特·雪莱
Gone With The Wind《飘》/ Margaret Mitchell 玛格丽特·米切尔
Gulliver's Travels《格列夫游记》/Jonathan Swift 乔纳森·斯威夫特
Hamlet《哈姆雷特》/ King Lear《李尔王》/ Othello《奥赛罗》/Romeo and Juliet《罗密欧与朱丽叶》/William Shakespeare 威廉·莎士比亚
Heart of Darkness《黑暗之心》/ Lord Jim《吉姆老爷》/Joseph Conrad 约瑟夫·康拉德
How the Steel Was Tempered《钢铁是怎样炼成的》/ Nikolai Ostrovcky 尼古拉·奥斯特洛夫斯基
Iliad《伊利亚特》/Odyssey《奥德赛》/ Homer 荷马
Invisible Man《隐形人》/ Ralph Ellison 拉尔夫·埃里森
Ivanhoe《劫后英雄传》/ Sir Walter Scott 沃尔特·司各特
Le Rouge et Le Noir《红与黑》/ Stendhal 司汤达
Leaves of Grass《草叶集》/Walt Whitman 沃尔特·惠特曼
Les Miserables《悲惨世界》/ Victor Hugo 维克托·雨果
Lolita《洛丽塔》/ Vladimir Nabokov 弗拉迪米尔·纳博科夫
Madame Bovary《包法利夫人》/ Gustave Flaubert 居斯塔夫·福楼拜
Middlemarch《米德镇的春天》/George Eliot 乔治·艾略特
My University《我的大学》/ Maxim Gorky 马克西姆·高尔基
Oliver Twist《雾都孤儿》/ David Copperfield《大卫·科波菲尔》/Great Expectations《远大前程》/A Tale Of Two Cities《双城记》/ Charles Dickens 查尔斯·狄更斯
On the Origin of Species《物种起源》/ Charles Darwin 查尔斯·达尔文
One Hundred Years of Solitude《百年孤独》/ Gabriel Garcia Marquez 加布里尔·加西亚·马尔克斯
Paradise Lost《失乐园》/Milton 米尔顿
The Pilgrim's Progress《天路历程》/John Bunyan 约翰·班扬
The Arabian Nights《一千零一夜》
Pride and Prejudice《傲慢与偏见》/ Jane Austen 简·奥斯汀
Pygmalion《卖花女》/ Bernard Shaw 萧伯纳

Rebecca《蝴蝶梦》/Daphne Du Maurier 达夫妮·杜穆里埃
Remembrance of Things Past《追忆似水年华》/Marcel Proust 马赛尔·普鲁斯特
Slaughterhouse-Five《第五号屠场》/Kurt Vonnegut 库尔特·冯内古特
Sons and Lovers《儿子与情人》/D. H. Lawrence 大卫·赫伯特·劳伦斯
St. Augustine Confessions《奥古斯都忏悔录》/Saint Augustine 圣·奥古斯丁
The Adventures of Huckleberry Finn《哈克贝利费恩历险记》/ The Adventures of Tom Sawyer《汤姆历险记》/ Mark Twain 马克·吐温
The Canterbury Tales《坎特伯雷故事》/Geoffrey Chaucer 杰弗里·乔叟
The Catcher in the Rye《麦田里的守望者》/J. D. Salinger 杰罗姆·大卫·塞林格
The Day of the Locust《蝗虫之日》/Nathaniel West 纳撒尼尔·韦斯特
The Divine Comedy《神曲》/Dante Alighieri 阿利盖利·但丁
The Gadfly《牛虻》/Ethel Lilan Voynich 艾·丽·伏尼契
The Grapes of Wrath《愤怒的葡萄》/John Steinbeck 约翰·斯坦贝克
The Great Gatsby《了不起的盖茨比》/F. Scott Fitzgerald 弗·司各特·菲茨杰拉德
The Histories《历史》/Herodotus 希罗多德
The Adventures Of Robinson Crusoe《鲁滨孙漂流记》/Daniel Defoe 丹尼尔·笛福
The History of the Peloponnesian War《伯罗奔尼撒战争史》/Thucydides 修西得底斯
The Prince《君主论》/ Niccolo Machiavelli 尼古拉·马基雅维利
The Sound and the Fury《喧嚣与骚动》/ As I Lay Dying《我弥留之际》/ William Faulkner 威廉·福克纳
Things Fall Apart《分崩离析》/Chinua Achebe 钦努阿·阿契贝
To the Lighthouse《到灯塔去》/ Mrs. Dalloway《达罗维夫人》/ Virginia Woolf 弗吉尼亚·伍尔夫
Tom Jones《汤姆·琼斯》/Henry Fielding 亨利·菲尔丁
The Social Contract《社会契约论》/Jean-Jacques Rousseau 让-雅克·卢梭
Tropic of Cancer《北回归线》/ Henry Miller 亨利·米勒
Ulysses《尤利西斯》/James Joyce 詹姆斯·乔伊斯
War and Peace《战争与和平》/Anna Karenina《安娜·卡列尼娜》/Leo Tolstoy 列夫·托尔斯泰

5.4 缩略语

AAL 美国文学会
AAAL 美国艺术与文学学会
AG 作协
AN 天方夜谭
ASCAP 美国作曲家、作家与出版商协会
ARSL 英国皇家文学学会准会员
BI 黑冰
BOF 文件开始
CAA 加拿大作家协会
CALT 远程语言教学
CFLAC 中国文学艺术界联合会
cm 普通格律
D. A. B. 美国人名词典
EI 工程索引
euph 委婉语
fig 比喻用法
fml 正式用语;书面语
GQ《绅士季刊》
infml 通俗用语;口语
idm 习语
JR 流水账[日志]记录
joc 戏谑语
L. B. 文学士
MS 手稿，原稿
NBC 全国图书委员会
NEB 新英文圣经
NFAL 全国文学艺术基金会
NPF 全国诗作基金会
OPP 相对的;对立
P. B. 祈祷书
par (文章的)段
PSA 美国诗社

RSR 评审总结报告	WP 工作底稿
SA 作家协会	Xn 基督的
U. S. P.《美国药典》	XXX X 级片或内容

6 比读体悟

6.1 鸟的天堂

① 起初四周非常清静。后来忽然起了一声鸟叫。朋友陈把手一拍，我们便看见一只大鸟飞起来，接着又看见第二只，第三只。我们继续拍掌。很快地这个树林变得很热闹了。到处都是鸟声，到处都是鸟影。大的，小的，花的，黑的，有的站在枝上叫，有的飞起来，有的在扑翅膀。

② 我注意地看。我的眼睛真是应接不暇，看清楚这只，又看漏了那只，看见了那只，第三只又飞走了。一只画眉飞了出来，给我们的拍掌声一惊，又飞进树林，站在一根小枝上兴奋地唱着，它的歌声真好听。（巴金）

Birds' Paradise

① At first it was very quiet all around. And suddenly, a twittering of birds arose. Chen clapped his hands and we saw a huge bird taking wing and flying up, and then we saw a second and a third following suit. We kept clapping hands and soon the forest became noisy. You heard birds' chirpings everywhere; you saw birds' shadows everywhere. There were big ones, small ones, colored ones and black ones. Some perched on the branches, singing, some flying in the air, and some fluttering their wings.

② I watched them, but my eyes were not quick enough to follow them. When I saw this one, I lost sight of that one, and when I spotted that one, a third one flew off. And then a song thrush appeared, but the next moment it was startled back to the tree by our clappings. It alighted on a thin branch, singing songs that were pleasant to the ear.（刘士聪 译）

6.2 四喜忧国

朱四喜在完成了《告全国军民同胞书》的那天晚上用大牙撬开一瓶红标米酒，忽然间觉得精神抖擞起来。他的老婆仍像平日一样隔着甘蔗板向外间屋抛送鼾声，并且不时将竹床压得咿哑作响；他的小儿子来宝在窗下吹塑料口琴；来宝的三个哥哥来福、来财和来寿则围坐在饭桌的另外三边打瞌睡、念英文，以及赞美小耶稣。这些声音都扰不着朱四喜，他把斟冒了沿儿的酒汁从桌面上吸吮入腹，觉得世界真是饱满来劲儿。一切仿佛正要重新开始。"这就对了!"他顺手拂开面前散落的花生壳儿，捧起文告来，环视一圈他的四个儿子，点点头，又强调了一遍："这就对了。"（张大春）

Lucky Worries about His Country

On the evening he finished his "Proclamation to Soldiers, Civilian and Countrymen," Lucky Zhu opened his bottle of red-label rice wine with his teeth. He suddenly perked up. As usual, his wife was sending out snores from the bedroom behind the cane-fireboard partition, and from time to time the bamboo bed creaked under her weight. His youngest son, Treasure, was playing his plastic harmonica by the window. Treasure's three brothers, Bliss, Fortune, and Longevity, were sitting around the other three sides of the table, dozing, studying English, and praising Baby Jesus respectively. None of these noises disturbed Lucky Zhu. He slurped up the spilled wine from the table and felt that the world was wonderful indeed, as if everything was about to start anew. "Yes, that's good!" He whisked off the peanut shells scattered on the table, picked up his proclamation and held it in both hands, then took a look at his four sons around him. "Yes, that's good!" he repeated emphatically and nodded in approval.(朱志瑜 译)

6.3 五柳先生传

①先生不知何许人也,亦不详其姓字。宅边有五柳树,因以为号焉。闲静少言,不慕荣利。好读书,不求甚解;每有会意,便欣然忘食。性嗜酒,家贫不能常得,亲旧知其如此,或置酒而招之。造饮辄尽,期在必醉,既醉而退,曾不吝情去留。环堵萧然,不蔽风日。短褐穿结,箪瓢屡空,晏如也。常著文章自娱,颇示已志。忘怀得失,以此自终。

②赞曰:黔娄之妻有言:"不戚戚于贫贱,不汲汲于富贵。"极其言,兹若人之俦乎?衔觞赋诗,以乐其志。无怀氏之民欤?葛天氏之民欤?(陶渊明)

A Biography of Mr. Wu Liu

① It is unknown where this gentleman comes from and what his name is. As there are five willows by his cottage, he calls himself Wu Liu (five pronounced wu in Chinese, and willow liu-trans.). He is, by nature, a quiet and reticent man, uninterested in fame and fortune. He takes delight in reading, but he does not bother much about minor details as he reads; when he awakens to some understanding, he so rejoices that he forgets his meals. Though he is fond of drinking, he cannot afford to drink as often as he wishes owing to domestic circumstances. His relatives and friends, aware of his plight, will invite him over for a drink from time to time. He will go and drink as much as to get tipsy. Being tipsy, he frankly takes leave of his host, not caring what they think. His small cottage with its dilapidated walls can hardly provide shelter from weather. His short coat of coarse cloth is patched over and over, and he often finds himself without enough food to eat and, yet, he takes it philosophically. He takes to writing and he writes for pleasure and expression of his will. He wishes to live the rest of his life by putting out of his mind worldly worries about gains and losses.

② A supplementary remark: the ancient scholar Qian Lou's wife once said of her husband: "He is not worried about poverty and inferiority, nor desirous of fortune and rank." A careful interpretation of this remark shows that this Qian Lou was the likes of Wu Liu, wasn't he? As he drinks to please himself and writes to express his will, don't you think he is like someone from the good old days of the legendary Emperor Wu Huaishi? Or someone from the good old days of the legendary Emperor Ge Tianshi?(刘士聪、余东 译)

6.4 The Song of the Lark

Mrs. Kronborg believed that the size of every family was decided in heaven. More modem views would not have startled her; they would simply have seemed foolish — thin chatter, like the boasts of the men who built the tower of Babel, or like Axel's plan to breed ostriches in the chicken yard. From what evidence Mrs. Kronborg formed her opinions on this and other matters, it would have been difficult to say, but once formed, they were unchangeable. She would no more have questioned her

云雀之歌

克朗伯格太太相信每个家庭的人口多少是由上天决定的。一些更为时髦的观点或许不会令她感到吃惊,因为她会觉得那简直就是傻里傻气的胡说、毫无意义的瞎聊,就像建造通天塔的那些人的夸夸其谈,或者说像她儿子阿克塞尔想在鸡圈里养鸵鸟的打算。克朗伯格太太凭什么根据对这事

convictions than she would have questioned revelation. Calm and even tempered, naturally kind, she was capable of strong prejudices, and she never forgave. When Dr. Archie came in to see Thea, Mrs. Kronborg was reflecting that the washing was a week behind, and deciding what she had better do about it. The arrival of a new baby meant a revision of her entire domestic schedule, and as she drove her needle along she had been working out new sleeping arrangements and cleaning days. (Willa Cather)

或那事形成自己的看法,这恐怕很难说清,但她的看法一旦形成就不容改变。她从不会怀疑自己的信念,就像她从不会怀疑神的启示一样。她平和,冷静,天性仁慈,能容忍别人极深的成见,可她绝不会姑息养奸。当阿奇医生来看西娅时,克朗伯格太太正在想一周前就该洗的衣物都还没洗,正在决定她对此应该怎么办。一个婴儿的降生意味着她得全盘修订家务日程,她一边飞针走线,一边在盘算新的床位安排和打扫清洁的日子。(曹明伦 译)

6.5 The Author's Account of Himself

① I was always fond of visiting new scenes, and observing strange characters and manners. Even when a mere child I began my travels, and made many tours of discovery into foreign parts and unknown regions of my native city, to the frequent alarm of my parents, and the emolument of the town-crier. As I grew into boyhood, I extended the range of my observations. My holiday afternoons were spent in rambles about the surrounding country. I made myself familiar with all its places famous in history or fable. I knew every spot where a murder or robbery had been committed, or a ghost seen. I visited the neighboring villages, and added greatly to my stock of knowledge, by noting their habits and customs, and conversing with their sages and great men. I even journeyed one long summer's day to the summit of the most distant hill, whence I stretched my eye over many a mile of terra incognita, and was astonished to find how vast a globe I inhabited.

② This rambling propensity strengthened with my years. Books of voyages and travels became my passion, and in devouring their contents, I neglected the regular exercises of the school. How wistfully would I wander about the pier-heads in fine weather, and watch the parting ships, bound to distant climes — with what longing eyes would I gaze after their lessening sails, and waft myself in imagination to the ends of the earth!

③ Further reading and thinking, though they brought this vague inclination into more reasonable bounds, only served to make it more decided. I visited various parts of my own country; and had I been merely a lover of fine scenery, I should have felt

作者自述

① 我总喜爱游览新奇美景,观赏奇风异俗。幼年之时,便四处漫游,走过不少地方,深入故土的穷乡僻壤,作一番探索。为此,父母常感惊恐,不过公告传报员却受益不少。及至少年,观察范围更趋广泛。每逢假日下午,便畅游四周。由此,历史上或传说中的著名地方,无不知晓。哪里有过凶杀抢劫,哪里出现过幽灵,我均能一一告知。我去邻近的村庄,观察其风俗习惯,与贤明之士和不凡人物交谈,从而知识大增。在一个漫长的夏日,我甚至远走他乡,爬上一座高山,极目远眺,凝视尚未去过的陌生地带。目睹我所居住的地球广阔无垠,惊叹不已。

② 我年岁愈增,愈加喜欢漫游。种种游记书籍,令我爱不释手,读得废寝忘食,以致把学校日常功课忽略。我多么渴望在风和日丽之际,漫步码头,看只只船儿远去。我心驰神往,凝视它们愈来愈小的风帆,想象随之漂向天涯海角。

③ 此种爱好,当时不过朦朦胧胧;以后读书更多,思想更广,爱好亦更具有理性,更加明确。我到美国各地游览。但我并非仅喜爱美丽风光——果

little desire to seek elsewhere its gratification, for on no country have the charms of nature been more prodigally lavished. Her mighty lakes, like oceans of liquid silver; her mountains, with their bright aerial tints; her valleys, teeming with wild fertility; her tremendous cataracts, thundering in their solitudes; her boundless plains, waving with spontaneous verdure; her broad deep rivers, rolling in solemn silence to the ocean; her trackless forests, where vegetation puts forth all its magnificence; her skies, kindling with the magic of summer clouds and glorious sunshine; no, never need an American look beyond his own country for the sublime and beautiful of natural scenery. (Washington Irving)

真如此,便无须去国外旅游,因自然赐予美国的妩媚,并不少于其他国家。美国有辽阔的湖水,银波闪闪;有巍峨的群山,色彩鲜明;有富饶的山谷,植物茂密,鸟兽众多;有巨大的瀑布,在幽静的山中隆隆作响;有广袤的平原,草木青葱起伏,天然而成;有深广的河流,庄严肃穆地流向海洋;有人迹罕至的森林,宏伟壮观;有蓝蓝的天空,夏日彩云飞舞,阳光灿烂,魅力无穷。是的,美国人若欲观赏壮丽美景,本国已绰绰有余,无需他求了。(刘荣跃 译)

6.6 Hamlet(Act Ⅲ Excerpt)

To be, or not to be: that is the question:/ Whether'tis nobler in the mind to suffer/The slings and arrows of outrageous fortune,/Or to take arms against a sea of troubles,/And by opposing end them. To die, to sleep — /No more — and by a sleep to say we end/The heartache and the thousand natural shocks/That flesh is heir to! 'Tis a consummation/Devoutly to be wished. To die, to sleep —/To sleep — perchance to dream: ay, there's the rub,/For in that sleep of death what dreams may come,/When we have shuffled off this mortal coil,/Must give us pause. There's the respect/That makes calamity of so long life;/ For who would bear the whips and scorns of time,/The oppressor's wrong, the proud man's contumely,/The pangs of despised love, the law's delay,/The insolence of office, and the spurns/That patient merit of the unworthy takes,/When he himself might his quietus make/With a bare bodkin? Who would these fardels bear,/To grunt and sweat under a weary life,/But that the dread of something after death,/The undiscovered country, from whose bourn/No traveler returns — puzzles the will,/And makes us rather bear those ills we have/Than fly to others that we know not of? /Thus conscience does make cowards of us all,/And thus the native hue of resolution/Is sicklied o'er with the pale cast of thought,/And enterprises of great pitch and moment,/With this regard their currents turn awry/And lose the name of action. — Soft you now,/The fair Ophelia! — Nymph, in thy orisons/Be all my sins remembered. (William Shakespeare)

《哈姆雷特》第三幕选段

哈姆雷特:生存还是毁灭,这是一个值得考虑的问题;漠然忍受命运暴虐的毒剑,或是挺身反抗人世的无涯的苦难,通过斗争把它们扫清,这两种行为哪一种更高贵?死了;睡着了;什么都完了;要是在这一种睡眠之中,我们心头的创痛,以及其他无数血肉之躯所不能避免的打击,都可以从此消失,那正是我们求之不得的结局。死了;睡着了;睡着了也许还会做梦;嗯,阻碍就在这儿:因为当我们摆脱了这一具朽腐的皮囊以后,在那死的睡眠里,究竟将要做些什么梦,那不能不使我们踌躇顾虑。人们甘心久困于患难之中,也就是为了这个缘故;谁愿意忍受人世的鞭挞和讥嘲、压迫者的凌辱、傲慢者的冷眼、被轻蔑的爱情的惨痛、法律的迁延、官吏的横暴和费尽辛勤所换来的小人的鄙视,要是他只要用一柄小小的刀子,就可以清算他自己的一生?谁愿意负着这样的重担,在烦劳的生命的压迫下呻吟流汗,倘不是因为惧怕不可知的死后、惧怕那从来不曾有一个旅人回来过的神秘之国,是它迷惑了我们的意志,使我们宁愿忍受目前的磨折,不敢向我们所不知道的痛苦飞去?这样,重重的顾虑使我们全变成了懦夫,决心的炽热的光彩，被审慎的思维盖上了一层灰色，伟大的事业在这一种考虑之下，也会逆流而退，失去了行动的意义。且慢！美丽的奥菲利娅！——女神，在你的祈祷之中，不要忘记替我忏悔我的罪孽。（朱生豪 译）

6.7 推荐读物

(1)陈宏薇，高级汉英翻译，外语教学与研究出版社2009年版。
(2)胡卫平，高级翻译，华东师范大学出版社2011年版。
(3)李明，英汉互动翻译教程，武汉大学出版社2006年版。
(4)刘宓庆、章艳，翻译美学理论，外语教学与研究出版社2011年版。
(5)刘重德，文学翻译十讲，中国对外翻译出版公司2000年版。
(6)马红军，翻译批评散论，中国对外翻译出版公司2002年版。
(7)马会娟，奈达翻译理论研究，外语教学与研究出版社2003年版。
(8)毛荣贵，翻译美学，上海交通大学出版社2005年版。
(9)熊俊，英汉互译简明教程，武汉大学出版社2011年版。
(10)许渊冲，翻译的艺术，五洲传播出版社2006年版。
(11)张保红，文学翻译，外语教学与研究出版社2011年版。

7 课后练习

7.1 分析题

(1)试用所译和比读材料分析文学翻译的特点。
(2)品读窍门，试用其对诗歌翻译的重点作一探讨。
(3)试用你最欣赏的译文，分析文学翻译中审美的再现。

7.2 实训题

7.2.1 荷塘月色

路上只我一个人，背着手踱着。这一片天地好像是我的；我也像超出了平常的自己，到了另一世界里。我爱热闹，也爱冷静；爱群居，也爱独处。像今晚上，一个人在这苍茫的月下，什么都可以想，什么都可以不想，便觉是个自由的人。白天里一定要做的事，一定要说的话，现在都可不理。这是独处的妙处，我且受用这无边的荷香月色好了。

7.2.2 Poor Relations

He reviveth past situations to institute what he calleth — favourable comparisons. With a reflecting sort of congratulation, he will inquire the price of your furniture; and insults you with a special commendation of your window-curtains. He is of opinion that the urn is the more elegant shape, but, after all, there was something more comfortable about the old teakettle — which you must remember. He dare say you must find a great convenience in having a carriage of your own, and appealeth to your lady if it is not so. Inquireth if you have had your arms done on vellum yet; and did not know till lately, that such-and-such had been the crest of the family. His memory is unseasonable; his compliments perverse; his talk a trouble; his stay pertinacious; and when he goeth away, you dismiss his chair into a corner, as precipitately as possible, and feel fairly rid of two nuisances.

7.3 思考题

(1)文学翻译与非文学翻译有何区别?
(2)文学翻译的原则是什么?
(3)何人适合从事文学翻译?
(4)文学翻译何时可能胜过原作?如何把握?
(5)文学翻译如何重塑原文中的形象?
(6)文学翻译如何传递原文的情感?
(7)意境可译吗?如何译?
(8)文学翻译中如何重显意象?
(9)文学翻译如何重构意境?
(10)文学风格可译吗?如何翻译?
(11)散文翻译如何做到形散而神不散?
(12)诗歌翻译的原则有哪些?
(13)小说翻译如何追求叙事性?
(14)戏剧翻译如何反映表演性?
(15)如何认识文学翻译的形与神及其关系?

第 20 课 艺术

导 译

艺术是一种文化现象,用能激发他人思想和感情的形态或景象来表达现实。其根本在于不断创造新兴之美,浓缩和夸张生活,借此宣泄内心的欲望与情绪。音乐、舞蹈、绘画、雕塑、工艺、建筑、戏剧、影视、书法等任何可以表达美的行为或事物,皆属艺术。艺术的本质特点,就是用语言创造出虚拟的人类现实生活。艺术发生的基础是人类的语言,有效的艺术创造必须完全借助于语言。人类有什么样的语言形式,就会有什么样的艺术形式。不借助语言的所谓艺术创造,只能算是普通的游戏创造。

艺术翻译是为艺术作品进行的翻译,属于专业翻译范畴,包括戏剧翻译、影视翻译、美术翻译等。艺术翻译是目的性极强的跨文化交流实践,充当着服务发展、引领发展的重要角色,具有重要的理论意义和深远的战略意义。

本课主要涉及以下艺术翻译理论与实践内容:戏剧翻译、歌曲翻译、绘画翻译、影视翻译等。将借鉴跨文化交际和全译理论,通过实例训练艺术作品的翻译过程,主要训练其中与语言密切相关的内容。

练笔 1 课前练笔

1.1 京剧

京剧是融合了歌曲、舞蹈、表演和杂技的舞台艺术。但我们在京剧舞台上看到的并不是对真实生活的模仿。比如,京剧在人物形象的塑造上使用特殊的表现手段。所有的角色都按其性别、个性、年龄、职业和社会地位类型化。"行当"就是对京剧中角色类型的说法。

1.2 宫廷建筑

据史料记载,秦代的阿房宫、汉代的未央宫、唐代的大明宫都是宏大的建筑群,有宽阔的庭院、宏伟的殿堂,以及亭台楼榭等。目前现存的帝王宫殿是明清两代的北京紫禁城、沈阳故宫。紫禁城完工于明永乐年间的1420年,从整体布局到具体结构和细节装饰,完全按照中国传统宫殿的要求建造,代表了古代宫廷建筑技术和艺术的顶峰。

1.3 **Film as Art**

① Movie making has become an art form in its own and there are many films that are recognized as classics. Sir Laurence Olivier's portrayal of Shakespeare's "Hamlet" is one of the great films in this category. In the world of musical films, Julie Andrews in "Sound of Music" is known and appreciated, as one of the best musicals ever made. In the field of drama, Humphrey Bogart's "Casablanca" and the "African Queen" are also regarded as "great" classics.

② While most films are recognized because of their leading actors, the real credit goes to the people who have the vision to make and direct the story. The director controls every aspect of film making, from the photographic angles, the special effects, the performance of the actors, and right through to the final editing. There have been several outstanding actors who have gone into directing. Charlie Chaplin was one of the most famous, but others such as, Orson Wells, Clint Eastwood and Kevin Costner have been both actor and director of their own films.

1.4 **The Classics and Modern Music**

① Classical music, generally, applies to the style of compositions originating in the 17th and 18th centuries. Although there are many variations in the performance of classical music, it is, probably, best associated with large orchestras which combine all forms of instruments. Classical music remains very popular today and has been perpetuated by continuous generations of musicians and composers, who carry on the tradition.

② By the late 1800s a new type of music began its evolution and, gradually grew in popularity. Jazz, Ragtime and the Blues spread throughout the world as the genius of the Afro-American musicians made their mark. With the development of films came the age of "pops" and the emergence of the big "baths" with Glenn Miller and Tommy Dorsey backing up crooners, such as Bing Crosby and Grank Sinatra. By the 1950s, electronic music had arrived and this ushered in the new sound of Rock and Roll.

2 课前批评

2.1 传统中国绘画 Traditional Chinese Paintings

① 中国人绘画采用毛笔蘸墨汁或颜色，灵巧地挥洒纸上。画家用深、浅、浓、淡的点和线构成一幅图画。在优秀画家的手里，毛笔和墨汁非常具有表现力，他们不仅是绘画的工具，也是画家艺术追求的象征。

① The Chinese do paintings with brushes, dipping their brushes in ink or paint and then skillfully wielding them. Painters produce on the paper pictures with lines and dots — some heavy, and some light, and some deep, and some pale. In the hands of a good painter, brushes and ink can be highly expressive. Because of this, they served not only as tools for drawing pictures, but also as a collective symbol of artistic pursuit.

② 与水墨画相比，源于宫廷的工笔重彩的特点是其细腻的画法、对细节的绘画，以及丰富的色彩。宫廷画盛行于宋代，当时全国的优秀画家都云集宫廷画院，并采用与朝廷命官同样的方法，按照其各自在绘画方面的成就排序。

② In comparison to ink and wash painting, fine brushwork, minute attention to details and rich, elaborate coloring characterize traditional Chinese paintings of a style known as gong bi zhong cai that originated from palace paintings. Palace paintings thrived in the Song Dynasty. The country's best painters were grouped in the imperial academy of paintings, where they were ranked the same way as officials according to their artistic accomplishments. For a time in the dynasty, there were schools of calligraphy and paintings to bring up painters and calligraphers qualified for work in service of the imperial family and ranking officials. (董玉国 译)

2.2 The Film Industry and the Evolution 电影产业及其发展

① The film industry is the greatest form of mass entertainment ever conceived by man. Even from its beginnings as silent films, in black and white, it captured the imagination of the public. The industry has evolved into one of the great art forms of modern times and will continue to enthrall people in every corner of our world.

① 电影业是人类所创造的最重要的一种大众娱乐形式。甚至从早期的黑白无声电影开始，它就引起了人们极大的想象。电影艺术现已经发展成为重要的现代艺术形式之一，并且会继续吸引世界各地的观众。

② Film making has come a long way form the days of black and white movies. Today, almost every film is

② 自黑白电影问世以来，电影拍摄技术取得了巨大的进步。

in colour, with a liberal dose of special effect and the obligatory sound track, to provide background music. The industry has progressed, along with the development of better quality photographic film and, is now moving into the field of digital recording. (Paterson, G.)

今天,几乎所有的电影都是彩色的,运用大量的特技,并配有专门音轨,以提供背景音乐。随着电影胶片质量的不断提高,电影产业也在不断进步。现在,我们正进入了数码拍摄时代。(张满生 译)

3 全译知识 艺术翻译

艺术是用形象反映现实但比其更具典型性的社会意识形态,包括文学、绘画、雕塑、建筑、音乐、舞蹈、戏剧、影视、曲艺等。除文学外,兼有文学成分的主要是戏剧,影视、歌曲等综合性艺术。艺术翻译在此主要指歌曲译配、影视译制和戏剧翻译。

3.1 歌曲译配

歌曲译配,指译原歌词以配原曲的翻译活动。歌曲译配时,曲调已定型,歌曲的旋律、节奏和节拍已由作曲者框定,译出的歌词必须服从原歌的旋律、节奏和节拍,力求译词和原曲完美结合。歌当诗译,但受曲限。试唱中华人民共和国国歌并品味歌曲译配的艺术:

① 义勇军进行曲	**March of the Volunteers**
起来!不愿做奴隶的人们!	Arise, you who do not want to be slaves!
把我们的血肉,筑成我们新的长城!	Using our flesh'n' blood, we shall build a new Great Wall!
中华民族到了最危险的时候,	Th' Chinese Nation's facing the grav'st danger of all;
每个人被迫着发出最后的吼声。	In desperation, everybody cries out the last call.
起来!起来!起来!我们万众一心,	Arise! Arise! Arise! Be united as one!
冒着敌人的炮火前进!	Brave the enemy's gunfire, march on!
冒着敌人的炮火前进!	Brave the enemy's gunfire, march on!
前进!前进!进!	March on! March on! On!

歌曲译配最大特点是信守译文与原文音节等数的原则。原文歌词一音节,汉译歌词一汉字,原则上原词一个音节占一音符,译词也应在一个音符下安一汉字;原词如果一个语言音节占多个音符(拖腔),译词则亦步亦趋。另外,译文词语的声调必须和乐曲旋律的音调相吻合,这是译歌不同于译诗的根本之处。

3.2 影视译制

影视即电影与电视的合称，是傲立于戏剧、文学、雕塑、音乐、绘画、摄影艺术之林的“第七艺术”。影视译制指影视剧本的翻译与制作，包括翻译、译制导演、演员配音等。影视剧本常分为文学剧本、分镜头剧本、对白台本、完成台本等。其中对白台本是用于演员对白或旁白的剧本，是影视译制的主要用本。

对白台本翻译要考虑影视语言的聆听性、综合性、瞬间性、通俗性、无注性等特点，最重要的是合口型。影视译制不能改变原作画面中的口型，因此受到其严格限制。换言之，译文口型需要同原文口型保持一致，具体有二：其一，译文台词的总字数应与原文台词的总音节数保持一致，至少是大致相同；其二，译文台词的首尾两字的口型应保持一致，至少要大致相同。如果实在难以实现，只能保“首”弃“尾”。如：

② Well, figure he knows only two people here. You and me. Me, he's running from. You're nice run into. Have you seen him? 我想他在这里只认识两个人——我和你。我是他想躲的，你是他想见的。看见他了吗？

③ A stay of execution by the order of the Lord Chancellor.

【译文Ⅰ】：你改为死缓，大法官下的命令。

【译文Ⅱ】：大法官下令了，你改为死缓。

例②台词较长，力求对口型，尤其是首尾的口型。例③虽然两种译文口型基本相对，但语义上译文Ⅱ比译文Ⅰ更符合汉语逻辑。

3.3 戏剧翻译

戏剧翻译实际上是剧本翻译，要译好剧本，必须掌握台词的特点，即口语化、个性化、生动、鲜明、洗炼。这些与文学翻译基本同理。

戏剧翻译最要注意的特点是力量性。剧本通过台词发展情节，要求台词能够句句入耳入心，否则就会失去戏剧的力量。从舞台来看，演员化妆更浓，声音更大，舞台性更强，有些夸张。正因为戏剧是舞台艺术，其假定性很强，戏剧是演员在舞台上说给剧场各个角落的观众听的。因此，对白台词一定要强化处理，即表演过程中演员必须有意识地提高声调，说出的台词一定要响亮、清晰，观众也能接受这种有别于现实生活对话的“舞台腔”。因此要求译文语言音量音强上夸张，口型到位，咬字准确，字字有力。试比较三种戏剧翻译：

④ Haste still pays haste, and leisure answers leisure;
Like doth quit like, and Measure still for Measure.

【英若诚译】：种瓜得瓜，种豆得豆，天网恢恢，疏而不漏！

【朱生豪译】：一个死得快，一个也不能容他缓死，用同样的处罚抵消同样的罪，这才叫报应循环！

【梁实秋译】：迅速永远要报答迅速，迟慢报答迟慢，同样的事受同样的报应，怎样衡量人也将怎样被人衡量。

上面是莎士比亚《请君入瓮》的三种译文。英若诚巧用汉语成语，紧凑传神，具有舞台性，便于演出，也便于观众接受。另两个译本略显松散，会影响戏剧表演效果。

4 全译窍门

4.1 字幕翻译的变通

影视剧字幕翻译就是为影视剧对白提供同步说明的过程。影视剧字幕翻译是一种特殊的语言转换类型，是对原文予以浓缩的书面译文。字幕通过视觉传递给观众，观众既要看画面，又要看字幕，所以字幕翻译要考虑到观众的接受能力，要有可视性、可读性，在保证准确的同时，做到简练。一些语气词、一些重复的词句如在上下文中没有特殊的功能，可以省略。字幕翻译时，要避免使用生僻词汇，还应注意少用多音字以免引起歧义。字幕翻译的原则是信息传递准确、译文通俗畅达、句式结构简单、文字与画面协调统一。

字幕翻译的方法有缩译（只译出原文信息的主要内容）、阐译（用较为简短的句子解释性地译出原文）、摘译（有选择性地略去某些内容不译）等。

4.2 译出艺术的美感

京剧剧本作为一种文学体裁，具有深厚的美学内涵，因此英译时要注重保留其音韵、形式等方面的美感。

比如，《凤还巢》第八场，朱焕然赞美程雪娥“如花似玉”，魏丽莎将其译为 as beautiful as flowers and jade。虽然 she is beautiful 也可表达此意，但上述的译文更能使外国观众深刻地体会到中国文化赞美的表达方式。再如：

朱焕然：岳母！	ZHU: Esteemed Mother-in-law!
程夫人：贤婿！	MADAM: Esteemed Son-in-law!
朱焕然：再“咸”，我就吃不得了。	ZHU: There is enough steam around here to cook my goose!
程夫人：事到如今，有什么长策无有？	MADAM: Now that things have come to such a pass, have you an inspiration?
朱焕然：这会儿，甭说长策，我连个短策都没有了。	ZHU: An inspiration? No, just a lot of perspiration!

译文中 esteem（尊敬）和 steam（蒸汽）与原文一样运用了谐音，相当于原文中“贤”与“咸”。英语中 to cook one's goose 译为“把人毁了”，达到了喜剧效果。而 inspiration（灵感）与 perspiration（汗液）则传达出原作中“长策”、“短策”的对比意蕴与喜剧风趣来。《凤还巢》是一出喜剧，格调清新，幽默诙谐，对成语、歇后语运用很巧妙，把这些语言准确地英译并保留其原有诙谐幽默的风格，对于保持原作美感很重要。

4.3 语篇跨语重构

面对应用型语篇，译者务必根据译语的语篇习惯调整原作的行文思路，而不是一味地局限于原作。以艺术活动介绍宣传单为例，翻译时必须明确译文的沟通目的，根据译语读者的阅读心理措词组句，做到"得意忘形"，适当重建行文方式，以便较为清晰地传递原文体的主旨信息。

Destination on the third	请回顾三层展厅
Art of Passion	"激情舞动"
Richard Young	理查德·杨
Exhibition period: From now till 30th April 2008	展览时间：由即日起至四月三十日
Exhibition venue: 3/F The Landmark	展览场地：置地广场三楼
Near the entrance of Three Sixty	邻近 Three Sixty 入口
"Art of Passion" is a series of art pieces which is full of lively dancing elements. It comprises the artworks drawn by a talented artist, Richard Young.	"激情舞动"展出才华横溢的 Richard Young 一系列以舞者为题的作品，尽现舞动的美感。

此处将英语展览名称"Art of Passion"译作"激情舞动"主要依据了标题（即艺术活动的醒目"广告词"）表达方式和习惯不同的特征。当然，这些方面往往会根据不同语篇情景，由译者做出合理性的翻译决策。无论是从艺术家的创作形式及主题范围，还是各类文体的沟通目的来看，艺术活动宣传单、画家简介、作品介绍等美术翻译可能涉及的语篇类型是难以设定界线的，译者涉及的语篇种类可能五花八门、无所不包。但无论遇到什么文本语篇，只要根据它涉及的基本沟通要素进行相应的信息构建，就能进行比较有效的沟通。

4.4 片名跨文化再造

片名可视为影视剧的商标、广告，有导视推介的作用，是影视剧取得成功的重要因素。片名译得好，能够为影视剧增色添彩，画龙点睛。片名翻译力求形神兼备，既要保持原片的信息内容、文化意义、主题特色，又要符合译语文化特征，富有吸引力和感染力。片名翻译还要考虑观众的接受能力、审美要求、欣赏水平和商业价值。常见译法有：

直译 译文最大限度地保持原片名的内容和形式，有时语序也与原片名一致，如：Kung Fu Panda《功夫熊猫》、Harry Potter《哈利波特》、Notting Hill《诺丁山》等。

意译 通过增补、删减的手段，传达原片的内容与特色，如：Dance with Wolves《与狼共舞》，A Good Woman《良家妇女》，The Piano《钢琴课》等。

直意兼译 通过直译传达原片名的字面之意，通过意译补充隐含之意，如：Madison Country Bridge《廊桥遗梦》，The Fugitive《亡命天涯》等。

仿作 根据作品内容和原片名另造一名，如：Gone with the Wind《乱世佳人》，Leon《这个杀手不太冷》，You Can't Take It With You《浮生若梦》等。

5 话题词汇

5.1 音乐

哀乐 funeral music
伴奏音乐 background music
标题音乐 program music
唱片音乐 disc music
抽象音乐 abstract music
传统音乐 traditional music
纯音乐 absolute music
丛林音乐 jungle music
打击乐 percussion music
电声音乐 electrophonic music
动人音乐 emotional music
复调音乐 polyphony
歌剧音乐 operatic music
宫廷音乐 court music
古典音乐 classical music
管弦乐 orchestral music
合奏乐 part music
交响乐 symphony
爵士音乐 jazz
军乐 martial music
室内乐 chamber music
alterative rock 另类摇滚乐
ceremonial music 礼乐
chorus troop 合唱团
continental music 欧洲大陆音乐
decadent music 颓废音乐
fugue 赋格曲
folk rock 民歌摇滚乐
folk music 民间音乐
graduation recital 毕业汇报演奏会
harmonist 和声作曲家
instrumental music 器乐
keyboard music 琴乐
light music 轻音乐
lounge music 休闲音乐
lyric writer 作曲家
ethnic minority music 少数民族音乐
musicians association 音乐家协会
pop music 流行音乐
progressive country 现代乡村音乐
sentimental music 伤感音乐
solemn music 庄严音乐
sombre music 忧郁音乐
sopranist 女高音歌手
soul music 灵魂音乐
soul rock 灵歌式摇滚乐
tenorist 男高音歌手
theatrical music 戏剧音乐
tuner 调音师
variations 变奏曲
vocal music 声乐

5.2 美术

表现派 expressionism
笔法 brush style
抽象派 abstractionism
城市风景画 cityscape
插图作家 illustrator
处女展 premiere
滴画法 drip technique
底色 field
风俗人物画 genre painting
风景画家 landscape painter
风俗画家 genre painter
个人作品展览会 one-man show
国画 Chinese painting
国家美术馆 national art gallery
画布 canvas
具象派 representationalism

蜡染画 batik
立体派 cubism
人体模型 manikin
调色板 palette
直线笔 ruling pen
Chinese ink 墨
composition 构思
contour style 勾勒法
drawing easel 画架
epic representation 史诗画
fake drawing 赝品
figure painting 人物画
fresco 壁画
futurism 未来派
grounding 绘画打底
iconophile 美术品欣赏家
imagism 形象派
imitating 临摹
living model 真人模特
master painter 绘画大师
modernist 现代派画家
naturalism 自然派
neo-impressionism 新印象派
painting exhibition 画展
private view 预展
realist school 写真派
retrospective exhibition 回顾展
sketchbook 素描本
stereographer 立体画家
stereography 立体画法
thinner 颜料稀释液
tube 颜料管
utility brush 通用画笔
watercolour brush 水彩笔
watercolour painting 水彩画

5.3 影视

爱情片 love story film
布景设计人员 set designer
悲剧片 tragedy film
电影译制厂 film dubbing studio
电影剧本 script
电影发行公司 film distribution
电影场 open-air cinema
导演 director
功夫片 kung fu film
获奖电影 awarded film
剧情 story
配音室 dubbing studio
摄影棚 filming hall
摄影师 camera man
同音摄影机 sound camera
荣誉奖 honorary award
入口处大厅 lobby
影片公司 motion picture company
新发行的影片 recently released film
background music 背景音乐
captioning 加字幕
cinema production 影片生产
climax 高潮
collage 胶片衔接
complimentary ticket 免费门票
costume 服装
director in chief 总导演
dubbing a film 电影配音
dubbing machine 配音机
evening show 夜场
film association 电影协会
film synopsis 电影内容简介
film projector 电影放映机
first run 首轮放映
lady minor role 女配角
lead 主角
make-up 化妆
newsreel 纪录片
nomination 评奖提名
Academy Award 奥斯卡金像奖
road show 新片特约放映
showbill 电影海报
sound stage 有声电影摄影棚
special camera 专用摄影机
stage setting 舞台布景
suspense 悬念

test shot 试拍
title 电影字幕
voice-over 旁白

5.4 戏剧

编剧 playwright
传统戏 traditional play
唱戏 acting in an opera
独白演员 soliloquist
大歌剧 grand opera
改编 adaption
古装剧 costume play
歌剧团 opera troupe
歌剧演员 operatic singer
歌剧剧本 word book
歌剧院 opera house
化妆师 make-up man
京剧 Peking opera
剧本 playbook
剧团成员 trouper
人物 figure
戏剧家 dramatist
戏剧协会 dramatists association
哑剧演员 pantomimist
演唱 singing
art director 艺术指导
artistry 艺术性
back curtain 背幕;底
backdrop lights 背景灯
black comedy 荒诞喜剧
comedian 喜剧演员
dance drama theatre 舞剧院
dramatic critic 戏剧评论家
dramaturgy 编剧法
dresser 服装员
dressing room 化妆室
finale 最后一幕
front stalls 正厅前座
guest performer 客串演员
histrionic ability 表演能力
local drama 民间戏剧
mobile drama company 流动剧团
modern drama actor 话剧演员
modern opera troupe 话剧团
main line 主线
play 话剧剧本
poetic play 诗剧
realistic drama 现实主义戏剧
reserved lounge 贵宾休息室
set piece 成套布景
soap opera 肥皂剧
star role 明星角色
theatre 话剧院
tragicomedy 悲喜剧
vision 幻镜

5.5 舞蹈

长鼓舞 long-drum dance
传统舞蹈 traditional dance
大舞厅 ballroom
儿童舞蹈 children's dance
宫廷舞蹈 court dance
交际舞女 ballroom dancer
交际舞 ballroom dancing
集体跳舞 group dancing
紧身衣 maillot
练习服 practice clothes
民族歌舞团 nationalities song and dance ensemble
民间歌舞协会 folk dance and song society
桑巴舞曲 samba
舞伴 dancing partner
舞曲 dance music
舞蹈协会 dancers association
舞蹈团 dance company
舞厅 dance hall
秧歌队 yangko troupe
中央民族歌舞团 Central Nationalities Ensemble
acrobatic dance 杂技舞蹈
ballet 芭蕾舞

ballet company 芭蕾舞团
ballet dancer 芭蕾舞演员
chasse 快滑步
contemporary dance 当代舞蹈
dance pose 舞蹈造型
dancer 舞蹈家
dancing shoe 舞鞋
dancing team 舞蹈队
disco girl 迪斯科女郎
discotheque 唱片夜总会
gigolo 舞男
hustle 哈斯尔舞
jazz hound 爵士舞迷
jazz dance 爵士舞
jazz 爵士舞曲
jig 吉格舞曲
lantern dance 灯舞
modern dance 现代舞蹈
polka 波尔卡舞曲
polonaise 波洛奈兹舞
rumba 伦巴舞曲
rock and roll 摇滚舞曲
skate dancing 冰上舞蹈
touch dancing 触身舞蹈
toe dance 足间舞
waltz 华尔兹舞曲
western dance 西方舞蹈

5.6 雕塑

冰雕 ice carving
半身石像 stone bust
宝石 precious stone
冰灯 ice lamp
冰雕品 ice carvings
半圆雕刻刀 scoop
碑刻 carved stone inscription
瓷雕 porcelain carving
大理石雕 marble carving
电铸 electroforming
雕塑风格 modeling method
雕塑台 modeling stand
点刻刀 stipple graver
雕刻品 carvings
雕塑用合金 statuary bronze
浮雕板 modeling board
浮雕花纹 decorative patterns
汉白玉 white marble
金刚石 diamond
熟石膏 plaster
armature support 人体架
artistic ceramics 美术陶瓷
atelier 雕塑室
bone carving 骨雕
bone carvings 骨雕品
boxwood 黄杨木
bust 半身雕像
cameo 多彩浮雕
carved furniture 雕花家具
clay sculpture 泥雕
color engraving 彩雕
colossal figure 巨型雕像
contour knife 轮廓线刻刀
embossment 浮雕
fire marble 火红大理石
flat chisel 瓶口雕塑刀
hammer 雕刻用锤
ice pavilion 冰阁
modeling 造型
modeling clay 型塑用泥
modeling skill 雕塑技术
motion 人物姿势
multiple graver 多刃雕刻刀
nudity 裸体雕像
relief 浮雕作品
relief carving knife 浮雕刀
shell carving 贝雕
stone tablet 石碑
whole-length statue 全身雕像
wood block 木刻块木

5.7 书法

笔力刚劲 writing in bold hand
笔触 inspiration
败笔 faulty stroke
草书 cursive script
春联 spring festival couplets
草体 running hand
点 point
对联 distich
仿宋体 imitation Song-Dynasty type
勾 stroke with a hook
古体 ancient style
横轴 horizontal scroll
横 horizontal bar
卷轴题词 inscrolling
楷书 regular script
隶书 official script
书写能手 calligraphist
宋体 Song typeface
现代书法家 modern calligrapher
amateur calligrapher 业余书法家
calligraphic art 书法艺术
curlicue 抖笔
epigraph 题字;铭文;碑文
famous calligrapher 著名书法家
genuine handwriting 真迹
graphomaniac 书写迷者
inscription 题词
large size vertical scroll 字画
neat regular script 工楷
Ouyang Xun's style 欧体
official script 金文
powerfulness 雄健
poster 标语
stone tablet 石碑
square scroll 斗方
seal 图记
sign board 招牌
signature on scroll 题署
strawing hand 字迹潦草
tadpole script 科斗文
vigorous strokes 骨力
vigorousness 苍劲
vertical scroll 条幅
writing rapidly 走笔
writing big character 写大字
writing small character 写小字
wild script 狂书
original handwriting 手迹

5.8 缩略词

AME 自动缩微胶片编辑装置
AS 艺术科学
BAFTA 电影和电视艺术学院
BB 爵士乐团
BF 蓝电影,性电影;黄色电影
BG 低音电吉他
BGM 背景音乐
BP 背景放映
BP 最低音歌手
BS 低音萨克管
CB 低音大提琴，任何最低音的乐器
CD 创作总监
CFA 中国风尚大典
CG 照相枪
DAM 数字式自动乐曲
FH 雾笛
FS 全景摄影
HS 拍摄头部
MF 中强
OVA 原创动画录影带
PIR 综合剧本
RAB 富于节奏的一种美国黑人音乐
SFX 特技效果
SO 交响乐团
TDA 黑色艺术
3DS 三维摄影室

体悟 6 比读体悟

6.1 高墙中的宁静

① 与古希腊建筑街区间有机的结合不同,中国传统建筑强调的是通透和情调,展现的是丰富的变化,并用无数流畅的线条表达出含蓄的情调。

② 高大、坚固的围墙不仅有保护宅院的功能,也营造了宁静的气氛。院墙挡住了外部的喧嚣,保持了家宅的安静,从而为居住者创造了安宁。

③ 隔离物,诸如栏杆、通透的石雕或砖雕,以及花窗都起着疏离的作用。内部与外部的链接是中国传统建筑所采用的艺术手法之一。可以借助竹帘、门窗来达到疏离与连接相结合的效果。花窗、门和窗户在疏离的效果中有着理想的结构,可以将外部景致分隔成不同的部分。

④ 简约和典雅之美是中国传统居民的主要特点。多数的居所没有天花板,横梁与椽都暴露在外。栏杆的结构配之以有些角落的装饰,在第一层展示出来。房舍的外部通常是朴素的砖墙。木制的屋檐也很少粉刷,只是涂上桐油起到防潮的作用而已。(李霞)

Tranquil Interior Surrounded by Solid Walls

① Unlike Greek architecture, which is an organic combination of blocks, Chinese traditional architecture emphasizes unobstructedness and tone, and displays the rich variance and connotation of the tone with innumerable flowing lines.

② Large, solid walls not only function as a protective surrounding defense, they also embody tranquility. Secluding the residence from the outside world, the thick, solid walls block noise from outside and keep the inside quiet.

③ Partitions such as railings, pierced stonework or brickwork, and window lattices act as frames and agents of distancing. Connection between the exterior and the interior is one of the artistic methods used in Chinese architecture. The combination of partition and connection can be achieved with a bamboo curtain, a door or a window. The lattices in partitions, doors and windows make ideal frames, separating the outside scenery into several sections.

④ Simple and elegant beauty is a major feature of the traditional Chinese residence. Most dwellings have no ceilings, and the beams and rafters are exposed. The railing structure is shown even on the ground floor, accompanied only with some decoration in certain corners. The exterior usually consists of plain brick walls. Wooden eaves are seldom painted, but only coated with tung oil as a damp-proof treatment. (董玉国 译)

6.2 中国电影

① 1896 年电影进入中国,但是在差不多10年后才有了第一部中国电影《定军山》。而直到1913 年中国正式的电影业才出现,当时郑振秋和张石川拍摄了中国第一部真正意义上的电影《患难夫妻》。

② 中国第一部有声电影是《歌女红牡丹》(1913),由当时的"电影皇后"胡蝶出演。20 世纪 40 年代,电影制作处于一种无序状态,一些奸商借机拍摄色情

Chinese Movie

① Motion pictures were introduced to China in 1896, but it was almost a decade before the first local attempt at filmmaking with Conquering Jun Mountain (1905). But the Chinese film industry didn't officially begin until 1913 when Zheng Zhenqiu and Zhang Shichuan shot the first Chinese film The Difficult Couple (1913).

② China's first "talkie" was The Songstress Red Peony (1931) played by the then "film queen" Butterfly Hu (Hu Die in Chinese). In the 1940s, filmmaking was in a chaotic state and some profiteers seized the chance to shoot pornographic and

电影和粗劣的恐怖电影。然而这一时期也出现了一些优秀的电影,比如有蔡楚生和郑君里拍摄的《一江春水向东流》(1947),有陈白尘和郑君里拍摄的《乌鸦与麻雀》(1949),由沈浮拍摄的《万家灯火》(1948)。

cheap horror films. However there were still some wonderful films being made, such as Spring River Flows Eastward (1947) by Cai Chusheng and Zheng Junli, Crow and Sparrow (1949) by Chen Baichen and Zheng Junli and Light of Million Hopes (1948) by Shen Fu.

③ 中华人民共和国建国到文化大革命的 17 年间,拍摄了 603 部电影,包括 1960 年拍摄的第一部宽银幕电影。1966 到 1972 年,中国电影业的发展受到了极大的制约,这期间没有一部电影问世。到了 20 世纪 80 年代,电影工作者们又一次打破艺术的禁锢。1984 年,主要由北京电影学院的毕业生们创作了《一个和八个》,陈凯歌的《黄土地》将第五代导演群体推向公众。这些人包括:吴子牛,田壮壮,何平等。张艺谋第一次凭借《红高粱》(1987)获得国际电影奖。20 世纪 90 年代,国产电影工业蓬勃发展,与此同时,1995 年,政府开放了外国影片在中国的上映。

③ In the 17 years between the founding of the PRC and the Cultural Revolution, 603 feature films were produced, including the first wide-screen film in 1960. The film industry was severely restricted and no film was shot in the period 1966—1972. In the 1980s, filmmakers again began to probe the boundaries of their art. In 1984, One and Eight made mainly by the graduates of the Beijing Film Academy, and Chen Kaige's Yellow Earth (1984) introduced the public to the fifth generation of filmmakers, including Wu Ziniu, Tian Zhuangzhuang and He Ping. Zhang Yimou first won an international prize with Red Sorghum (1987). In the 1990s, the domestic film industry prospered, coinciding with a government decision to allow the showing of foreign films from 1995. (董玉国 译)

6.3 奇妙的书法

The Art of Calligraphy

① 毛笔是中国的传统书写工具。笔尖由羊毛、黄鼬毛或兔毛制成。先要精心选择毫毛,将一端修剪成尖的形状,然后将另一端固定在竹子或木制的笔管上。毛笔的毫毛既软又有弹性。毛笔外部的毫毛稍短,使它更易吸收墨汁。尖端用较长的毛,以形成笔尖,这样可以轻易地写出点或线的形状。

① The brush is a traditional Chinese writing tool. Its tip is made of soft hairs from a sheep, a weasel or a rabbit. The carefully selected hairs are tied together, trimmed into a tapering shape and fixed onto one end of a bamboo or wooden holder. The hair is both soft and elastic. The outer layers of the brush are shorter, making it easier to absorb ink. The tip end has longer hairs which come to a tiny point, so that both wrinkle dotting and line drawing can be done easily.

② 墨是由桐油燃烧后的煤烟与松木炭加上明胶和一些草药及香料混合而成。墨汁是将坚固的墨块与水一道在砚台上反复研磨而成的。中国有“(黑)墨有五色”之说,因为中国的画家们精心地用墨调和出各种层次的阴影。

② Chinese ink is made by mixing soot from burning tung oil and pine tar with gelatin, Chinese herbs and spices. Ink is produced by grinding the solid ink with water against an inkstone. There is a saying that "(black) ink has five colors," because Chinese painters use ink meticulously to produce a number of subtle shades.

③ 宣纸最初是唐代时产自安徽省的宣州。宣纸的质地紧密、具有韧性,可以防虫咬。此外,在这样质地的纸上书写,笔画轻重缓急皆可。由于有这么多的长处,宣纸取代了曾经常用作绘画材

③ Xuan paper was originally produced in Xuanzhou in Anhui Province in the Tang Dynasty. Xuan paper has a close texture, making it pliable yet tough, and resistant to moth damage. In addition, this kind can be achieved with heavier or lighter strokes, or when the stroke is quickened or slowed

料的丝绸。丝绸的吸附力低，但是它更适合于细致的线描和重彩。

down. With so many advantages, Xuan paper largely replaced the silk fabric which had been used for painting before. Silk is not absorbent, but is suitable for meticulous line drawing and applying heavy colors. (董玉国 译)

6.4 The Television

电视

① The first TV presentations were black and white but, it wasn't long before colour was introduced. In most cases, the initial broadcasts were government-funded, although the commercial application of TV was always obvious. Initially, most TV was broadcast free to the audience, except for the payment of a license fee to the Governments. Gradually, the license fee was dropped and the commercial stations relied on their advertising revenue. Eventually, pay TV evolved, offering a wider range of stations for a monthly subscription.

① 最先投入应用的是黑白电视，但没过多久，彩色电视就走入了我们的生活。尽管电视的商业应用价值是显而易见的，但最初的电视播放是由政府资助的。起初，大部分电视免费向观众播放，支付政府一些播映许可费用。后来费用逐渐地下降，商业电视台开始依靠他们的广告收入。最后，付费电视出现，提供了大量的各种各样的电视台节目，观众可以每月预订这些节目。

② TV programs come in a wide range, from talk shows, to sitcoms, murder and mystery, documentaries, musical performances and films. A large majority of these programs are produced in the United States and, has resulted in a dominating influence of American culture. Most countries try to set quotas for programs that are produced locally, in an effort to sustain a home grown industry and counter this domination.

② 电视节目的内容相当广泛，从脱口秀到情景喜剧、凶杀侦探片、纪录片、音乐剧、电影等等。这些节目的绝大多数都是由美国制作的，这也导致了美国文化的盛行。许多国家都为本国生产的电视节目制订了一定的任务要求，以便扶持本土电视业的发展。

③ The higher the rating for a TV station, or a particular program, the greater attraction it presents for advertisers. This, in turn, directly impacts on the revenue earned through the sale of advertising time. The rating is measured from selected viewers in the major cities. These measurements are, therefore, biased to the heavily populated areas because, they represent the majority of customers.

③ 一个电视台或某个特定电视节目，其收视率越高，那么它对广告商的吸引力就越大，这直接关系到广告时段的销售收入。收视率是通过从大城市中选取观众来测定的，也就是说收视率的测定主要是集中在人口密集的地区，这主要因为大城市的人口代表了主要的消费群体。(张满生 译)

6.5 The Fine Art — the Measure of Civilisation

绘画——文明的标尺

① When anyone takes a brush in hand or, applies colour to a surface, to portray something, they are participating in the art of painting. That applies to the pre-historic cave man as much as it does to the most gifted artist. A painting is appreciated on many levels but, in the case of a "masterpiece," it is a combination of the skill of the artist, the subject of the painting, and the feelings expressed.

① 任何人只要拿起画笔，把色彩涂抹在某个平面上，来画些东西，那他就是在从事绘画创作。对于史前穴居人类是这样，对于那些最具天赋的绘画艺术家们来说也是这样。同样一幅绘画作品，人们可以从很多不同层面来欣赏。不过，对于经典艺术杰作来说，它应该是艺术家的绘画技法、绘画

作品的主题，以及绘画作品所要表达的意境的完美结合。

② Like all arts, the scope of sculpture is limitless. It is unrestricted in size, materials, colours or shape, as is verified by the relics found throughout history. Some claims of modern sculptors tend to stretch the definition of the art. Wrapping natural objects in plastic sheeting and, declaring this to the artistic, is questionable. Sculpture has the ability to generate instant reactions, possibly more than any other art.

② 就像所有的艺术形式一样，雕刻艺术的范围是无限的，不会被尺寸、材质、色彩、形状等所限制，这一点，各个历史时期所发掘的雕刻作品便是很好的证明。现代雕刻家的某些论调有夸大这门艺术定义之嫌。比如，把天然的东西包裹在塑料布中就说是艺术，这就有点儿不靠谱了。雕刻艺术的特点在于，它能让观众即刻产生共鸣，在这一点上是其他任何艺术形式都无法相比的。

③ While music is familiar to, virtually, everyone it is an art, about which, everyone has an opinion. What defines " great" music is, very much, a personal issue. There is " great" music in every style but, what is popular does not always define the quality. Music is a joint effort between the creator and the performer and one cannot exist without the other.

③ 尽管音乐对每个人来说，都再熟悉不过了，但是几乎每个人对这门艺术都有自己的看法。什么音乐算是好的音乐，这是见仁见智的。各种音乐风格都有自己的经典音乐作品，流行的并不完全等于经典的。一部好的音乐作品，是创作者和演奏者双方共同努力的结果。（张满生 译）

6.6 推荐读物

(1)刘宓庆，文体与翻译，中国对外翻译出版公司 2006 年版。

(2)刘秀芝等，北京世界文化遗产人文景观介绍翻译研究，光明日报出版社 2008 年版。

(3)麻争旗，影视译制概论，中国传媒大学出版社 2005 年版。

(4)Steiner, G. 通天塔之后：语言与翻译面面观，上海外语教育出版社 2001 年版。

(5)Basil, H. & Mason, I. Discourse and the Translator, Shanghai Foreign Language Education Press, 2007.

(6)Nida, A. E. Language and Culture Contexts in translation, Shanghai Foreign Language Education Press, 2006.

(7)Nord, C. Translating as a Purposeful Activity, Shanghai Foreign Language Education Press, 2001.

练习 7 课后练习

7.1 分析题

(1)试用所译和比读材料分析艺术作品翻译的特点。

(2)试析翻译中文与非文字作品形式的相配问题。

(3)结合比读材料归纳,掌握艺术作品翻译方法。

7.2 实训题

7.2.1 唐三彩

① 唐三彩出现时最主要的用途是随葬冥器。它的产生同唐代的政治制度和墓葬仪式密切相关。

② 唐三彩是唐代彩色釉陶器的总称,它的釉色包括黄、绿、褐、蓝、黑、白等,而以黄、绿、褐三彩为主。

③ 由于古人把阴阳二界都视为自己的生活空间,因而唐三彩的器形多样,涉及社会生活的各个方面,包括生活用具、人物和动物、家具、车马、山水和建筑物等。其中最为精美的是人物俑和动物俑。

7.2.2 Opera and Musicals

The stage has been a traditional venue for the performing arts over many centuries and music has been at the heart of all these performances. Opera and Ballet are stories told through dance, acting and singing and originating from the creation of musical scores by composers. Films have generated huge audiences for the "musical" by transposing traditional stage presentations onto the "big" screen. A completely new genre of "musical" was created by composers, such as, Gilbert and Sullivan, Irving Berlin and Rogers and Hammerstein.

7.3 思考题

(1)影视字幕翻译特有的文化处理手段有哪些?

(2)影视字幕翻译如何保持口型基本一致?

(3)《功夫熊猫》翻译如何体现了口语性?

(4)影视专题片的翻译有何显著特点?

(5)美术翻译的基本特点有哪些?

(6)美术翻译中重构译本语篇的依据是什么?

(7)如何提升美术翻译译文的语体品味?

(8)艺术作品标题的翻译处理手段有哪些?

(9)摄影图片说明的翻译特点有哪些?

(10)话剧台词翻译应如何保持警句性?

(11)戏剧翻译需要考虑的因素有哪些?

(12)怎样翻译歌名及影视片名?

(13)歌曲翻译的标准有哪些?

(14)歌曲翻译过程中韵律如何保持?

(15)歌词翻译的创造性有没有范围的限制?

第21课 体育

导 译

随着2008年奥运会的成功举办,人们的体育热情日益高涨。运动观念深入人心,体育事业蓬勃发展。人们积极参与体育活动强健体魄,愉悦身心,如球类运动、水上运动、冰雪运动等。与此同时,竞技体育也受到前所未有的关注,人们通过新闻媒体了解国内外体育赛事。

全译作为最基本的翻译技能,力求保证原作语用意义和语用价值不变的前提下,用译语准确通顺地表达原文的信息,讲究的是信息转换的完整性,既包含内容的完整性,也包含形式和风格的完整性。全译追求译文与原文"相似性"的最大化,即意、形、风格的"极似"。

英语体育新闻中的句型丰富多彩,生动活泼,字里行间凸显了运动的魅力。句子结构一般紧凑,简短而富有表现力;常用一般现在时以克服一般过去时所带来的陈旧感,使读者亲临其境,精彩赛事历历在目。为了最大限度地再现体育英语的风格,译者须明确语义;熟知一定的背景词汇、缩略语;炼字炼句以展现体育运动的魅力与动感;灵活选用时态以改变一般过去时固有的陈旧感,以增加新鲜感和现实性,置精彩纷呈体育赛事于观众眼前。

为服务于跨语言、跨文化的双语交际,在了解全译的标准与体育英语的特点的基础上,熟练掌握不同运动项目的专业词汇与各种运动项目的基本知识(如比赛规则等),译者当从英语、汉语和体育专业知识三个方面下工夫,力求译文与原文最大限度的相似。

1 课前练笔

1.1 游泳

一些科学家认为，人们有一种与生俱来的本能，就是用胳膊和腿来保持身体漂浮在水中。然而，这种本能在出生几周后消失。而在他们以后的生活里，很多孩子和成人开始学习游泳则是为了在水中能更安全，也更有趣，还有就是参加比赛。

1.2 赛龙舟

关于赛龙舟的起源，说法一直是众说不一。有人认为龙舟竞渡是为了纪念中国历史上的屈原。屈原是战国时期楚国人，中国历史上著名的文学家，位居高官，但是因为痛恨奸佞小人当道，受奸臣排挤而遭流放。于公元前278年五月初五投汨罗江而死。据说，屈原死后，当地民众自发组织起来，竞相划船营救。此举相沿成习发展成了龙舟竞渡活动。

1.3 The French Open

All tennis fans know about the French Open. It is one of the four Grand Slams, which are the biggest tennis championships in the world. Over the years, tennis stars have risen and fallen at the French Open. Older champions are beaten, and young new stars come on the scene and change tennis history. The French Open runs from late May through early June at the Roland Garros stadium in Paris. Therefore players find it one of the most challenging tournaments because the courts are different from most.

1.4 Rugby

① The game of rugby is said to have been played for the first time in 1823 in England when a William Webb Ellis picked up the ball during a game of football and ran with it.

② While football is played with a round ball, rugby is played with an oval ball. Following tackling, a tunnel or scrum is created by players of both teams. The ball is then thrown into the scrum and as watch pushes against each other, the ball is forced out of the scrum and into play.

③ Points are scored when a player places the ball on the ground behind the goal line of the opposite team re kicks the ball over the crossbar of the goalpost.

2 课前批评

2.1 太极拳

Tai Chi Chuan

① 由于慢动作的招式,太极拳常被认为是仅与老人相关的运动。然而,太极拳适合任何人学习,不受年龄、性别或体质的限制,所以在许多看重健康的年轻人中也流行起来。

① Because of the slow movements, tai chi chuan, also known as Taijiquan or shadow boxing, is frequently associated (linked) exclusively with senior citizens. Lately (Recently), however, the traditional martial art, which is in fact suitable for all people regardless of (without distinction of) age, sex (gender) and physical attribute (physique), has been in vogue among (has become popular with) health-conscious young people as well.

② 太极拳是建立在控制呼吸、规律的动作、达到身体平衡这三项原则的基础上的。它通常也包含了冥想,强调气血的循环,以及身体的协调,却不特别强调肌肉的锻炼。

② The exercises are based on the principles of controlled breathing, rhythmic movement and equilibrium (balance) in various part of the body. They typically involve meditation, emphasizing cardiovascular circulation and alignment (coordination) of the body instead of muscular development.

③ 太极拳和其他武术不同的地方,是它基于道家的哲学思维。太极主张阴阳调和,提倡万物一体的概念,并通过控制身体姿势,有效引导出内在的力量。

③ What makes tai chi chuan different from (distinguishes tai chi from) other material arts is that is has (takes) roots in Taoist philosophy. The name tai chi (Tai chi's very name) suggests a harmony between the principles of yin and yang, advocating the concepts of universal oneness (harmony/connectivity) and the perfect (ideal) channeling of inner strength (inner strength channeling) through the control of [physical] posture (through posture control). (黄源深、韩忠华用例)

2.2 A Passion for Sport

对体育的热爱

① Australians have always loved sport, and excelled at it. Even before Federation in 1901, "Australia" was competing internationally as a nation. Despite its relatively small population, Australia has consistently had world champions in most sports.

① 澳大利亚人一贯热爱体育,擅长体育运动,甚至在1901年成立联邦以前,“澳大利亚”就作为一个国家参加国际体育竞赛。澳大利亚人口规模相对较

小,但已在大多数体育项目中获得世界冠军。

② The most recent example of Australia's sporting prowess is its athletes' success at the Sydney 2000-Olympic and Paralympics Games. Finishing in fourth place overall in the Olympic competition, Australians won 58 medals. Australia gained first place in the Paralympics, with a total of 149 medals.

② 在2000年悉尼奥运会和残疾人奥运会上,澳大利亚运动员大获成功,这是澳大利亚体育实力的最新范例。在2000年奥运会上,澳大利亚共赢得58枚奖牌,总体排名第四。在残疾人奥运会上,澳大利亚共赢得149枚奖牌,总体排名第一。(黄源深、韩忠华用例)

知识 3 全译知识 翻译工具

翻译工具泛指用于翻译的工具,包括各类翻译词典(翻译学词典、翻译方法词典、译例词典、专名词典、专业双语词典等)、翻译百科全书、翻译手册、翻译索引、翻译书目、翻译行规、翻译指南等,还包括中外文网络。翻译离不开词典,理解阶段和表达阶段使用词典各有特色,更可以利用现代化网络便捷地深入理解,促进转化,确定译案。

3.1 各类词典

理解阶段 查阅词典的顺序一般是:双语语文词典→双语详解词典→原语词典→原语详解词典→原语词组词典→各原语专科词典(专名词典、科技词典等)→原语百科全书等。

表达阶段 查阅词典的顺序一般是:译语语文词典→译语详解词典→译语同义词词典→译语倒序词典→译语专科词典→译语百科全书等。

3.2 各类网站

词典总是落后于语言实践,一个词从产生到进入词典要经过时间的考验,但这个过程不可能妨碍人们对新词的运用,正是运用频率的高低决定了该词最后能否进入词典,这一频率一般可以借助网络和语料库来判断。当今时代,利用网络辅助翻译已成为一种重要的翻译能力。现列举一些有助于翻译的网站:

www. bartleby. com/65
www. All-Refer. com
www. xh. 5156edu. com
www. webster. com
www. onelook. com
www. baidu. com
www. encarta. msn. com
www. wikipedia. org
www. humanum. arts. cuhk. edu. hk/Lexis / Lindict
www. ldoceonline. com
www. google. com
www. baigoogledu. com

www. yeeyan. org　　　　　　　　　　www. fane. cn/forum. asp

译前查阅　译前可利用网络迅速查阅与原文相关的背景知识。如果作者健在，还可与其直接取得联系，更有助于深入理解原作的思想。

译中查证　译中可利用网络查询和验证译文，即遇到比较难译的词语和句子，可查网上现存的译文，以资借鉴。主要采取"双语并举"的搜索方法，即在搜索框中同时输入原文词语和译文可能包含的关键词，然后搜索。如要英译"历史长河"，将"历史长河"与译文关键词 history 输入 Google 搜索框，可得三种主要译法：in the long history、in the long river of history 和 in the long course of history。接着验证译文，其依据主要是相关译法的网络使用频率。三种译文中第一种省略了原文的比喻，暂不考虑；将后两种输入 Google 进行精确查询（即加上引号查询），分别获得 3 万和 8 万余条结果，表明后者远比前者常用。为求译文地道，将搜索范围缩至英国网页（只在搜索框中搜索对象后加上 site：uk 即可），分别获得 40 和 200 余条结果。至此可以确定，英语中与 history 的地道搭配是 course 而非 river，所以"在我国历史的长河中"可译为 in the long course of China's history。

译后润色　译后可利用网络润色译文，主要是在修改阶段利用网上平行文本提高译文的通顺程度，在多种方案中优中选优，可以优化译文。一种方式是直接利用同类材料的平行文本，另一种是利用精通译语者直接判断几种译法的优劣，从语感上确证译文的地道与否。

窍门　4　全译窍门

4.1 巧译时态

在体育英语的翻译中，特别是体育新闻报道或现场直播，为使表达变得生动、有效，经常使用一般现在时代替一般过去时。如：

① The final score is 98 to 82. 最后得分 98：82。

② Kong Linghui beats Waldner 5 to nil at the end of the firsting. 孔令辉在第一次发球权结束时，以 5：0 领先瓦尔德内尔。

③ He's on his second strike. 他已打出两个好球了。

④ When he takes turns，he tries to keep his boat flat，that is，esp the mast vertical. 他在拐弯时，尽量保持帆船平稳，也就是尽量使桅杆保直。

一般现在时可以突出已发事件的现实感和新鲜感，拉近作者与阅读对象的情感距离。为了让读者与体育赛事的结果产生共鸣，为自已看到的乐意的结果欢喜雀跃，为体育比赛中的爆冷发出感叹等等，……在体育新闻标题中现在时更是几乎所有新闻标题选用的时态。

⑤ Fu knocks out O'Sullivan in thriller. 傅家俊惊险"击"败火箭奥沙利文。

⑥ Nene makes an emotional return for Nuggets. 掘金众将喜迎内内回归。

⑦ Youzhny stuns Nadal for Chennai title. 尤兹尼横扫纳达尔清奈折桂。

⑧ Bosh doubles up to help Raps defeat Knicks and recapture sixth place. 龙王两双助猛龙击败尼克斯重夺东部第六。

4.2 善用被动

体育英语中被动语态的使用频率高于其他文体。一般来说，越靠近句子前端的部分越容易引起注意，导致被动语态使用率高。如：

⑨ Juande Ramos, former Tottenham and Sevillacoach, was appointed as the coach of Madrid by Real sports director Pedja Mijatovic. 皇家马德里董事米贾托维奇指定托特纳姆和塞维利亚队前教练胡安德·拉莫斯为皇家马德里教练。

例中 Real sports director Pedja Mijatovic 是句子的重点，而教练的名字 Juande Ramos 很容易被读者忽略。但就本条新闻来说，其惹人眼球的地方在于这位新上任的教练 Juande Ramos 身上，所以使用被动语态能够突出此信息。

体育英语中被动语态常用来表达主动意义。如：

⑩ He is well qualified for a forward. 他完全具备做前锋的素质。

⑪ A game is won by the first player to score 21 points. 首先得 21 分的一方为胜。

⑫ A penalty stroke may be awarded for offence in the shooting. 射门区犯规可能要罚点球。

4.3 义随境迁

一词多义如何选取最恰当的词义，唯一的依据是语境。同一词语在不同运动项目中有不同的译法。如 system：low repetition system 少重复法（举重），scoring system 记分系统（船艇运动），training system 训练体制，one-setter system5—1 配备、五攻一传（排球），rotation system（双打）轮转配合打法（羽毛球），seven system 七人密集队形（橄榄球），open system 开放式氧气装备（登山），4—2—4 system 4—2—4 阵形（足球）。又如 play：medal play 击数比赛（高尔夫球），off-table play 远台打法（乒球），unfair play 犯规动作（球类运动），offence play 进攻战术（篮球），shadow play 不用球的练习（棒球），strong-side play 强侧配合（篮球），body play 身体冲撞（棍球），decisive play 决定性进攻（足球），finger play 手指技术（击剑）。

体育英语有很多术语和特殊表达方式，汉译时不可望文生义，要根据语境定义。如：

⑬ England, who have not won the World Cup for four decades, were fortunate to emerge with 1—0 win in Frankfurt, relying on an early own goal by Paraguay captain Carlos. 英格兰已经 40 多年没有取得世界杯了，但它依靠巴拉圭队长卡洛斯的一记乌龙，在法兰克福幸运地以一比零战胜了对手。

⑭ Queensland attack, Danny Herbert passes to Tim Horan who scores a try. 昆士兰队进攻，丹尼·赫伯特将球传给蒂姆·霍兰，霍兰持球触地得分。

⑮ Dive all the way to the other side of the basket using the right or left hand with proper English on the ball. 用右手或左手适当转动球，直冲篮下的另一侧。

例⑬中 own goal 是足球、曲棍球等项目中的专有名词，字面义为“自己的球”，实际上是"乌龙球"。例⑭中普通词 try 在橄榄球比赛中意为"持球触地得分"。例⑮中 English 既非"英国人",也非"英国人的",而是"转动球"。根据篮球比赛中运动员常采用的技巧,可以断定句中在讲述球受控于某一球员,他做转动球的假动作,以掩饰他准备切入上篮的真实动作。

4.4 译出力度与动感

体育集激情和美于一身。运动乃体育之魂,没有动,就谈不上体育。体育英语使用 roar, stun, storm, beat, start, conquer 等动词的频率很高,有时连一些介词或副词也颇具动感,汉译选词时要注意力度和动感。如下例中 strike, over 等词的汉译透出了力度和动感,运动性跃然纸上,显得活力十足。

⑯ Supersub Podolsiki strikes to save Bayen. 波王子一击救拜仁。

⑰ Djokovic ends Fish's dream run to clinch Pacific Life Open title. 小德大师赛力克天王杀手,获赛季第二冠。

⑱ Roddick clinches third San Jose crown. 罗迪克第三次圣何塞折桂。

⑲ Noah's career night leads Bulls over bucks. 诺阿爆发助公牛顶翻雄鹿。

4.5 译出诙谐幽默

体育报道的收视有一个特点,即观众的广泛性,这要求译文尽量通俗易懂。因此,在译文易播报、易懂的基础上,译者应准确使用体育术语提高观众的欣赏水平,并适当使用诙谐的行话调节气氛,发挥信息本身的娱乐效果以迅速抓住读者眼球。如:

⑳ In the 64th minute Owen came on as a substitute and scored an immediate brilliant go. 欧文在第 64 分钟时作为替补出场,随即漂亮地踢进一球。

㉑ Arsenal should win when they play Benfica at home, bur the second leg could be a different story, away games are always much more difficult. 阿森纳队在主场应该能击败本菲卡队,但第二阶段比赛就不一定了,客场比赛总是很难打的。

5 话题词汇

5.1 球类

足球

black whistle 黑哨
by-line 边线
close-marking defense 盯人防守
cheer team 拉拉队
corner ball 角球
crossbar (球门)横梁
defender; fullback; back 后卫
defense line 后线
deny a goal 判进球无效
doping test 药检
elimination match 淘汰赛
extra time 加时赛
free kick 任意球
forward/striker attacker 前锋
goalkeeper 守门员
goal post 球门柱

hand ball 手球
header 头球
Manchester United 曼联
mid-field 中场
off-side 越位
own goal 乌龙球
penalty corner 罚点球
penalty kick 点球
punt 凌空踢球
Real Madrid 皇家马德里
round robin 循环赛
slide tackle 铲球
stationary ball 定位球
substitution 换人
swerving ball 弧线球
take a dive 假摔
throw-in 界外

网球

澳大利亚公开赛 Australian Open
大满贯 Grand Slam
戴维斯杯网球赛 Davis Cup
抽球 drive
吊球 dink
法国公开赛 French Open
发急转球 kicking service
发球区 service court；service
发旋球 twist service
红土球场 clay court
混合双打 mixed doubles
高压球 smash
观众 dedans
截击球 volley
锦标赛 championship
男子单打 men's singles
男子双打 men's doubles
女子双打 women's doubles
女子单打 women's single
切球 chip；cut
球童 ball boy
塑胶球场 synthetic court
球网 net
网带 net cord
网球场 tennis court
网球大师系列赛 Tennis Masters Series
网前截击 net interception
温布尔登公开赛 Wimbledon Open Cup
韦特曼杯网球赛 Wightman Cup
邀请赛 invitational match；match point
削球 to slice；to chop；
巡回赛 circuit
一局中的决胜球 game ball；game point
一场中的决胜分；赛点 ice-cream point；money point
暂停 suspension
baseline（网球场）底线
base-liner 底线球
break points 破发点
cord ball 擦网好球
double faults 双误
faulty service 发球失误
serve 发球
service ace 发球得分
unforced error 非受迫性失误

篮球

advanced guard；forward 前锋
attacking half；front court 前场
baseline；end line 底线；端线
centre 中锋
chaser 钉对方主力的队员
combined offence 进攻混合防守
defensive end；back court 后场
defensive player 防守队员
defensive fast break 防守快攻
dunk 扣篮
dribbling on the run 行进间运球
fast break 快攻
flash post 中场区
free thrower 控球罚球队员

free throw lane; 3-second lane 三秒区
second shot 补篮
jump shot 跳投
line-up 阵容
loose man; open man 无人防守的进攻队员
man-for-offence 进攻人盯人防守
midcourt line; division line 中线
offensive player 进攻队员
off wing; offside wing 弱侧
pass 传球
rebound block 抢篮板球
shot 投篮
sideline 边线
steals 断球次数
slow offence 慢攻
standing dribble 原地运球
spin dribble 运球转身
to catch 接球
to intercept 抢球
to block a shot 盖帽
zone offence 区域进攻

棒球和垒球

棒 球 baseball
边线 foul line
护盔 helmet
垒球 softball
垒线 baseline
垒位填补 base coverage
队长席 dugout
防守率 fielding average
击球区 batter box
界内区 fait territory
内场 infield; diamond
内曲线球 in-curve; inshot
飘球 floater
替换投手 derrick
外场 outfield
外曲线球 out-curve; swerving pitch
障碍球 blockball

高尔夫球

blind hole 盲穴
caddy 球童
fairway; undulation 球道
guiding post 标志杆
golfer; golf player 高尔夫球运动员
hitting area 击球区
hole 高尔夫球洞
lip 穴沿

羽毛球

baseline game 底线球战术
block 接杀挡网
backhand 反拍
bodyline ball 追身球
cut 切球
defense and fight back 防守反击
drive 接杀抽球
forehand 正拍
half court; service court 发球区
foul hit 击球犯规
fault serving 发球违例
full spike 全力击球
hook 勾球
lunge stroke 搓球
line 压线区
lob 挑高球
preliminary feint 假动作
recovery 被动救球
scoop 挑球
short low service 发短球
serving position 发球位置
smash 抽击
Sudirman Cup 苏迪曼杯(混合团体)
Thomas Cup 汤姆斯杯(男子团体冠军赛)
Uber Cup 尤伯杯(女子团体冠军赛)

5.2 水上运动

游泳

澳大利亚式爬游 Australian crawl
蝶泳 butterfly
动作形式 movement pattern
花样游泳 synchronized swimming
混合泳 medley
划水动作类型 stroke pattern
竞技游泳姿势 competitive stroke
竞技游泳 competitive swimming
潜泳 underwater swimming; diving
蛙泳 breast stroke
仰泳 backstroke
泳姿 stroke
自由泳 freestyle

跳水

acrobatic dive 特技跳水
alternative 替补队员
butterfly dive 蝶式跳水
crouched jump 抱膝跳水
dash 最后冲刺
deep dive 深水跳水
diving boards 跳板
crawl 爬泳
diving 潜泳
diving tower; platform; stage; 跳
dive 立定跳水
exhibition dive 跳水表演
figure competition 规定动作比赛
fancy swimming 花式游泳
goggles 游泳护目镜
heat 预赛
lane 泳道
pike dive 屈体跳水
routine competition 自选动作比赛
synchronized swimming 花样游泳
springboard diving; board work 跳板跳水
twist dive 转体跳水
top diving 跳台跳水
water ballet 水上芭蕾

花样游泳

Albatross 信天翁式
castle 城堡式
Catalina 卡塔里纳式
crane 鹤立式
degree of difficulty 难度系数
diving boards 跳板
dolphin 海豚式
dolpholina 海豚里纳式
duet 双人项目比赛
figure competition 规定动作比赛
fishtail position 鱼尾式
flamingo 火鹤式
Gaviaa 加维亚太式
heron 苍鹭式
high tower 高塔式
kip 基普式
Knight 骑士式
porpoise 鲸鱼式
preliminary routines 自选动作预赛
reverse crane 倒立鹤式
routine competition 自选动作比赛
solo 单人项目比赛
Subilarc 萨比拉克式

船艇运动

beam wind 横风
backwash 逆流
canoeing 皮划艇运动
course 航向
ceiling 船底垫
cabin 船舱

current 水流
catamaran 双体帆船
catboat 独桅帆船
crew 全体船员
channel 航道
dead water 静水
displacement 排水量
reef 暗礁

钓鱼

抄网 hand net; land net
钓具 fishing tackle
钓竿支架 rod rest
底层鱼垂钓 bottom fishing
钓鱼竿 rod
浮子 float
接钩绳 cast
划艇渔船 fishing boat
铅垂 lead; lead weight
饵料 bait
饵针 bait needle
撒网 to cast net
三角钩 triangle
线圈 coil
鱼篓 fish basket
鱼钩 angling

5.3 田径运动

背越式跳高 back layout
撑竿跳高 pole jump; pole vault; vault; to vault
对抗赛 dual meet;match
短跑练习 sprint training
犯规线 foul line
径赛场地 track
立定跳远 standing broad jump; standing long jump; standing leap
力量型跳远 strength jump; strength take-off
链球 hammer; chain ball
耐力训练 endurance training
铅球运动员 shot putter; weight putter
铅球 shot
七项全能比赛 heptathlon
三项全能比赛 triathlon
三级跳远 triple jump; hop, step and jump
十项全能比赛 decathlon
沙坑 landing pit; landing area
速度型跳远 velocity take-off
田赛场地 field
推铅球 shot put
铁饼 discus; disc; platter
投掷速度 velocity of throwing
踏跳板 take-off line; scratch line
弹跳力 spring
投掷项目 distance throw; throwing events
跳远 long jump; broad jump
五项全能比赛 pentathlon
训练量 training burden

田赛

助跑道 runway
掷铁 discus throw; to launch the discus
助跑 approach run; run-up
做准备活动 to limber up; to warm up
蹲踞式跳远 knee-tuck type; float style
掷标枪 javelin throw
走步式跳 hitch-lick; stride-in-air type step walk; run-in-the-air
自由式跳高 free-style high jump

径赛

公路赛 road race
加速跑 acceleration sprint;
径赛 track event
竞走 race walking; competitive walking; walking
跑道竞走 track walking
最后弯道 home turn; home bend;
越野赛跑 cross-country race; cross-country running
障碍栏 dry hurdle
终点冲刺跑 dash; sprint; spurt
中距离赛跑 middle-distance race

5.4 冰雪运动

滑雪

短雪橇 luge; luge tobogganing
飞跃区 jumping hill
滑雪道;坡 slide
滑雪旅行 ski tour
滑雪服 anorak
滑雪鞋 ski boots
沙地滑行 sand skiing
上山缆索 skit tow; rope tow
山地滑雪 alpine skiing
上坡;坡道 uphill
速度滑雪 cross-country; langlauf; stepping
凸型地带 convex
U 型轨道 U-rail
无雪滑行 snowless skiing
雪炮 snow gun
助滑道 inrun; Take-Off Track

速度滑冰

British style 英国式
backward skating 倒滑
blade 冰刀
curve technique 弯道技术
compulsory dance 规定舞蹈
curved end; corner 弯道
crossing line 换道区
double skating 双人滑
footwork 步法
figure skating 花样滑冰
figure dance 冰上舞蹈
free dancing 自选舞蹈
free glide; free slide 自由滑行
goal line 终点线
ice rink; ice stadium; skating rink 冰场
ice ballet 冰上芭蕾
inner curve 小弯道
individual skating 单人滑
moderate pace 中速
maximum rate 最大速率
maximum effort 极限运动
optional routine 自选项目
skating step 滑行步
separate race 分道比赛
sprint championships 短道速滑锦标赛
speed skating track 速滑跑道
short track speed skating 短道速滑

冰球

airborne pass; lift pass 传凌空球
body cover 身体掩护
crossover 压步
drop pass 留球
face-off alignment 争球阵式
fake shot 虚射
flip pass 挑传
flip shot 挑射
follow shot 跟进射
forward 前锋
hard pass 劲传
headman 主力队员
hoister 后卫
ice hockey 冰球
kick shot 踢射
long stride 长滑步

offensive play 进攻型阵式
offensive- side trap 进攻型战术
off-side through 传球越位
screen shot 掩护射门
shooting lane 射门路线
shot 射门
sliding 滑倒挡球
speedy shot 快速射门
snap shot 弹射
streamline hockey 流线型进攻法
tip shot 补射
to intercept the puck 断球
off-side position 门外球

5.5 缩略语

中国网球协会 CFA
中国田径协会 CAA
中国足球协会 AFC
中国游泳协会 CSA
中国龙舟协会 CDA
中国摩托艇运动协会 CMSA
中国皮划艇运动协会 CCA
中国钓鱼协会 CAA
中国滑雪协会 CSA
中国雪橇车协会 CBTA
中国冰球协会 CIHA
中国击剑协会 CFA
中国体操协会 CGA
中国射箭协会 CAA
中国马术协会 CEA
中国篮球协会 CBA
中国羽毛球协会 CBA
中国保龄球协会 CBA
中国技巧协会 CSAA
中国武术协会 CWA
IAPT 国际职业网球协会
IFFA 国际足球协会联合会
FIFA 国际足球联合会
ISF 国际游泳联合会
UEFA 欧洲足联
FINA 国际业余游泳联合会
IPC 国际残奥委会
PGA 职业高尔夫球员联盟
ECIOC 国际奥委会执行委员会
IOC 国际奥委会
UIPM 国际现代五项联合会
WAC 世界田径锦标赛
IAAF 国际业余田径联合会
FIFCA 国际田径教练员协会
AAAA 亚洲业余田径联合会
AFC 亚洲足球联合会
IBA 国际篮球联合会
ABA 美国篮球联合会
NBA 美国全国篮球协会
ILTF 国际网球联合会
WIRE 国际女子网球联合会
FINA 国际业余游泳联合会
YAA 美国帆船驾驶员协会
STAGB 英国航海训练协会
ICF 国际抛钩钓鱼联合会
ISRA 国际滑雪竞速赛协会
IFS 国际雪橇运动联合会
FIBT 国际雪车联合会
IIHF 国际冰球联合会
FIE 国际击剑联合会

体悟 6 比读体悟

6.1 体育促进和平与发展

Sport for Peace and Development

①体育运动是人类的共同语言，是促进和平与发展的重要因素。自远古时

① Being a common language [of mankind] (As a universal language), sport is an important factor in the

代起，体育运动就已超越种族、肤色、文化的差异，承载起人类对和平美好世界的向往与追求。诞生于两千多年前的奥林匹克精神，就是这一追求的具体体现。

promotion of (spot is a vital element in fostering) peace and development. Ever since ancient times (Since days long past), sport has transcended (disregarded) differences in race, color or (and) culture and given expression to (expressed/embodied) mankind's aspirations for and pursuit of a peaceful and better world, as evidenced in the Olympic spirit that came into being more than 2,000 years ago.

② 自19世纪顾拜旦先生首创现代奥运会以来，世界人民对和平的向往和对奥林匹克理想的追求从未动摇。联合国的成立及《联合国宪章》宗旨与原则的确立，在维护世界和平、促进社会发展的同时，也推动了奥林匹克精神的传播与发扬。

② Since [Mr.] Pierre de Coubertin founded the modern Olympic Games at the end of the 19th century, (Since the end of the 19th century when Pierre de Coubertin) revived the notion of Olympic Games, the people of the world have (the world/global community has) been determined to follow (pursue) the Olympic ideals. The founding (birth) of the United Nations and the establishment (creation) of the purpose and principles of the UN Charter have not only contributed to maintenance of world peace and social development, but also facilitated the spread [and further development] of the Olympic spirit.

③ 在21世纪的今天，世界各国仍应继续坚持《联合国宪章》的宗旨和原则，积极倡导奥林匹克精神，增进不同文明间的对话与交流，推动世界社会经济不断向前发展。

③ [In our times] in the 21st century (In the 21st century) the countries (nations) of the world should continue to uphold (should maintain) the UN Charter's purposes and principles and actively advocate (energetically endorse) the Olympic spirit so as to enhance the dialogue and exchanges (intercourse) among civilizations and promote (stimulate) steady (sustained) economic and social progress throughout the world.（黄源深、韩忠华用例）

6.2 奥运会与北京市发展

The Olympic Games and the Development of Beijing

① 由于筹办奥运会在城市基础设施、生态环境、电子技术等方面提出大量的建设性需求，使得筹办过程对整个城市的经济发展产生巨大的带动作用。例如，韩国在筹办1988年汉城奥运会期间，从1981年到1988年经济增长速度年均提高到12.4%；1985年至1990年，人均国内生产总值从2 300美元增加到6 300美元，实现了从发展中国家向新兴工业国的转变。因此，人们有理由相信，2008年的北京奥运会也将对这座城市的经济发展产生巨大影响。

① The preparations for an Olympic Games accelerate the host city's economic development as they greatly increase the demand on the construction of the city's infrastructure, ecosystem, electronic technology and other capabilities. A case in point is South Korea. During its preparations for the 1988 Seoul Olympic Games, its economy enjoyed an annual growth rate of 12.4% from 1981 to 19881, and its GDP per capita increased from $2,300 to $6,300. Boomed by the Olympic Games, South Korea realized the transformation from a developing country to an industrialized economy. In light of this, we have every reason to believe that preparation for the 2008 Beijing Olympic Games will also have a significant impact on the economic development of the city.

② 北京申奥成功后，许多专家就举办2008年奥运会对首都经济增长的促进作用作了不少分析。据估计，2002年至2007年，因奥运引起的投资和消费需求，将拉动全市国内生产总值增长速度平均每年提高约1.67个百分点。到2007年，全市国内生产总值可达到5 900亿元左右，人均国内生产总值达到6 000美元，接近汉城20年前举办奥运会时达到的水平。

② With Beijing's successful Olympic bid, many experts have anticipated the almost certain positive effects the Games would have on Beijing's economic growth. It is estimated that the investment and consumption demand spurred by the Olympic Games will lift the capital's GDP growth by an additional annual rate of 1.67% on average between 2002 and 2007. By 2007 the city's GDP is expected to reach RMB 590 billion, and the GDP per capita around $ 6,000 — approaching that of Seoul's when it hosted the summer Olympic Games in 1988.

③ 实施《北京奥运行动规划》后，北京市在基础设施和生态环境等方面的建设投资不断增长。在环境保护方面，2002年建成了120平方公里的绿化隔离带，完成了"五河十路"366公里的绿化工程，搬迁了40家污染严重的企业；新建了包括菖蒲河公园，明城墙遗址公园在内的16处大绿地，占地104公顷；新增草坪362万平方米，总面积已达到5 000万平方米。清河、凉水河等综合整治污水处理系统进展顺利，生态环境保护工作取得了显著的成果。

③ Since the Beijing Olympic Action Plan was approved, construction-related investments on infrastructure and the ecosystem have been increasing steadily. With respect to environmental protection, a 120km^2 green belt was built in 2002, and the green projects alongside 5 rivers and 10 main roads were also completed. More than 40 high-pollution factories were moved out of the city proper, and 16 forested areas were built, with a total area of 104 hectares. In addition, there are now over 3.63 million square meters of new lawns, increasing the capital's total lawn area to 50 million square meters. Furthermore, the city's efforts in cleaning the Qing River and Liangshui River have already produced positive results in environmental protection.

④ 在交通建设方面，四环路全线开通。投资14.5亿美元的地铁5号线预计2006年建成通车，在2008年前新建8条轨道交通线，使全市的轨道交通线路总长达到300公里。

④ With respect to transportation infrastructure, the newly constructed Fourth-Ring Road is already open to traffic. The No. 5 subway line, with a total investment of $ 1.45 billion, will be completed and put to operation in 2006. By 2008 an additional eight light railway routes will have been completed, extending the total length of the intra-city rail network to 300 km.

⑤ 在文物保护和文化建设方面，近几年，北京市拨款20多个亿用于文化设施建设，在未来5年中，北京市政府还将陆续投资7 500万美元，用于城市遗址遗迹的保护和修缮。

⑤ Progress has also been made in the preservation of historical and cultural relics and sites. In the past few years, the Beijing municipal government has invested over RMB 2 billion in the construction of cultural facilities. In the next 5 years, an additional $ 75 million will be contributed exclusively to the preservation and renovation of historical and cultural relics.（黄源深、张春柏用例）

6.3 The Pleasure of Walking

步行的乐趣

① Walking gives us back our senses. We see, hear, and smell the world as we never can when we ride. No matter what vehicle, it is the vehicle that is moving, not ourselves. We are

① 步行唤起我们的知觉，我们看到的，听到的，闻到的世界与我们坐车时感知到的世界绝对不一样。无论乘

trapped inside its fixed environment, and once we have taken in its sensory aspects — mainly in terms of comfort or discomfort — we turn off our perceptions and either go to sleep or open a magazine and begin dozing awake.

坐什么车,运动的是车,而不是我们自己,我们被困在车内固定的环境里,一旦接受了它所给予我们的感觉——主要是舒适与否的感觉——我们就关闭了自己的知觉,不是睡觉,就是打开一本杂志,睁着眼睛打起盹来。

② But when we walk, the environment changes every moment and our senses are continuously being altered. Around each corner of a city block, around each bend in a country road, there is something new to great the eyes, the ears, the nose. Even the same walk, the one we may take every day, is never the same from one day to another, from one week and season to another.

② 可是当我们步行的时候,周围的环境每时每刻都在变化,我们的知觉不断地为外界事物所激活,在城市街区的每一拐角处,在乡间道路的每个拐弯处,总有什么新的东西映入我们的眼帘,窜入我们的耳朵,扑入我们的鼻子,即使我们日复一日,年复一年走同一条路,但是,我们感知的事物却没有一次是完全相同的。这种情况不仅在乡村如此,而且在任何地方也是如此。纽约城里,有几位公司主管,天天早上结伴从各自家里步行到办公室。一路上,他们先是沿着古旧的褐色石头铺成的寂静街道向前走,经过一个全市最古老的街区,继而跨过布鲁克林大桥,穿过支撑着蛛网般得钢缆的教堂式桥拱,最后步入大楼巍然耸立的金融区。

③ This is true not only in the country, but anywhere at all. In New York City, a group of executives who meet every weekday morning walk from their homes to their offices. Their way takes them through quiet streets of old brownstones, one of the oldest neighborhoods in the city, then up and over the Brooklyn Bridge with its cathedral arches supporting the web like drapery of cables, then down into the skyscraper canyons of the financial district. . On their daily route they see, hear, and smell the city in all its seasonal changes, under bright and cloudy skies. Only the most inclement weather stops them — suitably dressed, they can walk with pleasure in spring rains, autumn drizzles, the sunlight of a summer morning or a soft winter snowfall. The river waters roll by below their feet, sullen or sparkling. Tugboats chug past, shoving and hauling their variously laden barges; on a shrouded morning, foghorns hoot and moan. The famous skyline of lower Manhattan rises before them, glittering in sun, afloat in mist, against a backdrop of sky never twice the same.

③ 每天在途中,他们用整个身心感受着这座城市的阴晴冷暖,四季变化,只有极其恶劣的天气才会阻止他们步行。他们衣着得体,惬意地行走在蒙蒙春雨之中,步行于秋日的毛毛细雨里,漫步在夏日清晨的阳光下,或徜徉于冬天鹅毛般的飘雪间,河水在他们脚下滚滚流过,或阴沉凝滞,或闪闪发光。拖船突突驶过,拖着载满各色货物的驳船。在大雾茫茫的早晨,雾号时而嘟嘟叫嚣,时而呜咽呻吟。在变化万千的天幕衬托下,曼哈顿著名的天际线在他们面前升起——在阳光中闪烁着,在雾霭中漂浮着。(黄源深、张春柏用例)

6.4 Cheerleading Safety

Cheerleading safety efforts have led to modest reductions in the number of serious injuries in recent years, according to a new report about college and high school sports and cheerleading mishaps. But cheerleading continues to cause more serious and deadly injuries by far than other sports. Researchers have long known how dangerous cheerleading is, but records were poorly kept until recently. An update to the record-keeping system last year found that between 1982 and 2007, there were 103 fatal, disabling or serious injuries recorded among female high school athletes, with the vast majority (67) occurring in cheerleading. The next most dangerous sports: gymnastics (nine such injuries) and track (seven). Today, the National Center for Catastrophic Sports Injury Research at the University of North Carolina at Chapel Hill released its 26th annual report on the topic. The latest figures are from the 2007—2008 academic year for college and high school sports, male and female. The report defines catastrophic injuries as any severe or fatal injury incurred during participation in the sport. The new numbers are for the 26-year period from the fall of 1982 through the spring of 2008.

拉拉队安全

最新一项针对大学和高中学校体育运动和拉拉队重伤事故的报告指出,近些年来,拉拉队安全保障措施已使重伤事故数量有所降低。但到目前为止,与其它体育项目相比,拉拉队所导致的严重和致命伤患仍然比较多。研究人员早就知道拉拉队运动有多危险,但是以往的受伤记录保存不善,直到最近才有所改观。去年,对记录跟踪系统的更新显示,在 1982 年至 2007 年间,高中女运动员中发生了 103 起致命、致残或重伤事故,而其中大多数(67 起)发生在拉拉队员身上。体操(9 起)和田径(7 起)分列第二、三大危险项目。北卡罗来纳大学教堂山分校的国家严重体育伤患研究中心于今日公布了第 26 期关于此问题的年度报告。最新的数据是从 2007 至 2008 学年度的大学和高中男女体育项目中统计而来的。该报告将严重伤患定义为在参与体育项目期间遭受的任何严重或致命伤害。最新数据是自 1982 年秋季至 2008 年春季以来共 26 年间统计而来的。在此期间,共发生了 1 116起严重伤患事件,其中高中和大学分别占 905 起和 211 起。

6.5 推荐读物

(1)王屏,陈家刚,体育英语,科学文献技术出版社 2003 年版。

(2)冯庆华等,汉英翻译基础教程,高等教育出版社 2008 年版。

(3)黄源深,全国翻译资格(水平)考试指定教材英语笔译实务三级,外文出版社 2005 年版。

(4)龚学众,英汉翻译一本通,中国人民大学出版社 2010 年版。

(5)马国力,体育英语第六册,清华大学出版社 2004 年版。

(6)宁翠叶,体育英语词汇手册,复旦大学出版社 2010 年版。

(7)田华实等,用英语说中国,科学普及出版社 2008 年版。

(8)许建平,英汉互译与技巧,清华大学出版社 2007 年版。

(9)徐宪光等,英语翻译四级笔译,外语教育出版社 2008 年版。

(10)曾诚,实用汉英翻译教程,外语教学与研究出版社 2002 年版。

7 课后练习

7.1 分析题

(1)试析某一翻译工具的具体使用方法。

(2)试析体育翻译中的文化现象。

(3)品读窍门,试验析比读材料中的翻译技巧。

7.2 实训题

7.2.1 北京2008奥运会会徽

"舞动的北京"是一方中国之印。这方"中国之印"镌刻着有着13亿人口和56个民族的国家对于奥林匹克运动的誓言;见证着一个拥有古老文明和现代风范的民族对于奥林匹克精神的崇尚;呈现着一个面向未来的都市对奥林匹克理想的诉求。它是诚信的象征,它是自信的展示,它是第29届奥林匹克运动会主办城市北京想向全世界、全人类做出的庄严而神圣的承诺。

7.2.2 Golf: The Best Sport in the World

① When most people think of golfs, they probably think of Tiger Woods jet-setting to golf courses around the world winning prestigious tournaments and making a lot of money.

② It is generally agreed that golf was first played in Scotland in the 15th century. Its popularity spread throughout the 16th century, and the first international gold match took place in 1682 between players from England and Scotland. Clubs began forming soon after, and concrete rules of the game were established.

③ Golf was made an Olympic sport in 1900, by which time there were already more than 1,000 gold courses in the United States. The famous PGA (professionals Golfers Association) was formed in 1916, and by 1944, the equally famous PGA tour consisted of 22events and was held throughout the year.

7.3 思考题

(1)体育英语翻译有哪些特点?

(2)体育英语多用动词,汉译如何处理?

(3)体育新闻标题翻译应注意哪些问题?

(4)试归纳体育英语新闻标题中时态的翻译技巧。

(5)如何突出体育英语翻译的"动感"?

(6)如何译出体育术语的力度?

(7)如何译出体育文本中的语势?

(8)如何译出体育文本中的节奏?

(9)试总结体育英语翻译原则。

(10)试总结体育赛事比分的翻译规律。

(11)如何理解体育英语的简洁性？汉译如何体现？

(12)试比较英汉时间、地点、方式状语顺序及其互译规律。